The New NETSCAPE & HTML eXplorer

The New NETSCAPE & HTML eXPLORER

Urban A. LeJeune

CORIOLIS GROUP BOOKS

Publisher	*Keith Weiskamp*
Editor	*Toni Zuccarini*
Cover Design	*Anthony Stock*
Interior Design	*Bradley O. Grannis*
Layout Production	*Dorothy Bungert*
Proofreader	*Shelly Crossen*
Indexer	*Nicole Stock*

The Coriolis Group
7339 E. Acoma Drive, Suite 7
Scottsdale, AZ 85260
Phone: (602) 483-0192
Fax: (602) 483-0193
Web address: www.coriolis.com

ISBN 1-883577-91-8 : $39.99

Printed in the United States of America

10 9 8 7 6 5 4 3 2 1

CONTENTS

INTRODUCTION

Since the publication of the first edition of this book, a lot has happened in the universe of Netscape and the World Wide Web. Thousands of new Web sites have sprung up almost overnight; new technologies have emerged, like Shockwave, VRML, and RealAudio, to help developers create more interactive Web sites; new Web development languages like Java and JavaScript have been released; and Netscape has set the world on fire by introducing powerful additions and improvements to their new Netscape Navigator including JavaScript, Java applets, frames, plug-ins, mail, CoolTalk, and new HTML extensions.

The problem with Netscape Navigator and the Web is that they are both fast moving targets. As soon as one version of Navigator is released, another one is waiting in the wings to be unveiled on the Web. And new technologies for displaying and accessing content like multimedia files are constantly being introduced and improved. But amidst this sea of change remains a stable plethora of tips and techniques for using Netscape and exploring and publishing on the Web. So my goal in creating the new edition of this book is to show you the best that Netscape and the Web have to offer, demonstrate Web publishing techniques you can put to work immediately, and bring you up-to-date with the latest Netscape and HTML features. With the information presented in this book, you'll be able to master the art of customizing Netscape and turning your area on the Web into a much more dynamic electronic publishing center.

Who This Book Is For

If you are the kind of person who wants to get the most out of the software you use, this book is for you. It isn't just another Web tour guide with screen shots of my favorite places on the Web. It is a hands-on, in-depth guide written to show you how to harness the power of the new Netscape Navigator, how to use the Web to access as much of the Internet as possible, how to create dynamic Web pages using HTML and other features including Java applets and JavaScript, and how to find especially useful information and resources on the Web for publishing and Web development with JavaScript, Java, and HTML.

What's Inside

We'll start our journey in Part 1 by looking at how we can put many of the new Netscape features to work, including Netscape plug-ins, mail, CoolTalk, and Netscape's new built-in email and news features. In Part 2 and Part 3 we'll immerse ourselves in the world of Web publishing. Getting your stuff published on the Web is an exciting proposition, and the ease with which you can create dynamic and interactive Web pages will surprise you. I'll explain in detail how HTML works and I'll introduce all of the new and key HTML features with plenty of examples to go around. After we get our bearings with HTML, we'll move on and learn the ins and outs of creating interactive Web pages with JavaScript. If you have never used a scripting language before, you'll be amazed at what you can accomplish with just a little bit of JavaScript code. Throughout Parts 2 and 3 I'll be showing you how to perform a number of useful tasks including:

- How to add Java applets to your Web pages
- How to create simple but useful CGI scripts
- How to add JavaScript code to HTML pages
- How to design and set up different types of Web pages
- How to use the more powerful JavaScript features, including objects, events, and methods
- How to create more dynamic and useful Web pages using tables and visual forms
- How to make your HTML forms more interactive using JavaScript
- How to use frames to make visually interesting Web pages
- How to use Netscape's HTML editor and Netscape Gold

To round out the publishing section of the book, I've also included detailed reference guides on both HTML and JavaScript. You can refer to these reference sections in the back of the book whenever you are creating Web pages and you need to look up the format of a particular HTML tag or JavaScript instruction.

Everything in this book is designed to give you an easy and painless introduction to the ever-changing world of Netscape, HTML, and the World Wide Web. However, there is also enough advanced information here to make your Web site a truly multimedia experience. This book is really for anyone interested in Netscape and HTML, from the beginner to the more advanced user. So jump on in and explore the ever-expanding world of Netscape and the World Wide Web.

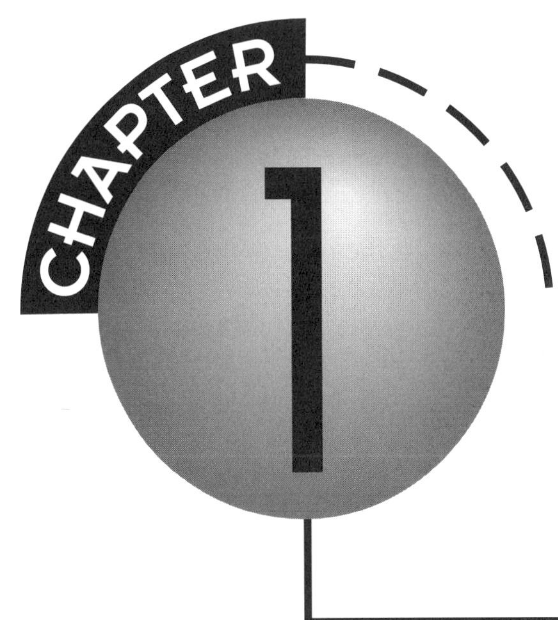

Harnessing the Web with Netscape

The World Wide Web—the great electronic publishing center of cyberspace—is waiting for you. All you need is a little know-how and Netscape to explore its potential.

When I wrote the first edition of this book (almost one year ago), the World Wide Web was just starting to be discovered by thousands of users who were being introduced to Netscape at a record pace. Of course, the Web had been around for quite some time, but Netscape turned the complexity and vastness of the Web into an intuitive visual format. Since the first beta release of Netscape, this software has evolved so fast that most users find they can't keep up. In fact, it seems that a new release is introduced weekly sporting new features that turn the Web into a much more dynamic and eye-catching place.

Fortunately, within this sea of change, you'll find a number of things that aren't moving quite at the speed of light. Once you master many of the key techniques for using the Web and creating Web pages, you'll easily be able to apply what you know—even if Netscape sneaks in another new feature while you are not looking. Unlike most books that just explain the basic features of a particular software product, this book emphasizes the important concepts and techniques you'll need to know to use Netscape to harness the Web. My goal is to help you acquire the kind of knowledge that you can use as the universe of Netscape continues to evolve.

At the time of this writing, Netscape has introduced a number of powerful features, which Web users are scrambling to learn more about. As we start our journey in this book, you'll get a chance to explore many of these new technologies including frames, JavaScript, Java Applets, plug-ins, new HTML tags, a new mail system, and much more. We have a lot of ground to cover, so let's fire up our browser and get to work.

NETSCAPE—A BROWSER FOR THE REAL WORLD

Netscape and its siblings are called *browsers* because one of their main jobs is to help us navigate through the dizzying maze of information that we call the Internet and the World Wide Web. In fact, a key reason for the rapid rise in the popularity of browsers is that they helped tame the Internet by providing an interactive visual interface to the World Wide Web and other Internet services. The simple idea of a unified visual platform to be used throughout the Internet brought a lot of order to a world that was getting pretty chaotic, even for experienced Internet users.

The visual Internet browser concept helped reorganize the Internet for the masses, largely by including a graphical user interface (GUI) that mere mortals could understand and use. Netscape is easy to use and increasingly easy to configure. I'll show you how to make the most of your Internet and World Wide Web travels using the powerful Netscape browser—that is one of the main goals of this book.

This is an interesting time in the history of both the Internet and the Web. Usage is growing exponentially—new Web pages are being published daily. If you learn to use Netscape as a Web tool now (and focus on how the Web works and how you can publish on the Web), you'll be building skills that will enable you to deal with some of the many changes guaranteed to be coming down the information superhighway.

USING THIS BOOK

This book is divided into three parts. The first part provides you with a hands-on exploration of Netscape's features and the Internet in general. In the second part, you'll learn all about the techniques for publishing home pages and other

Web pages with HTML. The third part covers more advanced Web publishing techniques, such as frames, JavaScript, Java applets, and designing with Netscape Gold.

Explorations and Base Camp Briefings

You'll find two types of chapters along the way. The first (of which this chapter is one) I call an *exploration*—because that is simply what it is: A get-out-there-and-run Web surf-session that goes somewhere in Webspace and does something interesting. Each exploration, or small group of explorations, is followed by what I call a *base camp briefing*. Just like the explorers of old, we'll talk about what we've seen so that we can put it into context and (with some luck) keep it all straight in our heads.

Each exploration in this book has a two-fold purpose: To take an interesting journey somewhere in the Internet universe, and to illustrate a particular set of Internet tools and Netscape features. HTML, frames, JavaScript, Java applets, electronic mail, and other hot Netscape topics are "tried out" and discussed. We have to warn you up front that the Internet changes hour by hour, and there's no guarantee that any particular journey we take will still be available by the time you read this book. Internet sites come and go like TV series, except that how popular they are doesn't seem to have much connection with how long they live. (Some Internet sites, in fact, have proven so popular that their hosts have had to shut them down—but that's another story altogether.) Still, the techniques I demonstrate will be just as valid, and if you have to type a different URL (more on those later) and confront a different set of words and images, well, are you an explorer or what?

The first mission of this book is to *make* you an explorer, so that you can head out into the weird, wired wilderness solo and bring back the biggest game cyberspace has to offer. This will help you learn enough so that you can become your own Web publisher if you desire.

Installing Netscape

At the back of this book you'll find an Appendix that presents the details required to install Netscape on your PC. However, some Internet service providers are giving their subscribers pre-configured disks that are simple to install. You might never have to do the dirty work of installing Netscape or another Web browser from scratch.

If you are one of those lucky subscribers, or if you're one of the many other fortunate users who are in a business or university setting with a system administrator who handles these details for you, your major interest will probably be to learn what you can do on the Web rather than how to install Internet and Web browser software.

Connecting to the Internet

In any event, using Netscape requires that you connect directly to the Internet. However, the type of connection required to run Netscape may not be as complex and costly as you've heard. The server of choice used to be Unix, but Windows NT has become increasingly popular, which is good news for those of us who like the ease of a Windows environment. If you have some experience installing Windows software, you could have Netscape up and running in an hour or less, assuming you start from scratch. If you use the software supplied on the companion CD-ROM it should only take you a few minutes. To learn more about installing Netscape, go to Appendix D.

What You Should Know before We Begin

This book assumes that you understand the basics of using Windows applications. A great depth of knowledge is not required, but it would be helpful for you to understand basic Windows terminology, such as double-clicking, the desktop, menu bars, and the like. Understanding path names and directories is desirable, as is the ability to use some form of plain text editor. (A great Window's Notepad replacement editor is supplied on the CD-ROM.) But you don't really need to have any great knowledge of the Internet or communications technology. Any Internet, Web, or Netscape-specific terms that we use will be defined on their first appearance in the book.

Starting Your Web Browser

It's time to get out and see the world via the World Wide Web. To do so, you'll need to start up your Web browser. Running your Windows-based Web browser is as simple as double-clicking on its icon.

To start Netscape, click on the icon that looks something like this:

The catch: Running Netscape requires that your computer has the ability to "speak" *Transmission Control Protocol/Internet Protocol* (TCP/IP). TCP/IP is the language used when computer networks speak to each other. TCP/IP is in a very real sense the universal language of cyberspace. The Instant Internet software (also known as Chameleon) supplied on the companion CD-ROM speaks TCP/IP. With TCP/IP installed, your PC can connect to the Internet and speak to the world's multitude of networks on their own terms.

To run any of the Windows-based Web browsers, you first must run some type of TCP/IP software (often called a *TCP/IP stack*), and use it to connect to your Internet provider. Exactly how this is done will vary depending on who your provider is and what TCP/IP stack you're using. Your provider will have to tell you precisely how to log into their host system. It usually involves a password (or sometimes two passwords) and may also involve one or more numeric addresses that will need to be entered into your software. It's not really all that difficult—and once done, it doesn't have to be done again.

Running Netscape will initiate some disk activity. With Netscape, you'll know when Netscape is processing by the shooting stars displayed within the Netscape logo in the upper-right corner of the Netscape window. If you haven't changed the default Netscape configuration, you will soon see the Netscape home page on your screen, as shown in Figure 1.1.

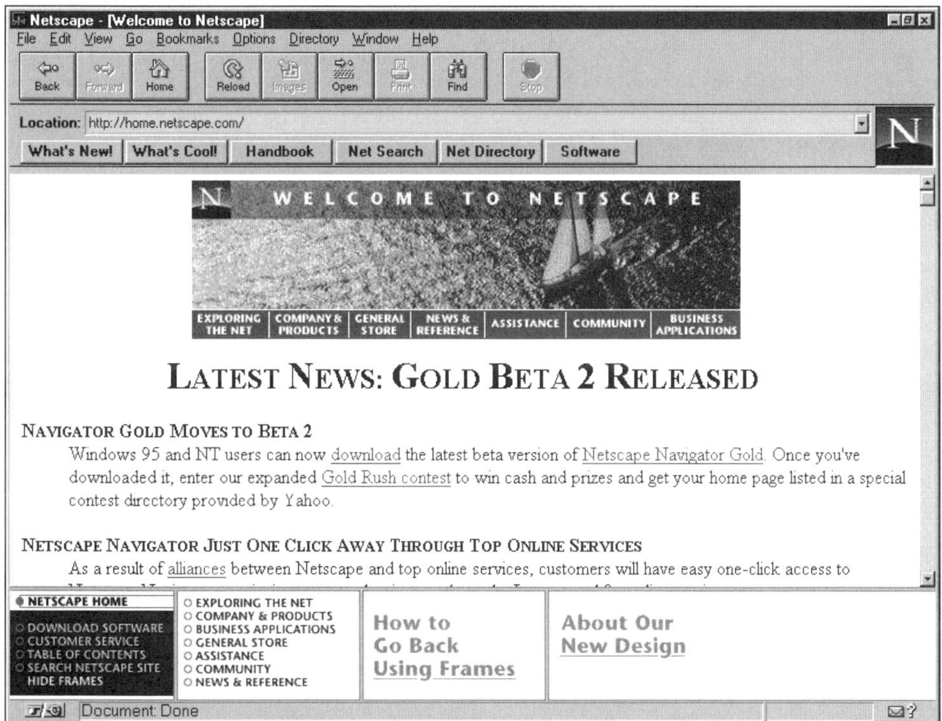

Figure 1.1 *Netscape's home page.*

Starting Netscape at its home page is not without its drawbacks. With hundreds of thousands of users downloading Netscape and accessing its home page all the time, the site is sometimes too busy to accept additional connections. Pointing Netscape to another startup location may make a lot of sense. We'll be discussing this option in a later chapter.

A Client and a Browser

Netscape, shown displaying the Netscape Communications home page in Figure 1.1, is an Internet information browser and World Wide Web (or simply Web) client. A *client* is a program that receives information from another program called a *server*, located somewhere else on a network. Documents readable from your browser may be located anywhere in the world. Assuming that there is in fact a connection between the client and the server, how far apart they are really doesn't matter.

Much as a word processor lets you view a document having special formatting features, such as boldface and underlining, Web browsers let you view Internet-based documents having similar special formatting. Web documents may contain plain text, graphic images, frames, video clips, sound files, animation, or any combination of these and other goodies.

If graphic images do not display when you run Netscape, there is no need for concern. Someone may have set the Netscape menu item Options | Auto Load Images to off. Image display is frequently turned off to accelerate Netscape performance. Graphics may take a long time to transmit over your modem line, as you'll discover very early in your career as a Web explorer. Options | Auto Load Images is a *toggle;* that is, you click on it to change it to its alternate state, much like the ON/OFF button on your TV set.

Turning off the inline image display will result in an "image" icon appearing where a graphic image would normally be displayed. (Another reason that images don't display is that Netscape may not be able to locate a particular image. I'll tell you how to handle this in a later exploration.)

Manually Loading Images

If the Auto Load Images option is turned off and you want to display a specific image without turning the option back on, click on the Images button in the toolbar. Next, click on the Reload button in the toolbar to make the image appear.

The Netscape Desktop

If you're familiar with Windows applications, you will recognize most of the features of Netscape shown in Figure 1.1.

The top line, called the *title bar*, contains the title "Netscape - " plus the title contained in the viewed document enclosed within the "[ ]" bracket pair. The title of the application used in Figure 1.1 is "Welcome to Netscape," therefore the entire title is Netscape - [Welcome to Netscape]. The standard Windows minimize, maximize, and close buttons appear on the right side of the title and Netscape's application icon appears to the left of the title.

The second line from the top contains the Netscape *menu bar*. When you click on a menu bar term, a drop-down selection menu displays. The third line is the *toolbar*, which contains a series of buttons that initiate commonly used features. Immediately below the toolbar is the *Uniform Resource Locator (URL)* Location: text box. A URL is a pointer to a Web document or service. I'll tell you everything you need to know about URLs in this book. Below the Location: text box is a row of six directory buttons that provide Netscape services and information. The big "N" Netscape logo appears to the right of the Location: text box and directory buttons. Netscape shows you it is busy working by displaying a night sky with shooting stars behind the "N." You'll know exactly what I mean soon enough.

The bottom line is the *status bar*. The status bar gives progress reports when information is being transferred, and it will also give valuable information while reading a displayed page. In Netscape parlance, the *document viewing area* is the portion of the screen between the URL display area and the status bar. Netscape has further divided this area by using a new feature called *frames*. Frames allow viewers to see different areas of a Web site at one time. You'll see how useful frames are when we discuss them in detail in a later chapter.

Figure 1.2 shows a portion of the Netscape home page with the "General Store" anchor underlined. If you point to this anchor with your mouse, the URL for the General Store will be displayed in the status bar as shown in Figure 1.2. (More on anchors later.)

The right side of the document viewing area, and occasionally the bottom of the document viewing area, contains the familiar Windows scroll bars. A vertical scroll bar is included if the displayed document is longer than a single screen page. Likewise, a horizontal scroll bar is included only if the document is wider than a single screen. The display of the toolbar, Location: text box,

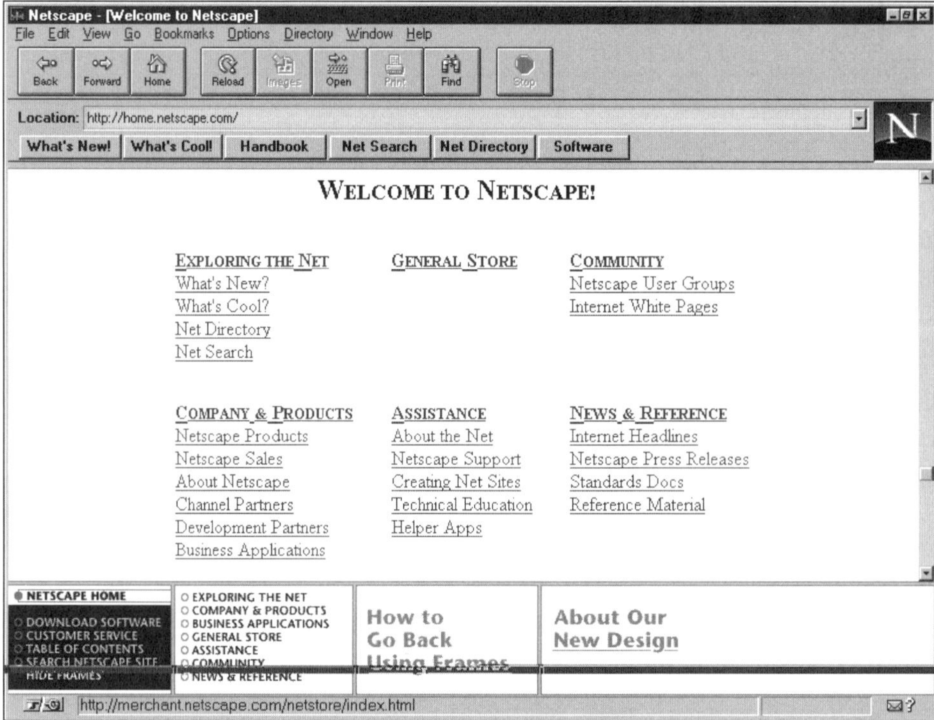

Figure 1.2 *Displaying a link's URL in the Netscape status bar.*

directory buttons, frames, and status bar are user configurable and may or may not be displayed on your screen.

Figure 1.3 shows another view of the Netscape home page. The graphic icon in the top center of the page indicates that either the Options | Auto Load Images option has been turned off (unchecked), or that the image was not received. Although the non-image mode of Netscape is not as pretty or as fun as Netscape with brightly colored graphical images, it is substantially faster. Additionally, a non-displayed image is only two mouse clicks away from being displayed.

Web Pages

Netscape is a Web browser designed to display hypermedia documents called *pages*. Hypermedia pages are created and stored in *Hyper Text Markup Language (HTML)*. We'll cover HTML in much more detail later in this book. Netscape can also display Gopher menus and documents, FTP directories and files, Java applets, and many other formats. Netscape also has built-in support for newsgroups and email services.

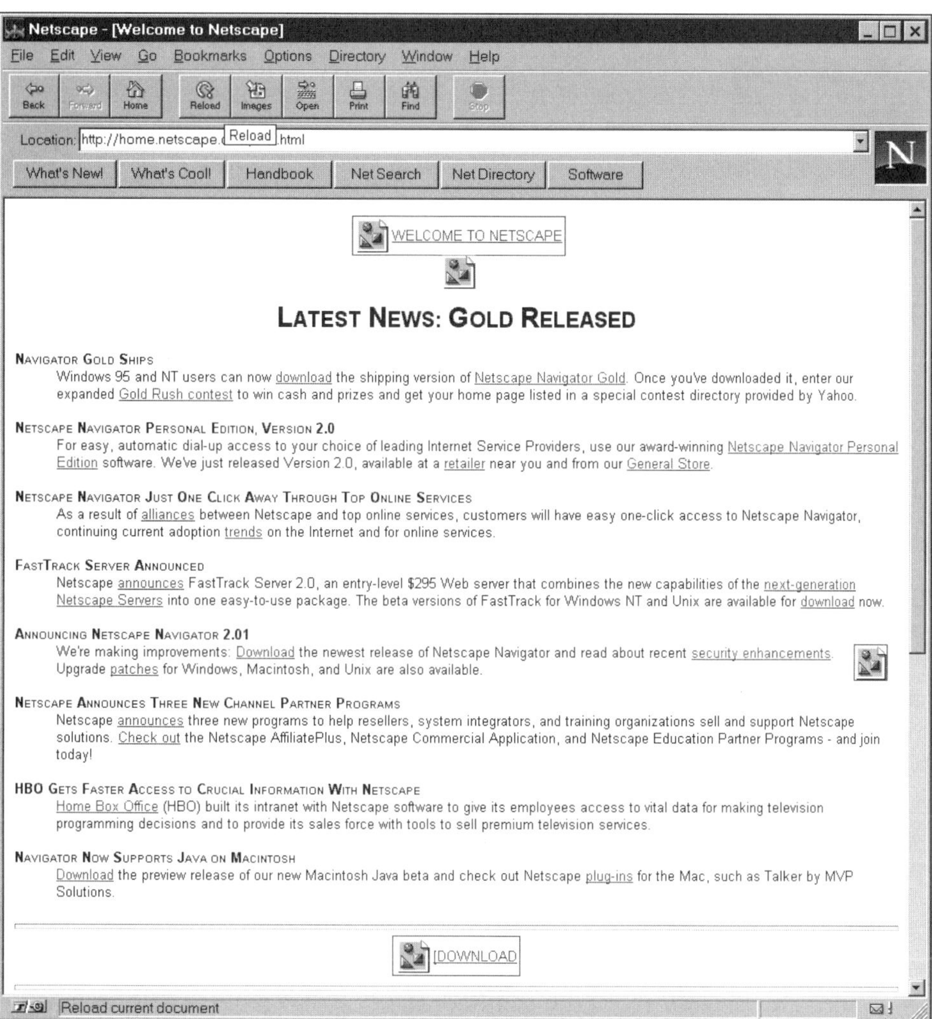

***Figure 1.3** Netscape's home page with the Auto Load Images option turned off.*

The choice of the term "page" for a Web document is unfortunate. Most computer users associate a page with what they see on the screen. Such is not the case with most Web "pages," which may be quite long. Substitute the word "document" in your head when you see the term "page," at least until the whole Web world begins to make sense. You may move through the page, as you would with any other Windows document, by moving the scroll bar pointer with the mouse or by pressing the Page Up or Page Down keys, depending upon which direction you wish to travel.

Taking Your Browser for a Spin

In this project, we'll start Netscape and test some hyperlinks. Using Netscape's search button, we'll take you to a popular Web site called Yahoo.

Depending upon the version of Netscape that you're using, you'll see that certain areas of text in the document view area are underlined, have a different color, or both. These items are *links* (technically, *hyperlinks*) to other resources and locations. These other resources may be textual or they may contain multimedia information. The purpose of these document links is to provide a nonlinear way for you to access information. Gone are the days of sequential processing and presentation. Now you can go where your interests lead you.

A hyperlink has two components: an *anchor* and a *reference*. The anchor is the displayed screen presence of the link (which may be either text or graphics) whereas the reference is the full network URL of the document or service. You see the anchor whenever the page is displayed, but the reference remains hidden. When the cursor strays over an anchor, its reference can be read in the status bar at the bottom of the screen (as we saw in Figure 1.2). When you click on a displayed anchor, Netscape will read the URL shown in the status bar, fetch the Web site, and automatically display the document, play the audio, show the movie, access the newsgroup, show the animation, or display the graphic.

Testing a Link

The row just under the Location: text box contains six directory buttons. Click on the button labeled Net Directory. Use your mouse to move the pointer across the screen. Notice that the shape of the pointer changes from an arrowhead to a pointing hand as you move to an anchor link area. To see how the hand works, scroll down the page and place the cursor in the Yahoo link. As you move the mouse pointer over the underlined Yahoo link, notice that the status line shows the complete URL link information—the reference portion—of the anchor to which the mouse is pointing. Activate the link with a single click on the underlined anchor area. Clicking on the anchor will start the process of retrieving the remote document and displaying it on your monitor. Figure 1.4 shows the Netscape display after clicking on the Yahoo anchor. The big "N" should be displaying with the "nightscape" backdrop and shooting stars, the Stop button should be temporarily red, and away we go.

With a single mouse click we have connected to another Web site, transferred the hypermedia document that was located in California, and displayed it on

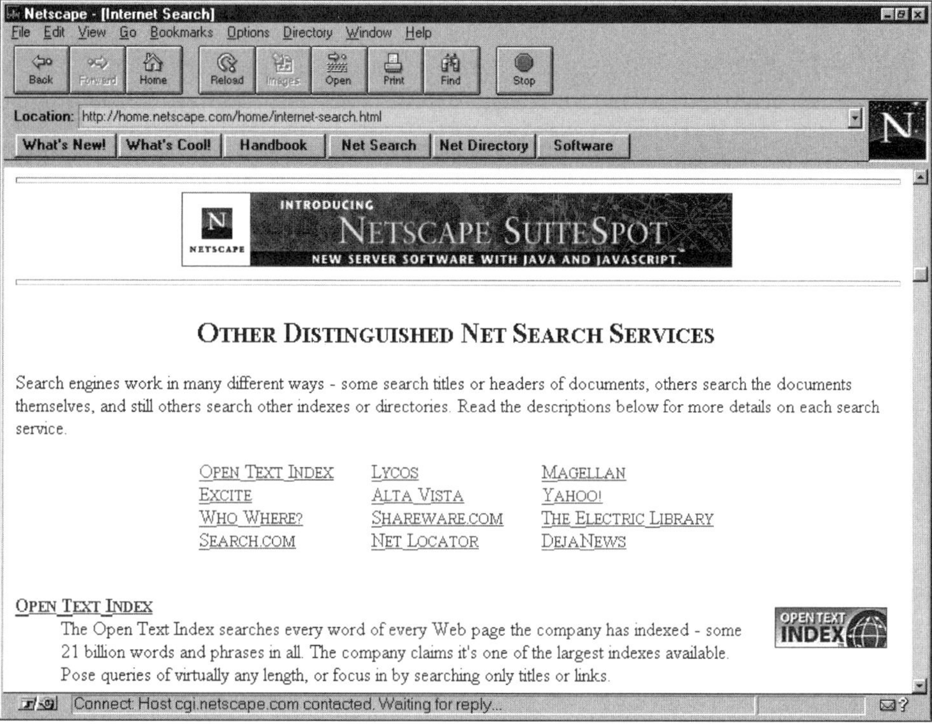

***Figure 1.4** Using Netscape's Net Directory button and the Yahoo link.*

the screen. The document could have been located anywhere in the world. Figure 1.5 shows the Yahoo document entitled "Yahoo."

The Yahoo page is one of the greatest resources on the Web. It contains pointers to thousands of sites, and seemingly grows by the minute. As you can see from Figure 1.5, the Web pointers are arranged by category. We'll spend more time with our friend Yahoo and other search engines in later explorations.

You may, of course, start to follow the links that appear on the Yahoo page. You might undertake a little side-exploration of your own. Go ahead. Feel free to explore at any point in this book, I'll always be ready and waiting for you to pick up where we left off.

Heading Home

Upon finishing an exploration, we typically want to return to our starting point and brag a little about our recent discoveries. Netscape makes it easy. The icon bar has a little stick house icon that, when clicked, returns us to the home page, the first location visited when we started the current session of

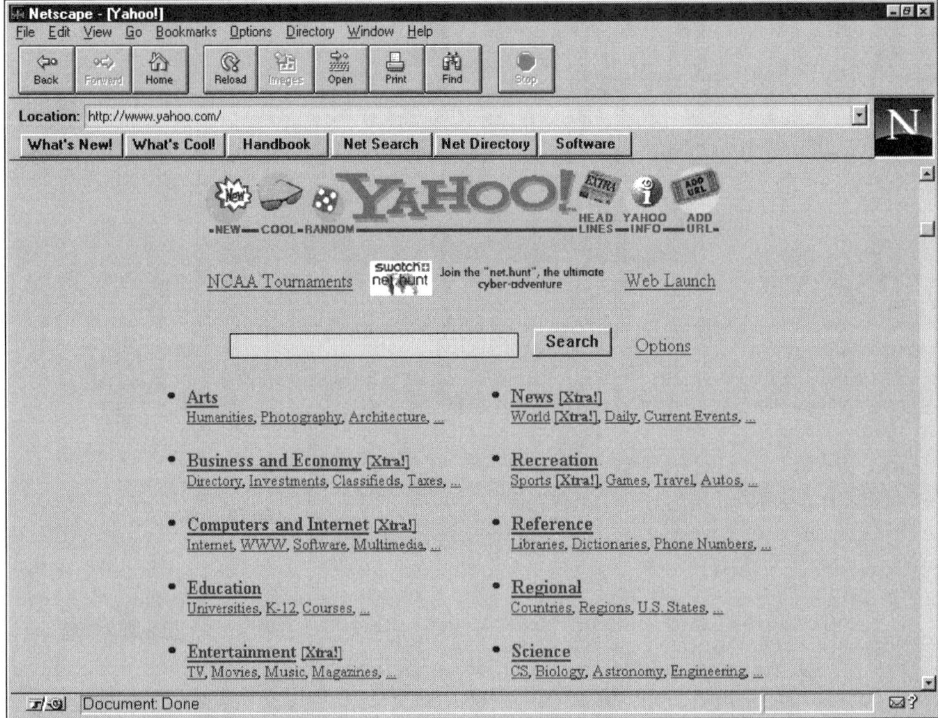

Figure 1.5 *Yahoo's home page.*

Netscape. As you might expect, we could also go directly to any intermediate stop in one step. We will explore pointing Netscape to a specific location and using "bookmarks" in Chapter 3.

We could also backtrack one step at a time, because Netscape leaves a trail of invisible breadcrumbs for us to follow. Clicking on the left pointer icon in the toolbar will take us back to the document that immediately preceded the document currently being displayed. Once we have moved backward, we may click the right pointer icon to move forward again by one document. Keep in mind that the two arrow icons can only be used to navigate along a trail you've already blazed; if you're at either end of the trail, the arrow pointing beyond trail's end will not work. Figure 1.6 shows the Back, Forward, and Home buttons.

Figure 1.6 *Netscape's Back, Forward, and Home toolbar buttons.*

NETSCAPE CONFIGURATION

Netscape is highly configurable and customizable. Frequently changed user preferences may be modified using the Options menu. (I'll have much more to say on the Options menu in later explorations.) Newer versions of Netscape have simplified the world of configuring your browser to a great degree. In the past, there was a great deal of configuring your "ini" file. The netscape.ini file is a simple text file, albeit a pretty big one. You can inspect and edit it with any text editor, including Windows Notepad or DOS EDIT. Most of what it contains is of little interest to you, the user. For the most part, netscape.ini can be transparently modified by executing menu sequences and setting your preferences on subject cards.

Netscape Preference Cards

Let's take a look at a preferences subject card. Execute the Options|General Preferences sequence, then click on the Appearance tab, if necessary. The Appearance card displays as shown in Figure 1.7.

Take a look at some of the options this card allows you to set. This should give you a better idea of some of the information that is changeable in a Netscape preferences card. Notice in Figure 1.7 that Netscape is configured to display the Netscape home page at the start of every session. After using

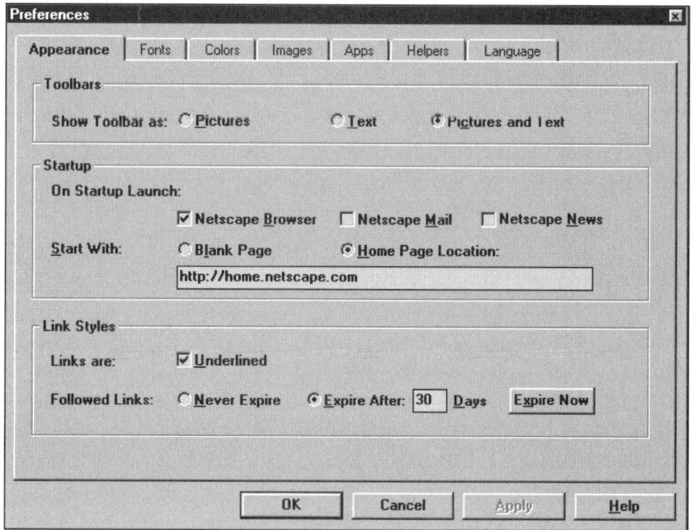

Figure 1.7 Netscape's General Preferences—Appearance card.

Netscape a few times, you may want to change your home page. We'll discuss all of Netscape's preferences cards in this book so you can customize your browser to suit your needs.

Mail and Newsgroup Features

Netscape's Mail and Newsgroup features provide a framework that simplifies your electronic communication—after reading the Mail and Newsgroup chapters, you're going to want to use Netscape as your interface to meet all your mail and news correspondence needs. Not only will you be impressed with Netscape's ease-of-use features, but you won't have to worry about switching programs while you are online because Netscape will truly become your one-stop shop.

Using the various Netscape windows you can send and retrieve messages, as well as organize your mail messages, newsgroups, and news postings. Using Netscape's mail feature you can easily send mail messages containing hypertext documents and links to Web sites. In fact, sending someone a link to your favorite Web site has never been easier. Netscape also provides an Address Book that you'll find handy and easy to use.

Frames

Frame technology was developed by Netscape in an attempt to help people as they navigate through the Web. As you will see, it is often difficult to follow where you are on the Internet as you click from link to link. Sometimes you'll lose sight of your original document. Frames help keep your feet grounded on a particular site, so to speak. The Netscape home page is a great example of frames. Click on a topic in the lower left frame, and the larger frame above reflects the information. For example, click on the Table of Contents link in the lower-left frame. The Table of Contents page should display as shown in Figure 1.8.

Notice the lower frames stay put while the upper frame changes to reflect our link selection. The lower-left frame continues to display the other available links, with the Table of Contents link boxed, serving as a "You Are Here" arrow. Without frames, the "other available links" would be nowhere to be found—clicking on a link would have taken us away from our original page. You would have to return to the original page, Netscape's home page in this example, to see the links.

Other uses of frames are sure to arise. Some examples are already out there, such as displaying graphics, animations, or video clips in one frame and text

Figure 1.8 *Netscape's Table of Contents page.*

in another. We'll be discussing frames in detail in later chapters; you'll get a good feel for how frames can be used and what to expect in the near future.

HTML, Java Applets, and JavaScript

Hyper Text Markup Language, HTML, has long (well, long in Internet terms) been the coding source for Web documents. We'll discuss how to create, view, and read HTML coding later in this book. We owe formatting and linking features on the Internet to HTML, and it is worthwhile to learn a little about it. Don't be intimidated by its appearance, HTML is really rather simple and easily learned. In fact, you'll probably soon be feeling comfortable enough to create your own HTML documents, which I'll show you how to do in Part 2.

Java is the newest programming language on the netblock. It's the hot topic, and it's no wonder why. Java will be opening new doors for everyone, and its effects are sure to create changes across the board. So far only two browsers contain the Java Virtual Machine, which allows the browser to read Java coding. Netscape is one, and the other is the SUN Microsystem's browser, Hot

Java (which makes sense, because James Gosling, the designer of Java, heads the technology arm of SUN's Java development operation). On the simple level, Java applets can grant small favors like animated text or interactive illustrations (such as a site with a circuit simulator instead of a circuit diagram). Figure 1.9 shows a neat animated Java applet that is used on the Coriolis Group's "Get a Jump on Java" Web site. Of course, you can't see the animation effects on a static printed page, but take my word—it's really cool. (To see the Java applet yourself, go to http://www.coriolis.com/java).

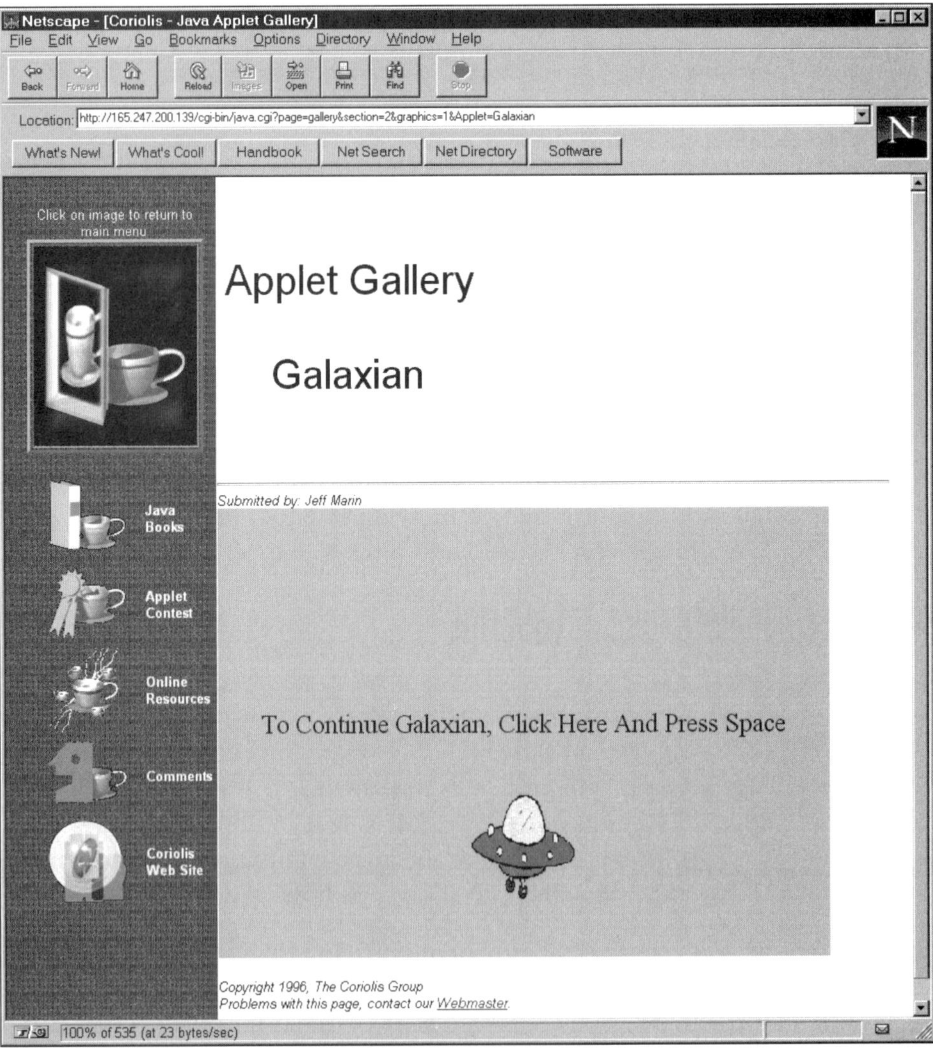

Figure 1.9 *An animated applet from Coriolis Group's "Get a Jump on Java" Web site.*

Java applets can be strung together to provide real time graphics, applications, and information, such as the Wall Street Web site showing a moving graph of the activity on Wall Street. JavaScript, a derivative of the Java programming language, allows you to build simple scripts that can perform calculations or configure your browser within Netscape. With Java, Web servers can send more than static HTML pages; they can also send full-fledged applications. You'll be hearing a lot more about Java and the Java Virtual Machine in the future, so it is important that we discuss Java in this book. I think you'll find the chapters on Java applets and JavaScript fascinating.

Plug-Ins

One of the key new Netscape features that everyone is talking about on the Web, next to Java applets and JavaScript, is plug-ins. Plug-ins give you the ability to turn Netscape into your own custom software package. In fact, you can think of Netscape as simply a shell that you can add to and create your own individualized browser. By downloading and installing different types of plug-ins, you can have Web-surfing abilities that your entire neighborhood will be jealous of.

Shortly after Netscape introduced plug-ins, hundreds of them starting appearing on the Web. Currently, you can find plug-ins for a myriad of tasks including playing multimedia content, viewing Acrobat files, playing animation files, developing and displaying visual presentations, and much more. Figure 1.10 shows you what one plug-in looks like. Prior to the new Netscape, most plug-ins ran as helper applications and didn't operate within Netscape itself. The new plug-ins work in conjunction with Netscape, and Netscape will automatically access the plug-ins when it needs them. As you can guess, this gives you powerful features that were not available in the past.

In Chapter 5 I'll show you how to download plug-ins from the Web and use them to supercharge your version of Netscape. I'll also introduce you to the leading plug-ins that are available today.

A PEEK AT THE FUTURE

Netscape has given us a peek into their future with the new release of Atlas, a preview release of a new version of Netscape. Atlas is in the very early stages of its existence, but some of what it offers will change the way we think of the Internet. One of its most important features is called CoolTalk,

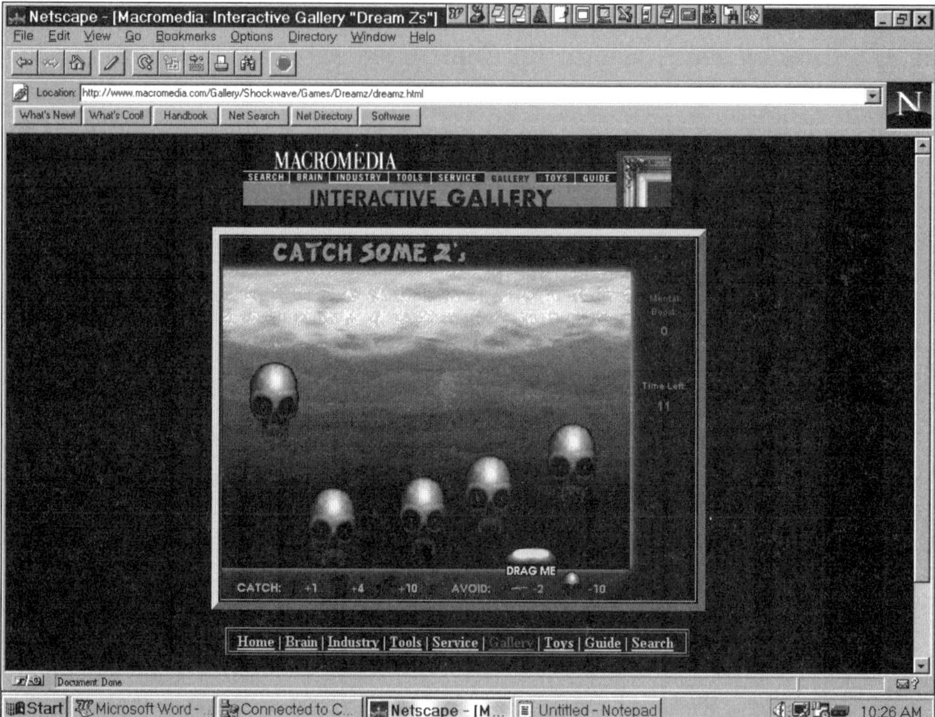

Figure 1.10 The Macromedia plug-in for Netscape.

which I'll tell you more about in Chapter 6. CoolTalk allows Netscape users to talk to each other across the Internet. Not just send messages, but actually talk, using microphones or a keyboard chat feature. It even has a whiteboard, so you can send copies of your latest work of art and talk about it with your friends at the same time. Figure 1.11 shows what CoolTalk looks like.

Many people have predicted that Web browsers like Netscape will change the way we use the Internet. Of that there can be no question. Taking the prognostication just a bit further, I believe that the World Wide Web will change

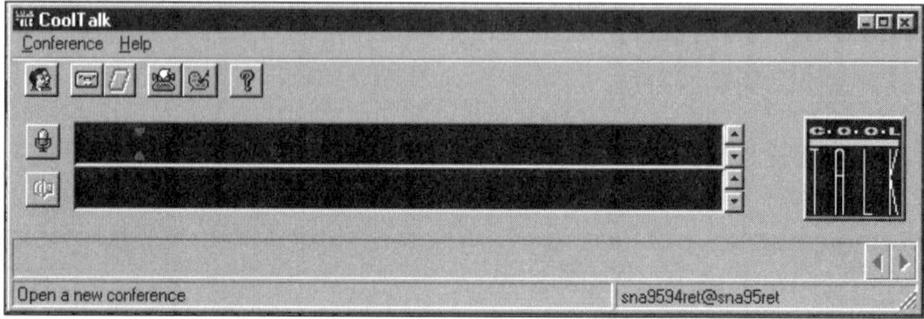

Figure 1.11 The CoolTalk window.

the very way people live. Our society, and our educational system, has in the past highly rewarded people who could perform repetitive tasks. The economy of the United States, as well as that of most other industrialized countries, has switched from being chiefly product-based to being service-based. In other words, many of us no longer make things so much as we *do* things. More and more, creative problem solvers are a highly sought-after commodity.

No doubt history will confirm that the World Wide Web is the future of the Internet, and that browsers like Netscape will become required applications of Internet-based information. The emergence of the Web has ushered in the era of online information for the masses. Now technological advances like Java scripting are blazing new trails for Internet usage. Who can fathom where all of this will take us in 5 years—or in the next 6 months, for that matter.

LET'S REVIEW

Netscape is a Web browser designed to display the hypertext documents that comprise Web pages. Web browsers and the Web itself are often confused as being the same thing—which they are not. Think of the Web as a conceptual world-spanning hypertext document, and Netscape as the tool used for viewing and navigating the world-wide document. Each Web site consists of multiple text files connected by hyperlinks (generally shortened to "links") that are pointers to other documents or locations on the Internet. The Web may be read non-sequentially by following links as need or interest requires.

Netscape can be launched by double-clicking on its icon. You'll automatically see the Netscape Communication's home page when Netscape starts (unless you have modified your Preferences).

Links consist of a visible anchor, which is a text string or an image (such as a button), and a reference, the URL or address pointer to another hypertext document. The shape of the mouse pointer will change from an arrow to a pointing hand as it moves over an anchor. The URL of the link under the pointer will be displayed in Netscape's status bar. Clicking once on an anchor will display the referenced file.

Movement within a document can be accomplished a line at a time using the up or down arrow keys, a page at a time using the Page Up and Page Down keys, or in sections using the scroll bars to navigate through the document at will.

Clicking on the home page icon (the "stick house") will redisplay the home page that started the session. Unless Netscape was modified by you, another user, or your Internet provider, the defined home page will be Netscape's home page. The left and right arrow icons allow navigation over a path that has been traveled at least once.

HTML provides the background information that Netscape needs to display the pages and graphics of Web sites. You can create your own HTML documents and view HTML source codes using the Netscape browser. Netscape is currently one of only two browsers capable of viewing Java programs called *Java applets*. Java allows the transmission of animated, interactive, and real time graphics and applications. Netscape also now supports the JavaScript language developed by the creators of Netscape.

With all the new technology bolting through our modem lines, we need to remember to get a firm grasp on the basics—it will keep our lives considerably simpler in the long run. Therefore, the goal of this book is to provide you with a solid foundation for using Netscape and the Web, but, with the way things are changing, I recommend you keep one eye on this book and one eye on your monitor—you never know what's going to happen out there next!

Getting Your Bearings on the Web

Before making any further explorations on the Web, you'll want to read this chapter to understand where Netscape and the Web have come from and where they are headed.

Now that you've seen Netscape in action and had a little taste test of the Web, you're probably anxious to spend the rest of the day surfing the Web. Once you get started, you'll get so consumed by the seductive power of the Web that you won't want to return to the day-to-day world of spreadsheets or tax programs. But before we get into the fun explorations such as searching the Web, creating home pages with HTML, and creating multimedia publishing projects, we need to get some concepts and terminology under our belts.

Many book authors like to tell you a lot more than you want (or need) to know about a particular topic. I'll try not to be guilty of this sin. However, one lingering fact remains: We are dealing with a sometimes highly technical topic—to wit, computer networks and very sophisticated software. When you run Netscape, it sometimes seems to have a mind of its own. How much detail do you need to become a Netscape user who is able to surf the Web with ease and eventually learn the art of Web publishing?

Which technical details of the Internet do we cover and which do we leave out? Well, the answer lies somewhere between what I know and what you need to know to become a contented Web surfer and publisher. I promise to find the right mix. If it's really important, I'll include it in one of our base camp briefings, of which this is the first. If it's nice to know, but not a matter of urgent need, I'll place it someplace else, probably in an appendix.

Now that the campfire is ablaze and I've struck a jargon deal with you, let's get down to business.

A Brief History of Netscape and the World Wide Web

Every age has a major development that ushers in a new way of living and thinking. The invention of the printing press, the commercialization of electricity, and the introduction of the automobile come to mind as such landmark developments. I believe future historians will record that the introduction of the World Wide Web and browsers like Netscape and Mosaic were the seminal developments ushering in the age of near-instantaneous information search and delivery for the masses.

Netscape, and its predecessor Mosaic, were designed to satisfy the need to provide a friendly interface for accessing organized information on the Internet. The Internet has always contained an incredible amount of information. However, it was almost impossible to find anything of value except by word of mouth. Before the advent of the Web and Gopher (a menu-oriented information finding utility), the organization of information on the Internet might charitably be described as chaotic. There were few real lists of information, and organization was a concept that didn't seem to apply. Someone would send you an email message extolling the features of a new program, or a new source of data, and away you'd go to find it. Sometimes you would be successful, but other times the object of the quest had vanished in cyberspace before you reached it. As a result, frustration was the order of the day.

It's been a long road from there to here. Let's take a look at the route.

In the Beginning: FTP

The Internet has always been a vast depository of information, assistance, and software. The problem, until a few years ago, was that people couldn't find what they wanted. Although no one person knows where everything is, the gap between knowing something might be "out there" and actually finding where it is has narrowed considerably.

Almost from the beginning, a person using the Internet could transfer files between networks. Cooperating networks would agree upon a protocol allowing file transfer; this protocol eventually came to be called *FTP (File Transfer Protocol)*. Internet insiders often use lowercase letters for the FTP acronym, so if you see "ftp" in the literature (this book and others) it's not a typo—just a holdover from Unix, where somebody once decided that capital letters were déclassé. A *protocol* is simply a set of rules governing digital communication, specifying certain commands, appropriate responses, and what these commands and their responses mean in different contexts. Most human interaction involves protocols of one sort or another. An auction is a fairly simple protocol for both establishing a market price and making a sale, all at the same time. You might even say that the protocol for this book is the English language. The Internet is really a catalog of protocols governing how various sorts of client programs interact with their appropriate server programs in the cause of orderly location and retrieval of data.

You may have already used FTP to get a file, or program, from a distant site. If you haven't, don't worry. You can use Netscape or another browser to retrieve files from FTP servers, even if you don't know a thing about FTP. (That's one of the seriously cool things about Netscape.) But one problem that occurs frequently is that you know file abc.xyz is exactly what you need—but you don't know where it resides. How can you find it?

Hello, Archie

Archie was the first major attempt to organize Internet information that was otherwise scattered with no apparent pattern. If there was an organizational model in the storage of files reachable via FTP, it certainly escaped most mere mortals. A group of dedicated people at McGill University in Canada designed Archie, and the transition from Internet chaos to organization was launched.

Today, an Archie server periodically searches up to 3,100 publicly available, anonymous FTP server sites and can build a database of over 7 million records containing unique file names and associated information, such as the home of the FTP server and the directory in which the file resides. You can then use an Archie client program to query the Archie database about the location of file abc.xyz. We will use Netscape to find and then retrieve a remote file through FTP in a later exploration.

While Archie was a big step forward, it didn't fully solve the problem. If you knew the name of the file, you were home free, but if you didn't know the name, you were out of luck, since Archie doesn't know about file contents, only file *names*.

If you don't know that file n32e20.exe is the latest Windows 95 version of Netscape 2.0 and its associated support files (or that n16e20.exe is the latest version of Netscape 2.0 for Windows 3.1), you're clueless as to Netscape's whereabouts.

Giving Teeth to the Internet: Gopher

About four years ago (a lifetime in Internet terms), two ambitious attempts to organize Internet information were independently initiated. One, called Gopher, began its life at the University of Minnesota. The second, called the World Wide Web (or simply the Web), emerged from the European Laboratory for Particle Physics (CERN, the French acronym) in Geneva, Switzerland.

Both Gopher and the Web (in fact, most Internet services of any kind) are *client/server* systems requiring a client program on the user side and a server program on the "big" system side where the "served" information resides. The client and server programs engage in a dialog over the Net, usually defining what information the client's user wants. The server then serves up the requested information in a form that the client can in turn present to its user.

Gopher is a hierarchical menu-structured organizational technique, defined in a set of protocols for client and server software. Cooperating Gopher sites organize their information in the format defined by the Gopher protocols and supported by Gopher server software. The result is an intuitive interface that yields as much information and detail as the organizers desired. The first Gopher site was brought online in 1992.

Most Web browsers (including Netscape and Mosaic) understand the Gopher data protocols, and Gopher sites can be accessed effectively from those browsers.

The World Wide Web

Now, the biggie. The Web is a system for organizing, transmitting, and retrieving information of all types. As mentioned earlier, the Web was originally conceived and developed at the CERN laboratory in Switzerland.

Central to the idea and organization of the Web are *hypermedia documents*. A hypermedia document is one that may be traversed in a non-linear fashion, via links from one place in a document to another, or between entirely separate document files. A hypermedia document may contain pointers to another hypermedia document, which also may contain a pointer to another document, and so on. Another hallmark of hypermedia documents is that they may contain non-textual material as well as plain text. An example of non-textual material could be a graphic image, a sound file, or a video clip.

So seamless are the links between different hypermedia documents that users literally follow these pathways all over the world without ever knowing the actual location of the information—unless choosing to stop to ask. Although these documents are truly hypermedia, since they may contain various information, they are almost always called hypertext documents in the literature. In this book, I will use the term "hypertext." But remember that Web-based documents are always hypermedia in nature.

We saw an example of non-linear reading of a hypertext document in the first exploration in Chapter 1. When we clicked on the Net Directory button we arrived at Netscape's "Exploring the Net" page. The first option was the "Excite" link. If we search using that link, we are connected to the Excite database. This site has more than 1.5 million Web page links arranged by categories. An added bonus is that the database is searchable. (There is an entire future exploration devoted to searching.) If we see something we like, we just click on the anchor link to retrieve the information. Think what a breakthrough this concept represents! If we are reading a book and find a topic on which we need additional information, we must first mark our current spot, then go to the index and find the location within the book of the desired information. Next we must go to the selected supportive information, and finally, go back to our original starting point. The search process is even more difficult if the desired level of detail is not contained in the same book.

Now look at the wonderful capability provided by Netscape: When we desire additional information on a topic, we click on the link that points to the supplemental knowledge, read the more detailed information, maybe even going down multiple levels for progressively more detailed information, and then automatically return to the original starting point. The additional information may reside halfway around the world or in the next room. Where it actually exists simply doesn't matter.

The Web, along with hypermedia servers and clients, predates Netscape and even Mosaic. The first browser developed at CERN was a character-based (that is, non-graphic) implementation. CERN wasn't being lazy for doing text-only processing. Virtually all Internet-related programs were character-based until very recently. The reasoning was strictly practical because almost everyone accessing the Internet was using a non-graphical (text-based) terminal over a relatively slow serial line.

That character-based Web browser from CERN was not a lot of fun to use and tended to be cryptic in operation. As a consequence, few network administrators put their information into Web-browsable format until the official introduction of Mosaic in early 1993. Upon Mosaic's release, there were perhaps 100 Web servers in the world. Since that day, there has been an explosion in the number of Web server sites and in the volume of information contained on those sites. Web-related Internet traffic has been growing at a phenomenal rate. One demographic survey revealed that of the 37 million people aged 16 and over in the United States and Canada who have access to the Internet, 18 million have used the Web in the past three months. And as far as browsers for the Web go, despite Mosaic's early start, Netscape is the overwhelming browser of choice for most Web users. The Netscape home page alone receives 40 million hits per day, which is more than 1 billion hits a month.

Birth of a Browser

Development of Mosaic took place at the National Center for Supercomputing Applications (NCSA) located at the University of Illinois, Urbana-Champaign. Federal grants were the primary source of Mosaic project funding. As a tip of the hat to this government largess, NCSA Mosaic, while copyrighted by the university, is distributed without cost.

In addition to the development and enhancement of Mosaic, NCSA also maintains an up-to-date group of documents. The "NCSA What's New" page is a frequently accessed page in Web-land. We will be showing you how to load a URL (Web document address) shortly, but in case you already know the technique, the URL for NCSA's "What's New" page is:

```
http://www.ncsa.uiuc.edu/SDG/Software/Mosaic/Docs/whats-new.html
```

The URL for the NCSA home page is:

```
http://www.ncsa.uiuc.edu/General/NCSAHome.html
```

Most Netscape sessions start at the Netscape home page (http://home.netscape.com), as we explained in Chapter 1. Any location that you desire may become your starting point by changing one field in your Netscape preference menu. Changing the starting location is not a bad idea since sometimes it can be difficult to connect to Netscape due to the high demands placed on Netscape's computers. If you get strange error messages when starting your Netscape session, it may be the system's convoluted way of telling you that you are receiving a Netscape busy signal.

Both Netscape and Gopher are frequently touted as do-all to end-all data management clients. In actuality, they are just the glamorous and highly visible pointers to information resources stored on the Internet. The genuinely incredible part of the Web and *gopherspace* (the system of menus that the Gopher client understands) is the underlying organization of the information. In less than two years, informational structure replaced chaos. The Internet's amazing growth can be easily attributed to the information organization coupled with user-friendly access.

The evolving profile of the average Internet user reflects the impact of the Internet's organized information and easy access. Four years ago, it was almost impossible for someone who was not an academic, corporate researcher, or government contractor to get an Internet account. Indeed, as recently as the summer of 1992, I taught at a college that would not generally give its own students Internet accounts. The new wave of Internet users tends to be less sophisticated in the use of the arcane ways of the old guard and their beloved Unix command-line prompts. Mastering the difficulty of information access used to be a badge of honor. The new breed of user has demanded the same ease of Internet accessibility and user friendliness that they have come to expect from their windowed Mac and PC environments. When time is at a premium, the value of information becomes a function of the ease with which it may be obtained. Long live the new breed!

Not only has the number of Web and Gopher servers increased geometrically, the amount of information stored on most of these servers has seen an astonishing increase. To give you some idea of the rapid growth of graphical Web browsers, virtually all Internet books bearing a 1993 copyright don't even mention Mosaic!

An Explosion of Browsers

Although Netscape and Mosaic get most of the Web browser glory, it's only fair to point out that the first release of Mosaic and the first release of Cello (a browser from Cornell University) were very nearly simultaneous. Cello was a more modest effort, but it does many of the same things that Mosaic does.

After those two browsers proved the concept, the deluge began. NCSA licensed the Mosaic source code through a company called Spyglass, and several firms began developing commercial offshoots of Mosaic. The best-known of these is AirMosaic, which became part of a suite of Internet client utilities offered as a commercial product from Spry, Inc.

Both Netscape and Mosaic require a fair amount of memory (ideally, at least 8MB) to function well. To cater to people whose machines have only 4MB of memory, the WinWeb browser was released in mid-1994. Both Cello and WinWeb were created to be tight with system resources, although they lack some of the functionality of "bigger" browsers like Netscape and Mosaic.

Mark Andreesen, the NCSA lead programmer who created the original Mosaic program, left the University of Illinois in the spring of 1994 and helped to start a firm, Netscape Communications, to capitalize on the emerging market for Web servers and browsers. In a remarkably short period of time, the Netscape browser appeared, with more speed and more features than recent versions of Mosaic while requiring neither more memory nor the awkward Win32s subsystem. Nicknamed "Mozilla" (after Netscape's cartoon dinosaur mascot), the browser is distributed free (to employees of academic institutions, non-profit organizations, and for evaluation purposes) from Netscape's Web site. Netscape's main product line is a full service browser offering links to services such as email, gopher, ftp, netnews, and a number of Web servers with necessary commerce-oriented features like encrypted credit card transfer and digital cash transfer. With features like secure credit card shopping built into the Netscape Web browser, Andreesen and Co. (frequently called NCSA West on the Web) are hoping that broad free distribution of the browser will generate demand for their big-money Web server line.

Another player is InternetWorks, a Web browser designed from the outset as a one-stop entry point for all Internet services, including NetNews, email, Gopher, ftp, chat, and (of course) the World Wide Web. InternetWorks is also available in free form with some of its features disabled. More and more products that began simply as Web browsers are adding more features. Conversly, popular online services such as America Online, CompuServe, and Prodigy now offer Web browsers as part of their packaged services. More and more products are converging on the ideal of *one place to stand for all Internet access.* That is, one program to run, not a dozen.

Where in the World Are We Going?

The past has shown us a world of explosive growth for the Web and interactive browsers. New operating systems like Windows 95 have Web browsers built right in. Even popular Windows programs like Word for Windows can support Web browsing. So what's in store for the future?

New software applications like the Coriolis Group's NetSeeker™ are designed to give you another glimpse of the future. These applications, called *intelligent agents*, are designed to sneak out to the Web as you are performing other tasks and locate software and other goodies for you. Then, they bring located software back to your computer and install it. As the Web grows in complexity and the day-to-day traffic increases, these types of intelligent agents will certainly become much more valuable.

UNIFORM RESOURCE LOCATORS [URLs]

When viewing a web document with Netscape or any other Web browser, the links (displayed underlined and in blue under Windows) contain hidden information pointing to the actual location and type of data at the far end of the link. This information is contained in an address called a *Uniform Resource Locator*, or URL.

Think of a URL as a standardized pointer to an Internet resource. The resource might be a graphic, sound, or just a plain text file. URLs are also used to initiate Gopher, Telnet, and FTP (File Transfer Protocol) sessions. A URL may fetch the latest postings from favorite newsgroups. URLs can also point to queries, which are documents stored deep within a database.

In many cases, it's convenient to conceptualize a URL as the network equivalent of the standard DOS pathname and filename. In fact, a URL can point to a file on our PC. A URL can also point to a specific file in a specific directory on a remote network machine. A target file may reside on a Web server located anywhere in the world. The general concept underlying a URL is, "If it's somewhere out there on the Internet, we can point to it." In this section we will explore some of the more common URLs.

I showed the Netscape home page in Chapter 1 (see Figure 1.1). The figure has the URL for this document displayed in the URL viewing area, located below the line containing the toolbar with the Netscape icons.
By entering the following URL

```
http://home.netscape.com/
```

we would bring back the Netscape home page. Let's look at a few fundamentals.

A URL has several components. The first part tells the browser what type of document is being requested. This is the "http://" prefix in the URL shown above. The acronym "http" stands for *hypertext transport protocol.*

The "http" determines the protocol used by both the Web server and client. (Recall that Netscape is a Web client.) A protocol is a standardized method of communication that we humans call a language. If you speak French and don't understand English and I speak English and don't understand French, we can't communicate very well. Turning up the volume or trying very hard doesn't help.

The idea behind a protocol is to have one language that is common to all parties. Some of the common Web protocols, in addition to http, are gopher, telnet, ftp, news, and file. A colon separates the protocol from the remainder of the URL.

The second part of the URL, "home.netscape.com" in this example, is the Internet address that contains the server software. This address contains several levels. The "com" part in this example is called the *top-level domain* and indicates that the site is a commercial organization. The "netscape" portion is commonly called the *domain* and indicates that this site is Netscape Communications located in California. The "home" portion indicates a specific network at the Netscape domain, the Web network at Netscape Communications.

Some URLs continue with a name of the *directory structure* and the actual file name of the target file. For example:

```
http://home.netscape.com/home/internet-directory.html
```

In this example, "/home" is the directory structure, and "/internet-directory" is the file name. The "html" extension is the convention for a file that is in Web standard hypertext. The acronym *HTML* stands for *HyperText Markup Language*, and it is a document standard allowing fancy formatted hypermedia text to be expressed in plain text characters. We will talk more about HTML later.

Using the "/" in a URL

Some Web servers strictly enforce the URL standard that states that a URL should be terminated with a "/" slash. If your browser chokes when given a URL as shown above, append a "/" at the end. For example:

```
http://home.netscape.com/home/internet-directory.html/
```

You will frequently see an http:// type of URL without a file name at the end. Most Web servers (the software on the sending end that interfaces with your browser) are configured to look for a file named "index.html" (or "index.htm" on a PC server without Windows 95) if no file name is specified. Keep this in mind when you create your own home page.

The protocol designation, http in this case, is case-independent as is the URL's domain name. However, the path and file names are case-sensitive if the target resides on a Unix-based machine. When copying a URL, it is best to enter the URL exactly as you see it in the original.

Certain characters may not appear in a URL; the most notable prohibited character is a blank. To overcome this problem, there is a special encoding scheme used to represent prohibited characters. The scheme begins with a percent sign "%" followed by two hexadecimal digits (0..9, A..F). As an example, the code for a blank is "%20". (You technical types will recognize that hex 20 is ASCII 32, both of which indicate a blank.)

Watch Your Case

Before we go any further, I have a few words of warning about URLs. As you know, a URL has several components. What you may not know is that entering the components can be a source of potential error, especially for DOS users. Pathnames usually contain the names of directories, subdirectories, and file names. A DOS pathname might be:

```
C:\WINDOWS\NETSCAPE.INI
```

which points to the file NETSCAPE.INI in the directory \WINDOWS on drive C:. DOS commands are not case sensitive, so you may type the above path as:

```
c:\windows\netscape.ini
```

When you are accessing URLs on the Web, life is not so simple. All lowercase pathnames may not work on the Web if the Web server is running the Unix operating system (and most Web servers do). Unlike DOS, Unix is case-sensitive. Take a look at the following URL.

```
http://home.netscape.com/escapes/index.html
```

Unix will allow you to use uppercase or lowercase letters in domain names (such as home.netscape.com in the above example) because domain names are *not* case sensitive. However, path names (escapes, in this example) must be entered exactly as they appear on the Web page. To a Unix-based server, "Escapes" and "escapes" are not the same thing. If you receive some type of error message after manually entering a URL, check your entered case very carefully.

Understanding Network Ports

All networks connected to the Internet have a series of ports. Conceptually, ports have been compared to apartment unit numbers in postal addresses—specifying a unit number (port) for your Uncle Ebb directs your correspondence directly to Ebb's mailbox, bypassing all other residents in his apartment complex. Ports also specify what type of correspondence you want to send. Are you logging in? transferring files? sending email? Network ports are very much like the serial communication ports on your PC. You may have a mouse connected to COM1 and a modem connected to COM2. Your serial controller card expects rodent-type things on COM1 and telephone-type things on COM2.

The default port for the http protocol is 80. It is not necessary to explicitly declare port 80. If the desired http port is something other than 80, it must specified. Each protocol has a different default port. Let's assume that the HTML document gems.html resides on port 1213 of network www.state.pen.edu in the directory /you-call/we-haul. Its URL would be:

```
http://www.state.pen.edu:1213/you-call/we-haul/gems.html
```

http URLs

One of the most common of all URLs is http, which stands for Hypertext Transport Protocol. http servers are common because they deliver hypertext documents using a low-overhead protocol that takes advantage of the fact that a link pointer may be embedded directly in http documents. The embedded pointers are efficient since http doesn't have to support full features, such as those employed by FTP and Gopher.

The general form of an http URL is:

```
http://host[:port][/path-name][/file-name]
```

Remember that the port is explicitly specified only if it is something other than 80—its default. Many times the pathname and filename are omitted, such as:

```
http://www.charm.net
```

If no path is specified, the server looks in the defaulted path. As stated previously, if a file is not specified, the server initially looks for a file named "index.html" in the specified, or default, path. The advantage of unspecified path and file names is that the location of the start-up file, and subsequently read files, may be moved to another location without the necessity of changing the URL sent by the client.

ftp URLs

FTP stands for File Transfer Protocol. Cooperating networks have dedicated portions of their disk storage system for anonymous public access. Anonymous access simply means that you can download a file from an FTP server even though you do not have an account on the host network system. A Web browser, such as Netscape or Mosaic, makes what is otherwise a fairly arduous process a snap. We will have a future exploration dedicated to FTPing. The general form of an FTP URL is:

```
ftp://[userid[:password]@]host[:port][/path-name][/file-name]
```

The default port for FTPing is 21, which does not have to be explicitly specified unless it is something other than 21.

Entering an FTP URL without a trailing file name causes the display of the path's directory contents. This may be a big help if you know the directory but you are not sure of the name of the latest version of the desired file.

The prevalent FTP mode is anonymous. An anonymous session is initiated by entering "anonymous" (must be lowercase; however, "ftp" usually works) as the user name followed by entering the user's full Internet email address as the password. (Usually "userid@" is enough since the FTP server knows the domain name of the connected network.) If the [userid[:password]@] portion of the FTP's URL is omitted, anonymous mode is assumed. There are FTP servers that require something other than "anonymous" as a userid. Additionally, if you actually have an account on a remote network, you may perform an FTP login using your real login name and password. Let's assume that Jane Doe has an account on network "big.deal.com"; let's additionally assume that Jane's userid is janedoe, her password is 123abc, and that her home pathname is /home/janedoe. Jane's FTP URL would be:

```
ftp://janedoe:123abc@big.deal.com/home/janedoe
```

While running Netscape, the above entry would produce a listing of her home directory. Since she would have read and write privileges in her home directory, she could send and receive files. If either the userid or password is specified, the "@" character must be included.

gopher URLs

Gopher is a text search and retrieval system named after the mascot of the University of Minnesota, where Gopher was created. (Aren't you glad you didn't go to this school and have to wear their T-shirts?) A Gopher server treats the hierarchy of Internet databases, directories, and files as a series of menus, which you can browse through to find specific information. Of course, the easiest way to access Gopher sites is by using a gopher URL.

The general form of a gopher URL is:

```
gopher://host[:port]/document-type[/path-name][/file-name]
```

Gopher's default port is 70 and it does not have to be explicitly specified, unless it is something other than 70. The document type tells the Gopher server what file type is expected by the client. As an example, a document type of "1" represents a top-level menu. Once you get below a top-level menu, the gopher URL will have a file name and most likely a path name. The URL for the top-level menu at the University of Minnesota—where Gopher was invented—is:

```
gopher://gopher.micro.umn.edu/1
```

The URL to get to the New Jersey menu on the University of Illinois at Urbana-Champaign weather Gopher is:

```
gopher://wx.atmos.uiuc.edu/11/States/New%20Jersey
```

Note the "%20" encoding method to overcome the blank prohibition in a URL.

telnet URLs

Telnet is a remote logon protocol. In its simplest form Telnet allows "live" connections to another network. An account on the remote system is typically required. Your initial login sequence looks exactly as it would if you were logging into the system from a local terminal. More advanced uses of Telnet, such as logging into a remote library, may require an account or password. Telnet is more powerful than FTP because it lets you do more than just access files from a remote computer. With Telnet, you can actually log into a network and run programs and other services available on the network. Unfortunately, Telnet is text-based so it might seem a little in need of a graphical facelift—especially after you've used Netscape.

The general form of a telnet URL is:

```
telnet://[userid:[password]@]host[:port]
```

Telnet's default port is 23 and need not be explicitly specified. A very common use of Telnet is to do an Archie search for a file name that exists somewhere out there in cyberspace. The URL for the Rutgers University Archie server is:

```
telnet://archie.rutgers.edu
```

You would log in as archie (no caps) when prompted for a login name. Technically, you should be able to enter

```
telnet://archie@archie.rutgers.edu
```

avoiding the entry of a login name. Unfortunately, most Telnet clients do not support this form of the telnet URL. Try it and see if your client supports login names and passwords. Some Telnet clients tell you to enter "archie" as a login name, others just ignore the "archie@" prefix.

Another great Telnet server, at least for ham radio operators, is the Amateur Radio Callbook at the University of Buffalo. The URL for this service is:

```
telnet://callsign.cs.buffalo.edu:2000
```

Notice that port 2000 is explicitly stated.

A practical note: When you Telnet from a Web client such as Netscape, the browser passes the information concerning the host and port information to a "helper" program called a Telnet client. The Telnet client supplied with the Netmanage Internet Chameleon package that's included on the enclosed CD-ROM works fine with the port as shown above. However, the Telnet client supplied with the Chameleon sampler, which is also supplied on the enclosed CD-ROM, expects a space between the host name and the port number. The Chameleon sampler's Telnet client does not resolve the host domain name lookup when entering the URL as shown above. The workaround, if your Telnet client behaves in this fashion, is to enter the URL with a space in place of the ":", such as:

```
telnet://callsign.cs.buffalo.edu 2000
```

It's not a legal URL (no spaces allowed) but it fakes out Chameleon.

Usenet Newsgroup URLs

If you've spent any time at all on the Internet, you've probably heard about Usenet newsgroups. Usenet is a really massive networked collection of newsgroups, which in turn refers to special-interest forums where Internet users get together to share common interests. Newsgroups have sprung up for just about any topic you can think of from archery to Zen and the art of computer programming. Once you start using newsgroups, you'll be hooked for life.

The URL format used to retrieve a Usenet newsgroup is different from those we have previously seen. To "point" to a newsgroup, use the following format:

```
news:group-name
```

As an example, the URL to retrieve the newsgroup comp.internet.net-happenings would be:

```
news:comp.internet.net-happenings
```

Netscape, and other browsers that I have tested, will not let you specify a news server as you might expect, such as:

```
news://[news-server]/news-group
```

The Netscape configuration file netscape.ini does not initially specify a news reader so you may not be able to activate a newsgroup at this point. There will be a large section on using Netscape as a newsreader in a later chapter.

Partial URLs

Once you have successfully retrieved a document located somewhere on the Web, you can use a partial, or relative, URL to point to another file on the same network or in the same directory. To illustrate, assume we have read the Netscape home page, having entered the URL:

```
http://home.netscape.com/
```

The file images/home_igloo.jpg contains the large graphic image at the top of the Netscape home page. Therefore

```
images/home_igloo.jpg
```

would be a valid partial URL following the initial retrieval of home.netscape.com.

It is a shorthand notation for:

```
http://home.netscape.com/images/home_igloo.jpg
```

Partial URLs are an important consideration when creating, or modifying hypertext documents. A group of hypertext documents, residing in a common directory, may reference one another using only file names. These documents are said to be hyperlinked. The normal information, such as access method, hostname, port number, and directory name, are assumable based on the URL used to reach the first document.

file URLs

Finally, let's discuss file URLs. First, let's assume we have copied the Netscape home page to a disk on our local computer. (We'll do exactly that in a later exploration.) Let's additionally assume that the name of our local hard disk file is "netscape.htm" and that it resides on drive "D:" in directory "WWWfiles". To have Netscape load the local file, the entered URL would be:

```
file:///D:/WWWfiles/netscape.htm
```

There are several points worth noting in this example. There are truly three consecutive slash characters "/" following "file:"; it's not a misprint. Remember from our URL introduction that protocols are delineated by a colon followed by a double slash, then the network host information, followed by a single slash. Three consecutive slashes indicate that the network host information is absent (or null as computer techies like to say); therefore, the remainder of the path name is on the local computer, not on a remote host. Technically the designation for a file read from a local disk is:

```
file://localhost/
```

Most browsers are forgiving when using the "///" in place of the "//localhost" designation. However, when breaking apart URLs, as with many other factors, browser mileage requirements may vary.

The DOS path and file names' URL separators are also "/" not "\". Information component separators contained within a URL are delimited by a forward slash; the backward slash (used as a delimiter in DOS) is a reserved character in URL-speak because of its Unix heritage.

DOS path and file names are case-independent. I like to intermix upper- and lowercase for clarity and readability.

HYPERTEXT MARKUP LANGUAGE (HTML)

Although it will be a good while before we start to develop our own hypertext documents, let's take a peek ahead. By doing so, you'll have a much better idea how hypertext links work. Hypertext might seem like magic, but it's really little more than some carefully placed formatting and linking codes within an ordinary text document—nothing mysterious at all.

We'll examine a portion of the Netscape home page on the Netscape Web server. In future explorations, we'll actually bring some of these documents home to roost on our PCs. We'll change some of the reference pointers so that frequently accessed documents can reside on our PCs. If we load these documents from copies stored locally on our own hard disks, rather than fetching them from their remote home, we'll save both network bandwidth and the amount of time it takes Netscape to display them.

Let's get a taste of HTML documents by looking at a small portion of the Netscape home page file. Have Netscape display its home page, or look back to Chapter 1's Figure 1.1, as you examine the following HTML fragments.

Click on the View menu item on Netscape's menu bar. Next, click on the item in the drop-down menu named Document Source. In the future we will indicate this sequence as View|Document Source (first click on the View menu and then select the Document Source option).

Figure 2.1 shows a portion of the Netscape home page source document. This is the home page as seen by your browser.

HTML commands, usually called *tags*, are typically paired and enclosed between < and > characters. The second tag of a pair contains a forward slash / and closes the sense of the tag pair. Often a pair of tags acts on the text that falls between them. The first line in this segment of the HTML file is

```
<CENTER>
```

indicating that everything until the closing **</CENTER>** tag is to be centered on the page. Centering is a Netscape enhancement to HTML; the effect will not be reproduced on most other browsers. If you are using a non-Netscape browser to follow this exploration, don't think something is wrong when items do not appear centered on your browser's desktop. The next three lines are used to display information for a file named home_igloo.jpg, which is the graphic displayed as the first item in the document viewing area. The **<P>**

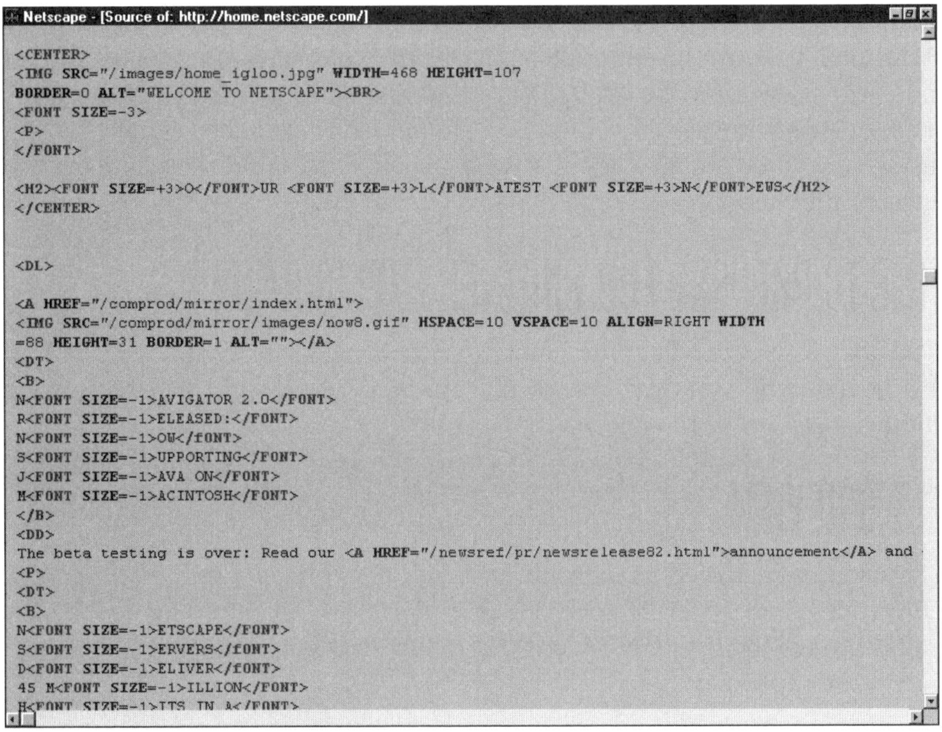

```
Netscape - [Source of: http://home.netscape.com/]

<CENTER>
<IMG SRC="/images/home_igloo.jpg" WIDTH=468 HEIGHT=107
BORDER=0 ALT="WELCOME TO NETSCAPE"><BR>
<FONT SIZE=-3>
<P>
</FONT>

<H2><FONT SIZE=+3>O</FONT>UR <FONT SIZE=+3>L</FONT>ATEST <FONT SIZE=+3>N</FONT>EWS</H2>
</CENTER>


<DL>

<A HREF="/comprod/mirror/index.html">
<IMG SRC="/comprod/mirror/images/now8.gif" HSPACE=10 VSPACE=10 ALIGN=RIGHT WIDTH
=88 HEIGHT=31 BORDER=1 ALT=""></A>
<DT>
<B>
N<FONT SIZE=-1>AVIGATOR 2.0</FONT>
R<FONT SIZE=-1>ELEASED:</FONT>
N<FONT SIZE=-1>OW</fONT>
S<FONT SIZE=-1>UPPORTING</FONT>
J<FONT SIZE=-1>AVA ON</FONT>
M<FONT SIZE=-1>ACINTOSH</FONT>
</B>
<DD>
The beta testing is over: Read our <A HREF="/newsref/pr/newsrelease82.html">announcement</A> and
<P>
<DT>
<B>
N<FONT SIZE=-1>ETSCAPE</FONT>
S<FONT SIZE=-1>ERVERS</fONT>
D<FONT SIZE=-1>ELIVER</fONT>
45 M<FONT SIZE=-1>ILLION</FONT>
H<FONT SIZE=-1>ITS IN A</FONT>
```

Figure 2.1 *HyperText Markup Language.*

command indicates that a new paragraph is to be started following the displayed graphic.

Moving down toward the bottom of the page, the items under **<DD>** represent plain text with a Web link thrown in for good measure (**<A>** markers represent link anchors). The greater part of most Web documents is plain text.

At the heart of most hypertext documents is the link, which is the mechanism by which a browser moves to another document or another place within the same document. As explained earlier, an HTML hyperlink has two components, the anchor and the reference. Look at the next to last long line displayed in Figure 2.1. The portion of the line containing

```
<A HREF="/newsref/pr/newsrelease82.html">announcement</A>
```

illustrates the practical application of these two components. The **<A>** and **</A>** pair encloses the two components. The 'HREF="/newsref/pr/newsrelease82.html" ' portion is the reference. The 'announcement' portion is the anchor and it displays as underlined text on the screen.

There is certainly much more, but let's hold off on the inner workings of HTML until we can work through a full-blown exploration after you've gained more experience on the Web. Don't be concerned if this HTML business seems a little fuzzy at this point. The confounded documents actually start to make sense after you've read a few and gained a little more Netscape experience on the Web.

TIME TO PREPARE FOR ANOTHER EXPLORATION

Well, the glow of the campfire embers is starting to dim. It's time to wind up this briefing and get some rest so that we can journey into the Internet for another Netscape exploration.

LET'S REVIEW

The Internet coalesced as a group of linked networks at large corporations, universities, and especially government installations. All parties agreed to pass traffic through their systems on the way to other systems, taking off the stream only what applied to them.

The File Transfer Protocol (FTP) was implemented very early, allowing people to transfer files over the Internet from other systems on the Internet. The main problem was finding files. The Archie utility was the first general means of searching for material on the Internet. Later, the much more ambitious Gopher protocol was designed, which treated Internet files as hierarchical menus.

The most wide-reaching advance in Internet navigation was the World Wide Web, a protocol treating material on the Internet as linked hypertext—and as a bonus, adding standard support for multimedia data like sound and video. The Web was mostly a curiosity until the release of graphical browsers such as Mosaic and Netscape. The graphical browsers allowed for easy "surfing" of the Internet and included services like FTP and Gopher. A special document format, the HyperText Markup Language (HTML), was adapted from an earlier markup spec (SGML) for use in formatting Web documents.

Behind the general usefulness of Netscape, Mosaic, and other Web browsers is the idea of the Universal Resource Locator (URL), a standardized addressing scheme for all types of Internet data and services. Our discussion of URLs is by no means complete. There are several other URL types that are not used often enough to justify inclusion in this overview.

In the most unlikely event that this overview has piqued your interest, here are several URL references in URL format:

A Beginner's Guide to URLs
`http://www.ncsa.uiuc.edu/demoweb/url-primer.html`

Uniform Resource Locators
`http://www.w3.org/hypertext/WWW/Addressing/URL/`

For a more advanced treatment of URLs try:

Universal Resource Identifiers in WWW
`http://www.w3.org/hypertext/WWW/Addressing/URL/uri-spec.html`

Now that we have covered the basics, let's set sail and explore some of Netscape's browser features.

Navigating with Netscape

Now that you've learned how to use Netscape and the Web, it's time to learn how to roam cyberspace, and how to mark your trail with bookmarks.

Do you remember the early navigators such as Christopher Columbus, Lewis and Clark, and Ponce de Leon? When they set out on their travels, they didn't know where they were going or what to expect. They successfully carved their paths by mastering the navigational tools available to them, developing their own tools, and charting their courses.

As you start to explore the Web using Netscape, you too will need to chart your paths and learn how to use the powerful navigational tools available to you. The more you know about URLs, History lists, bookmarks, frames, and your Netscape mail address book, the better you'll be at traveling around on the Web. In this chapter, I'll introduce you to the basic Netscape navigational tools, including a detailed exploration of bookmark lists.

TEACHING NETSCAPE TO POINT

Since you don't always want to be following someone else's path, you must be able to steer your Netscape navigational system on your own. An amazing number of Web sites await exploration once you know how to get around. The trick is knowing how to find these sites, and once you find them, you need to know how to chart them. The Web is tremendously dynamic. Hundreds of new sites are being added each week, and that number is increasing. The contents of existing sites are also being constantly improved and expanded.

Making a Stop at Baltimore's Charm Net

Baltimore's Charm Net has a great home page. This unique Web site, which is the pride of Maryland, has a wonderful assortment of HTML document information and pointers to all types of interesting places. Enough said; let's go explore.

Pointing Particulars

You can easily get to a particular Web site with Netscape once you know its location or URL. Recall that the URL is the Uniform Resource Locator—a special Internet address for a Web page. Every Web resource, such as a document or graphic image, has its own unique Internet address (URL). Let's start our first exploration with a visit to Baltimore's Charm Net. This will show you how to use URLs to navigate the Internet seas. Fortunately, a net-surfer acquaintance supplied the URL for the Charm Net home page, which is:

```
http://www.charm.net/
```

Note the "/" at the end of this URL. Technically speaking, the "/" is a required URL terminator. However, most browsers, including Netscape, allow you to specify a URL without using the / terminator. Some browsers, notably NetCruiser, require the terminator.

There are a few ways you can get to Charm Net using Netscape. I'll show you all of them so that you can quickly learn different ways to navigate. A simple way to travel to a new Web site is to type a URL in the Open Location dialog box. To open this dialog box, you click on the File item in the menu bar and select the Open Location command (File|Open Location). Once the Open Location dialog box displays, you simply type in the URL and click the Open button. Figure 3.1 shows the Open Location dialog box.

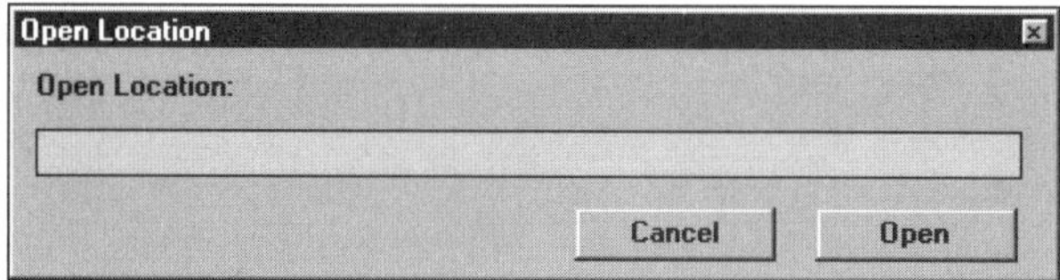

Figure 3.1 Using the Open Location dialog box.

An alternative to using the File menu to enter a URL is to click on the toolbar's Open folder icon. (Look for the icon displayed to the left of the Print icon on the toolbar.) Clicking on the Open folder icon brings you to the Open Location dialog box displayed in Figure 3.1.

A third way to access the Open Location dialog box is to press Ctrl+L. (Hold down the Ctrl key while you press the L key.)

Finally, my favorite method of pointing to a Web site is to bypass the Open Location dialog box and simply type the URL in the Location text box on the screen (just below the toolbar). To do this you use the mouse to highlight the current URL in the Location text box, type in a new URL to replace the highlighted URL, and press Enter to activate the link. In addition, you can save time by highlighting and replacing only the parts of a URL that are different. For example, there is a good chance that both the new and existing URLs begin with the characters "http://www.". In this case, you could simply position the cursor after the "www.", press Ctrl+Delete to remove everything to the right of the cursor, and type in the remainder of the new URL. This editing feature is especially handy when much of the current URL is usable.

Now, lets take a quick trip to Charm Net. Select one of the methods we just discussed, and type in the URL http://www.charm.net to display Charm Net's home page as shown in Figure 3.2.

Charm Net's opening display includes a giant emerald. The Charm Net "Emerald on the Matrix" symbolically represents the city of Baltimore. If you like the Charm Net home page as much as I do (it has great lists of links to other places on the Web), you may want to make it easy to return to for later explorations. Netscape makes return trips easy, and I'll show you how after a little background information.

BOOKMARKS: EXTRAORDINARY TOUR GUIDES

Once Lewis and Clark blazed their trails, they became guides for others. Similarly, you can chart your paths across the Web and create guides for yourself—

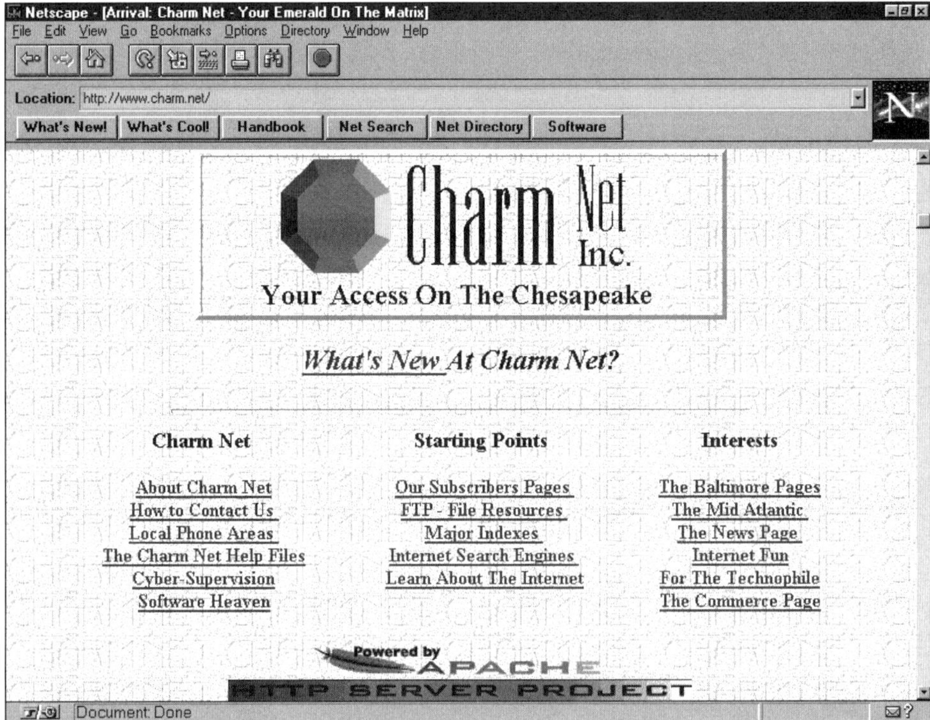

***Figure 3.2** Our first exploration—Charm Net's home page.*

marking Web sites instead of landmarks and creating bookmark lists instead of maps. Netscape's navigational system provides all the tools you'll need for your exploratory adventures. We have already seen that Netscape permits us to navigate the Web, either by clicking on links provided in a home page or by manually typing URLs to takes us to the sites where the good stuff resides. Now it is time for us to venture further into the wilderness.

Like any good explorer, I like to veer off the beaten trail with the hope of discovering obscure things and out-of-the-way places. So it is not surprising that this is also how I like to explore the Web. Netscape can be extraordinarily helpful in this regard. With Netscape's linking and searching capabilities, you can easily link a trail of 15 or 20 URLs in less than an hour. Netscape is so helpful, in fact, that you may suddenly realize that you have no idea what path you've followed to get to that cool Web site displaying on your monitor. Fortunately, Netscape provides a handy feature called *bookmarks*.

A bookmark is an electronic record that you make of a Web site address. It is very similar to a rolodex card, except that a bookmark stores Web site addresses as opposed to street addresses or phone numbers. Without bookmarks our computer work areas would probably be covered with a sea of yellow sticky notes containing all the great URLs we've found along the way.

A bookmark has two main components, a URL and a descriptive title. Look at the Charm Net page in Figure 3.2. Its bookmark is the URL shown in the Location: text box. Its title—[Arrival: Charm Net - Your Emerald On The Matrix]—is displayed on the top title line, just after "Netscape -". The title is supplied by the document's creator.

Netscape provides a couple navigational tools utilizing bookmarks. First, Netscape automatically records a History list of any and all locations you visit during your current trip (notice I say "during your current trip"—bookmarks in a History list are temporary). The first two icons on the toolbar make use of the history list. The Back arrow button, the left arrow icon that is the first icon on the left of the toolbar, will take us back to the preceding site, provided we are not at the very first stop on our trek. The Forward button, the right arrow icon just to the right of the back arrow icon, will take us forward, provided we have backed up at least once.

Another navigational tool is the Go menu option on the toolbar. Clicking on the Go menu displays the Back, Forward, and Home commands, as well as a list of the URLs you have recently visited. This list is in the form of a stack, or what accountants call "last in first out." The History list helps you avoid excessive clicking on the arrows to back up to a URL you recently visited. Using the History list, you can leap over multiple URLs in a single bound. It's time to take a look at how the History list works, but first, we need to set the stage.

For this exploration, we'll assume that you are using the Netscape home page as your home page, or starting point (you can create your own personalized home page, but more about that in a later chapter). Lets view Charm Net's home page (www.charm.net), click on The News Page anchor, and from the News page scroll down, then click on What's New Yahoo. (Yahoo is an incredible site; we'll talk about it shortly.) If we then open the Go menu, it will appear as shown in Figurc 3.3.

The lowest portion of the Go drop-down menu is the history of our current session. The most recently visited site, in this case What's New Yahoo, is at the top of the list. Charm Net Current Events Information is the site visited immediately before the current site. If we press the left arrow, we would go to the item under the current site. Last on the list, Netscape's Home Page, is where it all started. If we type a *3* we'll return to the Netscape Home Page.

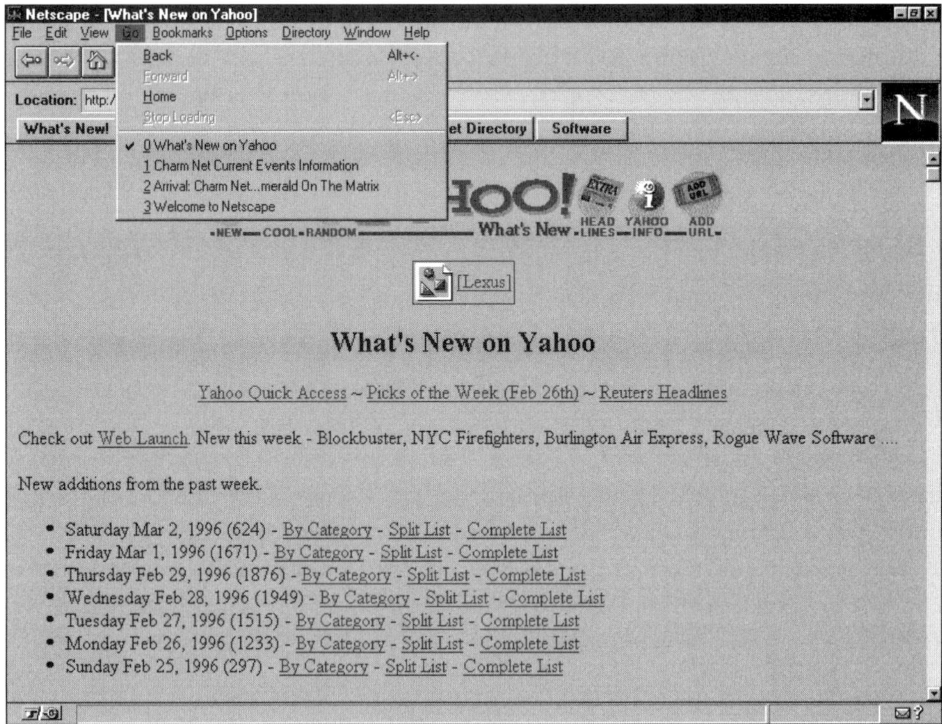

Figure 3.3 *The Go drop-down menu shows visited sites.*

In this example, we've been viewing the title portion of the history bookmarks. You can also view the URLs associated with the bookmark titles by clicking on Windows|History or pressing Ctrl+H. This feature is shown in Figure 3.4.

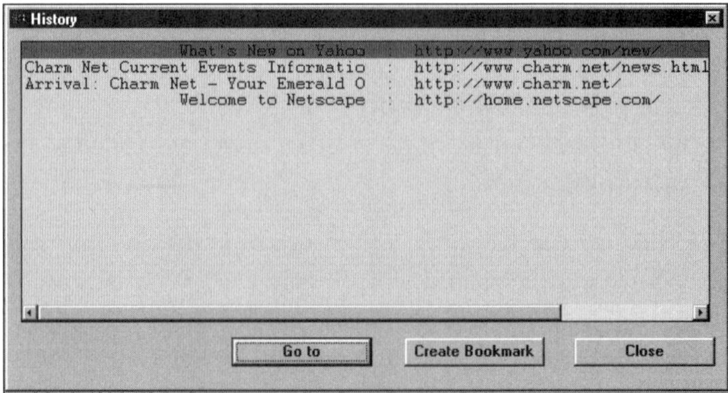

Figure 3.4 *Netscape's History of the current session.*

The History list shows both the titles and their associated URLs. You can scroll to the right to see more of the URLs. You can also activate the highlighted bookmark by clicking on either the Go to button or clicking on the bookmark of your choice.

So we can jump around and return to sites previously visited during the current session at will. "Big deal," you might reply, "how about tomorrow?" Enter permanent bookmark files.

Send Pointers, Not Documents!

An excellent way to share information with friends or colleagues is to send them one of your favorite bookmarks, bookmark files, or a subject portion of a bookmark file. A group of bookmarks is better than sending actual documents, since a file contains pointers to the documents as they are maintained by their owners. (This also eliminates any possible copyright violations inherent in copying someone else's documents.) A mailed document may be older than the version of the document available on the server where it resides, and thus may be obsolete before the recipient even gets it. Finally, sending a bookmark, bookmark list, or a portion of a list, as opposed to sending the entire document, is a far more efficient use of network resources.

The Care and Feeding of Bookmark Lists

You can create a collection of your favorite bookmarks by making a bookmark list. A Netscape *bookmark list* is a file of stored Web sites. A URL link and its description are stored for each bookmark entry. A Netscape bookmark file also maintains the date the bookmark was initially added to the list and the most recent date the site was visited. A bookmark entry may also contain an optional user-defined description. Bookmark files may contain folders and submenus. Functionally, the bookmark organization can be used to create a hierarchical menu system.

The name of Netscape's initial bookmark file is bookmark.htm. It is a text file. Actually, it is an HTML file that uses Netscape HTML enhancements. Unfortunately, Netscape does not supply an initial bookmark file to help with the navigational process.

Adding Your Own Links

Although serendipity may rule the day while exploring the Web, it can be difficult to make serendipity happen twice in a row. When you find something really interesting on the Web, you certainly don't want to depend upon your memory to get you back to it.

Navigating the Web is like navigating a maze—actually, it's worse, since there may be many paths for getting to any Web site. I don't know about you, but I have a hard time remembering where I put my car keys 15 minutes ago, much less where in the Web I found that great location for brownie recipes. What we need to accomplish symbolically is to sprinkle some crumbs along our path so that we can find our way back. (It's our problem if we don't make it back before the birds have eaten all our crumbs.)

Adding a New Link to a Bookmark List

New links may be added to an existing bookmark list at any time. For this project, let's go visit Yahoo, which is one of the great Web Sites. Yahoo is a database of searchable net resources. We'll add its link to our bookmark list.

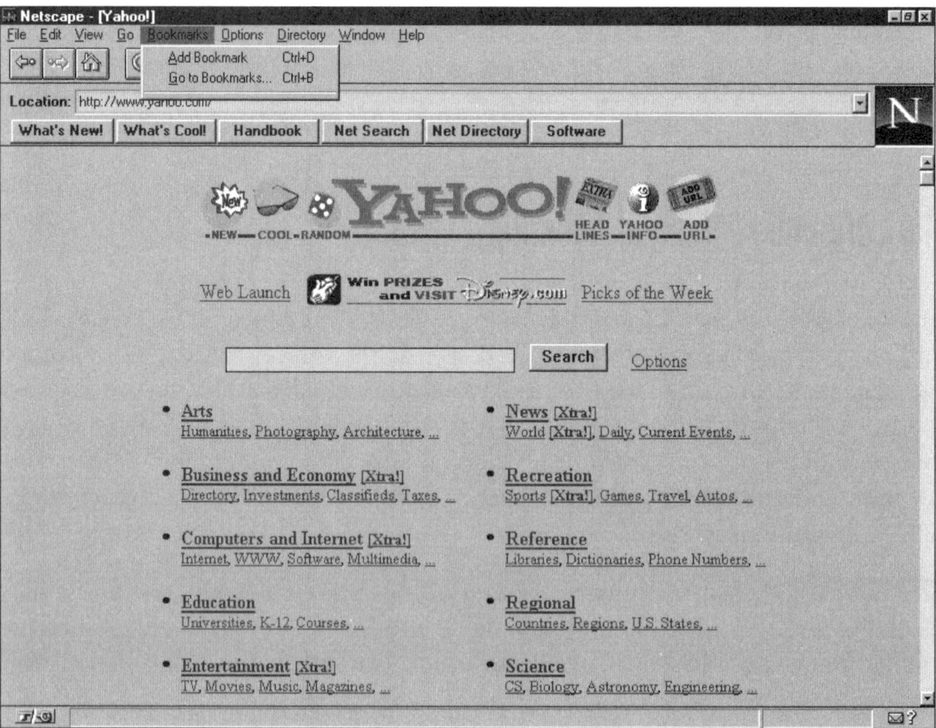

Figure 3.5 The Bookmarks drop-down menu.

Using one of the techniques described earlier in this chapter, enter the URL:

```
http://www.yahoo.com
```

Once the document is displayed, its URL and title can be added to a bookmark list. Click on Bookmarks on the menu bar. Notice that the bookmark drop-down menu, as shown in Figure 3.5, only has the two items, Add Bookmark and Go to Bookmarks.

Later, as we add bookmarks, our top-level bookmark entries will show up below Go to Bookmarks. Clicking on the Add Bookmark item will add the title and URL of the currently viewed document to the bookmark list. We could also press Ctrl+D to add the current document to the bookmark list. Figure 3.6 shows the results of opening the Bookmarks menu after Yahoo has been added. We may return to visit Yahoo at any time by opening the Bookmarks menu and clicking on Yahoo. Congratulations, we've just placed our first navigational crumb.

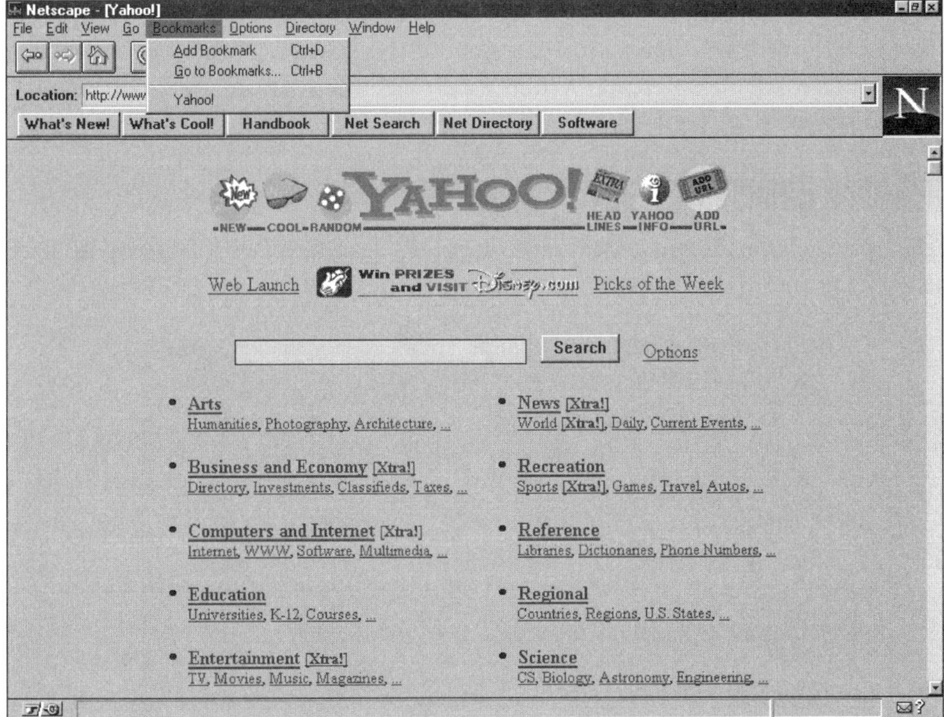

Figure3.6 *Yahoo has been added as our first bookmark.*

Let's enter the URL for my home page at Charm Net; it's:

```
http://www.charm.net/~lejeune
```

Notice the little character between the "/" and "lejeune". It's called a tilde, and it's usually on the key just to the left of the 1 key. After displaying my home page, execute the sequence Windows|History, which brings up the History dialog box as shown in Figure 3.7.

Any item in the history can be turned into a bookmark. Highlight Urb's Home Page by clicking once on any part of the title or URL; next click on the Create Bookmark button. Finally, click on the Close button to exit the History dialog.

Open the Bookmarks menu again and—presto!—you'll have two bookmarks, as shown in Figure 3.8.

You can bring back good old Yahoo or Urb at any time by opening the bookmark menu and clicking on your choice. When you exit Netscape, your bookmarks wait patiently for your next exploration. You can continue in this fashion to add interesting sites to your bookmark file until you fill up the screen with entries. When you see a note at the bottom of the screen stating "more bookmarks," it indicates you're ready for a little more sophistication in the management of your bookmarks.

Modifying Bookmark Lists

Netscape provides three different techniques for modifying bookmark lists and adding menu and submenu items. Here they are in ease-of-use order:

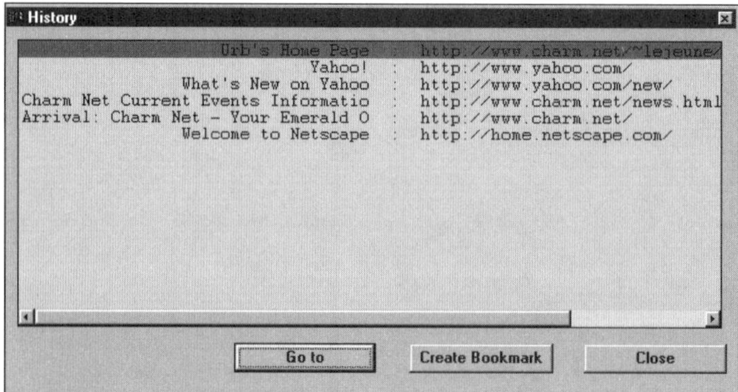

***Figure 3.7** Setting up the History dialog box to save a bookmark.*

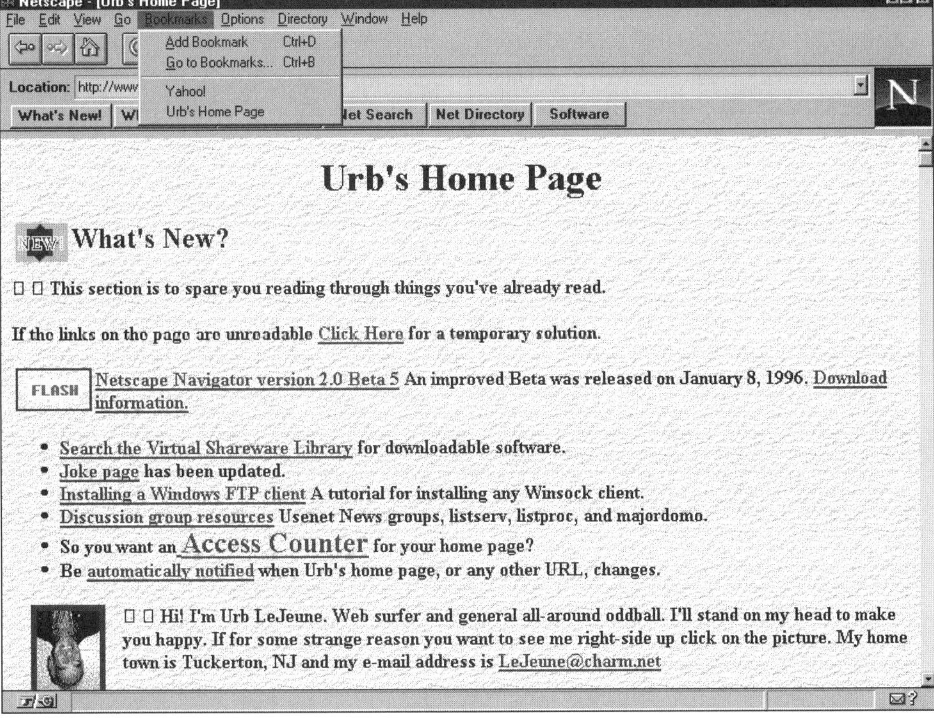

Figure 3.8 *There are now two bookmarks available for instant recall.*

- Click on the Bookmarks|Add Bookmark option, press Ctrl+D, or click on Windows|History|Create Bookmark to add the currently viewed document's URL and title to your bookmark list.
- Use Netscape's bookmark editor by clicking on the Bookmarks|Go to Bookmarks option, press Ctrl+B, or click on Windows|Bookmarks.
- Modify the file bookmark.htm, or any other bookmark file, using a text editor.

The first option simply lets you add the URL and title of the currently displayed document to a bookmark file—just as you added the Yahoo bookmark in the previous exercise. The information is appended to the currently specified bookmark HTML file as a top-level entry. I'll show you how easy this is to do in the next project. The second option, using Netscape's bookmark editor, by contrast, lets you add, delete, and edit bookmarks as well as add, delete, move, and edit URL links and their titles.

The third option requires a little bit of manual work but it gives you the most control. A Netscape bookmark file is actually stored as a standard HTML file—

with a few wrinkles. (As you will soon realize, Netscape doesn't do anything without a few wrinkles.) To change a bookmark file with an editor, you'll need to understand some of the basics of HTML. Therefore, we'll hold off the discussion of manually editing bookmark files until a later chapter.

Keeping Abreast of Net Happenings

There is a Usenet newsgroup called comp.internet.net-happenings, and, as the name implies, it is a gold mine of new and interesting things happening on the Internet. Gleason Sackman, the moderator of the list, seems to be posting new and exciting things 24 hours a day. (I wonder if he ever sleeps.) The list is a great source of new URLs waiting to be explored.

If you don't have access to a Usenet newsreader, there is also a listserv list called net-happenings that distributes the same information. To subscribe to the list, send an email message to:

```
majordomo@is.internic.org
```

In the body of the message place the following one line of text:

```
subscribe net-happenings <your-first-name> <your-last-name>
```

Shortly, you will receive a message proclaiming your acceptance to the inner circle. Read the message carefully because it tells you how to get off the list. This may become important if you have trouble keeping up with your daily flow of email!

Starting a New Bookmark File

The best way to see how bookmarks are created and manipulated is to build and change a Netscape bookmark file. First we will create a new bookmark file. Creating a new bookmark file is as easy as creating a blank Word document and saving it with an .htm extension, such as:

```
C:\NETSCAPE\my-menu.htm
```

I recommend you save your bookmark htm file in your Netscape folder so it will be easy to find later. Once you create the htm file, open Netscape, then click on Bookmarks|Go to Bookmarks to open the bookmarks editor. Next, click on File|Open, find the htm file you just created, and click on the Open button. You have now designated the main bookmark file. Any bookmarks you save will be saved to this file until you change the designation.

Creating a Bookmark Hierarchy

Now that we have a new bookmark file, let's start building a hierarchical system with a three-topic menu. We'll include these three items at the top level:

- Business
- Resources
- Computers

To start, click on the Bookmarks|Go to Bookmarks option. This command displays the Bookmark list editor screen view. Click on Item|Insert Folder to display the Bookmark Properties dialog box, as shown in Figure 3.9.

Type Business in the Name: text field to name your first top level category. As you can see, Netscape's bookmark hierarchical system is similar to Windows in that it uses folders to prioritize and categorize bookmarks. Let's repeat this process and create folders for our Resources category and Computers category. Make sure that you highlight the Main Bookmarks header before you insert each new folder, otherwise you might insert a subdirectory folder instead of a main folder. Also, if you want to have a little extra fun, after you create the three folders you can highlight them and select Item|Sort Bookmarks—now your folders appear in alphabetical order. Your screen should now look like the one shown in Figure 3.10.

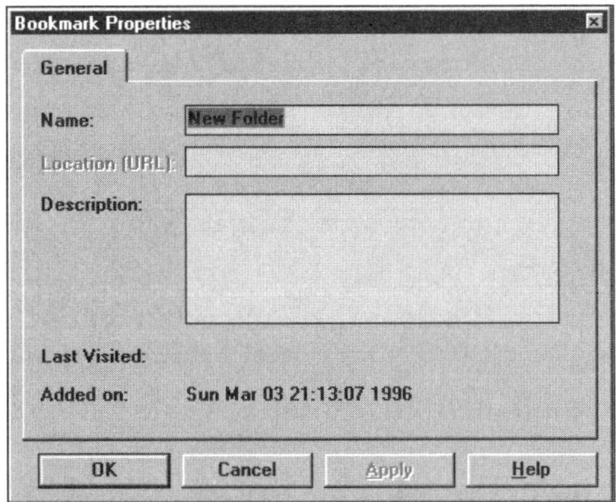

***Figure 3.9** The Bookmark Properties dialog box.*

Figure 3.10 *The new Bookmark folders in alphabetical order.*

Now let's add some subdirectories to our top-level directories. To accomplish this, we simply highlight a top-level menu and click on Item|Insert Folder. The subdirectory folder appears slightly indented below the top-level directory folder. Let's add Accounting, Marketing, and Finance subdirectory folders under the Business directory; PC, Mac, and Unix folders under the Computers directory; and an Online subdirectory under the Resources directory. After you add the subdirectories, your screen should look like the one shown in Figure 3.11.

You now know more about Netscape's bookmark structure than 80 percent of the people using Netscape. On the Netscape discussion list there are more questions asked about bookmarks than any other subject. With our newfound expertise, let's go forth and multiply. What good is a menu hierarchy if the structure doesn't contain anything of interest?

Adding URLs to the Bookmark Structure

One morning, my perennially overflowing electronic mailbox contained a message about a Web site with an interesting-sounding document called

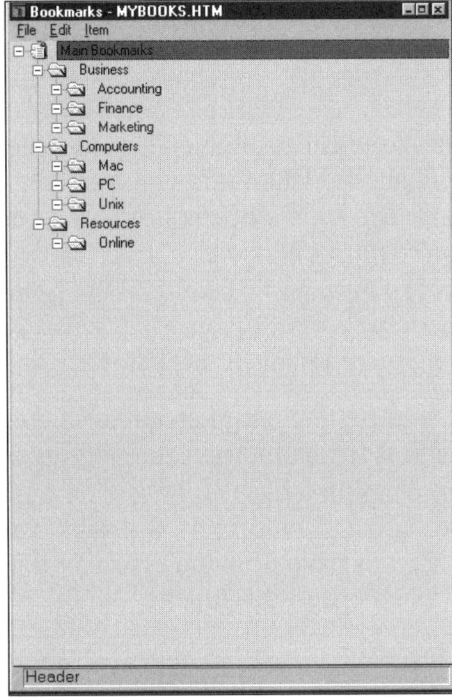

Figure 3.11 The Bookmark list with subdirectories.

"Internet Training Resources." The message contained the URL of the site, which is exactly what we need to access the site. The URL is:

```
http://www.brandonu.ca/~ennsnr/Resources/Welcome.html
```

Snagging a Useful URL with Windows

For this project, we'll use the Windows clipboard to copy and paste a URL that points to an interesting Web site for Internet training material. This technique will illustrate how easy it is to use Windows to try out a new Internet resource and add the URL to our bookmark list.

Now let's see how the Windows clipboard can be used to help us transfer the URL from my email message to Netscape. This technique can save you a lot of keystrokes and keep you from making typing mistakes as you transfer cumbersome URLs.

If you are copying a URL address from an email, you must first use your mouse to highlight the URL in the email message. Then, you can copy the

URL to the clipboard by using the Copy command with your email program. (Virtually all Windows applications have an Edit menu that contains Copy and Paste commands.)

After copying the URL to the clipboard, you'll need to get into Netscape. From within Netscape, highlight the URL in the Location: text box by dragging the cursor across the URL. (The Location: text box is the one normally displaying the current document's URL.) Choose Edit|Paste or press Ctrl+V to copy the contents of the clipboard into the URL field. Then, press Enter to activate the URL. Figure 3.12 shows Brandon University's Internet Resources home page. It's a great resource if you're relatively new to Web surfing.

The contents of the "Internet Training Resources" are indeed impressive. We could print a copy of this document for future reference. However, there are two disadvantages to creating a hard copy version of this document: one, it will quickly become outdated, and two—a prospect totally abhorrent to a lazy guy like me—you will have to manually enter the URLs whenever you want to access the document in the future. The maintainer of the list, Neil

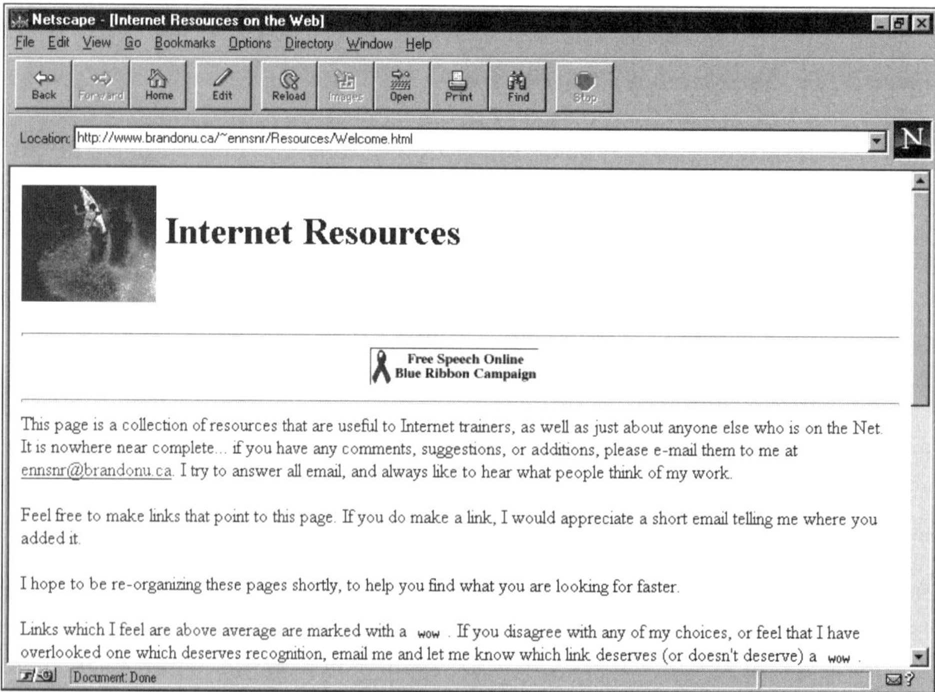

***Figure 3.12** Brandon University's Internet Resources.*

Enns of NetSurf Technologies, keeps the list current by adding new information and changing existing information as needed. By creating a bookmark pointer to the document, we will have continual access to the latest version.

Let's save the Internet Training Resources Web site as a bookmark. Click on the Bookmarks | Add Bookmark option to add the information as a top-level menu item. This is just what the doctor ordered if you feel this URL is important enough to warrant top-level status. However, we're talking about a menu subsystem, and top-level items defeat the structure concept. Let's pick a category and place the item in the corresponding menu level.

The easiest way I've found to add a bookmark to a category is to use the copy and paste method. To use this method we must first copy the URL in the Location: text box. Next, we click on Bookmarks | Go to Bookmarks to display the bookmarks editor window. In this case, I think we should add this bookmark to our online category under the Resources top-level menu. To do this, click on the Online folder, then click on Item | Insert Bookmark. The bookmark appears as an item in the Online subdirectory of the Resources folder.

Now let's add a bookmark and use the bookmark editor drag and drop feature to place a URL in an appropriate category (technically it is a drag and drop feature).

If you are into investing, you might be interested to know that the SEC maintains its filings online so that you can search them. They call the system EDGAR. A search engine I find very useful is:

```
http://www.town.hall.org/cgi-bin/srch-edgar
```

Enter the URL into Netscape's Location: text box and press enter to activate it. You can then search using the name of your favorite company to see what they've been telling the SEC lately. This site is a for-sure site to come back to, so let's save it as a bookmark. Make sure you are at the EDGAR home page, then click on Bookmarks | Add Bookmark. Now let's look at our Bookmarks drop-down menu. There's EDGAR—added as the last top-level menu item. We would probably have better luck finding this bookmark again if we filed it under our Finance subdirectory. To accomplish this move, we need to return to the bookmark editor window. Select Bookmarks | Go to Bookmarks. Once we are in the Bookmarks list editor, all we have to do is select EDGAR and

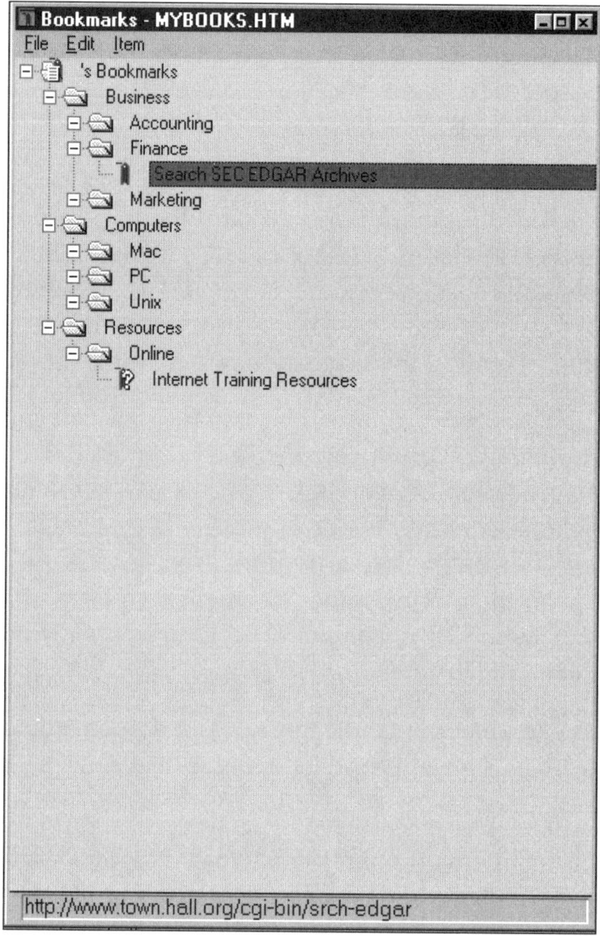

Figure 3.13 *You can have as many folders and subfolders as you need.*

drag the bookmark icon up to the Finance subdirectory. When the Finance folder is highlighted, click on Finance. The drag and drop feature is one of the great improvements included in Netscape 2.0. Your bookmarks editor screen should look like the screen in Figure 3.13.

Deleting Bookmarks

Deleting bookmarks and bookmark directories from within Netscape is easy. While in the Bookmark editor window, highlight the bookmark or bookmark directory you want to delete, then click on Edit|Delete or hit the Delete button.

Keep in mind that when you delete a directory or subdirectory, you are deleting all the bookmarks (and subdirectories) contained in the folder. If you want to save selected records, I recommend that you copy or drag the bookmarks out of the folder before you delete.

Using Item Separators

A plain line may be inserted between entries to create emphasis or make logical separations in the Bookmarks menu list. To do this, go to the bookmark editor view and highlight the item you want to appear just *above* the separator. Click on Item | Insert Separator and a bookmark icon appears with <separator> appearing as the icon title.

Creating a Separator That Has a Label

If you want a logical separator to contain a title, create a bookmark entry without a URL. You won't get a response if you click on the title separator, but no harm is done.

Moving Bookmarks Directories

Often, there are times when you would like a subdirectory to become a temporary top level directory. Maybe you are going to do some serious searching and need a submenu to store some of your findings. (Web surfing is not all fun and games.) Netscape's drag and drop feature makes directory management easy. Click on Bookmarks | Go to Bookmarks to display the bookmark editor window. Select any subdirectory, then drag and drop it into the Main Bookmark file at the top of the window. You can also drag and drop bookmarks from one level to another (even making it a top-level entry if it is a URL you use often). After you finish rearranging your bookmarks and bookmark directories, click on the Bookmarks menu in Netscape's main window to view your changes.

Importing Menus

The Import Bookmarks button is quite useful if you want to import bookmarks from another HTML file. To use this feature, go to the Bookmarks list editor and click on File | Import. Select the HTML file containing the bookmarks you want to import, and Netscape will do a great job of extracting the URLs and titles from within the document and importing them as a group at the bottom of the currently specified bookmark file.

CREATING MAILING LINKS

One of the features of Netscape Mail is the Address Book. An entire chapter in this book is devoted to Netscape Mail, but I think this is a good place to mention the Address Book because it is very similar to the Bookmarks list. The Address Book simplifies the process of sending emails by keeping track of addresses and groups of addresses for you. To display the address book, click on Window | Address Book. At this point, your Address Book is probably empty and appears as the window shown in Figure 3.14

We will show you how to fill in this window later in the book. Basically, we will use the same methods as we did to fill our bookmarks window—using many of the same features, as well as designating mailing groups.

USING FRAMES

Frames are one of the newest features of Netscape. Frames allow net surfers to view the content of links on a Web page, without losing sight of the original document. Frames also present the opportunity to unify Web pages with fixed banners and navigation bars. Each frame on a Web page has its own URL, which means that you can change the view in one frame without affecting the others. Probably the best visual example of frames can be

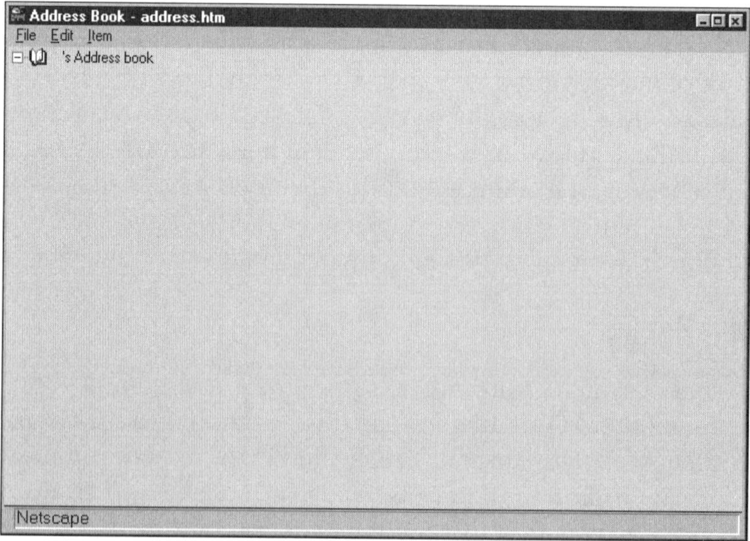

***Figure 3.14** The Netscape Address Book.*

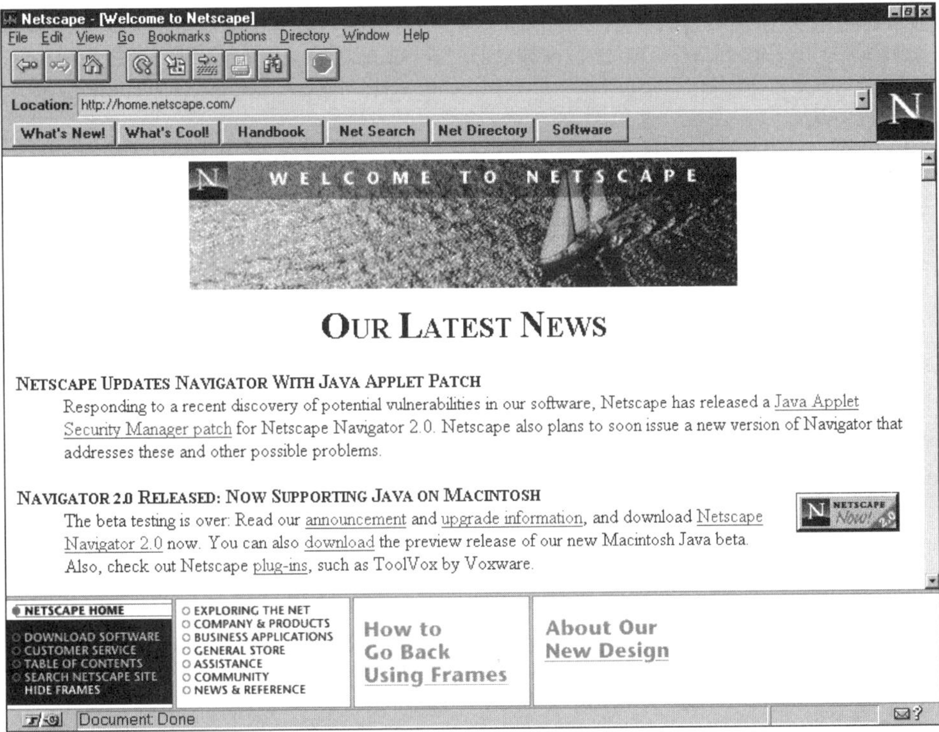

Figure 3.15 *Netscape's home page features frames at the bottom.*

found on Netscape's own home page. We'll be having an in-depth discussion about Frames later in the book, but for now, let's whet our appetites by taking a quick look at Netscape's home page frames as shown in Figure 3.15.

Notice the smaller frames along the bottom of your screen. These frames contain jump items and other information. Click on Table of Contents in the lower-left frame. Notice how the lower frames remained intact while the larger, viewing frame displayed the linked information.

If you really can't wait until our discussion on frames, you can read Netscape's brief overview of understanding frames at:

```
http://home.netscape.com/navigate/understanding_frames.html
```

LET'S REVIEW

A Netscape bookmark list is functionally a folder containing pointers to Web sites or other Internet services. Bookmark lists are completely user configurable.

Netscape's initial default bookmark list is named bookmark.htm and is found in the same directory with all the other Netscape files. The name and location of the bookmark list may be changed at any time. Bookmark lists can be created, deleted, and renamed. Individual bookmark items can likewise be added, deleted, copied, and moved. Selecting the menu sequence File | Open Location or clicking on the Open icon are common routes to the Open Location dialog box. Another method of activating a URL is to edit it directly in the Location text box.

The sequence in which you visited Web sites during the current Netscape session is displayed in the History list. Select the menu item Window | History. Highlight the desired item and click on the Go to button to return to a previously visited site. You can also double-click on any history item to return to the document or service it describes. Another option is to choose the Go menu, which lists the last few sites you visited.

The currently displayed document or service can be added to your bookmark list by executing the sequence Bookmarks | Add Bookmark. You can also use the shortcut Ctrl+D.

The Netscape mail address book is organized in the same manner as the bookmarks list. You use the Address Book to simplify the process of addressing the email you send.

Frames are a new feature of Netscape Navigator 2.0. Frames aid in the presentation of information and make navigating net sites easier.

AND ONWARD!

Bookmark navigation is one of the most powerful features of Netscape. Take some time to get comfortable with the concepts behind bookmarks. Just because Christopher Columbus didn't know where he was going is no reason for us to assume that good things will automatically happen if we just wander out on the open sea. Not all explorers are as lucky as Chris.

Setting Netscape Preferences and Helpers

Netscape is highly configurable, and with the right tips you can make it work the way you want. If Netscape can't do it, you can install a helper program that can.

In most cases, flexibility equals power. The more flexible a tool is, the more you can use it—kind of like that all-purpose thingamajig that hammers nails, tightens screws, cuts wires, and clubs rattlesnakes—all depending on how you snap it together. The snag, of course, is that flexibility can also equal difficulty, and, at worst, total obscurity. If a tool becomes so flexible that it grows obscure, it loses its utility for most people. (Unix is a lot like that. You can do almost anything with Unix except understand it.)

Netscape is a Web browser of extraordinary power, mainly because you can set it up in a number of different ways. That's what this chapter is about: configuring Netscape. Fortunately, Netscape has made configuring your browser easy. The greater part of Netscape's configurability does not require editing a very large, frighteningly obtuse configuration file. (Earlier versions of most Web browsers required the scary process of editing an INI file.)

However, you'll work (and sleep) easier if you take a few precautions before jiggering Netscape's configuration and the configuration file netscape.ini:

- Always make a backup copy of netscape.ini before making major configuration changes or editing the file (if you discover you need to).
- If you change the INI file, comment out parameters; don't delete them.
- Make changes to the INI file one parameter at a time, and test the results of that one change before making any additional changes.

If you follow these three simple steps, there is nothing to fear, since you can always return to a copy of your original netscape.ini set up as it was before you began to fuss with it. Also, keep in mind that Netscape reads netscape.ini only when it starts up, therefore you'll need to exit and restart Netscape to see the effects of some of your configuration changes.

Now, before I scare you off with INI files, let me show you how easily we can meet most of our configuration needs by using Netscape menu options.

USING THE OPTIONS MENU

Let's start by exploring the most straightforward configuration menu options first. A few common preferences can be changed simply by clicking on Netscape's Options menu as shown in Figure 4.1.

If we ignore the top section in the Options menu for a minute, we can see that we use the Options menu to control whether we want to display or hide:

- Netscape's toolbar
- the URL (Location:) text box
- Netscape's directory buttons
- Images while loading a Web page

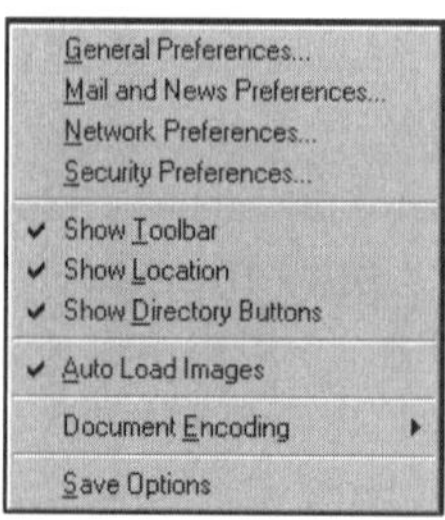

Figure 4.1 *Netscape's Options menu.*

If any of those four items has a checkmark next to its name, you'll know the option has been selected. To turn off an active option, simply select it and the checkmark will disappear. Keep in mind that any changes you make using the Options menu only affect the current session unless you execute the Options | Save Options command.

If the Auto Load Images option is selected, all images will be displayed when you download a Web page. If this option is not selected, images may not be displayed when you download a Web page. Instead of an actual image, you'll get a small built-in icon placeholder where the graphic normally displays. Often, netheads will turn off the Auto Load Images option to save transmittal time (we'll talk a little more about hiding images in Chapter 8 when we cover different home page options). To fetch and display a hidden image, click on the icon placeholder with the right mouse button, then select the Load this Image option.

Making More Room for Netscape

One of the options you might want to turn off is Show Directory Buttons. The What's New and What's Cool buttons provided with the group of displayed buttons are interesting in the beginning, but they take up space that could otherwise be used to view documents. And after all, the URLs underlying the directory buttons are also available as selections on either the Directory or Help drop-down menus.

Finally, before we move on to the preferences menus, notice the command for Document Encoding. If you click on the arrow, you will see a list of encoding languages as shown in Figure 4.2

You can select an encoding language from this quick menu, or, as we'll discuss in the next section, you can choose and set preferences for an encoding

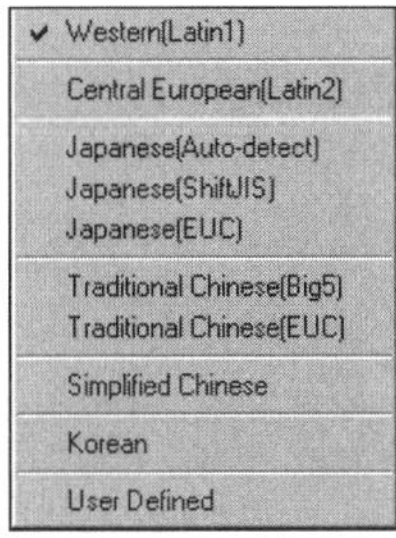

***Figure 4.2** The Document Encoding language Options list.*

language using the Appearance Card in the General Preferences dialog box. Netscape's default encoding language is Western(Latin1).

USING THE WONDERFUL PREFERENCES MENUS

There was a time in the evolution of Netscape (a few versions ago) when all the useful Netscape configuration options needed to be set by changing the netscape.ini configuration file. Fortunately, the later versions of Netscape allow you to change settings directly from within Netscape. The best part is, you can do most of the configuration work by selecting options with the mouse.

Netscape provides four preferences menus:

- General Preferences
- Mail and News Preferences
- Network Preferences
- Security Preferences

Let's look at these preferences groups one at a time. To select a particular preferences group, select Options, then click on the name of a preferences group. After you access the group's main Preferences dialog box, you will have to click on tabs to display various topic cards. You'll see what I mean as we work our way through each of the preferences groups.

General Preferences

Execute the Options | General Preferences sequence to display the General Preferences dialog box. Figure 4.3 shows the General Preferences dialog box with the Appearance card displayed.

Notice the seven topic cards included in the General Preferences dialog box. The topic cards are: Appearance, Fonts, Colors, Images, Apps, Helpers, and Language.

Appearance

The Appearance card is divided into three sections: Toolbars, Startup, and Link Styles. The Toolbars section consists of three radio buttons controlling how your toolbar displays. Toolbars can display as pictures, text only, or as a combination of the two—the default. The advantage of the first two options is that they allow more space for displaying documents.

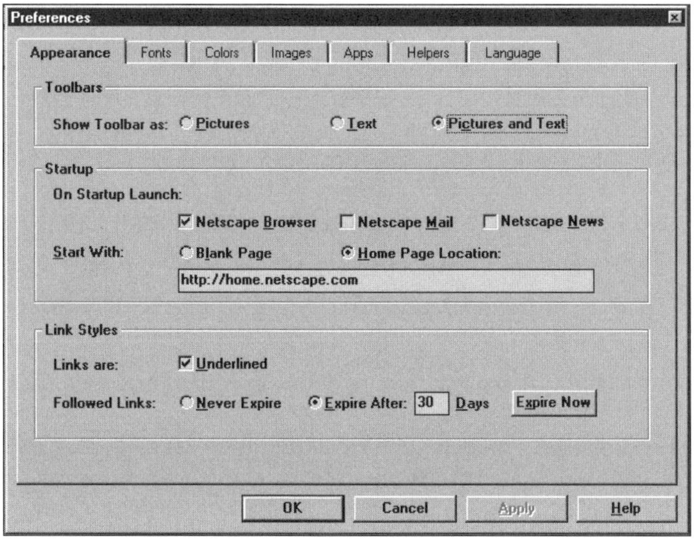

Figure 4.3 The Appearance card.

The second portion of the Appearance card specifies which applications to launch and which document to display at startup. You have a choice of launching any of Netscape's windows as your startup window, either the Netscape Browser, Netscape Mail, or Netscape News window. The default, as configured by Netscape, is to launch your Netscape browser and to display Netscape's Home Page. You can specify any startup page you want by entering its URL in the Home Page Location: text box. I start my Netscape session by displaying my menu of over 300 frequently visited sites. You can even load a starting page document from your hard disk to speed up the startup process (we'll have a more detailed discussion about customizing your startup page location later in Chapter 8). If the Blank Page radio button is selected, the specified home page document won't display at startup, but it may be retrieved at any time by clicking on the toolbar's Home icon.

Finally, the third portion of the Appearance card, titled Link Styles, configures how you see links. Your documents will load faster if the Links are: Underlined option is not selected. Why? Because Netscape won't need to display underlined text for all the links in your documents.

Another useful option you can set in the Link Styles section is the Followed Links: option. Netscape "remembers" all the sites you visit for a specified amount of time. Netscape's default setting is to remember a site for 30 days after that site has been visited. Links visited within the specified time frame appear in a different color on your screen. This makes traveling down new paths, or revisiting interesting sites, easier. Clicking on Never Expire means your links will appear as followed links until you click on Expire Now. Clicking on Expire Now erases the history file and reverts the links back to their original color, without changing the retention parameters.

When you are finished with the Appearance card, click OK to accept any changes or click Cancel to revert back to the original settings.

Fonts

The Preferences dialog box Fonts card is shown in Figure 4.4.

This dialog box has one section, named Fonts and Encodings. Encoding is the mapping of glyphs (such as character symbols) to computer codes (such as hexadecimal digits). The Encoding drop-down list isn't really useful unless you are viewing documents in Japanese, Korean, or Chinese. Latin1 is the default encoding.

The other two options, Use the Proportional Font and Use the Fixed Font, are used to determine the font style and size of text associated with the default encoding character set. The proportional font is used to display portions of documents, including scaled headings. The fixed font is used for special effects such as Gopher menus, FTP listings, and forms. The default settings for Latin1 is the proportional font of Times 12 and the fixed font of Courier 10.

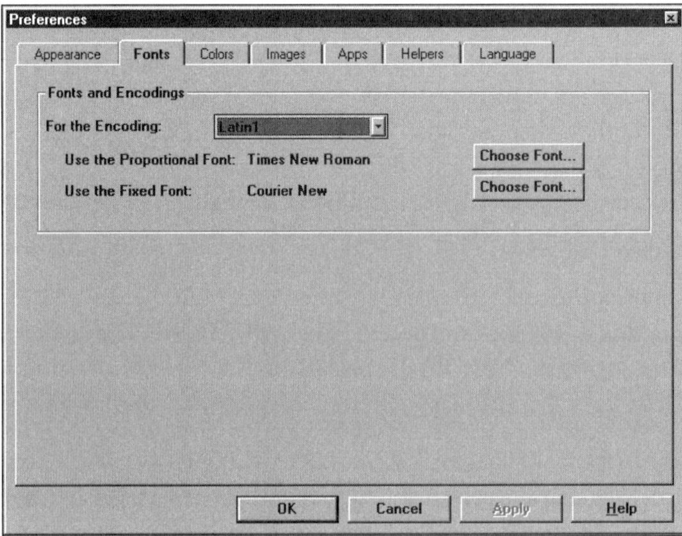

Figure 4.4 *The Preferences Fonts dialog box.*

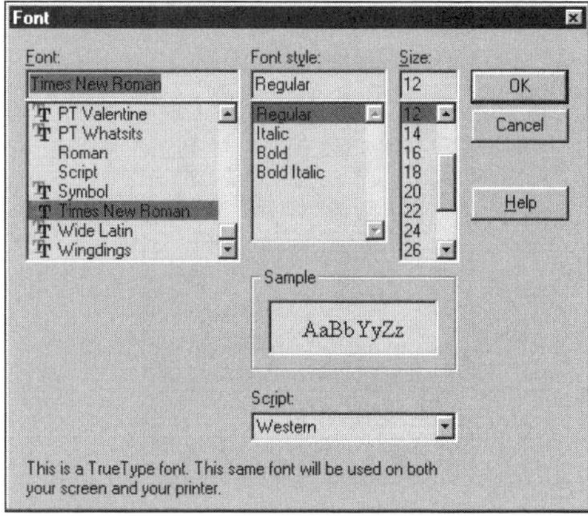

***Figure 4.5** The Choose Font dialog box.*

You can select a different font or font size for proportional and fixed font styles by clicking on the desired Choose Font button. Figure 4.5 shows the Choose Font dialog box.

Scroll through the Font selections or the Size options to adjust specifications. Changing fonts periodically tends to add a little spice to Web browsing. If you're spending too much time surfing the Web and you have a hard time seeing the small print, you may want to increase the font size. On the other hand, you may want to decrease the font size to display more information on each Web page.

Colors

The next card in the Preferences dialog box is the Colors card, which is used to customize how Netscape displays documents.

The first four selections on the card, to the left of the Choose Color buttons, determine the color of links, followed links, text, and the background. An actual swatch of the specified color is displayed to the right of the word Custom. Clicking on a Choose Color button brings up the initial Color dialog box as shown in Figure 4.6.

Clicking on the Define Custom Colors option expands the dialog box to include a color palette as shown in Figure 4.7.

Select a Basic Color by clicking on the color of your choice. Select a Custom Color by clicking somewhere in the palette or by editing the color numbers. You can lighten or darken the shade of your preferred color by moving the arrow to the right rectangular box. If you select a custom color, add it to your

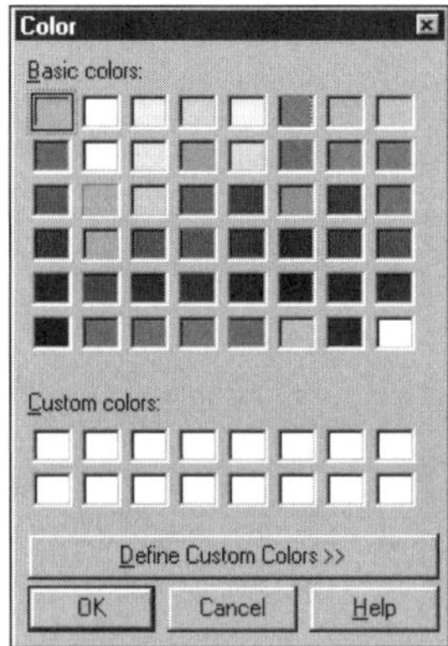

Figure 4.6 *The Color dialog box.*

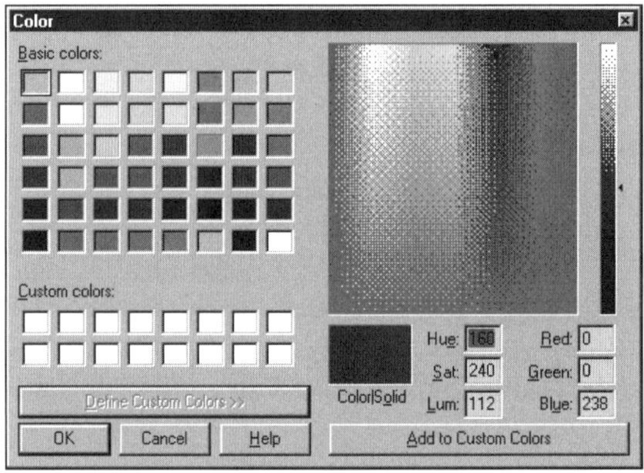

Figure 4.7 *The Color dialog box with the color palette displayed.*

color repertoire for future use by clicking on Add to Custom Colors. The custom color will then appear in one of the Custom Colors boxes.

Getting the Best Contrast

Most people prefer to display text using as much contrast as possible. If you've spent any amount of time surfing with Netscape, you've seen the result of ill-conceived background color schemes. To get the most contrast possible, use black text on a white background. Try changing the default gray background to white and see if it doesn't make viewing easier. If you decide you prefer the original gray color, just select the Background Default radio button.

When selecting background and text colors, don't choose closely related colors. Low color contrast can make long-term viewing tedious. You can always choose black text on a black background when you get tired of viewing (grin).

The next item on the Colors card is Image File. If you have seen a background image you like (not a background color) you can use it for all your documents by downloading the image to your hard disk and specifying its name and location in the text box. Even though you select an image file, you must still select the radio button to the left of the Image File prompt for it to take effect.

Finally, the checkbox at the bottom of the card is used to indicate if your color preferences should override the colors specified in a document. I suggest you let the document settings override your customized settings. A Web author like yourself may spend hours getting a document just right, and you don't really want to miss out on all this hard work, do you?

As usual, click on OK to accept any changes or click on Cancel to revert back to the original settings.

Images

The next Preferences card is the Images card. Frankly, I don't see much difference among the Automatic, Dither, or Substitute Colors radio button choices. Theoretically, basic differences are that Automatic attempts to determine the appropriate type of image display, while selecting Dither or Substitute Colors tries to closely match your computer's available colors. If you choose Dither, your images may offer the closest match to an image's intended colors, but it will probably take longer to display. You might want to experiment with the settings on your system.

Having images displayed While Loading or After Loading is again a matter of personal preference. I like to watch my images being displayed as they are loading. But then again, maybe I'm just weird.

Apps

The Apps (Applications) card is used to specify where applications that support Netscape are stored on your computer system. The applications on this card provide Netscape with connection and page formatting utilities. There are four supporting application fields on this card: Telnet application, TN3270 application, View Source, and Temporary Directory.

Telnet applications provide you with the means to connect to other computers using standard Internet protocols. You use the Telnet Application: text box to specify the location of your Telnet application.

The TN3270 text box is used to specify where your TN3270 application resides. TN3270 is used for Telnet connections to IBM mainframes.

A View Source application displays a Web page in plain text embedded in HTML formatting commands (kind of a behind the scenes look at what makes the page look the way it does). If you do not specify the location of a Viewer application, your platform will probably use a default viewer. To view the source of an HTML document in Netscape, you execute the sequence View | Document Source. If you specify an HTML editor, as opposed to letting Netscape display the document, you have the advantage of modifying and saving the document. The disadvantage is longer loading times.

Finally, specifying a folder in the Temporary Directory: text box tells Netscape where to store helper applications while they are being used. Whenever a helper application executes, Netscape temporarily stores the application files to disk. After you exit the helper application, Netscape deletes the files. You can indicate where you want Netscape to store and delete temporary files.

Helpers

The Helpers card in the General Preferences dialog box is shown in Figure 4.8.

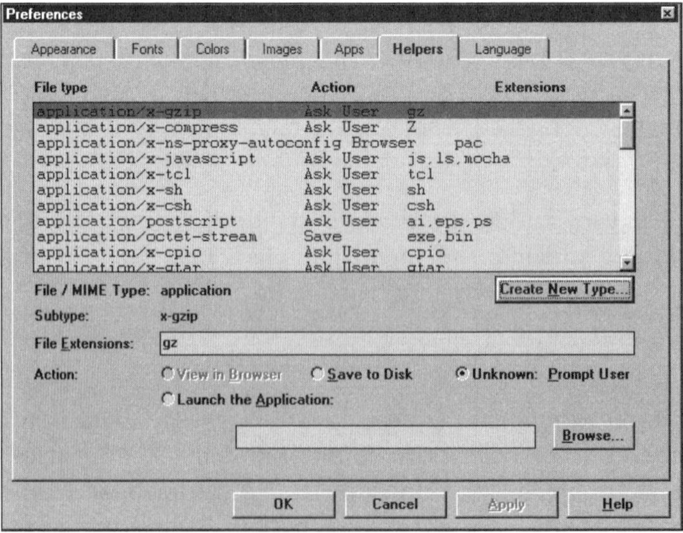

***Figure 4.8** The General Preferences dialog box–Helpers card.*

It is no secret that documents scattered across the Web point to text files, images, sound files, movies, and potentially any kind of data you can store in digital form. When a link points to a resource Netscape cannot process internally, the file is "displayed" using an external viewer. The term "viewer" may be slightly confusing when used in a Web context. To Netscape, a viewer is a program that presents to the user (most people still say "views") an external file that Netscape cannot process internally. Viewers display graphics, run animated clips, and play sound files—you can see why "viewer" isn't exactly the best word. More and more people are calling them *helper applications*.

When Netscape, or any other Web browser, receives a file from a Web server, the server identifies the file's MIME (Multipurpose Internet Mail Extensions) type. The server furnishes a MIME code, which is a standardized method for defining a group of different file types. When a browser receives a file of some sort from a server, the browser determines if the file can be processed by the software's built-in capabilities. If the browser can't handle the file format, a helper application (assuming one is available) is executed to "view" the file. The concept is the same for all browsers. (Keep in mind that browsers differ in their capabilities to process file types internally—that is, without having to resort to a viewer.) Netscape retrieves files with formats that Netscape cannot read, then it attempts to use an external helper application to read the file.

The Helpers card lets you examine and configure how a file's format maps to a helper application. The card contains several fields and buttons used to specify MIME file types, helper applications, and associated actions.

Configuring Helper Applications requires a reasonable degree of support material. I think it is probably best if we hold off discussing Helper applications in-depth until a later chapter.

Language

You can inform servers of your language preferences using the Language card in the General Preferences dialog box. For example, you can specify that you would like to receive a document in English, but a Spanish version of the document would be an acceptable second choice. When you set your preferences on the Language card, your language priorities are sent as a part of the http header.

In some instances, you can specify a language and region code. For example, English/United States [en-US], specifies the English language in the United States region. You can either select a language and region code from the Language/Region list, or you can specify another language in the User define: text box.

Let's build a short language priority list. First, click on English/United States [en-US] in the Language/Region list. Then click on the arrow key pointing toward the Accept List text box. English/United States [en-US] appears as your first language preference in your Accept List. Select Spanish [es], then click on the arrow key pointing toward the Accept List. Next, click in the User define: text box, type Latin, then click on the arrow pointing down toward the Accept List. Your language priority list should look like the one on the Language Card illustrated in Figure 4.9.

We've now looked at the cards found in the General Preferences dialog box. The next preferences menu under the Options command is the Mail and News Preferences dialog box.

Mail and News Preferences

The Mail and News Preferences dialog box contains five topic cards: Appearance, Composition, Servers, Identity, and Organization. Let's take a quick look at each of these cards.

Appearance

The Mail and News Preferences Appearance card is shown in Figure 4.10.

You use the Appearance Card to customize font styles displayed in Mail and News windows. You can select either Fixed Width Font or Variable Width

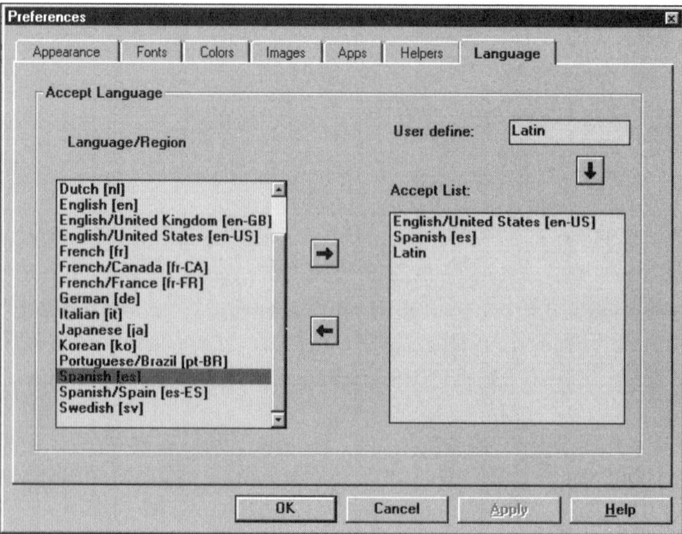

Figure 4.9 The Language Card—language priority list.

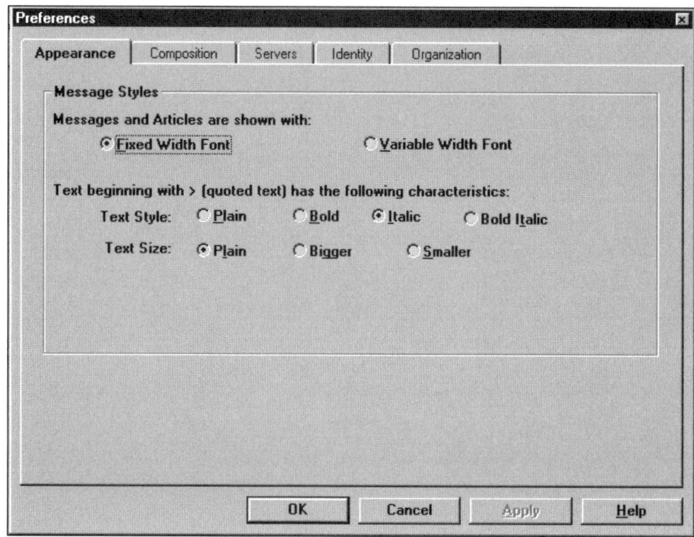

***Figure 4.10** The Mail and News Preferences dialog box–Appearance card.*

Font by using the radio buttons located in the top section of the card. Using the radio buttons located below the font width buttons, you can specify the text style and the text size of quoted material.

Composition

In the top section of the Composition Card, you can opt to compose mail and news messages using the 8-bit or MIME-compliant option. The Allow 8-bit radio button selection is the default, and it accommodates the widest range of email servers in the United States and Europe. Unless you are into MIME encoding, you should keep the Allow 8-bit option selected as your default.

The next section of the Composition Card helps you retain copies of mail and news messages. Enter an email address in either the Mail Messages or News Messages field if you want to email a copy of mail or news messages you send. You can also automatically store copies of mail or news messages to a file or disk. Netscape's default is to copy mail messages to the Sent Mail file, as shown in Figure 4.11.

Finally, notice the option at the bottom section of the Composition Card named Automatically quote original message when replying. This check box is used to restate original messages in your mail or news message (preceded by the > symbol). Remember, when you are extracting lines from the original message, you should delete nonrelevant lines so your messages are not unnecessarily long.

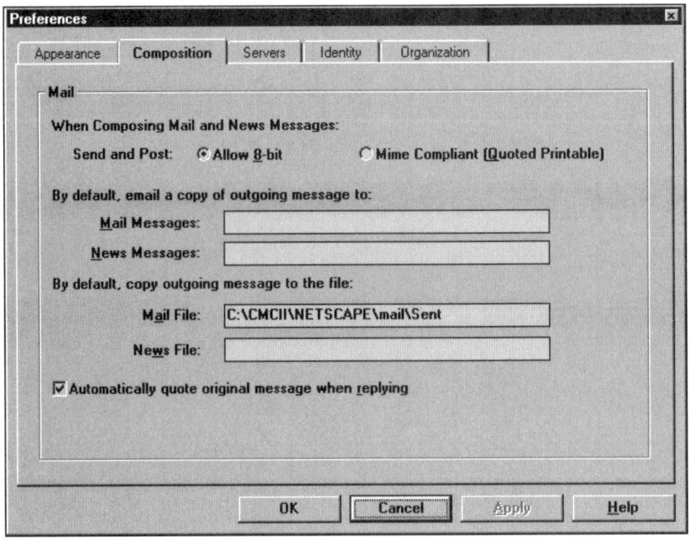

Figure 4.11 The Mail and News Preferences dialog box–Composition card.

Servers

The top of the Servers Card in the Mail and News Preferences dialog box is titled Mail. This section assists you in setting up your email preferences. To send email, Netscape must be able to make the appropriate connection to a Simple Mail Transport Protocol (SMTP) server. To receive mail, Netscape must be able to make a connection to a Point of Presence (POP) server. Usually the Outgoing Mail (SMTP) and the Incoming Mail (POP) servers are the same. If you don't know the name of your mail server, you can ask your Internet provider or Network administrator. You use the Servers Card in the Mail and New Preferences dialog box to provide Netscape with the information it needs to make the connections for you. This card also has some useful options such as how often to check for messages and how long messages should remain on the server.

The lower section of the Servers Card, titled News, has three entries dealing with News. If you don't read news using Netscape, you can skip this section. The name of your News Server, as with the Mail Server, is provided by your Internet provider or Network administrator. The News RC Directory is a directory path where Netscape keeps news related items. I like to keep life simple and keep all my Netscape-related files in the same directory as the executable program.

The last entry, Get Messages at a Time, is the limit of how many news messages are transferred in a single block. The default is set at getting 100 messages at a time, but that number can be replaced with any number up to 3500. Keep in mind that the larger the number, the longer it takes to complete the transfer of the messages.

Identity

The Identity card supplies information used to identify you in email messages and news articles. The text fields are fairly self-explanatory. Your name is what your parents hung on you or what you choose to call yourself. Netscape uses your name entry when constructing a bookmark file title and a mail heading. Your email address is the user identification given to you, or selected by you, when you opened your account, followed by "@" and your provider's domain name. There are never any spaces in an email address. Your Reply-to Address is an alternative email address (if you have one) for receiving replies to your email. Your Organization is typically your work affiliation if you choose to use one.

Identity Using the Correct Email Address

Be very careful when entering your email address in the Identity Card text boxes. If you make a mistake when entering your address and someone subsequently replies, the returned message will not reach you. It's a good idea to send mail to yourself and then select "Reply" (if your mail reader supports the function) to ensure everything is OK.

Many people like to have a small message appended to their mail messages. The message—called a sig block—may be a cute little saying or, heaven forbid, quasi-commercial. You too can personalize Netscape mail by creating your own sig block. Create a file using a text editor and type the text you would like included with your signature. Save the file, then specify its name and path in the Signature File: text box on the Identity Card. Good taste dictates holding a signature block to five lines or less.

Organization

You use the Organization card in the Mail and News Preferences dialog box to arrange the display of your messages. The Organization card is shown in Figure 4.12.

Notice the checkbox at the top of the card. If you click on the Remember Mail Password check box you will not have to enter your password each time you open the Mail window.

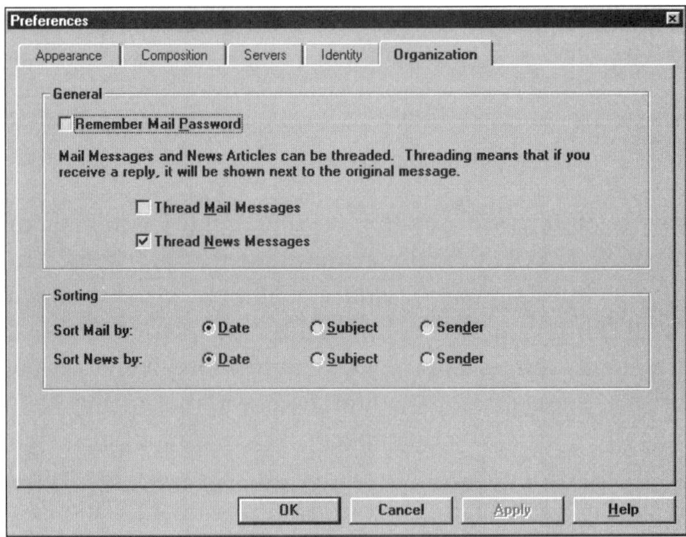

Figure 4.12 *The Mail and News Preferences dialog box–Organization card.*

Below the initial checkbox item, you can choose to organize your mail and news messages by threading, or listing messages of the same topic together. By default, Netscape threads news messages, but not mail messages. Without threading turned on, news and mail message are listed in the order received. You can also sort your messages by date, subject, or sender. By default, both mail and news are sorted by date.

Once again, click on OK to accept any changes or click on Cancel to revert to your previously saved settings. This completes our survey of the Mail and News Preferences menu options, let's move on to the third preferences menu —Network Preferences.

Network Preferences

The Network Preferences menu consists of three card topics: Cache, Connections, and Proxies.

Cache

Since this section is somewhat complicated, you might want to leave the options at their default setting.

The idea behind caching is to hold things that might be used again in the future in main or disk memory. If a required file is held in cache memory, Netscape does not need to fetch it from the Internet. That's the good news;

the bad news is that caching takes both disk and main memory space. Memory Cache specifies how much memory will be set aside for caching. Unfortunately, memory dedicated to cache memory cannot be used for anything else during an active Netscape session. Disk Cache, on the other hand, is used to specify the size and location of space on your hard disk used to hold stored files between Netscape sessions.

If you look at the directory specified as the Disk Cache Directory, you will see many files with an .MOZ extension. Most of these files are actually the GIF files that were loaded when you visited various sites.

Viewing Stored GIF (MOZ) Files

Paint Shop Pro, included on the companion CD-ROM, comes with a program called PSP Browser, which is a very clever and useful utility. If you run PSP Browser and point it to your Disk Cache Directory, it recognizes which files are GIF images despite the .MOZ extension. PSP Browser gives you thumbnail sketches of all your image files. Be careful of copyrights and ask for permission before using any GIF you find in your cache. I have never had anyone tell me no when I asked for permission to use an image—I've had people ignore my request, but then again, I don't always answer all of my mail.

The first time a page is requested, Netscape downloads the page from the Internet. Each page you retrieve is temporarily stored in a cache. If you subsequently request a page you have previously acquired, Netscape checks to see if the page is available in the cache. If you click on the Back button, you'll notice that cached documents are displayed much faster than when you first displayed the document.

There are times when you don't want to use cache retrieval. The page you fetched initially may have changed. If this happens, you typically want to see the updated page, not the original. This is especially noticeable when you perform multiple searches. When you click on a link, choose a bookmark, enter a URL, or press the Reload button, Netscape checks to see if an update has occurred before loading a page from cache. If a change has occurred, the new version is fetched. If no change has occurred, the faster loading cache version is retrieved.

Netscape does not check for different versions when you choose a history item or press the Back button. If you have reason to suspect a document has changed (you may have changed it yourself), click on the Reload button, which manually overrides the process.

Caching sizes are a tradeoff between processing speed and maximizing memory resources. Memory cache sizes between 200 and 400 Kilobytes are typically used with computers having 4 megs of main memory, and 600 Kilobytes to the-sky-is-the-limit are used when you have more memory. I would recommend you select the Once per Session radio button in the Verify Documents section. Disk cache sizes are typically set to about 2,000 to 8,000 Kilobytes (2 to 8 megs).

There may be times when you suspect your cache is acting incorrectly, or maybe you just want to free up some memory space. The caches are clearable by clicking the Clear Memory Cache Now and Clear Disk Cache Now buttons.

Connections

The Connections card of the Network Preferences dialog box specifies your system's maximum number of simultaneous connections made to the Internet. The text and each image on a Web page are distinct files. Netscape can display multiple files (both text and graphic) simultaneously by opening more than one connection to a server. You can see this simultaneous transmission in action whenever you watch a graphic coming in while text is being placed.

The Network Buffer Size option specifies the number of kilobytes allotted in memory for data transmissions. Netscape's Connections card defaults are 32 Kilobytes of network buffer size for Windows and 4 simultaneous network connections. These are fine parameters for most uses. You don't really want to be using more than 4 simultaneous connections if you're using a 14.4 Kb modem.

Opening Multiple Netscape Windows

Netscape provides the ability to have multiple windows open simultaneously. This can be a major advantage when you are FTPing a large file or you want to rapidly switch between sites to make a comparison. To open another window press Ctrl+N or select the File | New Web Browser option. A new window always starts by opening your designated home page. (A good reason to load it from local disk.) After your home page is displayed, you can select a different URL. To switch between windows, press Ctrl+Tab. To close a window press Ctrl+W or select File | Close.

Moving right along, click on OK to accept any changes or click on Cancel to revert to the saved version of your Connections preferences.

Proxies

Normally, Netscape does not require proxies to interact with external network services. However, in some networks, the connection between Netscape and the remote server is blocked by a firewall. Firewalls protect information in internal computer networks from external access. Unfortunately, firewalls also might limit Netscape's ability to exchange information with external sources.

If you already know about proxies, you don't need me to tell you about them. If you are accessing the Internet using a standalone PC, you definitely don't need to use proxies.

Let's leave proxies well enough alone and move on to Security Preferences.

Security Preferences

The Security Preferences dialog box has two topic cards: General and Site Certificates. The General card offers optional Security Alerts such as notifying you when you are entering or leaving a secure document. If you are running Windows 95 this also allows you to choose whether you want to disable Java (more about Java later). The Security Preferences Site Certificates card represents a not-so-subtle commercial reminding us that Netscape Communications supplies secure servers.

EDITING NETSCAPE.INI

Windows configuration files, frequently called initialization files, are essentially lists of program directives. One of the most important files on your entire system is the Windows initialization file. This file resides in your main WINDOWS directory. The initialization file that Netscape uses is netscape.ini. It's a good idea to become as familiar as you can with both of these files so that you can better troubleshoot any problems that might occur with Netscape. My first rule of computer management is, "Don't try to understand how things should work after they don't."

> *Note: Never edit netscape.ini while Netscape is running. Netscape only reads netscape.ini when it starts, and overwrites the original version when it finishes. Any editing done in the interim is lost.*

Saving Backup Copies of netscape.ini

Before manually editing any configuration file, I suggest you make a copy of the INI file using its actual name and an extension of "ORG" (for original). Alternatively, you can do what I do and number your versions using the scheme, netscape.000, netscape.001, and so on. This technique allows you to return to older versions at any time.

I also include the following lines in my autoexec.bat file:

```
copy c:\autoexec.bat c:\*.org
copy c:\config.sys c:\*.org
copy c:\windows\win.ini c:\windows\win.org
copy j:\netscape\netscape.ini j:\netscape\*.org
```

You get the idea.

Here are a few other points to consider. Use comments to notate original lines and make changes one at time. Any line beginning with REM (or rem) is considered a comment. If you are going to change something, first copy the line to be changed. Next, put a "rem" in front of one of the lines. Lastly, edit the uncommented line. After each change, test the INI file. If something goes wrong, it's easy to determine where the problem occurred.

INI files have a common structural theme. They are grouped into sections. For example, the Netscape section in win.ini is:

```
[Netscape]
```

Each new section contains a label enclosed in square brackets.

INI files also contain what are called *embedded program directives*. These directives allow you to include parameters to define values. Here's the format:

```
keyword=replacement-value
```

Where Is netscape.ini?

If you search your hard disk for netscape.ini files, you may find several. Which is the one Netscape reads when it starts? The answer can be found by looking at the main Windows configuration file, win.ini. Within this file is a special Netscape section as shown here:

```
[Netscape]
ini=J:\NETSCAPE\NETSCAPE.INI
```

Essentially, this tells Windows where to look for the file—in the directory \netscape. I once spent three days working on a problem with a friend. He kept changing the netscape.ini file and restarting Netscape, but couldn't solve his problem. Finally, it dawned on me; he was editing the wrong file.

When you install a new version of Netscape, the installation program looks for an existing netscape.ini. If it finds one, it does not overwrite the original. Earlier versions of Netscape installed netscape.ini in the c:\windows directory. Check win.ini to see which one you are using. It is also a good idea to check the netscape.ini that comes with a new release. As we'll see in a minute, the file frequently contains troubleshooting comments.

Let's look at a netscape.ini section.

```
[User]
User_Name=Urb LeJeune
User_Addr=lejeune@acy.digex.net
Sig_File=J:\NETSCAPE\SIG.TXT
User_Organization=
```

Recognize these settings from our Preferences editing? Sections may come in any order and frequently get rearranged when the program rewrites the file. However, all the components for a specific section must occur within that section.

Netscape.ini File Comments

Recall that INI files use the keyword REM or rem to indicate a comment line. The netscape.ini file for version 2.0, for example, starts with the following comment:

```
rem  This is the default initialization file for Netscape.  Netscape
rem  will look in win.ini in the [Netscape] section for the ini
rem  entry and expect this file to be there.  Failing that, Netscape
rem  will look in the directory where it was launched for this file.
rem
rem  If you install Netscape in a directory other than c:\netscape
rem  you should make sure that you update the "History File"
rem  and "File Location" (under "Bookmarks") to be pointers to
rem  files in valid directories that Netscape can write to or
rem  else you won't get global history or bookmarks across
rem  sessions.  In addition, you should make sure the directory
rem  specified by "Cache Dir" exists and is writable.
rem
rem  If you are having winsock problems you should try setting
rem
rem     [Network]
rem     Use Async DNS=no
rem
rem  you might also need to set
rem
rem     [Network]
rem     Max Connections=1
rem
```

Had my friend read the first section, about where Netscape looks for netscape.ini, he would have saved both of us three days of aggravation.

There are a few settings that are not changeable from within a preferences dialog box. In the history section, the location of the history file, as shown next, cannot be modified from within a preferences dialog box. The Expiration setting, however, can be modified.

```
[History]
History File=j:\netscape\netscape.hst
Expiration=30
```

The Network section contains the Use Async DNS setting, which can cause the problem described in the remarks section above. If you are having DNS problems, try changing the Use Async DNS=yes and Max Connections=4 settings to:

```
[Network]
Use Async DNS=no
Max Connections=1
```

Finally, if the **<BLINK>** tags in Web pages drive you crazy, you can change the Blinking parameter in the Settings section from Blinking=yes to:

```
[Settings]
Blinking=no
```

So there you have configuration in all its glory, or is it gory? It wasn't all that scary, was it?

Using Editors

You can edit netscape.ini using one of the following text editors: Windows Notepad, DOS EDIT, or any other ASCII editor such as an HTML editor. Notepad is probably the most convenient to use. You can also use a full-featured word processor like Word for Windows or WordPerfect, but you'll need to make sure that you save any files you change as text files. The native format for a word processor contains all sorts of binary information that will be appended or prefaced to netscape.ini, and this will prevent Netscape from reading and using the file.

INSTALLING HELPER APPLICATIONS

Implementing a helper application is a four-part process:

1. Obtain the program from the companion CD-ROM (if it is available) or FTP it down to your PC.
2. Install the helper on your PC.
3. Tell your browser where the helper resides.
4. Tell your browser the extensions associated with each helper.

Steps 3 and 4 are performed very easily by using the Netscape Preferences dialog box. Earlier versions of Netscape frequently required editing of the program's initialization file, which could be quite tricky.

To illustrate the viewer concept, we might want to tell Netscape to send a file with a .JPG extension to a helper program called lview.exe, which is a commonly used image viewer. Likewise, the program wham.exe can play audio files. Helper programs are not restricted to multimedia files.

Netscape's use of external programs for handling specific data types is configurable by entering the required information in the General Preferences dialog box. Fortunately, Netscape is configured to recognize quite a few file and MIME types. Don't settle into complacency, though, for you will undoubtedly run into situations where you will have to tell Netscape how to read a particular file.

All the helper programs mentioned in this chapter are contained on the companion CD-ROM. I've also listed some FTP sites containing the helper files, since helper programs are periodically updated.

You do not necessarily have to use the specific viewers mentioned in this chapter. You can use any viewer capable of processing the desired file type—and new viewers appear all the time.

Netscape Viewers List and WinSock Client Listing

Netscape maintains a list of viewers tested and known to work with Netscape. The URL for this page is:

```
http://home.netscape.com/assist/helper_apps/windowhelper.html
```

The document also has anchors containing the full FTP URLs for the listed programs so you can easily click and download the ones you want.

Obtaining Current Helper and WinSock Information

Current and comprehensive information on helper applications and WinSock-compliant programs is available from a few different sources. Forrest H. Stroud maintains a set of online documents called "The Consummate WinSock Applications List". One URL where you can find the CWSApps list is:

```
http://cws.wilmington.net/cwsapps.html
```

Figure 4.13 shows a portion of The Consummate WinSock Apps Site List.

Each location listed provides access to invaluable documents that help you find the most current Web browsers and support applications. Notice our friend Charm Net is listed next to the Maryland header. If you click on Charm Net, you will see Charm Net's Stroud's page. Click on the large blue graphic at the top of the page and you will find yourself at Charm Net's CWSApps display page. The CWSApps page is your connection to applications, tips, browsers, and other interesting netware. Notice the links to Audio Apps, Critical Winsock, and Multimedia Viewers among the topics, as shown in Figure 4.14. You could spend quite a bit of time investigating this page, so you may as well make it a bookmark. You can come back to this apps page later, but right now I want to take you to another helpful netstop.

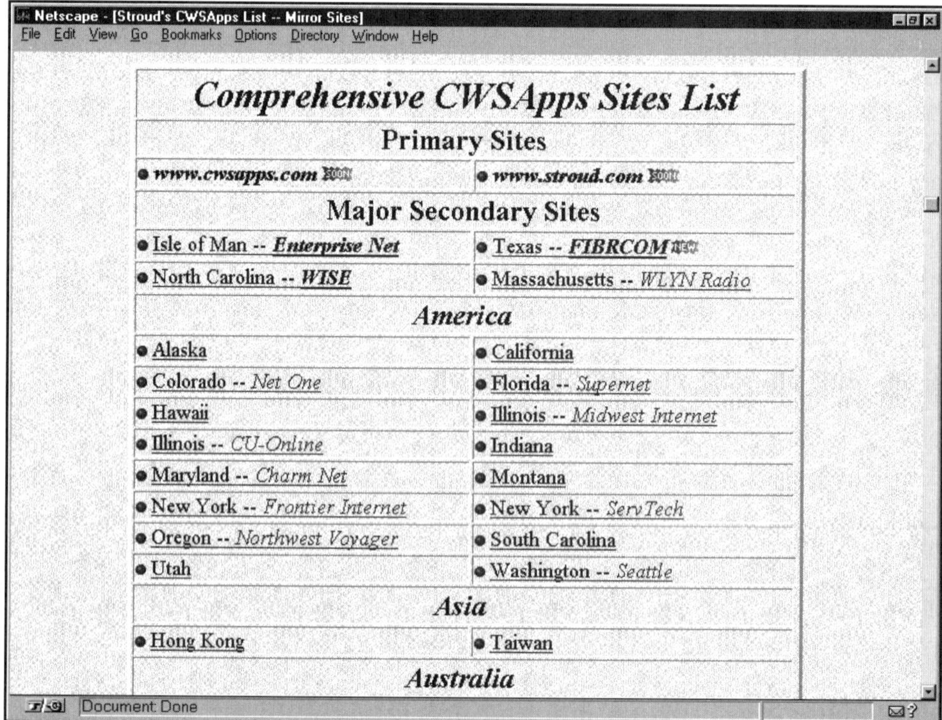

Figure 4.13 *Stroud's Comprehensive CWSApps Sites List.*

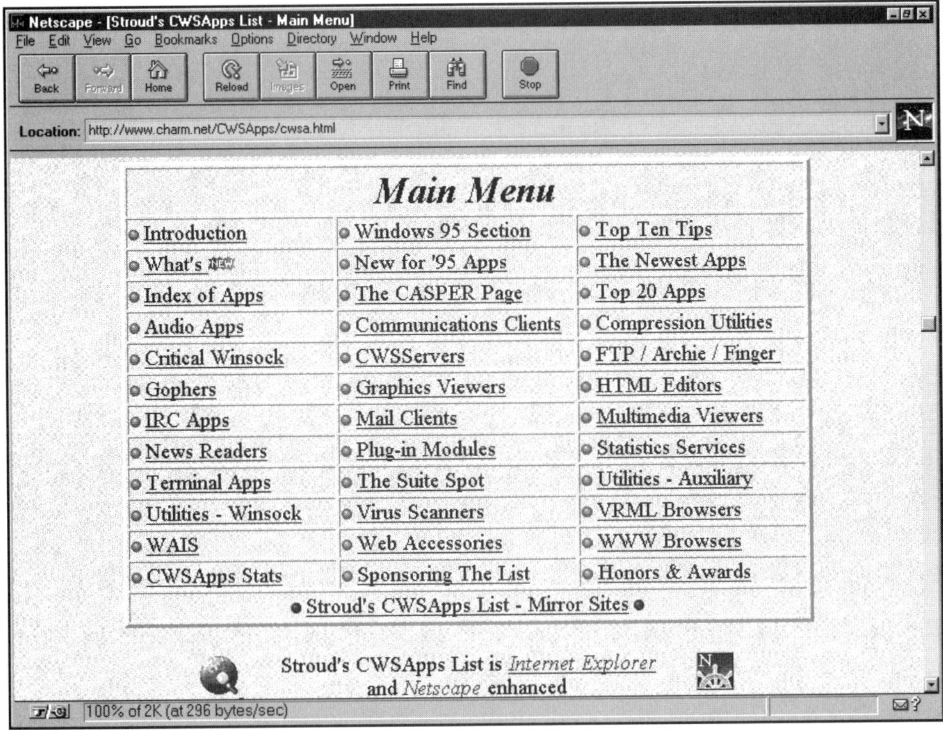

***Figure 4.14** Charm Net's CWSApps page.*

Another excellent site containing a list of available apps is the Tucows site, which has over six million visitors each month. If you want join the crowd, the URL is:

```
http://tucows.phx.cox.com/index.html
```

Scroll down a little and you will see a group of buttons. If you click on the Apps Index button, you will see more helper applications than you probably knew existed. You'll find all the basic apps plus a slew of lesser-knowns. I think it is time to make another bookmark, don't you?

Finally, I want to take you to one more net site before we get down to serious business. The site is SuperNet, and the URL is:

```
http://www.supernet.net
```

Once you are on the home page, click on Go to the SuperNet Hot List and then the Software & Freeware link. Scroll down and you'll see a link to Stroud's

WinSock list and The Ultimate Collection of WinSock Software (which is the Tucows site). As you were scrolling you probably noticed a few other interesting topics. Go ahead, I'll wait while you add a SuperNet bookmark. Now it's time to install some of these helper applications.

INSTALLING HELPER APPLICATIONS

Here are the steps used to install a helper application:

1. Create a new directory to hold the program files.
2. Copy the file from the CD-ROM or FTP the file to your new directory.
3. Uncompress the file (which is typically inside a ZIP archive).
4. Enter the helper information in Netscape's Helper Applications Preferences dialog box.
5. Test the helper application.
6. Delete any unneeded files.

If you obtained a helper via FTP download, you might also archive the downloaded program onto diskette for safekeeping.

We'll perform a fairly detailed installation of Lview Pro shortly. (This is a must-have viewer and all-around image program.) The Lview installation process can then be used as a template for installing additional viewers.

There are two possibilities for installing any program under Windows. Simple programs often require nothing more than unzipping them into a home directory. More complex programs often have their own setup.exe or install.exe programs that handle the creation of directories and any possible install-time configuration. It isn't always possible to tell which sort of installation a program will need just by looking at its ZIP archive; very often you will have to unzip the archive into its directory and then double-check the read.me file. The presence of a file named setup.exe or install.exe and most files existing in the form abc.ex_ (with the underscore as the last character) are good tipoffs that the program needs to be installed through an included installer utility.

For this chapter's discussion, I've compiled information about helper applications into tables. Each table suggests a directory to hold the program, and recommends files to delete after the program is installed and tested. In some cases the ZIP file is deleted; in others, an entire temporary directory of files can be deleted. In the latter case, the use of a directory in the form of c:\temp shows the purpose of the directory and also serves as a reminder that the directory, along with its contents, can be deleted after installation.

The tables use the following format:

Program Name:
Version:
Path on CD-ROM:
FTP URL:
Status:
Download to:
Netscape Preferences **File Type:** **Extensions:**

The first four table entries are self-explanatory. The fifth, Status, will indicate whether a program is freeware or shareware, and if it's shareware, how much it costs. If the program uncompresses into files requiring additional uncompression and installation with a SETUP program, the suggested download directory is c:\temp. Call it what you like (and put it where you like), but I suggest that you use a directory named \temp. If no additional uncompression is required and there is no SETUP program, the download directory can be the program's final resting place.

The entries for Netscape Preferences represent the File Type and Extensions that are selected from the Helper Applications Preferences dialog box. The majority of multimedia files you will encounter on the Web are preconfigured in the Helper Applications dialog box. The default actions for these file types are either Ask User, Save to disk, or use Netscape, which is shown as Browser in the text box. The purpose of the preference configuration is to associate helper applications with MIME types and file extensions. The process will be much clearer when we actually configure Lview Pro.

Configuring Viewers

After a viewer is installed, Netscape must be informed of its location and the types of files it views. Netscape looks to its configuration file, netscape.ini, for this information. Fortunately, all viewer configuration is accomplished directly from the General Preferences dialog box on the Helpers card, as shown previously in Figure 4.8.

AN INSTALLATION TEMPLATE

The next section is a detailed set of instructions for installing Lview Pro. This Netscape image helper will serve as a model for other helper applications.

GIF and JPEG Viewer Lview Pro

Program:	lviewp1c.zip	
Version:	Version 1.C	
Path on CD-ROM:	x:\helpers\lview\lviewp1b.exe(16-bit) x:\helpers\lview\lviewpro.exe(32-bit)	
FTP URL:	http://www.ncsa.uiuc.edu/SDG/Software/ WinMosaic/Viewers/lview.htm	
Status:	Shareware, $30 plus shipping	
Download to:	c:\lviewpro	
Netscape Preferences	**File Type:**	**Extensions:**
	image/gif	gif
	image/tiff	tiff, tif
	image/jpeg	jpeg, jpg, jpe

Lview and Lview Pro are two widely used GIF, JPEG, and Targa file viewers. Lview is a freeware program that has been available for quite some time. Lview Pro is the professional version of Lview (with more features), and is shareware.

Now let's go through the process step by step. You'll perform the same steps for installing other simple helpers.

Step 1 - Create a directory to hold the program. Create the directory shown in the table's entry "Download to."

Step 2 - Copy or FTP the file into the directory. Simply copy the files from the \helpers\lview directory on the CD-ROM to the new directory if you want to use the version from this book's CD-ROM. If not, click on Lview Pro on the NCSA page listed in the previous table, and you will be presented with the Save As dialog box, as shown in Figure 4.15.

NCSA also maintains an FTP directory for helper applications if you want to FTP a file to your hard disk; its URL is:

```
ftp://ftp.ncsa.uiuc.edu/Web/Mosaic/Windows/viewers/
```

To FTP an application from the NCSA site, you must first access the appropriate FTP directory, click on the application, and choose Save to Disk when Netscape prompts you for directions to process the file. This will bring up the Save As dialog box as shown in Figure 4.15. Select the target directory for the program and you're set.

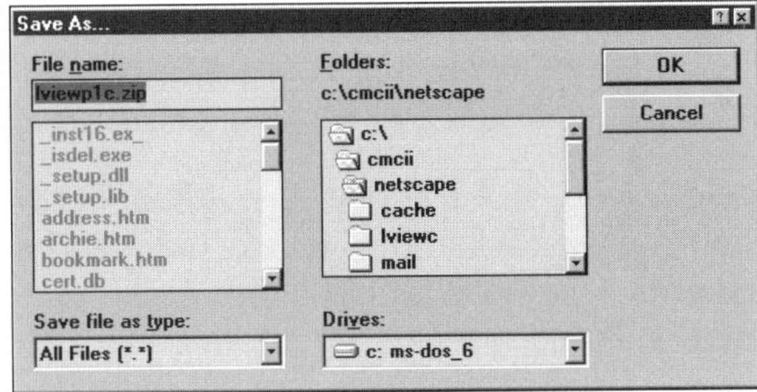

Figure 4.15 The Save As dialog box.

Step 3 - Uncompress the file. Unless you have a Windows-based uncompression utility (and Nico Mak's WinZip shareware product is excellent in this category), shell to DOS by clicking on the MS DOS icon in the Main group, and uncompress the file lviewp1c.zip from the command line. Make c:\lviewpro (or whatever directory you used) the default directory, and enter:

```
C:\LVIEWPRO>pkunzip lviewp1c.zip
```

Step 4 - Configure Netscape to use the program. Execute the sequence Options | General Preferences then click on the Helpers tab. This will bring up the Helper Applications card as shown in Figure 4.8. Use the scroll bars in the large text box to bring the line containing the file type image/gif into view. Click on the item to highlight the line. The items in the Extension Column will appear in the File Extensions: text box in the middle of the screen. The radio button in the Action area below the File Extensions: text box corresponds to the entry in the Action column.

Next, click on the Browse button located in the lower-right corner of the Action frame. This will bring up the Select an appropriate viewer dialog box as shown in Figure 4.16.

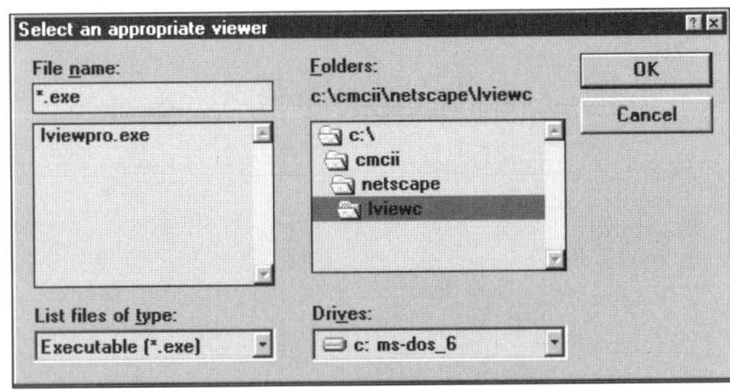

Figure 4.16 The Select an appropriate viewer dialog box.

Adjust the Drives and File Name fields until you get to the path holding the recently installed Lview Pro. In this example, the path is c:\cmcii\netscape\lviewc. Highlight the file lviewpro.exe and then click on OK to accept the entry.

The helper program's icon (if it has one) should appear below the Action: radio buttons when you get back to the Helpers preferences card. Repeat the process described above for JPEG and TIFF file types. Click on OK to complete the configuration of Lview Pro.

Even after installing Lview Pro, Netscape displays JIF files. However, if you click on the image with the right mouse button and then select View This Image, the image displays from within Lview Pro. You can then do any of the wonderful image manipulations Lview supports.

Step 5 - Test the program. You can't be sure your helper installation is complete until you go on the Web, download a file, and see (or hear) it presented correctly by the new helper. Two excellent sources of test files exist. The first is "Multimedia File Formats on the Internet: A Beginner's Guide for PC Users." This was created by Allison Zhang, azhang@admin.stmarys.ca, a graduate student at Dalhousie University in Halifax, Nova Scotia. The URL for this document is:

Figure 4.17 *Multimedia File Formats on the Internet: A Beginner's Guide for PC Users.*

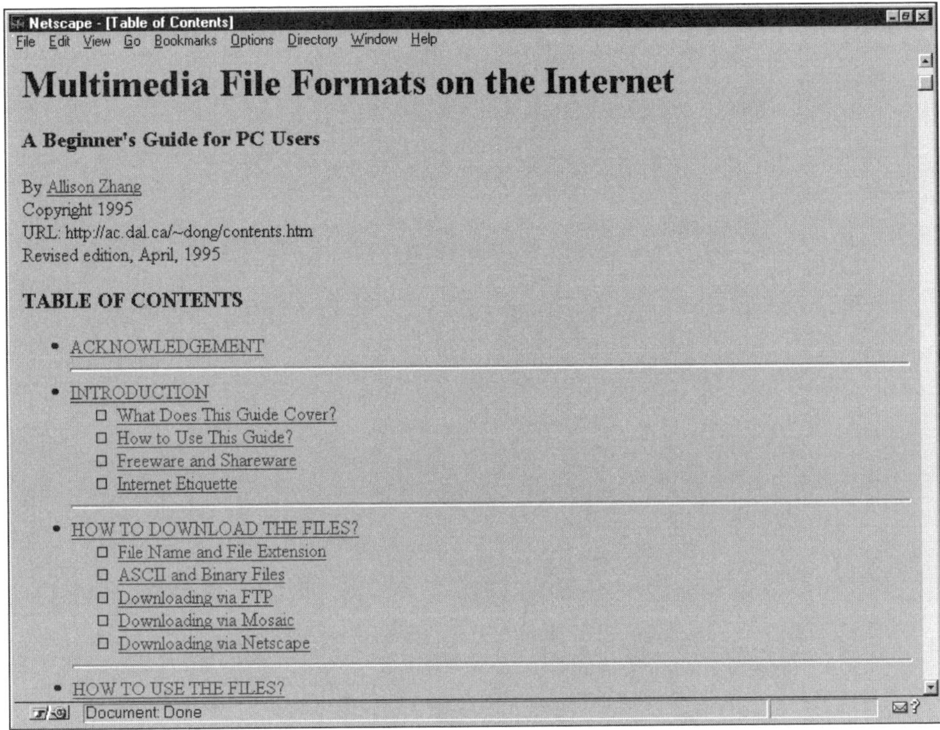

***Figure 4.18** The Table of Contents for the Beginner's Guide.*

```
http://ac.dal.ca/~dong/contents.htm
```

Figure 4.17 shows the first page of this outstanding document, while Figure 4.18 shows the first page of the Table of Contents.

If you want to learn more about multimedia documents, this is *the* place to be. I consider it one of the most outstanding resources on the Web.

The second excellent test site is reachable at:

```
http://www-dsed.llnl.gov/documents/WWWtest.html
```

The home page for this document is entitled, "WWW Viewer Test Page." The first page of this test suite is shown in Figure 4.19. You can test 29 different types of file formats using this document, which is maintained by the Lawrence Livermore National Laboratory.

Step 7 - Delete any unnecessary files. If the program works correctly, the last step in the installation process is the "Action After Installation" section of

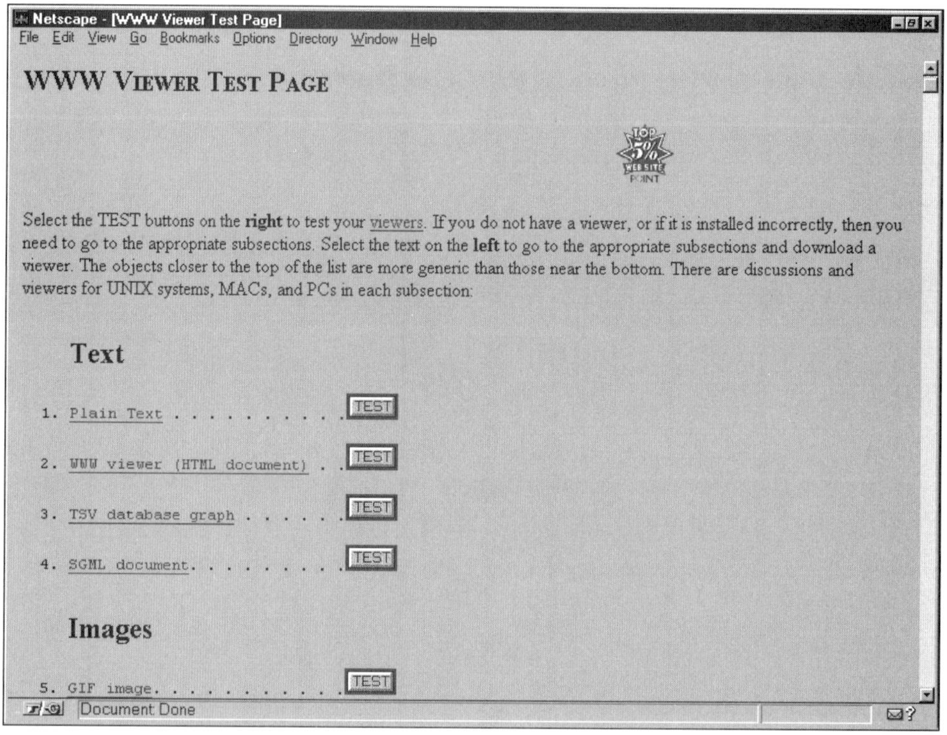

Figure 4.19 *The WWW Viewer Test Page.*

the table. In this case, delete the lviewp1c.zip, the original ZIP file. If you downloaded the program from a remote site, you might archive the ZIP file onto diskette for safekeeping before deleting it from your hard drive.

ONE-STOP SHOPPING FOR VIEWERS AT NCSA

NCSA maintains an FTP directory containing some external viewers tested with Mosaic, which should all work with Netscape. The URL for this viewer site is:

```
ftp://ftp.ncsa.uiuc.edu/Web/Mosaic/Windows/viewers
```

Figure 4.20 shows the contents of this directory.

The following is a partial list of the Netscape helpers available at NCSA.

Lview Pro (lviewp1b.zip and lviewp1c.zip), a shareware image viewer for GIF, TIFF and JPEG graphics images.

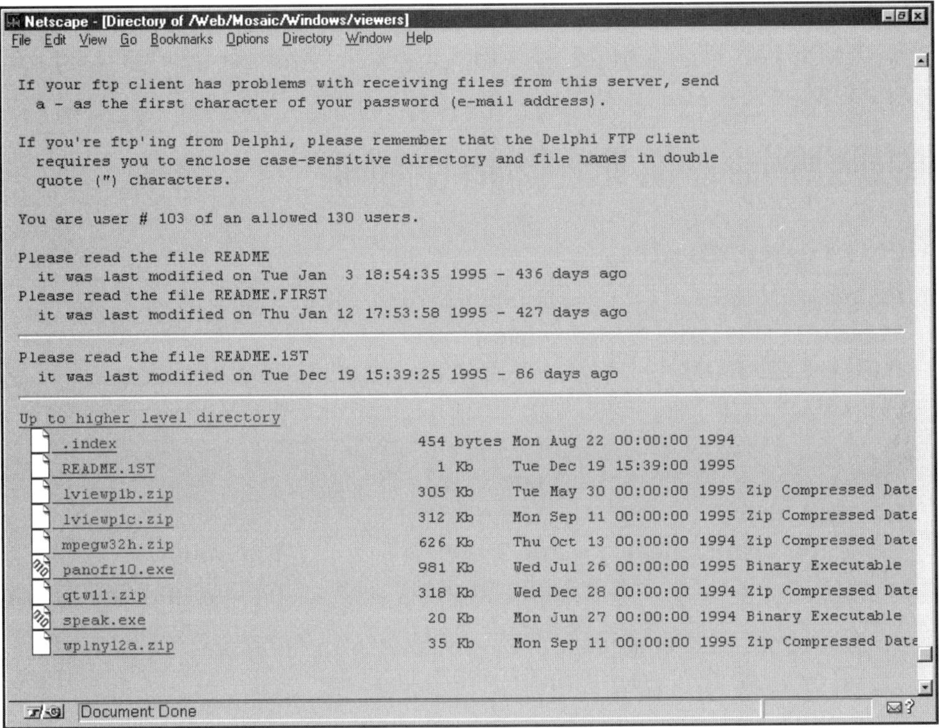

Figure 4.20 *CSA's viewers directory.*

MPEGPLAY (mpegw32h.zip), a shareware MPEG viewer. MPEG is designed for viewing animated image or movie files. At present the MPEG file format doesn't support audio.

Panorama Free (panofr10.exe), the first SGML browser for the World Wide Web. You can view SGML (Standard Generalized Markup Language) documents with Panorama Free.

QuickTime (qtw11.zip), the necessary files that will allow you to run QuickTime movies (a format owned by Apple Computer) with the Windows Media Player.

Speaker (speak.exe), a PC speaker driver produced by Microsoft, free to licensed users of Windows. This driver helps you get more than simple tones and beeps from the standard PC speaker, although it cannot rival even a minimal sound board.

Wplany (wplny12a.zip), a freeware audio player that works well with Netscape. Think of this one as Windows Play-Any. When Netscape passes an audio file to this application, you hear the file without having any control over the playback. If you want control over the playback, you will need WHAM (described below).

Installation Tables for Other Helper Programs

MPEG Viewer MpegPlay

Program Name:	mpegw32h.zip	
Version:	Version 1.65	
Path on CD-ROM:	x:\helpers\mpegpla\setup.exe	
FTP URL:	ftp://ftp.ncsa.uiuc.edu/Mosaic/Windows/viewers/mpegw32h.zip	
Status:	Shareware, $25	
Download To:	c:\temp	
Netscape Preferences	**File Type:**	**Extensions:**
	video/mpeg	mpeg, mpg, mpe

Note: This is a 32-bit application. If you are using Windows 3.1, Win32s must be installed before running the program.

QuickTime Video Player for Windows 95

Program Name:	qtinst.exe (16-bit) qt32inst.exe (32-bit)	
Version:	Version 2.1.1 beta 2	
Path on CD-ROM:	x:\helpers\quiktime\16bit\qtinstal.exe x:\helpers\quiktime\32bit\qt32instal.exe	
FTP URL:	http://quicktime.apple.com/qt/sw/downw.html	
Status:	No charge for personal use	
Download To:	c:\quick-tm	
Netscape Preferences	**File Type:**	**Extensions:**
	video/quicktime	qt, mov

WHAM Sound Player

Program Name:	wham133.zip
Version:	Version 1.33
Path on CD-ROM:	x:\helpers\wham\wham.exe
FTP URL:	ftp://gatekeeper.dec.com/pub/micro/msdos/win3/sounds/wham133.zip

Status:	Donation-ware	
Download To:	c:\wham	
Netscape Preferences	**File Type:**	**Extensions:**
	audio/x-wav	wav
	audio/x-aiff	aiff, aif, aifc
	audio/basic	au, snd

Note: WHAM requires the presence of a hardware sound card.

Future MIME Types

Netscape has the ability to support MIME types not currently in use or even in existence. In the unlikely event a new document type is developed—and a helper application is available—prior to the release of a new version of Netscape, it can be configured quickly.

In the more likely event that a new extension is added to an existing MIME type, take the following actions:

1. Execute the sequence Options|General Preferences, then display the Helpers card.
2. Highlight the MIME type from the File type column.
3. Add the new extension immediately after the current extensions in the File Extensions: text box.
4. Click on OK.

To add an entry that is a completely new MIME type, follow these steps:

1. Execute the sequence Options|General Preferences, then display the Helpers card.
2. Click on the Create New Type button, which will bring up the Configure New Mime Type dialog box as shown in Figure 4.21.
3. Enter the new MIME type into the Mime Type text box. Text and Audio are MIME types.
4. Enter the MIME subtype into the Mime SubType text box. HTML is a subtype of Text and x-wav is subtype of Audio. Click on OK.
5. Enter the new extension in the File Extensions: text box and designate an action.
6. Click on OK.
7. Configure the helper application for the new MIME type exactly as you did before.

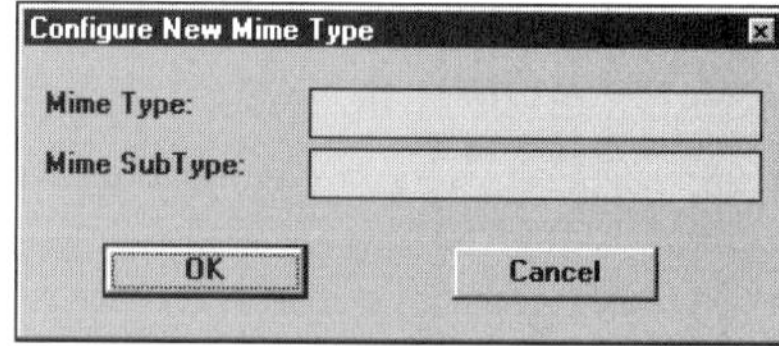

Figure 4.21 Configuring the new MIME type.

LET'S REVIEW

Most Netscape user-modifiable parameters are modified using a series of Preferences dialog boxes. These parameters let Netscape adjust to your preferences rather than the other way around.

The notion of modifying Netscape's configuration file netscape.ini is unnerving to some people, but there is truly nothing to fear if you follow the golden rule, "Always make backups." Before editing any configuration file (and this could apply to any Windows INI file) follow these three simple rules:

- Make a backup of the file you are about to edit.
- Comment out parameters, don't delete them.
- Make changes one parameter at a time and test the result before making additional changes.

INI files typically have section names enclosed between square brackets. Sections may come in any order but individual items must be in the proper section. Within sections, there are parameters typically having the form:

```
Parameter=replacement-value
```

Replacement values may sometimes be a simple "yes" or "no". The replacement value may also be a file name or a server name. The URL used for the starting home page would be another example of a replacement value.

To accommodate new data types that will invariably emerge as the Web evolves, Netscape and most browsers support a system that allows new data types to be presented to the user through a helper program. When a file comes down from a Web server, the browser looks up the file extension in a table, and if a helper is available to support that file extension, launches the helper application with the name of the file as the first parameter.

Newer Web servers type a file using the MIME (Multipurpose Internet Mail Extensions) system. Helper applications can be configured for any MIME type, including those that haven't been developed yet.

Netscape Plug-Ins

Do you feel like you're missing something when you're surfing the Net? Well, you could be if you don't have plug-ins.

Recently, a friend of mine came over to my house while I was surfing the Web. He sat down next to me and watched as pages loaded with dazzling animation, cool sounds, and even video. "What software is this?" he asked. "Netscape," I replied. "That doesn't look like *my* Netscape," he grumbled. "Well, I've souped it up dramatically with all sorts of plug-ins," I answered.

What many people don't realize is that the new Netscape is not simply an application, but a skeleton on which you can build your own individualized browser. By downloading and installing different types of plug-ins, you can have Web-surfing abilities that your entire neighborhood will be jealous of. Not improving Netscape with plug-ins is like having a Christmas tree without any lights or ornaments.

Now that I've gotten you excited about getting all the latest and greatest plug-ins, I'll cover some key plug-in basics and then give you a rundown of the best plug-ins available on the Web.

PLUG-IN BASICS

Downloading plug-ins is actually very easy; you simply find the URL for your desired plug-in and go download it. (I'll be explaining more about downloading files in Chapter 9.) Make sure that you're downloading the correct version for your operating system. There are different versions of plug-ins for Windows NT, 95, and 3.1, not to mention Macs and other systems. Also make sure that you surf through the entire site to capture any installation instructions and tips, license agreements, or example URLs, and see if there is an email list for update announcements. It's worth spending some time at the site now, so you won't have to return when you can't figure out why the plug-in isn't working.

Installing Plug-Ins

Almost all of the plug-ins that I've dealt with come ready to install. When you download the file, you simply click on the EXE file and it launches an install program. For example, with the RealAudio plug-in, you simply download the file to c:\netscape\plugins, and after it's downloaded click on the ra16_20.exe file. It gives you a choice between "express" and "custom" installation (I would choose express, unless you're an expert at configuring your computer) and that's it, you're ready to explore Netscape with your new plug-in.

Even though most people think it's a waste of time to read the README.TXT files, I strongly recommend that you read them for plug-ins. Since so many plug-ins are distributed as Beta software (software that's still in the development stage), the README files tend to be crucial in plug-in installation.

Tips for Installing Plug-Ins

1. Always read the readme.txt files.

I said it once, but it's worth saying again—read the documents that come with the plug-ins! It might help you discover why your browser keeps crashing.

2. Check for instructions on the Web site, too.

Sometimes there are instructions about downloading and installing the plug-in right there on the site. Be sure to read through the site carefully—sometimes they don't include a readme.txt or install.txt file.

3. Regularly check for plug-in updates.

Most things on the Net seem to get revised every few months, and plug-ins are no exception. Check your plug-ins frequently to make sure you've got the latest version. Many companies now have email alerts that help to keep you abreast of the latest details.

4. Make sure the plug-in is compatible with Netscape.

There are other browsers out there, most notably Microsoft's Internet Explorer. Make sure you read the fine print to see if the plug-in you're downloading is for Netscape (and also for your version of Netscape). In addition, don't forget to check to see whether it's for Windows, Unix, or Mac.

5. Check to see how many sites use them.

Some plug-ins are so new that there's not much you can do with them—no one is using them yet. The first thing I do when I spot a new plug-in is surf around and see how many sites are using it to enhance their site. If there aren't many sites using that plug-in, I wait until there are more before I download it.

6. Look for plug-in collections.

It's just a matter of time before more companies bring out collections of key plug-ins for Netscape on CD-ROM. Just think of how much time and money you could save by purchasing just a few good collections instead of surfing around trying to find exactly what you want.

7. Regularly check plug-in index sites.

I've listed some sites that keep you updated on new plug-ins. As new plug-ins become more frequent, it's going to take regular checks to see if something new and useful is available to add to your collection.

8. Don't delete your plug-ins!

It seems like I download a new version of Netscape Navigator every week. Since Netscape updates their program so frequently, it's a good idea to keep versions of the original plug-in (or a zipped copy) in case you have to reinstall it.

Using Plug-Ins

Prior to the new Netscape, most plug-ins ran as helper applications and didn't operate within Netscape itself. The new plug-ins work in conjunction with Netscape, and Netscape will automatically access the plug-ins when it needs them.

Developing Web Pages with Plug-Ins

This chapter concentrates on using plug-ins to enhance your Web-surfing experience, but inevitably you're going to want to build your own Web site (more on this in Part 2). Since you'll already have used plug-ins in your wanderings, you'll probably want to offer enhanced features on your site by taking advantage of plug-ins.

The problem is that many plug-ins are reader applications and don't help you to create content for your Web page. For example, the Shockwave plug-in doesn't help you create Shockwave files, it just reads and executes the files; so you'll need to talk to the developer of the technology to find out what tools you need to build sites containing their technology. This is where developers make their money. RealAudio sells the products that encode the audio files, and the server software to distribute them over the Net, for thousands of dollars.

THE BEST OF THE PLUG-INS

There are seven key plug-ins that should form the core of your first plug-in acquisition adventure, they are Acrobat Amber, Corel Vector Graphics, Crescendo, RealAudio, Shockwave for Director, VDO Live, and QuickTime. The following are brief summaries to explain what each one does.

ACROBAT AMBER
Produced by Adobe Systems
Address: http://www.adobe.com

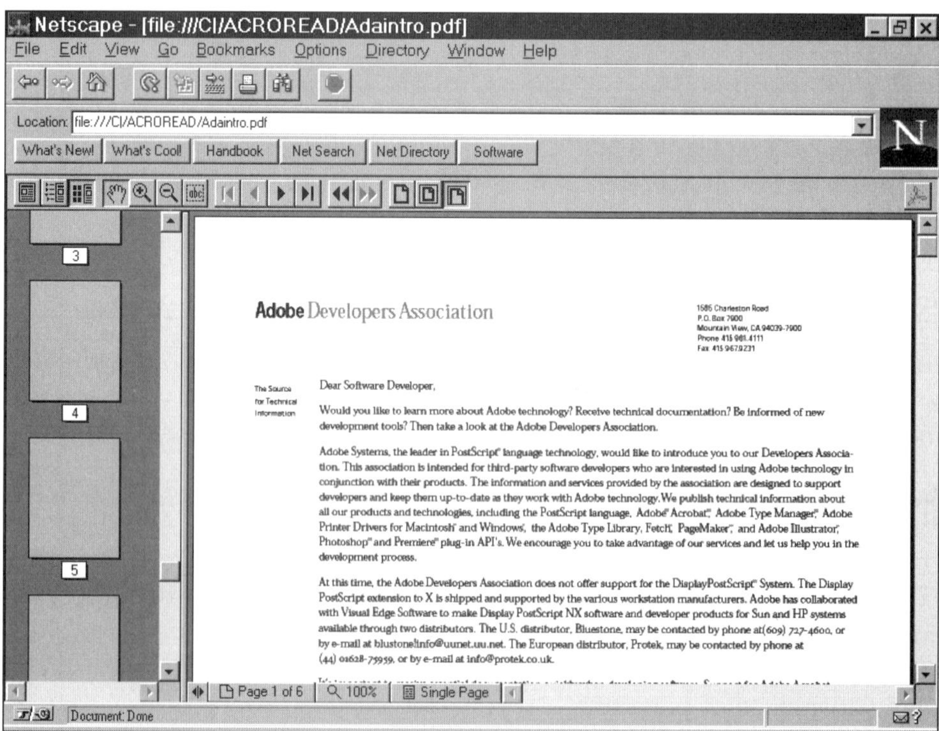

Figure 5.1 Adobe Acrobat Amber plug-in.

Adobe Acrobat Amber allows you to view Acrobat PDF files directly in the Netscape environment. PDF files are extremely compact, platform-independent, and easy to create. They offer design control, print-ready documents, and an endless array of authoring applications.

COREL VECTOR GRAPHICS
Produced by Corel Corporation
Address: http://www.corel.com

With Corel Draw, Corel is the king of vector graphics software packages. So it's no wonder that for one of their first plug-ins they built one that allows you to view different types of Corel vector drawings online.

CRESCENDO
Produced by LiveUpdate
Address: http://www.liveupdate.com

Crescendo is to Midi Files what RealAudio is to WAV files. With this plug-in installed, MIDI files embedded in Web pages will automatically play when you enter the site.

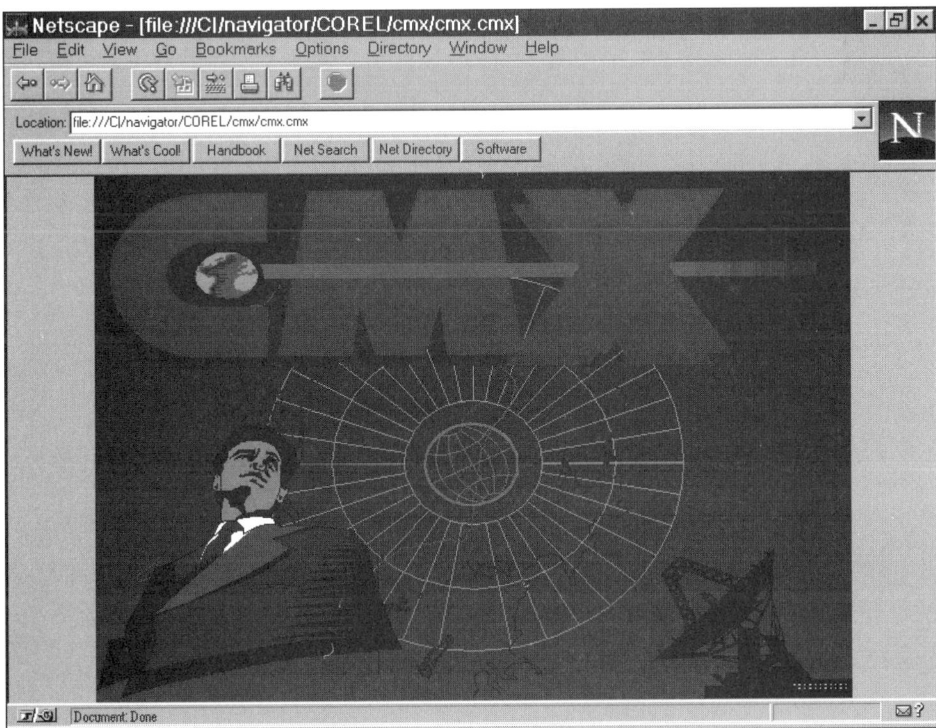

Figure 5.2 *Corel Vector Graphics' plug-in.*

REALAUDIO
Produced by Progressive Networks
Address: http://www.realaudio.com

RealAudio is one of the most famous plug-ins around. It provides live and on-demand real time audio over 14.4Kbps or faster connections to the Internet. The current version is available for download and features good quality sound.

There are several other major audio technologies available to you on the Web, and all of them work similarly to RealAudio. RealAudio is currently the best of the bunch because of its popularity—everyone's using it. But it's good to know what else is available, so I created Table 5.1 to provide you with a complete breakdown of the major real time audio technologies and plug-ins.

SHOCKWAVE FOR DIRECTOR
Distributed by Macromedia
Address: http://www.macromedia.com

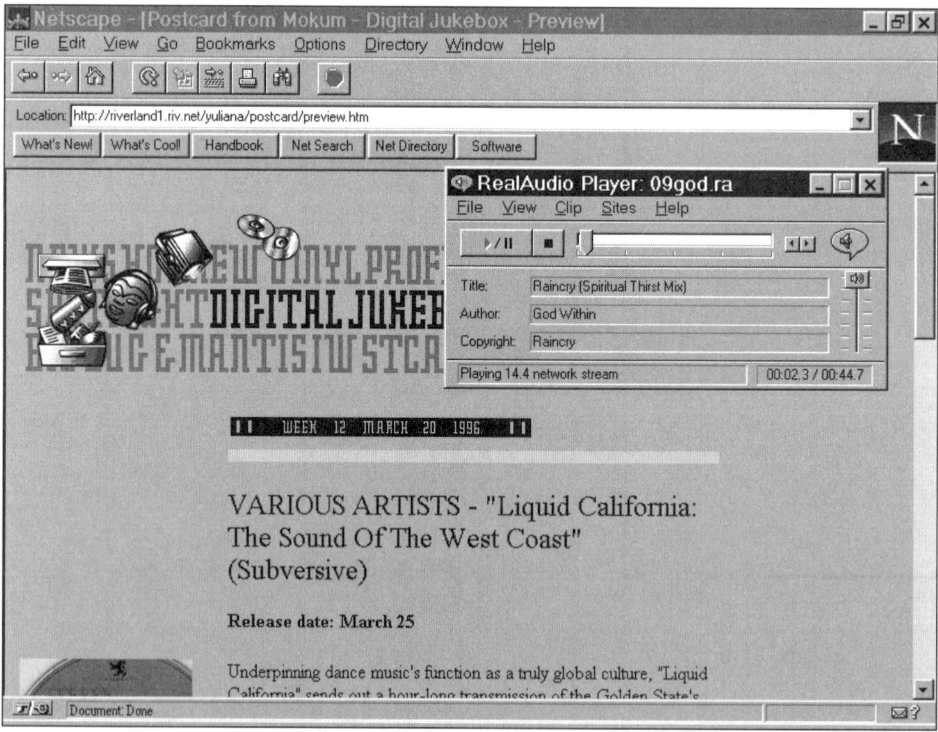

Figure 5.3 RealAudio's plug-in.

Table 5.1 Key Audio Streaming Technologies and Plug-Ins

Title	Where to Find	Plug-In	Minimum Connect Speed	Quality	Encoder? Server Needed?	Cost of Player
ToolVox	http://www.voxware.com	Yes	9,600	Great for Speech.	Encoder is free. No server needed.	Free
Internet Wave	http://www.voceltec.com	No	9,600	Very good for music, not great for speech.	Encoder is free. No server needed.	Free
StreamWorks	http://www.xingtech.com	Yes	9,600	Good for both	Encoder is free. Special server software needed, costs several thousand dollars.	Free
RealAudio	http://realaudio.com	Yes	21,600	Speech is good, music is excellent.	Encoder is free. Special server software needed, costs several thousand dollars.	Free
TrueSpeech	http://www.dspg.com	Coming Soon	14,400	Great for speech, music is good.	Encoder is free. No Server needed.	Free

Next to RealAudio this is perhaps the best plug-in to have. Director is a program that developers use to create dynamic multimedia programs, some so extravagant that they become off-the-shelf retail games or CD-ROMs. In 1995 Macromedia brought out Shockwave, which allows Director programmers to create Internet applets using Director.

The Shockwave plug-in lets users interact with Director presentations right in a Netscape Navigator window. Animation, clickable buttons, links to URLs, digital video movies, sound, and more can be integrated to deliver a rich multimedia experience.

VDOLIVE
Distributed by VDONET
Address: http://www.vdolive.com

When I first heard about VDOLive, I said I'll believe it when I see it. VDOLive compresses video images without compromising quality on the receiving end, and with a 28.8Kbps or higher modem, VDOLive can deliver real time video at 10 to 15 frames per second. You have to see this plug-in at work to believe it!

QUICKTIME
Distributed by Apple
Address: http://www.apple.com

As of the writing of this book, Apple still hadn't finished their QuickTime plug-in, but once it's done you'll have the ability to view QuickTime movies directly inside a Web page.

Figure 5.4 *The Shockwave plug-in.*

THE BEST OF THE REST

Just in case you run across some Web pages that use plug-in technology that isn't included as one of the "best," here's a rundown of some of the more interesting plug-ins I've seen in my travels.

SIZZLER
Distributed by Totally Hip
Address: http://www.totallyhip.com

Sizzler is a plug-in that helps create streaming animation files to be delivered over the Web. With Sizzler you don't have to wait for an animation to download before viewing it, it updates the animation directly as new information streams in. Sizzler can also convert popular multimedia formats, such as QuickTime movies and PICS files, into Sizzler files.

SVF PLUG-IN
Distributed by SoftSource
Address: http://www.softsource.com/softsource/

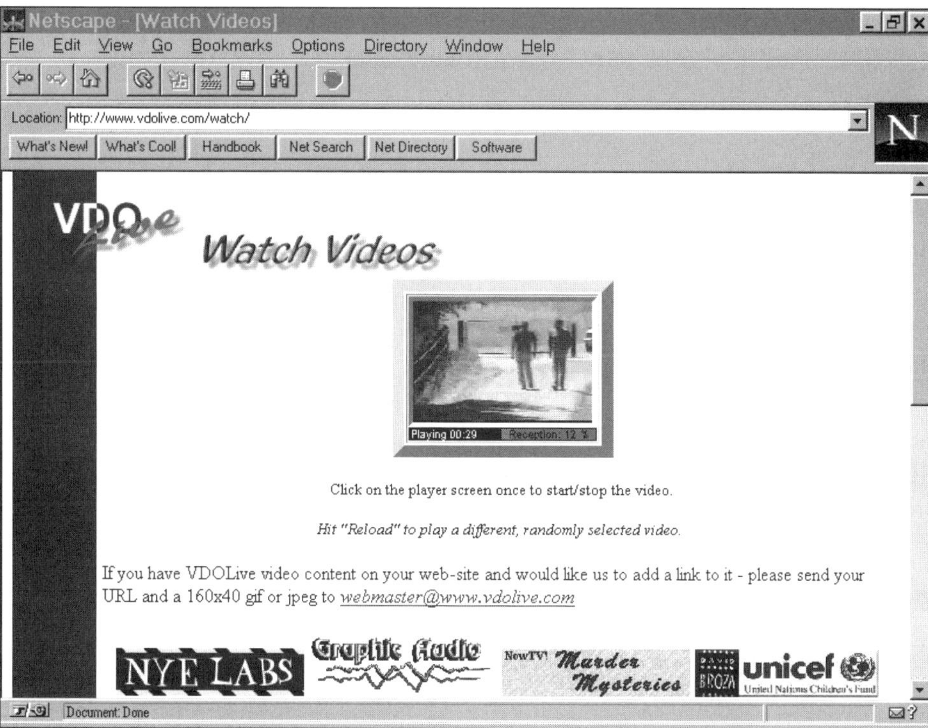

Figure 5.5 *VDOLive's plug-in.*

The SVF plug-in is an inline viewing product for looking at CAD files in the Simple Vector Format. You can pan and zoom an SVF image, as well as hide and display layers. The SVF plug-in also lets you include HTML hyperlinks (either URLs or textual annotations) in an SVF file.

PREVU
Distributed by Intervu
Address: http://www.intervu.com/prevu.html

PREVU is a plug-in which allows any MPEG video file to be played back in a Web page without MPEG hardware or video servers. When you surf to a page featuring an embedded MPEG file, PREVU provides a first-frame view right in the Web page, then it streams the video while downloading it (though not in real time), and then plays it at full speed off your hard drive when it's done.

ASAP WEBSHOW
Distributed by Software Publishing Corporation
Address: http://www.spco.com

With this plug-in you can view, download, and print presentations created by the ASAP WordPower presentation software package.

ASTOUND WEB PLAYER
Distributed by Gold Disk
Address: http://www.golddisk.com

This plug-in from Gold Disk allows you to access multimedia slideshows created with their Astound or Studio M software. The documents you download can include sound, animation, graphics, video, and interactive hooks like hotspots.

CHEMSCAPE CHIME
MDL Information Systems
Address: http://www.mdli.com/

For the mad scientist in the house, this plug-in lets you display 2-D and 3-D structures of your favorite chemical substances within an HTML page.

DWG/DXF PLUG-IN
Distributed by SoftSource
Address: http://www.softsource.com/softsource/

This plug-in is an inline viewer for AutoCAD (DWG) files and 3DStudio (DXF) wireframes. You can pan and zoom as well as hide and display layers.

EARTHTIME
Distributed by Starfish Software
Address: http://www.starfishsoftware.com

From the company started by former Borland executive Phillip Kahn comes EarthTime, a simple plug-in that tells you the time around the world without having to switch out of Netscape. EarthTime displays the local time and date for up to eight different locations from a selection of 350 world cities.

ENVOY
Distributed by Tumbleweed Software
Address: http://www.twcorp.com

Envoy is similar to Adobe's Acrobat plug-in because you can view documents exactly as they would appear on a printed page, complete with all the fonts, graphics, and layout options. Tumbleweed Software offers Tumbleweed Publishing Essentials for publishing Envoy documents, and the Envoy Software Developer's Kit for creating a customized Envoy document viewer.

FIGLEAF INLINE
Distributed by Carberry Technology/EBT
Address: http://www.ct.ebt.com

With the FigLeaf Inline plug-in you can zoom, pan, scroll, and rotate multiple graphics formats within a web page. FigLeaf Inline supports GIF, JPEG, PNG, TIFF, CCITT, GP4, BMP, WMF, EPSF, Sun Raster, and other popular bitmap formats, plus CGM, the first vector MIME standard.

LIGHTNING STRIKE
Distributed by Infinet OP
Address: http://www.infinop.com

This plug-in is designed to provide browsers with a new scheme for viewing graphics within their Web page. Right now JPEG is used to display large complex graphic files over the Internet, but with the Lightning Strike plug-in you can load graphics significantly faster, due to a much higher compression ratio.

WORD VIEWER PLUG-IN
Distributed by Inso Corporation
Address: http://www.inso.com

The plug-in allows you to view Microsoft Word 6.0 and 7.0 files inside Netscape. It also lets you copy and print Word documents with all the original formatting intact.

VRML PLUG-INS

VRML (Virtual Reality Markup Language) is a new aspect of the Web that does for 3-D objects what HTML has done for text. When coupled with a VRML-capable plug-in or browser, users can walk through 3-D scenes or manipulate 3-D objects via the Web.

VRML is too complex a technology to cover in just two paragraphs—there are entire books written about it. But for now I thought I'd list a few VRML plug-ins so you can begin to explore the world of VRML.

VR SCOUT VRML PLUG-IN
Distributed by Chaco Communications
Address: http://www.chaco.com

This plug-in gives you a fast VRML viewer that conforms to the 1.0 standard of VRML.

VREALM
Distributed by Integrated Data Systems
Address: http://www.ids-net.com

VRealm is a full-featured VRML plug-in and supports object behaviors, gravity, collision detection, and multimedia hooks.

WIRL VIRTUAL REALITY BROWSER
Distributed by VREAM
Address: http://www.vream.com

VREAM is a leading developer of VRML technology. With their WIRL Virtual Reality plug-in you can explore a number of VRML-capable sites.

LIVE3D
Distributed by Netscape
Address: http://home.netscape.com

This plug-in features interactive, multiuser VRML applications written with Java, 3-D text, background images, texture animation, morphing, viewpoints, collision detection, gravity, and RealAudio streaming sound.

EVEN MORE PLUG-INS

I've only covered a handful of the major plug-ins available for Netscape; more debut every day. There are so many new plug-ins that it's almost a daily chore to keep up with the latest and greatest. The best way to keep up is to first gather the major plug-ins that I've listed, and then scan a few of the Web sites and other resources listed below to build up your collection.

LET'S REVIEW

With the new version of Navigator, Netscape has taken the program and re-engineered it from being just a simple application to being a complete platform that other people write applications for. Some people have said that this new version positions Netscape Navigator as a sort of "Internet Operating System," much like Windows is a computer operating system.

Right now the plug-ins are all relatively simple: view this document, listen to this audio file. In the future, however, there'll be plug-ins that are word processors or databases, all connected to each other over the Internet. Plug-in technology may seem unimportant, but it opens perhaps the most important new aspect of computing over the Internet since the invention of the Net itself.

PLUG-IN RESOURCES

Netscape's Plug-In Page:

```
http://home.netscape.com/comprod/products/navigator/version_2.0/plugins/
index.html
```

Yahoo's Guide to Netscape Plug-Ins–contains a good listing of Netscape plug-ins:

```
http://www.yahoo.com/Computers_and_Internet/Internet/World_Wide_Web/Browsers/
Netscape_Navigator/Plug_Ins/index.html
```

Netscape Mail and CoolTalk

The new versions of Netscape have an added attraction—email! It's time to learn the art of sending and receiving messages at the push of a button.

Imagine being a scribe, carefully copying texts with a flowing quill onto parchment, working into the wee hours of the morning by candlelight. Then one day, moveable type printers revolutionize the printing process—quills are set down, tweezers picked up, and typesetters begin to patiently drop tiny letters into printing frames. Fortunately, pencils and pens, offset printers, and, best of all, the computer came along to help us put words on a page (or screen).

In the meantime, as printing became easier and easier, we created more and more written documents. The problem of delivering the words then arose. (I'm sure you can see where I'm going with this.) Carrier pigeons, while amazing, were a lot of work and not very reliable (they never did get their union organized), so we devised a mail system—our postal system. If you think about it, being able to drop a letter in a mailbox and having it arrive 3,000 (or more) miles away at the correct house is an astonishing feat of cooperation.

Unfortunately, mailing a letter takes a few days, and the advent of computers has brought us to the age of immediacy. With computers, we can accomplish the even more astonishing feat of sending information around the world in a matter of seconds. Electronic mail gives everyone the ability to transmit information rapidly. In this age of immediacy, people are demanding electronic mail—and not just any electronic mail, but mail that can show viewers graphics or take them to Internet links. This chapter will show you how Netscape expands the capabilities of your email service to provide you with the latest and greatest in email technology.

NETSCAPE MAIL

Netscape now comes equipped with a mail manager as part of the package. Netscape's mail manager makes it possible to send and receive messages and attachments without ever leaving the comfort of your favorite browser. As with most Netscape features, you can customize your mail manager to suit your needs. You can create and maintain an easy-to-use Address Book, as well as organize copies of the messages you send and receive. You can attach Internet pages and disk files to your mail or include fully formatted HTML pages within your message. Electronic mail, or email, is today's hottest communication medium, so, what do you say? Want to find out a little more about it? You've come to the right place.

SETTING YOUR MAIL PREFERENCES

Before you can send or receive mail messages, you have to tell Netscape where to find your email program and where to store your mail—you have to set your preferences. (Sound familiar? As you are probably starting to realize, "setting your preferences" is the secret to maximizing Netscape's capabilities.) In Chapter 4 we took a look at each of the cards found in the Options|Mail and News Preferences dialog box. The five subject cards found in the Mail and News Preferences dialog box are the Appearance, Composition, Servers, Identity, and Organization cards. If you want to refresh your memory on any of these cards, flip back to Chapter 4 and I'll wait here patiently. Once you are back we'll take another look at the Servers card, because that is the card you need to set up your Netscape mail feature. When you are ready, execute Options|Mail and News Preferences, then click on the Servers tab. The Servers card should appear similar to the one shown in Figure 6.1.

As we discussed earlier, you have to indicate to Netscape your outgoing (SMTP) and incoming (POP) mail servers. SMTP stands for Simple Mail Transport (or

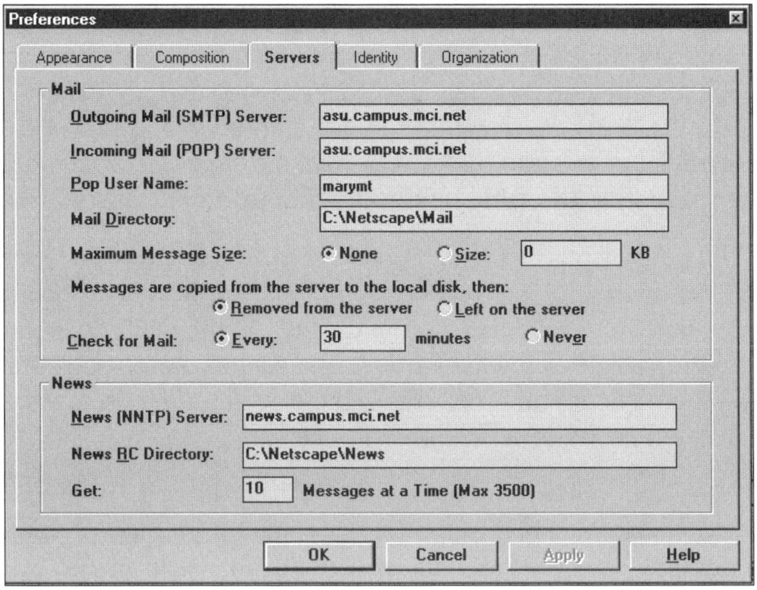

Figure 6.1 *The Servers card.*

transfer) Protocol, and POP stands for Post Office Protocol. Simply put, POP is the transfer protocol used between your computer and your mail server—kind of like the relationship between your house and your neighborhood post office. The SMTP is the transfer protocol that servers use to communicate with other servers—similar to the network of post offices around the world. Of course the mechanics of SMTP and POP are much more complicated than that, but we can leave those musings to our service providers or network administrators. Take a look at the SMTP and POP fields shown in Figure 6.1. Notice that my SMTP and POP are the same. This is usually the case. If you don't know the names of your mail servers, you can call your Internet provider or check with your network administrator.

Below the mail server information is a text box where you can enter your POP user name. In layman's terms, it means to enter your email name—the part that comes before the @ in your address. For example, if your email address is jeffc@aok.com you would type jeffc into the POP User Name: text box.

You now have the most important informational pieces in place for using Netscape's mail feature. Netscape knows your name and address (or at least your email name and how to contact your mail servers). Technically, at this point you could send and receive mail, but there are a few options you need to choose so you can customize your settings. A few are found on the Servers card, so let's continue where we left off.

Below the POP User Name: text box is the Mail Directory: text box. You use this area to point Netscape to the file where you want to store your messages. As you can see in Figure 6.1, I've told Netscape to save my mail messages in C:\Netscape\Mail. My personal preference is to keep all my Netscape documents together, but you can direct your mail messages to be saved anywhere you want (except on the table next to the front door, of course).

The last three mail options on the Servers card are relatively self-explanatory. You can limit the size of any message you receive under the Maximum message size option. You can delete your messages off the mail server after you've received them, or you can leave your messages out there. I delete mine as a courtesy—there's an awful lot of email chatter going on these days, so I don't want to add excess noise where it isn't necessary.

Finally, there is an option on the Server card to indicate how often you want Netscape to check your mail server for new mail. Netscape performs a periodic "behind-the-scenes" check for you. You can see in Figure 6.1 that I've indicated that Netscape should check my mail server every 30 minutes. You can enter any length of time that you want, or you can select never. If you select never you will have to check for mail manually while you are in the Netscape Mail Window (more about that in a later section).

Let's look at one more preference before we create a mail message. You can tell Netscape to "remember" your email password every time you open Netscape. This is a convenient option because it eliminates having to retype your password. (Of course, if you are in an office environment, you may not want to choose this option because passwords provide a measure of confidentiality.) Click on the Organization card in the Mail and News preferences dialog box. This card should appear similar to the card in Figure 6.2.

In the General section, there is a check box next to the words Remember Mail Password. Click in the box if you want to select this option.

Ok, details taken care of, let's send some mail.

SENDING MAIL

Netscape provides two main Mail windows—one for sending mail and one for viewing mail. To select the window for sending mail, execute File|New Mail Message; or execute Window|Netscape Mail, then click on the To Mail button in the button bar; or click on the small envelope and question mark displayed in the lower right corner of your Netscape screen, then click on the

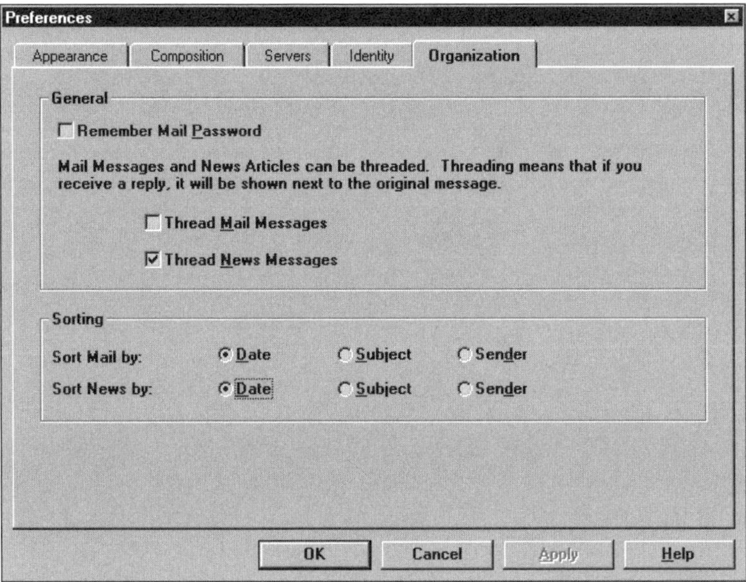

***Figure 6.2** The Organization card.*

To Mail button in the button bar (once again, you are on your own to pick your preference). The Netscape Message Composition window is shown in Figure 6.3.

The message composition window is made up of a menu bar, a button bar, header text fields, and a message creation field (the large area at the bottom of the screen). The most pertinent information at this time is probably the header text fields. The text fields provide important header information, such as the email recipient's name and address, and the subject line. Figure 6.3 shows only a small selection of available text boxes. Click on View | Show All, then maximize your window for easy viewing. Your Message Composition window should now appear similar to Figure 6.4.

View menu items are all toggle options. You can display or hide each field by clicking on it in the View menu. The field options are as follows.

From: displays your email address.

Reply To: displays the email address where you want replies to your email sent. This is the address used when a mail recipient chooses the reply option to respond to your original message.

Mail To: displays the email address of the person (or persons) to whom you are sending the message.

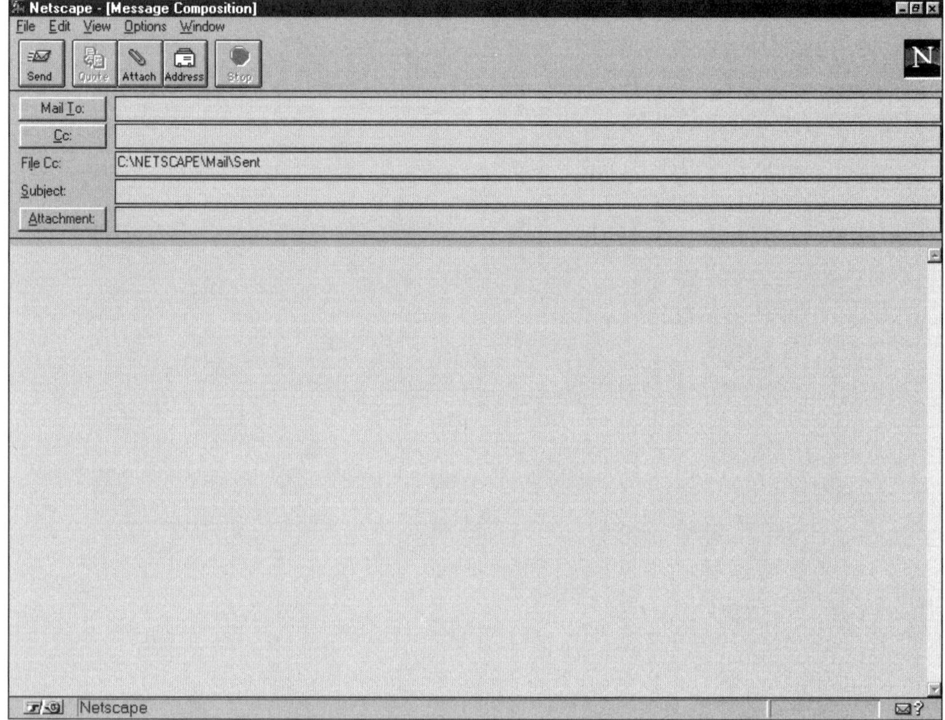

Figure 6.3 Netscape's Message Composition window.

Cc: displays the email address of the person (or persons) to whom you are sending a copy of a message.

Blind Cc: displays the address of the person (or persons) to whom you are sending a blind copy of a message. Blind copy addresses aren't displayed to the other recipients of the message.

File Cc: displays the location where you want to store a copy of the messages you send. By default, messages are stored in a Sent directory in the folder you specified in the Options | Mail and News Preferences | Servers card.

Newsgroups: displays the name of the newsgroup where you want to send your news message. If you are creating a message from a newsgroup listing or message, this field is preset with the name of the newsgroup (see Chapter 7 for more information on Newsgroups).

Followup To: displays the name of the newsgroup where you want replies to your message posted.

Subject: displays a description of your email or newsgroup message. If you're responding to an email or newsgroup message, this field is preset.

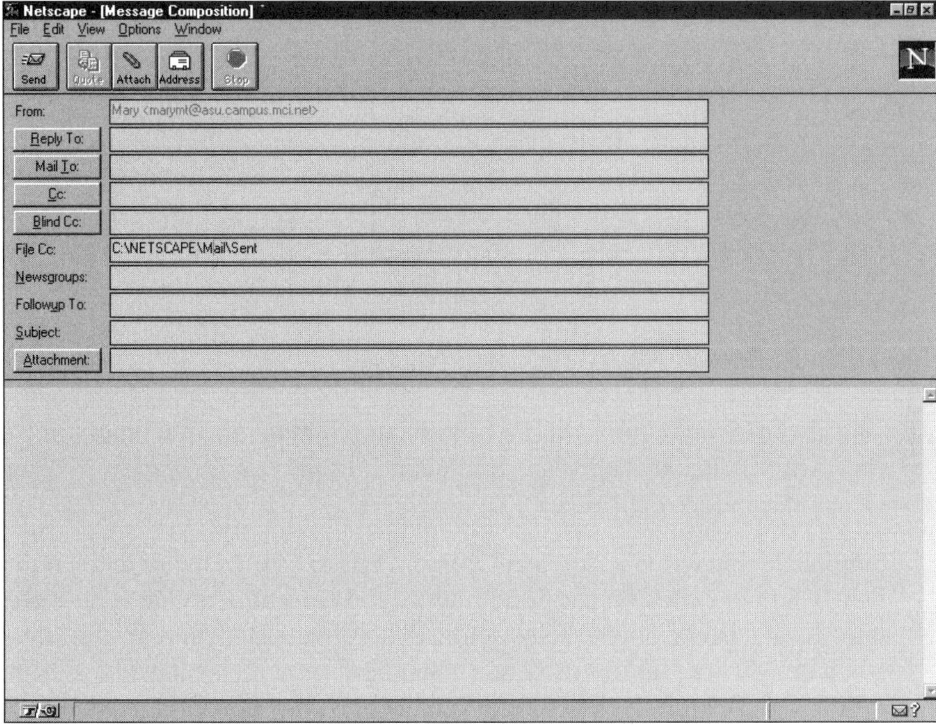

Figure 6.4 Netscape's Message Composition window showing all the heading field options.

Attachment: displays the page name or file name of any attachments you've included with your message.

Let's hide some of the fields we don't need to create a basic email message. Click on the View menu option. The View menu is shown in Figure 6.5.

Click on From. Notice that the From: field is removed from your message composition window header section. Click on the View menu option and you'll notice that the checkmark does not appear next to the From option. Turn off Reply To, Mail Bcc, Newsgroups, and Followups To. Your message composition window should again look similar to Figure 6.3.

Notice that the Mail To, Cc, and Attachment text box headers appear as three-dimensional buttons. If you click on any of those buttons you will be taken to a menu box. Clicking on Mail To: or Cc: will take you to your Address Book—we'll set up your Address Book a little later in this chapter. Clicking on the Attachment button will take you to the Attachments dialog box—an area where you can specify Internet URLs, copies of web pages, or personal files to be sent with your email message.

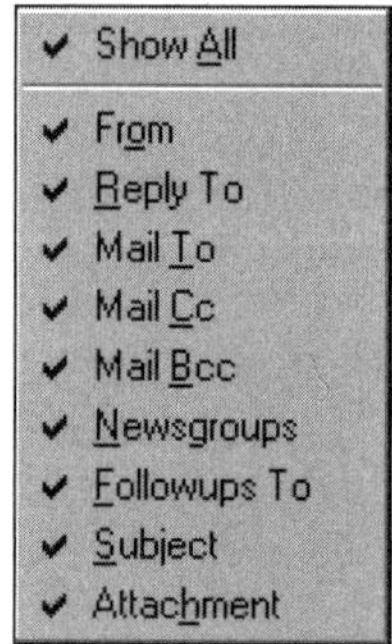

***Figure 6.5** The View menu with all the field options turned on.*

You can also use the buttons on the button bar to create an attachment or call up your Address Book. There are five main buttons on Netscape's message composition window button bar.

Send available when you select Options | Immediate Delivery in the menu bar. When you click on the Send button, the current message is delivered into the network. If you select Option | Deferred Delivery on the Menu bar, a **Send Later** button displays (a Send button with a small clock on it). When you click on the Send Later button, the current message is saved in the Outbox folder on your disk for distribution at a later time. Execute File | Send Mail in Outbox when you are ready to send the deferred message.

Quote changes the current message into quoted text format (indicated on the Mail and News Preferences—Appearance card).

Attach assists you in sending Internet or file documents along with your email message. When you click on the Attach button, the Attachments preferences dialog box appears, as shown in Figure 6.6.

Address displays your Address Book.

Stop halts the transmission of the message being sent.

Let's create a sample email message using the following addresses. The person we want to mail a message to is named Shiela, and her address is shiela@netcom.com. We want to send a copy of our message to Archie, and his address is archie@aok.com. Let's make the subject line read *Test Message*. Type a short message. Your composition window should look similar to Figure 6.7.

A little later we'll attach a file to this email, so let's store this message until then. To store your message, execute Options | Deferred Delivery. The Send Later button should display in your button bar. Click on the Send Later button

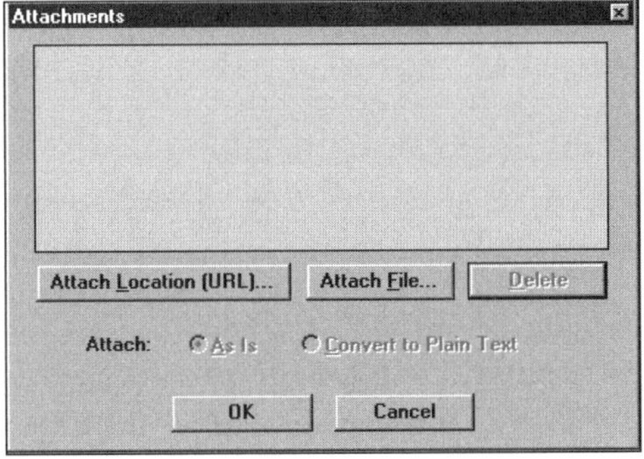

Figure 6.6 *The Attachments dialog box.*

to save the message in your Outbox. We'll check for it when we check our mail—and now is as good a time as any.

VIEWING YOUR MAIL

As I mentioned earlier, Netscape has two main Mail windows. We've just covered the message composition window—the window used for creating and sending messages. Now let's talk about the message viewing window—the window where your read and organize your mail messages. To display the mail message window, execute Window | Netscape Mail or click on the small mail envelope located in the bottom right corner of the Netscape window. If you

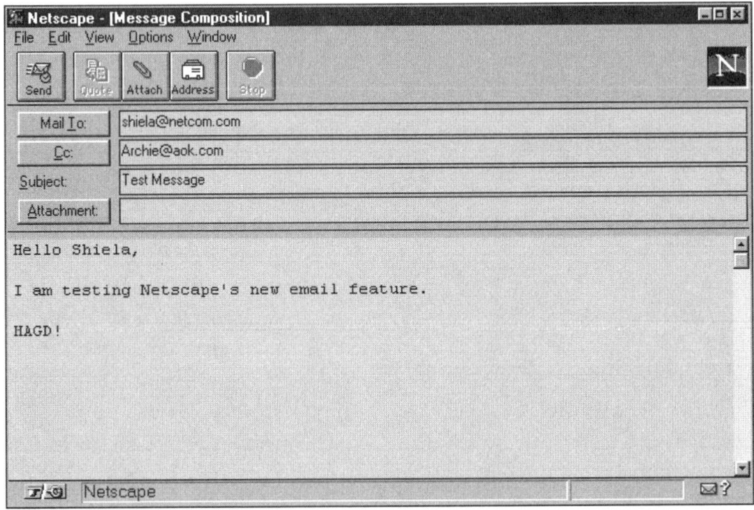

Figure 6.7 *Our sample email message.*

didn't tell Netscape to remember your password earlier in this lesson, you should receive the Password Entry dialog box shown in Figure 6.8.

Type your password in the text box (use the password that you established with your Internet service provider or your system administrator), then click on the OK button. You should now see Netscape's message viewing window, as shown in Figure 6.9.

Notice that you already have one message in your inbox and one message in your outbox. You know what the message in your outbox is all about (it is the one you created earlier in this chapter). But what about that message in your inbox? Well, the kind folks at Netscape included a default email message for you so you wouldn't feel lonely. Actually, if you click on your Inbox, you will see that you have a message from Mozilla (Netscape's trademark lizard). The message subject line reads "Welcome!" This is a good document for reviewing some of the Mail features. Included are some links to helpful resources. For

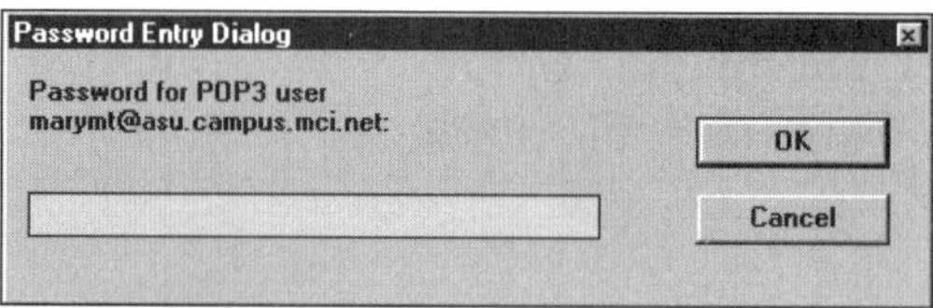

Figure 6.8 *The Password Entry Dialog box.*

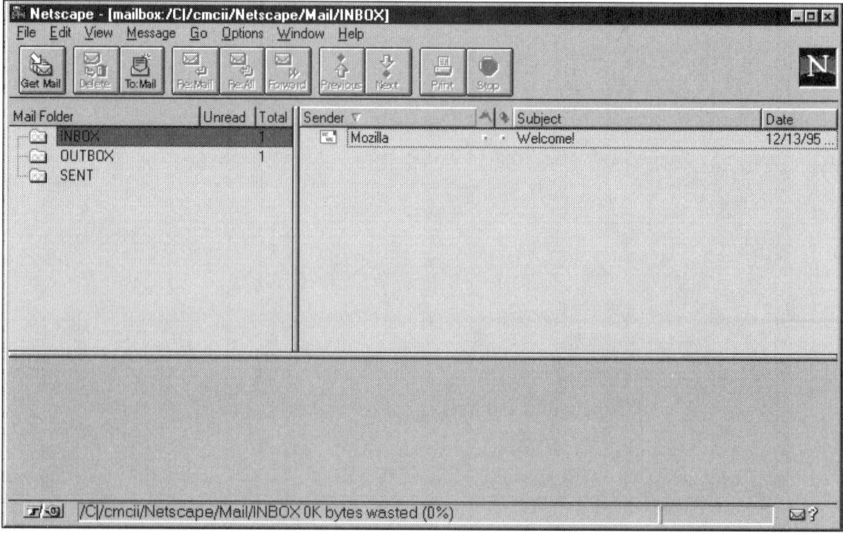

Figure 6.9 *The message viewing window.*

example, if you scroll down, you will see a link to Netscape's Navigator Handbook under the Learn More about Netscape Mail heading.

When you open your Mail window, Netscape automatically checks the server and retrieves any new mail you may have. As we saw earlier on the Mail and News Preferences—Servers card, you can tell Netscape to periodically re-check the server for new messages. Once the Mail window is opened, Netscape does not automatically retrieve the messages it finds, but it will automatically check for you.

Fortunately, getting your mail is as simple as clicking on a button. To get your new mail, you can click on the Get Mail button located on the far left end of the button bar, or you can click on the small envelope icon, which tells you when you have mail. For example, if the envelope has a question mark beside it, Netscape cannot automatically check the mail server. The question mark usually appears when you first open Netscape or if you haven't supplied your password. The envelope alone means that there are no new messages. An exclamation point appearing adjacent to the envelope indicates that a new message is available for retrieval.

The message viewing window is made up of three frames: the mail folder frame, the message header frame, and the message content frame.

Your mail folder frame should list your Inbox, Outbox, and Sent message folders. There are four Netscape-generated folders that can appear in this frame: Inbox, Outbox, Sent, and Trash. Using the File | New folder... sequence, you can add custom folders to help organize your mail. There are also three columns in this frame: Mail Folder, Unread, and Total. The Mail folder column shows the name of the folder, the Unread column displays the number of unread messages in each folder, and the Total column lists the total number of read and unread messages within a folder.

The message header frame contains three headings and two toggle columns. The red flag toggle is for your own use—you can click in the flag icon column to turn on a flag to designate a message as noteworthy. The diamond icon toggle, located just to the right of the flag toggle column, appears if a message has not yet been viewed. The frame also contains Sender, Subject, and Date columns. You can sort your email messages by any one of these three options by clicking on the column heading.

The third frame, the largest of the trio, is the message text frame. This is the frame where the message contents display. All three frames can be resized by dragging the borders. Click on your Inbox, if necessary, and highlight the

Mozilla message. Netscape's welcome message displays in the message text frame, as shown in Figure 6.10.

Like most windows, the message viewer window contains buttons and menu items. The buttons and menu items in the mail window are used to view, store, create, and delete mail messages. I'll give you a quick overview of the buttons and some of the menu items found in this mail window (many definitions are excerpted from Netscape's Handbook). If you would like a complete listing, refer to Netscape's online Navigator Handbook. It's located at:

```
http://home.netscape.com/eng/mozilla/2.0/handbook
```

Here's a quick overview of the buttons in the message viewer window.

Get Mail - imports new messages from the mail server and places them in the inbox.

Delete - moves the currently selected message into the Trash folder.

To: Mail - displays the Message Composition window used for creating and sending new mail messages.

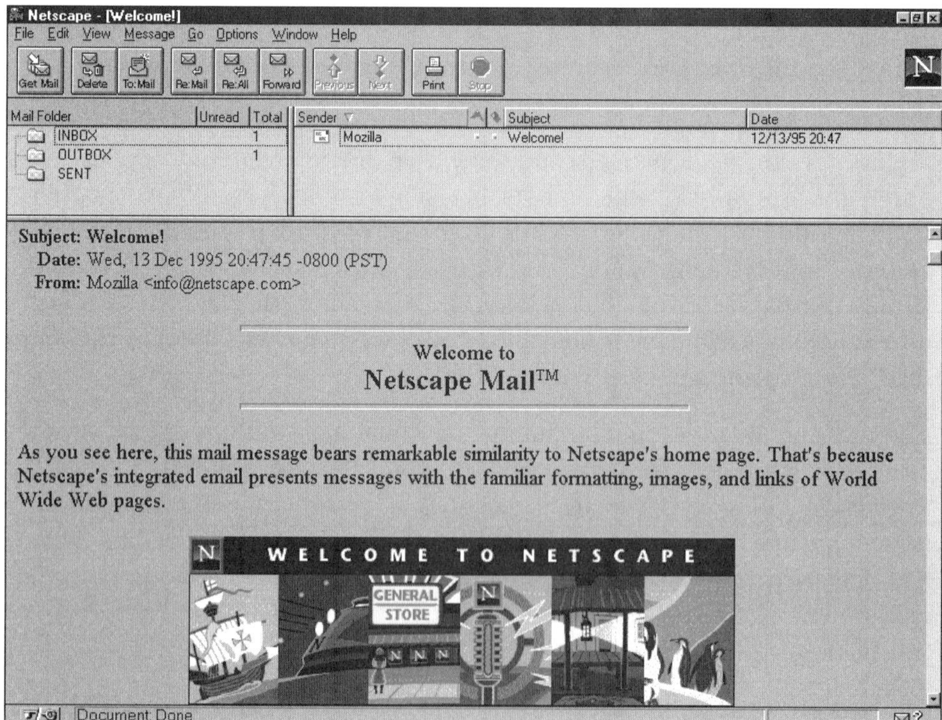

Figure 6.10 Netscape's welcome message displayed in the message text frame.

Re: Mail displays the Message Composition window used to reply to the currently selected message. The To: and Subject: fields are preset with the original sender's address, and subject line prefixed with Re:.

Re: All displays the Message Composition window and presets the To: field with the original sender's address, as well as the addresses of other recipients of the original message.

Forward displays the Message Composition window for forwarding the current message as an attachment. The Subject field is preset with the original subject line prefixed with Fwd:.

Previous displays the previous unread message in the message list.

Next displays the next unread message in the message list.

Print prints the message currently selected in the message heading frame.

Stop halts any ongoing transmission of messages from the mail server.

Above the button bar is the Menu bar. Many of the Menu options are standard options, such as Close and Find, as well as the options found under the Go, Window, and Help menus. I won't reiterate the basics here—there are plenty of mail-specific menu options to keep us busy for the moment. Following is a list of some of the mail menu items. (Remember, as I said earlier, if you would like a complete list of menu items, refer to Netscape's online Navigator's Handbook.)

File | New Mail Message displays the Message Composition window.

File | Save As produces a dialog box used for saving the current message as a file.

File | Get New Mail retrieves your messages.

File | Send Mail in Outbox sends your deferred outgoing messages that have been stored in your Outbox.

File | Empty Trash Folder permanently removes messages in the Trash folder.

File | Compress This Folder recovers disk space from deleted messages.

Edit | Select Thread selects all the messages in the currently selected thread.

Edit | Select Flagged Messages selects messages in the current thread that are flagged.

Edit | Select All Messages selects all messages in all threads.

View | Sort arranges messages in the message heading frame according to Date, Subject, Sender, or Message Number.

View | Unscramble (ROT-13) decodes a certain type of message in which the sender has shifted the message's characters.

View | Load Images displays the images of the current message if they have not been automatically loaded.

View | Attachments Inline when this option is selected, you view a page attachment as part of the message. If the sender has included an HTML document as an attachment, the formatted page is appended to the message body.

View | Attachments as Links when this option is selected, you access a page attachment using a link. If the sender has included an HTML page as an attachment, a link to the formatted page is appended to the message body. Clicking on the link displays the page in the message content pane.

Message | Reply displays the Message Composition window used for writing a response with the Send To: and Subject: fields preset.

Message | Reply to All displays the Message Composition window used for writing a response with the Send To: field preset to the sender, as well as to the other recipients of the message.

Message | Forward displays the Message Composition window used for sending the current message as an attachment with the Subject: and Attachment: fields preset.

Message | Forward Quoted displays the Message Composition window used for sending the current message as quoted text in the message content area.

Message | Mark as Read designates that the current message has been viewed.

Message | Mark as Unread designates that the current message has not been viewed.

Message | Flag Message distinguishes the current message with a small flag in the flag column.

Message | Unflag Message removes a flag marker.

Message | Add to Address Book creates an Address Book entry for the sender of the current message.

Options | Show All Messages when checked, displays both read and unread messages in the message header frame.

Options | Show Only Unread Messages when checked, displays only unread messages in the message header frame.

Options | Show All Headers when checked, displays full header information, including Return Path, Received, Message ID, and Content Type. When unchecked, the message content frame displays only the basic address fields.

Options | Document Encoding lets you select which character set encoding a document uses when document encoding is either not specified or unavailable.

Before we move on, let's take a quick look at our document in the Outbox. We'll be able to see how the document will be viewed by Shiela. Click on your Outbox folder in the mail folder frame. Notice the mail message we put on hold appears in the message header frame on the right. Click on the message. The message text displays in the large content frame under the two upper frames. Your screen should look similar to the one displayed in Figure 6.11.

We now know how to create and view mail messages. You can also print and save your mail messages, just as you would any other document.

SAVING AND PRINTING MAIL MESSAGES

Saving and printing your mail messages are easy. You perform both operations while in the Mail window. Let's save a couple of messages to disk first, then we'll print the message we are storing in our Outbox.

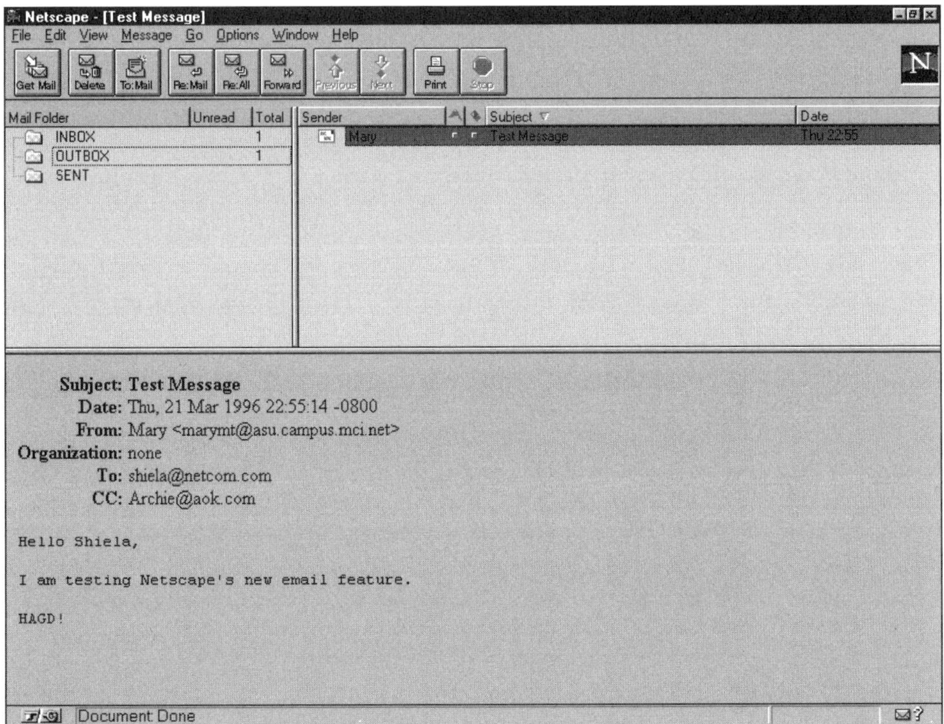

Figure 6.11 Viewing our Test Message.

Let's save the message from Mozilla to our hard disk. First we need to select the message by clicking on the Inbox folder, then clicking on the Mozilla message. After the message displays in the content box, execute File | Save As. Netscape will display the familiar Save As dialog box. Highlight the word "inbox" in the File name: text box and rename the document. I'm going to call my message Mozilla.doc and direct Netscape to save the document in my C:\Netscape\Mail folder on my hard drive. Your Save As dialog box should look similar to the one shown in Figure 6.12.

Click on the OK button to save the message to disk. Let's follow the same procedure to save our test message in our Outbox. I'll save mine as test.doc in my C:\Netscape\Mail folder. Now that we've saved our messages to disk there are two ways we can view them. The first way would be to simply open the file. Let's open the test message file from our hard drive. Your saved message should look similar to the one shown in Figure 6.13.

Aside from the extra information appearing in the header, the basic message appears the same. Now let's open our Mozilla.doc message. It should appear as shown in Figure 6.14.

Notice that the HTML coding shows up in the text form of this message. You can weed your way through the HTML tags or you can view the saved document using the Netscape browser as a viewer. To use Netscape to view a saved message, open Netscape and type the location of your message in Netscape's Location: text box. In my case, I would type c:\netscape\mail\mozilla.doc. The message should appear in the Netscape browser as shown in Figure 6.15.

You can view and access the links on this page as if you called up a Web site (of course, the links won't work unless you are connected to the Internet). Scroll down the page and move your cursor over the Netscape Navigator

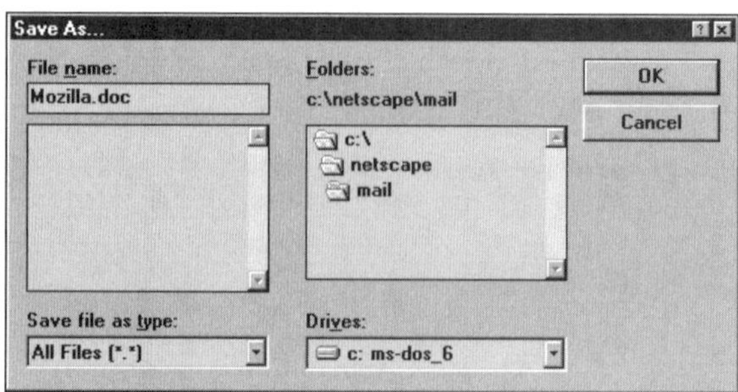

Figure 6.12 *Saving a mail message to your hard drive.*

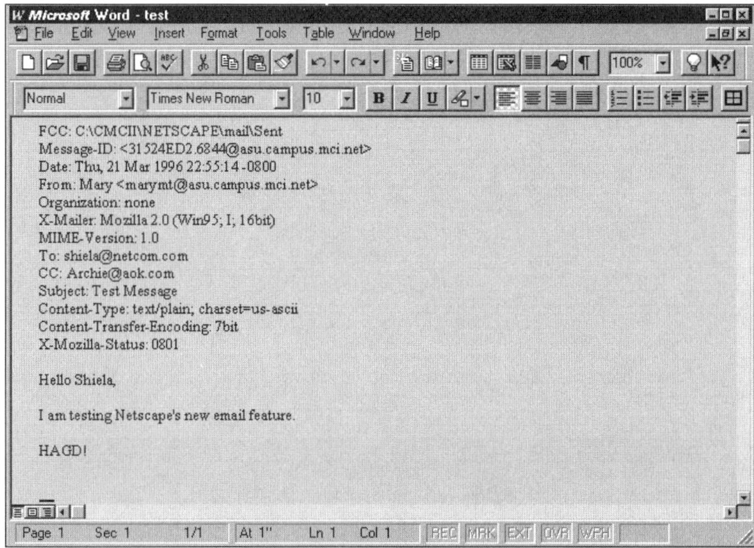

Figure 6.13 *Viewing a mail message saved on the hard drive.*

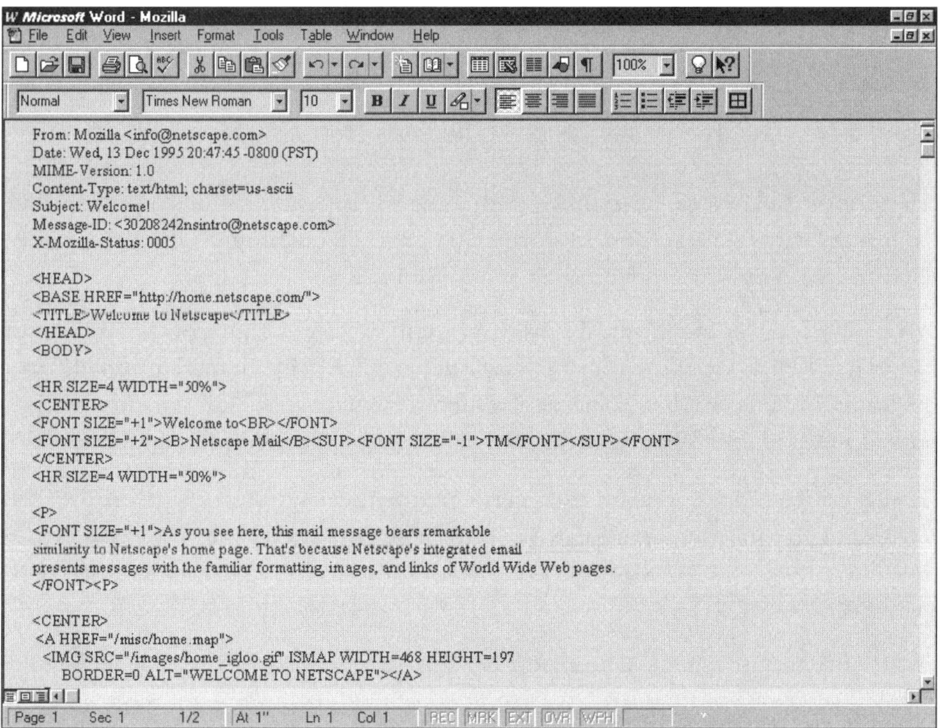

Figure 6.14 *Viewing a mail message with HTML coding saved on the hard drive.*

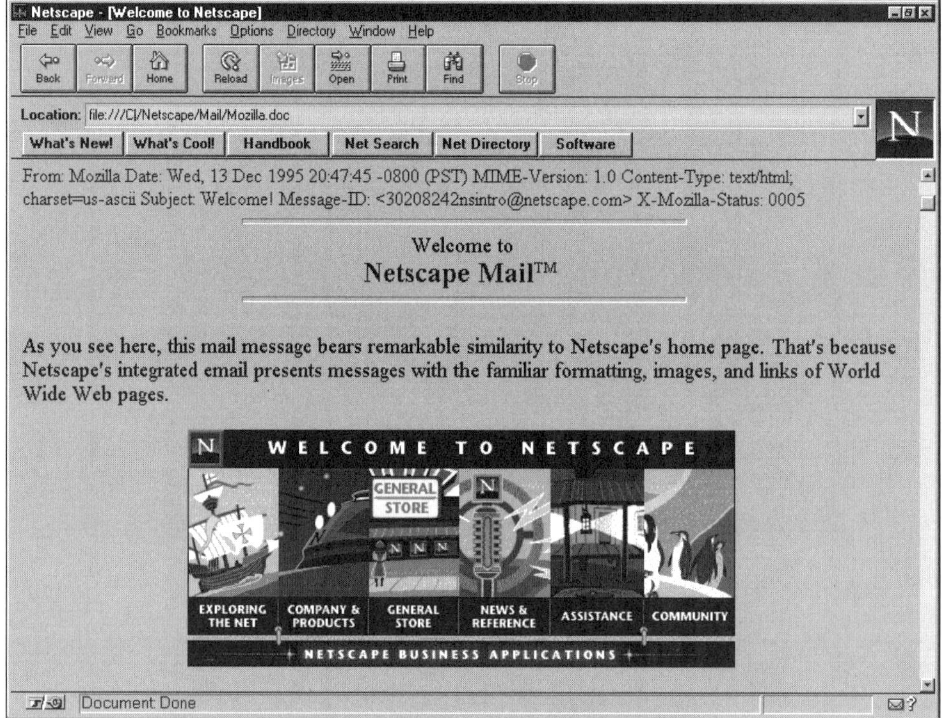

Figure 6.15 *Viewing a saved mail message with HTML coding using Netscape.*

Handbook link. Notice the link's URL address appears in the status bar at the bottom of your screen. You can print this page by clicking on the print toolbar button as if you were printing a typical Web page.

You are probably comfortable printing mail messages that you have saved to your hard disk, so let's take a look at how to print a mail message from Netscape's Mail window. You can return to Netscape's Mail window without closing Mozilla.doc by executing the Window|Netscape Mail sequence.

Printing a message is easy. You can open a message and click on the print button in the toolbar, or you can use the File menu command. If you choose the File menu command, you will see two printing options: Print Message(s) and Print Preview.

You can preview a message before you print it using the File|Print Preview option. Open your Outbox and select your test message. After it displays in the content window, execute the File|Print Preview command. Move your cursor over the page display. Your cursor arrow should change to a magnifying glass. Click once on the document page to zoom in on the text of the message. Your screen should look similar to Figure 6.16.

You can also click on the Zoom In button located at the top of the Print Preview window. If you click on the Zoom In button the document view becomes larger, and the Zoom In button becomes gray while the Zoom Out button becomes bold. If you click on the Zoom Out button twice, your view should now show the page as it originally appeared in print preview mode. Other options in the print preview toolbar are Next Page, Previous Page, display Two Pages at a time, and Close. Click on Close.

We've viewed our message as it will appear when we print it, but we haven't printed it yet. Click on File | Print Message(s). You should receive the Print dialog box shown in Figure 6.17.

The Print dialog box gives you the option of printing all the pages of a message, printing selected portions of a message, or printing selected pages. Select the All option, then click on the OK button. You can also use the Print dialog box to set up your printer options by clicking on the Setup button. Remember, if you want to print an entire message, it is easiest to select the message and click on the Print toolbar button.

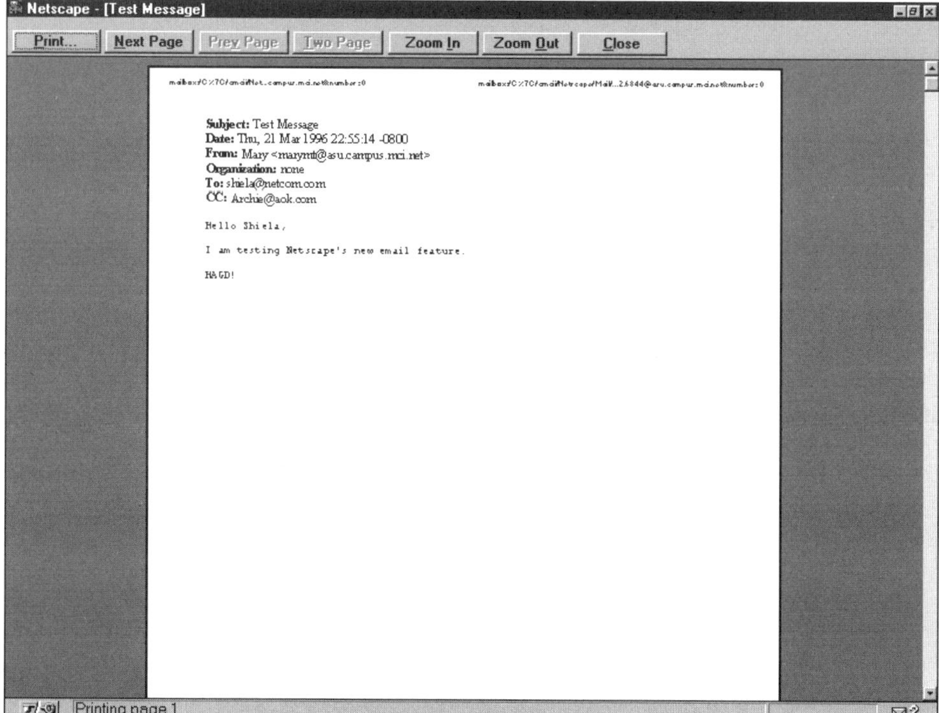

Figure 6.16 *A message displayed in Print Preview mode.*

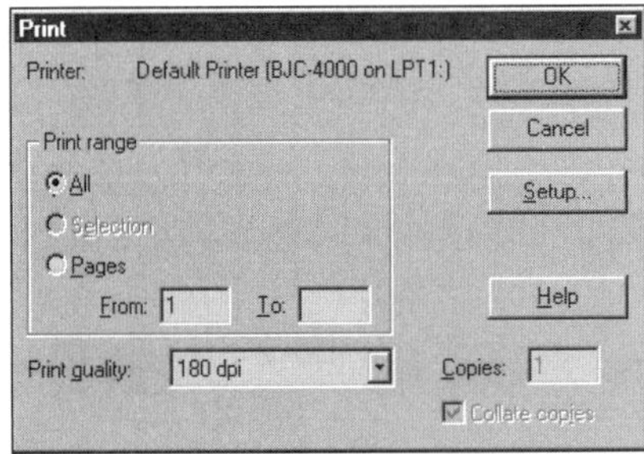

Figure 6.17 The Print dialog box.

We've created, viewed, saved, and printed mail messages. We're ready for a flurry of correspondence…or are we? Maybe we should set up an Address Book for ourselves, to make our lives easier. Let's look into that….

MANAGING YOUR ADDRESS BOOK

Setting up and using your Address Book is similar to creating and using your bookmark list. Your Address Book is designed as an HTML document in your Netscape folder. You can create any number of Address Books, and you can organize your addresses within each Address Book using individual address icons and mailing list books. Individual icons are listed first, followed by any mailing list books you may create. We'll create a basic Address Book here just to get you started.

There are a few different ways to add addresses to your Address Book. Let's start by opening the Address Book and adding Shiela's address. Click on Window | Address Book. Your empty Address Book should appear similar to the one shown in Figure 6.18.

Notice the default file name, address.htm, appears in the title bar. We'll use the default file name for now; later you may want to save your Address Book as a different file. If you decide to save your Address Book as a different file name, remember to save it as an HTML document.

To add an address, execute Item | Add User. You will get the Address Book Properties dialog box as shown in Figure 6.19.

The Address Book Properties dialog box provides text boxes where you can enter a nickname, name, email address, and description. Let's enter Shiela's information. In the nickname text box, type *shiela*. (Note the lowercase "s."

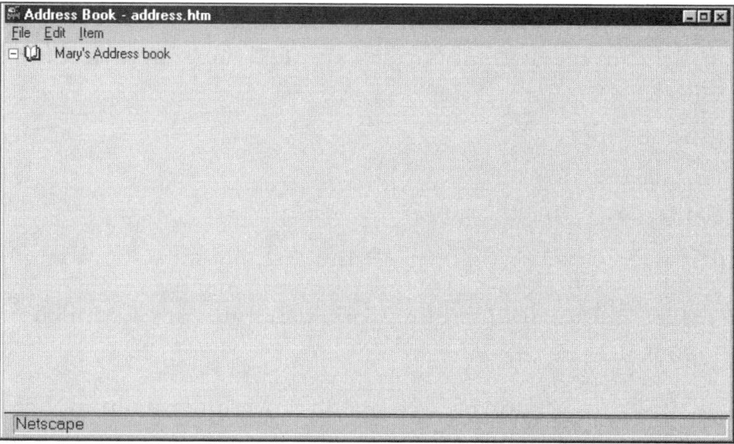

***Figure 6.18** The empty Address Book.*

Nicknames must be entered in lowercase letters.) Nicknames are handy because by the time we are done adding Shiela to our Address Book, we won't ever have to enter her email information again. The next time we send Shiela some mail, we'll only have to type Shiela in the Mail To: text box; Netscape will take care of the rest of our addressing worries. Enter the following information:

Name: Shiela Mills

E-Mail Address: shiela@netcom.com

Description: Recipient of the test message.

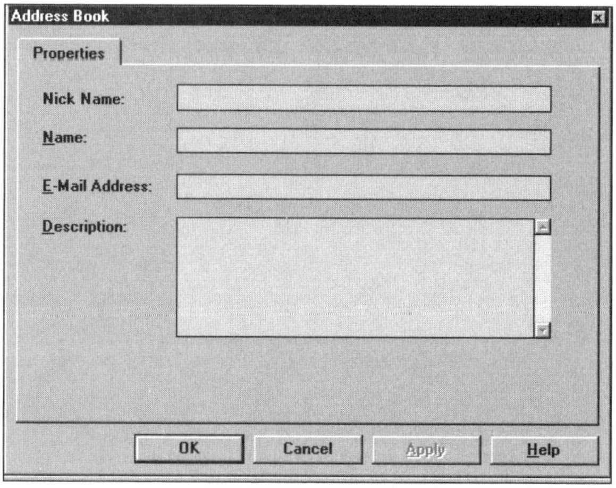

***Figure 6.19** The Address Book Properties dialog box.*

Click on the OK button. Let's add Archie's address to our Address Book, too. (Archie was the one receiving a copy of our test message.) Archie's information is as follows:

Nick Name: archie

Name: Archie Lee

E-Mail Address: archie@aok.com

Description: Recipient of a copy of the test message.

Click on the OK button. Your Address Book should appear similar to the one shown in Figure 6.20.

The Address Book automatically arranges your addresses in alphabetical order. By now you should feel comfortable adding addresses using the Item | Add User option in the Address Book. If you ever need to change the properties on an address, you can right click on the entry and the Address Book Properties dialog box for that entry will open. Let's move on now—close your Address Book, and I'll show you another way to add an address.

Open your Netscape Mail Window, then display the message in your inbox from Mozilla. There are two ways you can add Mozilla's email address to your Address Book. First, you can use the Message menu bar option by executing the Message | Add to Address Book command. But there is an even easier way. Move your cursor over the content frame, then right click. You will get a quick menu with the Add to Address Book option. An Address Book Properties dialog box appears with the name and email text boxes completed. You

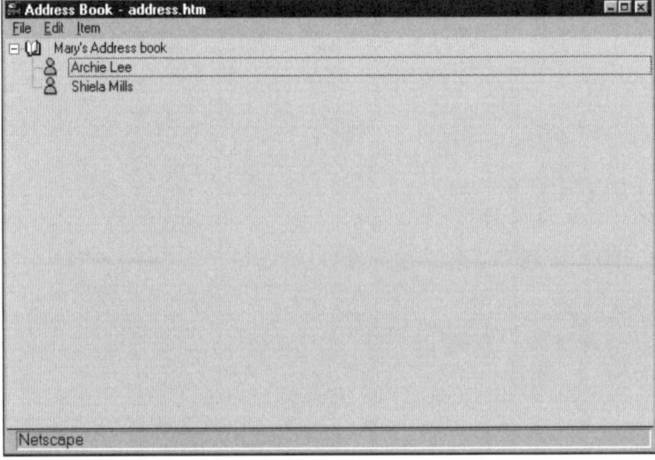

***Figure 6.20** The Address Book with two sample addresses.*

can add a nickname or description here if you want. Click on the OK button. Reopen your Address Book. Notice Mozilla appears between your Archie Lee and Shiela Mills entries. This is a quick and easy way to beef up your Address Book.

While we're in our Address Book, let's create a mailing list that includes Archie and Shiela.

To create a mailing list, execute the Item | Add List command. You will receive a property box for the mailing list folder. Highlight the default folder name (New Folder), type *Test Messages*, add *testing* as the nickname, then click on the OK button. An Address Book icon should appear below your Shiela Mills entry as shown in Figure 6.21.

We now need to add Archie and Shiela's addresses to our mailing list. When you create a mailing list, the list contains aliases to individuals in your Address Book. Each individual in a mailing list is also represented by an icon outside of the list. To add an address to a mailing, simply drag and drop the individual icon onto the mailing list book. The individual icon remains in place, and the alias is stored in the mailing list folder. Click on Shiela Mills, then drag and drop it into the mailing list book. Drag and drop Archie Lee into the mailing list, as well. Once again Netscape alphabetizes your entries. Your Address Book should now appear as shown in Figure 6.22.

Our test Address Book is completed. Let me show you how easy it is to address an email to Archie and Shiela now. Close your Address Book, and

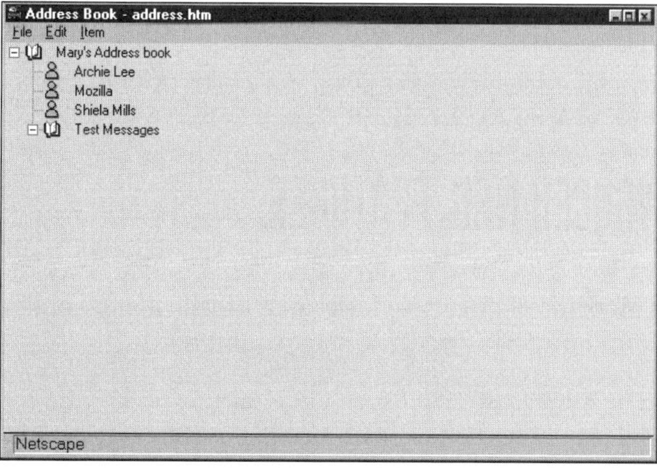

Figure 6.21 *Adding a mailing list to an Address Book.*

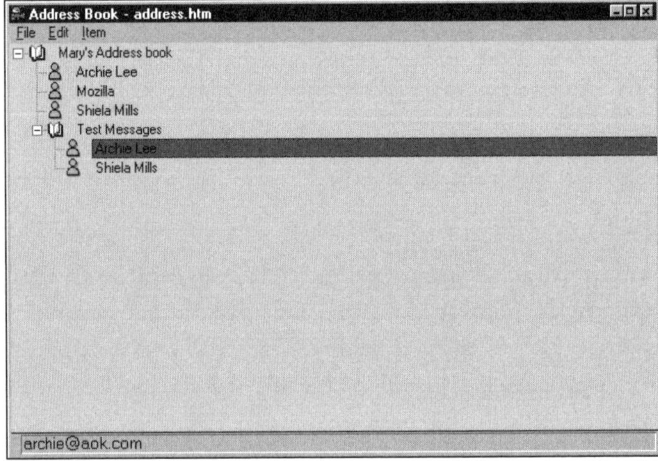

***Figure 6.22** The completed test Address Book.*

open the New Mail Message window (you can use the Ctrl+M shortcut). Type "archie" in the Mail To: text box, then tab to the next field. Notice Archie's address is automatically inserted. Click on the Cc: button, and your Address Book will appear. Click on Shiela Mills, click on the Cc: button, then click on the OK button. Shiela's nickname appears in the Cc: text box. Tab to the Subject text box, and Shiela's full email address displays in the Cc: text box.

Other ways to access your Address Book are to click on the Address button in the toolbar or execute the Window|Address Book sequence. You can also address a new message by highlighting a name in your Address Book, then selecting File|Mail New Message. You'll receive a New Message window pre-addressed to the recipient you highlighted in your Address Book.

Don't close the new message you just created (to: Archie, cc: Shiela), we're about to add an attachment to the message.

USING ADVANCED MAIL FEATURES

In this section we will cover sending and viewing attached documents and passing links. Accomplishing these tasks aren't really that complicated—we've just called them "advanced" because they sound hard.

You can send attachments with a message that can be viewed as inline components or as links. Inline components appear as fully formatted HTML pages appended to the message body or as plain text. Links appear as links on the mail message that the receiver can click on. You can send multiple attachments on an email. Let's send an attachment to Archie and Shiela showing our bookmark.htm file. Let's also send them a link to the Charm Net home page. First, we'll attach our bookmark.htm file as an attachment.

Return to the message you created to send a message to Archie and Shiela. Type "Testing Attachments" in the subject line. Next, click on the Attachment button next to the Attachment: text box. The Attachments dialog box displays as shown in Figure 6.23.

The Attachments dialog box gives you the option to attach either a URL or a file. First we are going to attach our bookmark file. Click on the Attach File button. The Enter file to attach dialog box appears, as shown in Figure 6.24.

Find your bookmark.htm file on your hard drive, then click on the OK button. As you can see in Figure 6.24, my bookmark.htm file is stored in my c:\netscape folder. After you click on the OK button in the dialog box, Netscape returns you to the Attachments dialog box. Notice the file address displays in the dialog box. We now have two options: sending the file As Is or Convert to Plain Text. We are going to assume that Archie and Shiela have the capability

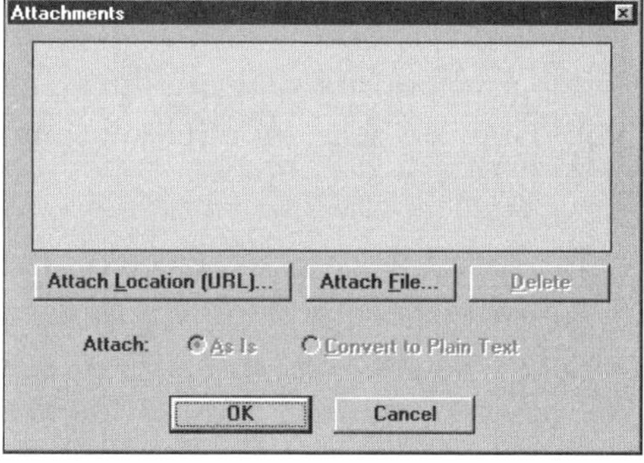

Figure 6.23 *The Attachments dialog box.*

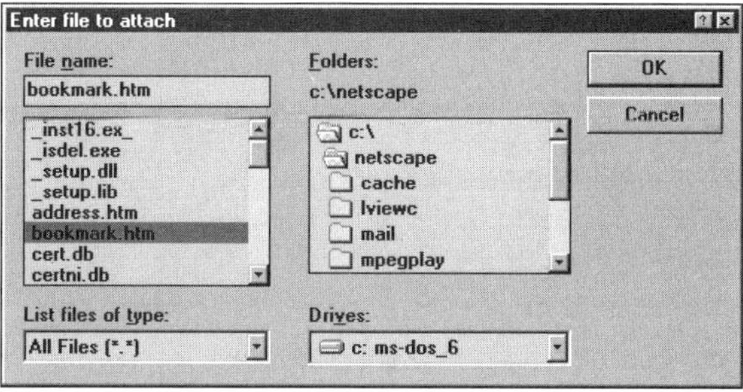

Figure 6.24 *The Enter file to attach dialog box.*

to view HTML documents in their email program (they, too, are using Netscape!). Let's click on the As Is radio button. Click on the OK button, and we are now back to our New Message window.

Now let's add another attachment to the Testing Attachments message. This time, we'll attach a Web page. Instead of typing the path in the Attachments dialog box, let's call up the Web page and have Netscape type the path for us. First, we need to call up Charm Net's home page. To do this, type Charm Net's home page URL in Netscape's Location: text box. Charm Net's URL is:

```
http://www.charm.net
```

View your New Message Window again and click on the Attach button in the toolbar. The Attachments dialog box appears again (this time with your bookmark file attachment listed). Click on the Attach Location (URL) button. The Please Specify a Location to Attach dialog box appears with the Charm Net address inserted in the text box, as shown in Figure 6.25.

This feature is especially handy if the attachment you are sending sports a long, complicated URL address. Click the OK button twice. Finally, let's complete our mail message by typing a short introductory sentence or two in the content frame. You can type whatever you want; I'm keeping it simple. When you are done typing, your New Message should look similar to the one shown in Figure 6.26.

Make sure the Options|Deferred delivery is selected, then click on the send button in the toolbar. Your message should now appear in your Outbox. Let's verify that your message found its way to your outbox. Click on Window|Netscape Mail to access the Mail window. Notice there are now two files in your Outbox. Before you view the message you just created, execute the View|Attachments Inline sequence. Open your message, and you will see the contents of both your bookmark file and a reproduction of Charm Net's home page. Your message should look similar to the one shown in Figure 6.27.

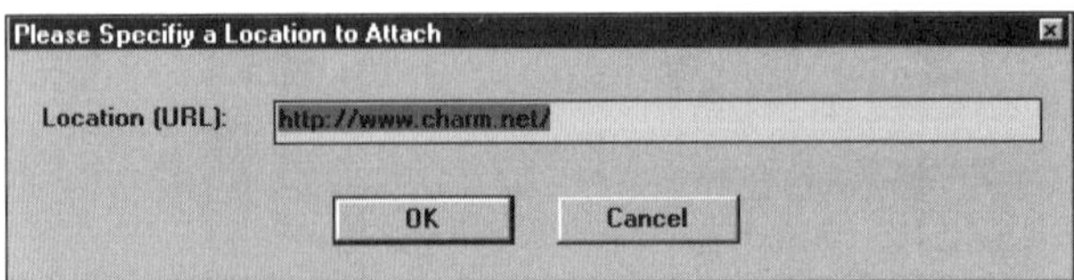

Figure 6.25 *The Please Specify a Location to Attach dialog box.*

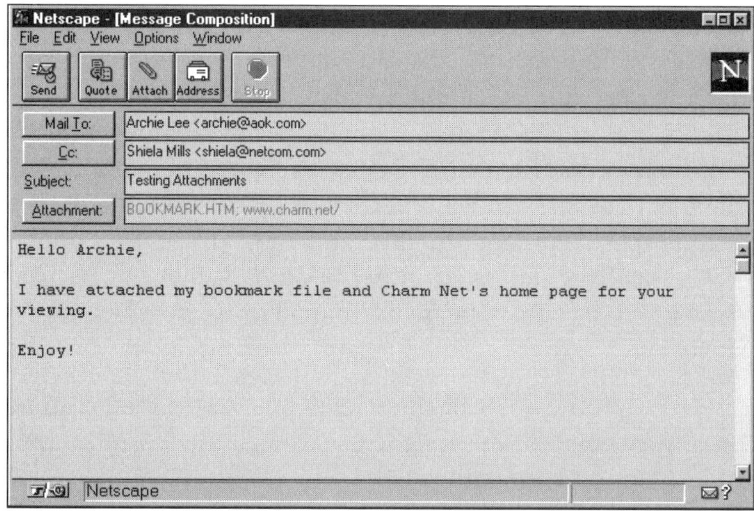

Figure 6.26 Our newly completed message with an attachment and a link.

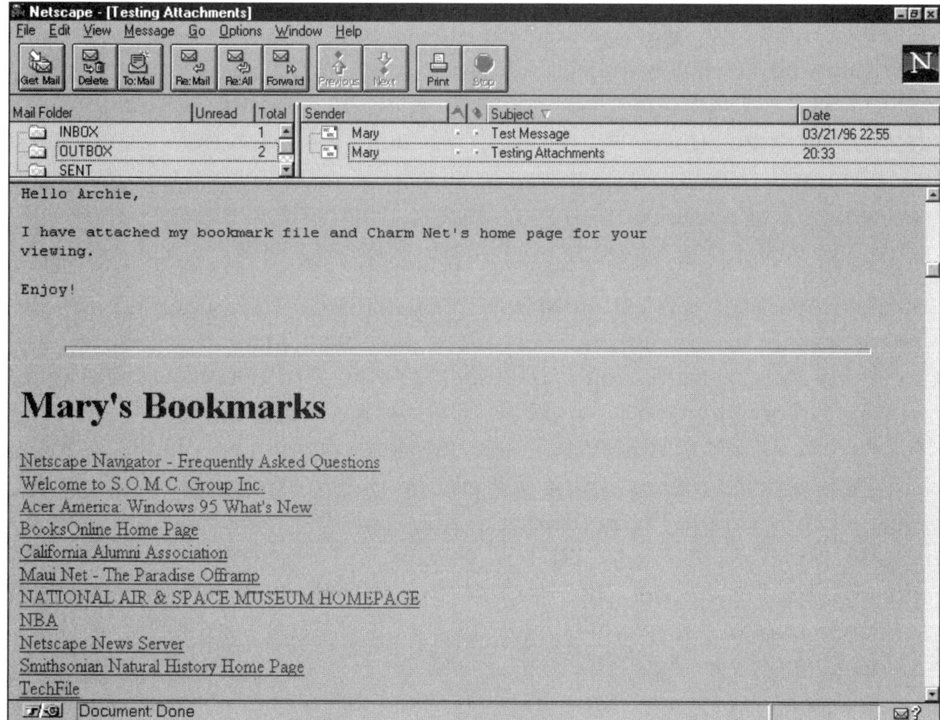

Figure 6.27 Viewing a message with the attachments inline.

If the recipient of the message does not want to view the attachments as inline components of the message, she can execute the View|Attachments as Links command. Go ahead and execute the View|Attachments as Links sequence. When the links option is activated, the viewer can see the name, type, and encoding information of the file. In either case, when the viewer displays the attached document as an inline component or by clicking on a link, any links included within the document are alive and well. (In other words, if Archie wants to view the NBA site listed in my bookmark file—all he has to do is click on the NBA entry as it appears in his mail message—Netscape will take him to the site.)

Good work—you are now email proficient. Netscape's mail feature has expanded email way beyond the basic text message. Have fun swapping lines and links with your favorite netheads!

CoolTalk

Netscape's new Mail feature is a great timesaver and asset, but what do you do if you really prefer to talk to someone, instead of just sending them an email message. Until now you would have to pick up the phone and call whoever you wanted to talk to—and pay a hefty long distance charge. But a new preview release from Netscape, called Atlas, is changing that. Atlas is a very early test of a new version of Netscape. There are many new and exciting features included in the program, but one of the most interesting is CoolTalk.

No doubt everyone has caught themselves talking to their computer at one point or another (usually in a not-very-nice tone!). Well, imagine talking (nicely) to your computer and having it talk back to you. Or better yet, talking into your computer and having another Internet user talk back to you. With Netscape's CoolTalk, Internet communication goes beyond email into the realm of multimedia messaging. With CoolTalk, an online conference can include business card swapping (complete with photographs), whiteboard charts and graphics, audio discussions, URL transmittals, and interactive text communication. CoolTalk provides Internet users with high-quality audio and chat communication features, as well as a full-featured whiteboard. The CoolTalk window is shown in Figure 6.28.

You use the CoolTalk window when you are conducting voice conferences. You can also access CoolTalk's other features from this window. Using the six buttons in the top toolbar, you can set up a conference, turn your answering machine on and off, check your messages, open the chat feature, open the

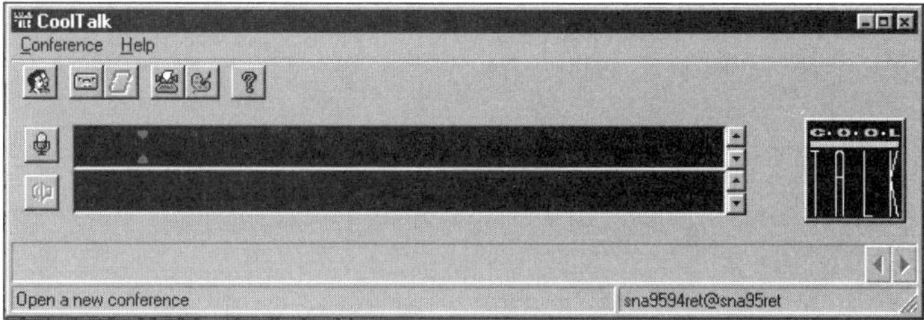

Figure 6.28 The CoolTalk Window.

whiteboard feature, and access CoolTalk's Help files. Let's take a quick look at CoolTalk's audio, chat, and whiteboard features. Since we're already viewing the Audio window, let's look at audio communication first.

Making an Audio Connection

Real-time audio messaging is one of the new kids on the Internet block. Netscape makes using audio easy by including the CoolTalk application as part of the browser's setup. Basically, CoolTalk allows you to send and receive audio messages using a microphone and speakers attached to your soundcard. During a conference, CoolTalk automatically switches between send and receive modes, creating the effect of seamless communication. There are two ways you can become involved in an audio conference. You can be called, in which case your CoolTalk window will automatically display on your screen along with a dialog box asking you to accept or reject the call. Or you can place a call to another user. To place a call, you need to know the receiver's address. You can use the CoolTalk phonebook search page to find active CoolTalk users. You can reach CoolTalk's phonebook search page using the following URL:

```
http://live.netscape.com
```

Live.netscape.com is Netscape's audio server. CoolTalk's phonebook search page appears as shown in Figure 6.29.

You can sort by real name, user name, domain, or status, and you can search by real name, user name and hostname. Let's keep it general by leaving the options blank and clicking on the Begin Search button. We've opted to display all the active CoolTalk users, sorted by their real names. Your display should appear similar to Figure 6.30.

If you click on a Real Name link, such as Alex in Figure 6.30, Netscape will automatically launch CoolTalk and dial the person's number. You should hear

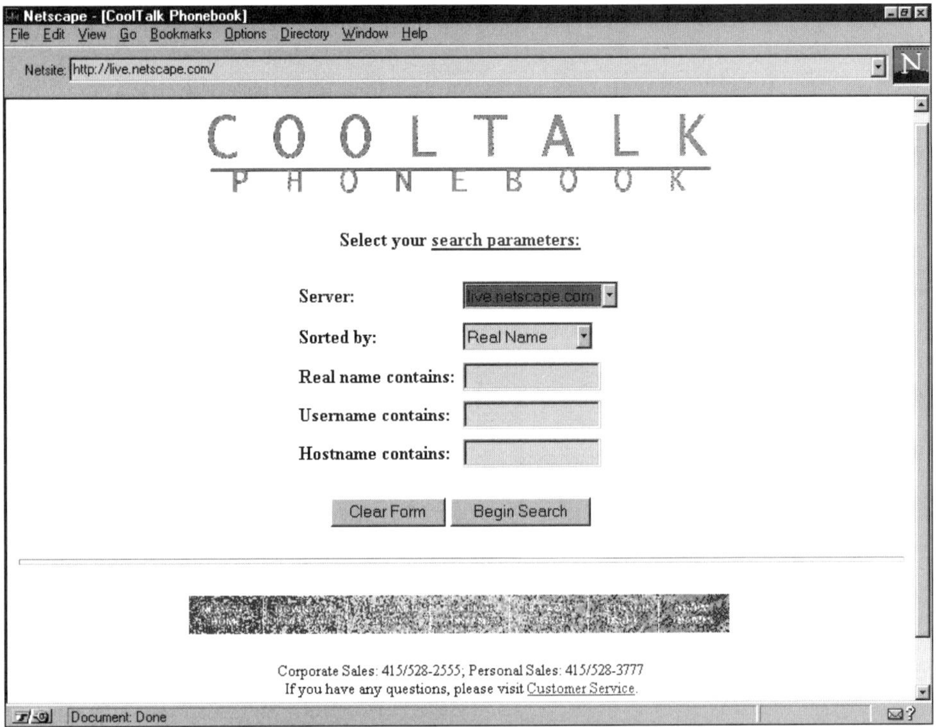

Figure 6.29 *CoolTalk's phonebook search page.*

a couple of ringing tones, and then the receiver will "pick up" and say hello (if they are friendly). If your system is properly configured, you can talk to the other person using your microphone, type messages using the chat feature, or draw illustrations on the whiteboard. I have found that most people using CoolTalk make good accomplices when trying to learn how to use this new feature. If you don't have a particular contact at first, try randomly clicking on a name—most likely you'll find a friendly voice on the other side willing to help you navigate your way around the CoolTalk neighborhood.

Using the Chat Tool

CoolTalk's chat tool provides Internet users with a text-based communication feature accompanying the audio capabilities. The chat tool can be used to send and receive text files, as well as to type messages to conference members. One benefit of providing typed messages is that the text can be saved to disk. To access the chat feature, click on the Chat button in the CoolTalk toolbar (it's the fourth button from the left). The Chat Tool window appears similar to the one shown in Figure 6.31.

Figure 6.30 *The search results in CoolTalk's phonebook.*

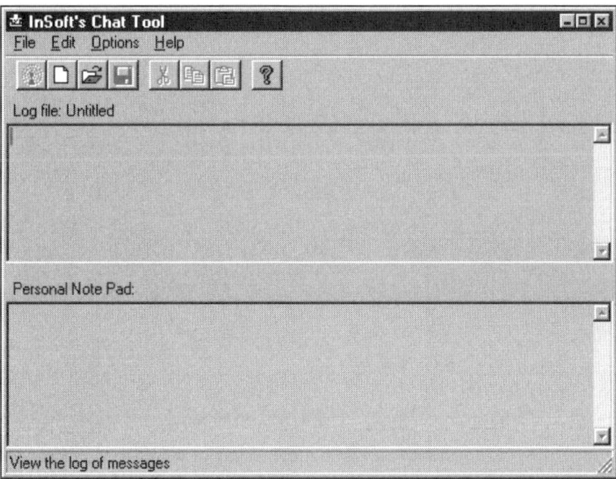

Figure 6.31 *CoolTalk's Chat Tool.*

Type your messages in the lower frame, then click on the Post button (the leftmost button on the toolbar) to send the message. Your posted message will appear to both you and the other conference members, who are listed in the upper frame. You can use the toolbar buttons to post messages; clear the log (upper frame); open and attach text files; save the log to disk; cut, copy, and paste text; and access help files. The chat tool is similar to email, with the added bonus that you can talk to each other while you write or transmit documents.

Using the White Board Viewer

The third major component of ChatTalk is the White Board feature. The White Board enables viewers to share and edit images during a conference. The White Board includes a variety of markup tools, many similar to those found in popular paint programs. To access the whiteboard feature, click on the White Board toolbar button (fifth button from the left). The White Board viewer is shown in Figure 6.32.

Notice the familiar tools located along the left side of the White Board window. In addition, toolbar buttons and menu commands display above the White Board drawing area. You can use the Open File icon in the toolbar to

Figure 6.32 CoolTalk's White Board.

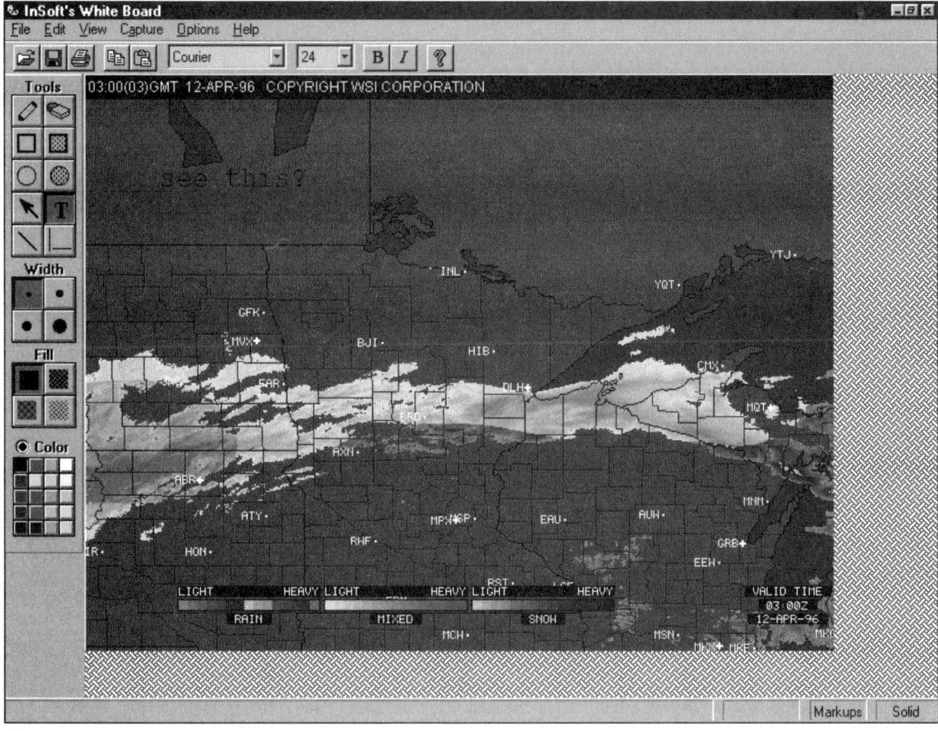

Figure 6.33 A weather map displayed on the White board.

attach graphics. To clear your White Board area execute the menu command Edit | Clear White Board. Figure 6.33. shows a map sent to me from a Web designer in Minnesota—they were experiencing their first thunderstorm of the year at the time.

CoolTalk Summary

Well, those are the basics of CoolTalk. The more you use it the easier it will become—I promise. The best part of CoolTalk is that it comes packaged with Netscape. Therefore, the appropriate application window opens as you need it. In other words, if someone calls you, CoolTalk opens. If someone sends you a Whiteboard graphic, your whiteboard opens. It is all very convenient, but you are bound to have a question or two now and then. Fortunately, there are a few helpful URLs that you can visit in search of CoolTalk answers. Both of the following sites are provided by Insoft, the makers of CoolTalk. To analyze your system for CoolTalk compatibility use:

```
http://ice.insoft.com/cgi-bin/SystemCheck.cgi
```

For support go to:

```
http://ice.insoft.com/support/CoolTalkPS.html
```

And don't forget to check out Netscape's release notes and handbook entries. Of course, my all-time favorite tactic for garnering information is to dial up a user and ask away. As a matter of fact, I've made five new netfriends tonight while writing this section!

LET'S REVIEW

Before you can do anything with Netscape's mail feature, you have to tell Netscape your email information. To do this, you must set the preferences on the Servers card in the Mail and News Preferences dialog box.

There are two main windows in Netscape's mail feature: the New Message(s) window and the Netscape Mail window. You use the New Message(s) window when you are sending mail, and you use the Netscape Mail window when you are viewing or sorting your mail messages.

Mail messages can be saved to disk and printed in the same way that you print and save most documents. Messages containing HTML codes can be viewed using the Netscape browser as a viewer. Netscape expands your email capability by adding the benefit of transmitting HTML documents and web pages as inline components or links on a mail message.

Managing your Address Book is simple using Netscape's Address Book feature. You can create individual icons for each address, and you can compile mailing lists by combining aliases of existing addresses. Addresses are easily added and deleted—without having to resort to white-out and erasers! You can also create nicknames for each address to help you quickly fill out New Message(s) headers.

The more you use Netscape for processing your email, the more comfortable you'll feel taking advantage of all the features. Once you are comfortable with the advantages, you're not going to want to send and receive email any other way.

CoolTalk is a real-time audio conferencing and data sharing tool specifically designed for the Internet. CoolTalk includes audio and text conferencing, as well as a full-feature whiteboard.

The real-time audio feature is the newest communication tool on the Web. CoolTalk makes connecting easy. You need a microphone to plug into your soundcard before you can transmit audio messages, but you can receive audio messages using your basic speakers and soundcard (you can send text messages in response to audio messages until you purchase your microphone).

Another feature offered with CoolTalk is the Answering Machine. The Answering Machine can be turned on or off using the toolbar button. Like a telephone answering machine, messages are recorded from users whose calls you missed, and you can pick up a call while the other user is leaving a message. The Answering Machine saves the other user's Business Card along with the message, making the return call as easy as clicking on a button.

Finally, the CoolTalk White Board can load and save many popular image formats, including GIF, JPEG, Windows Bitmap, and TIFF. Simultaneous use of audio and whiteboard applications can be accomplished in CoolTalk without any degradation of audio or visual quality.

Netscape News

Where can you find all kinds of information, and put your two cents in? In newsgroups, of course, and now Netscape has a Usenet News function built right in.

In any race, sooner or later the leaders break away from the pack. It's been the same with Web browsers. Mosaic kept its lead for a surprisingly long time. Then, a challenger named Netscape came out of nowhere and grabbed the crown of King Browser in a crowded field. (Well, not exactly out of nowhere. The guy who wrote Netscape is the same guy who wrote Mosaic. Not many people have the opportunity to do something that important twice!) In countless tests, about 75 percent of the people connecting to major Web sites are using Netscape. (A server can determine the connecting browser's brand and version.)

The speed of the transition is what makes this revolution surprising. In Web circles, technological half-life is being measured in months, not years. There has never been a time in the history of the world when a technology has increased as quickly as Web utilization. Television and the telephone were snails by comparison.

In this chapter we'll take a look at one of Netscape's useful features, a powerful Usenet newsgroup reader. If you are not reading Usenet News, you're missing out on a lot of fun and information.

NETSCAPE'S USENET NEWSREADER

Even in its very first release, the Netscape browser improved on Mosaic by incorporating a powerful Usenet newsgroup reader. Such utilities are called newsreaders. Before looking at the specifics of this newsreader, a little background is in order. Usenet newsgroups have a long history on the Internet that goes back to the very early days and Bitnet. There are currently about 13,000 newsgroups, and new ones are being added every week. Newsgroups are much like electronic bulletin boards, and are very similar to the popular public forums on CompuServe. You can post a message to the group (that is, on the "board") and others who peruse the newsgroup can read your message at their leisure. Readers of your message can, in turn, reply to your posting, and their messages are logically associated with yours so that people reading the newsgroup understand that one follows another. A series of such cascading postings is called a thread.

When you decide you want to read a newsgroup regularly, you tell your newsreader the name of the group, and it "subscribes" to the group for you. This means that the name of the group is held by the newsreader, and when you want to read the group, you need only click on the newsgroup's name. Because some of the names of the groups are long and (as with the alt.barney.dinosaur.die.die.die newsgroup), subscribing is simpler than typing the whole name every time you want to read a group.

Using Netscape to read postings to newsgroups is much like reading an elaborate version of your email. Instead of clicking on your inbox or outbox to view email messages, you click on a newsgroup name to view postings to the newsgroup. The core difference between email and newsgroups is that email is distributed on a person-to-person basis, while news postings are distributed on a publication-for-all basis.

Compared to other documents, newsgroup offerings have advantages and disadvantages. News messages organized by topics into threads is a major advantage. You have the ability to post your own contributions to either the individual originating the message or to the entire group, another advantage. Another advantage is that you may be able to begin what might become your own thread. Disadvantages of newsgroups include the fact that you might find yourself spending a few too many hours reading and responding to interesting newsgroup postings.

Netscape has many newsreader features; however, the program doesn't help you to get started, other than subscribing you to three start-up groups: news.announce.newusers, news.newusers.questions, and news.answers. Unless you're content to participate in these three newsgroups, you have to find other groups that intrigue you.

Setting Your Newsgroup Preferences

The names of Usenet newsgroups are organized in a hierarchical structure. The hierarchical structure lists news servers first, categories next, then newsgroups. Before you can access Usenet news, you need to tell Netscape the name of your top level—your news server (NNTP). To do this, execute Options|Mail and News Preferences, then click on the Servers tab to display the Servers preferences card. Click in the News (NNTP) Server: text box, then type in your news server information. You can get this information from your Internet service provider. Your Servers preferences card should look similar to the one shown in Figure 7.1.

Notice the News RC Directory: text box located directly below the News (NNTP) Server: text box. The "RC" stands for "read command." These files are much like Windows INI configuration files. You should select a path for your News RC File. When Netscape is initially installed, the file newsrc is placed in c:\. I prefer keeping all related files in the same path as the executable program, so I indicated that my RC files should be saved in C:\netscape\News. If

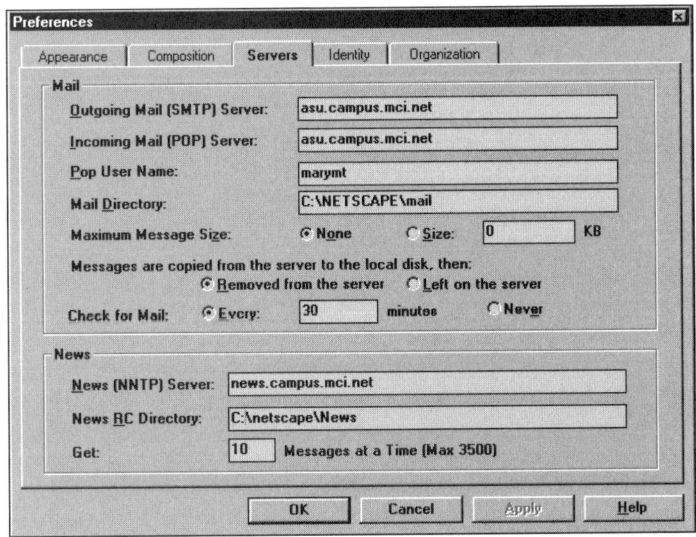

Figure 7.1 A completed Servers Preferences card.

you want to specify a path for your news RC file in this step, copy newsrc from c:\ to the specified directory. Click on OK to accept your entries.

The final news groups setting on the Servers preferences card is the Get option. You use the Get: text box to tell Netscape how many news messages you want to view at one time. You'll see how this affects your viewing in just a minute. I like to keep this number relatively low because the more messages you display, the longer you'll have to wait to view them. Notice in Figure 7.1 that I indicated to only "get" 10 messages at a time; you can pick any number up to 3500 that you want.

OK, preferences set, we are now ready to explore the Newsgroup window.

Netscape's Newsgroup Window

Before you can view newsgroups and participate in the fun, we should discuss some of the features of Netscape's newsgroup window. To open the newsgroup window, execute Window | Netscape News. Your Netscape news window should look similar to the one shown in Figure 7.2.

As mentioned earlier, the top-level of the newsgroup's hierarchical structure is the news server. Notice that your server appears as the default server folder in

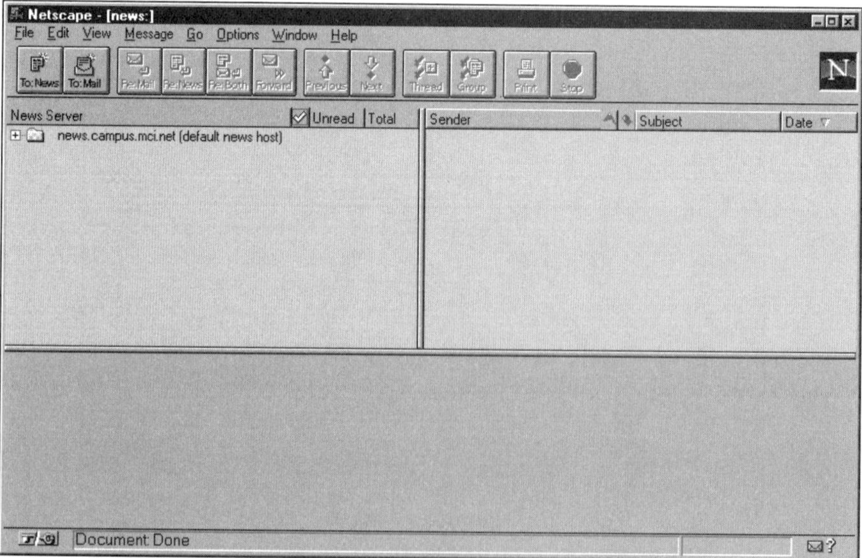

Figure 7.2 *Netscape's News window.*

the left pane of the News window. Typically, you'll only be connected to one news server at a time, and you'll only have one top-level folder.

If you have no previous News file, Netscape creates one for you that contains three newsgroups designed for new users: news.announce.newusers, news.newusers.quesions, and news.answers. To view the full set of available news categories and newsgroups execute Options | Show All Newsgroups. You can tell the difference between newsgroups and news categories, because news categories display with a folder icon and an asterisk in the folder's name. A category folder contains newsgroups sharing the same prefix. To display the newsgroups in a category, just click on a category folder.

The top left frame in the newsgroup window contains four columns. The first column lists the names of the news server, newsgroups, and news categories. The second column consists of check boxes indicating whether you want to subscribe to a newsgroup. The check box is a toggle. To subscribe to a newsgroup, you click on the check box and a checkmark displays. To discontinue your subscription to a newsgroup, you simply click on the checkmark in the check box and the checkmark disappears. The next column is the Unread column. This column shows the number of unread messages in each newsgroup. Finally, the fourth column, named the Total column, shows the number of read and unread messages in each newsgroup.

The top right frame in the newsgroup window contains five columns. The Sender column shows the name of the sender of the news message. The Flag icon is a toggle icon showing whether a message is noteworthy (you control when and where you want the flags to appear). The read icon (diamond shaped), is also a toggle icon, and it shows if a message has been viewed (if you view a message but want to come back to it, you can redisplay the read icon to ensure that the message displays the next time you view the newsgroup's messages). The Subject column shows the subject line of each message. Like all columns in the newsgroup window, the subject column can be sized to accommodate viewing the text by dragging the column edge one way or the other. Finally, the fifth column, the Date column, shows the date and time each news message was posted.

As we discussed earlier, newsgroups are threaded by default. You can change this setting by executing Options | Mail and News Preferences, then clicking on the Organization tab to display the Organization preferences card as shown in Figure 7.3.

Notice the check mark options in the General area of the Organization card indicating to thread mail and news messages. Netscape's default is to thread

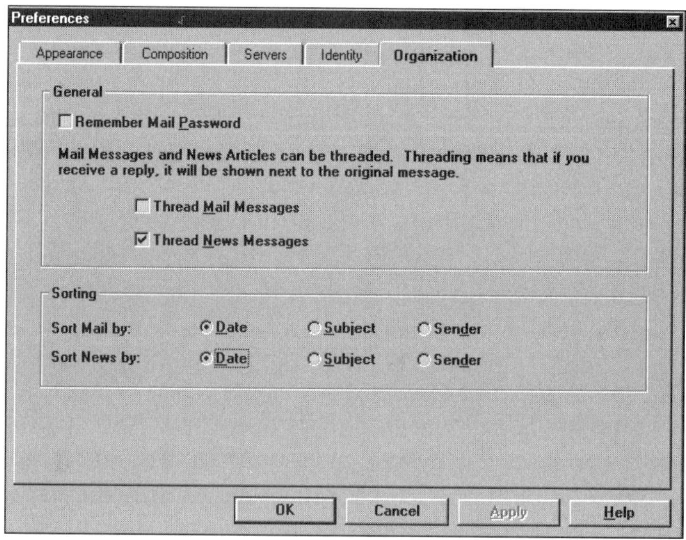

Figure 7.3 *The Mail and News Preferences—Organization card.*

news messages. Under the General area is the Sorting area. Mail and News items can be sorted by date, subject, or sender. Netscape's default is to sort by date for both mail and news items. For news items, you can change your sorting preference here, or you can click on the column heading in the top right frame of the newsgroup window. Close the Organization preferences card, and open your newsgroup window. Notice the downward pointing arrow in the Date column heading. Click on the Sender column heading. The sort arrow now displays in the Sender heading, and you have just changed your preferences (if you don't believe me you can pull up your Organization card, where you'll see the radio button next to sender is now selected). All the messages should now be organized in alphabetical order by sender.

The third frame in the newsgroup window is what I'll call the Message window. This is the window that displays newsgroup messages, along with the Subject, Date, From, Organization, Newsgroups, and References information. You view news messages in the Messages window. Like the other two frames, this area can be enlarged or reduced by dragging the frame border in the appropriate direction.

By now you should be starting to feel a little more comfortable with your newsgroup window. I know I promised that we'd get to the fun part soon, but bear with me for one more minute. Let's do a quick run through of the buttons on the button bar shown in the newsgroup window and briefly discuss the menu selections, then we'll be off to get the news. The buttons on the newsgroup window's button bar include the following:

To: News displays the Message Composition window used to create a news message.

To: Mail displays the Message Composition window used to create a mail message.

Re: Mail displays the Message Composition window used to reply to the currently displayed message's sender. You will notice that the **To** field is pre-addressed for you.

Re: News displays the Message Composition window used to reply to the currently displayed news thread.

Re: Both displays the Message Composition window for replying to the current news message thread and replying by mail to the message's sender.

Forward displays the Message Composition window for forwarding the current news message as an attachment. You will notice that the subject field is prefixed with **Fwd**.

Previous displays the previous unread message in a thread.

Next displays the next unread message in a thread.

Thread marks messages in the thread as read.

Group marks all messages in the group as read

Print prints the currently selected message in the message field.

Stop stops a transmission of messages from the news server.

Above the buttons bar, there is the familiar-looking menu bar. Many of the News menu items are familiar to you. Commands such as Undo, Close, and Paste don't need to be reiterated here. Other commands, such as those found under the Go, Window, and Help menu items, are self-explanatory. Following is an list of some useful menu items, excerpted from Netscape's online Handbook. The URL for Netscape's complete list of the News menu items is:

```
http://home.netscape.com/eng/mozilla/2.0/handbook/docs/mnb.html#C9
```

File|Open News Host prompts you to specify the news server to access and add to your news server list.

File|Remove News Host deletes the selected news server from your list.

File|Add Newsgroup lets you select a new newsgroup to add to your subscription list.

File|Get More Messages lets you retrieve an additional group of news messages.

Edit | Select Thread selects all messages in the current thread.

Edit | Select Flagged Messages selects messages in the current thread that are designated in the message heading pane.

Edit | Select All Messages selects all messages in all threads.

Edit | Find searches for text in the current message.

Edit | Find Again searches for the same text as the previous search.

Edit | Cancel Message removes the selected message you've sent to the newsgroup.

View | Sort lets you arrange the position of messages in the message heading field according to Date, Subject, Sender, or Message Number and can specify Ascending order. Choose Again to sort again. Choose Thread Messages to sort messages so that messages and their responses are grouped together.

View | Unscramble (ROT-13) lets you decode a certain type of message in which the sender has shifted the message's characters.

View | Load Images displays the images of the current message if they have not been automatically loaded.

View | Refresh redraws the current message.

View | Reload brings the message from the server again.

View | Document Source produces a View Source window showing the current page in HTML format.

View | Attachments Inline, when checked, lets you view a page attachment as part of the message. If the sender has included an HTML page as an attachment, the formatted page is appended to the message body.

View | Attachments as Links, when checked, lets you access a page attachment using a link. If the sender has included an HTML page as an attachment, a link to the formatted page is appended to the message body. Clicking on the link displays the page in the message content pane.

Message | Post Reply displays the Message Composition window for writing a response with the Send To: field pre-addressed to the newsgroup of the previous message.

Message | Post and Mail Reply displays the Message Composition window for writing a response to the current message thread and replying to the message's sender.

Message | Mail Reply displays the Message Composition window for replying to the current message's sender. The To: field is preaddressed.

Message | Forward displays the Message Composition window for forwarding the current news message as an attachment. The To: field is blank. The original Subject: field is prefixed with Fwd.

Message | Forward Quoted displays the Message Composition window for sending the current message as quoted text in the content area.

Message | Add to Address Book creates an address book entry of the sender of the current message.

Options | Show Subscribed Newsgroups, when checked, displays only newsgroups in your subscription list.

Options | Show Active Newsgroups, when checked, displays only subscribed newsgroups with new messages.

Options | Show All Newsgroups, when checked, displays all available newsgroups from your news server.

Options | Show New Newsgroup, when checked, displays only newsgroups new since you previously connected to the news server.

Options | Show All Messages, when checked, displays all messages of the selected newsgroup.

Options | Show Only Unread Message, when checked, displays only unread messages.

Options | Show All Headers, when checked, displays full header information, including Return Path, Received, Message ID, and Content Type. When unchecked, the message pane displays only the basic address fields.

Options | Add from Newest Messages, when checked, displays the most recent messages first.

Options | Add from Oldest Messages, when checked, displays the oldest messages first.

Options | Document Encoding lets you select which character set encoding a document uses when the document encoding is either not specified or unavailable.

Options | Save Options preserves any changes made to your menu settings for subsequent sessions (excluding the preferences [Organization card] panel items, which are saved by pressing OK).

Feel free to use the above list as a quick reference while you're manipulating your news messages. Another way to access many of these commands is to position your mouse over the right or bottom news frame and click with your right mouse button. Right-clicking displays a pop-up menu of shortcut commands. We'll use the pop-up shortcut menu when we post a reply message later in this chapter.

Well, you've finally made it. You've read the newsgroup details, now joining a newsgroup and getting the news will be a breeze. Let's go!

Searching for Newsgroups on the World Wide Web

There are a number of places where we can look for and call up newsgroups. Recall that when we were testing helper applications, one of the test sites was named Multimedia File Formats on the Internet: A Beginner's Guide for PC Users. If you were being especially observant when we were testing our music helper application, you probably noticed newsgroups listed on the music page. Let's go back to that site, and I'll show you what I mean. The URL for the Multimedia File Formats site is:

```
http://ac.dal.ca/~dong/contents.htm
```

Click on the Table of Contents link, scroll down to the Sound and Music section heading, then choose Selected Sources. The next screen displays music topics, including newsgroups. Figure 7.4 shows the music sources web page.

If you click on any of the newsgroup names, your Netscape News window will open and the selected news group will be added to your list of newsgroups. As you navigate the web, you will notice that many sites list newsgroups for you to join. Finding newsgroups "by accident" is always fun, but you also have the option of searching for newsgroups that interest you. I present to you the tile.net news service, an index service for Usenet newsgroups. tile.net's URL is:

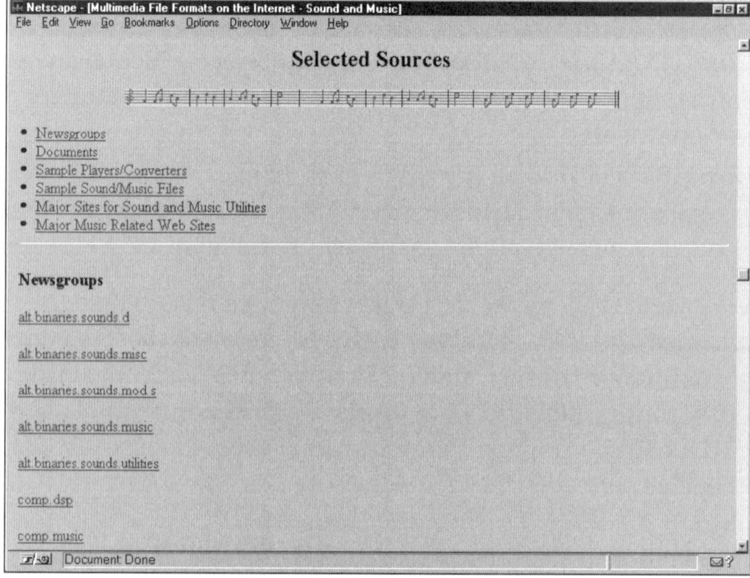

Figure 7.4 A list of music-related newsgroups.

```
http://www.tile.net
```

tile.net's home page is shown in Figure 7.5.

Not long ago, there was no truly general newsgroup search capability using a Web browser. If tile.net seems a little awkward at first, remember that this site is a great improvement over Usenet search services in the past. Click on the /news link. Figure 7.6 displays the tile.net /news page.

On the tile.net /news page, you can search by Index, Description, or Newsgroup Hierarchy. (You can also choose Search in the top menu bar, but this basically brings you to a search service, such as Excite or Yahoo. I'm not discounting this search feature, by any means—it is extremely useful—but we'll go into more detail about using search engines in another chapter.) Since we're using the Netscape Navigator, let's search for a newsgroup on sailing. Click on Index, then choose S, then click on Sailing. You should now be at the search result page where two newsgroups on sailing are listed. Figure 7.7 shows the results of our search for sailing newsgroups.

Click on alt.sailing.asa, and you will bring up a fact page on the alt.sailing.asa newsgroup. This page gives you information on the number of readers and new messages posted per day, among other statistics. Click on the alt.sailing.asa link to the newsgroup. Clicking on a newsgroup automatically opens your Netscape News window and temporarily adds the newsgroup to your list

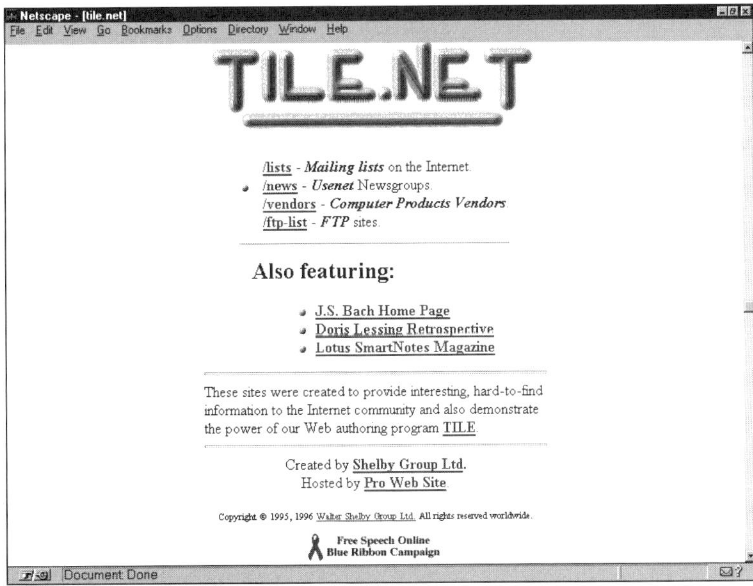

Figure 7.5 *tile.net's home page.*

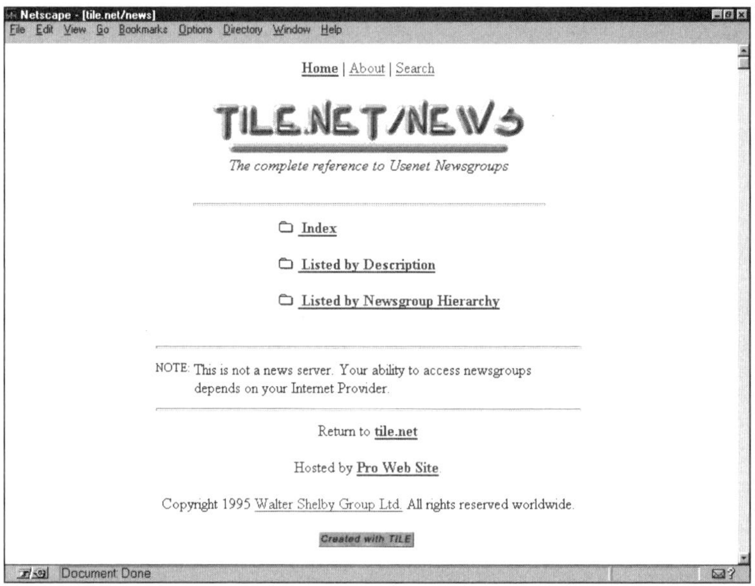

Figure 7.6 *tile.net's /news page.*

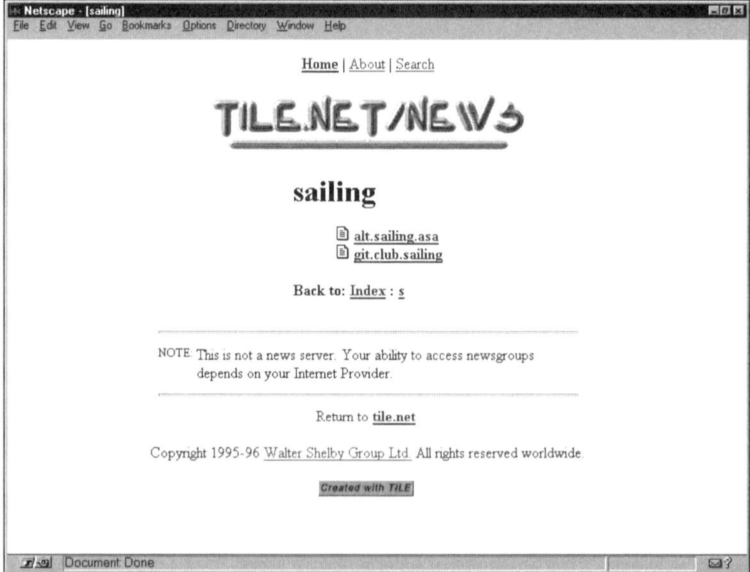

Figure 7.7 *tile.net /news' results of the "sailing" search.*

(don't worry, you won't permanently add a newsgroup to your list unless you officially "subscribe" to it by placing a checkmark in the check box). Your Netscape News window should appear as in Figure 7.8.

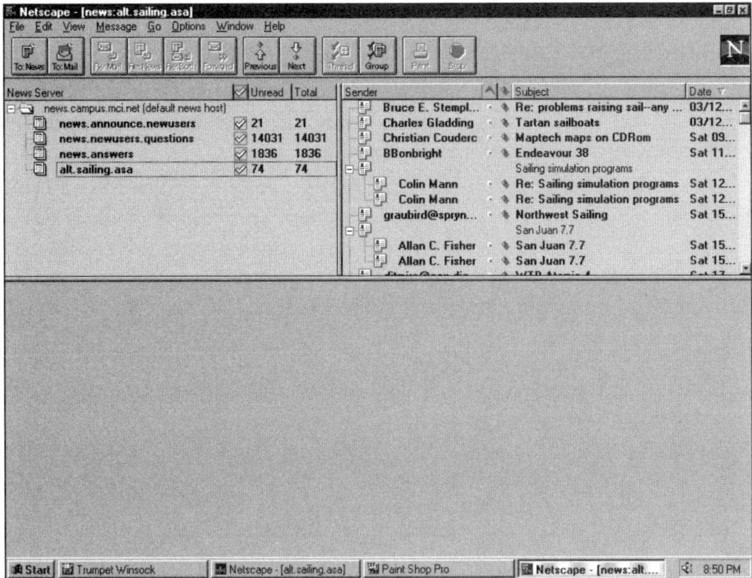

Figure 7.8 ***Looking at the alt.sailing. as a newsgroup.***

Notice the file hierarchy displayed in the right frame. Primary messages are shown furthest to the left. Replies are indented and have a subject line that starts with Re:. Let's look at one of Colin Mann's replies in our example. If we click on Mann's second Re: Sailing simulation programs message, we see the reply message as shown in Figure 7.9.

There are a few additional items to note at this point. Notice that the read icon is removed. Also notice the header information in the message frame, which includes Mann's email address, a link back to the newsgroup, and the number 1 in the References section. Numbers that appear in the References section are links to other messages in a thread. In this example there is only one other message in the thread—the original message. If we click on the number 1, we can see the originating message as shown in Figure 7.10.

Notice that Jorma Hannula, from Finland, is looking for more sailing newsgroups (also notice that we would have to scroll right to view the entire text of the message). Colin Mann, in his reply shown in Figure 7.9 mentions two other sailing newsgroups, rec.boats.racing and rec.boats.cruising. Lets say we want to visit the rec.boats.cruising newsgroup. How do we get there from here? The answer is simple. Execute File|Add Newsgroup, and you will open the Netscape User Prompt dialog box as shown in Figure 7.11.

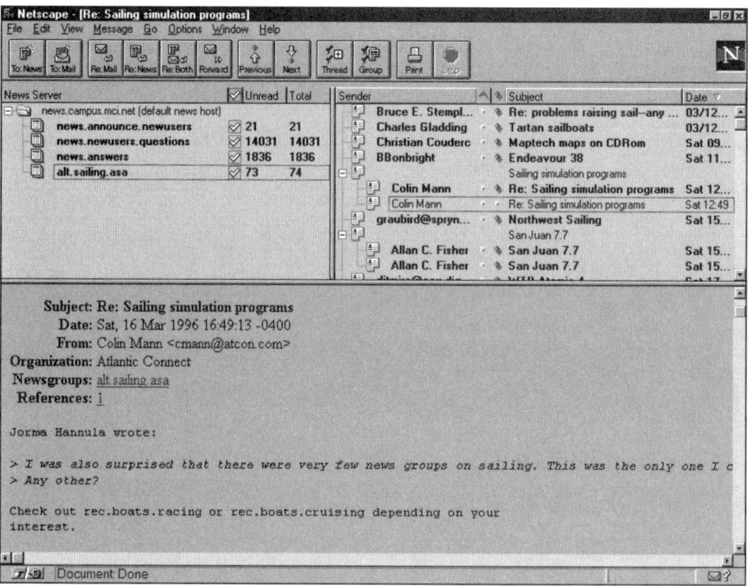

Figure 7.9 *A sample reply to a news message.*

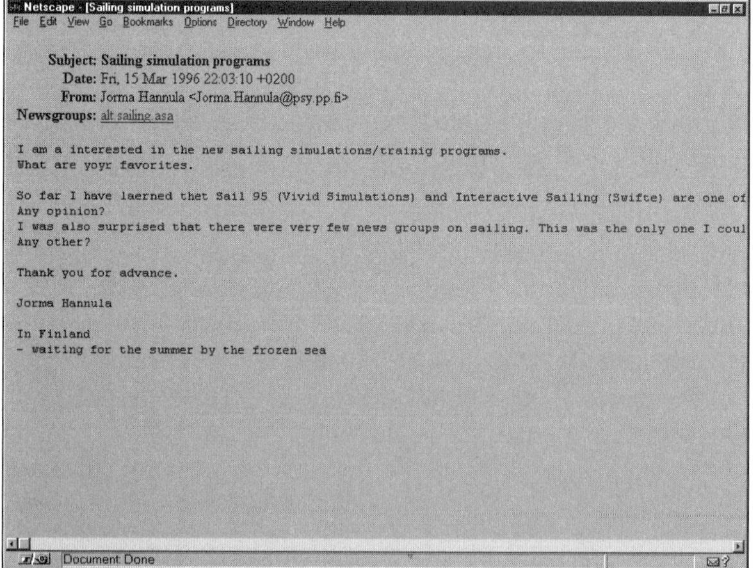

Figure 7.10 *The original news message.*

In the Type in a Newsgroup to add to the list: text box, enter the address of a newsgroup; in this example we would enter rec.boats.cruising. Entering a newsgroup address in this dialog box results in the same action as clicking on a newsgroup link. The newsgroup displays in the left frame of your

Netscape User Prompt
Type in a Newsgroup to add to the list:
OK
Cancel

Figure 7.11 The Netscape User Prompt dialog box.

newsgroup window, and the messages display in the right frame. Remember, the newsgroup won't be saved unless you subscribe to it by clicking in the check box.

Finally, before we move on, I want to mention another good source for finding newsgroups. Ohio State University provides a listing of newsgroups that have FAQ documents. While many newsgroups don't have FAQ documents, those that do probably represent about 95 percent of all the newsgroup subscriptions. Use the following URL to access the Ohio State server:

```
http://www.cis.ohio-state.edu/hypertext/faq/usenet/FAQ-List.html
```

The Ohio State FAQ List page is shown in Figure 7.12.

Congratulations, you can now find and view newsgroup messages. But the best part of newsgroups (and probably the easiest part) is yet to come—participating in the discussion.

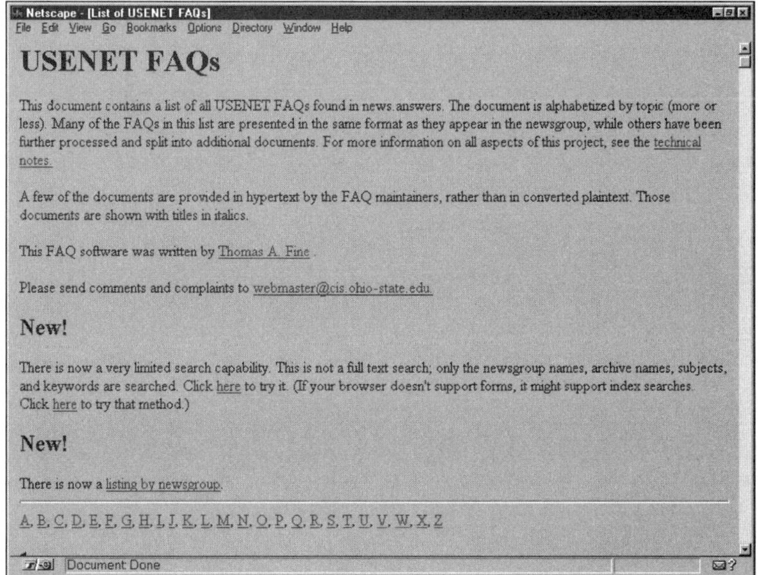

Figure 7.12 The Ohio State FAQ list.

Responding to a Posted Message

For illustrative purposes, let's reply to Colin Mann and Jorma Hannula, and tell them about a newsgroup named alt.sailing.fans (I made that newsgroup name up, so don't try to find it on the net). To respond to Mann's message, you can use your right-click shortcut. You can either right-click directly on Mann's message in the top right frame of the newsgroups window, or you can open the message you are responding to and right-click in the message window. In either instance, select Post Reply to respond to the message. When you select Post Reply you will get a message box as shown in Figure 7.13.

You can type your reply below the message as shown in Figure 7.14. Notice that the text you type does not follow a > on each line. A > indicates quoted text from another message. Your final step (which we won't execute here so we don't send Colin and Jorma on a wild goose chase searching for a nonexistent newsgroup) is to send the reply. This is easily accomplished by clicking on the send button, or executing File | Send Now. It's that simple.

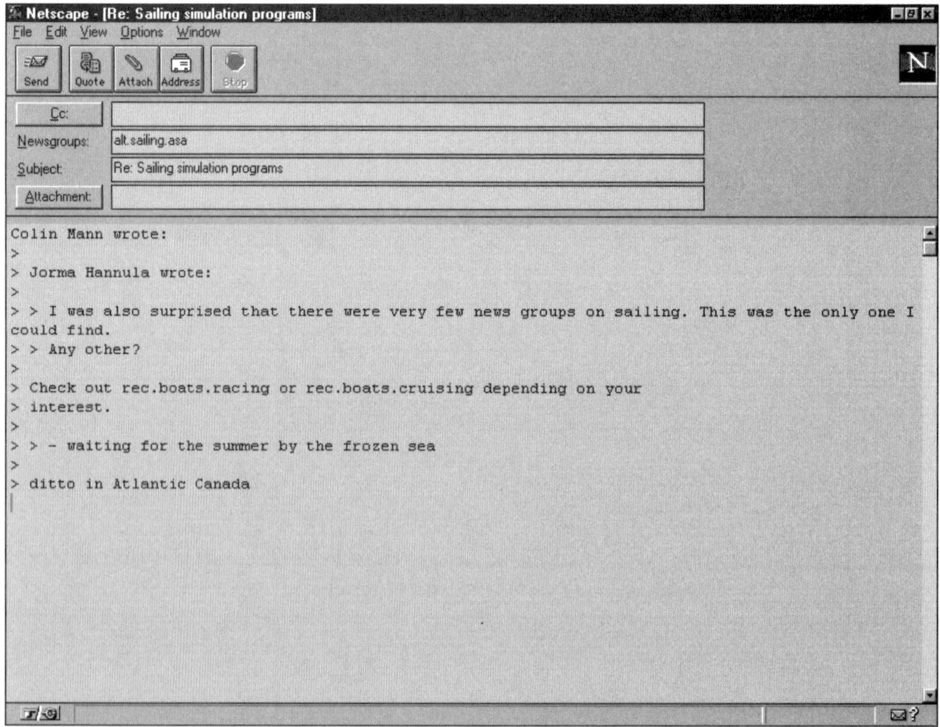

Figure 7.13 The Post Reply message box.

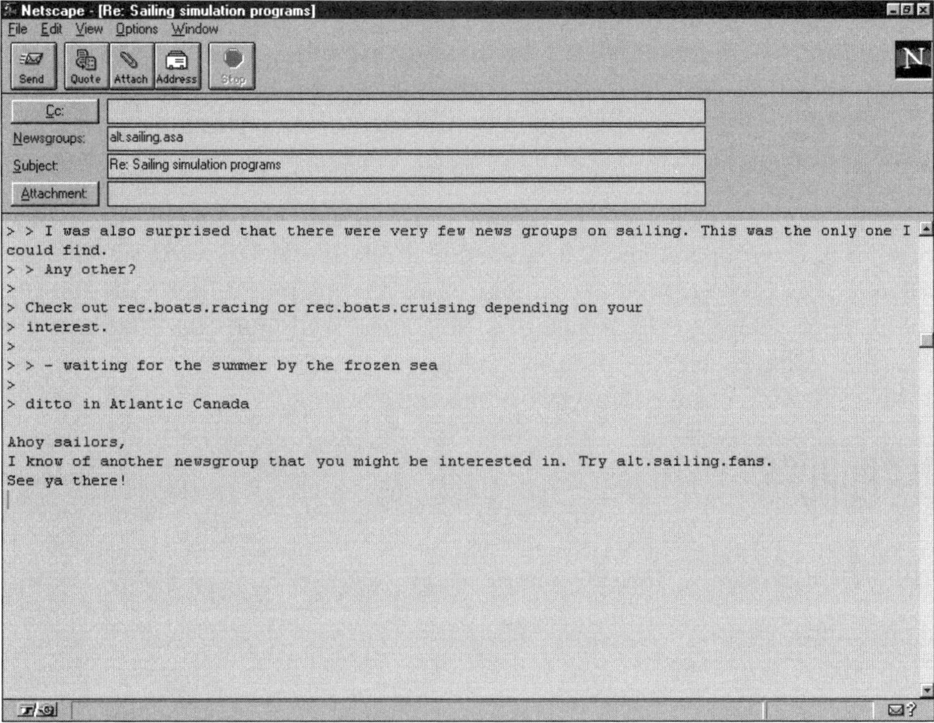

Figure 7.14 *Replying to a newsgroup message.*

Subscribing to Several Newsgroups

One last note—you can subscribe to several groups in one shot. The "*" character may be used as a wild card when subscribing to newsgroups. For instance, I know there is a top level geographic hierarchy of newsgroups beginning with "nj", so subscribing to the entire list of New Jersey newsgroups with "nj.*" will let me know what's there and I can prune the list down to size at my leisure.

Well, I think this would be a good time for you to try out a newsgroup that sounds interesting to you. Read some messages, decide if you would like to subscribe, and maybe send your first response. I'll still be here when you get back, and we can pick up where we left off.

LET'S REVIEW

Netscape contains a powerful newsreader feature for subscribing to and reading Usenet newsgroups. Newsgroups are a distinctive Internet protocol, similar in concept to CompuServe's public forums. Articles are posted to a newsgroup, where they may be read by anyone who reads the newsgroup. Follow-up articles may be posted to the newsgroup and they are logically connected to the articles that they follow by Netscape. The logical progression of associated articles is called a thread.

Subscribing to a newsgroup is as simple as clicking on a checkbox, which logs the newsgroup's name into a local disk file named newsrc. This allows you to read a newsgroup by clicking on an anchor rather than entering the full name of a newsgroup, which may be complex and difficult to remember. Netscape contains button controls and menu item selections used to view, store, send, and retrieve newsgroup messages.

RESOURCES

Reading and Posting Usenet News
`http://www.duke.edu/~mg/usenet/reading-news.html`

tile.net/news
`http://www.tile.net/news`

Internet Newsgroups
`http://www.w3.org/hypertext/DataSources/News/Groups/Overview.html`

A Newsgroup FAQ
`http://www.lib.ox.ac.uk/internet/news/faq/news.groups.html`

Netscape's Guide to News Menu Items
`http://home.netscape.com/eng/mozilla/2.0/handbook/docs/mnb.html#C9`

MaasInfo.UseGroup.html - Helpful Information for Finding Newsgroups
`http://pip.shsu.edu/MaasInfo/MaasInfo.UseGroups.html`

Netscape Presentations

Speeding up Netscape is simply a matter of learning how to download time-intensive Web pages. In the process, you'll discover that Netscape is also a great presentation program.

I'll bet this scenario sounds familiar: You call up a friend or family member and the line is busy. After trying over and over you decide that something has "gone wrong." You then call the phone company or, if you're really paranoid, the police. Almost always the problem isn't an equipment glitch; it's the fault of the person you're trying to reach who has caught a bad case of wind-bag-itis.

The Internet equivalent of this telephone scenario typically occurs when you try to connect to a very busy computer such as Netscape's or the NCSA computer that Mosaic calls home. These computers are probably the two busiest computers on the Internet. Many monthly surveys show Netscape's home page is the most frequently accessed Web document, closely followed by the NCSA home page. Typically, the NCSA What's New page is in fourth or fifth place on the Web hit parade.

Equipment and practical considerations limit access to these popular sites to a finite number of users. Forget trying to FTP from Netscape during prime time. After a major new version release it may be difficult making an FTP connection to Netscape Central for several weeks. Many other Web sites have also imposed access restrictions. Don't forget that most of these computers have "real jobs" and their primary purpose in life isn't just to serve you information and entertainment on the Web.

The Web equivalent of a busy signal is usually a cryptic non-descriptive message. (Cryptic error messages are a carryover from the old days when systems programmers tried to fake out less sophisticated users.) If you have received an "Unable to connect to HTTP Server!" or "SOCKET: Connection has been refused" message, you've received a busy signal and most likely nothing is wrong with your Netscape installation or Internet access. Unfortunately, the connectivity problem is going to get worse because Web users are increasing faster than the facilities available to service their needs. NCSA specifically requests that Web users specify a startup site other than the NCSA home page to help reduce the strain on its network.

In this chapter I'll give you some alternatives to initially connecting to the home page of one of these busy sites. One of the techniques, loading copies of Web documents to your local hard drive, uses the fact that Netscape, in addition to being a great Web browser, is also an outstanding stand-alone presentation program.

TAKING THE STRAIN OFF THE WEB

You can easily reduce the strain on the prime Web machines when you start Netscape, or any other Web browser, by using one of these three methods:

- Start Netscape without displaying any document.
- Load a home page document from somewhere other than Netscape.
- Load the Netscape home page or any other document from your hard drive.

Let's examine these options one at a time. The last technique, loading from your hard disk, presents other interesting possibilities.

NO DOCUMENT ON STARTUP

Netscape, as originally configured, loads its home page document from this URL:

```
http://home.netscape.com
```

The fastest way to speed up the loading of Netscape, and save valuable Internet resources, is by starting the program without displaying a home page. You can do this by executing the following sequence: First, choose Options | General Preferences. Then, select the Appearance card if it's not already selected. Figure 8.1 shows the Appearance card of the Preferences dialog box.

Notice the radio buttons used to start Netscape with a blank page or a unique home page location. A startup URL can be entered even if the Blank Page radio button is selected.

If you select the Blank Page radio button and you have Netscape's home page URL (or any other URL) in the text box, you can bring up the home page at any time in the session by clicking on the toolbar's home page icon.

Turning off the display of inline images is another method to speed up the process of loading Web pages. The graphics associated with a Web document are typically much larger than the text portion of the file. In addition, a graphic must be uncompressed and displayed, which takes additional processing time at the browser end. To get Netscape to turn off automatic graphics display, open the Options menu and uncheck Auto Load Images. Thereafter, a locally supplied little graphic will appear wherever transferred graphics would normally appear. Figure 8.2 shows the Charm Net home page without any graphics.

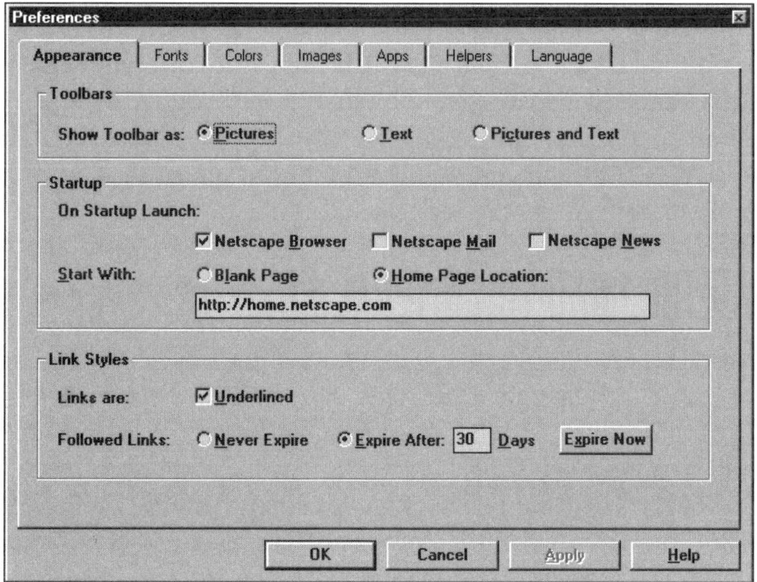

Figure 8.1 *The Appearance card of the Preferences dialog box.*

***Figure 8.2** The Charm Net home page without graphics.*

You can display the full graphic of an individual iconized image by clicking on it using the right mouse button, which brings up an options menu. Click on Load this Image to display the individual image. You can also click on the Images icon on the toolbar to display all the document's images. After unchecking Auto Load Images, you can then turn image display back on by reversing the process.

SHIFTING THE LOAD TO SOMEONE ELSE

The second alternative for saving wear and tear on busy computer sites is to shift the burden to someone else. This does not save network bandwidth since you are still going to fetch a document, and maybe a graphic or two, but it will make the people at NCSA happy. (If no one called NCSA for a full day, do you think they would start checking their equipment?) I get the feeling that the Netscape people, unlike the folks at NCSA, enjoy a captive audience. They may not be happy if you don't call on a regular basis.

If you've discovered a nifty starting point for Netscape, by all means use it. I start my Netscape sessions with a large menu loaded directly from my local hard disk. More on this technique in a minute. To load a different starting home page, copy the URL for your favorite site and insert it in the Home Page Location: text box on the Appearance card in the Preferences dialog box. To do this, execute Options|General Preferences and click on the Appearance tab, if necessary. Then, in the Start With: section on the Appearance card, paste the URL into the Home Page Location: text box. Finally, click on OK to activate your new home page location. A site with many well-maintained pointers to interesting places is a great Netscape starting point. An outstanding example of such a document is "Subject Based Information" on the University of Maryland, Baltimore Campus, machine. It contains an extensive list of Web site pointers. Categories are alphabetically arranged. The URL for this wonderful document is:

```
http://umbc7.umbc.edu/~jack/subject-list.html
```

If you are going to change the Home Page document, it's a good idea to save the Netscape home page URL as a bookmark before making the change. There may still be times when you want to call up Netscape.

To configure Netscape to display the "Subject Based Information" document at startup, follow these steps:

1. Load the document.
2. Select the document's URL in the Location: text box using the mouse.
3. Copy the highlighted URL to the Windows clipboard by pressing Ctrl+C.
4. Execute the sequence Options|General Preferences.
5. Select the Appearance tab in the Preferences dialog box, if necessary.
6. In the Start With: section, highlight the URL in the Home Page Location: text box.
7. Press Ctrl+V to paste in the new URL from the clipboard, and verify that the Home Page Location: radio box is turned on.

Loading Netscape from Local Files

If you want to become a good net citizen, but you also like the look and convenience of the Netscape home page when Netscape starts, all is not lost. You can still reduce both your use of net bandwidth and the strain on the Netscape machine by first storing a document you normally retrieve from the Net on your hard disk. After you have brought all its associated files, if any, to roost on your computer, you can start Netscape and display the page by loading any files from your locally stored copies. Is this the best of all worlds or what?

Netscape, in addition to being a great Web browser, is also a great presentation program. You can use the techniques I'll present next to create your own presentations with the same look and feel that Netscape provides when you connect to the Web. The only difference in the operation of Netscape is that URL links point to your hard drive instead of somewhere out in Webspace. I frequently give Netscape presentations, using the Netscape home page, without using a modem or a phone line. All the required components, including graphics, are loaded from my laptop's hard disk. Extending the no-Internet-connection concept, I have developed Netscape presentations that have nothing to do with the Internet or the Web. Netscape's ability to present documents in a non-linear fashion is a major presentational advantage.

Having Netscape load hypermedia documents from your hard drive, instead of fetching them from Webland, is a two-part process:

1. Transfer the desired document from its host site.
2. Make any necessary changes to the links.

Let's look at each of these processes.

Downloading to Your Hard Disk

Ideally, you could load the Netscape home page directly from a hard disk. However, the page uses frames. The concept of frames is that each frame has a separate URL so you can click on a link in one frame and view the corresponding information in another frame. We'll be exploring frames a little later in this book, but for now let's use a simpler home page so that we won't have to deal with the complexities of frames. For our example, we'll download the University of Maryland's Subject Based Information (UMD) page to disk for easy retrieval. Having the ability to load the UMD page from your hard disk requires transferring the UMD's main HTML document to your hard disk. Fortunately, you can easily download files from a Web site to your local disk using Netscape.

Start the process by creating a directory on your hard disk to hold Web documents. I keep all my Web documents in a directory called c:\WWWfiles. You may, of course, keep your files anywhere you choose.

Getting the University of Maryland's Subject Based Information Page

Let's go out and get the file for the University of Maryland's Subject Based Information page. Once you have this file, you can view it from your own PC.

Start by connecting to the UMD URL at:

```
http://umbc7.umbc.edu/~jack/subject-list.html
```

Save the Web page you are currently viewing by executing the sequence File | Save As. (The shortcut key for this process is Ctrl+S.) This action brings up the Save As dialog box as shown in Figure 8.3.

The actual name of the file is subject-list.html. Let's save this document as subject.htm in the directory c:\WWWfiles.

Since the file name has more than eight characters, the default transfer file name will truncate to eight characters. The file extension will also default to the first three characters of the original extension. It truncates because DOS file names can only contain eight characters, and DOS extensions only three. Unix file names can be substantially longer and may also have multiple periods. Although DOS limits you to using eight characters, use a meaningful file name. After you enter the path and file name for your download in the Save As dialog box, click on the OK button or press Enter to start the transfer.

EXPLORER TIP

Getting Organized

If you plan on building a library of hard disk hypermedia documents, you may want a separate directory for each site from which you download files. As an example, you could create a subdirectory called Netscape immediately under c:\WWWfiles to store the files for various Netscape pages and graphics. Without such organization, you'll find it difficult to associate files with Web sites.

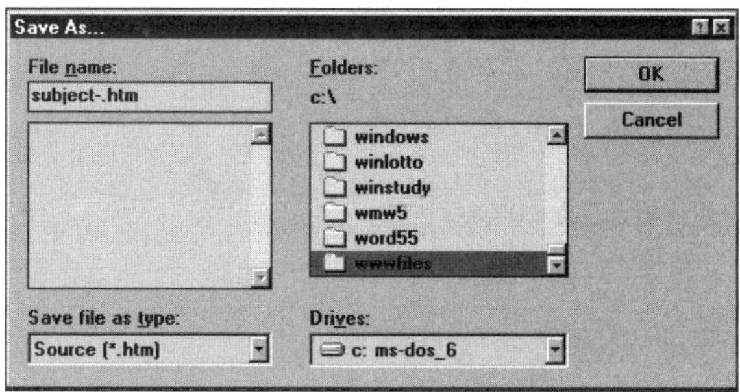

Figure 8.3 The Save As dialog box.

In most cases, you'll need to download GIF graphical files that are associated with the Web pages you download. You'll also need to modify internal links that the documents use so they can be loaded from your local hard drive. We'll get to these more exotic examples in a few minutes, but for now let's take our newly loaded document for a spin. Assuming the file was saved to your PC as c:\WWWfiles\subject.htm, enter the following URL:

```
file:///c:/WWWfiles/subject.htm
```

Note several things in this URL. First, notice that *file:* replaces the *http:* prefix. This change tells your browser to search for a file instead of using hypertext transfer protocol (http) to visit a Web site. Next, note that there are three forward slashes ("/"), not two. If you recall our earlier URL exploration in Chapter 2, we usually place a domain name between the "http://" and the "/". Since we are reading the file from a local hard disk, we don't need to include a domain name. Some browsers may require the URL to be entered as:

```
file://local-host/c:/WWWfiles/subject.htm
```

But you don't need to do this with Netscape.

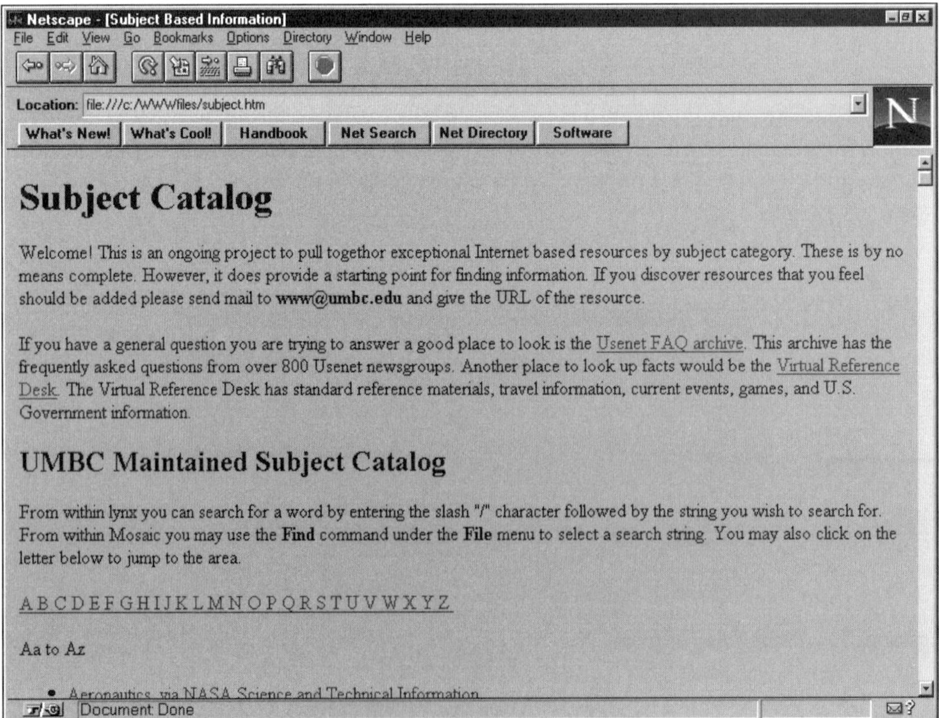

Figure 8.4 *The document loaded from the hard disk.*

The third formatting issue to take note of is that the forward slash "/" (not the standard DOS backward slash "\") is used to specify the directory path for the file. Browsers are designed to speak Unix—not DOS—and Unix uses "/" instead of "\". Netscape will actually accept "\" slashes in the DOS portion, but most browsers are not as accommodating.

Figure 8.4 shows the document displayed after being loaded from my hard disk.

When you load from your own hard disk, notice the relative speed between loading a document from disk as opposed to loading it from the Net. The difference is especially pronounced when loading graphics.

Congratulations, you have just completed a major step. You might be surprised how often the question of how to load documents from disk comes up on the various discussion lists.

Getting Your Local HTML Documents to Load

Now that you've discovered one of Netscape's best kept secrets—it can load and interpret HTML documents stored on your hard drive—you might be tempted to use this feature often. Because you may be loading files without being connected to the Internet, you might encounter occasional problems. The first, and easiest problem to fix, is when your local HTML documents might try to access other documents that aren't available on your hard disk. In this case you'll need to either download the files to your computer or make sure that you are connected to the Internet.

The other trick in loading local files is that you should make sure that your TCP/IP stack software is loaded in memory so Netscape will operate properly. This software performs the work of connecting your computer to the Internet. You don't actually need to dial to your provider and connect to the Internet; you just need to load the TCP/IP software so that Netscape will not give you any error messages.

Essentially, here's how Netscape operates. As it performs certain operations, it calls special functions that are stored in a file named winsock.dll in some directory accessible in your Path variable. These functions are known as the *WinSock API*. If the TCP/IP software is not loaded, some versions of Netscape and other browsers such as Mosaic may not be able to locate the WinSock API functions. If this happens, you'll receive an error message indicating that your browser could not find winsock.dll. To fix the problem, run the TCP/IP software you use to connect to the Internet and minimize it—the stack doesn't have to be logged into anything. You don't have to actually connect to your provider, only load the software. I'll cover TCP/IP software in much more detail later in this book.

Another alternative, especially attractive if you are using Netscape on a laptop and never connecting to the Net via a modem, is something called a *NULLSOCK*. It's essentially a "fakeout" piece of software. Netscape, and many Netscape mirror sites, provide a program file named mozock.dll. This file is included on the companion CD-ROM for you to use. You can also get the latest version of this file by FTPing to the same site you would normally use to obtain Netscape. It may be in the same directory as the Netscape browser or it may be in another directory. The URL for FTPing mozock.dll directly from Netscape is

```
ftp://ftp.netscape.com/unsupported/windows/mozock.dll
```

Copy mozock.dll to the same directory containing Netscape. Rename mozock.dll to winsock.dll and you won't need TCP/IP software to use Netscape to view Web pages stored on your hard drive. When you want to use Netscape to go back online to the Web, you'll need to change the name of winsock.dll back to mozock.dll.

Loading the Charm Net Home Page to Disk

Let's practice what we've learned and pick up a few new techniques by downloading the Charm Net home page. This is the Web site we first explored in Chapter 3.

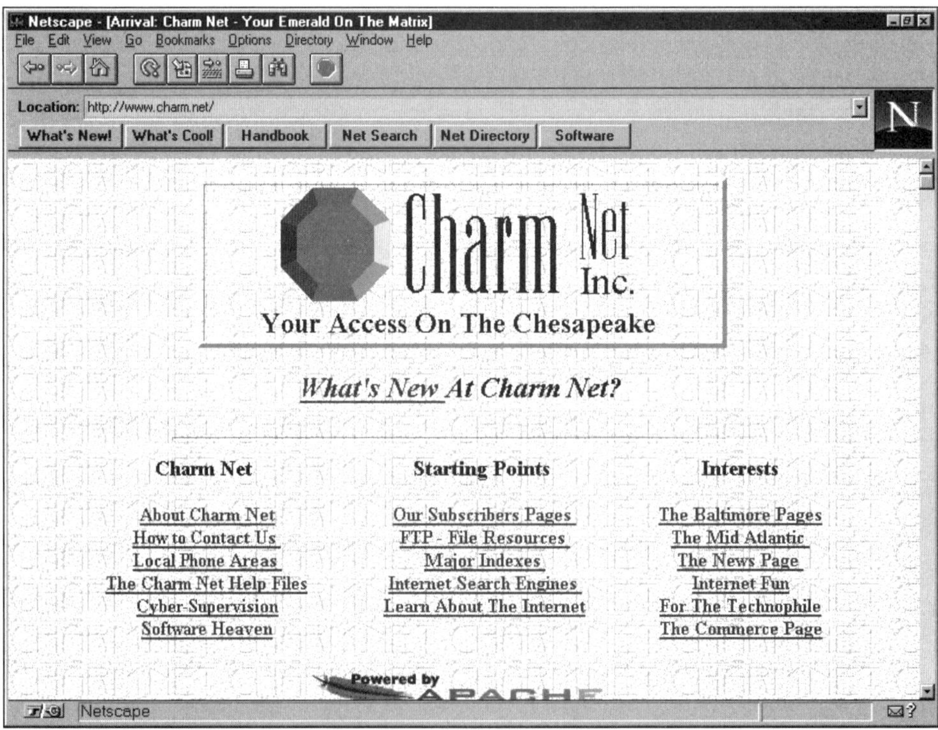

Figure 8.5 *The Charm Net home page.*

Previously, we saved Charm Net's home page URL as a bookmark. If you still have it in your bookmark list, activate it now. If not, type http://www.charm.net/ in Netscape's Go To: text box. The Charm Net home page appears as shown in Figure 8.5.

Now let's save the Charm Net home page to our hard disk. First we need to bring up the Save As dialog box by either executing File | Save As or pressing Ctrl+S. Next, let's save this document as charmnet.htm and place it in the same directory as our subject.htm home page (in my case, I created a c:\WWWfiles directory). We now have a local copy of the Charm Net home page on our hard drive.

The actual HTML document used to produce the Charm Net home page is displayable using the View | Document Source sequence. You must click on the option, Document Source in this example. Figure 8.6 shows how the charmnet.html source document is displayed when you select View | Document Source.

Let's dissect the following portion of the eighth line (you may have to scroll to view all of the html text):

```
Netscape - [Source of: http://www.charm.net/]

<html> <! --Created by Nicole  webmistress@charm.net - Updated 12/28/95 --->
<head>
<title>Arrival: Charm Net - Your Emerald On The Matrix </title>
</head>
<body BACKGROUND="bkgnd.gif" >
<P>
<CENTER><TABLE BORDER=4 WIDTH=60%><TD  ALIGN=center >
<H2><A HREF="http://www.charm.net/doc/charm/help/theme.html"><IMG ALT="Charm Net"  border=0 SRC=
<BR>Your Access On The Chesapeake
</TD></TABLE></H2></CENTER><P>

<CENTER><H2><STRONG><I><A HREF="whatsnew.html">What's New </A> At Charm Net?</A></I></STRONG></H
<hr size=2 width=500>

<CENTER> <TABLE  WIDTH=90% COLSPAN=1 ><TR ALIGN=center VALIGN=top><TD>
<H3>Charm Net </H3>
<STRONG>
<a href="charminfo.html">About Charm Net</a><br>
<a href="contact.html">How to Contact Us </a><br>
<A HREF="http://www.charm.net/doc/charm/help/phone.local">Local Phone Areas </A><br>
<A HREF="http://www.charm.net/doc/charm/help/index.html">The Charm Net Help Files</A><br>
<A HREF="http://www.charm.net/doc/charm/censor/">Cyber-Supervision</A><BR>
<a href="http://www.charm.net/CWSApps/">Software Heaven</a><br>
</STRONG>
</TD>
<TD>
<H3> Starting Points </H3>
<STRONG>

<a href="charm/local/index.html">Our Subscribers Pages </a><br>
<a href="ftp.sites.html">FTP - File Resources </a><br>
<A HREF="bigtrees.html">Major Indexes </A><BR>
<a href="info.search.html">Internet Search Engines </a><br>
<a href="learning.html">Learn About The Internet</a><br>
```

Figure 8.6 *Charm Net's source document.*

```
<A HREF="http://www.charm.net/doc/charm/help/theme.html"><IMG ALT="Charm Net"
border=0 SRC="/nlogo2.gif"></A>
```

The first part, '<A HREF="http://www.charm.net/doc/charm/help/theme.html">,' is called an *anchor reference.* If you click on the logo for Charm Net, a document named theme.html will be loaded. The second part, '<IMG ALT="Charm Net" border=0 SRC="/nlogo2.gif">' is a pointer to an image (.GIF file) having the name nlogo2.gif in this case. Let's download the GIF to our local hard drive, and then we'll return to this HTML statement.

Close the HTML source document by either clicking on the close window icon or clicking on the Netscape logo to the left of the document name, then choosing Close from the drop-down list. When the Charm Net home page is again displayed in the document area, click on the large emerald logo graphic with the right mouse button. This will bring up a menu with a few options, as shown in Figure 8.7.

Just below the bottom third divider is an entry, View this Image (nlogo2.gif). Viewing the image will simply display it all by itself on a page. This option would be handy if we had the Auto Load Images unchecked. However, we

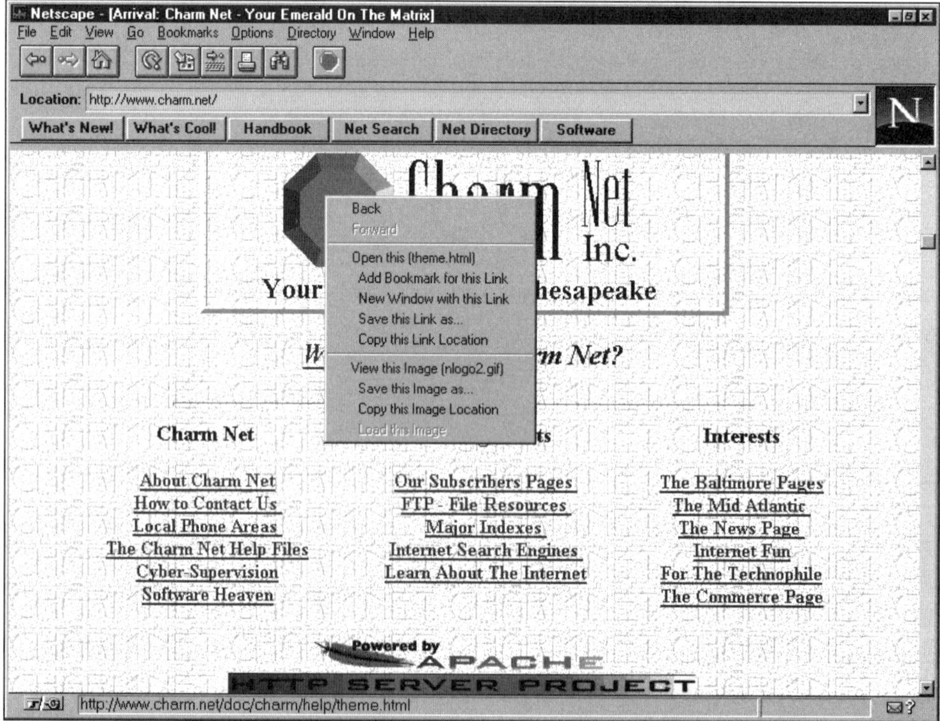

Figure 8.7 *The right mouse button menu.*

already know what the image looks like so let's download it. Click on the option, Save this Image as, and the familiar Save As dialog box will appear. Save the image as nlogo2.gif in the same directory where you saved a copy of the Charm Net home page document.

Changing Pointers

Let's return to the HTML statement we were looking at earlier:

```
<A HREF="http://www.charm.net/doc/charm/help/theme.html"><IMG ALT="Charm Net"
border=0 SRC="/nlogo2.gif"></A>
```

The link reference for the GIF document is in a form called a *relative reference.* The link does not specify a particular path for the file, nlogo2.gif, so the browser expects to find the GIF file and the anchor reference in the same directory. Because we stored our copy of the Charm Net home page and the nlogo2.gif file in the same directory on our hard disk, the anchor reference and the GIF file have no problem finding each other. Now, notice that the anchor reference contains the complete path pointing to the theme.html Web page.

theme.html is dynamic—it's modified frequently, reflecting the rapidly changing nature of Webspace. We could download the theme.html document onto our hard disk, but it is not normally good practice to download dynamic documents to a local computer, unless you are creating a demonstration of some type. There are many dynamic documents associated with the Charm Net Web site, therefore our next step will be to change the pointers on our local copy of the Charm Net home page so we can fetch documents from the Charm Net server.

Taking a close look at the charmnet.htm document source shows many references having the appearance of the following:

```
<a href="charm/local/index.html">Our Subscribers Pages </a><br>
<a href="ftp.sites.html">FTP - File Resources </a><br>
<A HREF="bigtrees.html">Major Indexes </A><BR>
<a href="info.search.html">Internet Search Engines </a><br>
<a href="learning.html">Learn About The Internet</a><br>
```

Notice that the references do not include pointers to the Charm Net server. Before we can view any of these documents from our local home page, each of these documents must either be downloaded or the reference must be changed. As I mentioned before, unless you're doing an entire presentation using local documents, you will most likely want to change the pointers. The easiest way to change pointers is to use an HTML or text editor.

If your favorite text or HTML editor has a global find and replace function, the task is easy. If your editor doesn't have a global find and replace, you may want to try the Windows Write editor. If you use Write, it will ask if you want to convert to Write format (.WRI extension) when you load the file charmnet.htm; reply, "No Way." When saving the edited file, make sure that it's saved as a text file. The same rule applies if you use a word processing package such as Word to perform the search-and-replace task—*make sure you save the file as a text file.*

To change the reference pointers, we simply need to prefix all the references with the Charm Net server's original home page URL:

```
http://www.charm.net/
```

Go ahead and load charmnet.htm in your seek-and-destroy editor, then search for:

```
href="
```

Selectively replace that string with the following pointer to Charm Net's home page for the references that don't include the pointer information (Be careful. As you've already seen, some references, such as the anchor reference for theme.html, already contain the pointer information). The Replace With text should be:

```
href="http://www.charm.net/
```

Remember to be selective while replacing text. For example,

```
<A HREF="http://www.charm.net/doc/charm/help/theme.html">
```

remains unchanged since it already contains the Charm Net home page address information, but

```
<a href="charm/local/index.html">Our Subscribers Pages </a><br>
```

becomes

```
<a href="http://www.charm.net/charm/local/index.html">Our Subscribers Pages </
a><br>
```

adding the Charm Net home page address information to the reference.

My favorite HTML editor is Web Spinner. (It's included on the companion CD-ROM.) This editor has a search and replace option, making it easy to perform the above task. Highlight the text to be used for the search. Then, execute the sequence Search|Replace to display the Replace dialog box. The Find What text box is filled in with the highlighted text. Fill in the Replace With text box with the replacement text. Next, continuously click on Find Next and Replace to modify the links as necessary.

The modified charmnet.htm file should now look like Listing 8.1

Listing 8.1

```
<html>
<head>
<title>Arrival: Charm Net - Your Emerald On The Matrix </title>
</head>
<body BACKGROUND="bkgnd.gif" >
<P>
<CENTER><TABLE BORDER=4 WIDTH=60%><TD  ALIGN=center >
<H2><A HREF="http://www.charm.net/doc/charm/help/theme.html"><IMG ALT="Charm
Net" border=0 SRC="/nlogo2.gif"></A>
<BR>Your Access On The Chesapeake
</TD></TABLE></H2></CENTER><P>

<CENTER><H2><STRONG><I><A HREF="HTTP://WWW.CHARM.NET/whatsnew.html">What's New
</A> At Charm Net?</A></I></STRONG></H2></CENTER>
<hr size=2 width=500>

<CENTER> <TABLE  WIDTH=90% COLSPAN=1 ><TR ALIGN=center VALIGN=top><TD>
<H3>Charm Net </H3>
<STRONG>
<a href="http://www.charm.net/charminfo.html">About Charm Net</a><br>
<a href="http://www.charm.net/contact.html">How to Contact Us </a><br>
<A HREF="http://www.charm.net/doc/charm/help/phone.local">Local Phone Areas </
A><br>
<A HREF="http://www.charm.net/doc/charm/help/index.html">The Charm Net Help
Files</A><br>
<A HREF="http://www.charm.net/doc/charm/censor/">Cyber-Supervision</A><BR>
<a href="http://www.charm.net/CWSApps/">Software Heaven</a><br>
</STRONG>
</TD>
<TD>
<H3> Starting Points </H3>
<STRONG>

<a href="http://www.charm.net/charm/local/index.html">Our Subscribers Pages </
a><br>
<a href="http://www.charm.net/ftp.sites.html">FTP - File Resources </a><br>
<A HREF="HTTP://WWW.CHARM.NET/bigtrees.html">Major Indexes </A><BR>
```

```
<a href="http://www.charm.net/info.search.html">Internet Search Engines </a><br>
<a href="http://www.charm.net/learning.html">Learn About The Internet</a><br>
</STRONG>
</TD>
<TD> <H3>Interests</H3>
<STRONG>
<a href="http://www.baltimore.com/">The Baltimore Pages</a><br>
<a href="http://www.charm.net/baltwash.html">The Mid Atlantic </a><br>
<a href="http://www.charm.net/news.html">The News Page </a><br>
<a href="http://www.charm.net/fun.html">Internet Fun</a><br>
<a href="http://www.charm.net/technophile.html">For The Technophile</a><br>
<a href="http://www.charm.net/biz.html">The Commerce Page</a><br>
</STRONG></TD></TR>
</TABLE><CENTER>

<P>
<CENTER><A HREF="http://www.apache.org/"><IMG BORDER=0 ALIGN=BOTTOM
SRC="apache.gif" ALT="Apache Powered"><BR><IMG BORDER=0 ALIGN=BOTTOM
SRC="apach.gif" ALT="HTTP Server Project"></A></CENTER>

<!———————————— Logo Table ———————— —>

<CENTER><TABLE>
<TR> <TD COLSPAN=3> <hr size=1 width=100%> </TD> </TR>
<TR> <TD ALIGN=CENTER>
         <A HREF="http://www.charm.net/charminfo.html"><img border=0 src="/
           minilogo.gif"></A>
         </td>
     <TD ALIGN=CENTER><text>
          Charm Net, Inc.,  Internet Service for Maryland, DC, and No.
            Virginia<br>
          <font size=-2>
          2228 East Lombard Street,  Baltimore, MD 21231 <br>
          (c) 1995 <br>
          <hr size=.5>
          </font>
          </td>
     <TD ALIGN=CENTER>
          <A HREF="http://www.charm.net/charminfo.html"><img border=0 src="/
            minilogo.gif"></A>
          </td>
     </tr>

<TR>
     <TD ALIGN=CENTER COLSPAN=3> <font size=-2>
          TEL:  (410) 558-3900 -
          FAX:  (410) 558-3901 -
          DATA:  (410) 558-3300 or (703) 790-5054<br>
          Charm Net's <A HREF=http://www.charm.net/setup/prices.html>FEES</
            and online
          <A HREF=http://www.charm.net/register.html>REGISTRATION</A> form.
          </font>
          </td>
     </tr>
```

```
</TABLE></CENTER>

<CENTER><FONT COLOR="#FF0000"><font size=1>This Page Was Last Modified On 1/12/
96 </font></CENTER>
</body>
</html>
```

Notice I didn't add Charm Net's home page pointer to the reference with the www.baltimore.com pointer. This is because that reference already points to a Web site, www.baltimore.com.

Also, don't be concerned if you find the HTML listing for the Charm Net home page slightly intimidating right now. We will discuss HTML coding later in this book. At that point, you will be able to return to the Charm Net home page and decipher the coding. You'll see that it's really very simple once you know what the codes mean.

Great job! You're now ready to create your own hypertext home pages and presentations. How does it feel to be a creative artist?

LET'S REVIEW

You can reduce the strain on the Web computers and be a good Net citizen using one of three different methods:

- Have Netscape start without displaying any document.
- Load a home page document from somewhere other than Netscape.
- Load a document, complete with graphics, from your local hard drive.

The method you choose is a matter of personal preference.

Building a local copy of a starting home page, or any other HTML page, typically downloaded from a remote host, is a five-step process:

1. Capture the HTML text of the desired page to a local file with an .HTM extension.
2. Change the appropriate pointer by executing Netscape's Options|General Preferences|Appearance command. Type the URL of your choice, either a site on the Web or the location of a local file in the Home Page Location: text box.
3. If the local file contains references to a non-text file, such as a graphic image, download the referenced file.
4. Change any links referencing downloaded non-text files so they point to the location of the local files.

5. If links to frequently changing sources do not contain external pointers, they must be added.

To save the displayed HTML document to disk, execute the sequence File | Save As. (You can also use the hotkey Ctrl+S.) This will bring up the Save As dialog box. Enter your desired file and path names.

To save an image file, click on the image with the right mouse button, which brings up an options menu. Click on the Save this Image as option. This will bring up the Save As dialog box where you should enter your file name and path preferences.

After loading a home page or any document from your hard disk, check your links very carefully. Drag across all anchors in the displayed document to insure that they will not try to fetch a file that isn't there.

Well, there you have it, Netscape fans. What could be better than speeding up your Web surfing while simultaneously reducing net traffic? If you come up with interesting ways to use Netscape as a presentation tool, I would sure like to hear about them.

CHAPTER 9

Finding and Retrieving Files

There are thousands of free files out there on the Net, just waiting to be downloaded. The trick is finding them...but with a little help from some searching tools, you'll be able to find what you want in no time.

One of the joys of being connected to the Internet is the ability to download the latest programs and other goodies from a seemingly inexhaustible supply. Indeed, new files and programs are being placed "out there" faster than anyone could possibly hope to download and evaluate them.

Many of these downloadable programs are absolutely free and others are low cost "shareware" that may be tested before you buy. (More on the notion of shareware shortly.) The process of first finding and then downloading files can be frustrating unless someone has told you the precise location of a particular program and its exact file name. This chapter will do just that.

In this chapter I'll take you out into these uncharted waters and direct you through the process of finding and downloading files from remote sites in cyberspace. Don't despair! The process seems complicated at first, but it becomes second nature as you continue to fill up your hard disk with goodies.

FILE COMPRESSION PROGRAMS

Programs that compress and uncompress files have gone from an exotic luxury to an absolute necessity in recent years. Stac's patent infringement suit against Microsoft, over a compression utility, was page one news in the mainstream press, and the battle was frequently mentioned on national TV during the 11 o'clock news. Until a few years ago, only aficionados of online services even knew about file compression. Then, along came Windows and its voracious memory appetite—and a market was born.

Why File Compression?

My first word processor was WordStar. I think it was version 3.0, if my rapidly failing memory serves me correctly. WordStar ran very nicely on a two diskette XT machine; 360Kb diskettes at that. Disk swapping was required only when I wanted to spell check or do something else really out of the ordinary. Not being content to swap diskettes simply because I wanted to run a different program, I installed a hard disk.

My first hard disk was a Seagate ST232, a 32MB workhorse that changed consumer attitudes about hard disks. After installing this behemoth drive, I was king of the hill, since all my friends only had 10 or 20 MB hard drives. To put 32MB of hard disk space into perspective, a few years earlier I was providing mini-computers with 12MB of disk space to businesses with 50 or so employees. We did everything on those machines, including payroll and many thousands of inventory items.

I think I paid about $500 for my 32MB drive plus another $50 for a controller. I remember thinking, "I'll have enough disk space to last for years." Now, neither WordPerfect for Windows nor Microsoft's Word for Windows would fit on that ST232 hard disk, if they were installed with all the accompanying bells and whistles. Worse yet, a quick look through *Computer Shopper* shows dozens of listings for gigabyte (that is, *billion*-byte) drives that can be purchased for far less than I paid for my beloved "232" and its controller.

The arrival of Windows, coupled with the desire to have lots of software and especially graphics on one's disk, accelerated both the need and development of compression techniques. As a consequence, almost all files stored on BBSs or at FTP sites are in a compressed form. The only exceptions are typically very small text files. Without going into the gory details, compression reduces a file's storage requirements, often by as much as half, and sometimes by up to 80 or 90 percent. That's the good news...the bad news is that a compressed file is absolutely useless unless you can uncompress it. Another piece of bad news is that there often seems to be an infinite number of compression techniques—and at least ten more at any given time than you know how to handle. As many of my online friends would say, `:-(`

Have a Smiley Day

As a short aside, *smileys,* like the one I dropped at the end of the last paragraph, frequently embellish email. Smileys are a group of ASCII keyboard characters designed to evoke an emotion in an otherwise emotionless medium. For example, `:-)` is a smiley face (look at it from the side) while `:-(` is an unhappy face. Look for The Unofficial Smiley Dictionary home page (Figure 9.1) at:

```
http://www.nova.edu/Inter-Links/bigdummy/eeg_286.html
```

There are loads of smileys out there, some of them so obscure or arcane that even grizzled old net veterans like myself have a tough time figuring them out. Unless you want your readers to do a lot of head scratching, stick with the obvious ones.

The most commonly used compression scheme is one developed by a company named PKWARE ("PK" for Phil Katz, the company founder). Files compressed using their technique have a file name with a .ZIP extension, and are typically called "ZIP files" or simply "ZIPs." Let's start our FTPing career by finding a specific file located somewhere "out there," and then we'll transfer that file to our Internet-connected PC. The file that we'll use in this exploration (actually a group of files) is WinZip, a suite of utilities used to create and manipulate ZIP files. The most popular programs for ZIPping and UNZIPping files are WinZip and PKZIP and PKUNZIP, the original ZIPping programs.

Other Compression Schemes

If life were simple, we would only need to concern ourselves with the ubiquitous ZIP-compressed files. As you might suspect, life is not that simple. Before you can uncompress a file, you must know the compression technique used to compress the file in the first place. Although ZIP compression predominates, there are hundreds of different file compression methods in use on the Internet, and you'll encounter many of them if you cruise the world's FTP sites regularly.

This implies a problem: How are you ever going to navigate the "compression seas" and figure out the compression method employed by a given file, where

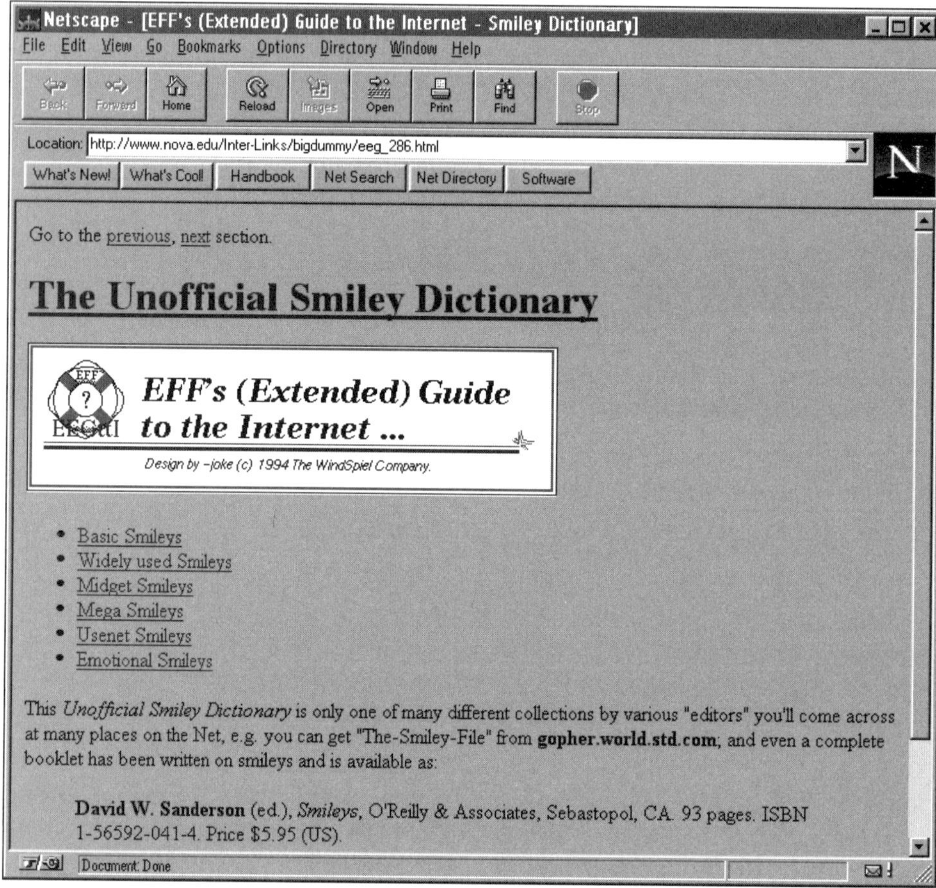

***Figure 9.1** The Unofficial Smiley Dictionary.*

it isn't obvious from the file extension? Most FTP directories have a read.me or index file (or something similar) listing all the files that are in that directory. Some considerate FTP site administrators have created expanded read.me files that include information about the compression method utilized. Some *exceptionally* considerate administrators even tell you where to obtain the software needed to uncompress the files.

Failing specific uncompression instructions, look at the file extension of a stored archive file. Table 9.1 shows some of the most popular extensions that you may find during your visits to FTP sites worldwide. The list also shows the transfer modes needed to retrieve files with these extensions and which uncompression software package you will need to uncompress the retrieved files. The list, derived from "The EFF's Guide to the Internet," is by no means all-inclusive, but it should cover about 98 percent of the FTPable files you will find.

Table 9.1 Commonly Used File Extensions on the Internet

Extension	Mode	Transfer Comments and Uncompression Program, If Needed
.doc or .DOC	ASCII	A common extension for text documents. However, .doc and .DOC extensions are also used for Microsoft Word documents, which must be transferred as binary files. Try previewing the file with a plain ASCII editor, such as DOS's EDIT. If you see strange graphic-like characters, it's a binary file.
.gz	Binary	This is a Unix version of a ZIP file and is uncompressed with a program named gunzip. At the Unix command line enter: `unix% gunzip filename.gz`
.hqx or .Hqx	Binary	Macintosh compression format requiring the BinHex program to uncompress.
.LZH	Binary	A DOS format in widespread use.
.ps or .PS	ASCII	A PostScript document that does not need uncompressing. You may print this file on any PostScript capable printer or use a special program called GhostScript. PostScript is Adobe's page description language.
.shar or .Shar	Binary	Another Unix compression scheme. Use unshar to uncompress.
.sit or .Sit	Binary	A Macintosh format requiring StuffIt to uncompress.
.tar	Binary	Yet one more Unix compression scheme that is frequently used to compress many related files into one large file. Unix systems typically have a program called tar to uncompress or, as the Unix types say, "un-tar," these files. The "tarred" file could be compressed with the .gz compression method. You first have to use uncompress and then tar.
.txt or .TXT	ASCII	A file with a .txt or .TXT extension indicates that the file is a document rather than a program. It does not need uncompression.
.Z	Binary	A Unix compression method. To uncompress a file with a .Z extension, enter the following from within a Unix shell account: `unix% uncompress filename.Z`
u16.zip		A DOS program that uncompresses downloaded .Z files on your PC. A Mac-equivalent program is called MacCompress.
.zip or .ZIP	Binary	Uncompress using PKUNZIP or WinZip. You may uncompress a ZIP file from within a Unix shell using a program called unzip.
.zoo or .ZOO	Binary	These extensions may be either a Unix or a DOS compression scheme. To uncompress use a program called zoo.

Fortunately, most uncompression software is either public domain or shareware. Public domain is free but shareware authors expect you to send some money for the program (typically less than the commercial counterpart) if you decide to keep and use the program on a regular basis. Thankfully, most uncompression software is available for FTPing.

FILE TRANSFER PROTOCOL (FTP)

There are currently over 1,200 Internet sites making files available for downloading by people who do not have accounts on these remote systems. The downloading (and uploading, if you have write privilege on the remote site) is accomplished by a protocol named FTP, for File Transfer Protocol. This transfer process by system "outsiders" is called *anonymous FTP* because you don't need an account on the host system to avail yourself of their largess. You simply log in as user "anonymous" and enter your email address as your password.

Just so you don't get the idea that FTPing is a minor undertaking, there are over 2.5 million unique filenames out there in cyberspace, consuming over 200 gigabytes of storage space. (That's 200,000,000,000 bytes.) CICA, one of the major software depositories, adds about 20 new programs a day! The database holding information on all available FTPable files, complete with file and path names, requires about 400MB of storage space for the reference material.

What Time Is It in Tokyo?

Consider the following information before connecting to an external Internet computer. Most Internet resources (like FTPable files) reside on computers primarily engaged in other activities. Most employees would be annoyed to discover their paychecks are late because their employer's computer was busy servicing FTP requests from people on the other side of the world. Internet services on these machines have a very low priority. Many sites that normally allow anonymous FTP will not permit, or severely limit, outside access of their systems during normal local business hours. Even those permitting the service may be very sluggish during periods of high "local" activity.

Much of the traffic on the Internet moves at close to the speed of light. Limitation in traffic flow is usually the result of low priority rather than low transmission speeds. Resource-intensive tasks frequently complete more quickly when connected to a system on the other side of the earth, when the local inhabitants are fast asleep—even though it's 3:00 in the afternoon where you live.

The sun rises in the East, so remote time—that is, the time as perceived by the other person—gets progressively farther ahead of local time as we go east. The rate is approximately 45 minutes for every 1,000 miles. London is five hours ahead of New York and eight hours ahead of San Francisco. The time on the opposite side of the earth is 12 hours different from local time. Keep that in mind the next time you want to transfer a large file from an FTP site.

It's a Shareware World. Although there are only 90,000 different programs available at these depositories, compared to over 2.5 million files of all sorts available for FTPing, depository programs represent about 99 percent of all FTP downloads. Major software depositories have four distinguishing characteristics:

- They're designed to hold large numbers of programs and files.
- They have user-friendly directory structures.
- They have an index file in each directory containing a one-line plain text description of each program in addition to the file's name and size.
- They have *mirror sites* (ideally at wildly different geographical locations) to minimize the distance files have to travel to any given requester.

A mirror site has the same files as the parent site and a similar (and often identical) directory structure.

Public Domain, Shareware, and Freeware

There is much confusion on the Internet, and elsewhere, concerning the difference between public domain, freeware, and shareware. There are no restrictions on the use or distribution of software placed in the public domain. You may do anything you choose with it, and may copy, sell, or modify the software as you like. Public domain software is frequently, but certainly not always, developed with government funding.

Freeware is software that is distributed without charge, but is nonetheless protected by the author's copyright. The owner of the copyright may state conditions for no-charge usage of the software, as in non-commercial applications, and may require some sort of license and fee for commercial use. Several Web browsers, including Netscape and Mosaic, fall into this category. Netscape may be used without charge by people affiliated with academic institutions or non-profit organizations, or by people evaluating the browser. There is currently a charge for people not falling into one of the above categories. I'm not aware of a time limit imposed upon the evaluation period.

Mosaic has a little less restrictive policy; individuals may use the software without charge. With most freeware, there is no charge for individual users but commercial users must often pay for the use of the software. As with most software, you may not sell or modify the programs without the written permission of the copyright owner.

Shareware is very much like regular commercial software, with a few twists. It is essentially commercial software that you pay for on the honor system. The full, non-crippled copy of the software is distributed widely, and you are encouraged to pass it along to as many people as you like. You may try shareware before you purchase it—but you are morally and legally bound to pay for the software if you retain it and use it regularly. The quality of shareware runs the gamut from poor to superior. (Why should the quality of shareware be different from the quality of commercial software?) But you're at least allowed to see how good it is (and decide whether you want to keep it) before you're actually out any money.

Shareware is different from "demo software." A demo copy is frequently limited or disabled in some way, and after you've played with the demo a while, you have the opportunity to upgrade to the full commercial product. Some demo software may not be able to print or save a file, or the product may only work for a short period of time or access a limited amount of data. The idea is to let you see clearly how the software works and what it can do, but not give you enough functionality to allow you to use the demo copy as though it were the product itself.

SEARCHING TECHNIQUES

A few years ago, there were only one or two ways to search for FTP files on the Internet. The most popular of these was Archie. Archie's still around, and I'll discuss how to do a search using Archie, but there are now many other, much faster, ways of finding the types of FTP files that you want.

FTP SEARCH ENGINES

While there are a number of different FTP search engines for you to choose from, their quality and ease of use varies. I decided to put all of the engines through a simple test. Since WinZip is such an important utility, I decided that I would download it. I also wanted to find as many different WinZip files as possible, so I could pick the version and FTP site that I wanted to download from. To keep it simple, I used the word "winzip" in all the searches.

The results of my test varied considerably in quality. I judged the various engines on how fast they searched and how many files they found. Here's a rundown of some of the best programs, from least to most successful.

Harvest Broker

If you aren't interested in paying someone for their program, then Harvest Broker is for you, because it only searches for freeware. It searches six of the largest and most popular FTP sites, including CICA, Garbo, UMich, and Hobbes, which among them contain over 35,000 freeware programs. You can find Harvest Broker at:

```
http://www.town.hall.org/Harvest/brokers/pcindex/query.html
```

Harvest Broker's search form is simple, too, as you can see in Figure 9.2. The form gives you one text box for entering information, and you can search for a filename or a description of the file. You can even restrict your search to one particular site. There are also three checkboxes that allow you to choose how your information is returned.

I used the default checkboxes that Harvest Broker presented me with and searched for "winzip." Harvest Broker returned two different versions of the program, one at Garbo and one at Oak. However, WinZip isn't freeware, so this result is pretty surprising.

shareware.com

shareware.com, which went online back in November 1995, is the new kid on the block. However, it was created using an existing system, the Virtual Shareware Library, which allows you to search over 160,000 software files. It searches some of the bigger FTP sites, such as CICA, Garbo, and Netscape.

The Quick Search uses a relatively simple form, as shown in Figure 9.3. The first pull-down menu offers a number of different platforms (Windows, DOS, etc.) to choose from, while the second allows you to limit or expand the number of files that will be displayed. shareware.com will return any files (up to your chosen maximum) that match the exact keywords you choose. The keywords are words or letters that you think will appear in either the description of the file or in the name.

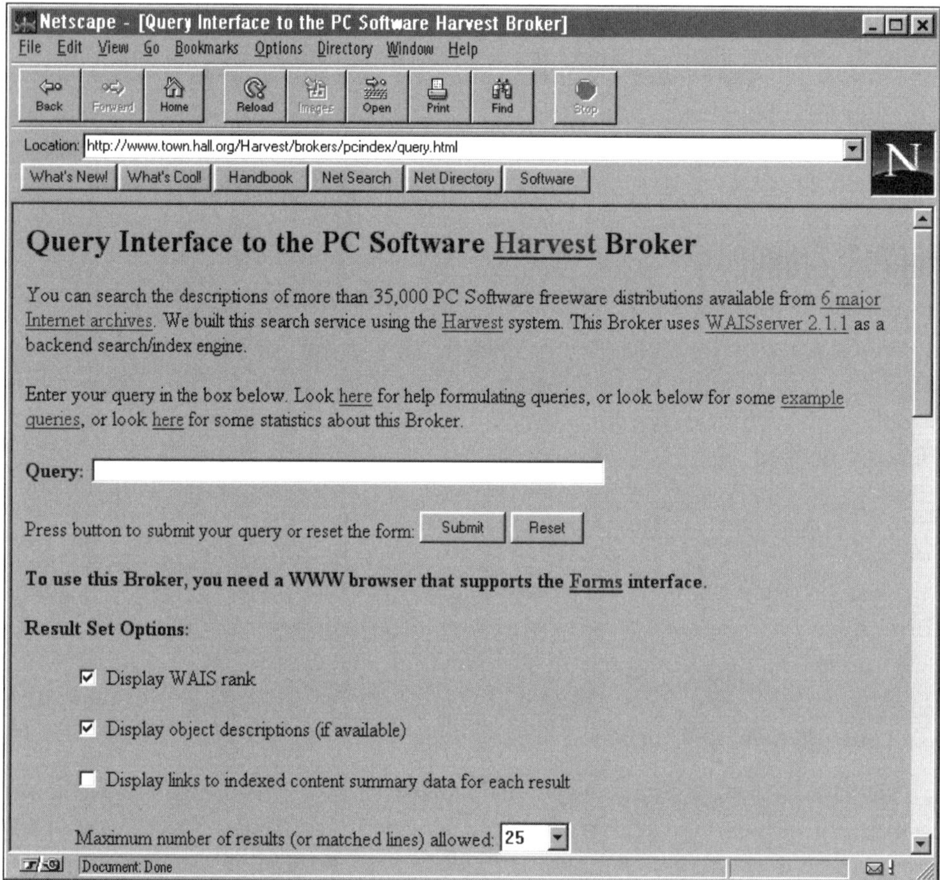

Figure 9.2 *Harvest Broker's search form.*

Even though the form is quite simple, the shareware.com site is not. If you are unfamiliar with navigating with frames, don't even try going to this site, which doesn't give you a frameless option. The first time I visited this site I was a frames novice, and I got so confused that I left before I found what I was looking for.

Because it is often difficult to find the right keyword, I had a hard time using shareware.com. I also think that the instructions are a little too concise. A search for "winzip" for all Windows platforms produced ten files, nine of which were actually WinZip. Since WinZip is one of the most popular downloadable files available, I thought there would be more matches. Thinking that perhaps I had been too specific, I decided to try another search, this time using wz (often the first letters of the WinZip program name). This time shareware.com returned 27 different files, but only 6 of them were actually WinZip.

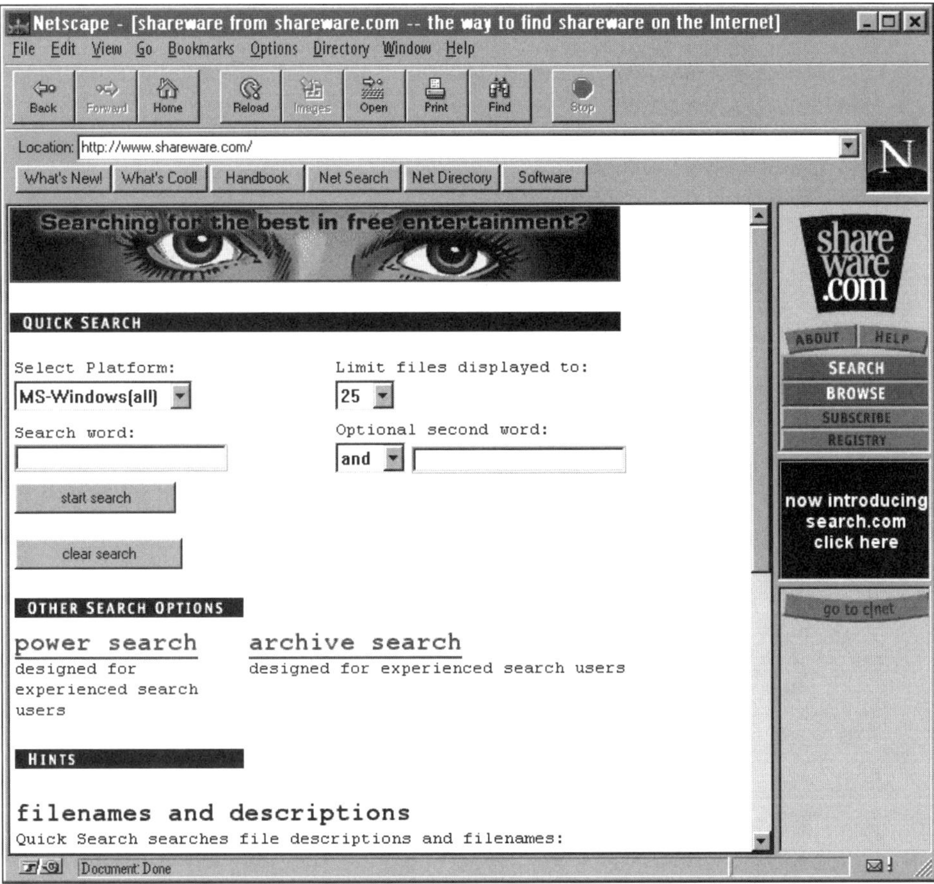

Figure 9.3 The shareware.com search form.

My recommendation: If you can't find what you're looking for elsewhere, try shareware.com. You can find shareware.com at:

```
http://www.shareware.com
```

Archie

Archie is the old reliable standby of FTP search engines. When I was researching this chapter, a few people told me that Archie was archaic and that no one used it anymore. However, Archie's search form gives you lots of choices (Figure 9.4), and a basic search for "winzip" came up with 23 choices. However, Archie can be incredibly slow, so if you're in a hurry, this may not be your best option.

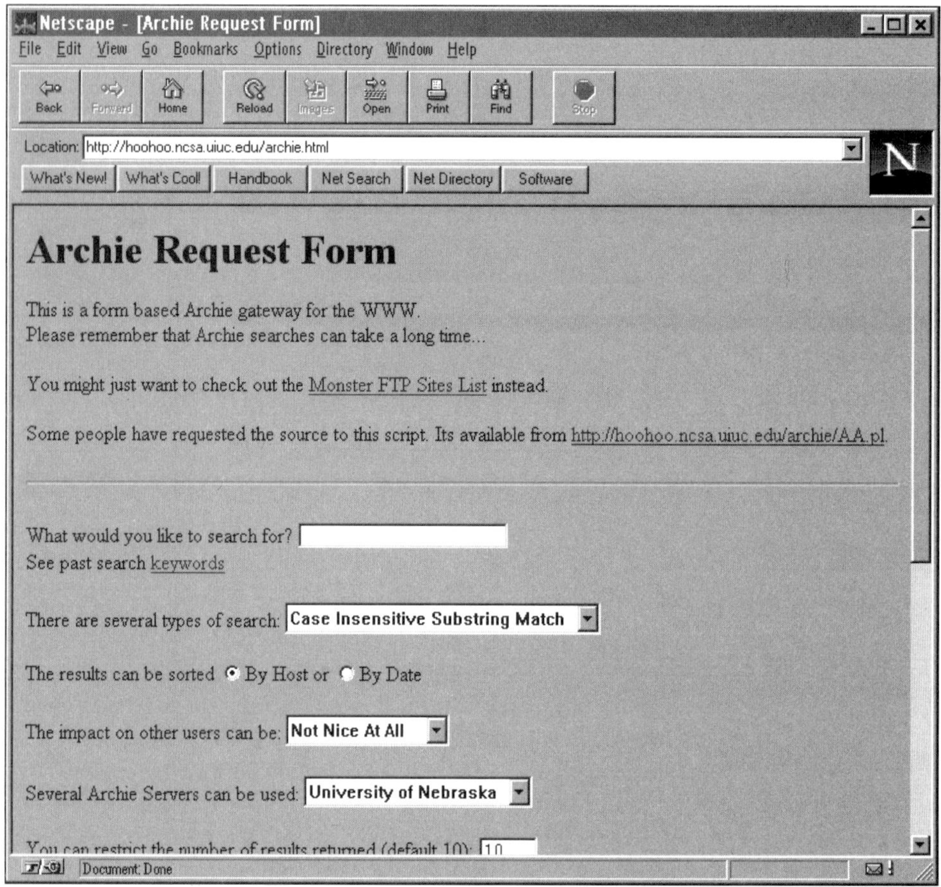

***Figure 9.4** Archie's search form.*

Archie has many addresses around the world. Its U.S. site is:

```
http://hoohoo.ncsa.uiuc.edu/archie.html
```

Snoopie

Snoopie searches its own database of almost six million FTP files and directory names. Even though it has such a large database to search through, it's extremely fast. Figure 9.5 shows that Snoopie's the simplest search engine, with just one textbox and nothing else.

Snoopie returned the best results from our WinZip test, returning 25 different files and directories containing WinZip. The result of the search contains a list of links to matching files and directories, each one showing the size and name

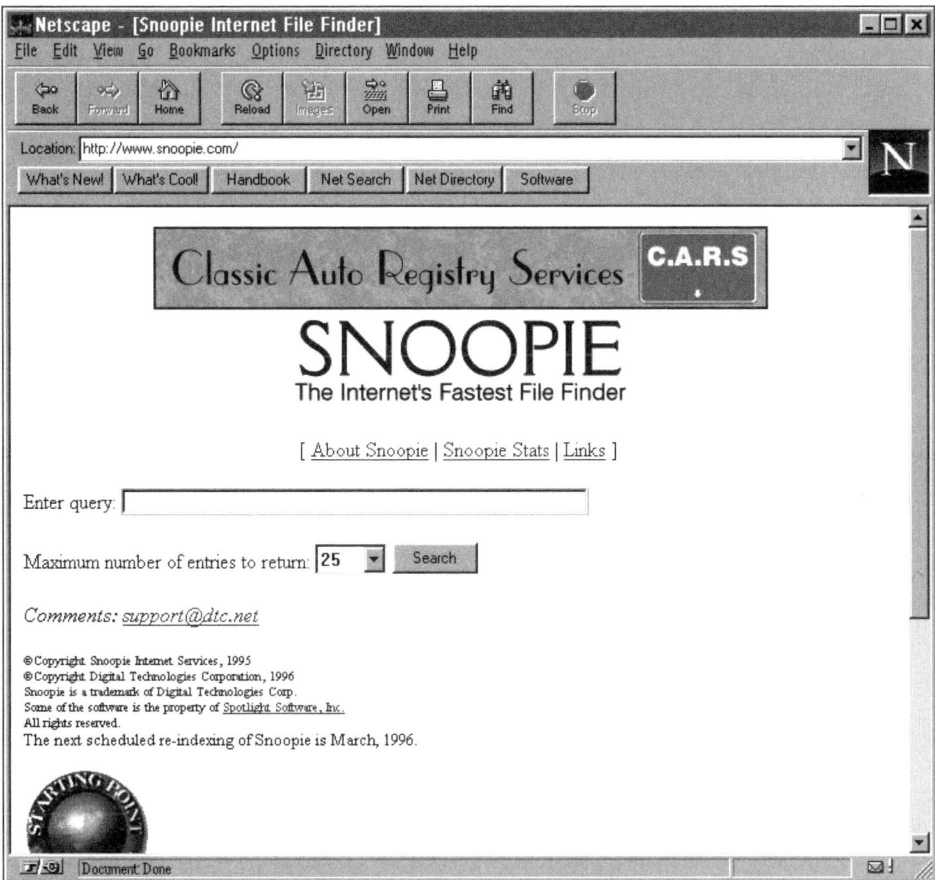

***Figure 9.5** Snoopie's search form.*

of the matching resource. In the search for a good FTP search engine, Snoopie is definitely the winner. Snoopie's address is:

```
http://www.snoopie.com
```

Other Options

There are many other ways for you to search for the particular downloadable file that you are looking for. Instead of using a search engine specifically geared toward FTP sites, you can use one of the general search engines that will hunt through the entire World Wide Web for your requested file. A search using Netscape's default search engine (Infoseek) turned up more links to pages containing WinZip than any of the attempts by the FTP search engines. I'll discuss searching for information on the Web in more detail in the next chapter.

All of the different search options that I mentioned above are perfectly valid, despite how well or poorly they performed in my little test. Each search engine has its own strengths and weaknesses, and each will give you different results, even for the same search. If you can't find what you want with Snoopie, by all means try Open Harvest or Infoseek; one way or another you'll find what you're looking for.

LET'S REVIEW

Locating programs and other useful documents and downloading these files to your PC makes the Internet both fun and rewarding. With a little practice you'll become an old hand at these complementary skills. Once you get the hang of ZIPping and UNZIPping files, everything else will be a breeze. Don't forget, you'll get different results from different search engines, so if you can't find what you want the first time, try, try again.

Searching the Web

Data doesn't become information until you know where to find it. It's time to hop in and rev up those search engines.

They say you can never step into the same river twice—the river flows by without pause, and the water you see today will be lapping at the shores of Arkansas tomorrow morning. The Internet is, in a sense, a river of data, updated continually and without notification. Items—nay—*whole sites* full of useful files come and go with regularity. Every time you fire up Netscape and venture forth for a short trip, you will discover something of interest, and perhaps something that will (when brought home) become a permanent part of your information landscape.

Initially, entertainment rather than knowledge rules the day. However, there comes a time when serendipity (that is, just tripping upon things) will no longer get you everything you want or need. A friend may ask if you can find information on obtaining a National Science Foundation educational grant. Your quiz-kid progeny may want to find out the Catholic population of Spain for a school project. Your boss walks into your office and admonishes, "Either you have that census data for me by this afternoon or I'll find someone who can." Just how do we go about finding the answers to such highly specific, Internet resource-related questions?

FINDING THINGS

Finding Internet information typically requires the use of a search engine to ferret out elusive data. Before jumping into the review of different search engines, let's first look at a few general concepts used when searching for information.

How do queries work? In detail, this depends heavily on the individual search engine you use. Each engine does things in its own way, but the broad strokes follow the same general principles.

Before getting into the arcane details of database searching, let's look at a real example. Execute the sequence Directory | Internet Search to begin a search using Netscape's default search engine, Infoseek. Notice the pulldown menu below the textbox. You can choose to narrow your search as much as you want, but let's just stick to searching the entire World Wide Web for now.

In the textbox, you should enter a keyword or keywords. A keyword describes exactly what you're looking for. Let's say you want to find out about that National Science Foundation grant. All you need to do is type in National Science Foundation Grant and click on Search Now. The search engine will take care of the rest.

More about Keywords

Most keyword queries search an established database. Databases are frequently constructed by parsing search strings into words based on space and punctuation boundaries. Each component word is frequently (but not always) converted to lowercase to facilitate searching—"Netscape" becomes "netscape." Checking parsed words against a "don't include" list eliminates those that are trivial or in other ways meaningless in the search context.

AND and OR

There are two possible ways of searching for multiple words. In a search with a two-word search key, you might want to find only those database entries containing *both* words, or you might be happy bringing home any entry containing either one word or the other. You generally have to tell the search engine what sort of search you want to do. This is an issue of Boolean logic in the query, and a matter of AND and OR. An AND search requires the presence of all stated keys; for example, to find entries on computer science you would search for "computer" AND "science" in the same entry. To search for items relating to DOS or Windows (which stand independently) you would want to do an OR search. AND is usually implied in the absence of an explicitly stated operator.

SEARCHING THE WORLD WIDE WEB

The World Wide Web has spawned a cornucopia of Web search engines. There are engines specifically designed to search Usenet news archives, shareware sites (see the previous chapter), and even an Electronic Library. Even those designed to search the entire Web aren't the same. Each uses its own techniques and each returns quite different results.

One of the best places to start your search is Netscape's default search page, which we used in the first example. If you scroll further down the page, you'll notice that Infoseek contains two lists. The first lists some of the most popular search engines on the Web and gives you a brief description of what each one does. The second list is an alphabetical list of all the search engines that Infoseek knows about.

As you can see, you have a lot of different choices. To help you navigate these navigational devices, I've searched for (and found) some of the best search engines on the Net. The five that I've listed below are really just a sampling of the most popular search engines available, in no particular order. This list is meant to be a starting point, be sure to try other engines as well.

Yahoo

Yahoo is one of the oldest Internet guides available, but it doesn't show its age. It's one of the most popular search engines on the Internet. Yahoo is different from most other search engines in that it doesn't send out a software robot to pick up millions of Internet resources. Instead, Yahoo has indexers (yes, humans!) who describe and index each site; so Yahoo is a great place for quality, if not quantity.

Yahoo is divided into categories, so you can go about your search in two different ways. You can search for a keyword, as described above, or you can navigate the category lists. Since Yahoo's category lists are what makes it stand out from the rest of the crowd, we'll confine our search to that aspect of Yahoo.

Let's see how Yahoo works. To get to Yahoo directly, simply type in their URL:

```
http://www.yahoo.com
```

As you can see from Figure 10.1, Yahoo's search page initially provides 14 categories to choose from. Let's say you're a high-school science teacher interested in finding out more about different science programs on the Internet. There are two obvious places to start on Yahoo's page: Science or Education. Education seems to fit our search more closely, so we'll start there.

Notice in Figure 10.1 that under each heading link there are several subheading links, which contain some of the more popular divisions of the topic. Since you're a high-school teacher, the K-12 link seems to be the best option.

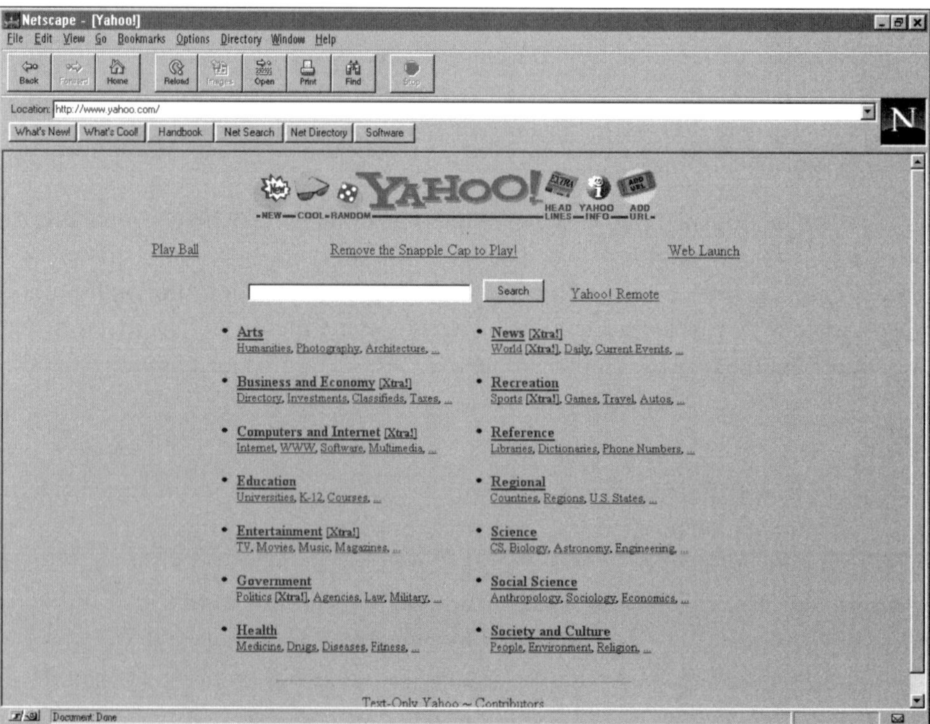

***Figure 10.1** Yahoo's home page.*

Click on that one. A new page appears with the Education: K-12 heading. Again, you have the choice of using a keyword to search the K-12 category or you can continue using the hierarchical lists.

Oh, look, there's a heading for Math and Science Education. That's exactly what we're looking for. But, you may be wondering, what are those numbers in parentheses after some of the links? Those numbers indicate the number of different pages that are located in that link. If you choose that link, you're at the end of Yahoo's list path, and all links after that will take you out of Yahoo. Math and Science Education doesn't have a number after it, so there are still more subheadings beneath it. Let's click on Math and Science Education and see what we come up with.

There it is, Figure 10.2 shows us exactly what we've been searching for, Science Education; and there's a number after it, which means we've finally reached the end of the link path. Click on Science Education and you'll find a long list of school science-related sites, as shown in Figure 10.3, just waiting for you to explore.

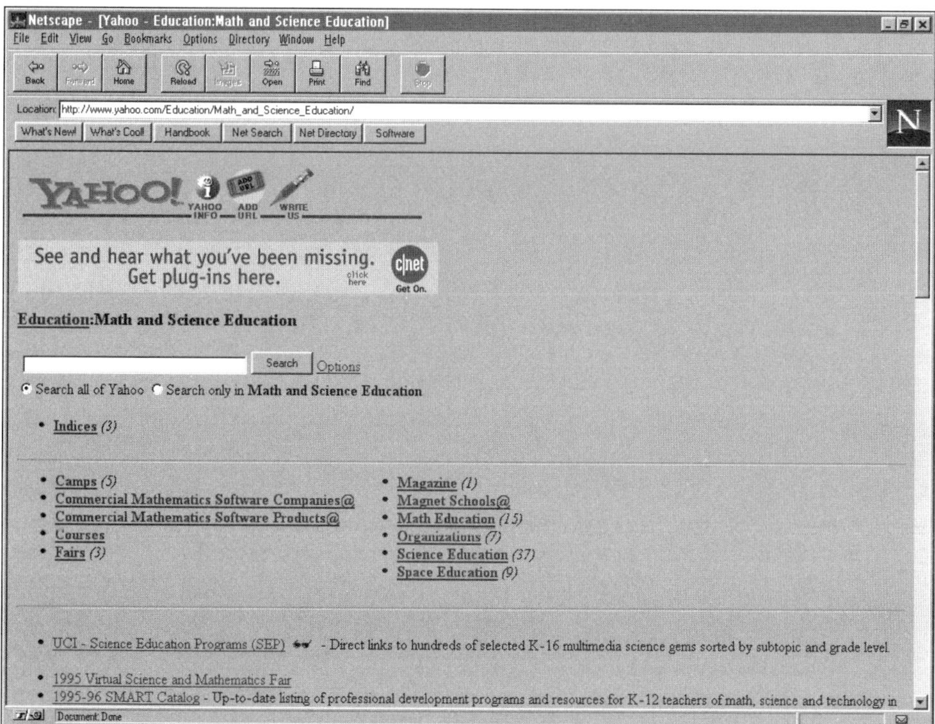

***Figure 10.2** Nearing the end of our search for Science Education.*

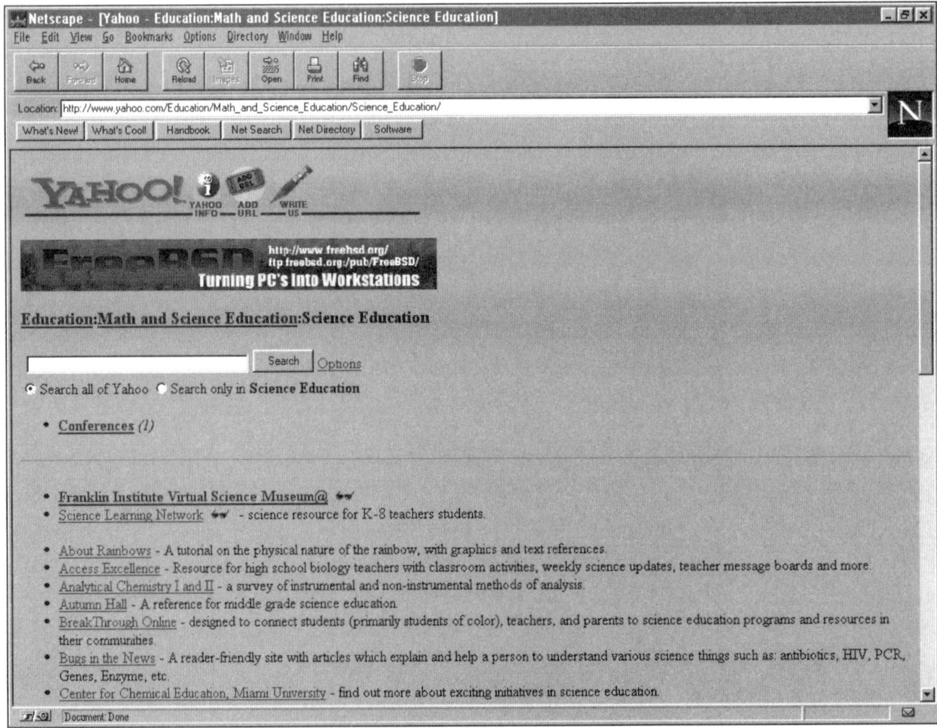

Figure 10.3 *Yahoo's list of links to Science Education-related sites.*

If we had simply used the search engine at the beginning of Yahoo, instead of using the links, we would have been given a whole list of science education subheadings, ranging from what we were looking for to Bill Nye, the Science Guy. Yahoo is different from most other search engines because of its links, and if you're going to use Yahoo, you might as well take advantage of them.

Lycos

Lycos is one of the most popular and largest Web search engines available. Lycos claims to be the biggest of the search engines, and it contains millions of URLs in its database and adds thousands each week. This is a good place to find what you're looking for. Let's take a look at Lycos' home page (Figure 10.4). Their URL is:

```
http://www.lycos.com
```

Notice that it, too, has a textbox at the top and a link directory at the bottom. Its link directory is called A2Z (cute, huh?). This is a new service offered by

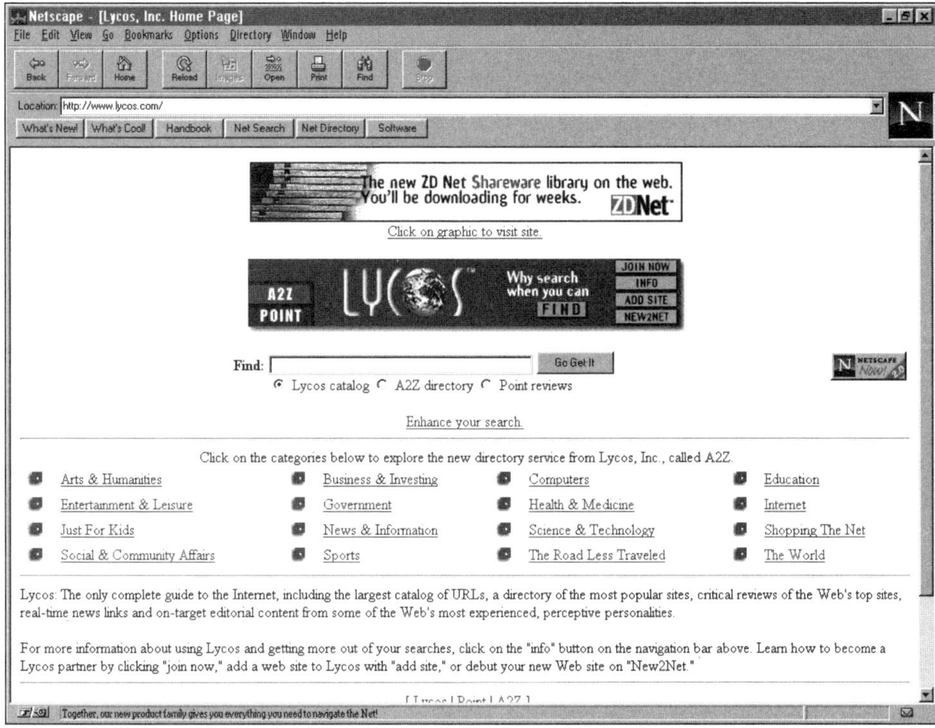

***Figure 10.4** The home page for the Lycos search engine.*

Lycos, to enhance their already popular searching service. Lycos also contains Point, which reviews the top 5 percent of Web sites on the Internet. However, what we're really interested in is Lycos' standard keyword search.

This time, let's search for something more specific. Let's stay with the science teacher idea, and look for information about the Hubble Telescope. Simply enter the words "hubble telescope" into the textbox and click on Go Get It. In a few seconds you should see a screen, similar to that in Figure 10.5, with the results of your search.

At the top of the screen you'll see a heading stating what we searched for, with the date directly below it. Next to the date is a link telling you how many URLs Lycos has searched through (over 34 million!). Below that it tells you how many different sites matched at least one of the keywords and Lycos also tells you that it's giving you the first 10 of however many documents matched both keywords—in this case nearly ten thousand—to a certain percentage of accuracy. If at this point you decided that you only wanted to look at sites containing the word "hubble" you could then click on that link and Lycos will change your search results.

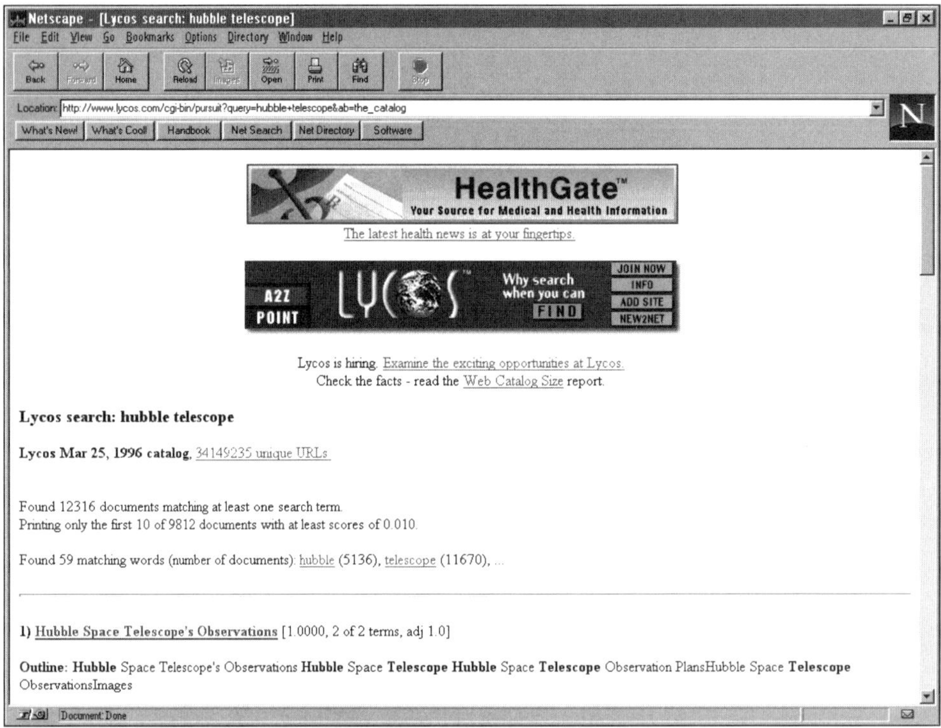

Figure 10.5 *The results of the Hubble Telescope search.*

However, since what we're interested in is information on the Hubble Telescope, let's start looking at the search results. Lycos returns the results of its search in descending order from what it deems the best match to your keywords on down the line, so somewhere within the first ten "hits" (Web search terminology for results) you should find what you're looking for. If not, you can simply click on the "Next 10 Hits" at the bottom of the page to see what else Lycos found. Or you can refine your search using the textbox at the bottom of the page.

Lycos makes it easy to see which particular site is the best by giving you an Abstract containing the first few lines that can be found on each Web. Now, with a simple click of the mouse, you can go directly to a site containing the latest Hubble pictures, or look at Hubble's Greatest Hits.

Alta Vista

While Lycos searches millions more Web sites than Alta Vista, Alta Vista searches the complete text of all the pages within a Web site, whereas Lycos only searches home pages. Their search engine gives you access to over 11 billion words in 22 million Web sites. Alta Vista searches Web sites and newsgroup messages at lightening fast speed. This site often finds information that other search engines, with their less comprehensive searching methods, miss.

To go to the Alta Vista site, shown in Figure 10.6, follow this URL:

```
http://altavista.digital.com
```

Notice that Alta Vista offers two pull-down menus that let you choose whether to search the Web or Usenet and how you want the results returned. (Personally, I couldn't see any difference between displaying the results in Standard form or in Detailed form.)

For the Alta Vista search, let's move to a different branch of high school science, biology. Many people don't like the idea of dissecting a dead frog, and that has caused some controversy in a few school districts. Maybe we could find a solution to this on the World Wide Web. Enter *frog dissection* in the textbox, click on the submit button, and Alta Vista should return results similar to those in Figure 10.7.

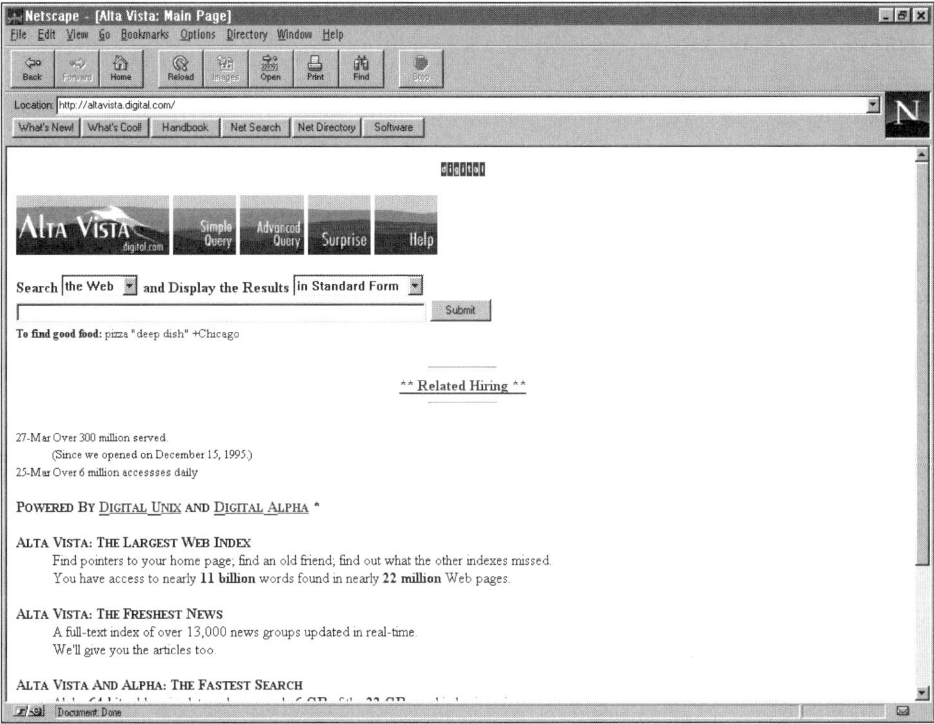

Figure 10.6 *Alta Vista's home page.*

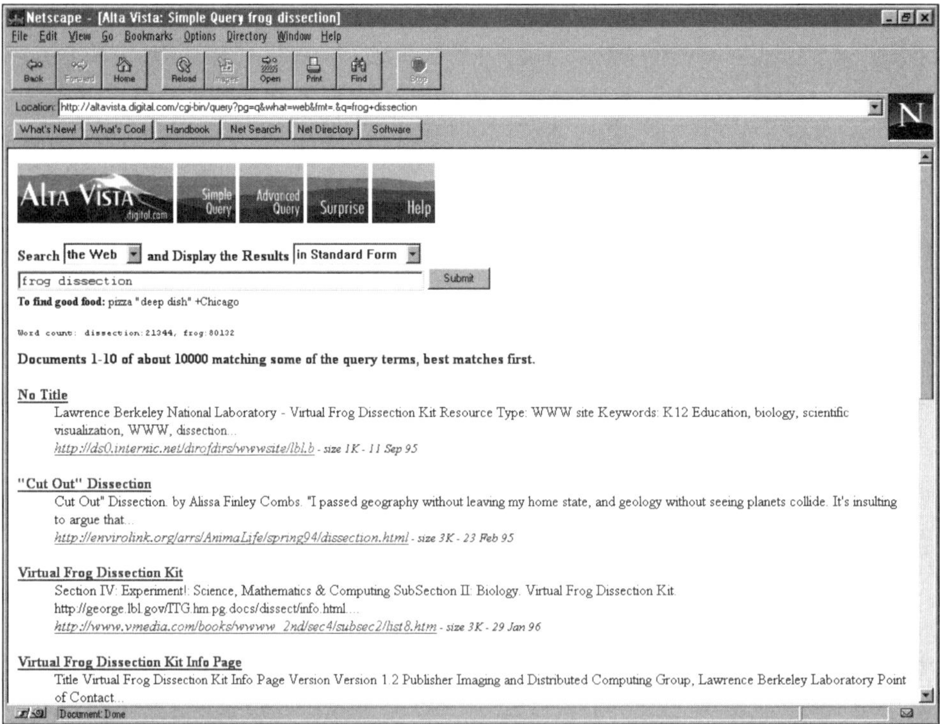

***Figure 10.7** The results of Alta Vista's frog dissection search.*

Similarly to Lycos, Alta Vista tells you how many matches they found for your keywords. Alta Vista also gives you the first ten hits on a page, and allows you to view more pages, as needed. One difference between Alta Vista and Lycos is that the descriptions beneath the links is much more condensed than in Lycos. However, it does explain quite adequately what is featured on each page.

Alta Vista also offers an Advanced Query search, which lets you specify a date range (the only Web searcher that does so) and other advanced parameters. However, if you're just surfing around the Net looking for items of interest, the advanced functions should be unnecessary.

Excite

Excite (http://www.excite.com) is one of the many new kids on the search engine block. As you can see by Figure 10.8, Excite gives you more choices on its search form than any of the other search engines that we've tested. Not only does it allow you choose where you want to search (including Usenet,

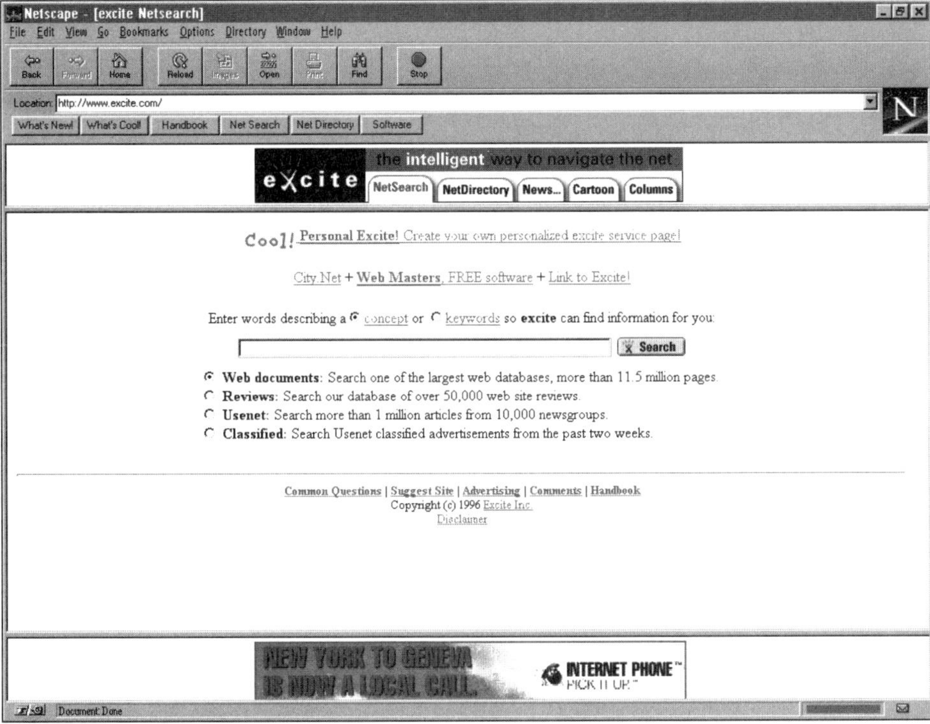

Figure 10.8 *Excite's search form.*

Web site reviews, and the entire Web), there are two different ways that Excite can search. It can search using the standard keywords, and Excite will search for the exact words you enter in the textbox. However, the aspect that makes Excite different is that it can consider the words as a concept. It will find what you mean, not just what you say.

Other differences surface when a search is completed. It's time to move on to another branch of science, earth science. Let's do a search for volcanoes and see what we come up with.

Like other search engines' results, Excite lists its results in hierarchical order, from best to worst. It even gives you a percentage to show how well Excite thinks it matched your request. The next thing you might notice is the little red graphic next to each link (see Figure 10.9). This graphic is one of the best features of Excite. If one of Excite's matches is exactly what you're looking for, simply click on the graphic, and Excite will give you a list sites that are closely related to that link. Excite refines your search to give you exactly what you're looking for. This feature alone makes Excite a great searching tool.

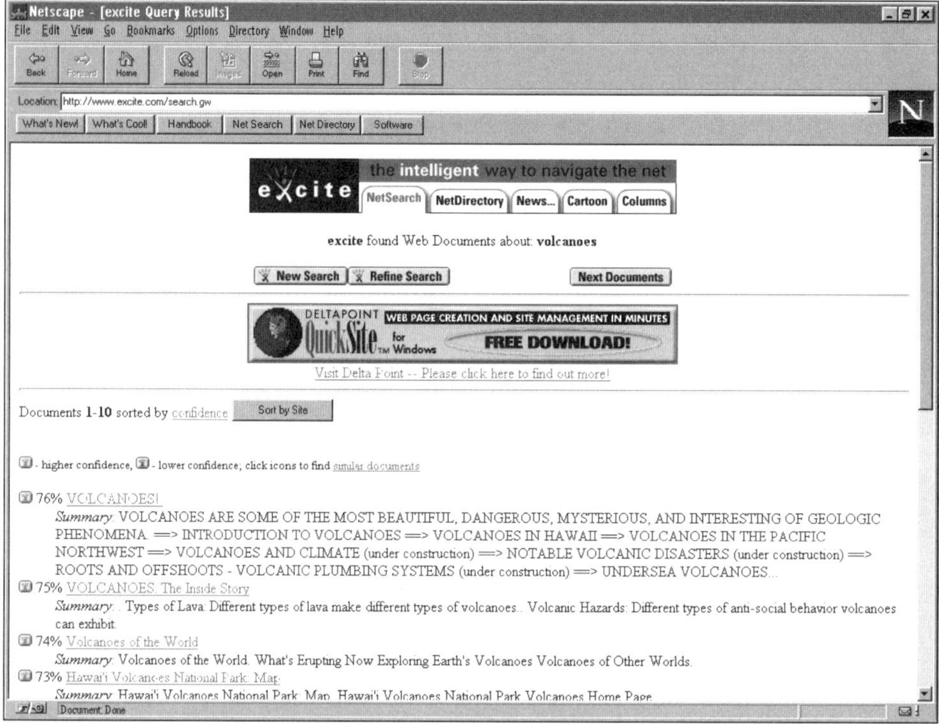

Figure 10.9 The explosive results of the volcano search.

Savvy Search

I have officially saved the best for last. If you don't feel like hunting around in different search engines to find what you're looking for, Savvy Search will do it all for you. Savvy Search queries all of the most popular Web search engines at the same time!

If you look at their search form, shown in Figure 10.10, you'll notice that it's the most complicated of the forms we've reviewed. However, we've seen most of these choices before. If you look at Figure 10.10, the one confusing aspect of the form is the checkboxes for sources and types of information. Savvy Search preselects WWW Resources for you, and then you can specify what other areas you are looking for, be they academic, entertainment, or software.

Even schoolteachers have to eat, so let's look for a good recipe for chicken marsala. First go to the Savvy Search home page. Their URL is:

```
http://www.cs.colostate.edu/~dreiling/smartform.html
```

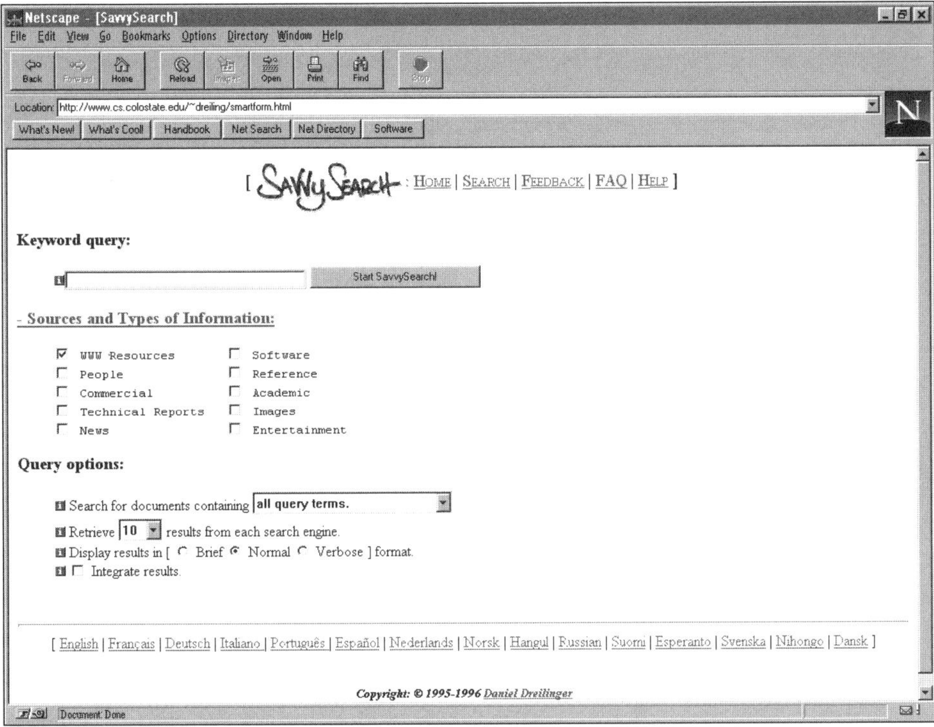

***Figure 10.10** The Savvy Search home page.*

Let's just use Savvy Search's default preferences, to keep it simple. Enter chicken marsala in the textbox, and away we go. You can see the results of my first search in Figure 10.11.

The results list the top 10 results from three different search engines. When you scroll to the very bottom of the page, you'll see a table telling you which engines they chose, and what other results are available (Figure 10.12). Savvy Search decides which search engines should produce the best results, and lists them in order in groups of three.

However, when I did a second identical search for chicken marsala, three completely different search engines were chosen as the best matches. I'm not sure that their ranking system is very accurate, so if you can't find what you want in the first set of results, scroll down to the bottom of the page and choose the next set of search engines.

Of course, there are drawbacks to using something as all-encompassing as Savvy Search. One of Savvy Search's biggest problems is that it can be very

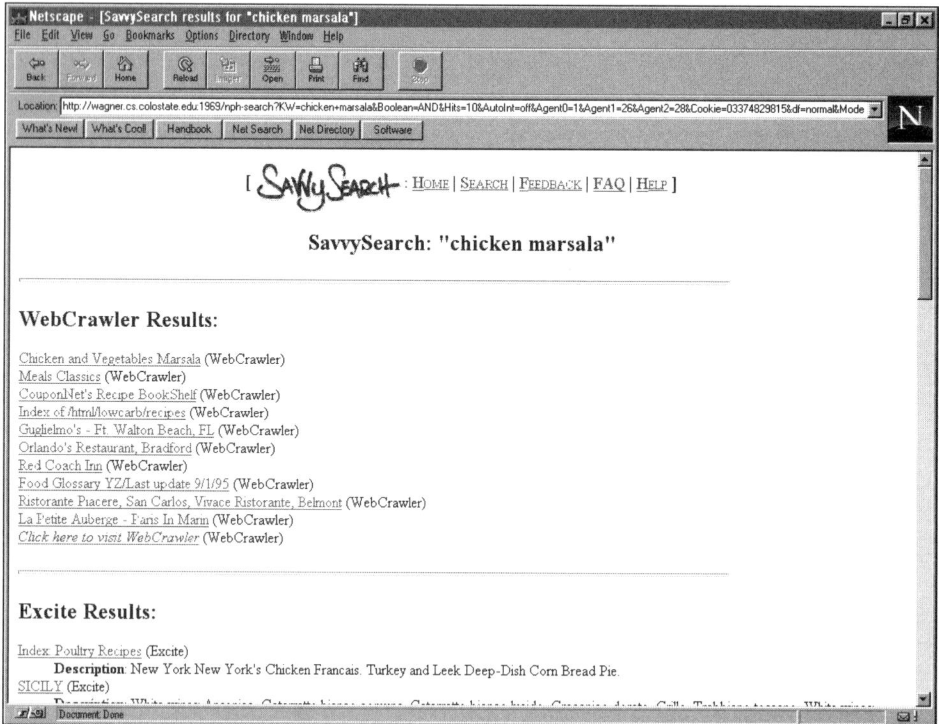

Figure 10.11 *The overwhelming results of our search for chicken marsala.*

slow, and sometimes it doesn't allow you to complete your search. However, if you're looking for a lot of information regarding one subject, and you want as many choices as possible, Savvy Search is definitely for you.

Other WWW Search Engines

Even though I only reviewed five of the more popular search engines, there are many, many more out there for you to explore. WebCrawler, Open Text, and Pathfinder are just a few of the other search engines available in an ever-growing field of contenders. When you begin to be more comfortable with searching on the Web, don't confine yourself to just one search engine. The more engines you use, the more sites you'll find to explore and that will make your explorations much more interesting.

SEARCHING OTHER AREAS

In the last chapter, we discussed the best engines to use to find FTP files on the Internet (including using WWW search engines). There are also other areas of the Internet to explore, and other search engines to explore them

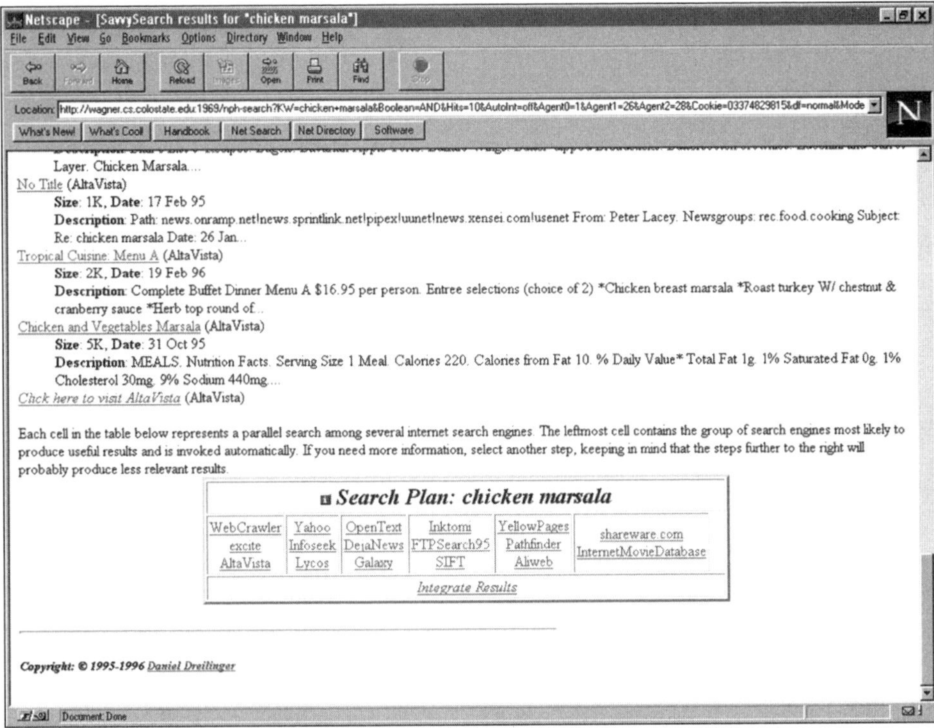

Figure 10.12 *The table at the bottom of Savvy Search's results page.*

with. For instance, The Electronic Library is a useful research tool for anyone writing a research paper. The Electronic Library searches 150 newspapers and newswires, almost 800 magazines and journals and around 3,000 reference works to find the information you're looking for. This is not a free service, you have to pay a monthly fee, but they will give you 100 free searches so you can decide whether or not you want to subscribe. Their URL is:

```
http://cgi.netscape.com/www_s/inserts/tel_srch_dist_ad.cgi
```

Another specialized search engine is DejaNews. This engine will search what DejaNews claims is the largest Usenet archive. If you're interested in finding out information from Usenet, then DejaNews is the place to start.

Finally, if you're trying to figure out what your friend's email address is, or what the URL is for the kid down the street's home page, WhoWhere? can help. WhoWhere? is a free service that helps locate people and institutions on the Internet. Simply type in the name of the person or organization you're looking for and WhoWhere? will give you a list of relevant matches. Their URL is:

```
http://www.whowhere.com
```

There are several other specialized Internet services available. Why not try doing a search for them?

SEARCHING TIPS

Now, what to do when your search produces no results at all? First, check your spelling! If that looks okay, then try to be less specific in your query. For instance, the query "molecular biotechnology DNA sequencing genetics chromosome human genome project" is probably a touch too specific. Very likely no one document contains all, or even most, of those keywords—as valuable as such a hypothetical document might be to your current line of inquiry. Don't jump in with an indiscriminate Boolean OR hoping to find sources containing at least one of the descriptors. Think about the range of documents, or even titles, containing the common words "human" or "project" or "molecular" or...I'm sure you get the point. Instead, try something like "molecular DNA sequencing."

Suppose your search produces too many results? Be more specific. Try to think of words that uniquely identify the object of your affection—without also identifying a lot of other things as well. Some words are of little value, because they will match many database indexes. The words "information" and "university", even when taken together, identify a lot of the entries in almost any database, and are of little value in trying to narrow down the search.

Search engine errors don't always mean that you made a mistake. Sometimes they can indicate that the engine is busy, or that the server in question is down for maintenance. Generally they don't indicate bugs in the software, so please be merciful about flaming the creators of a service—they're giving you an extraordinarily valuable service for free.

Be aware of characteristic terms or acronyms associated with your search goal. For instance, if you're looking for information on the band They Might Be Giants, you can search for "They Might Be Giants," or remember that insiders sometimes refer to the band as just "TMBG."

Some keywords pop up in many places. Ada is a programming language, but it's also an acronym for the Americans with Disabilities Act, the American Dental Association, and probably many other things. (Many search engines cannot discriminate based on case.) So instead of searching for "ADA" use something more descriptive such as "ada programming" or "ada computer".

LET'S REVIEW

After the initial rush from surfing the Web, your enjoyment tends to be a function of your ability to find the things you want, rather than simply accepting what's there as you explore. Make it a habit to use searches early and often in your Web journeys. The Yahoo search engine is an especially good place to start.

Successful searching requires practice, so experiment and try things—remember, you're an explorer. However, recognize that knowing the *nature* of what you search for is far more important than its name or where you choose to search.

Most search engines know a lot about Web information and documents, so it pays to make precise queries—within limits. You can, however, be too precise. Finding what you want frequently requires multiple queries—multiple spellings, perhaps, and certainly multiple approaches.

One final piece of pragmatic advice: As you become an expert in the fine art of information procurement, don't tell anyone. This goes double if you're within earshot of a high school or college student. If you're foolish enough to boast about your wizard status as a data snooper, be prepared to spend all of your spare time doing other people's homework. It happened to me. It can happen to you.

Fingers and FAQs

Fingers are a way to get information about users; FAQs answer common questions about almost anything. Together, they'll help you get the information you need to know.

Pat, my beautiful wife, frequently states that my life has become one big balancing act. Her observation usually occurs within a second or two following the sound of breaking china, as yet another of my spinning plates comes crashing to the ground. Surfing the Net is a lot like keeping a whole group of plates spinning on sticks, all at once. New things are happening all the time, and there is just so much "out there" requiring attention.

In Chapter 10, we explored ways of finding information through the use of search engines. We dealt with generalized searching and questions in the form of "What is...?" or "Where is...?" In this chapter we'll look at another category of information, the type of questions frequently asked in the form of "How do I...?" or "What's going on...?"

After the initial excitement of discovery begins to abate, it's fairly typical to sit back and reflect upon the gaps in one's knowledge base. How best to catch up? Can I go to a public forum and ask some questions without making a pain, or perhaps a fool, of myself? That's where FAQs, or Frequently Asked Questions, come into play.

As I stated in the previous chapter, the focus of this book is the quest for information. Information acquisition includes the techniques for finding information and retrieving things of value. In addition to finding information via FAQ pages, we can find users and retrieve information associated with them using finger programs. The finger program (which is actually a protocol; the finger programs themselves are nearly trivial) allows you to find information about the users on your host network, in addition to finding information about users having accounts on cooperating networks. As we shall see, users are not always people. They may also be interesting (if inanimate) things like Coke machines. Additionally, finger gives you a convenient method for posting information that may change frequently, in the fashion of an Internet billboard.

FAQS TO THE RESCUE

In the parlance of the Internet, a FAQ is a list of Frequently Asked Questions. There are FAQs for an amazing number of topics. These are not trivial or casual lists put together on a whim. Most FAQ lists have evolved over a period of years. Each of these lists represents a substantial body of topical knowledge, and collectively have become a set of encyclopedias available for our use while surfing the Net.

The two primary reasons for obtaining a FAQ for your specific area of interest are:

- being a good net citizen
- procuring the latest version of information that changes unpredictably

A common place to find FAQ lists are in Usenet newsgroups and listserv discussion groups. Logically enough, this is because newsgroups like to support and maintain FAQs pertaining to the specific interests of the group. There are several reasons for a group with common interests to support a FAQ. The first reason is somewhat obvious: People enter the Internet community at various points in time. If you're new to the Internet, any question that you might ask has probably been asked hundreds, if not thousands, of times. The quickest route to the answers for many of your questions lies in a FAQ. The Internet community is very collaborative; nevertheless, it does get somewhat trying when you read the same question several times a week or (as occasionally happens) several times in an afternoon. You don't want to be thought a pest or (gasp!) a perpetual newbie. Checking for FAQs first makes you a good netizen (net citizen) because you're not taking up a lot of Net bandwidth and other people's valuable time asking questions that have already been answered in detail.

FAQs are a great source of current information since updating takes place on a regular and ongoing basis. The currency of FAQs contrasts well with material contained in a book such as this. Any Internet resources listed in a book may well be out of date by the time you read the material. It's not always the case, obviously, but try as we might to pin it all down, the electronic universe changes all the time.

Many FAQs are available using the Web and Gopher, while others require FTP downloading. We'll start by looking at some online resources and then detail how to FTP interesting FAQ documents to your PC.

THE MIT FAQ DEPOSITORY

Many Usenet newsgroups have FAQs associated with their groups. There is a massive depository of these FAQs at the Massachusetts Institute of Technology (MIT). Thomas Fine, webmaster@cis.ohio-state.edu, a systems programmer at Ohio State University (OSU), has started taking the MIT depository and converting the FAQ documents to HTML. Hypertext FAQ documents ease the effort required when accessing a knowledge base as vast as the composite FAQ depository. The opening page of the Usenet FAQ processor is shown in Figure 11.1. The URL for the MIT Usenet FAQs list is:

```
http://www.cis.ohio-state.edu:80/hypertext/faq/usenet/FAQ-List.html
```

Notice that at the bottom of Figure 11.1 there is an alphabetized lookup listing. If your "how do I" question is fairly general and you don't know the name of an appropriate newsgroup, you can click on the *here* link located in the first *New!* Paragraph. This link takes you to the limited search dialog box shown in Figure 11.2.

OK, let's see what we can learn about FAQs by trying a search on "FAQs." If we enter the search term FAQ, the search results appear as shown in Figure 11.3. The search turns up a few unrelated FAQs, but look at the sixth entry down—FAQs on FAQs. That entry looks promising.

If you click on the FAQs about FAQs link, you should see something similar to Figure 11.4.

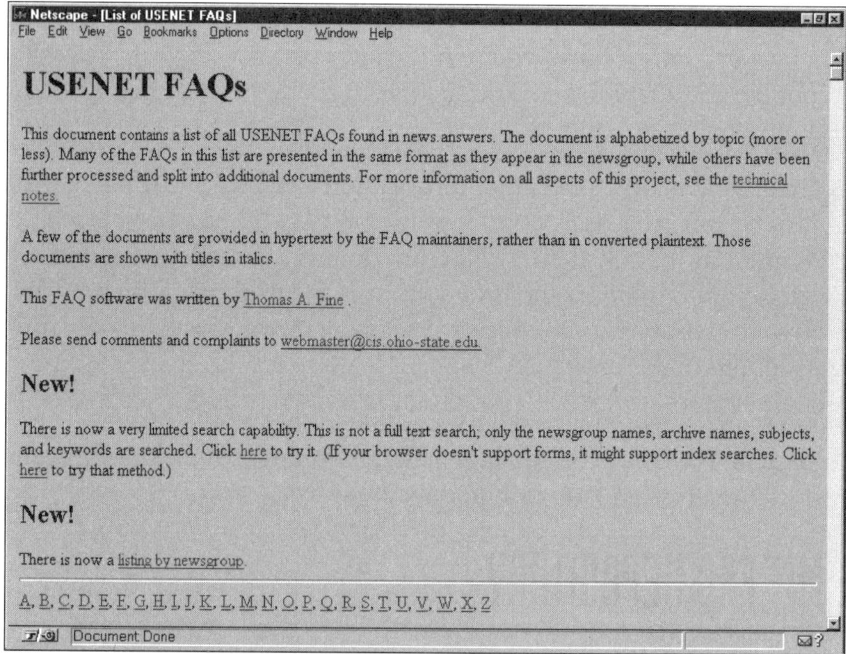

Figure 11.1 *MIT's Usenet FAQs list home page.*

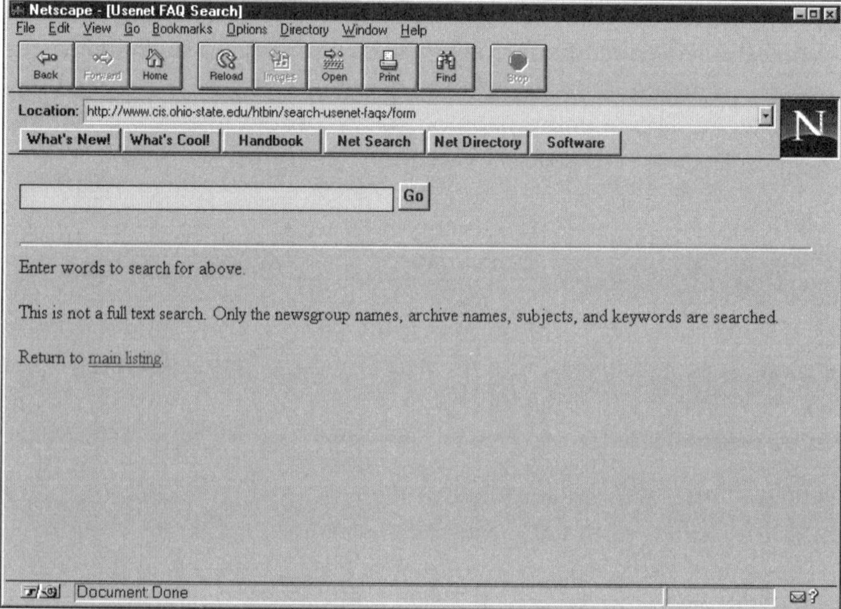

Figure 11.2 *MIT's Usenet FAQs search page.*

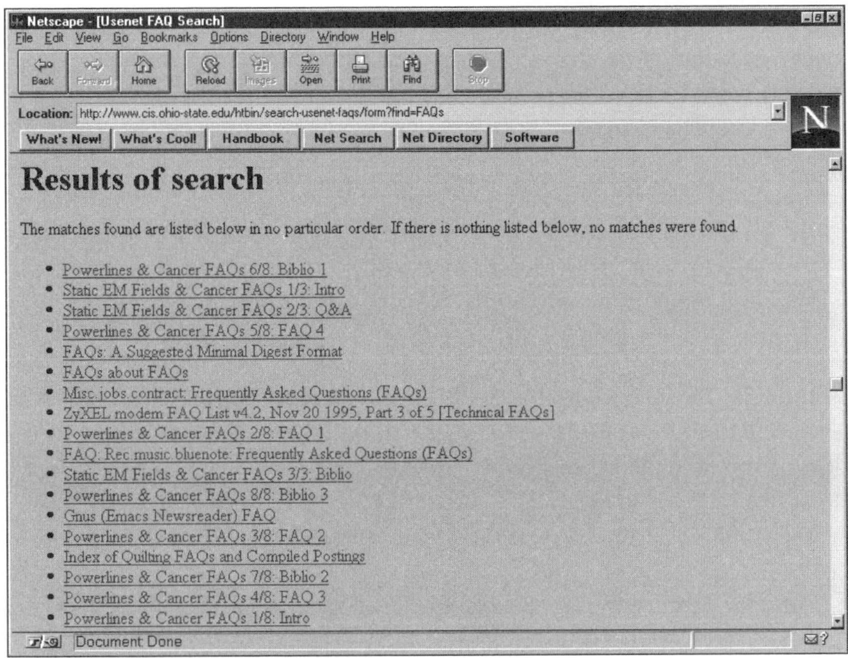

Figure 11.3 *The search results for "FAQs".*

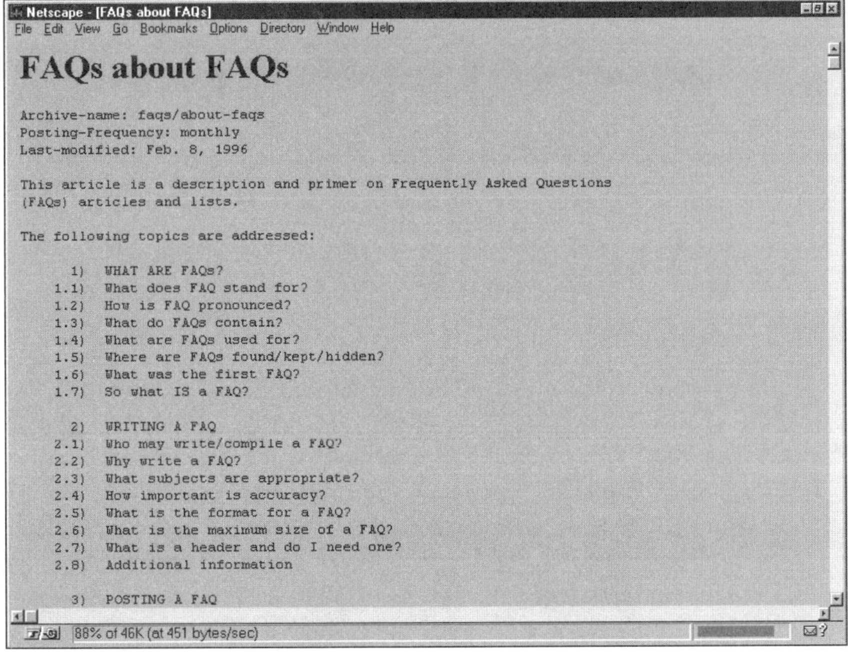

Figure 11.4 *The FAQs on FAQs home page.*

I suggest you take a quick look at this site (it won't take you long) to get an overview of what FAQs are all about and how you can post your own FAQ site. If you want to peruse another site about FAQs try the Jazzie site, shown in Figure 11.5. The URL for this site is:

```
http://www.jazzie.com/ii/internet/faqs.html
```

The Jazzie FAQs page provides links to all the sites you'll need to search for FAQ lists, as well as information to create and maintain your own FAQ page. Notice a link to Tom Fine's Hypertext FAQs Archive is listed.

Let's return to the offerings of the MIT FAQ list. Another feature of the FAQ list is that it maintains running statistics on database accesses. To get the latest version of the statistics, point Netscape at:

```
http://www.cis.ohio-state.edu/hypertext/faq/usenet/technical-notes/faq-doc-7.html
```

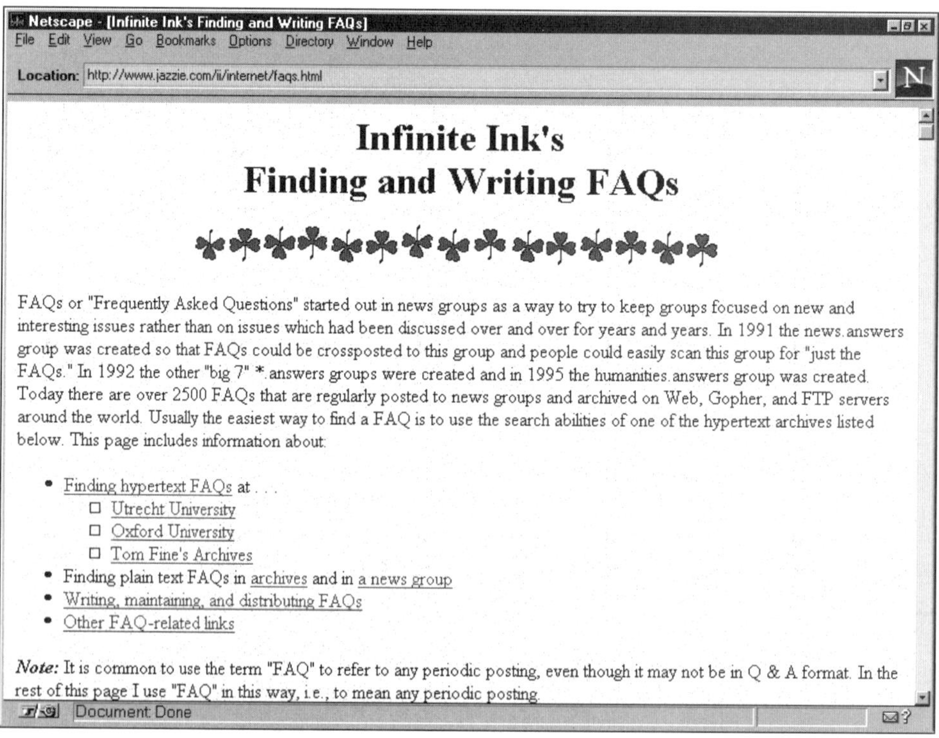

***Figure 11.5** Jazzie FAQs' home page.*

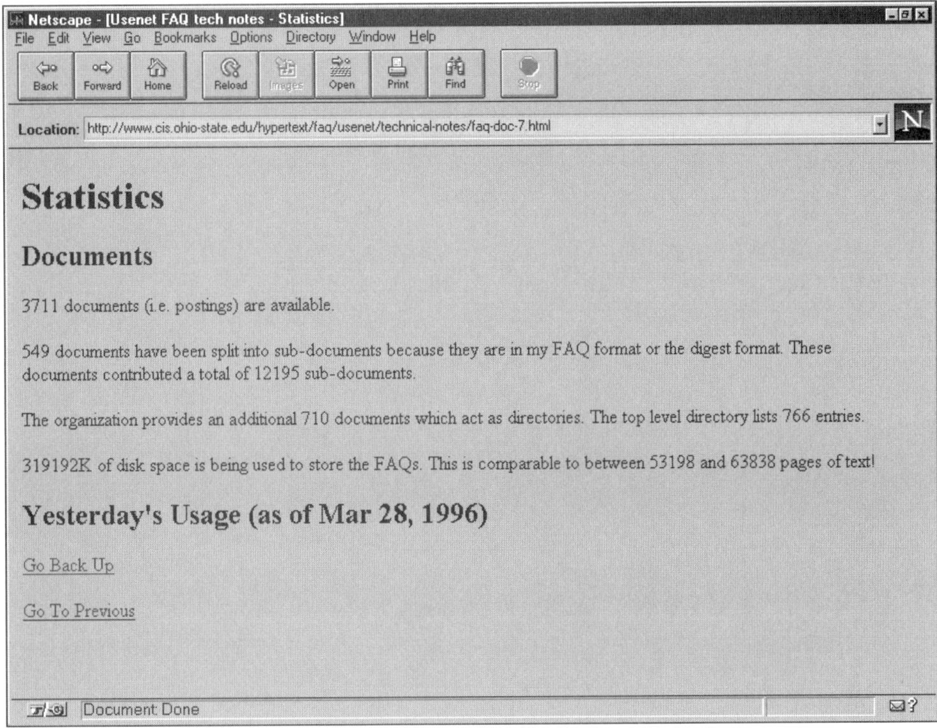

Figure 11.6 *Usenet FAQs' statistics page.*

Figure 11.6 shows a sample of the statistics page.

As of this writing, you only have 3711 documents to look over before you're up-to-date on the FAQs!

Finding FAQs about WAIS

WAIS is an acronym for Wide-Area Information Servers. WAIS, pronounced "wayz," is a powerful system for searching large amounts of information very quickly. WAIS resulted from a collaborative effort by Apple Computer, Dow Jones, and the Thinking Machine company. WAIS searching is rather difficult (much more difficult than it should be!) and space considerations preclude detailed WAIS coverage in this book. Let's take one last look at the Ohio State FAQ machine and its WAIS machinery before moving on.

Point your Web browser toward

```
http://www.cis.ohio-state.edu:80/hypertext/faq/usenet/FAQ-List.html
```

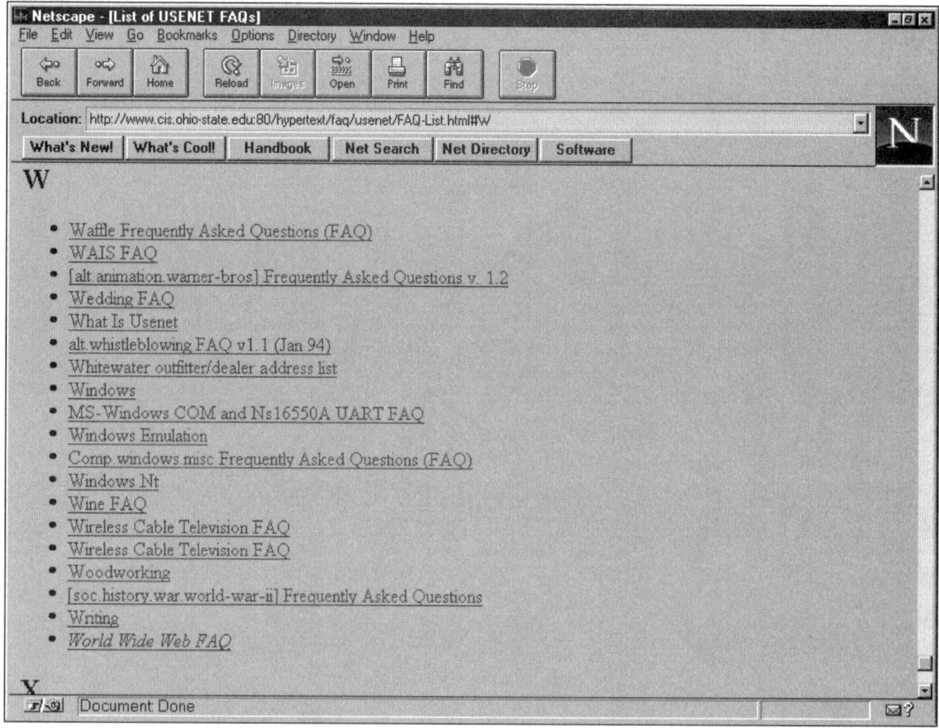

***Figure 11.7** The W index listing.*

to bring the OSU FAQ home page back to life. Select the "W" index listing, and the group shown in Figure 11.7 appears. (The Comp.windows.misc FAQ entry is also a great list.)

Follow the WAIS FAQ anchor, which brings up two pointers:

- freeWAIS-sf Frequently Asked Questions [FAQ] with answers
- comp.infosystems.wais Frequently asked Questions [FAQ] (with answers)

Selecting the first brings up the WAIS FAQ hypertext startup page. This FAQ is an excellent tutorial on WAIS, and a good example of hypertext spicing up dull plain-vanilla documents.

Of course you could get side tracked and click on the World Wide Web FAQ in the W index listing page (I did). The FAQ listing displays in italics because the site is a hypertext site. I recommend that you take this detour. If you don't have time now, here's the URL, you can visit the site later:

```
http://www.boutell.com/faq/
```

FAQs Via FTP

Not all of the available Usenet FAQ lists are on the OSU machine. If you want any excluded lists, or if you like your data in raw form, go directly to the source. Load the following URL into your favorite Web browser:

```
ftp://rtfm.mit.edu/pub/usenet/news.answers/
```

This is the FTP machine at MIT. The whole FAQ business, or so it's rumored, started when the early "flame wars" erupted on Usenet. The term flame is netspeak for an inflammatory remark. In the beginning, someone would ask a question that someone else considered stupid. The reader of the question would post a message to the effect of, "Read the fine manual;" that's not exactly what was said, but you get the idea. In time, all common usage phrases seem to get reduced to acronyms, and it happened that "read the - - - - ing manual" became RTFM. Note the machine name in MIT's URL above—and you thought engineers didn't have a sense of humor.

Figure 11.8 is the start of the "news.answers" directory at MIT.

```
Netscape - [Directory of /pub/usenet/news.answers]
File Edit View Go Bookmarks Options Directory Window Help
Location: ftp://rtfm.mit.edu/pub/usenet/news.answers/

Current directory is /pub/usenet/news.answers

Up to higher level directory
.message                639 bytes Mon Jul 17 00:00:00 1995
1996-olympics-faq        20 Kb    Sat Jan 06 03:22:00 1996
386bsd-faq/                       Thu Mar 28 14:53:00 1996 Directory
3b1-faq/                          Wed Feb 21 04:48:00 1996 Directory
3d-programmer-info       35 Kb    Tue Mar 26 14:29:00 1996
AOL/                              Mon Jul 24 00:00:00 1995 Directory
Arabic-software-map      48 Kb    Sun Dec 17 02:24:00 1995
AudioFAQ/                         Sun Mar 17 04:41:00 1996 Directory
C++-faq/                          Sat Mar 09 02:39:00 1996 Directory
C-faq/                            Fri Mar 15 14:40:00 1996 Directory
CAD/                              Sun Sep 17 00:00:00 1995 Directory
CPM-faq                  53 Kb    Fri Mar 22 02:16:00 1996
GNU-Emacs-FAQ/                    Sun Oct 15 04:30:00 1995 Directory
LANs/                             Thu Mar 14 06:39:00 1996 Directory
LEGO-faq                 47 Kb    Mon Mar 25 01:51:00 1996
Modula-2-faq             21 Kb    Tue Nov 14 23:44:00 1995
Modula-3-faq             65 Kb    Wed Aug 30 00:00:00 1995
Objective-C/                      Mon Mar 18 10:10:00 1996 Directory
PC-games-faq/                     Mon Nov 13 03:38:00 1995 Directory
PCsoundcards/                     Sun Feb 11 17:21:00 1996 Directory
Document Done
```

***Figure 11.8** MITs FTP news.answers listing—Page 1.*

Download the individual document if you like your FAQs in hard copy. The listings of FTPable FAQs use the following format:

```
rtfm.mit.edu/pub/usenet/news.answers/gopher-faq
```

The part preceding the first "/" is the domain name of the network hosting the resource. In this illustration "rtfm.mit.edu" is the domain name of the remote server. You would FTP to this site. The item to the right of the last "/" is the actual name of the file, in this example, "gopher-faq". The part between these two items is the directory path containing the resource, in this example "/pub/usenet/news.answers".

The site

```
rtfm.mit.edu/pub/usenet/news.answers
```

is the primary site for the Usenet FAQs. There are many "mirror" locations. It may be difficult to log onto an anonymous FTP server during certain times of the day. Use an alternative site or try during non-peak hours. There is, however, always the possibility that a mirror site may not have the latest version of the FAQ. If you doubt that you've cornered the latest scoop in a particular FAQ, perform a search and then compare file creation dates. This is always a good idea when downloading important files, especially when the download takes a significant amount of time.

FAQs and Fiction—Fun FAQs to Try

Not all your time on the Internet has to be spent on research and hard work. There are plenty of people out there enjoying themselves on the Web, and you should take the time to be one of them. Following is a short sample of some fun sites (meaning they could be entertaining, interesting, or just plain silly!). You can visit some of the ones I've listed, or you can hunt down your own—this list is just to give you an idea of the Web's multiple personalities.

```
http://www.cs.ruu.nl/wais/html/na-faq/tv-gilligans-isle-guide.html
```

This site tells you everything you ever wanted to know (plus a little more) about the Skipper and his little buddy Gilligan. The site comes complete with all the words to the theme song and a listing of the episode names. If you're interested in other TV shows—including Married with Children, Letterman, Mystery Science Theatre 3000, and Saturday Night Live—click on the rec.arts.tv.html link found on the Gilligan FAQs page.

http://www.cis.ohio-state.edu/hypertext/faq/usenet/music/classical-faq/faq.html

I am listing this URL to redeem ourselves after spending time with Gilligan, Peg, and the Church Lady. This FAQ page is an information source for Classical music newbies and enthusiasts alike, covering topics from major classical periods to "how to pronounce conductors' and composers' names."

http://www.cs.ruu.nl/wais/html/na-faq/movies-trivia-faq.html

You guessed it—a FAQ site for movie trivia buffs. You can link to other Internet Movie sites from this FAQ page, or you can spend huge amounts of time saying, "I never knew that!" to yourself as you read page after page of movie trivia. An example of some of the trivia on this FAQ page includes:

```
Annie Hall (1977)
- Alvy's ('Woody Allen' (qv)'s) sneezing into the cocaine was an unscripted
  accident.  When previewed, the audience laughed so loud that director Allen
  decided to leave it in, and had to add footage to compensate for people
  missing the next few jokes from laughing too much.
Blues Brothers, The (1980)
- Every time we see the window in Elwood's apartment a train goes past.
- When the police car flips over in the mall, the police officer says "Hey,
  they broke my watch!"  This line is repeated after every major car crash.
- Elwood never takes off his sunglasses, and Jake never takes off his hat.
- This film holds the world record for the number of cars crashed.
Star Trek II: The Wrath of Khan (1982)
- There are several books in the container that shelters Khan's followers on
  Ceti Alpha VI. Two of the titles are "Moby Dick" and "King Lear", and
  a lot of Khan's lines are directly taken from those books.
  In particular, the final monologue of Khan is identical to the last words of
  Captain Ahab from Melville's book.
```

http://www.cs.ruu.nl/wais/html/na-faq/internet-services-list.html

Don't blame me if you spend a few hours checking the links on this FAQs' page. This site lists the URLs for everything from botanical gardens to employment opportunites, the Library of Congress, yellow pages, financial information, games, chemistry labs, comics on the Web, and much, much more.

http://www.usatoday.com/leadpage/about.htm

Here's the FAQ page of the USA Today. Among other topics, this page tells you how you can subscribe to the newspaper, do the crossword puzzle online, and respond to the editor.

```
http://www.cs.ruu.nl/wais/html/na-faq/autos-sport-race-schedules.html
```

I'd be remiss not to mention that there is also an abundance of sports information out there (as if you couldn't guess!). This site is a monthly listing of upcoming race schedules.

```
http://www.cs.ruu.nl/wais/html/na-faq/mensa-faq.html
```

Finally, with all the information you going to be getting from the Web, maybe you should keep the Mensa FAQ page URL handy—you could become their newest member!

PUTTING YOUR FINGER ON THE WEB

You can put your *finger* on, or get information about, a Web user from within Netscape. The University of Indiana has a finger gateway at the disposal of Web citizens. A *gateway* is essentially an interconnection between two otherwise unrelated networks or protocols. You send a finger request to the University of Indiana, and it gateways your request to the appropriate network site. When some response occurs, the gateway then passes the information back to you. To use the Indiana finger gateway, enter a URL in the form

```
http://www.cs.indiana.edu/finger/host-domain-name/user-id
```

where *host-domain-name* is the host name to be fingered and *user-id* is the login name of the user you wish to finger. For example, if you wanted to finger me from within Netscape, you would click in the Location text box (the one displaying the URL for the current document), then enter the following URL

```
http://www.cs.indiana.edu/finger/acy.digex.net/lejeune
```

and as the last step, press Enter. My information sheet should display as shown in Figure 11.9.

A good example of the degree of diversity of applications that creative Internauts have discovered for finger is Cyndi Williams' Trivia Time. Finger Cyndi at

```
http://www.cs.indiana.edu/finger/magnus1.com/cyndiw
```

Figure 11.10 is the display of the first page of Cyndi's Trivia Time.

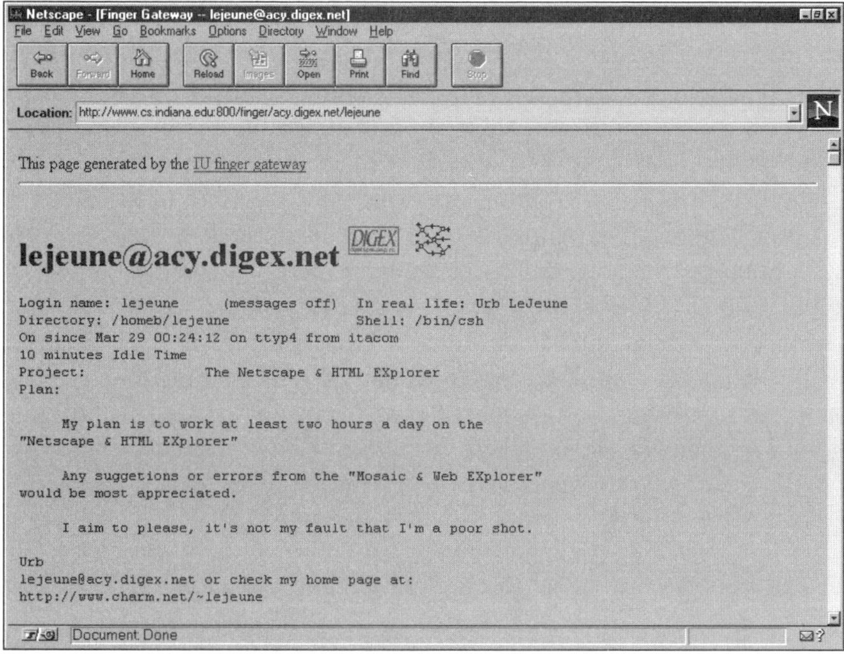

Figure 11.9 *The information page for Urb Lejeune.*

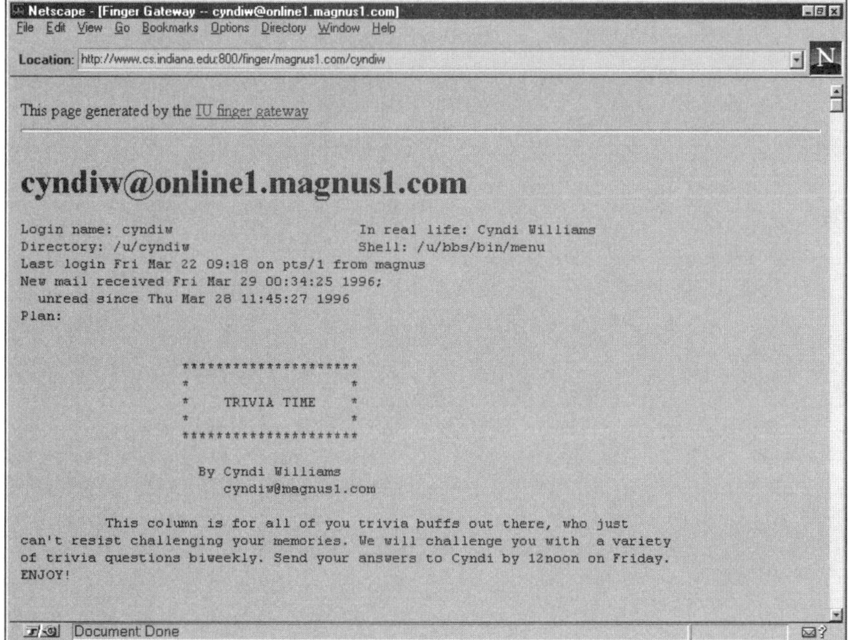

Figure 11.10 *Cyndi's Trivia Time.*

The list goes on and on, and, yes indeed, there are fingerable Coke machines on the Internet. The first Coke machine came "online" in the mid-1970s. It served the Computer Science department at Carnegie-Mellon University. Everyone knows that programmers need periodic caffeine fixes to help sort out those ones and zeroes. The Coke machine in question was located quite a distance from where many of the programmers were caged. Total frustration ensued when one of these guys, complete with pocket protector, trotted up a long flight of stairs, only to find that other caffeine-deprived programmers had already emptied the machine. Almost as bad, they might deposit their trusty quarter only to find that the forthcoming Coke was warm. Their solution was to make the machine a node on the Internet so that it could be interrogated remotely. The wonderful Coke machine at Carnegie-Mellon can be fingered, along with other Coke machines, at:

```
http://www.cs.cmu.edu/afs/cs.cmu.edu/user/bsy/www/coke.html
```

Figure 11.11 shows the Accessible Coke Machine Page.

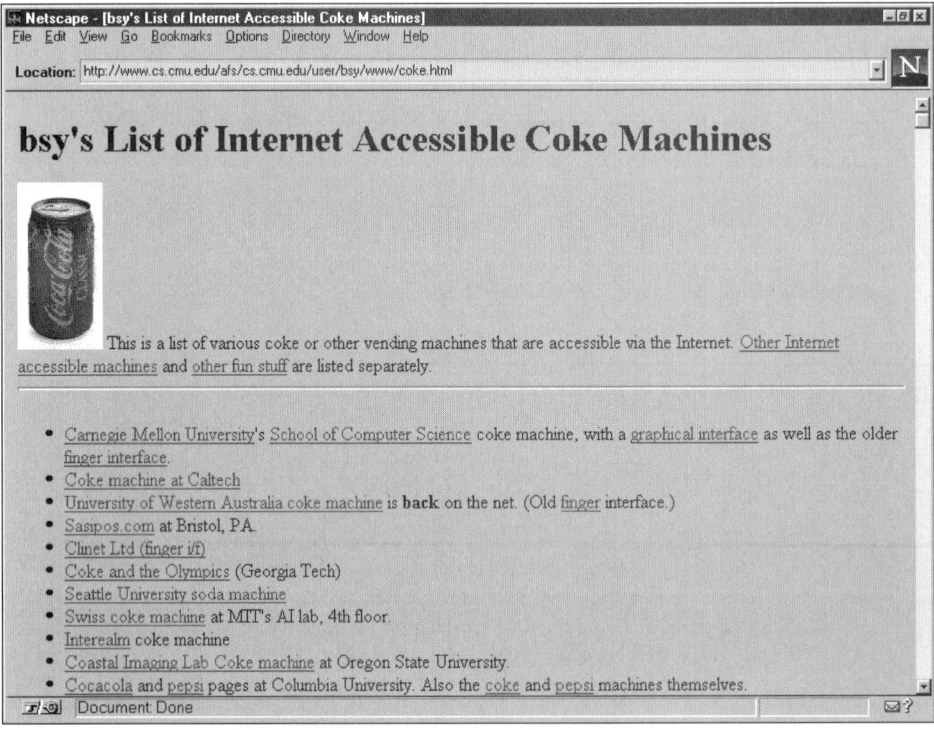

Figure 11.11 *The results from fingering Accessible Coke Machines.*

Other Interesting Sites

A couple other interesting finger sites are:

Events on This Day in History
copi@oddjob.uchicago.edu

Tropical Storm Forecast
forecast@typhoon.atmos.colostate.edu

Scott Yanoff's Internet Services List, usually known as the Yanoff list, has lots of interesting places to finger. If you access the World Wide Web version of Scott's list, you can activate the finger command right from within the document. The HTML list is available for Netscape browsing at:

```
http://www.uwm.edu/Mirror/inet.services.html
```

The Gopher version of the list has more finger entries. To retrieve the Gopher version enter the following URL

```
gopher://gopher.csd.uwm.edu
```

and then select Remote Information Services, then select Special Internet Connections (Yanoff List).

A Home Page for (Almost) Everyone

The Netscape Web browser introduced an interesting feature that may create a universal "home page" capability, even for people without access to a Web server. A finger client, once it discovers the target of a finger request, looks for a file with the name ".plan". If the file is present and accessible, its contents are displayed by the finger client.

While browsing the Web using Netscape, try fingering someone via a finger gateway. If that person has created his or her .plan file as an HTML document, Netscape will display the document as it would any other HTML document, hotlinks and all. (Well not quite, formatting is somewhat different.)

Try it by entering this URL

```
http://www.mps.ohio-state.edu/cgi-bin/finger
```

and fill in the form with the email address of the person (or Coke machine) that you want to finger.

If your network system allows external fingers, you can now have a home page. Power to the people!

LET'S REVIEW

Frequently Asked Questions (FAQs) represent the collective wisdom of the Internet, gathered into the well-known question-and-answer format. The topical broadness of the subject material practically guarantees that answers are waiting to virtually any question you might have about almost any topic held as interesting by more than three people in the Internet community. The instantaneous availability of the large database makes accessing this information easier now than in the past.

Most FAQs have come about through the efforts of people participating in Usenet newsgroups, which are "asynchronous cocktail parties" of people with common interests posting messages of interest to the group where subscribers to the group can read them. Many FAQs are distillations of the discussions of these groups gathered over a period of years.

There is a list of FAQs available in HTML format, for viewing with your favorite Web browser, at:

```
http://www.cis.ohio-state.edu:80/hypertext/faq/usenet/FAQ-List.html
```

The primary site for the MIT collection of FAQs is:

```
rtfm.mit.edu/pub/usenet/news.answers
```

You can finger a user from within a Web browser, taking advantage of the finger gateway at the University of Indiana. Enter a URL in the following form:

```
http://www.cs.indiana.edu/finger/host-domain-name/user-id
```

where *host-domain-name* is the host name to be fingered and *user-id* is the login name of the user you wish to finger.

If a user has created his or her .plan file as an HTML document and you are using Netscape, try the finger gateway at:

```
http://www.mps.ohio-state.edu/cgi-bin/finger
```

Since many administrators consider finger to be a security risk, they have disabled finger servers, or at least disabled them to outside users. Don't be surprised if you receive a message

```
Connection Refused
```

in response to a finger request. It's the price we pay when people abuse the system.

Exploring the Power of Web Publishing

Get ready—the fascinating world of Web publishing is just around the corner. And it's easier than you think.

Now that we've mastered the art of exploring the Web with Netscape and using features like URLs and bookmarks, it's time to turn the corner and start our Web publishing explorations.

In a previous chapter, we learned how to prune and tune Netscape's home page so that Netscape could read it—including its embedded links—from your local hard disk. We've also pulled apart URLs in a recent chapter. This experience should give you the background you need so that you can jump in and learn how to create your own Web publishing documents and eventually publish on the Web.

In many ways, you'll be surprised at how easy it is to create your own Web pages, including a home page, and become a cyberspace publisher. If you have a talent for graphics and design, you'll really feel at home. But you don't need to be an artist, designer, or professional author to publish on the Web; you just need something interesting to tell the world.

I'll start Part 2 of this book by discussing what Web publishing is all about. You'll learn how to take advantage of this exciting medium by looking at the kinds of documents you can and cannot publish. After this introductory chapter, we'll start by creating a home page and then we'll learn how to use most of the key HTML features—including formatting codes, hyperlinks, and tables—to create exciting and useful Web pages. The more you learn about HTML, the more you'll appreciate the flexibility of this publishing tool.

Here are some of the questions that I'll answer in this chapter:

- What is Web publishing and what can be published on the Web?
- Why is Web publishing becoming so popular?
- What is the difference between a home page and a Web page?
- What exactly is a Web server?
- What is an HTML document?
- How are Web pages created?
- What is needed to publish on the Web?
- What does it cost to set up a publishing operation on the Web?
- What is involved in setting up a Web server?

THE WORLD OF WEB PUBLISHING

From using Netscape and surfing the Web, you already know that the Web is an interwoven network of computers and documents. With the powerful technique of hyperlinking, many different kinds of documents—from online newspapers to catalogs to complete electronic books—can be linked in interesting ways. New content and links can be added at any time and adding features like "point and click" navigational maps and interactive forms to Web publications makes them more interactive and useful.

The best part about Web publishing is that you don't have the kinds of limitations that you face with traditional publishing. Some of these limitations include:

- The high costs of paper and printing
- The cost and challenge of wide distribution (especially if you are a small publisher)

- The logistics problem of receiving feedback from people who read or view your publications
- The significant amount of time required for publishing and distributing material

Web publishing removes these obstacles because it is an electronic medium—a medium supported by the dynamic, global nature of the Internet. You don't need to be in any specific place in order to publish on the Internet. Also, the people who read or view what you've published don't have to go to central distribution centers, such as bookstores or newsstands, to get your latest publication. All they need is an Internet connection and access to the Web.

As the Web is becoming more widely used, more and more companies and individuals are setting up publishing operations. In some cases, material published on the Web can't be found in any other medium, including newspapers, magazines, or TV. Some companies are even using the Web to showcase new publications and get feedback from their audience before they publish their products in a printed or recorded format. For example, The Coriolis Group—the publisher of this book—often puts early chapters of some of their books on the Web before the book is printed and distributed. This allows readers to get information quickly and check out a book in advance.

A NEW KIND OF PUBLISHING

If anyone tells you that publishing on the Web is just a new form of desktop publishing or that it's just like creating online documentation, tell them you have ocean-front property in Arizona to sell them. Web publishing requires a completely different approach to designing and creating publications. Whether you want to publish an electronic newsletter or a catalog, your audience will have a completely different set of expectations. The information or *content* that you publish should be interactive, contain links that access other content, be up-to-date and as dynamic as possible, and should use different media—text, sound, images, video, and so on—whenever it makes sense to do so. Let's take a closer look at these different aspects of Web publishing.

Interactive Publishing

Many users look for an interesting home page with links to click on in order to access more information, or fill out a form. Often, users will be able to navigate by clicking on a visual map or icons. This gives the users the feeling that they can easily interact with the content they are exploring.

In traditional publishing, the audience is passive. They can't send a message to the author, ask a question, or click on a "link" to get more information. If you haven't worked with the interactive element before, this takes some getting used to. You need to learn how to design your publications so that your audience won't get easily bored or distracted and wander off to check out another site. Whether you are creating newsletters, books, magazines, newspapers, or personal content, the goal is to attract the reader's attention and keep it focused on your publication by offering the reader things to do. Some of the more useful techniques for accomplishing this include:

- Provide a set of links to other sites of interest so that your users can easily explore other places.
- Include features that users can click on to see more of a subject. For example, let users click on an image that will display a complete photo gallery.
- Add forms that users can fill out to send you comments or ask questions. (If you include features like this, make sure you set aside some time to respond to your users.)
- Provide searching features so that users can easily look up information.

Some of these interactive features require special skills to incorporate. However, as the Web is becoming more interactive, more and more tools are being developed to help publishers create interactive Web pages. And the best part is that many of the tools are free or very inexpensive. One useful system now available for setting up a "chat mode" feature is called WebChat. As shown in Figure 12.1, you can create a set of Web pages where users can come and leave messages for each other.

To learn more about WebChat or try out a live demo, use this URL:

```
http://www.irsociety.com/webchat/webchat.html
```

Publishing on Demand

People who are in traditional publishing businesses (books, magazines, newsletters, and so on) often talk about the ability to publish information "on demand." The underlying issue here is that most people don't need an entire book or magazine when they are interested in learning something new. Usually, they are looking for specific information and they end up having to purchase an entire book just to get access to one chapter they need. For example, let's say you are creating Web documents with HTML and you are

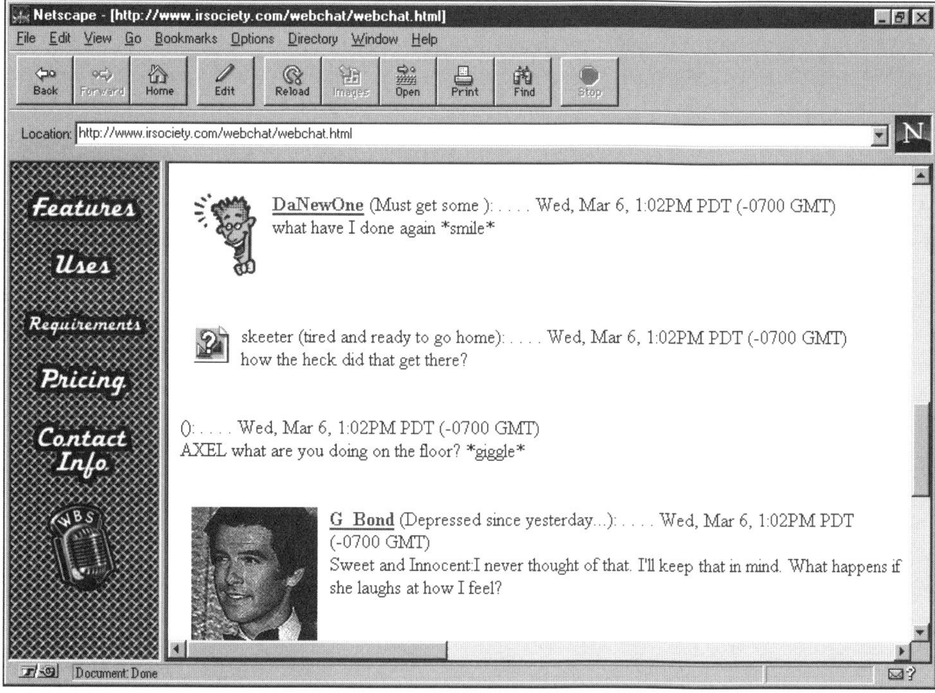

Figure 12.1 *One of WebChat's chat rooms.*

interested in learning more about the newer features that have been added to HTML. Instead of buying a complete book on HTML that covers most of what you already know, what you really need is a straightforward guide with examples of the new features.

The Web easily makes this kind of publishing possible because of the "on demand" nature of Web pages. As you gain more experience publishing on the Web, you can even set up features such as a database of articles that your users can query to access important information.

ME MAGAZINE

The following article about the future of publishing appeared in the Oct/Nov 1994 issue of *PC TECHNIQUES* Magazine. In it, the author, Jeff Duntemann, discusses a new approach to publishing designed for the future. If you think about it, some of these ideas are starting to appear now.

> The Internet is a lot like NASA in some ways. It's a gigantic testbed for technologies we're going to need someday to serve the general

public. Client/server is one of these, and the more I play with the Internet, the more possibilities I see in really *really* sophisticated client/server publishing systems—systems good enough to put me out of a job.

In 2005 I see a new model for periodical publishing. The press syndicates have gone electronic and absorbed the editorial function. Writers sell *them* articles now, and the syndicates do the copy editing and proofing. Finished pieces are indexed and categorized and stored on a server on our information superhighway.

Publishers have mutated away from content generation toward a niche once filled somewhat gamely by clipping services. Subscribers subscribe to a *publisher,* not to any specific magazine. Each publisher has a very clever client application that maintains a subscriber interest profile and uses it to search the syndicates for articles, columns, and cartoons that seem to fit the subscriber profile.

Each month, or two months, or every 33 or 41 days (or whatever), the client goes out and finds as much stuff that fits the profile as the reader has requested and paid for. If, for example, I can only read 40 pages every month, I get 40 pages. If I know I'm going on vacation, I can request that the July issue be 70 pages long instead.

The profile is detailed indeed. I can request articles on any topic I'm interested in. I can ask for *Dilbert* and *Outland;* trends in copper prices; photos of classic Chevelles; and new recordings of music by Percy Grainger, Ralph Vaughan Williams, and Leslie Gore. The client digs up what it can, and then arranges it in a tidy if plain page layout and sends me the file. I can read it on the screen or print it to paper to take to the beach.

The free market works well here. If the publisher I subscribe to delivers stuff that I think misses the profile, I take my profile to a different publisher. The publisher prospers on the strength of its client application. The price I pay for my subscription depends on what percentage of ads I allow the publisher to sprinkle into my periodical, and how expensive the stuff I request happens to be. The publisher charges the advertisers to advertise in my periodical by how "valuable" my demographics are to them. Authors are paid by the request, and the more people who request their material, the more they get paid.

It's an *extremely* efficient system, especially with regard to wasted paper. About 50 percent of all magazines are never sold and go right from stores to landfills. (Sooner or later, the environmentalists are going to find out about that.)

Multimedia Publishing

If you think multimedia is one of those publishing buzzwords coined by computer people years ago to sell more computers, you're probably half right. Many brilliant people in the computer and publishing industries have made all kinds of predictions and promises over the past five years about multimedia; unfortunately, this technology hasn't quite taken over. One of the biggest problems with multimedia is that multimedia applications are difficult to develop and test. In addition, many users easily get bored with multimedia because it often offers nothing more than boring "point and click" slide shows.

Multimedia publishing on the Web offers something very important that can't be done with other publishing vehicles such as CD-ROMs—new content can easily be added. You can design Web pages that offer multimedia features such as sound, video, images, and so on, and then you can continually update your links so that your users don't get bored by seeing (or hearing) the same thing over and over.

The other major benefit of multimedia publishing on the Web—and one that is making it grow rapidly—is that it's easy to do. You don't need any special multimedia languages or engines to add multimedia links to your Web pages. In addition, you can easily create multimedia pages that can be "viewed" by users of a wide variety of computer platforms—from PCs to Macs to Unix machines.

Resource Publishing

When was the last time you bought a computer book or magazine, only to be disappointed that the publication didn't come with a disk or CD-ROM loaded with goodies for you to play with or try out? Although the costs of duplicating disks and CD-ROMs are decreasing, it's still an expensive proposition to produce them and get them in the hands of your users. Web publishing attacks this problem head on by offering users the ability to automatically download software, multimedia files, text, and other resources by simply clicking on a link.

This "dynamic download" feature opens up all kinds of new possibilities for publishing. Instead of displaying everything in your publications, you can easily provide links that will send material to the user's computer when selected. This approach can save you time and resources. The challenge is to determine what to display and what to include as a resource link.

Growth of Web Publishing

Here's one of the most commonly-asked questions on the Internet and in computer magazines these days: How fast is the Web growing? Nobody knows for sure, but hundreds of new Web sites are emerging daily. And the main reason most of these sites get set up in the first place is to publish material for others to explore.

Although Web traffic still accounts for only a small percentage of Internet activity, the Web is growing faster than any other Internet service. Popular Web sites that feature newly-published home pages have become so popular that your chances are better at getting a parking place at the mall on Black Thursday than being able to connect to one of these sites.

This means the competition is heating up for people who want to publish on the Web and get others to view their publications.

What Can You Publish on the Web?

Since you've been surfing the Web with Netscape, you probably are already familiar with a few of the types of publications that can be successfully distributed. Here are a few suggestions, some of which you might not have encountered yet:

- **Specialty Newsletters.** The Internet is a great place for people with similar interests to get together. In fact, many people who have unique hobbies or professions join newsgroups so that they can share information—new ideas, gossip, horror stories, and so on. Newsgroups are one of the most widely used features of the Internet. As the Web is becoming more popular, specialty newsletters are being published that provide a useful supplement to newsgroups. These newsletters feature in-depth articles, interviews, tips and advice, and graphics and illustrations. To create your own specialty newsletter, all you need is a topic that you know something about and the ability to write, edit, or talk other people into writing and editing for you. Whether you are into hang gliding, stamp collecting, or traveling in foreign countries, you can turn your interests and knowledge into a publishing venture without spending a lot of money and resources on printing, paper, and postage.

- **Personal Profiles.** You might not have much to say about a particular topic, such as rock climbing, mountain biking, or gourmet cooking, but you should have a lot to say about yourself. Because of the high cost of traditional publishing, most people don't feel that they have the opportunity to share personal things with the world. Once you are on the Web, you can publish any type of personal information, including your resume or a collection of poetry or short stories. Who knows? Maybe someone will read your stuff and offer you a job or a book contract.
- **Electronic Books and Magazines.** Many commercial publishers who are looking for new and innovative ways to distribute their publications are turning to the Web. In fact, some of today's publications exist only in an electronic format. Some readers who get both a printed and electronic version of a publication prefer the electronic version because they can search for information and get up-to-the-minute corrections and updates. Many tools and converters are being developed to help traditional desktop publishers transfer publications created with programs like PageMaker to a Web page format. As the tools improve, more and more books and magazines are likely to appear on the Web.
- **Shopping Catalogs and Guides.** One concept with a very promising future in the Internet and the Web is the world of online shopping. Every day someone I know asks me, "Can you really buy things on the Internet?" Of course you can. In fact, you can buy anything from a luxury car to a wedding gift for a friend. If your company has products for sale, you can create electronic catalogs and brochures that feature pictures and descriptions of your products. You can even offer free samples by including links that your customers can click on. The best part about featuring products on the Web is that you can include ordering information so that customers can buy your products directly from you.
- **Directories.** The world is full of directories: white pages, yellow pages, *TV Guide, Literary Marketplace,* guides to U.S. colleges, lists of books in print, concert tours for rock bands, sports schedules.... The list goes on and on. The biggest problem with most of these printed directories is that they are quickly out of date. On the Web, you can publish electronic directories that can be updated weekly, or even hourly if you have a lot of free time on your hands. A good Web-based directory can easily link to other Web sites and resources to help the user better access referenced information.
- **Research Reports and Studies.** So many interesting studies and reports have been written about the world; unfortunately, many of these reports are hidden away in library basements. You can easily turn hard-

to-find information into interesting reports, complete with illustrations and photography. You can also include information about yourself or the author of the reports so that readers can send in comments and critiques. The Web could even be a good place for you to test out your college term papers.

- **Annual Reports or Company Profiles.** Companies trying to get the word out about how well they've done throughout the year or who plan to introduce new products or services are turning to the Web in record numbers.
- **Literature, Fiction, and Poetry.** This is one of the fastest-growing corners of the Web. There are some good, interesting sites devoted to original, contemporary literature. There are a number of very interesting "ezines," as electronic magazines are called. One good place to look is at eSCENE, which displays some of the best fiction on the Internet. Their address is:

  ```
  http://www.etext.org/Zines/eScene
  ```

  If you've got a literary bent and have always wanted to start a "small press" literary magazine, now's a good time to get your publishing operation going online. To exploit the full capabilities of the Web, be sure to include photos of authors, artwork, and links to other interesting literary Web pages.
- **Online Documentation.** The Internet is jam-packed with authors of shareware and freeware programs, and one of the main reasons these authors love the Internet is that they can publish their documentation online. Instead of having to run to the printer every time they add a new feature to a program, they can simply update their online manuals. This is a great way to introduce a product to the world and keep your manufacturing and support costs down.
- **Unique Projects.** Your Web publishing venture doesn't necessarily have to be oriented toward a traditional publication venue. Because the Web provides multimedia capabilities, you can provide anything from an online science experiment to an interactive game. The Web is rife with unique sites, from the outlandish (Talk to My Cat) to the fun (the URouLette) to the educational (Dissect a Virtual Frog). Just let your imagination guide you.

If you are still not sure what you want to publish on the Web, you should spend a little more time exploring what others have done. The best part is that you can easily check out the work of others to see the mistakes they've made and "steal" some of their better ideas.

WHAT EXACTLY ARE WEB PAGES?

Before I can answer this question, there are a few concepts and terms we need to discuss so that you can keep all of this new publishing technology in perspective. Here are the four important buzzwords of Web publishing:

- Web site
- Web server
- Web page
- Home page

Anything published on the Web must physically be located on a computer somewhere. This location is called the *Web site*. It could be anywhere in the world, from Hawaii to Australia. Three pieces of hardware are needed in order for the Web site to operate: a computer, a physical connection to the Internet, and a big hard disk. In order for users to be able to access the Web site at will, it must be connected to the Internet 24 hours a day.

Many Web sites that operate as major electronic publishing centers perform other operations as well. For example, you could connect up a computer to be your Web site and then use the same computer to run reports for your company at night. However, if your Web site gets really popular, your computer might be tied up all the time.

The Web site's mission in life is to broadcast (transmit) information and this is where a *Web server* comes in. Essentially, a Web server is specialized software that transmits information from a Web site to a user's computer. When you access a location on the Web such as Netscape's home page, you are sending a message to Netscape's Web server telling it that you want some information. The server responds by sending you back files that your Web browser can read and display.

What are the primary files that Web servers transmit? Web pages of course. All documents that are published on the Web are called *Web pages*. This term is a little misleading because a Web page is really not a page per se; it is simply a document—a text file with special formatting and linking instructions. The technical term for a Web document is the infamous *HTML document*. As you'll see shortly, HTML is the heart and soul of all Web documents, including home pages.

A *home page* is simply a Web page (or HTML document) that has a special function. It is the first document that is transmitted by a Web server when you access a Web site. Let's look at an example. If you give Netscape a URL such as

```
http://www.coriolis.com
```

the Coriolis Group's home page will be transmitted by a Web server to your computer. When the server determines you are asking for something, it says "I guess they want the home page, because they didn't ask for anything specific." Now, let's assume you use a slightly different URL:

```
http://www.coriolis.com/xyz.html
```

This time around, you'll get a different Web page—the file xyz.html, because that's the file you asked for.

People who publish on the Web use home pages as their front door. A good home page invites the user to come inside, look around, and spend some time.

What's a Markup Language?

We've been talking about HTML, but we haven't properly introduced it yet. HTML stands for *HyperText Markup Language*. Let me start by stating that a detailed reference guide on HTML appears in Appendix A. In this chapter, we'll explore just the basics of HTML so that you can start constructing a cool home page using a minimum number of HTML features. In later chapters we'll go a little deeper into HTML, and you'll learn how to create more powerful Web pages. After you've finished reading all of the HTML chapters, you'll have the knowledge to create many types of Web pages and publish many different types of documents on the Web, including documents that incorporate multimedia features.

HTML is based on a language called *SGML* (Standard Generalized Markup Language), which has been around for years. Many people in the typesetting industry use it in one form or another to prepare documents for publication. HTML is actually a subset of SGML. It contains the more useful commands, which are called *tags*, for specifying how documents should be displayed and processed in Web browsers like Netscape.

If you have ever looked at what's stored in a word processor file, you've probably noticed that the file's data looks much different from what you see when viewing the file with the word processor. Within the file, you'll find special encoding data to indicate that certain text should be displayed in bold, italic, large type, double space paragraphs, and so on. This type of file stores data that is tagged with a special markup language so that a particular program will know how to interpret the data. Netscape and other Web browsers are similar to your word processor; they read a markup file and display the results on the screen in WYSIWYG (What You See Is What You Get) format. But one major difference between Web browsers, such as Netscape, and your word processor is that browsers do not write to a file; they only read from plain ASCII text files and reformat the input to produce those dramatic display effects, including both text and graphics. The other difference is that the information displayed in Web browsers is "interactive"; users can click on things that in turn cause other actions to occur.

One common misconception about HTML is the belief that it is a page layout or page description language like PostScript. HTML is actually a much simpler language and is designed to describe how documents are organized and not just how they should be displayed. For example, HTML doesn't allow you to specify the fonts you want to use in a document. It also doesn't allow you to indicate the leading (spacing) for how lines of text should be displayed. You might at first think that this is a big limitation, but it's actually a benefit in disguise. The actual formatting of HTML documents is left up to the browser program that views the document. This allows HTML documents to be interpreted and formatted in a number of different ways. The main benefit with this approach is that HTML documents can be read by a wide variety of browsers (HTML readers) running on literally every type of computer in the world. For example, if a user has a text-based browser such as Lynx running under Unix, they would be able to view the same document that a Power Mac Netscape user could view. In this respect, you can think of HTML as the universal publishing language.

GETTING STARTED

Before you start writing HTML documents and setting up a publishing center, you need to carefully plan what you want to accomplish. Otherwise, you'll end up with an assortment of documents that aren't as effective as you'd like. Publishing on the Web is a "trial and error," time-consuming activity, so you want to plan as much as you can in advance.

What Do You Want to Publish on the Web?

Okay, so you know you want to create your own Web pages. And maybe you have a general idea about what you want to include at your Web site. But unless you're only planning to create a simple "one-page" home page with maybe a graphic or two and a few links to other people's sites, you still have a lot of planning ahead of you.

The best way to begin planning is probably among the most obvious: Take a close look at what's already on the Web. But don't approach this by simply touring five or six or even a dozen Web sites at random. Purchase copies of *Wired, Internet World*, and other magazines and books that review Web sites and publish URLs. Then go visit Web sites that sound interesting.

Again, don't check out just a few sites. If you haven't yet spent a lot of time on the Web, you might not realize how easy and fast it can be to visit several sites in a relatively brief period. In two to three hours, you can easily tour 50 or more Web sites. If you haven't visited *at least* this many Web sites, you haven't even begun your homework.

When you find a Web page that is especially well designed or that has unique design concepts, print or download the page for future reference. All the elements of your pages don't have to be 100 percent original. If you borrow design concepts from other Web pages and then incorporate the best ones into your own Web pages, your published work will almost certainly look unique. In fact, your pages will look derived only if you model them based solely on one or two other Web pages, so "borrow" from as many sources as you can find.

Designing for the Web

In print media—regardless of whether we're speaking of books, magazines, newspapers, or newsletters—designing a publication is a critical, essential step. This is also true for broadcasting, although the design approach used in print and in broadcasting are a bit different.

Book, magazine, and newspaper designers and layout artists typically begin with a "dummy," which is simply a rough layout of the different components of the publication. A dummy shows where headings, body text, artwork, and other components will be placed and in what size and appearance. Often designers will come up with several dummies, or design versions, and then either select the one that seems to work best or select different elements from each dummy and "mix and match" to incorporate the best concepts from each dummy into a single design.

In broadcasting, especially in TV advertising, designers use an approach called "storyboarding." A storyboard is much like a dummy, except that a collection of storyboards is created to show the sequence of events or scenes that will make up the complete broadcast. So storyboarding just takes the dummy approach a step forward to show sequential events. In other words, storyboards show how different events relate to one another and help designers and producers determine how the events will be arranged.

In designing effective Web pages, storyboarding is practically a necessity because the interactive nature of links will have your visitors jumping from one location to another in rapid-fire succession. You need to make sure you provide plenty of clear direction on how to navigate your Web pages so that your visitors don't become lost or frustrated between one link or page and another.

Remember, storyboards don't have to be fancy; they're just rough sketches that convey design and organization concepts. You can build your storyboards by using one sheet of paper for each Web page you want to create. For each page, a storyboard page should show what graphics are displayed on that page, what kinds of text are presented, any buttons or icons and what the buttons do, what kinds of links are on the page, and any check boxes or interactive forms that your visitors can fill in.

Then, you can shuffle your paper pages around to determine how you want to sequence your Web pages. You may find that you come up with new ways to combine pages. And, of course, your Web pages can have multiple links with each other. When you have an idea of what you want, create a smaller-sized, single-page version that shows all the pages with arrows indicating the links between pages and the direction of travel, as shown in Figures 12.2 and 12.3.

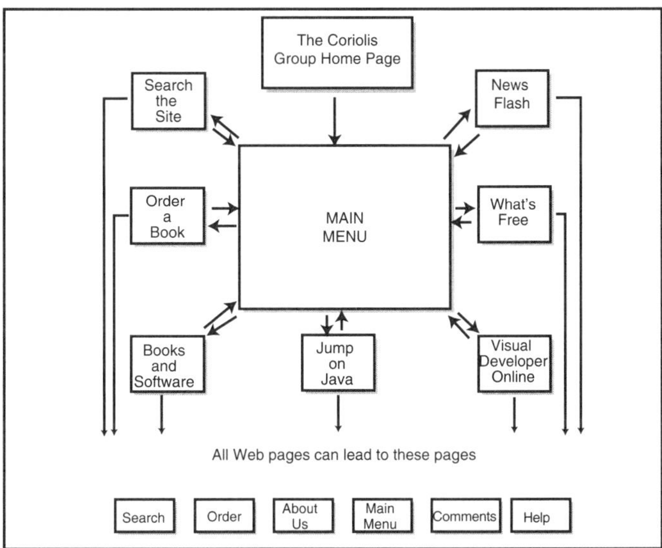

***Figure 12.2** The links at The Coriolis Group Web site.*

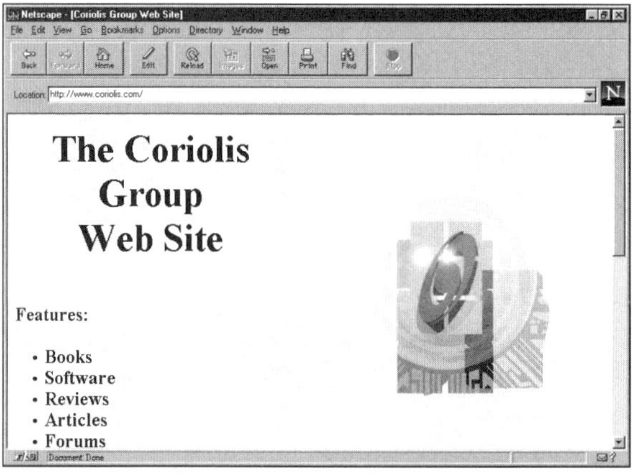

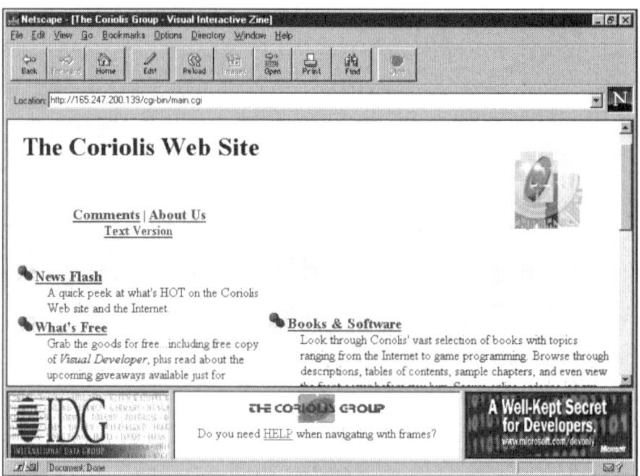

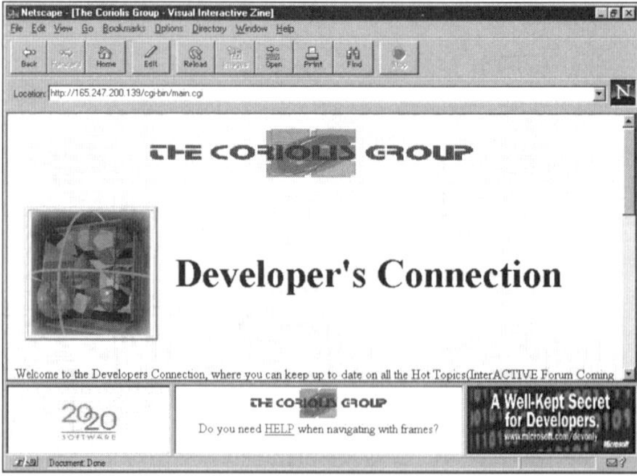

Figure 12.3 Some sample links at The Coriolis Group's site.

Time-Based Publishing

In broadcasting, each storyboard often includes a notation indicating how long the event or scene will last. (For instance, in broadcast advertising, commercials are typically 30 or 60 seconds in length. Each event has to be timed carefully and compactly.) In Web publishing, time is also an important consideration, but for a different reason: When you design Web pages, you need to consider how long it will take for each page to *load*.

This is critical! If you load up your pages with graphics, your site may become too time-intensive for most visitors to tolerate. Also, those visitors who choose to turn off the graphics will find that a graphics-intensive site typically looks flat, boring, and empty when its most important elements (all those darned graphics) are eliminated.

A better approach is to mix graphics and text carefully for an attractive balance. And keep your graphics small (in bytes, not necessarily in physical size) wherever possible, although an abundance of small graphics is just as bad as having a few large graphics.

For instance, suppose you use an attractive spherical button with a drop shadow as a link to a different page. The button is only 16 KB in size, so you figure that you're doing a good job in conserving space. Now suppose that button is the first "bullet" in a bulleted list of six items. That means you'll have six bullets for a total of 96 KB. At 14.4 Kbps, it will take about 6 to 7 seconds to load all of those bullets. That's not too terribly long a wait. But if you add the text and any other icons and graphics that you're planning to put on that page, the time begins to add up, visitor frustration mounts, and guess what? People visit your Web site once and never return. You also need to take into account that some servers are very slow during peak periods of traffic. So that 10-second maximum wait you've anticipated based strictly on baud rate and file size can double, triple, or quadruple on a slow server.

Space-Based Publishing

With print media, designers define the size of the publication up front. Because this size remains fixed, it's easy to design the layout of the publication within the specified height and width boundaries. Designing on the Web is not that simple. You need to take into account different screen sizes, because HTML tags do not include any provisions for adjusting your graphics content based on screen size. Web browsers will wrap text from one line to the next when the text reaches the right edge of the screen. But there's no way to wrap graphics, so logos and other large graphics need to be designed for small screens.

Let's say the graphical logo that appears at the top of your home screen was designed to fill the horizontal margins of a 17" monitor, and your logo reads "Great Ideas." That same logo on a 14" monitor might read "Great Id," because the right end of your logo won't fit on the screen. True, visitors can scroll to the right to read the remaining part of the logo, but they might not think to do so. Anyway, it's an annoyance to have to scroll horizontally across a screen. In general, you're safe if you design your Web pages to fit within a 14" screen.

It's also a good idea to make sure that large graphics will fit vertically on a single screen. If viewers have to scroll up and down to see different parts of a graphic, they lose the overall effect that you intended to create. It still amazes me to see so many otherwise well-designed Web pages that don't follow these simple guidelines.

Publishing with Levels

Depending on how you organize your Web pages, the links you create will either delight or confuse visitors. Because HTML makes it so easy to create links, it's just as easy for Web page designers to go a little bit overboard in the way links are placed. Sure, *you* know where each link takes you, but that's because you designed the links and the Web pages. For your visitors, the links will probably not be that intuitive. I can't tell you how many times I've visited a site and found myself linking to places I didn't want to go and being forced to use Netscape Forward and Back buttons to return to where I began and then try to find the link I *really* wanted.

This problem tends to be the most serious in Web pages that go overboard with links—where every graphic and every third word is a link to something. When you provide so many options, how can you expect your visitors to decide how to navigate effectively? They can't.

The key to effective organization of Web pages is to view the entire content of your Web site as representing a hierarchy, or series of levels. It's a lot like newspaper publishing. The first element in a newspaper article is the headline, which is designed to give readers a "feel" for what the article contains, using only a few carefully selected words to do so. After the headline comes the lead sentence, which includes general information that describes the who, what, where, why, and how of the article's content. Following the lead sentence, the most pertinent facts are presented, and the successive paragraphs contain less important and typically more specific information.

When you design the links for your Web pages, think in terms of these kinds of interest levels—moving from the general to the specific, from the most important information to the least important information. Your home page should provide general information about your Web site and briefly explain what's provided in lower-level pages. You'll then want to include links to the next two or three more specific pages at your Web site. Within these pages, you can include still more links to even more specific information or to other Web sites that provide related information.

The bottom line: Don't go crazy with links. There's an art to organizing links and Web pages, and most Web sites, unfortunately, demonstrate how few home page authors really understand this art. The key is to think like a visitor. Assume the role of a first-time visitor who knows nothing about the contents of your Web site. Then determine the easiest way to get this visitor from point A, to point B, to point C, and back to any previous page they've visited. Make sure your links and buttons are very descriptive so that your visitors know precisely where they're headed or where they're heading back to. Don't send them off to Japan when they really wanted to go to Australia.

Evaluating Your Costs

Creating a simple home page typically costs you nothing but the time it takes to design and test your work. Because most, if not all, of the software you can use to design and edit your Web pages is freeware or shareware, all you'll end up paying is the registration fee for any shareware that you decide to use on a regular basis.

However, after you've created your home page and its associated Web pages, you'll still need to store the files on a server. The big consideration at this point is whether you want your own computer to be the server or whether to locate your Web pages on somebody else's server.

Setting up a Web server on your own computer is hardly a no-brainer; in fact, entire books have been written on this topic alone. If you're just getting started in Web publishing, you probably won't feel ready to tackle the additional effort of setting up a server. Fortunately, other low-cost and free alternatives are available.

Many Web publishing entrepreneurs turn to their Internet access provider for help in establishing their Web pages. Increasingly, Internet access providers offer their customers space on their server for storing their Web page files. Although many providers will give you server space for free as an incentive to sign up or to remain with that service, this offer is typically limited to the space required to set up a single home page or a few simple Web pages. If your Web publishing plans are more elaborate than that, your provider will probably charge you a monthly fee to lease space on their server.

Unfortunately, most people who are new to Web publishing don't realize that there are a number of Web service bureaus in the U.S. and around the world whose main business is to provide server space for Web publishers. Often, these service bureaus can offer Web space at a lower cost than your own Internet access provider, and with more reliable results. Remember that you're publishing on the *World Wide Web,* so it doesn't matter where the physical server is located. It can be down the street or in Taipei, literally. Prices for server space on a service bureau's system typically begin at about $30 per month. That cost guarantees that your Web site will have uninterrupted, 24-hour access, and service bureaus can usually support many more incoming lines than a local access provider. (There's nothing more frustrating than dialing into *your own* home page stored on your local provider's server and receiving a "connection refused by host" message.)

Other costs can be incurred if you want to create elaborate Web pages that have a truly professional appearance. For this level of sophistication, you might want to enlist help from others. For instance, you might want to pay a graphic artist to help design your Web pages or to create your home page logo. The Web service bureaus mentioned above often also offer the services of professional artists and other designers to help you create your Web pages, but fees for this kind of assistance typically *start* at $30 per hour, totaling hundreds or even thousands of dollars. The question you'll want to ask is: "How much of this can I do myself and how much will require assistance?" With all the Web publishing tools now available, you'll find that you can create some fairly elaborate designs on your own.

Tools of the Trade

There are several tools available on the Web to help you create and edit Web pages, along with several tutorials and other resources designed to help new Web publishers. Most of the best Web publishing tools available are on the companion CD-ROM. For descriptions of these tools, see Appendix F. To find out about additional resources to create Web pages, take a look at Appendix D.

LET'S REVIEW

There are several benefits of Web publishing over more traditional print publishing media. When you publish on the Web, you provide a way for your audience to interact with your Web pages through links, buttons, forms, and multimedia effects. Also, you can publish on the Web with little or no assistance from others. And the cost to publish on the Web is often free or as little as the leasing fee that you pay to a company that provides you with server space. Another benefit of Web publishing lies in timeliness. You can update your Web pages at any time to ensure that they also contain the most timely and accurate information.

One great feature of the Web is that "anything goes." In deciding what to publish, remember that the Web doesn't limit you to simple text and graphics. With links, you can create a truly interactive page, and with sound and video capabilities, you can extend your publishing effort into the multimedia arena.

Designing effective Web pages takes careful planning and requires that you give some thought to the needs and expectations of your audience. Using storyboards to create rough designs for all your Web pages can be a tremendous aid in visualizing how your Web pages will be linked and how your pages can interact with your audience. And make sure you consider your visitors' hardware—especially limitations that stem from slower modems or smaller screens.

Even if you create some of the most artistic and professionally designed Web pages this side of cyberspace, they'll do you no good until you get your files up on a server system. The easiest approach is to talk to your Internet access provider about acquiring free or inexpensive space on their Web server. Also look into the possibility of leasing server space from a national or international service bureau. The costs for these services have been decreasing as competition heats up.

CHAPTER 13

The Easy Way to Create Your Own Home Page

Now that you've explored the publishing potential of the Web, it's time to learn how to grab a few moments of publishing fame by creating your own home page.

After you surf the Web for about five minutes, the next thing you'll want to do is put up your own home page. This urge seems to happen to everyone I know. I call it the *home page publishing obsession.* As soon as it happens to you, you'll start to frantically look around for information and tools to help you get your home page together.

First, you'll want to determine what you want to publish in the universe of Webspace. Perhaps you have an interesting story to tell or a great picture of yourself that you're dying to share with others. Or, you might want to put up a cool home page for your business. (In addition to acquiring fame, most Web users are frantically trying to figure out how they can make money or expand their business on the Web.) Once you gather the information for your home page, you'll need to figure out how to compose a home page document. This usually involves creating an HTML document with a text editor, but there is also a very quick way you can compose a basic home page.

Using the easy, step-by-step techniques presented in this chapter, you'll be able to create a home page in no time. Your home page can include text, images, your email address, and even links to other Web pages. The best part is that you'll be able to do all this without writing any HTML! (The program I'll present creates the HTML file for you.) You'll then be able to take your home page creations and view them with Netscape or put them on a Web server.

I'll begin this chapter by showing you a few different ways to design your home page. Of course, the techniques I'll present also apply to creating other Web pages. Then, we'll use our secret weapon—a custom program named HomePage Creator that will automatically create a home page for you. This program queries you for information and then automatically creates an HTML document. In the last part of the chapter, I'll give you a few tips to help you get your home page published on a Web server.

IS THERE A HOME PAGE IN YOUR FUTURE?

The challenging part of creating a home page is coming up with something interesting to publish on the Web. So, how do you get started? First, you'll need to get organized. Then, you'll want to create a storyboard as I suggested in the previous chapter. If you plan to eventually publish more than just a home page, you'll want to think through a rough design for all the other pages.

To get started with a simple, standalone home page, create an outline for your text and sketch out a page design for your layout. In this respect, creating a home page is no different from creating another type of document, such as a report or newsletter. The big difference with Web pages is that you have so much more to work with because of the interactive nature of the Web.

But don't get carried away. The best home pages are those that are simple and clean. I always like to get the basic structure of my Web pages up and running first, and then go back and refine them. As you are typing the text, links, and references for images into an HTML document, it's hard to visualize exactly how the finished product will look when viewed with a browser.

Of all the Web pages you create and publish, your home page is the most important. It is the front door to your Web publishing enterprise, and needs to get across a number of ideas at once, including:

- Who you are
- What you have to offer

- What you have to offer that's new (this is important in getting users to return to your home page)
- The links that you have to other Web pages
- How users can navigate with your home page and explore further
- The type of service or product you have to sell (this is required if you are a business)
- An email address for a contact person

Of course, you won't have much space to communicate all this information. If you're running tight on space, perhaps the most important information to emphasize is what's available from your home page, and an email address for a contact at your Web site.

One way to determine how you should set up your home page is to surf the Web for a while looking at examples. In fact, let's do that right now. We'll start with the simplest types of home pages and work our way up to more complex (and unusual) ones. I'll present different types of Web sites to give you some idea of the variety of Web pages that can be created. As you explore them, you might want to keep in mind how they address the six points I just explained about effective home page (and Web page) design.

Text-Based Pages (Resources)

These are the simplest kinds of pages to create. All you need is text. The benefit is that they are fast. Unfortunately, text-based pages are going the way of the dinosaur, especially now that Web publishing is becoming more commercialized.

Text-based Web pages are often used for academic sites or research groups. You can use a text-based page to publish papers, provide listings of available research grants, or even include online documentation for a product or service you provide. You could even publish your resume as a text-based home page in hopes that someone might read it and email you a job offer.

Figure 13.1 shows a good example of a text-based Web page. (This page actually provides one little image, so it's not entirely composed of text.) This page features useful links to all sorts of state agencies and departments across the U.S. This is not the kind of information you need to have at your fingertips on a daily basis, but when you need it, it's nice that one place has it all.

To explore this page, use the following URL:

```
http://www.law.indiana.edu/law/states.html
```

If you use a text-based approach like this, you must make sure that the information you present is high quality and that there is a good demand for it. Text-based pages typically serve as resource centers that are composed of links to other useful Web pages.

Typically, pages like the one shown in Figure 13.1 are organized as a hierarchical list. Publishing a document like this involves creating a simple but useful outline and then assigning links to some of the topics. If you take this approach, you'll need to make sure that you keep all of your links up to date. The main reason that users come to a Web page like this is that they believe they can quickly access reliable, up-to-date information.

Of course, the information you provide doesn't need to be boring. Here's a list of some text-based (or content-based) Web pages that provide great information with a twist.

- The TV home page with links to more TV-related sites than you could possibly surf in an evening:

```
http://www.cs.cmu.edu/afs/cs.cmu.edu/user/clamen/misc/tv/
```

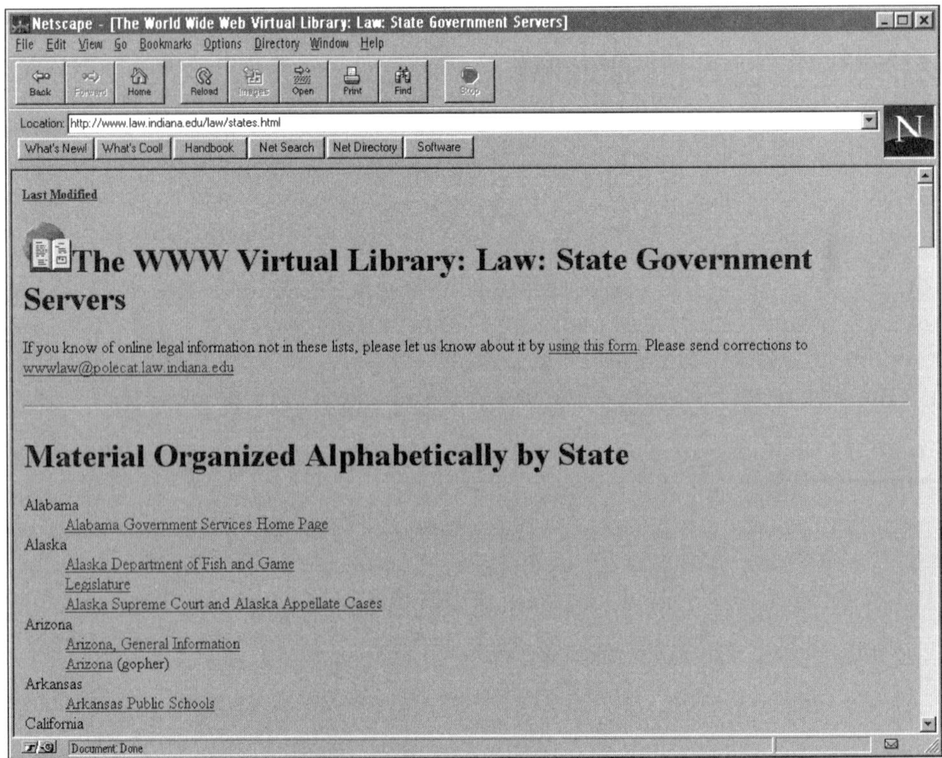

Figure 13.1 A text-based Web page.

- Zarf's list of Interactive Games on the Web (the name says it all) at:

```
http://www.leftfoot.com/games.html
```

- Interesting Places for Kids home page, which features the best resources for young Web surfers:

```
http://www.crc.ricoh.com/people/steve/kids.html
```

Personal Home Pages

Some Web publishers like to get personal. In fact, this was my approach in creating my home page, shown in Figure 13.2. Since this type of home page should make a personal statement, you can include whatever you like—photos of you, your bio, a picture of your house, the movies you've starred in, and so on.

One of the nice features about the Web is its informal and personal nature. I always enjoy surfing the Web and coming across pages by authors who have

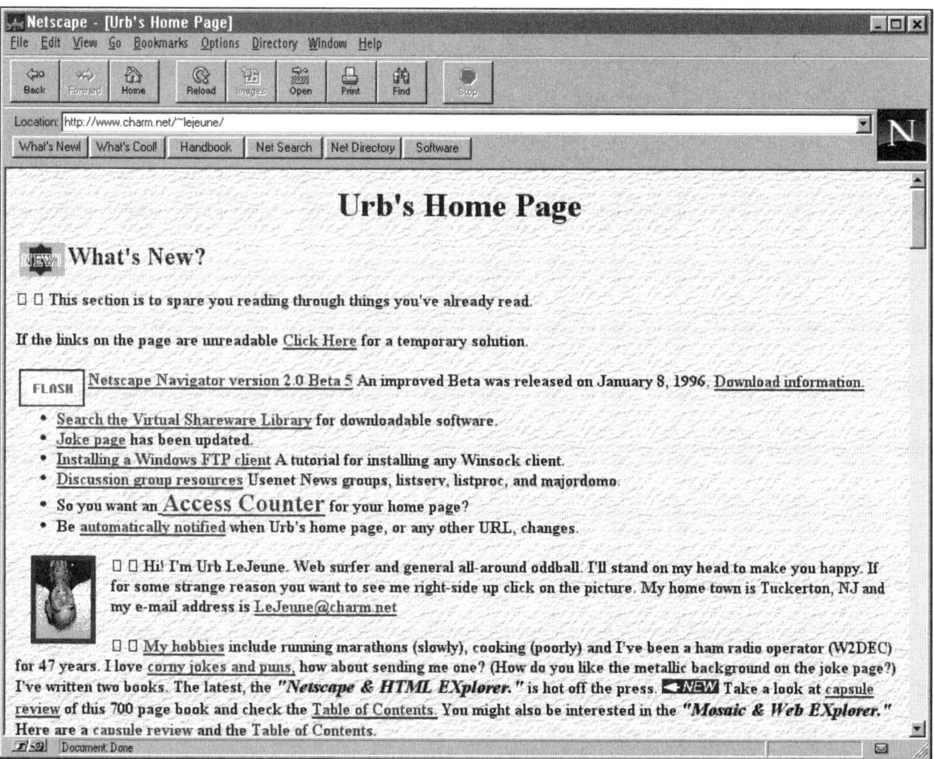

Figure 13.2 My home page.

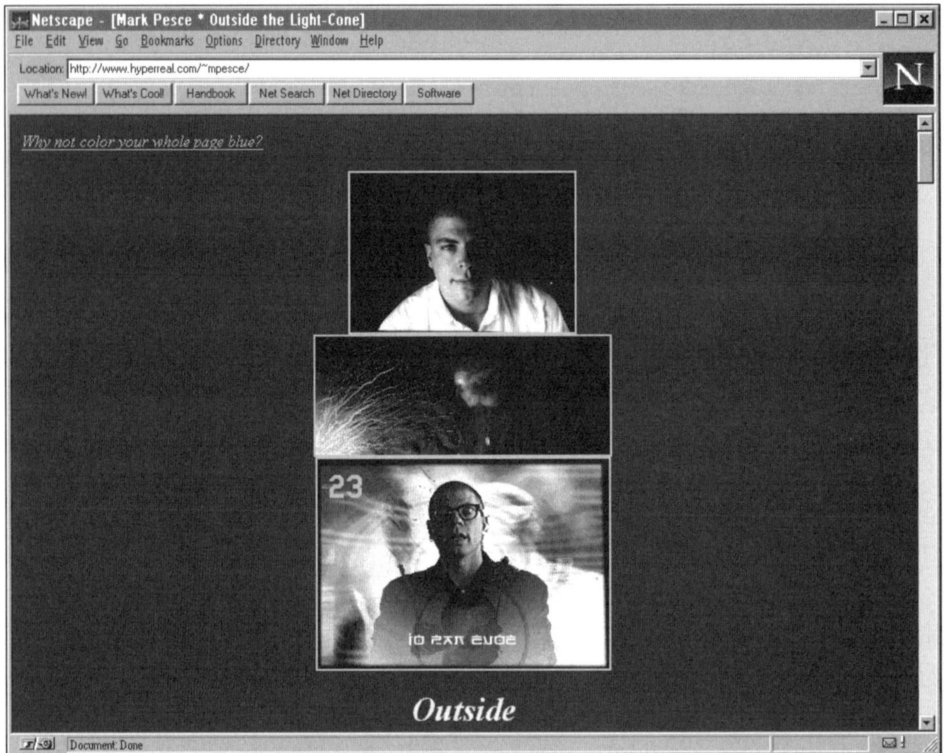

Figure 13.3 Mark Pesce's home page.

written other books or articles about the Web. Recently, I was looking into a new virtual reality language developed for the Web called VRML (http://vrml.wired.com/vrml.tech) and came across the home page of one of the developers and visionaries behind this technology. Figure 13.3 shows this home page, which you can explore by using the following URL:

```
http://hyperreal.com/~mpesce/
```

This home page works well and probably gets good traffic. Personal home pages like this typically provide links to other interesting Web pages, unusual pictures, and attention-getting writing.

Commercial Home Pages

Someone recently said that the Web is like the California gold rush. Everyone's trying to get his or her business on the Web to stake a claim and start raking in those fortunes. Commercial home pages are popping up like mushrooms. Some of them are really interesting, and others are big time-wasters.

If you want to publish a home page to promote your business or to serve as a vehicle to sell products, check out the competition. In creating this type of home page, it's important to make it clear what your business does (unless you're IBM or Microsoft). In many commercial home pages I've seen, I can't figure out for the life of me what the business does or what products or services they're trying to sell.

A commercial home page is essentially the sign in front of your business. If your business is tucked away down a side alley or the sign is not visible or attention-getting, not many people are going to walk through your door. If you're trying to get a lot of attention, you'll need good graphics and something interesting to give away or offer.

Figure 13.4 shows one commercial spot on the Web that's a big success—the Sega home page. Notice how this home page is designed to invite both new and repeat customers. The interface is very simple and friendly, the graphics are eye-catching, and it gives you the latest new right up front, to encourage customers to come back again and again. What more could you want?

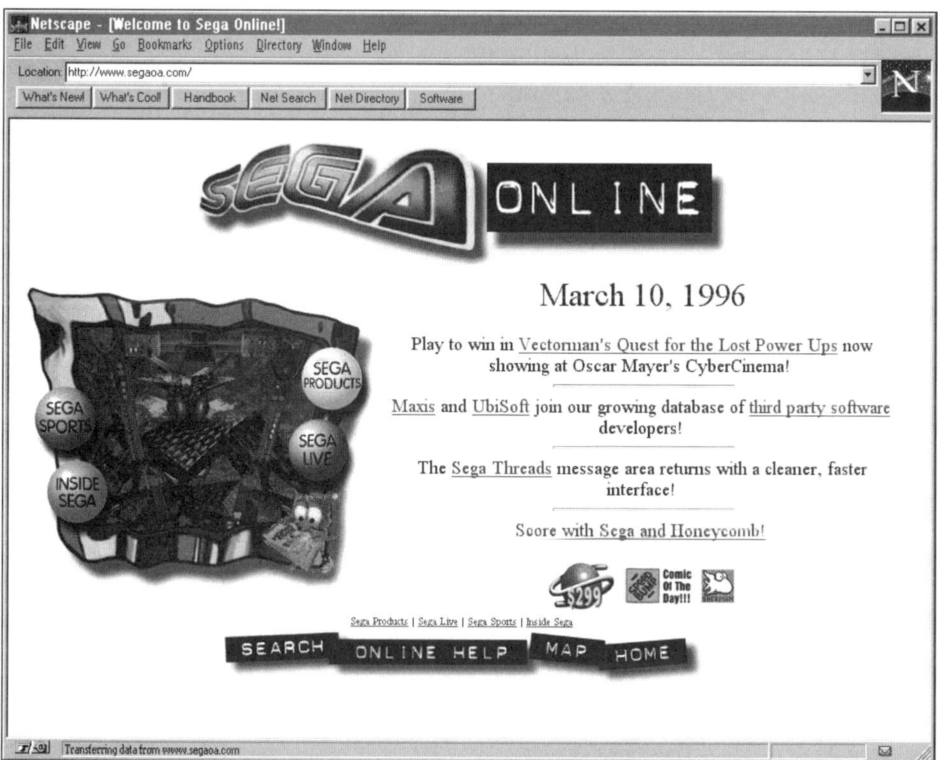

Figure 13.4 The Sega home page.

To check out the Sega home page, use this URL:

```
http://www.segaoa.com
```

Most commercial home pages provide a banner to display their company name and logo. Make this image as small as possible without losing your message. You should also consider including a short description about what your company does—but keep it as brief as possible. Some key points to broadcast include special offers you are giving (especially if you have free samples to give away or are running a contest), products or services that are new, and unique information about your products or services.

Service-Oriented Pages

You sent a package yesterday to an important client in New York. Unfortunately, the package didn't arrive in time. Where is it? Who signed for it? What

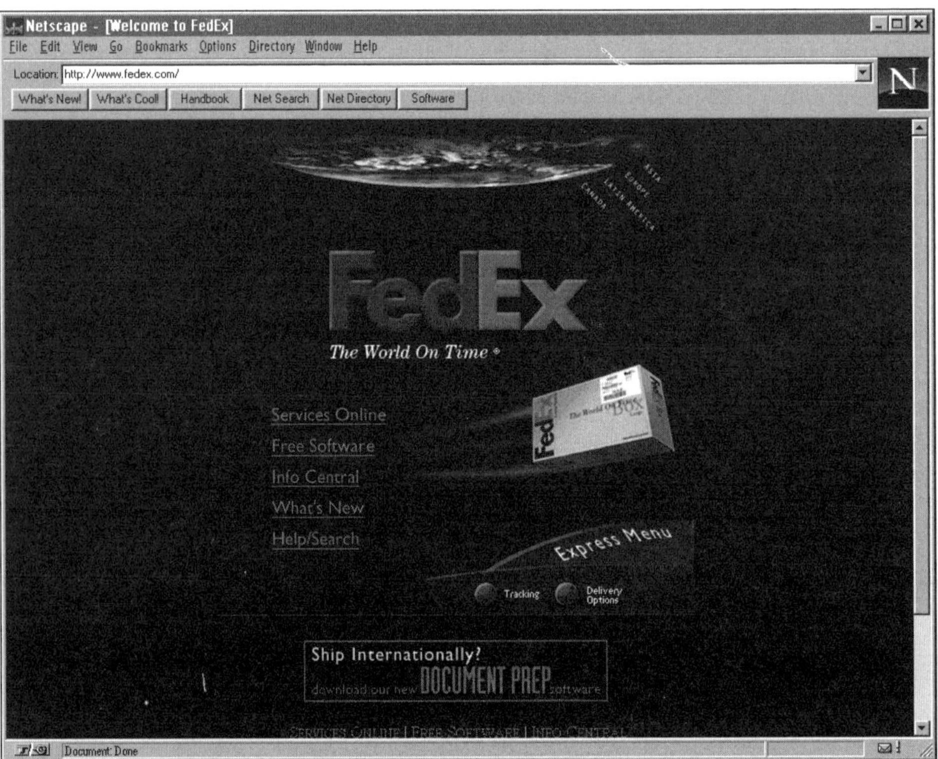

Figure 13.5 The Federal Express home page.

do you do? If you sent the package by Federal Express, you're in luck because you can go to their home page and put a trace on your package. I've used this feature many times and it really works!

Figure 13.5 shows the FedEx home page, accessible with the following URL:

```
http://www.fedex.com/
```

Typically, home pages that are designed for a service-oriented purpose are linked, in one fashion or another, to a database. They are relatively easy to design—however, they require some special CGI scripting (and possibly programming) features. For example, when you use the FedEx Web page to locate a package, a special script sends the airbill number of your package to the FedEx Web server. Then, the FedEx database is searched and a message is sent back to you.

Writing scripts for Web pages is a more advanced feature that we'll explore later in this book.

Resource-Oriented Pages

Although the Web is getting very popular with commercial enterprises, historically it was used by academic organizations. This means there are a lot of home pages that serve only one purpose—to provide free resource information for other Web users around the world. Although this category overlaps with the text-based home page category we just discussed, good resource-oriented home pages often feature navigational graphics.

One of the more helpful resource-oriented home pages is the AskERIC Virtual Library, shown in Figure 13.6. To get there, use this URL:

```
http://ericir.sunsite.syr.edu
```

Here you'll find easy access to electronic books through Project Gutenberg. Although this page uses just a few modest-sized images, they are handy navigation tools. Just click on one of them as you scroll through the page, and you'll be taken to a corresponding Web page to get more information.

Resource-intensive Web sites often incorporate visual maps, called *image maps*. In an image map, different parts of an image can link to different Web pages or sections within a Web page. This is a great technique for creating maps or visual clickable access guides to information on the Web.

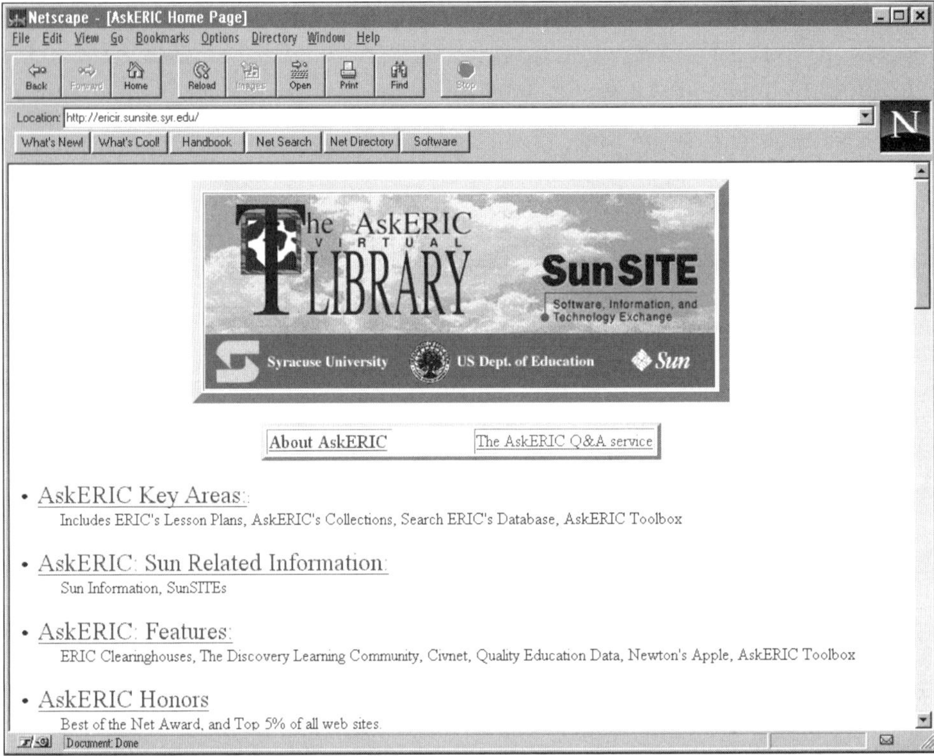

Figure 13.6 *The AskERIC Virtual Library.*

Let's look at an example. Open Text Corporation, a company with a popular search engine, uses an attractive and very functional image map on their home page, as shown in Figure 13.7. You can get to this home page by using the following URL:

```
http://www.opentext.com
```

The displayed image is a single GIF file. However, it is divided into clickable regions. For example, if you want to perform a search, you can click anywhere around the yellow arrow. If you want to see "Breaking News" on their Web site, click in the volcano image on the right hand side of the image map. And, if you're not comfortable using image maps, Open Text has corresponding text links for its users.

Image maps provide two benefits: They help make your home page more attractive and they help the user navigate. But don't fall into the trap that many Web page designers do—get caught up in the neat effects produced by

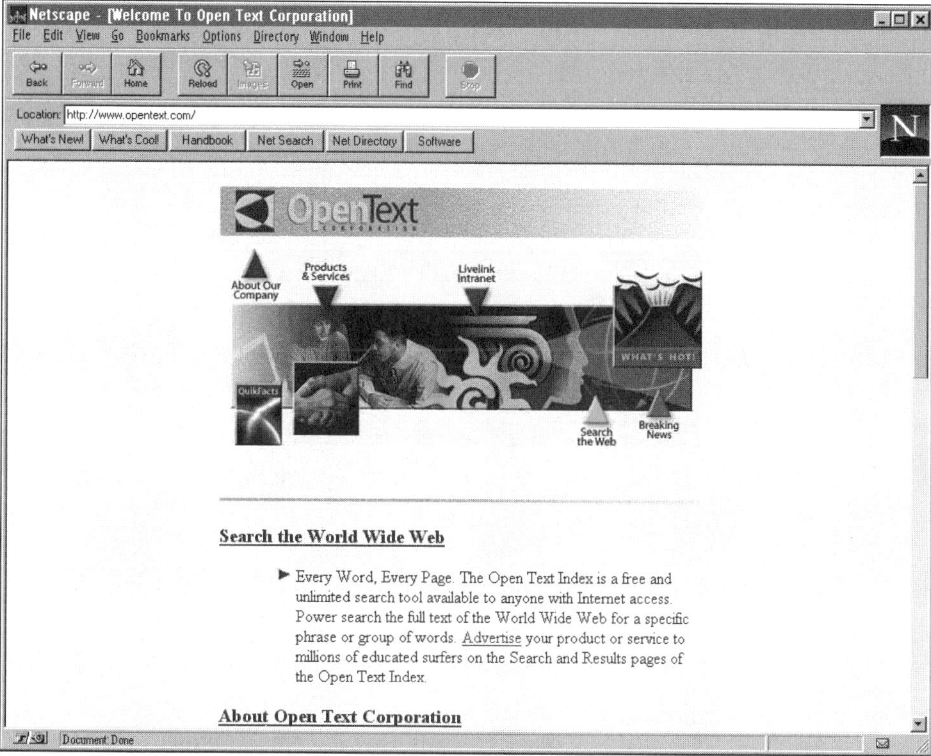

Figure 13.7 Open Text's image map.

image maps and make them way too large. I've also encountered countless image maps on home pages that are impossible to use because it isn't easily discernible what the different sections of the image link to. This defeats the whole purpose of using image maps.

Billboard Pages

In one sense, thinking of a home page as simply an electronic billboard is dumb. After all, the best feature of the Web is interactivity. On the other hand, if you have some incredible art and you want to show it off, go for it. Just keep in mind that many users won't wait for your very large images to download, especially if they've got a slow connection.

If you have the talent (and the time), you can go all out and create art that will knock people dead. Or, as one enterprising publisher thought of, you can exploit a certain celebrity and attract people to your Web site.

Entertainment and Multimedia Pages

This category is growing rapidly. The twist here is that entertainment and multimedia home pages contain multimedia goodies or run on computers that are connected to multimedia devices such as video cameras.

To create effective multimedia home pages, you need to make them as interactive as possible. You can have buttons (links) to play sounds, video, or even animation. The technology is in place for all of this now, and there are a number of home pages on the Web that provide multimedia features. The big problem is bandwidth. Many Web users are too impatient to even wait for a simple graphics image to download, let alone a video clip that could take over ten minutes to download and play.

One commercial home page that uses multimedia effectively is Windham Hill Records' home page. Its URL is:

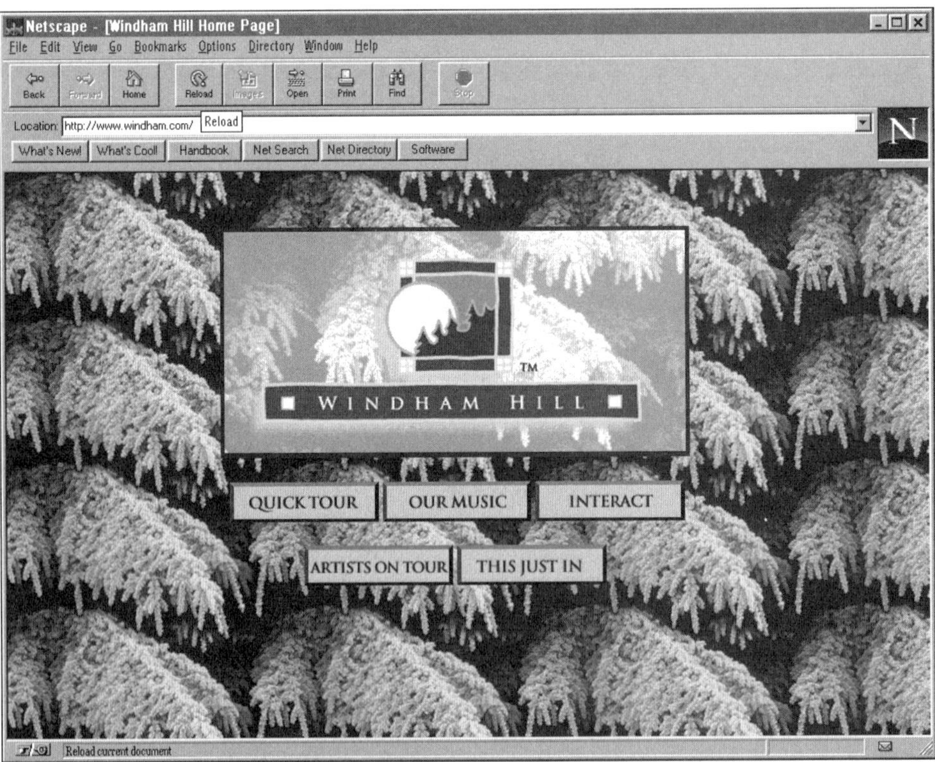

Figure 13.8 Windham Hill's multimedia efforts.

`http://www.windham.com/`

Windham Hill puts out popular CDs by talented recording artists. They are noted for having a unique "sound" in a business that doesn't always encourage creativity. Figure 13.8 shows the home page. Actually, this page doesn't directly include multimedia, but you can click on a link to select a particular recording artist. You can then listen to a sample from an artist's latest CD, or see a video clip of the artist in concert. This is the next best thing to having the artist come to your living room to put on a concert for you (if you don't mind waiting while large files are downloaded).

Another unique, emerging multimedia publishing approach combines interactive CD-ROMs with information published on the Web. The idea here is to link the relative static world of multimedia CD-ROMs that run on PCs with the dynamic universe of the Web. With this approach, you can run multimedia software on a CD-ROM and then have it access the Web to get additional content or to view dynamic Web pages. This approach to multimedia publishing opens up all kinds of design possibilities.

Humor-Oriented Home Pages

Everyone loves to have a good laugh, so why not use humor as the main theme of your home page? Here are some ideas that come to mind:

- Jokes page
- Cartoon-based page
- Humorous quotations page
- What's wrong with this picture page
- Outrageous headlines in the media page
- Political spoofs page
- Wacky (or really stupid) FAQs page

If you have a talent for drawing cartoons, funny pictures, or writing snappy copy, your home page could be a big hit. Figure 13.9 shows a very successful cartoon home page I came across recently. It's called *Where the Buffalo Roam* and features weekly cartoons created by Hans Bjordahl for the *Colorado Daily*. Here is the URL:

`http://plaza.xor.com/wtbr/`

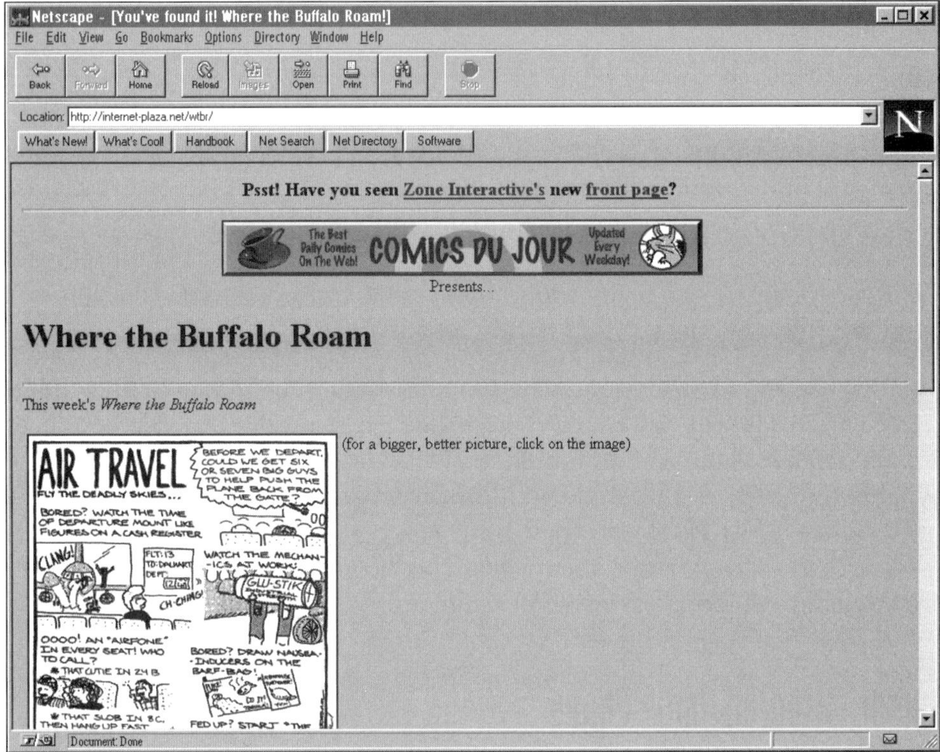

Figure 13.9 *Hans Bjordahl's weekly comic strip.*

Weird Home Pages

If you're looking to shock people, you'll need to come up with something *really* weird—the competition is stiff in this category. One popular, unusual home page is "Talk to my Cat." As the name suggests, this home page lets you talk to some guy's cat. Figure 13.10 shows the page created by Michael Witbrok. This home page allows you to type messages that are then spoken to Michael's cat. Evidently, the computer running this home page is hooked up to a speech synthesizer, which "speaks" the messages that users type. You can also read the messages that other users have posted.

To check out this home page, point your browser to:

```
http://queer.slip.cs.cmu.edu/cgi-bin/talktocat
```

What are the guidelines for creating a weird home page? The sky's the limit.

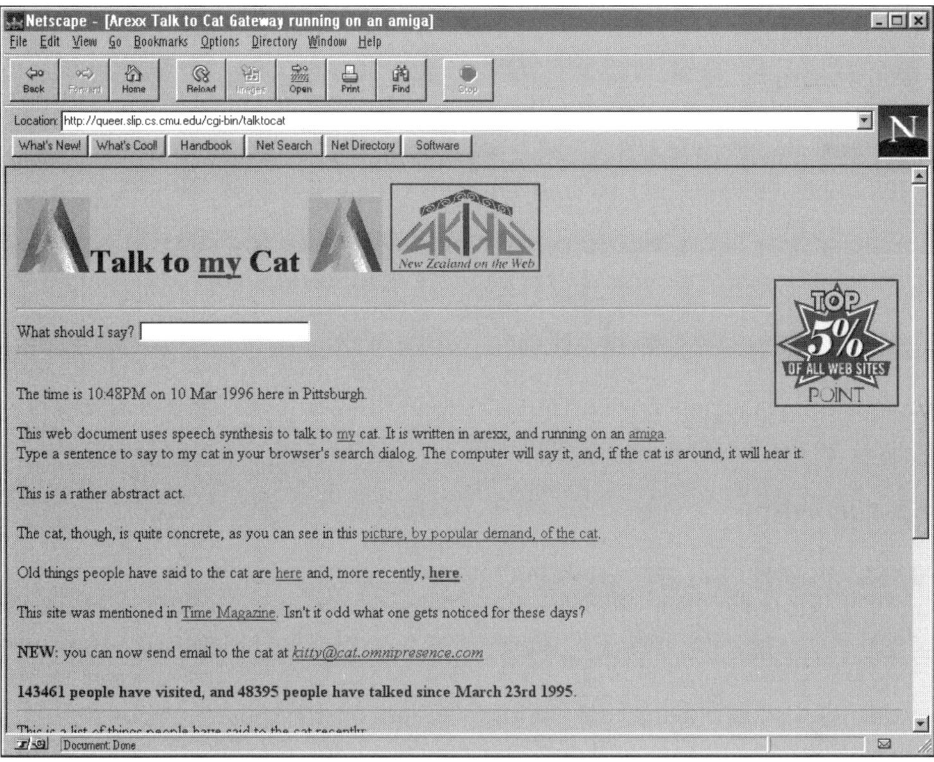

Figure 13.10 *Ever wanted to talk to a cat? Here's your chance.*

HOME PAGE DESIGN 101

A wise saying coined years ago by a great architect sums up what we've been discussing about creating effective home pages: "Form follows function." Because of the highly interactive nature of home pages in particular and Web pages in general, a good design must do double duty. It must interest the user *and* allow the user to do something. If people land on your home page and the information presented doesn't get their attention or they don't know what to do next, your home page has failed.

I don't pretend to be an expert home page or graphics designer. The one thing I know is that there are about as many different home page design styles as there are actual home pages, but if you surf the Web long enough, you'll start to notice some general design principles that really work. (And you'll notice some techniques that really turn people off!)

Simple Is Good

Your first attempt might be to include everything you can think of in your home page. Stop right there, especially if you want other people to spend time at your home page and come back. Experienced designers are fond of repeating this word to designer newbies: KISS. It stands for Keep It Simple, Stupid.

A home page is like a New York apartment. You need to make the most out of the small space you have. Don't clutter it with information or pictures you don't really need—save them for another Web page.

If you start with very little, you can always add more. If you start with too much, you'll get attached to the information or the *way the information looks,* and you won't want to take things out.

Focus Is Better

Don't try to cover too much ground with your home page or any of your Web pages. If you have a lot of information to present, use one Web page as an entry point to link to other Web pages you provide. Try to come up with one strong theme or message and stick with it. If you're not careful, your home page will be so confusing that people will just pass it by.

Fast Is Best

I can't think of anything that annoys Web surfers more than Web pages that are really slow to load. The more stuff you put on your home page, the longer it will take to download, the longer the user will have to wait, and the less often the user will come back to see your page.

When designing your home page, try to imagine your typical user surfing the Web at home on a 9600 baud modem (and during the commercial breaks of *Seinfeld* or at work when nobody's looking). If your home page needs to download ten minutes of data (text files, graphics files, and so on) when it first comes up, you're dead.

Many Web page publishers use fast connections, such as ISDN or T1, and they forget what it's like to access the Web with a slow modem. If you fall into this category, buy a 9600 baud modem and use it to test your home page. If it is too slow, simplify it.

If you can't simplify your Web page, offer a fast text-based version. Include a short message and link right at the top of your home page so that users can click on it and get the text version. But make sure you put the message and link before any graphics appear. Many home pages display a big, time-intensive image at the top of their home page and then they include a message at the bottom that says:

```
Click here for a text-only version.
```

Is this stupid, or what?

If You Provide a Text Version, Go All the Way

This tip comes from Vince Emery, author of *How to Grow Your Business on the Internet.* If your home page links to other Web pages at your site, don't just provide a text-only version of the home page. Otherwise, a user will access the text-only home page and click on a link to another Web page that contains a lot of graphics. The way to avoid this is to provide text-only versions of all your Web pages. This is more work, but your users will thank you by coming back.

Take a cue from magazine publishers. Years ago, magazine articles were long and very narrative. Today, most magazines provide much shorter articles with sidebars. Is it because people don't read any more? I don't think so. Publishers do this because people are overloaded with information, and prefer their information in bits and pieces.

Alternate Images and Text

If you use a lot of images, try my alternating method of first displaying a page with images, then a page that is text-based. For example, your home page could be displayed with a useful navigation image. When users click on a link, take them to a page that is more text-oriented. This way, users will see a much faster response time when they access the second page. Of course, to do this you'll need to first plan the organization of your links.

Truly inconsiderate designers create Web pages that display one time-intensive image after another. I hate clicking on a link after accessing a slow home page only to discover that I have to wait another five minutes to get to the actual information. Perhaps when *all* users are connected to the Web at high speeds, these issues will fade. But for now, do everything you can to get your user moving through your Web pages as quickly as possible.

Make Your Pages Readable

Netscape supports a feature called *backgrounds.* With it, you can add a neat background pattern to your home page. (I'll show you how to do this later in the book.) Unfortunately, Web publishers immediately went crazy and put backgrounds on everything. Overnight, already hard-to-read Web pages became *impossible* to read.

The moral of this story is *do everything you can to make your pages more readable.* Forget all of the neat visual effects if they get in the way of your message. For many people, text is difficult to read on a computer screen, especially when they have to scroll through pages and pages of small type.

Come Up with an Angle

If you want other people to visit your home page (outside of your immediate family), you'll need an angle. This means you need to think like a marketing person. The Web is becoming crowded with new home pages, and it's getting harder to attract people to a new site. And this electronic publishing traffic jam is bound to get much worse before it gets better.

Try to think of a strategy that no one else has considered. This is your chance to unleash your creativity. If you are really stuck and can't come up with a good angle, try my favorite standby of the three best attention-getting words in the English language: "Win Free Sex." Seriously, think marketing. If you're not good at this, befriend people who are; take them out to dinner (marketing people love to spend time in restaurants) and make them give you an angle.

Use the Newspaper Approach

Reporters and designers at newspapers understand the main principle of presenting lots of information without losing their readers' interest. Here's the principle: Information is hierarchical in nature. When you scan a newspaper, the first thing that gets your attention is a headline:

"Giant Toads to Inherit the Earth"

Then, you start to read on:

"Scientists today announced recent findings: the population of giant toads is increasing 400 percent per year—a growth rate that will allow them to take over the earth by 1997. Top scientists from around the world attended the Chicago meeting, which made public the finding of a recent two-year survey..."

The goal is to present information in descending levels of detail. The general attention-getting stuff comes first. Then, the story starts and some of the details emerge. As you continue reading the story, you'll learn about a bunch of other facts. Often, you don't really care about all of the details, so you stop after the first few paragraphs. When was the last time you read a newspaper article from beginning to end?

The hierarchical approach is a good way to set up your home page and other pages that you link to on your Web site. Most users who read your pages will read the highlights. A much smaller percentage will click on links and examine the details. But that's okay—you've designed your pages with that in mind. Right?

Don't Ignore Your Links

As we learned in the previous chapter, users who come to your home page may often be more interested in where your page can take them than what you have to say. Here are some tips to help give your users *more* of what they want:

Add new links as often as you can. To keep users coming back, you'll want to offer new links at least once a week. (Some sites that are really popular provide new links daily!) If you're not convinced, just think of the reason you drive across town to your favorite store at the mall—you want to see what new goodies they have to offer. If the store stopped adding new products, you'd probably find a better place to spend your money.

Don't provide links to the same Web pages everyone else links to. Try to come up with the best links you can. Sure, you might want to provide a few of the links to popular pages like What's Cool on the Web or Yahoo, but don't neglect newer, out of the way places that are useful or interesting. Every time you surf the Web and find something that really grabs your attention, link your home page to it for a while.

Keep your links up to date. Things move around on the Web about as often as political leaders change their position on an issue. Don't let your links get rusty. Test them regularly. Think of this as a "must-do" activity, like backing up your hard disk. If you don't come up with a system and follow it religiously, you're asking for trouble.

Provide a good description for each link. Every link should have a description—and the description should be accurate. Recently I came across a home page that provided a link labeled "Cool places to explore in Hawaii." I clicked on the link and up came some boring Web page about government offices located in the Hawaiian Islands. Did I feel ripped off or what? I thought I was going to get pictures of secluded beaches or tips on locating secret waterfalls. Instead I got a listing of the hours for the Department of Motor Vehicles in Maui—what's so cool about that?

List file sizes for links that download files. Many Web pages provide links that will automatically download a file when the link is selected. The only problem is that the user's time might be limited and he or she won't know how long the download will take before the link is selected. You can really make your users happy by using labels like this for your downloadable file links:

```
Transcripts from the O.J Simpson trial (200 Mb)
```

THREE WAYS TO CREATE A HOME PAGE

There are three techniques you can use to create your own home page:

- Use HomePage Creator. (This requires no knowledge of HTML on your part.)
- Find a Web page that's similar to the one you want to create, obtain the HTML document, and then change it to meet your needs.
- Start from scratch using a text editor or special-purpose HTML editor that automatically creates a shell document for you.

The method you use depends on your personal preference and, of course, the amount of free time you have. But I think it's a good idea to look at all three of these approaches to gain a better understanding of HTML and the techniques involved in creating Web pages.

In this chapter I'll show you how to use the first method. Although somewhat limited, it will get you started in a flash. After we create a home page in this manner, we'll dig in and start writing our own HTML instructions in the next chapter.

Creating Your First Home Page with HomePage Creator

When my good friend Demetris Kafas, kafas@mars.superlink.net, was starting to get interested in the Web, I told him about Web publishing with HTML. Coming from a programming background, he was soon fascinated with HTML. "Isn't there a program that creates a basic home page?" he asked innocently one evening. To my knowledge there wasn't a tool available. I really set the hook when I told him, "If you really want to learn HTML, write a program that

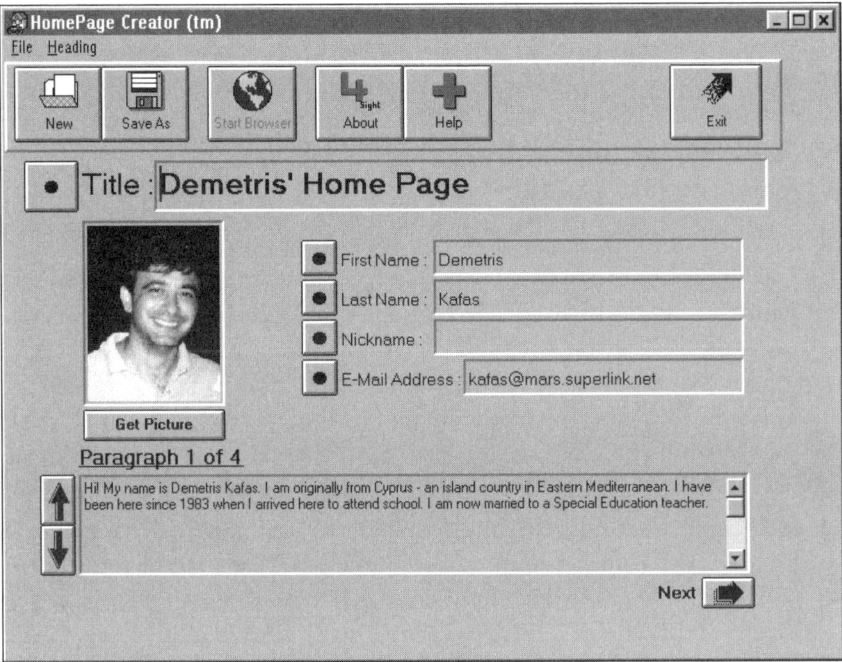

***Figure 13.11** The opening screen of HomePage Creator.*

creates an HTML document." Soon thereafter he created a program called HomePage Creator (HPC).

What does HPC do? It builds a simple home page without requiring you to write any HTML. The program queries you for information for your home page and then presto, it creates the HTML document for you. This is a good place to start, especially if you want to learn HTML. You can use HPC to create a basic home page (HTML document) and then modify the document to your liking.

HPC presents a series of text boxes for you to enter your name, email address, and so on. It also allows you to enter a GIF file name for displaying a picture as well as a few paragraphs to tell the world all about yourself. You can even include some of your favorite URLs to link to other Web pages.

Let's put this easy-to-use tool to work. First, you'll need to install it on your hard disk. To do this, run the SETUP.EXE program in the directory \tools\hpc on the companion CD-ROM. The setup program will ask you to provide the drive name where you want to install HomePage Creator. The setup program will then copy all of the files you need to your hard drive.

Start HPC by clicking on the program icon provided in the Windows Program Manager. Figure 13.11 shows the first screen that HPC displays. With this screen you can enter the following elements in your home page:

- A main heading
- A picture
- Your name
- Your email address
- Up to four paragraphs of plain text

If you make a mistake while entering information, don't worry—you can delete it and enter the text correctly. To get to the second page in HomePage Creator, click on the right arrow (Next) button displayed at the bottom of the window. Figure 13.12 shows the standard "favorite spots" default listing, which is displayed for the second screen. This is where you can add your own links to other Web pages. To change or insert a link, click on one of the buttons to the left of the site names that are displayed. HomePage Creator will then

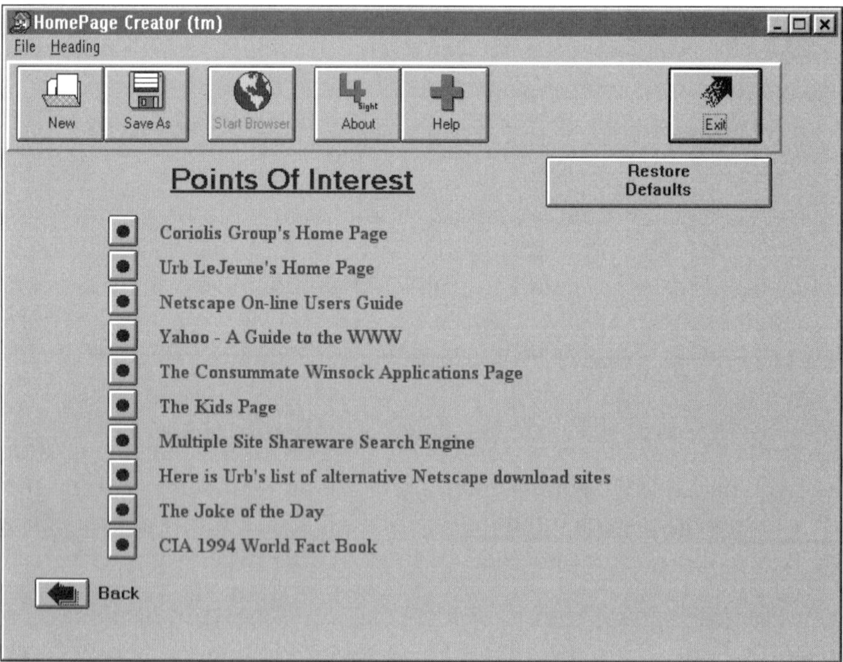

Figure 13.12 *The default favorite links page of HomePage Creator.*

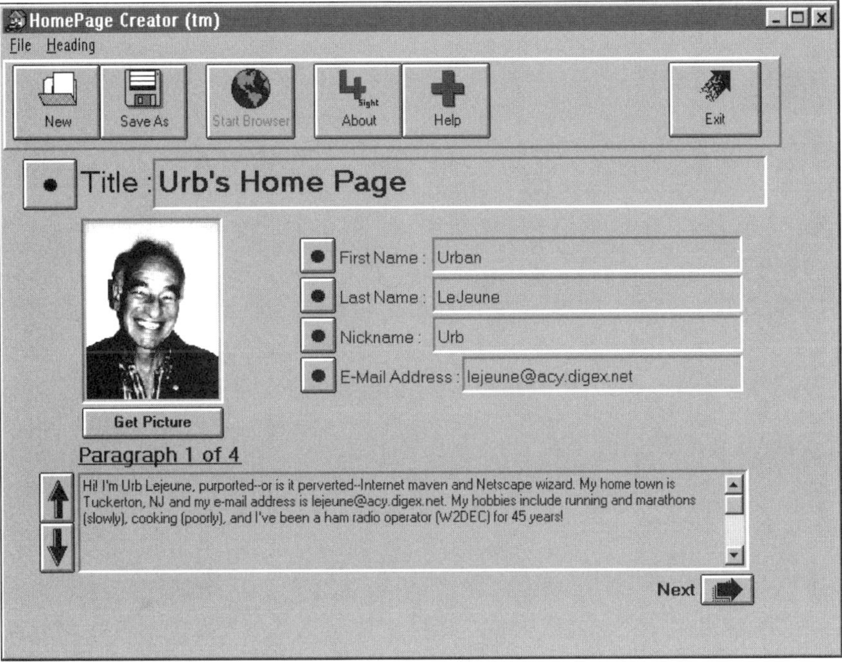

Figure 13.13 *Data just waiting to become a home page.*

display the Site Editor dialog box that you use to enter both a site name and its URL. That's all there is to it.

Let's go to the first screen and fill in enough information for a basic home page. First, click on the New icon button to clear all the existing fields. Next, you can add a picture by clicking on the Get Picture button. This action displays the standard Windows Open File dialog box. This is where you select the name of the GIF file you want to display.

Figure 13.13 shows all the data that I entered to create my basic home page, including some personal information, my GIF file name, my address, and an introductory paragraph. After you enter your information, click on the Save As button to bring up the standard Windows Save As dialog box. Make sure you specify a file name for your HTML document and save it by clicking the OK button. If you want to insert some of your own Web pages as links, make sure that you click on the Next button and use the Site Editor to put in the names and URLs for your links.

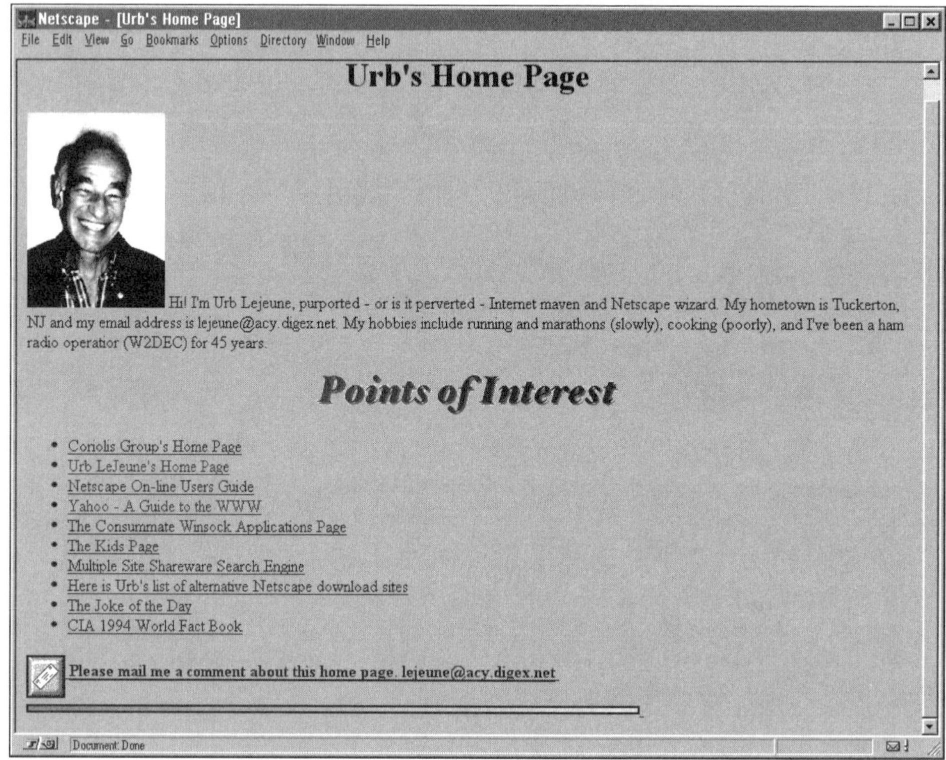

Figure 13.14 *The final product—my home page.*

Figure 13.14 demonstrates the output created by HPC. The GIFs, other than your picture, are included with the program. The actual HTML output created by HPC for my home page data is in Listing 13.1.

Listing 13.1

```
<HTML>
<HEAD>
    <TITLE>Urb's Home Page</TITLE>
  </HEAD>

  <BODY>

    <CENTER><H1>Urb's Home Page</H1></CENTER>
    <IMG ALT="Urb's Home Page's picture usually goes here" SRC="URB.GIF">

    Hi! I'm Urb Lejeune, purported - or is it perverted - Internet
   maven and Netscape wizard.  My hometown is Tuckerton,
   NJ and my email address is lejeune@acy.digex.net.  My
   hobbies include running and marathons (slowly), cooking
   (poorly), and I've been a ham radio operatior (W2DEC)
   for 45 years.
```

```
    <P>

    <CENTER><IMG SRC="poi.gif"></CENTER><P>
    <UL>
      <LI><A HREF="http://www.coriolis.com/">
          Coriolis Group's Home Page</A>
      <LI><A HREF="http://www.charm.net/~lejeune/">
          Urb LeJeune's Home Page</A>
      <LI><A HREF="http://home.mcom.com/home/online-manual.html">
          Netscape On-line Users Guide</A>
      <LI><A HREF="http://www.yahoo.com">
          Yahoo - A Guide to the WWW</A>
      <LI><A HREF="http://bongo.cc.utexas.edu/~neuroses/cwsapps.html">
          The Consummate Winsock Applications Page</A>
      <LI><A HREF="http://www.pd.astro.it/kids.html">
          The Kids Page</A>
      <LI><A HREF="http://www.fagg.uni-lj.si/cgi-bin/shase">
          Multiple Site Shareware Search Engine</A>
      <LI><A HREF="http://www.charm.net/~lejeune/get-net.html">
          Here is Urb's list of alternative Netscape download sites</A>
      <LI><A HREF="http://bazaar.com/Jokes/jokeoftheday.html">
          The Joke of the Day</A>
      <LI><A HREF="http://www.ic.gov/94fact/fb94toc/fb94toc.html">
          CIA 1994 World Fact Book</A>
    </UL>
    <A HREF="mailto:lejeune@acy.digex.net">
    <IMG ALIGN=CENTER SRC=mailbutt.gif>
    <B>Please mail me a comment about this home page.
    lejeune@acy.digex.net</B>
    <IMG SRC=line.gif>    </A>
  </BODY>
</HTML>
```

Is this a piece of cake, or what? We've just created our very own home page without needing to know any HTML. This is the way Web publishing should be. Unfortunately, HomePage Creator can't do everything for us. You can, of course, take the HTML file created by HomePage Creator and add more to it.

GETTING PUBLISHED ON THE WEB

Now that you know how to create your own basic home page, you're probably anxious to publish on the World Wide Web so that the rest of the world can view your information. For many Netscape users, this is a frustrating task. The Web is like the "wild west"—there are very few set standards for Internet service providers.

When I got into Web surfing, I lucked out. I was fortunate enough to have an account on Baltimore's Charm Net, where the forward-thinking folks managing this Internet provider allow all account holders access to a Web server so that they can show their home page to the world. The temptation to publish on the Internet was too much for me to resist, so I was up and running in no time.

To be "published" on the Web simply means that your HTML documents are available for other Web surfers to view. If you create a cool home page and just store it on your computer, no one will be able to view it unless you physically travel around the world and show it on your laptop computer. Obviously, you won't get very far with this approach. You'd be better off trying to find an Internet service provider to help you go public with your Web creations.

If your company has its own direct connection on the Internet, you'll need to talk to the person in charge of your system's administration. He or she should be able to tell you everything you need to do to get set up. If you ask nicely (sometimes a gift of chips and salsa does the trick), the administrator will probably set up everything for you. Usually, this is simply a matter of creating a directory on a Unix machine or Windows NT and uploading a few files.

If you are considering using a service provider, the first thing you should do is ask if they can supply you with a Web server. If they can't, you'll need to look elsewhere. If they provide server capabilities but want to charge you an arm and a leg to get your home page on their server, tell them you'll trade them server space for the Brooklyn Bridge. Putting up a home page on someone else's server shouldn't be expensive—all that's required is a little storage space and a few setup instructions. Don't let anybody tell you otherwise.

If your service provider allows you to put up your own home page, you shouldn't have too much trouble getting set up. Let me walk you through a typical setup so that you can see what is involved. Of course, the actual details will vary a little, depending on which service provider you are using.

Setting Up Your Home Page with a Service Provider

Most service providers (if they are at all organized) will supply you with a set of instructions for getting your home page up on their system. In fact, you might find a reference to such a document by viewing the service provider's home page. If you can't find the information you need, call them. (That's why they are there—to provide you with service!)

Your provider will likely charge you for the space that your HTML and other documents take up on their computer. So, if you are just doing this for fun, don't go wild with your GIF files—you might get a big bill at the end of the month.

Once you have your home page HTML file and other necessary files, you'll need to get them on your provider's computer. This usually involves three steps:

1. Create a directory under your home directory (on their computer) to store your Web documents. This directory might have a name like *public_html.* This is the place that the Web server goes to locate your files. The directory must be named properly and set up with the appropriate permissions. (Your service provider will fill you in on the details.)
2. You must name your home page using a predetermined name. Many servers use the file name index.html. (Remember, your files will probably be stored on a Unix computer and Unix uses different file name conventions than DOS.)
3. Upload your home page and other required Web documents to your newly created directory.

Keep in mind that these steps are typically completed by using Unix commands. The process involves logging on to your service provider's computer using your shell account and then executing some commands at a text prompt. Some service providers are even smart enough to give you a script to help you automate the process of setting up your Web document's storage area. For example, they might provide you with a script like

```
makehtml
```

which creates a directory for you and sets up the necessary server configuration so that you can be up and running in no time.

LET'S REVIEW

How's that for a crash course on creating a home page and getting it published on the Web? Of course, this is just a start—there are many other issues involved in creating HTML documents and Web publishing. Hopefully this is enough to whet your appetite so you'll continue to explore the other important HTML and Web publishing chapters in this book.

At its most basic level, Web publishing involves creating home pages, which in turn are written as HTML documents. HTML documents are text files that you can create with a text editor or a program like HomePage Creator.

Before you create your own home page, you'll want to create an outline for the content of your home page. A simple home page can include text, graphics, and links to other Web pages. With HomePage Creator, you can easily create your own home page (HTML document) by entering information into the program. The best part is that *you don't need to know any HTML to create a working home page.* HomePage Creator produces an HTML document, which you can use as is, or modify with a text editor or a special-purpose HTML editor.

To publish your home page on the Web, you'll need access to a Web server. Many Internet providers allow you to put up your own Web pages. To learn how to do this, you should ask your service provider for instructions.

Creating Web Pages with HTML

It's time to learn how to create your own Web pages from scratch, using HTML.

If you're like most budding Web publishers, you'll want to learn as much about HTML as possible so that you can publish better pages on the Web. Once you master the basics of HTML, you'll be amazed at how quickly you can create nice looking Web pages with hyperlinked text, graphics, and even multimedia features like sound, video, and animation. The best thing about working with HTML is that you can look at thousands of Web pages and easily examine the HTML used to create them. All you need is your Netscape browser and a little free time.

In this chapter, we'll take a close look at HTML from the perspective of creating Web pages. Actually, we'll return to the topic of creating the types of home pages introduced in the previous chapter. We'll explore how home pages can be created by either modifying other HTML documents or writing HTML documents from scratch. To start, we'll borrow an HTML document from another Web site.

As we build a new version of our home page, you'll learn about the structure of HTML documents and some of the basic HTML features, including character and paragraph formatting, headings, images, and hotlinks. You'll be surprised at how little HTML you need to know to get up and running. If you make a mistake during the process of creating your home page using HTML, no problem. You can easily fix it using your favorite word processor or special-purpose HTML editor and test your updated version with your Web browser. To make it easier for you to create and edit your HTML documents, I'll also show you how to use a visual HTML editor called HTML Notepad. This editor is very useful because it provides special features for creating HTML tags.

HTML FOR WEB PUBLISHING

When you first look at an HTML document like the one we created in the previous chapter with HomePage Creator, it's hard to see the correlation between the HTML instructions and a visual Web page. This takes some getting used to. As I mentioned before, HTML is not a language designed to describe page design or layout. Its strength is in describing how documents are organized and how they should link to other documents.

If your background is in traditional desktop publishing using programs like PageMaker, you'll need to adopt a different mindset to succeed with HTML. Basically, you need to keep in mind that HTML authoring involves working at a more basic command level. Many of the design and layout tasks that can be automated with programs like PageMaker require actual coding with HTML. For example, with PageMaker you can put a word in bold type by selecting the word and clicking on a bolding option. In HTML, you need to write a special instruction called a *tag* to put a word in bold type. In this respect, HTML is a step backwards in the evolution of electronic publishing.

Fortunately, due to the popularity of Web publishing, HTML is evolving very quickly. Many automated Web publishing tools are in development and new features are continually being added to the current HTML standard. Even if you eventually have an automated tool that creates all of the HTML documents you need to publish on the Web, you'll want to understand how HTML documents are structured and how to write your own HTML commands. After all, if you want to "borrow" ideas from other Web publishers, you'll need to be able to read and understand their HTML documents.

What Is HTML 3.0?

If you've done much surfing on the Web or spent any time hanging out with people who publish on the Web, you've probably heard the term *HTML 3.0*. HTML 3.0 is essentially HTML with added features. Whenever new computer languages' are unleashed on the world, those who use them come up with a million ideas for new features. Of course, HTML is no exception. Some of the new features include:

- Tables
- Mathematical equations
- Text that can flow around images
- Figures with captions
- More sophisticated links so that you can create "guided tours"

Remember, though, that if you use some of the HTML 3.0 features, such as tables and "flowable" text, not all Web browsers will support them.

Many of the HTML 3.0 features are so useful that I can't live without them. When I introduce them, I'll take special care to identify and point them out.

Learning HTML

The best way to learn how to create HTML documents (outside of using the HomePage Creator program introduced in the previous chapter) is to compose an HTML document that will become your home page. Even if you don't have access to a Web server yet, you can still view your home page with Netscape, or another browser such as Mosaic, and show it off to your friends. If you later get access to a Web server, all you'll need to do is upload your HTML files. (See the previous chapter for suggestions on how to do this.)

I'm a big believer in learning new things by looking at what others have done. After all, why reinvent the wheel? Fortunately, the Web is full of many great (and some not so great) examples of home pages and HTML documents. And the best part is that you can easily check out the HTML documents used for any Web pages you locate. When an interesting display technique catches your eye, you can view or save its HTML document by using Netscape. Before we create any of our own HTML documents, let's go out and get the HTML document for the Charm Net home page.

Charm Net HTML Here We Come

In this project, we'll travel to Charm Net's home page and save the HTML for this page as charmnet.htm. We'll also get the GIF files this home page uses and save them as well. This way, you can later view and modify the home page without having to go online to the Web. If you have already grabbed these files by following the projects in the previous chapter, you're all set.

The Charm Net home page uses a variety of interesting HTML styles and effects. To get this home page's HTML document, use the following URL:

```
http://www.charm.net/
```

Fire up Netscape and enter this URL in the Location: text box. When the document has loaded, execute the sequence File|Save As. Save the file as charmnet.htm. (Make sure you select the *.HTM option in the Save File as Type: selection box. If you save the file as a *.TXT file, the HTML tags will be removed and you won't be able to use them.) To work with the Charm Net home page, you'll also need to get the logos at the top and bottom, as well as the Apache logos. There are actually two GIF files in the Apache logo (apach.gif and apache.gif), so make sure you get both of them.

Click with your right mouse button on each of the images, then choose the Save This Image as: option, which will bring up the Save As dialog box. Accept the name of the file as it is given, and save it in the same directory where you saved the HTML document for Charm Net's home page, charmnet.htm.

Make a working copy of the HTML document by copying charmnet.htm to a file named index.htm. Figure 14.1 shows the Charm Net home page using our local disk document and GIFs. You'll want to refer back to this figure as you are making changes. (Your copy of the Charm Net home page doesn't have a background, because we didn't copy the GIF file associated with the background. We'll talk more about backgrounds in a later chapter.)

Before we do anything with Charm Net's HTML file, let's take a little side trip, a sort of HTML crash course. We'll explore some basics and then return to our newly downloaded Charm Net home page and turn it into your home page.

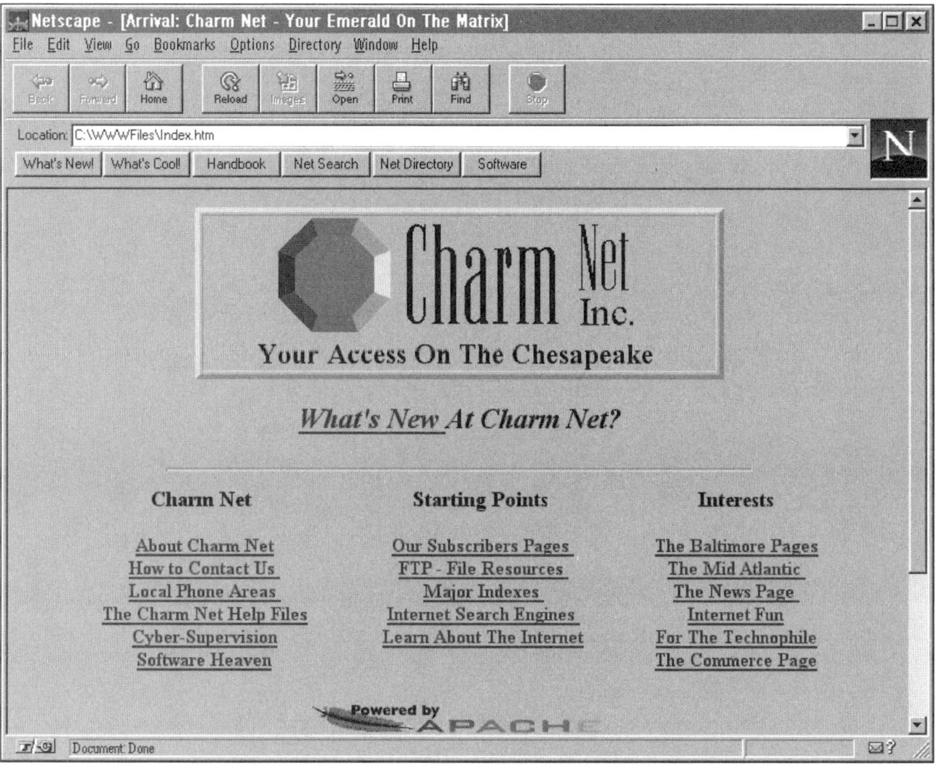

Figure 14.1 *Our saved Charm Net home page.*

Note: You can use any name you want to create an HTML file, as long as it has an extension of htm (for DOS) or an extension of html for other systems such as Unix. As a reference point for the remainder of this chapter, we'll call our evolving home page "index.htm". Let's assume that the Charm Net saved files and the files that we'll create will be stored on the "C:" drive in directory "WWWfiles."

HTML 101

You've captured your first HTML document. So, now what? Since HTML documents are readable text files, you can view them using your favorite word processor, text editor, or HTML editor. In the examples I present, I'll be using an HTML editor called HTML Notepad, which is a custom HTML editor that I like to use to create and edit HTML documents. I've included a version of this program on the companion CD-ROM for you to use. I'll explain more about HTML Notepad and other HTML editors later in the chapter when we create HTML documents from scratch.

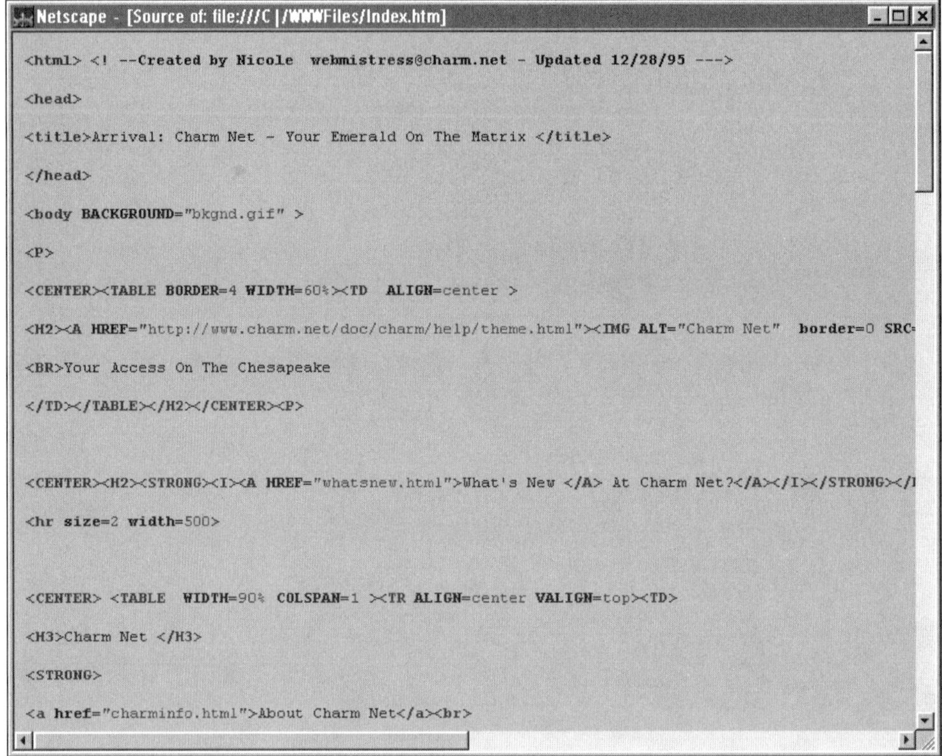

Figure 14.2 *The HTML code behind the Charm Net home page.*

Figure 14.2 shows the HTML tags for the index.htm file (the Charm Net home page). If you take a peek at the third line in this document, here's what you'll see:

```
<title>Arrival: Charm Net - Your Emerald On The Matrix</title>
```

This line actually reveals the essence of HTML. Look closely, and you'll see text inside angle brackets <>. These are called *tags*. Tags are what make this a "marked up" document. Text that has a special meaning is, for the most part, bracketed between a set of tags that have the same name. The trailing tag also has a slash between the "<" and the text inside the brackets. The text in this example is "Arrival: Charm Net - Your Emerald On The Matrix." The tag pair **<TITLE>** ... **</TITLE>** tells the browser how to treat the text between the tags. In this case, the text will be displayed as a title in the title bar for the Web page. Do you see how easy this HTML stuff is? Let's explore more.

Note: If you have any experience in graphic arts or typesetting, you can think of HTML tags as you would typesetting codes. In traditional typesetting systems, special codes are placed in front of words, sentences, and paragraphs to indicate how they should be printed. For example, a code such as <B> or <I> could indicate that text should be displayed in bold or italic, respectively. And this is exactly how HTML works!

A little further down in the index.htm file is this line of HTML:

```
<H3>Charm Net</H3>
```

This is the text for a heading. There are six tag pairs for headings; **<H1>** ... **</H1>** through **<H6>** ... **</H6>**. **H1** style headings are the largest and **H6** style are the smallest, providing nothing has been done to alter their size using Netscape's preference settings. Headings need not appear in any special order. Headings also generate a paragraph break; that is, the text that follows a heading will be displayed on its own line.

EXPLORER TIP

Centering Text with a Netscape HTML Enhancement

Netscape supports a useful HTML enhancement called centering. This feature is not part of the current HTML standard and is not supported by other browsers. In the Charm Net HTML example, you'll see that the heading "What's New at Charm Net" is enclosed within the **<CENTER> ... </CENTER>** tag pair. This tag tells the browser to center everything that appears between the two tags. Be aware that the center tags will be ignored by browsers other than Netscape. Part of the HTML standard states that unrecognized tags should be ignored—so there is no harm in using tags, even if the user's browser doesn't support them.

The text that is not a tag, or a component of a tag, is always considered plain text. A Web browser treats plain text as a continuous stream, which means that it continues to display the text using the currently selected format until a new format code is encountered. Embedded returns and multiple blanks are ignored. White space is also ignored. (White space can be a tab, a return, and the like.) You cannot split a line by simply pressing the Enter key. Line breaks and paragraphs must be explicitly specified. I'll show you how to do some neat formatting a little later.

The important thing to keep in mind about tags is that they usually come in pairs. The first tag tells your browser how to handle the text that is about to follow and the second tag in the pair tells the browser that no more text is coming and that it should stop formatting and look for another command. As an example, one widely used command pair is **<B>** ... **</B>**, which is used to display text in bold. In a sentence like this:

```
HTML is really <B>easy</B> to learn
```

only the word "easy" would be displayed in bold. If the second tag, **</B>**, were missing, your browser would continue to format all of the text that it found in the HTML document using bold type.

HTML has two components, plain text and formatting controls. The formatting tags control the way plain text displays although the tags themselves are not displayed by the browser.

HTML Consistency Check

When creating HTML documents, you cannot assume that everyone else will see your text exactly as you see it on your screen. The display window size may differ. Additionally, there are differences in the various Netscape versions. Mosaic users may also change the font and point size for any display type in their mosaic.ini configuration file. Or, if someone is viewing your files within another browser such as Mosaic, your HTML documents could look a little different.

What you see on the screen is a function of three things:

- The specific browser being used. (A browser such as Mosaic will have different display features than Netscape.)
- The size of the window in which the browser output is displayed.
- Netscape's configuration parameters, which are set using the Preferences menu.

The HTML Shell Game

Now that we've explored tags, the basic building blocks of HTML documents, what else is there to an HTML file? Fortunately, the actual structure of an HTML document is quite simple; we can reduce the universe of standard HTML files to a working template or shell. If you were writing an article, you could think of this shell as your outline. Here's the shell that I recommend:

```
<HTML>
   <HEAD>
      <TITLE>document-title-here</TITLE>
```

```
    </HEAD>

    <BODY>
        <H1>major-document-heading-here</H1>
             text and markup
         <A  HREF="url"> anchor-title</A>

        <ADDRESS>
              author and version information
        </ADDRESS>
    </BODY>
</HTML>
```

Since HTML is case insensitive, tags can be in either uppercase or lowercase letters. For example, **<title>**, **<Title>**, and **<TITLE>** all are treated the same. I use uppercase letters for things that do not change and lowercase letters for things that could be deleted or modified.

At the top and bottom of our template, we have the pair **<HTML>** and **</HTML>**. Everything inside this part of the file is the information that a Web browser will interpret when it reads the file. These tags tell the browser that the file is an HTML document. If you place text before the first tag or after the second tag, the text will be ignored. This area is a great place to put notes to yourself to document what your HTML files do. You could also include the dates when you created and modified the file.

If you look closely, you'll see that only two main sections are within the **<HTML>** tags: a header indicated by **<HEAD>** and **</HEAD>** and a body indicated by **<BODY>** and **</BODY>**. The header section tells the browser what title to display at the top of the browser's window. The body, on the other hand, is where all the action occurs. Anything placed within the body will be displayed by the browser. Mostly that means text, but it can also include images and even sound files, which are "displayed" by the browser by playing them on the system speaker. As we create our own home page, you'll learn how to put all kinds of different things in the body of an HTML document—including hotlinks.

Inside the body I've placed some of the more widely used HTML tags, including a heading, **<H1>**, anchor, **<A>**, and a documentation section, **<ADDRESS>**. As we work our way through this chapter, you'll learn how these important tags are used.

The advantage of using a template like this to create your own HTML documents is that you won't have to look up the basic HTML tags. (You could also include some of the other formatting tags that we'll be exploring in this chapter and the next.) The template will also help you remember the order of the main sections. You might save this template to a file, and each time you want to start a new document simply make a copy of the template. I use the name SHELL.HTM for my template file.

Note: Take advantage of the fact that browsers ignore white spaces and adopt a style and adhere to it in all of your documents. I like to have my starting and ending tags line up and everything in between indented two positions from the tag margin. It sure makes it easier to find things that have gone wrong.

Formatting Fun

You just saw how HTML is structured and how simple text is processed and displayed with HTML codes—in particular, titles for Web pages and headings. Of course, you can do much more with HTML, such as creating hypertext links, displaying images, formatting lists, setting up forms, and so on. We'll get into some of these techniques a little later, but for now, we need to take a closer look at some of the basics of formatting text.

In the document world, we can break things down into two levels: character formatting and paragraph formatting. At the character formatting level, you can format text like you would in a word processor. That is, you can put words or phrases in bold, italic, underline, and so on. Table 14.1 shows some of the more common HTML character formatting tags.

Let's look at a few examples:

```
<B>This is bold text.</B>
<I>This is italic.</I>
<B><U>This is bold and underlined.</U></B>
```

Here's how this text might look when it is displayed by a browser:

This is bold text.
This is italic.
This is bold and underlined.

Underlining is not currently supported by most browsers because underlined text looks too much like a link.

Notice that you can combine formatting tags for a single string of text. For example, the text in the third example is bold and underlined. When you combine tags, the order of them is not important. Just remember to include a closing tag for each starting tag you use. (The character formatting tags always come in pairs.)

Table 14.1 Basic Character Formatting Tags

Tag	Description
<B>...</B>	Bold
<I>...</I>	Italic
<TT>...</TT>	Typewriter style
<U>...</U>	Underline

You can also use character formatting tags with headings. But I recommend that you get in the habit of placing the character formatting tags inside the heading tags as shown here:

```
<H1><I>Welcome to the World of HTML!</I></H1>
```

In this case, the text would be displayed as a first level head in italic. I recommend putting the character formatting tags inside the heading tags because some older browsers may get confused if you do it the other way around.

Character formatting is the easiest HTML feature to master, although it limits you to simple display effects. Paragraph formatting is much more interesting and useful. Table 14.2 shows some of the basic formatting tags available for everything from inserting new paragraphs to creating lists to breaking a line of text within a paragraph.

We won't explore all of these now, but let's look at a few of them to get you started. As you work with paragraph formatting tags, the most important point to keep in mind is that browsers don't display text the way you format it within your HTML files. Text in an HTML file is treated as one big stream. The length of a line that a user sees when viewing a document in a browser is determined by the width of the screen or window. That means that the browser reformats the text to make it fit.

If you want to have your text displayed as different sections, such as headings, paragraphs, or lists, you'll need to put in some of the formatting tags. The most widely used tag, **<P>**, is not typically used as a tag pair. (There is a **</P>** tag, but it really doesn't do much.) This tag displays text as a new paragraph. For example, if you want to display two lines of text in a browser formatted as

```
HTML is easy to learn and use.

Let's start our HTML tour now.
```

Table 14.2 Basic Paragraph Formatting Tags

Tag	Description
 	Breaks a line
<DL>...</DL>	Creates a directory list (a list that's indented)
<H1>...</H1>	Creates a level 1 heading*
<HR>	Adds a horizontal rule in the displayed text
<LI>...</LI>	Creates a list item
<OL>...</OL>	Creates an ordered (numbered) list
<P>	Starts a new paragraph
<PRE>...</PRE>	Forces text to be displayed exactly as it is in the HTML document (this stands for preformatted)
<UL>...</UL>	Creates an unnumbered (bulleted) list

*Remember that HTML defines six different head levels, <H1> through <H6>.

the HTML version would look like:

```
<U>HTML is easy to learn and use.</U>
<P>
Let's start our HTML tour now.
```

If you omitted the **<P>** tag, both of these sentences would be run together.

How to Keep Your Lines from Wrapping

Because browsers ignore the format of text as it appears in an HTML document, text will wrap according to the width of the screen the user sees. In many cases, this is exactly what you want; however, there are times when you want to have more control over how text lines wrap.

The easiest way to get your text not to wrap is to use the **<ADDRESS>** ... **</ADDRESS>** tag pair. These tags are actually provided for documentation information, such as the author and revision dates, for an HTML document. But because they force text to appear exactly as it's written in the HTML document, with line breaks and line feeds as you've typed them, they are useful for controlling word wrap. The only limitation is that these tags force the text inside them to be displayed in italics.

Another tag pair you may want to try out is **<PRE>** ... **</PRE>**. Text placed between these tags will also keep its formatting as you entered it into the HTML file. But this time, it will force the text to a monospace font. This is useful for displaying computer source code or ASCII text, which is difficult to line up.

The tag **
** is another useful formatting tool. **
** causes a hard line break (carriage return). There is only a single **
** tag. The difference between the **
** and **<P>** tags is that the **<P>** tag causes a blank line while **
** simply advances to the beginning of the next line.

Displaying Images

One of the best things about Web pages is that they can display both text and graphics. Just think how boring the Web would be if you couldn't view pictures of things—it would be like reading a magazine without full color pictures.

As you learn more about HTML in this book, you'll discover a number of options for images in your Web pages including displaying:

- Full size images as standalone pictures
- Images as small thumbnails—a useful feature for minimizing the time it takes to display images
- Images as hyperlinks—when a user clicks on a hyperlinked image, he or she can be taken to another location in an HTML document or even to another Web site
- Images so that they can be used as navigational maps

Web browsers can easily display pictures if they are in a GIF format. If you have bitmap images in other file formats, such as PCX or BMP, you can easily convert them to GIF using a graphics imaging program. (In fact, I've included a program named Paint Shop Pro to help you convert your graphics files. We'll be using it in the next chapter.) The GIF file format is becoming so popular because it has been adopted as the standard by users of information services such as CompuServe, America Online, and of course, the Internet.

When browsers like Netscape and Mosaic first appeared on the scene, they didn't provide any special support to allow you to combine text with images. If you wanted to display a small picture to the left of a paragraph of text, you were out of luck. Fortunately, HTML 3.0 provides new features so that you can easily wrap text around images. Using HTML 3.0, you can also display captions with your images.

The easy way to display a bitmap image on a Web page is to use the **<IMG>** tag. Here's the actual format for this tag:

```
<IMG SRC="filename">
```

When a browser encounters an **<IMG>** tag, it will load the file that is specified by the "*filename*" part. The file name is specified as a parameter assigned to the "**SRC**" subtag, which effectively tells the browser the name of the bitmap graphics source file.

> *Note: When a browser reads a bitmap image and displays it, the image will be displayed using its original size. When you create your bitmap image files, you should make sure that you size them properly so that they will look good when they appear on a Web page. Most new Web page designers tend to make their images too big, and the user has to scroll quite a bit to completely see them. Small images also require less disk space and therefore load faster.*

The Magic of Hotlinks

Web pages really start to come alive when you add hotlinks. Hotlinks are essentially the text or pictures that you click on to take you to new Web-accessible locations or resources. For example, if you were creating a Web page that contained a list of your company's products, you could list each product with a small picture on one Web page. Each picture and product name could be set up as a hotlink. If a reader clicked on one of the product names or pictures, a new HTML document could be loaded to provide more detailed information.

Fortunately, hotlinks are very easy to create with HTML. Each hotlink you use on a Web page has two parts: an anchor and a hotlink location or resource. The anchor is the colored and underlined text or image that the user sees. The hotlink location is the place where your browser goes to fetch the next resource to display; typically, this hotlink location is a URL that references another HTML document. Since hotlinks can also be used to take a user to another location within the same HTML document, the hotlink location could be a tag that is placed somewhere else within the same document.

The more you know about anchors, the better you'll be at creating your own hotlinks. Let's explore the art of creating anchors with HTML. First I'll show you how to set up a link to a location within the same document, and then we'll create a link to reference a different HTML document.

Working with Anchor References

Anchor references are another pervasive HTML feature. Anchors are created by using the **<A>** ... **</A>** tag pair. This tag is easy to use; however, it will look a little awkward to you the first time you see it. Here is the general format for creating an anchor that allows you to set up a link to another location within the same HTML document:

```
<A HREF="#link-target"> anchor-text </A>
```

Notice that the formatting for an anchor tag is slightly different from the conventional <tag> ... </tag> pair. The first **A** tells the browser that it has encountered an anchor. The subtag, **HREF**, indicates that the anchor is linked to another location specified by the *link-target*. This is the location where the user will be taken when he or she clicks on the hotlink. Notice that you must place the character "#" at the beginning of the *link-target*, which can be any combination of letters. The "#" specifies that the address is on the same page as the link. That's all there is to the first part of the **<A>** tag. In the middle goes the anchor—the text you want to highlight or define as the hotlink. The final **</A>** terminates the anchor.

In order for this type of anchor to work properly, you must also place the link-target used in the anchor definition at another location in the HTML document. This is done by using another <A> anchor tag. This time the format is as follows:

```
<A NAME="link-tag"> target-text </A>
```

The **NAME** subtag tells the browser that this anchor is the location where the user should be taken when he or she clicks on its associated hotlink. Let's see an example:

```
This is our first Web page. It was a snap to create because
we had a great <A HREF="#htmllink">HTML guide</A> at our fingertips.
<P>
<P>
<P>
<HR>
<A NAME="htmllink">
<H2>The Easy HTML Guide</H2></A>
```

This is more actual HTML than we've written so far, but don't panic. It's actually very easy to follow. The first part is a paragraph of text that contains the hotlink or anchor "HTML guide." Then we have a few blank lines followed by a rule line. The last line is a level two head that is linked to the "HTML guide" hotlink. When the user clicks on the hotlink, he or she will be taken right to the level two head within the Web page. The target that ties both locations together is "htmllink." Wasn't that easy!

Linking to Another HTML Document

Setting up an anchor to link to another HTML document is similar to the technique we just explored; the only difference is that you must assign the path name of the target document to the **HREF** subtag. Here's the basic format:

```
<A HREF="file-pathname">anchor-text</A>
```

The *file-pathname* component can be a location on your hard drive or it can be a complete URL to another Web site.

To illustrate the use of an anchor tag that references another HTML document, let's use the URL for my actual home page, which is:

```
http://www.charm.net/~lejeune/
```

Now let's assume that you are creating an HTML document and want to say, "An interesting home page, demonstrating that one can be created by someone with marginal mental capability, is Urb LeJeune's. Another victory of perseverance over intelligence." Let's additionally assume that you want the text "Urb LeJeune's Home Page" to be the anchor. The body of your document might be:

```
<H2>The Original Big Dummy Creates Home Page</H2>

An interesting home page, demonstrating that one can be created by someone with
marginal mental capability, is

<A HREF="http://www.charm.net/~lejeune/">
   Urb LeJeune's Home Page</A>

Yet another victory of perseverance over intelligence.
```

What might show up on the screen is:

```
The Original Big Dummy Creates Home Page

An interesting home page, demonstrating that one can be created by someone with
marginal mental capability, is Urb LeJeune's Home Page. Yet another victory of
perseverance over intelligence.
```

Pointing to the anchor Urb LeJeune's Home Page will result in "http://www.charm.net/~lejeune/" being displayed on the status line in Netscape, and when you click on this anchor, up comes my home page to a display near you.

CREATING A HOME PAGE USING CHARM NET'S PAGE

As promised, we'll return to the Charm Net home page, which now resides on our hard disk as index.htm. (You'll see in a moment why we named the file index.htm.) I'll now show you a simple step-by-step procedure for turning this home page into your own home page. As you'll see, this is a good starting point for learning how to use some of the basic HTML tags. After we finish this project, we'll move up a level and create a home page from scratch using an HTML editor.

EXPLORER TIP

Using INDEX.HTM to Name Your Home Page

When you connect to a Web server using a URL that doesn't include a file name, the server will load a file named index.htm or index.html from the lowest order directory in the path name. Let's look at an example.

My main URL on the Web server I use is:

```
http://www.charm.net/~lejeune/
```

If you point Netscape to this location, my home page document, index.html, will be loaded. Essentially, I placed this HTML file in my main directory, /lejeune, on the Unix system I share with other users. The nice feature here is that Web surfers who come to my home URL don't need to specify a file name. The Web server automatically knows what to do, which is to load the file index.html stored in the current directory.

Step 1: View the File in an Editor

To start, load index.htm into your favorite editor. The first section of the file looks like this:

```
<html> <! —Created by Nicole  webmistress@charm.net - Updated 12/28/95 —>

<head>

<title>Arrival: Charm Net - Your Emerald On The Matrix </title>

</head>

<body BACKGROUND="bkgnd.gif" >

<P>

<CENTER><TABLE BORDER=4 WIDTH=60%><TD  ALIGN=center >
```

```
<H2><A HREF="http://www.charm.net/doc/charm/help/theme.html"><IMG ALT="Charm
Net"  border=0 SRC="/nlogo2.gif"></A>

<BR>Your Access On The Chesapeake

</TD></TABLE></H2></CENTER><P>
```

You might want to spend a few minutes looking over the file to get familiar with the different sections it contains. Since we are going to be changing the file, you might want to print the original to refer to if needed.

Step 2: Put in Your Own Title and Heading

Change the title and text between the **<HEAD>** and **<TITLE>** tags to reflect the page's new mission in life—your home page. Notice that the **<HEAD>** and **<TITLE>** are using the same text in between them. For my version, I use **<HEAD><TITLE>**Urb's Home Page**</TITLE></HEAD>**. You'll also need to change the text in the comment section **<!>**. (This is where you can put personal comments that won't appear on your page.)

This would also be a good time to change the main heading in the home page to make it your own. To do this, look for the **<H2>** tags and change the heading. I like to use the same text I use for the title. Thus, you would change "Your Access On The Chesapeake" to "Urb's Home Page." (It may be a little hard to find the **<H2>** tags, since they're buried in the code, but when you find the tags you'll see that the only text between them is "Your Access On The Chesapeake." We'll discuss the **<TABLE>** tags in a later chapter.) Here's the new version of the HTML with these changes made. Notice that I've changed the formatting slightly and removed the background and tables:

```
<HTML> <! —Created by Urb LeJeune—>

      <HEAD>
       <TITLE>Urb's Home Page </TITLE>
      </HEAD>
      <P>
      <BODY>
      <CENTER>
         <H2><A HREF="http://www.charm.net/doc/charm/help/theme.html">
               <IMG ALT="Charm Net" border=0 SRC="/nlogo2.gif"></A>
               <BR>Urb's Home Page
         </H2></CENTER><P>
```

Remember again, the text between the **<TITLE>** tags appears in the title area and the text between the **<HEADING>** tags appears in the document window area.

Better HTML Document Formatting

I like my HTML tags to be in uppercase to distinguish them from body text. I also like to use indenting to help keep track of how the HTML tags are being used. Although you can use whatever formatting techniques you like, this technique can help you better structure your HTML documents.

Step 3: Put in Your Own Image

The Charm Net home page displays a big green emerald. (This was the file nlogo2.gif that we retrieved and saved earlier.) Let's replace this file with one of our own.

In the first section of the HTML document, you'll find the following line of text:

```
<A HREF="http://www.charm.net/doc/charm/help/theme.html">
   <IMG ALT="Charm Net" border=0 SRC="/nlogo2.gif"></A>
```

This is a hotlink instruction. It might look a little confusing to you at this point because it contains three components: a URL, an alternate name for the image, and the file name for the image. A hotlink is built using the form:

```
<A HREF="url"> anchor-text</A>
```

In this case, the "anchor-text" is actually the graphical image nlogo2.gif. This indicates that it is a pointer to something. As you drag your mouse across the image, the URL "http://www.charm.net/doc/charm/help/theme.html" appears in the status bar. To put in our own image, just substitute your own GIF image file name for nlogo2.gif, strip out the anchor, and include an alternate label for the image. Here's the change I made to put in my image file urb.gif:

```
<IMG ALT="Urb's picture goes here" SRC="urb.gif">
```

You might also want to change the placement of the picture on the home page. I like to have my heading above the image. Here's how I rearranged the HTML tags to accomplish this:

```
<BODY>
      <CENTER>
         <IMG ALT="Urb's picture goes here" SRC="urb.gif">
         <H2>Urb's Home Page
      </H2></CENTER>
```

Again, this change is just a matter of personal preference.

Step 4: Add Your Story!

It's now time to tell the world all about yourself. Everyone has a unique story, and this is the place to tell it. Following the picture, insert a paragraph or two. Here's my version:

```
Hi! I'm Urb LeJeune, purported--or is it perverted--Internet
maven and Netscape wizard. My home town is Tuckerton, NJ and my
email address is <B><I>LeJeune@acy.digex.net</I></B>.
My hobbies include running marathons (slowly), cooking (poorly),
and I've been a ham radio operator (W2DEC) for 45 years. I also love
corny jokes and puns, how about sending me one. I've written two books
titled the <B>Mosaic &amp; Web EXplorer</B> and the <B>Netscape &amp;
HTML EXplorer</B>.
<P>
```

Notice that I've used a few of the character formatting tags presented earlier. I also included a blank line after my paragraph of text.

Step 5: Change Some of the Hotlinks

The Charm Net home page provides links to other Web sites. It is always a good idea to add links to your home page. You can leave the links as they are, change them, or add new ones.

For my version, I changed a few links in the Interests section of links in the original Charm Net HTML document. This section starts with the HTML instructions:

```
<A HREF="http://www.baltimore.com/">The Baltimore Pages</A><BR>
<A HREF="baltwash.html">The Mid Atlantic </A><BR>
```

Let's change them to point to the Yahoo database and the Cool Site of the Day home pages:

```
<A HREF="http://www.yahoo.com">Yahoo</A><BR>
<A HREF="http://www.infi.net/cool.html">Cool Site</A><BR>
```

At this point I also deleted most of the information at the end of the document, since it doesn't apply to me. I deleted everything from the first mention of the apache.gif to the end, making sure to leave in the **</BODY>** and **</HTML>**.

Step 6: Save the HTML Document

Before you can test the changes you've made to the HTML document with a Web browser, you'll need to save the document. If you are using your favorite word processor, make sure that you save the document as a text file. If you use another format, such as Word for Windows, your browser will not be able to read the file.

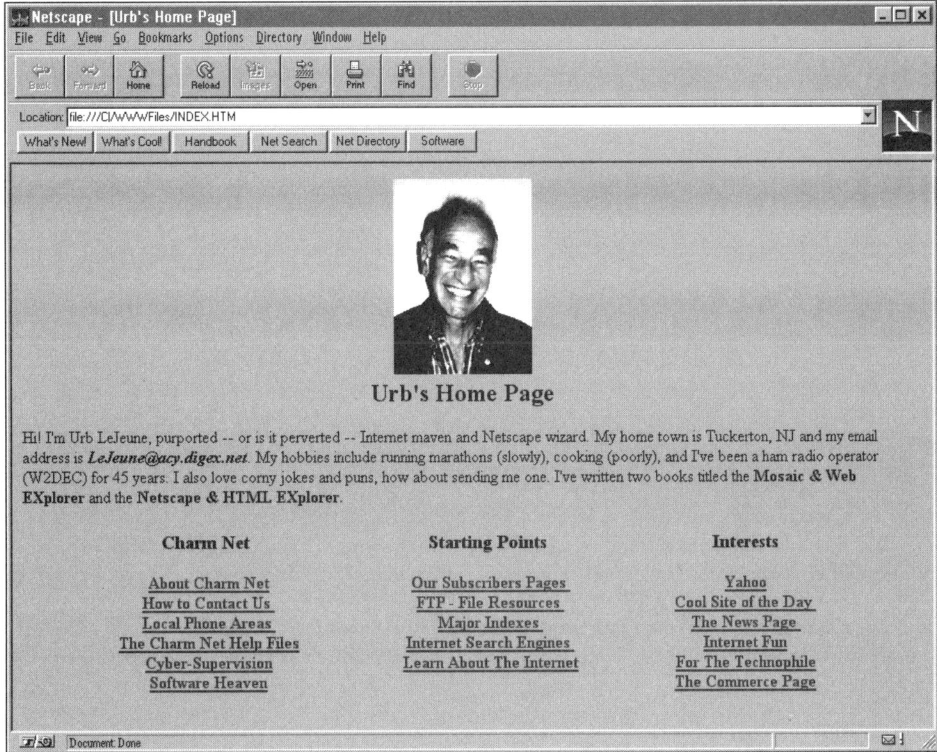

***Figure 14.3** Our new version of the Charm Net home page.*

Step 7: Test Your Creation

We've made enough changes for now. Fire up Netscape and load in the file using the instructions presented in the following section. Figure 14.3 shows how Netscape displays our altered version of Charm Net's home page. The actual contents of the index.htm document are shown here:

```
<HTML> <! —Created by Urb LeJeune—>
  <HEAD>
    <TITLE>Urb's Home Page</TITLE>
  </HEAD>
 <BODY>
  <P>
    <CENTER>
      <H2><IMG ALT="Urb's picture goes here" SRC="/nlogo2.gif">
   <BR>Urb's Home Page</H2></CENTER>

Hi! I'm Urb LeJeune, purported--or is it perverted--Internet maven and Netscape
wizard. My home town is Tuckerton, NJ and my email address is
<B><I>LeJeune@acy.digex.net</I></B>. My hobbies include running marathons
(slowly), cooking (poorly), and I've been a ham radio operator (W2DEC) for 45
years. I also love corny jokes and puns, how about sending me one. I've written
```

```
two books titled the <B>Mosaic &amp; Web EXplorer</B> and the <B>Netscape &amp;
HTML EXplorer</B>.
<P>

   <CENTER> <TABLE  WIDTH=90% COLSPAN=1 ><TR ALIGN=center VALIGN=top><TD>
   <H3>Charm Net </H3>
   <STRONG>
      <A HREF="charminfo.html">About Charm Net</A><BR>
      <A HREF="contact.html">How to Contact Us </A><BR>
      <A HREF="http://www.charm.net/doc/charm/help/phone.local">Local Phone Areas
         </A><BR>
      <A HREF="http://www.charm.net/doc/charm/help/index.html">The Charm Net Help
         Files</A><BR>
      <A HREF="http://www.charm.net/doc/charm/censor/">Cyber-Supervision</A><BR>
      <A HREF="http://www.charm.net/CWSApps/">Software Heaven</A><BR>
   </STRONG>
      </TD>
   <TD>
     <H3> Starting Points </H3>
      <STRONG>
      <A HREF="charm/local/index.html">Our Subscribers Pages </A><BR>
      <A HREF="ftp.sites.html">FTP - File Resources </A><BR>
      <A HREF="bigtrees.html">Major Indexes </A><BR>
      <A HREF="info.search.html">Internet Search Engines </A><BR>
      <A HREF="learning.html">Learn About The Internet</A><BR>
      </STRONG>
   </TD>
   <TD> <H3>Interests</H3>
      <STRONG>
      <A HREF="http://www.yahoo.com/">Yahoo</A><BR>
      <A HREF="cool.infi.net">Cool Site of the Day </A><BR>
      <A HREF="news.html">The News Page </A><BR>
      <A HREF="fun.html">Internet Fun</A><BR>
      <A HREF="technophile.html">For The Technophile</A><BR>
      <A HREF="biz.html">The Commerce Page</A><BR>
   </STRONG></TD></TR>
   </TABLE></CENTER>
 </BODY>/
</HTML>
```

Testing a Home Page

We're now ready to view the home page we've created. As you learned in the previous chapter, you can load an HTML file from your hard disk into Netscape by entering the URL in the Location: text box. You can also open an HTML file stored on your hard disk using File|Open File. When the standard Open dialog appears, locate and select the index.htm file we've been creating. Netscape will take over and process the HTML file for viewing.

Wait a second, we're getting ahead of ourselves. Recall that to load a local HTML file, your TCP/IP stack must be active in memory so that WinSock API calls can be made by Netscape. You can easily set this up by first running your TCP/IP stack application and then minimizing it. If your stack isn't anywhere in memory, Netscape may refuse to run. It'll give you an error message stating that it can't find winsock.dll.

You can view your local handiwork using Netscape even if you aren't connected to the Internet. Refer back to Chapter 8 for instructions on how to do this.

CREATING A HOME PAGE FROM SCRATCH

We now know enough to be dangerous with HTML and put a home page together without having to steal someone else's. Although there are a lot of HTML examples on the Web, you'll eventually get to the point where you'll be creating your Web page documents from scratch. You can do this using a word processor like Word for Windows, or you can use a custom HTML editor that will help you insert and modify HTML tags.

Whether you are just learning HTML or you have written hundreds of HTML documents, HTML editors can be a big help. Their advantage over conventional editors is that they make it easy to insert syntactically correct HTML tags in a document, which means that you won't have to memorize all of the HTML tags available. Most will allow you to view a document by launching a browser such as Netscape with the target document opened.

Some of the more popular editors that are available for Windows include:

- Hot Dog
- HoTMetaL
- HTML Assistant
- HTMLed
- HTML Notepad
- Web Spinner

I've included versions of some of these editors on the companion CD-ROM for you to try out and use. To locate them, look in the directory\tools. Some of them are shareware, so if you start to use them, please register them to support the developers of these great tools. I've also included another useful editor called Edit Master, which is a great Windows Notepad editor.

For the remainder of this chapter, I'll show you how to use one of these editors, HTML Notepad, to create a new HTML document and include features like formatted text, images, and links. Once you learn the basic techniques of writing HTML with HTML Notepad, you'll be able to easily use any of the other available HTML editors.

Creating a Home Page with HTML Notepad

For our final home page adventure, we'll create an HTML document with HTML Notepad that you can use as the foundation for your own home page. The home page won't look too much different from the page we created earlier; however, this example will show you the steps involved in creating a new HTML document using a special purpose editor.

Let's use the HTML Notepad editor provided on the companion CD-ROM.

To start the editor, run the program htmlnote.exe located in the \tools\htmlnote directory on the CD-ROM. To create a new document, click on the File | New option. The editor will create a skeletal document for you, as shown in Figure 14.4. To create a heading, place your cursor between the **<HEAD> </HEAD>** and type in what you want written at the top of your page. Figure 14.5 shows the text "Urb's Home Page."

To make your heading really stand out, go to the HTML menu and choose Headings. You'll get a choice of **<H1>** to **<H6>**. For this project, we'll choose the largest heading, **<H1>**. To center it, place **<CENTER> </CENTER>** on either side, producing this code:

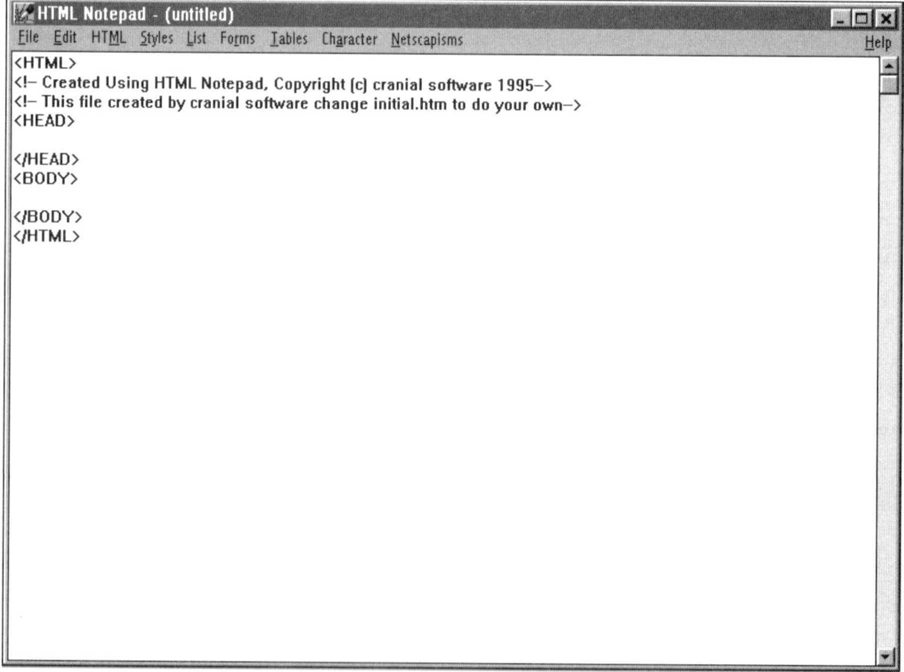

Figure 14.4 *A new document, waiting for more HTML coding.*

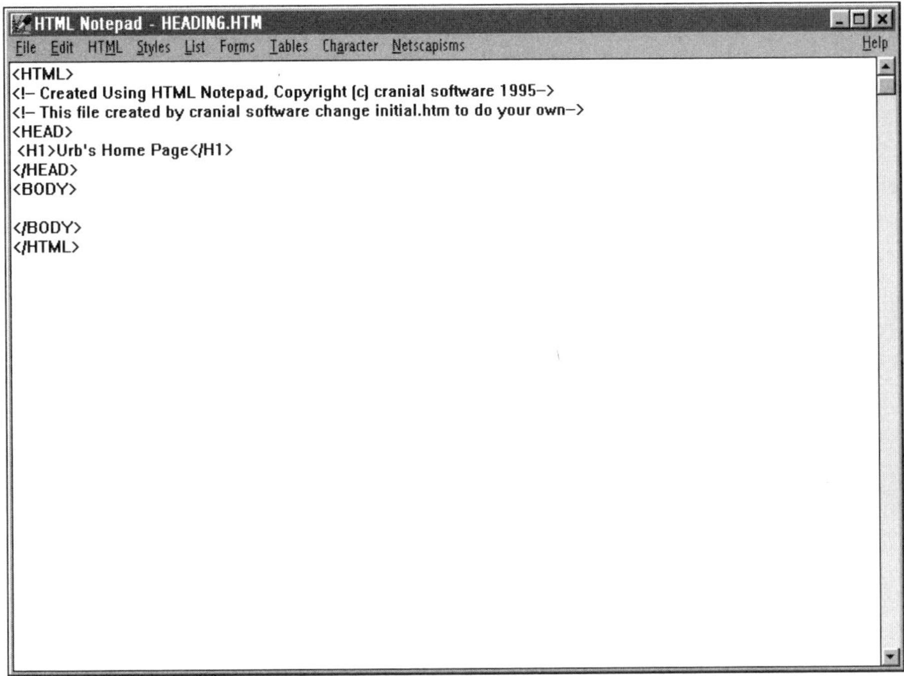

***Figure 14.5** The heading "Urb's Home Page".*

```
<CENTER><H1>Urb's Home Page</H1></CENTER>
```

This technique for creating HTML documents is great because it can save you from making annoying mistakes. If I had a dollar for every time I created an HTML document and used the bold tag **<B>**, then forgot to include the terminating tag **</B>**, I'd be rich. (By the way, when you make this mistake, everything in your document from the first **<B>** tag gets displayed in bold type!)

Once you've centered the main heading, insert a short paragraph in the between the **<BODY>** tags. This is your second time around, so make up a good story. I like to use a segment of text that contains my email address, and then I highlight the address. For example, to make "LeJeune@acy.digex.net" both bold and italicized, first highlight the address. Next, click on the Styles menu and choose Bold and Italic. HTML Notepad creates the following line:

```
<B><I> LeJeune@acy.digex.net</I></B>
```

Repeat this process for any other special formatting effects you want to include.

Once you are finished creating your home page, save it as an HTML document by selecting File | Save As. As mentioned previously in this chapter, you'll probably want to name the file index.htm so that later you can put it up on a Web site.

Now we can take this home page for a spin. The best part is that we can do it right from HTML Notepad! First you have to configure the program so it knows where to look for the Netscape browser. Click on the File menu and choose Browsers Setup. Then choose Add... and choose the Netscape.exe file. Then drag it into the Default Browser: box and click on the Set Default button and OK. For example, here's the path and file name I use to have HTML Notepad load Netscape:

```
C:\NETSCAPE\NETSCAPE.EXE
```

If Netscape isn't running, whenever you want to see one of your creations in progress go to the File menu and choose Test Page. If you're already viewing the document in Netscape and you want to look at your changes, just click on the Reload button on the toolbar.

Adding a Picture

After viewing the home page, let's return to HTML Notepad to add a picture. If you have a GIF of yourself, use it—if not, practice with the nlogo2.gif file we downloaded from Charm Net.

Recall that the **<IMG>** tag is used to display a picture—in this case the GIF file yourname.gif or nlogo2.gif. (Make sure that you have this file available on your hard disk; otherwise Netscape won't be able to display it when you view your home page.)

From the HTML Notepad editor, create a blank line where you want the graphic to appear above your paragraph. Next, execute the sequence HTML | Image. A Select Image Source dialog box will open, as shown in Figure 14.6. Choose the Browse button to find the nlogo2.gif file, then click OK. This will enter the name of your GIF in the box. This is a good place to put in Alternate Text and change the size of your image (in pixels), if you want. For now, just click on OK and an instruction like this

```
<IMG SRC="file:///c:/urb.gif" >
```

will be added to the document.

That's all you need to do. Of course, save your file and take it for a trial run.

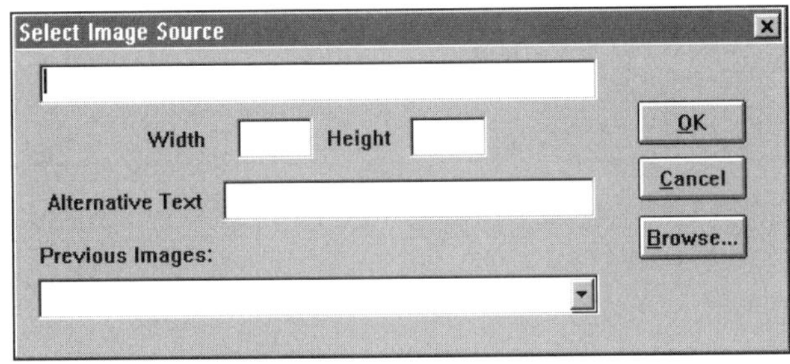

***Figure 14.6** The Select Image Source dialog box.*

My completed version, with all HTML tags, looks like this:

```
<HTML>
  <HEAD>
    <TITLE>
      Urb's Home Page
    </TITLE>
  </HEAD>
  <BODY>
    <CENTER><H1>Urb's Home Page</H1></CENTER>
    <IMG ALIGN=BOTTOM SRC="urb.gif" >
    Hi! I'm Urb LeJeune, purported--or is it perverted--Internet
    maven and Netscape wizard. My home town is Tuckerton, NJ and my
    email address is <I><B> LeJeune@acy.digex.net</B></I>.
    My hobbies include running marathons (slowly), cooking (poorly),
    and I've been a ham radio operator (W2DEC) for 45 years. I also love
    corny jokes and puns, how about sending me one. I've written two books
    titled the <B>Mosaic &amp; Web EXplorer</B> and the <B>Netscape &amp;
    HTML EXplorer</B>.
   <P>

  </BODY>
</HTML>
```

We'll add some more features as we expand this page in the next chapter. Congratulations—you're well on your way to becoming a HTML expert.

Figure 14.7 shows the results of our initial handiwork. Our home page doesn't do much yet, but it's a start. Save the URL to a Netscape bookmark link, since we'll be displaying the home page quite a bit as we change it.

Notice that the text between the **<TITLE> </TITLE>** tags appears in the title bar following "Netscape -". The heading displayed within the document display window requires a pair of heading tags. As you can see, mine is:

```
<H1>Urb's Home Page</H1><P>
```

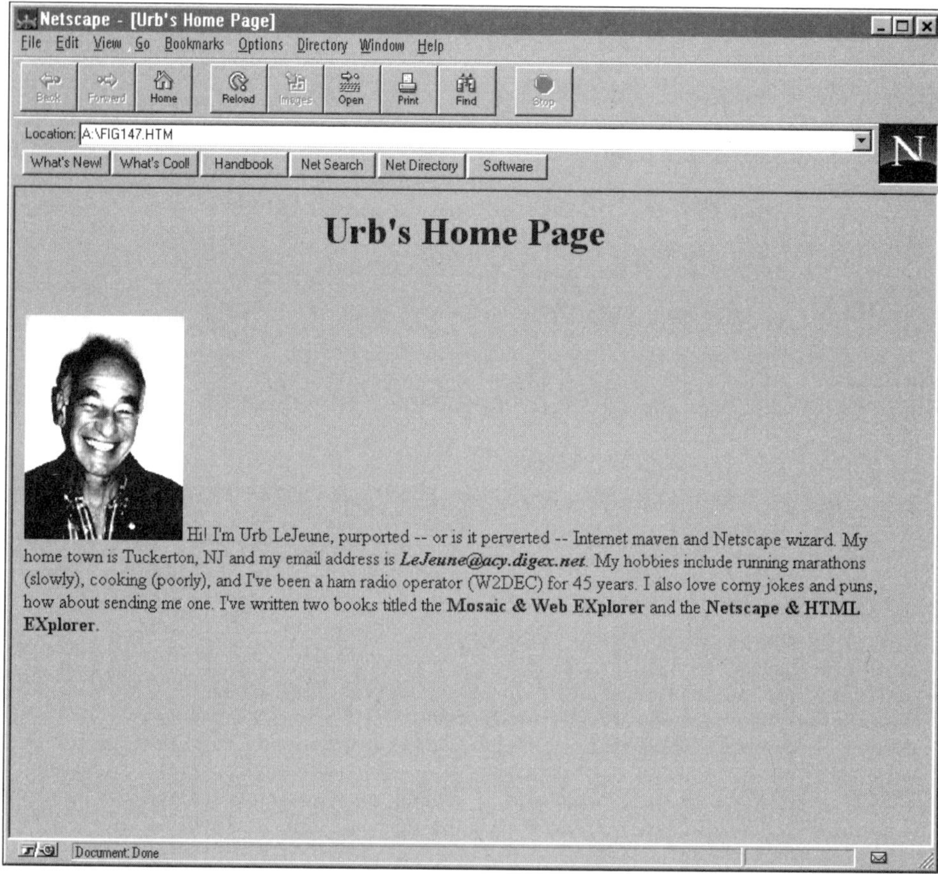

Figure 14.7 *My first homemade home page.*

The text line in INDEX.htm following the heading is:

```
<IMG SRC="file:///c:/urb.gif" >
```

Notice that it contains two parameters. The "IMG" parameter indicates an inline image, with the "SRC" parameter indicating the URL of the image file.

The **<P>** tag following the plain text is a "hard coded" paragraph. Recall that there is a corresponding **</P>** tag, but its use is optional since there is an implied **</P>** whenever encountering another **<P>** tag or a tag producing a formatting paragraph break such as a heading. Since the first paragraph has no **<P>** tag, the bottom of the first line of display text lines up with the bottom of the image. If you removed the **<P>** tag after the paragraph, the email address would end up directly beneath the paragraph, with no space between them.

Now that the HTML document is displayed in the browser, you can see first-hand the difference between how paragraph text is placed in the HTML document and how it is displayed in the browser. The word wrapping is taken care of automatically. If you resize your Netscape window, your text will be adjusted so that it fits in the window. Try this out.

Adding Anchors to Your Web Pages

What good is a Web page without a few anchors? A Web page that doesn't allow you to link to another Web document isn't a whole lot of fun, or very useful, for that matter. In my home page, I wanted four anchors that would link to additional documents in the same directory. (External Web document links will be covered in a moment.)

Naming Your Files

If your documents are eventually going to reside on a Unix server, your HTM documents will become html. Remember, Unix cares about case. Most Unix file names are lowercase, so it's a good idea to use lowercase when entering your DOS file names since DOS doesn't care. If your file extension is longer than three characters, DOS truncates. We can use DOS truncation to our advantage and specify all text file names as html. DOS will fetch the HTM version.

I want my first anchor, "My hobbies," to point to an HTML document named urbhobie.htm; the second anchor, "corny jokes and puns," should point to urbjoke.htm; the third anchor, "Mosaic & Web EXplorer," should point to mos-book.htm; and finally the last anchor, "Netscape & HTML EXplorer," should point to net-book.htm.

The HTML Notepad editor can easily help us add these new links. To do this, highlight the text to be used as the anchor. Then, execute the sequence HTML|Link HREF (Ctrl+H). Then in the top field, enter the file name urbhobie.htm or whatever document you want to link to. Click on OK and an HTML instruction like the following will be added to your document:

```
<A HREF="file:///c:/urbhobie.html">My hobbies</A>
```

In this case, "My hobbies" is the anchor or hotlink. When the user clicks on it, guess what happens? Up comes the HTML document urbhobie.htm. When you start entering the actual text for tags like anchors within a document, use some conventions to help you remember the document's "innards" when you return at a later time. I like having the individual components of an instruction on separate lines and I also indent the information two spaces to the right of the tag margin.

Figure 14.8 shows how Netscape displays these new changes with all the bells and whistles.

index.htm has evolved to:

```
<HTML>
  <HEAD>
    <TITLE>
      Urb's Home Page
    </TITLE>
  </HEAD>
  <BODY>
    <CENTER><H1>Urb's Home Page</H1></CENTER>
    <IMG ALT="Urb's picture normally goes here" SRC="urb.gif" >
    Hi! I'm Urb LeJeune, purported--or is it perverted--Internet
    maven and Netscape wizard. My home town is Tuckerton, NJ and my
    email address is <I><B> LeJeune@acy.digex.net</B></I>.
    <A HREF="urbhobie.html">My hobbies</A>
    include running marathons (slowly), cooking (poorly),
    and I've been a ham radio operator (W2DEC) for 45 years. I also love
    <A HREF="urbjoke.html">corny jokes and puns</A>,
    how about sending me one. I've written two books
    titled the<A HREF="mos-book.html">
    <B>Mosaic &amp; Web EXplorer</B></A> and the
    <A HREF="net-book.html"> <B>Netscape &amp; HTML EXplorer</B></A>.
    <P>

  </BODY>
</HTML>
```

There are a few items in the revised document worthy of note. First, I included the structural tags, such as **<HTML>**, **<HEAD>**, and **<BODY>** in this second version of the home page. Although they are optional, it's a good idea to get in the habit of using them because they can help you better structure your HTML documents and they will keep you out of trouble if someone is trying to view your document with a browser that requires them.

Notice that the IMG declaration has an added parameter **ALT**. This parameter is used to display a plain text alternative to the image for those people viewing the document with a character browser such as Lynx. The new line is:

```
<IMG ALT="Urb's picture usually goes here" SRC="urb.gif" >
```

Also note that parameters don't require enclosing quotation marks unless they contain embedded spaces. We'll explore this feature more in the next chapter.

Finally, notice the **<A>** anchor tags for each of four hotlinks. At this point, I suggest that you copy each of the four HTM files that this home page refer-

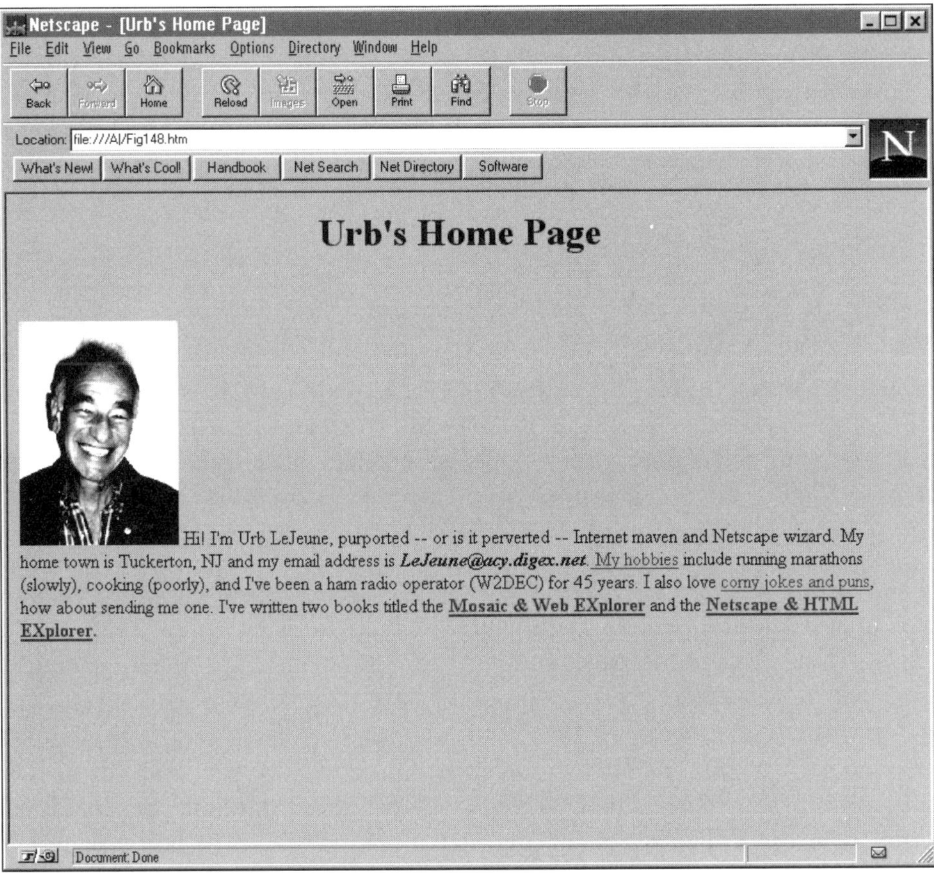

***Figure 14.8** My page with links inserted.*

ences from the companion CD-ROM to your hard disk, so that you can take this home page for a test drive. Make sure you also have the GIF file urb.gif. (You don't want to miss the chance to have my picture on your Web page!) In the next chapter, we'll take a closer look at these other HTML documents.

HTML STANDARDS

Before we leave our exploration of creating Web pages in this chapter, there are a few standards issues for HTML documents that we should discuss. (See the URLs at the end of this exploration chapter for further reference.) Unfortunately, not everyone builds documents adhering to the standards. Netscape, and most other Web browsers, *currently* let you get away with some sloppy construction techniques. For example, the HTML standard specifies that the portions of the document to be interpreted by a browser must be enclosed between the **<HTML> </HTML>** pair. However, all browsers that I have tested, correctly display documents that do not have the **<HTML>** tag pair. However, I don't think non-standard documents are a good idea if you are going to be serious about your HTML toils. There is no assurance that future version of Web browsers will ignore sloppiness and nonconformity. Let's produce standard documents while making life easy for ourselves.

LET'S REVIEW

So far, we've barely scratched the surface of available HTML mark-ups. Hopefully, you have seen that HTML documents are relatively easy to create and that you only need a handful of tags to produce nice-looking Web pages. Indeed, there is nothing stopping you from creating an HTML document without using HTML tags, but it wouldn't be much of a Web document if it didn't have hotlinks or special effects, such as graphics.

A simplistic group of HTML documents, such as the ones we've created here, can serve as your home page under construction, if you're lucky enough to have access to a Web server. If you don't have a server at your disposal, you can still create a home page, test it out, and refine it using Netscape. You just need to set up your HTML documents so that they can be loaded from your hard disk instead of an actual Web site. When I do a Netscape presentation, I find that interest always peaks when I demonstrate my own home page and tell people that they can easily do the same thing and publish on the Web.

To help you brush up on the HTML concepts we've explored so far, here's a quick summary.

The Hyper Text Markup Language (HTML) consists of three functional components:

- Plain text
- Tags that control the display and functionality of the plain text between the tags
- Hotlinks and the associated prompt enclosed by tag sets

HTML browsers do not recognize white space (multiple blanks, carriage returns, or tabs) embedded within plain text. Line breaks and paragraph breaks must be explicitly specified.

The basic form of an HTML tag is:

```
<tag>plain-text</tag>
```

where the tag determines the display characteristics of the plain text. The terminating tag is usually the same as the originating tag with the inclusion of the "/" between the "<" and the tag description. An example of a tag pair enclosing descriptive text would be:

```
<H1>This is Heading One</H1>
```

HTML tags are case independent; that is **<TITLE>**, **<title>**, and **<TiTLe>** are all acceptable.

An HTML document is enclosed between the tag pair

```
<HTML> . . . </HTML>
```

which is in turn constructed by these head and a body components:

```
<HEAD> . . . </HEAD>
<BODY> . . . </BODY>
```

The simple structure of a HTML document is therefore:

```
<HTML>
   <HEAD>
   </HEAD>
   <BODY>
   </BODY>
</HTML>
```

All of these tags are *currently* optional, allowing upward compatibility with older versions of HTML documents. However, you should get in the habit of using these structural tags so that your HTML documents will work correctly with all Web browsers.

The **<HEAD>** section of an HTML document typically contains the definition **<TITLE>** title-text **</TITLE>**. The title text appears in the Web page's Windows title bar.

There are two formatting tags that are not paired, the line break and paragraph break; **
** specifies a line break and **<P>** designates a paragraph break.

A hyperlink in an HTML document has two components, a reference address (URL) and an anchor. The general form of a hyperlink is

```
<A HREF=url>anchor-title</A>
```

where url specifies the complete location of the desired link and the anchor-title is the component that appears, usually underlined and colored, on the screen. Clicking on the anchor activates the URL. An example is the pointer to my home page:

```
<A HREF=www.charm.net/~lejeune/>Urb's home page</A>
```

A good way to learn about HTML concepts and expand your Web-publishing prowess is to be on the lookout for interesting effects as you surf the Web. When you find something that might prompt you to ask, "I wonder how they did that," take a minute to execute Netscape's View|Document Source sequence to look at the coding behind the display and find out how they did it.

Good luck with your home page publishing. Let me know when you get one up and going, I'd like to check it out.

HTML REFERENCE

A Beginner's Guide to HTML
`http://www.ncsa.uiuc.edu/General/Internet/WWW/HTMLPrimer.html`

The HTML Quick Reference Guide
`http://kuhttp.cc.ukans.edu/lynx_help/HTML_quick.html`

Information on the Different Versions of HTML
`http://www.w3.org/hypertext/WWW/MarkUp/MarkUp.html`

Composing Good HTML
`http://www.cs.cmu.edu/~tilt/cgh/`

HTML Specification Version 3.0
`http://www.hpl.hp.co.uk/people/dsr/html3/CoverPage.html`

HTML Editors
`http://akebono.stanford.edu/yahoo/Computers/World_Wide_Web/HTML_Editors/`

Resources for Converting Documents to HTML
`http://www.w3.org/hypertext/WWW/Tools/Filters.html`

An Archive of Useful HTML Translators
`ftp://src.doc.ic.ac.uk/computing/information-systems/www/tools/translators/`

HTML With Style

We've only scratched the surface of exploring the power of HTML. In this chapter, you'll learn how to use more advanced HTML features to create effective Web pages.

While trying to conceptualize this chapter, I experienced a conflict of sorts. On the one hand, an extensive overview of the HyperText Markup Language (HTML) at this stage might confuse you and it would be an overkill because Appendix A provides a detailed reference guide to the inner workings of HTML. On the other hand, presenting less than a major treatment of HTML would oversimplify and break the pattern of technical completeness from our previous explorations. Besides, you probably want to know as much as you can absorb about HTML so that you can add some of those neat effects to your Web pages that you see other people doing.

To me, the learning process is about 50 percent luck, 49 percent serendipity, and 1 percent skill. I taught computer programming at the four-year college level, and a former student recently reminded me of my opening monologue. "There's good news and bad news," I had started somewhat apprehensively. "The good news is that I'm an easy grader; the bad news is that you will be using Pascal to program your assignments and I don't know Pascal."

Serendipity helped me solve that educational dilemma. I learned Pascal that semester by helping students write and debug their programs. It was a great learning model—so why don't we use it here? Let's create more HTML instead of just describing more of its unique features. I'll cover as much as I can in the space available.

We'll begin where we left off in the previous chapter. We'll add more features, such as formatted text lists, to the home page we created. I'll also show you the contents of some of the other HTML files that my home page references. In the second part of this chapter, I'll introduce you to a useful HTML guide that I created as a Web page, which is called "HTML Style Guide & Test Suite." The guide is fairly complete, except that it doesn't cover HTML tables and forms. The guide is essentially one big HTML example that I've also included on the companion CD-ROM as the file styles.htm. I plan to keep this guide up to date and post it on my Web server for you to view.

CREATING LISTS WITH HTML

When the designers of HTML decided to support lists, they went all out. The end result is that HTML now supports five different types of lists: bulleted, numbered, menu, directory, and description. There are enough list options to let you get very creative with your Web pages, although not all browsers support all of these list types. You can count on most browsers to support unordered, ordered, and description lists.

Bulleted lists are actually called *unordered lists* in HTML. They are probably the most widely used list type since they are great for creating everything from simple lists to more complex menus. Each item in an unordered list is typically displayed on its own line with a bullet symbol. Numbered lists, on the other hand, are called *ordered lists*. They look just like unordered lists except that each item of an ordered list is displayed with a number, starting with 1. Here's an example of each of these list types:

```
This is an unordered list:
· This is item 1
· This is item 2

This is an example of an ordered list:
1. This is item 1
2. This is item 2
```

The best part about these two list types is that they can be nested. For example, a bulleted (unordered) list could be formatted as:

```
· This is the first element of level 1
   · This is the first element of level 2
   · This is the second element of level 2
· This is the second element of level 1
```

But if you use nested unordered or ordered lists in your HTML documents, keep in mind that not all browsers will indent the nested list items. In addition, some browsers use different bullet symbols to indicate the difference between inner and outer list members.

Menu lists and *directory lists* are special types of unordered lists. A menu list is actually a compact version of an unordered list. The idea behind it is that all items should fit on one line. If you are really into compactness, directory lists are the way to go. With these lists, all items should have no more than twenty characters. This restriction allows the items to be displayed in three or more columns.

The last menu type is the *description list*. This list is defined and formatted differently from any of the other lists. Instead of a bullet or number, each list item can be displayed with special text that you provide (like a glossary).

Just as you might guess, HTML provides tag pairs to define each of the five list types. Appendix A shows the tag pairs that are available. The techniques for using the first four of these list tag pairs are essentially the same. The **<DL>** ... **</DL>** pair works a little differently because description lists can have list items that consist of text for a description and text for the actual item itself.

Introducing the Basic List Structure

I'm not going to show you how to create every type of list format that HTML supports (Appendix A provides a complete reference for creating lists); however, here's a useful template you can use to create either unordered or ordered lists:

```
<list-type>


<LI> List item 1 goes here
<L1> List item 2 goes here
<LI> List item 3 goes here
...
</list-type>
```

The *<list-type> </list-type>* tags define the list type. This is where you use either the pair **<UL>** ... **</UL>** or **<OL>** ... **</OL>**. For example, a numbered, or ordered, list in HTML is enclosed between the **<OL>** ... **</OL>** pair. Within the *<list-type> </list-type>* tags, start the individual list items with the tag **<LI>**. There is no terminating **</LI>** since the end of a list item is implied by the next **<LI>** that starts a new list item, or by the terminating *</list-type>* tag that terminates the list. List items do not have to fit on a single line; individual items may contain **<P>** paragraph tags and **
** line break tags. Now that we have a good template to work with, let's create some lists.

The Return of Urb's Home Page

Just when you thought you've seen enough of my home page, it's back again, sporting new features. A different second screen of the home page is shown in Figure 15.1. In addition to a few different heading styles, the page uses an HTML unordered list. The list format I'm using here is exactly as it appears in the NCSA home page where there are four groups of identically constructed lists starting immediately under the heading "NCSA Mosaic Flavors."

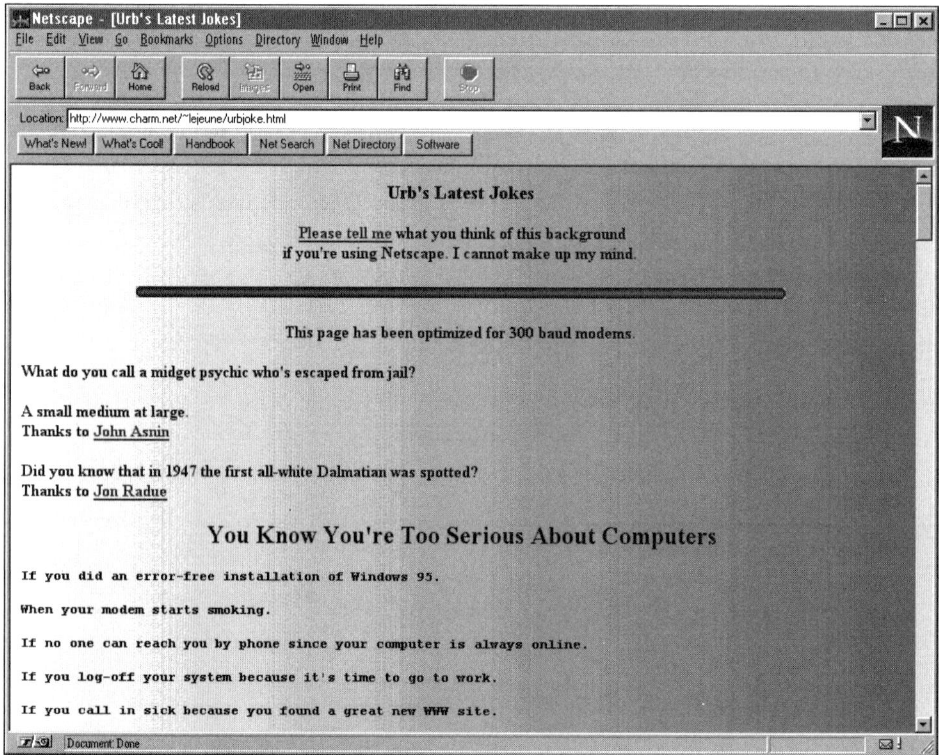

Figure 15.1 *The second page of my home page.*

Adding a Second Page

For our next HTML project, we'll add a second page to the home page we created in the previous chapter. To view this Web page yourself, all you need to do is add the HTML instructions shown next to the end of the body section of the HTML file index.htm.

The HTML text in index.htm producing the new page is:

```
<P><CENTER><IMG ALT="**********" SRC="line.gif"></CENTER>

    &#30; &#30;
    My beautiful wife Pat thinks all
    of us computer types belong in an institution, and not the academic
    type. What can you expect from a person whose first question, when
    shown a new application, is, "How do I get out of this thing?"

    <CENTER><IMG ALT="**********" SRC="line.gif"></CENTER>

    <P><CENTER><IMG ALT="**********" SRC="poi2.gif"></CENTER><P>
    &#30; &#30;
    Living close by, I usually start Web sessions checking on the
    <A HREF=
    "gopher://wx.atmos.uiuc.edu:70/00/States/New%20Jersey/
Metro%20Area%20Zone%20Fcst%20%28Atlantic%20Cty%29">
    Atlantic City Weather Forecast</A><P>

    <IMG ALT="*" SRC="green-ba.gif">
&#30; &#30;
    <B>What's New Pussycat</B><P>
&#30; &#30;
    To keep abreast of current net developments I frequently read postings
    to the newsgroup,
    <A HREF="news:comp.internet.net-happenings">
    comp.internet.net-happenings.</A><BR>
&#30; &#30;
    Another great source of new Gopher and WWW servers and all around
    resource information is the
    <A HREF="http://netlink.wlu.edu:1020/">
    Netlink Server at Washington & Lee University.</A><BR>
&#30; &#30;
    Let's not forget the
    <A HREF="http://www.ncsa.uiuc.edu/SDG/Docs/whats-new.html">
    NCSA What's New</A> document.<BR>
     <TABLE>
       <TR>
          <TD>
             <IMG ALT="*" ALIGN=CENTER SRC="cwsa.gif">
          </TD>
          <TD><B>
              For the latest on Winsock applications, (Web Browsers
              News Readers and the like) check out
             <A HREF="http://uts.cc.utexas.edu/~neuroses/cwsapps.html">
```

```
            The Consummate Winsock Applications Page</A></B>
         </TD>
      </TR>
   </TABLE>

    <TABLE>
      <TR>
         <TD>
            <IMG ALT="*" ALIGN=CENTER SRC="html2.gif">
         </TD>
         <TD><B>
          If you're into HTML, Forms, and CGI this may be the most valuable
          URL on the Net.
          <A HREF="http://WWW.Stars.com/">The
          Web Developer's Virtual Library</A> This is a gold mine!
          <IMG ALT="NEW" SRC="new-left.gif"></B>
         </TD>
      </TR>
   </TABLE><P>

   <CENTER>
   <H2><IMG ALT="*" SRC="redball.gif">
   Interesting Starting Points for Explorations</H2>
   </CENTER>
   <UL>
     <LI>My pick of interesting Internet visitation points.
         <A HREF="urb-menu.html"> Over 300 items arranged by category</A>
     <LI><A HREF="urb-menu.html#Browser-menu">
         <IMG ALT="*" SRC="ftp.gif">
         sites for downloading Web Browsers and helpers.</A>
     <LI><A HREF="get-net.html">
         <IMG ALT="*"  ALIGN=CENTER SRC="netscape.gif">
         Alternative mirror sites for downloading Netscape</A>

     <LI>The University of Maryland's (Baltimore County) great list of
         <A HREF="http://umbc7.umbc.edu/~jack/subject-list.html">
         Subject based information </A>
     <LI>The <A HREF="http://www.charm.net/"> Charm Net Home Page</A>
     <LI>Scott <A HREF="http://www.uwm.edu/Mirror/inet.services.html">
         Yanoff's List </A>of dynamite Internet sites
     <LI>The <A HREF="http://beta.yahoo.com"> Yahoo List</A>
         which is hierarchically arranged and has almost 40,000 links and
         growing by the minute. The list is also searchable, see the form just
         below. This may be the best URL on the Internet. BTW, the is the new
         format Yahoo is testing. <IMG SRC="new-left.gif">
     <LI>URouLette the University of Kansas'
         <A HREF="http://chef.sped.ukans.edu/cgi-bin/random">
         random selection of Web sites.</A>
         For details, or to enter your home page in go to
        <A HREF=
        "http://kuhttp.cc.ukans.edu/cwis/organizations/kucia/uroulette/
uroulette.html">
        URouLette Home Page</A>
        <P>
        <IMG ALT="**********" SRC="red-bar.gif">
        <P>
   </UL>
```

This HTML example is worth a close look because it uses many of the features that we covered in the previous chapter, such as anchors, multiple levels of heads, paragraph formatting tags, and character formatting tags. In a sense, you could say that it puts everything that we've learned into practice.

The first part of this section of HTML is simple enough: a new paragraph about my wife, some images, a few headings, a few anchors to link you to some hot places on the Web, and so on. The section where things get interesting starts right after the heading "Interesting Starting Points for Explorations." Here you'll find a bulleted list structure, which HTML calls an unnumbered list. Notice that it's enclosed within the **<UL>** ... **</UL>** pair. For your reference, here's what the start of the list looks like:

```
<UL>
     <LI>My pick of interesting Internet visitation points.
        <A HREF="urb-menu.html"> Over 300 items arranged by category</A>
```

In the actual list on the Web page, I provide eight options from which the user can select. In each list item, which is set up using the **<LI>** tag, I've also defined an anchor to serve as a hotlink. This is a great way to set up a text-style menu. (I didn't use a terminating **</LI>** tag to define each list item because the end of a list item is implied by another **<LI>**.)

Land Ho!

The end of my home page exploration is in sight. Figure 15.2 shows Netscape displaying my joke page. There are a few interesting things to pursue in this document and then we'll call it quits. (You might want to look at the other two HTML files used in my home page, urbhobie.htm and urb-book.htm, on your own.) Here's the complete listing of the urbjoke.htm document:

```
<HTML>
   <HEAD>
      <Title>Urb's Latest Jokes</Title>
   </HEAD>
   <BODY>
      <H6><B>Urb's Latest Jokes</B></H6>
      <P>
      <DIR>
         I bought the latest computer;<br>
         it came fully loaded.
         <P>
         It was guaranteed for 90 days,<br>
         but in 30 was outmoded!
         <P>
         <I>
```

```
        -The Wall Street Journal<br>
        From the Henry Cate, III Life Collection
       </I>
    </DIR>
    <P>
      Becoming proficient using the Internet is like playing Jai Lai;
      things move very fast, and you're constantly climbing the walls.
    <P>
      Why do cook books outsell sex books? You eat three meals a day!
      <P>
      <B>How about sending a joke to Urb at LeJeune@acy.digex.net?</B>
      <P>
      <A
        HREF=urbhome.htm>
         Back to Urb's home page
    </A>
    <HR>
    <ADDRESS>
       Urb LeJeune  LeJeune@acy.digex.net<BR>
       43 Willis Drive<BR>
       Tuckerton, NJ 08087
    </ADDRESS>
   </BODY>
</HTML>
```

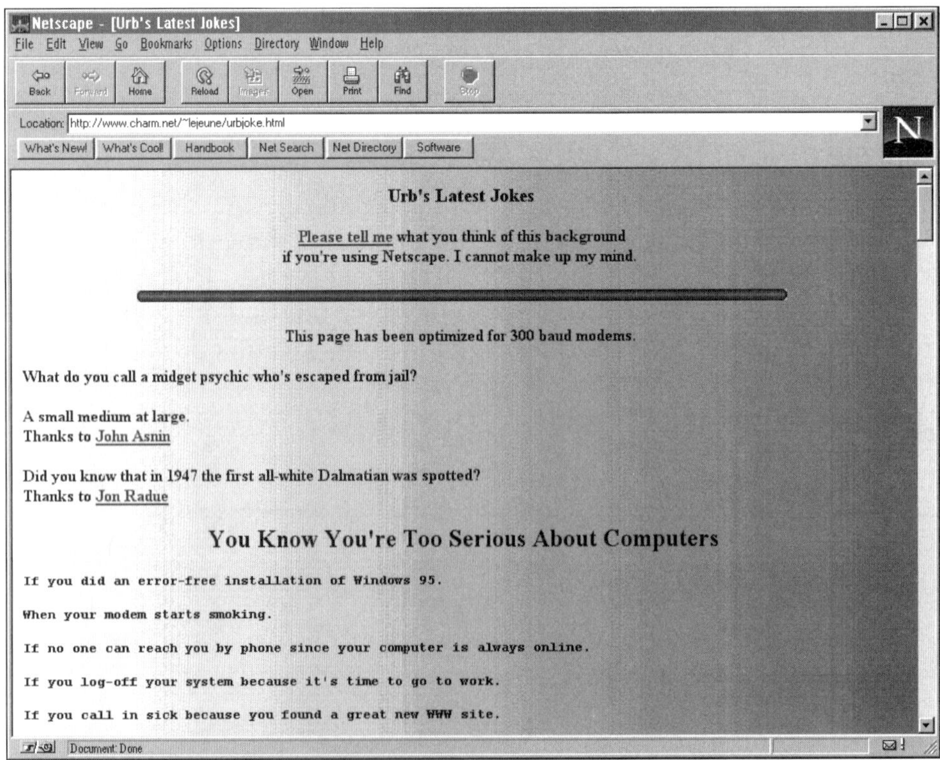

Figure 15.2 Displaying the joke page with Netscape.

Notice that I've put in another list type—the directory list. It is defined using the **<DIR>** ... **</DIR>** tag pair. This is a neat compact list that's also indented. This specific list has embedded **<P>** paragraph, **
** line break, and **<I>** italic tags. In this case, I'm just using this list style to format the initial text quoted from the *Wall Street Journal*.

The **<HR>** tag, which appears just above the **<ADDRESS>** section, inserts a horizontal rule graphic in the displayed text. The rule graphic nicely delineates the logical parts of this document.

WORKING WITH SPECIAL CHARACTERS

All the text we've used in our HTML characters has consisted of standard alphanumeric characters. That is, all of the basic characters that you can type in from your keyboard. But what do you do if you want to include a special character such as a copyright symbol or a symbol that is used by HTML as a coding symbol such as "<" or ">"? Fortunately, there is an easy way to get symbols like these in your HTML documents. In fact, you can see these characters with their codes displayed in the "HTML Style Guide & Test Suite" presented later in this chapter.

You can use one of two methods to display a special character: Specify the numeric code of the character or use a pre-assigned symbolic name. Here's an example of how the numeric approach works:

```
&#169;
```

This would display a copyright symbol: ©. (The numeric code for this symbol is 169.) To specify a numeric code for a character, you must include "&#" in front of the number as shown. You can also specify multiple characters by separating each code with a semicolon. For example, this unusual looking line of HTML would display three spaces on a page (160 is the numeric code for a space):

```
     
```

If you don't like using hard-to-read numeric codes, you can use a symbolic name to represent a special character. Actually, this method only works for four characters: ", &, <, and >. The symbolic names for these characters are quot, amp, lt, and gt, respectively. Here's an example of how the pair of brackets, <>, can be displayed using their symbolic names:

```
&lt; &gt;
```

A Little More on Images

In the previous chapter we only explored the basics of images. We experimented with the **<IMG>** tag to display bitmap images stored as GIF files. Recall that the format for this tag is

```
<IMG SRC = "gif-filename">
```

where *gif-filename* is the file name or the complete pathname and file name of the image to be displayed.

But there is much more to Web page images than this. You can also set up an image to be a hotlink just as you would set up a text hotlink. In addition, you can control the alignment of your images on a Web page by using special modifiers with the **<IMG>** tag. You can also include alternative text to be displayed if your image cannot be viewed.

The actual extended form of the **<IMG>** tag is:

```
<IMG [ALT = "alternative text"] [ALIGN=text-position] SRC = url-of-graphic>
```

Let's look at how these different features can be used to create more appealing Web pages.

Combining Images with Text

In most Web pages that you create, you'll want to combine images with text. With the first version of the HTML specification, you were not given a lot of options for displaying text with images. For example, you couldn't flow text around images like you would in a page layout program such as PageMaker. With HTML 3 features and a browser such as Netscape, you can now perform many types of text and image alignment features such as:

- Left, right, and center justify images and text
- Wrap text around left or right justified images using variable spacing
- Create variable-sized borders around images (or remove them altogether)

The important point to keep in mind when combining text with images is that an image does not force a paragraph break—all images are displayed inline with whatever text is displayed. Normally, any text in the same paragraph as an image will be lined up with the bottom of the image, and will wrap normally below the image. This works well if the text is essentially a caption for the image, or if the image is a decoration at the start of a paragraph. However, when the image is a part of a header, you may want the text to be centered vertically in the image, or to be lined up with the top of the image. In these cases, you can use the optional **ALIGN** parameter with the **<IMG>** tag to specify one of three settings: **TOP**, **MIDDLE**, or **BOTTOM**. As an example, the following HTML would display my picture with the bold text "This is me again" to the right of the picture, directly in the center of the picture:

```
<B>This is me again</B>
<IMG ALIGN=MIDDLE SRC = urb.gif>
```

If you wanted to display the text to the left of the picture and at the top, here's the HTML required:

```
<B>This is me again</B>
<IMG ALIGN=TOP SRC = urb.gif>
```

Later, when I present the HTML for our style guide, I'll show you what the different alignment effects look like as they appear on a Web page. I'll also show you how to use some of the more advanced features provided with the HTML extensions.

Using Multiple Images per Line

Since an image is treated in some ways as a single (rather large) character, you can have more than one image on a single line. In fact, you can have as many images on a line as will fit in a browser window! Of course, if you put too many images on a single line, the browser will wrap the line, and your images will appear on two or more lines. Therefore, don't specify a series of images that must be displayed on one line. Conversely, if you don't want images to appear on the same line, be sure to place a <**BR**> or <**P**> tag between them.

Displaying Text Instead of Images

You just created a fantastic HTML document with lots of images all designed to provide your user with important information. So what do you do if your user can only access your document with a text-only browser such as Lynx? You could either ignore them (and really annoy them) or you could be considerate and add text descriptions to your images. The user would then see the text descriptions and they'd at least get an idea of what's included in your HTML document. (Maybe if your descriptions are good enough, they would be enticed to view your document with a visual browser such as Netscape or Mosaic.)

To define an alternate text description for an image, you use the **<IMG>** tag with the **ALT=** subtag. For example, this statement will either display my picture if the user has a visual browser, or it will display the description "Urb LeJeune, author of Netscape and HTML EXplorer" if the image cannot be displayed:

```
<IMG ALT="Urb LeJeune, author of Netscape and HTML EXplorer" SRC="urb.gif">
```

You can use this feature with images you set up as hotlinks. (I'll show you how this is done shortly.) In fact, using the **ALT=** subtag is a good habit to get into for images that are either displayed as standalone pictures or as hotlinks. If an image is used as a hotlink, the text specified by the **ALT=** subtag will be the only thing a text-mode browser user will see. Without it, the user will miss out on the hotlink and they might get stuck somewhere in your document or not be able to access an important part of the document.

Using an Image as a Hotlink

Image hotlinks are set up just like hypertext links by using anchor tags **<A>** ... **</A>**. The only difference is that the image itself is used as the anchor text. Recall the format for defining an anchor:

```
<A HREF="file-pathname">anchor-text</A>
```

All we need to do is use the **<IMG>** tag to reference a picture in place of the anchor text. As an example, this anchor definition sets up the picture of you-know-who as a hotlink:

```
<A HREF = "UrbsBio.htm"><IMG SRC=urb.gif></A>
```

If you clicked on my picture, up would come the HTML document UrbsBio.htm. (Just what you need, more information about me!) The user can tell that the picture is a hotlink because it will be outlined in a color. Netscape will outline images that are set up as hotlinks in blue.

In the previous section, I showed you how to include alternate text with an image. Let's combine what we learned with the anchor definition. The result is this line of HTML:

```
<A HREF = "UrbsBio.htm"><IMG ALT="Urb LeJeune, author of Netscape and HTML
  EXplorer" SRC="urb.gif"></A>
```

If your user had a text-only browser, he or she would see the text assigned to the **ALT=** subtag as the hotlink. If this link were selected, the target document would still be displayed.

Linking a Picture to Itself

Here's a neat trick that many Web page designers incorporate into their Web pages. Define an anchor and link a picture to itself! I know this sounds weird, but follow along.

Here's how you can set up this type of anchor:

```
<A HREF=urb.gif><IMG SRC=urb.gif>
```

In this case, my picture is the hotlink. When the user clicks on the link, up I'll come. So why does it make sense to have an inline image point to itself? For one, many people turn off inline images to improve performance over a slow network link. If the inline image is an anchor for itself, they can then click on the placeholder graphic to see what they missed.

There is also an aesthetic issue at stake here. Some Web browsers do not "realize a palette" before displaying an image. Presumably this isn't a problem on a 24-bit display, but most of us have 256-color displays, and Windows maps the colors of inline images to the closest colors in the current palette. This can make for some funny looking images! If, however, the image is linked to itself, the readers can simply click on the image to load it into their favorite viewer, which will probably handle the colors much better.

Working with Thumbnails

A thumbnail is a small graphic image that points to a larger version of the same image. So why use them? They can help you save a lot of transmission and loading time of Web pages. Let's say that you are creating a Web page that will serve as a catalog of jewelry that your company makes. You could create a Web page and put a sizable picture of each piece of jewelry with a one-sentence description. The problem with this approach is that when Web surfers (and potential customers) access your page, they might have to wait a very long time for all of the images to be downloaded and displayed on their computer. They might lose interest and go check out someone else's Web site.

The better approach would be to use thumbnails—little pictures of each item that link to the bigger and better looking images. The users could then click on one of the small images of their choice to view the full-size image. This approach would give you a "visual" table of contents.

If this description of thumbnails sounds like I'm describing anchors or hotlinks, you're right. In fact, you use the anchor tag to set them up, as shown here:

```
<A HREF=larger-graphic-file><IMG SRC=thumb-nail-graphic-file></A>
```

As an example

```
<A HREF=urb.gif><IMG SRC=urbsmall.gif></A>
```

would load the image urbsmall.gif as a thumbnail link. When the user clicked on this link, the image urb.gif would be loaded.

Processing and Sizing Your Images

We've explored many of the fine points for adding images to your Web pages using the **<IMG>** HTML tag, but what you also need to know is how to get your image files ready for displaying. There are many techniques and tricks for processing images for electronic documents that you'll discover over time. Right now let's discuss a few to get you started.

The first thing you'll need is a good image processing program to help you work with your images. There are many programs available, both shareware and retail (and even a few freeware ones). I've included a powerful shareware program on the companion CD-ROM called Paint Shop Pro, as shown in Figure 15.3, to help you get started. I'll use it with a few of the image processing examples that I present here. If you have never used a program like this, I suggest you try it. You'll be amazed at many of the powerful image processing tasks you can perform, such as resizing and cropping images, editing your images, and saving them in different formats.

To display your images with Web pages, you'll need to make sure that they are converted to a GIF or JPEG format. Most PC images are stored in a TIF, BMP, or PCX format. Converting your images is a snap if you have a program like Paint Shop Pro. You can either open one image at a time and save it as a GIF format or use a batch conversion process to convert all of your images at once. The batch conversion feature can be selected from Paint Shop Pro by selecting File | Batch Conversion. A dialog box will appear. You can then select the files you want to convert and the directory where you want to save the converted files. Click the OK button and Paint Shop Pro will convert the files.

Another technique you'll need to know is how to resize your images. Most images you get from different sources will probably be full screen images and they will be much too large for your Web pages. Fortunately, if you have a program like Paint Shop Pro, images are easy to resize. First, load in the image using the File | Open command. Then, select Image | Resize to display the dialog box shown in Figure 15.4. The standard size for a typical full screen image is 640x480. (Paint Shop Pro uses units of pixels to represent image dimensions.) To make your image smaller, you click on the Custom Size radio button and then enter your new sizes for the image's width and height in the two text boxes. The sizes shown in Figure 15.4 will make the image approximately 1" by 1". If you want to keep the width-to-height aspect ratio of your resized image the same as the original, you should select the Maintain Aspect Ratio check box.

Having a program like Paint Shop Pro can be a real asset, especially if you plan to include a number of thumbnails in your Web pages and you need a way to produce small versions of your larger GIF files.

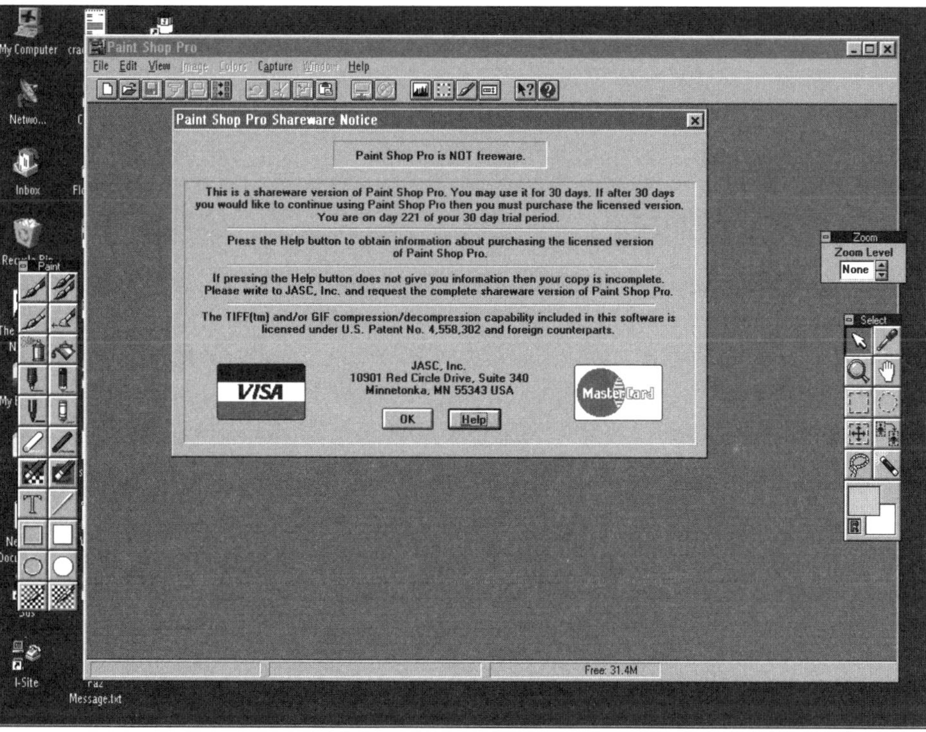

Figure 15.3 Using the Paint Shop Pro program to process images.

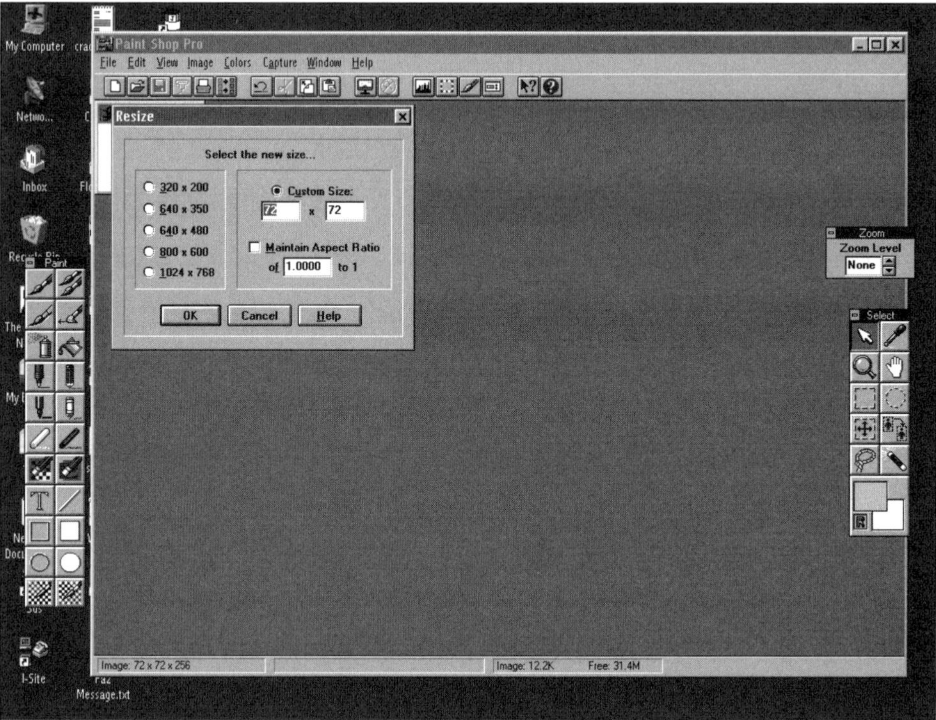

***Figure 15.4** Using Paint Shop Pro's image Resize dialog box.*

Working with Multimedia

In addition to displaying images and setting up hotlinks to images, you can use multimedia files with your Web pages to really make things interesting. Basically, you can define a hotlink to a video file or a sound file by using the anchor tag pair **<A>** ... **</A>**. When the user clicks on the hotlink, the file will be sent to his or her computer, which in turn will "play" the file.

As you work with multimedia files, keep in mind that most browsers can't actually play multimedia files. Browsers such as Netscape and Mosaic use what are called *helper programs* to load files that they can't internally read. For example, when you select a GIF file for viewing by clicking on a hotlink, Netscape calls a helper program to load and display the GIF image.

To set up a multimedia file as a hotlink, use the anchor tag pair **<A>** ... **</A>** as shown here:

```
<A HREF = "Gcanyon.wav">Sounds of the Grand Canyon</A>
```

When the users click on the text link, the WAV file Gcanyon.wav will be sent to their computer so that they can play it. Of course, you are not limited to just sound files; you can create hotlinks for all types of files, including video and animation.

Getting Smarter with Sound Files

One of the big problems with sound files is that they are typically very big and thus slow to download. If you include a sound file as part of a hotlink, the user must click on the link and then wait a long time for the file to be downloaded before it can be played. This is the kind of waiting that really turns off Web users—especially when the Internet has a lot of traffic.

One enterprising company, DSP Group, has created a program called TsPlayer, which is billed as the first World Wide Web real time sound player. TsPlayer lets you play any TrueSpeech sound file (WAV) while you are downloading the file. The sound file is actually played by your favorite sound file player, which is set up as the helper program. TsPlayer makes sure that the sound file starts to play as soon as you start the download. This means that your user can click on a hotlink that references a sound file, instantly start to hear the file, and then decide whether to continue downloading the file. What a dream!

I've provided the TsPlayer program on the companion CD-ROM. You can also download it using the following FTP site:

```
http://www.acs.oakland.edu/oak/SimTel/win3/sound/tsplay100.zip
```

Creating the HTML Style Guide

You're now in for a real HTML treat. We're about to embark on an adventurous Web document project to surpass all other HTML documents we've created so far. What we'll do is create an interactive document that presents all the essentials of HTML. This is our first major Web publishing project. What's unique is that we'll use all the knowledge we've acquired to create a useful reference guide. We'll call the guide "HTML Style Guide & Test Suite." It is stored in the file styles.htm on the companion CD-ROM. You can also access an "up-to-the-minute" version of the guide on the Web by pointing your browser to this location:

```
http://www.charm.net/~lejeune/styles.html
```

Of course, our HTML guide is not all-inclusive, nor will it provide detailed explanations of the HTML tags presented. The guide is mainly designed to be a quick reference. You'll find additional coverage of HTML topics, such as forms, in Chapter 19 and Appendix A. This appendix is an expanded guide to writing HTML. Our "HTML Style Guide & Test Suite" will be developed and discussed in twelve easy to follow sections; each section will represent roughly one page or screen of the guide. As we create the guide, I'll show you the section of the Web page in a Netscape screen along with the HTML that creates that particular page.

To get a real feel for HTML encoding, look at a listing of styles.htm while you are viewing Netscape's display of the file on your screen. Assuming that the file styles.htm is in the directory \WWWFiles on your C: drive, select the File | Open URL option from the menu line and enter

```
FILE:///C:/WWWFiles/STYLES.HTM
```

as the URL. If the file is stored on a different directory on your hard drive, make sure you specify the correct path name.

Without further fanfare, let's get started.

Screen 1—Creating the Table of Contents

Since our HTML guide provides a number of topics and scrollable pages, we'll need a table of contents for easy navigation. Figure 15.5 shows the first screen

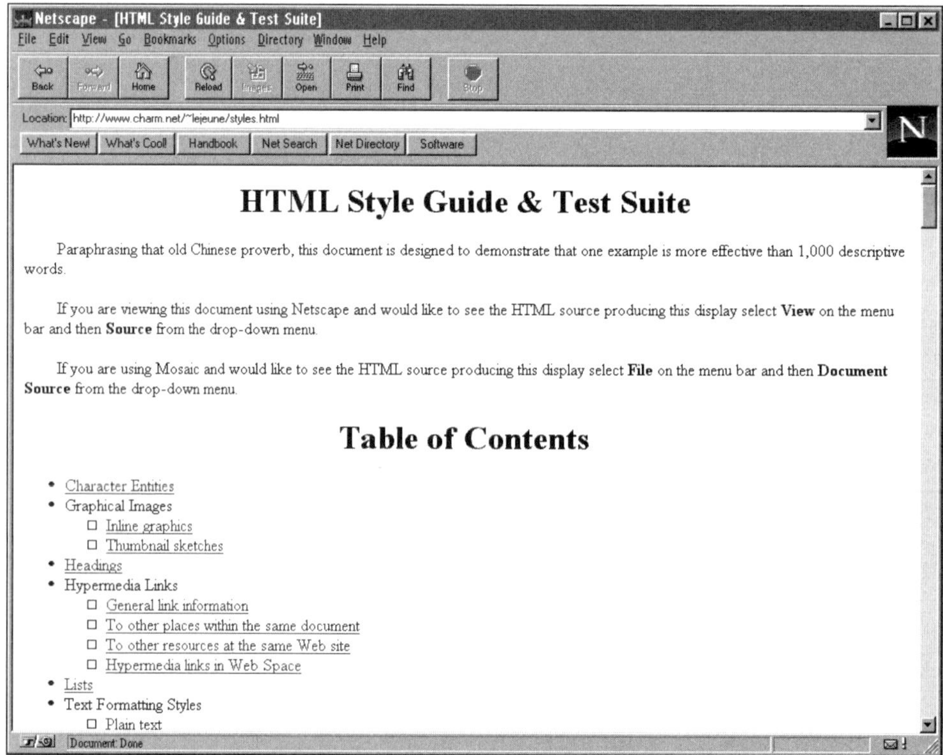

Figure 15.5 The Table of Contents for the HTML style guide.

of the style guide as viewed in Netscape. Notice that the guide provides a range of topics from using special characters to working with graphics images to applying text formatting styles.

As you might guess, the table of contents is set up as an unordered list with anchors. In fact, the table of contents contains nested unordered lists. (This is our first chance to put some of our advanced list creation experience to work in a practical application.) When the user clicks on any of the highlighted hotlinks, he or she will be taken to a location (another page) in the document that corresponds with the topic selected. How's that for a truly interactive document!

Enough of the overview, let's create the HTML that sets up the first screen:

```
<HTML>
  <HEAD>
    <TITLE>HTML Style Guide & Test Suite</TITLE>
  </HEAD>

  <BODY>
    <CENTER><H1>HTML Style Guide &amp; Test Suite</H1></CENTER>

    <! This is a comment and the four   below place four spaces
       at the start of the line. A comment ends with a greater than sign.>

           
    Paraphrasing that old Chinese proverb, this document is designed
    to demonstrate that one example is more effective than 1,000
    descriptive words.
    <P>
           
    If you are viewing this document using Netscape and would like to
    see the HTML source producing this display select <B>View</B>
    on the menu bar and then <B>Source</B> from the drop-down menu.
    <P>
           
    If you are using Mosaic and would like to see the HTML source
    producing this display select <B>File</B> on the menu bar and
    then <B>Document Source</B> from the drop-down menu.

    <A NAME="TOC"></A>

    <CENTER><H1>Table of Contents</H1></CENTER>

    <UL>
      <LI><A HREF=#SPECIAL_CHARACTERS>Character Entities</A>
      <LI>Graphical Images
      <UL>
        <LI><A HREF=#GRAPHICS>Inline graphics</A>
        <LI><A HREF=#THUMB>Thumbnail sketches</A>
      </UL>
```

```
<LI><A HREF=#HEADINGS>Headings</A>
<LI>Hypermedia Links
<UL>
  <LI><A HREF=#GENERAL>General link information</A>
  <LI><A HREF=#SAME>To other places within the same document</A>
  <LI><A HREF=#OTHER>To other resources at the same Web site</A>
  <LI><A HREF=#OUTSIDE>Hypermedia links in Web Space</A>
</UL>

<LI><A HREF=#LISTS>Lists</A>
<LI>Text Formatting Styles
<UL>
  <LI><A HREF=#PLAIN>Plain text</A>
  <LI><A HREF=#LOGICAL>Logical text styles</A>
  <LI><A HREF=#PHYSICALL>Physical text styles</A>
</UL>

<LI><A HREF=#NETSCAPE>Netscape enhancements to HTML</A>
<UL>
  <LI><A HREF=#CENTER>Centering Text and Graphics</A>
  <LI><A HREF=#BLINK>Blinking Text</A>
  <LI><A HREF=#FONTS>Font Sizing</A>
  <LI><A HREF=#BASE_FONT>Base Font Sizing</A>
</UL>
<P>
<LI><A HREF=#AUTHOR>The author of this document</A>
</UL>
```

The first part of the document takes care of all the required setup work. Here you'll find tags for the document's title, body, level one head, and so on. Notice that the special character code ** ** (space) is used to indent the introductory text over a few spaces. (Remember that Web browsers do not indent text, so we have to do it manually.)

Next, we get to the menu or contents section. This anchor kicks things off:

```
<A NAME="TOC"></A>
```

It defines the anchor target named "TOC". We need this target so that we can link back to the menu from any of the other sections. (This is the location the user returns to whenever he or she clicks on an anchor that is assigned **HREF=#TOC**.)

The actual navigation menu is created by using nested **<UL>** pairs. There's nothing tricky here, but keep your eye out for the anchor link targets that are being defined here, such as **#SPECIAL_CHARACTERS**, **#GRAPHICS**, **#THUMB**, and so on. You'll see these in action when we create the next sections.

One nice feature of the HTML style guide that we are building is that it contains information about some of the enhanced HTML features that Netscape supports, such as centering text and graphics, blinking text, and font sizing. These features will be placed in the section of the document that is referenced by the **#NETSCAPE** anchor.

Screen 2—Here Come the Headings

As Figure 15.6 shows, screen 2 of the HTML guide is used to display samples of each of the six HTML headings, **<H1>** through **<H6>**. Even without seeing the HTML for the main part of this screen, you can probably guess that it looks like:

```
<P>
The above table of contents is an unordered list. Each element
is a hyperlink in the form of:
<P>
&lt;A HREF=#branch-name&gt;branch-title&lt;/A&gt;
<P>
The target anchor is in the form of:
<P>
&lt;A NAME=#branch-name&gt;display-anchor-title&lt;/A&gt;

<H4><A NAME="HEADINGS">HTML Headings</A></H4>

<H1>Heading One &lt;H1&gt;</H1>
<H2>Heading Two &lt;H2&gt;</H2>
<H3>Heading Three &lt;H3&gt;</H3>
<H4>Heading Four &lt;H4&gt;</H4>
<H5>Heading Five &lt;H5&gt;</H5>
<H6>Heading Six &lt;H6&gt;</H6>
<P>
<A HREF=#TOC>Back to Table of Contents</A>
```

Actually, the first part of this HTML belongs with the previous section. It didn't all fit in the previous browser screen, so I'm showing it here. Basically, the text explains how the menu system was set up. If you look closely, you'll see the rather strange-looking line of HTML

```
&lt;A HREF=#branch-name&gt;branch-title&lt;/A&gt;
```

which gets translated into:

```
<A HREF=#branch-name>branch-title</A&>
```

Some people say that HTML is hard to read. If you had to read HTML lines like this all day, you'd probably agree. The code **<** represents the less than

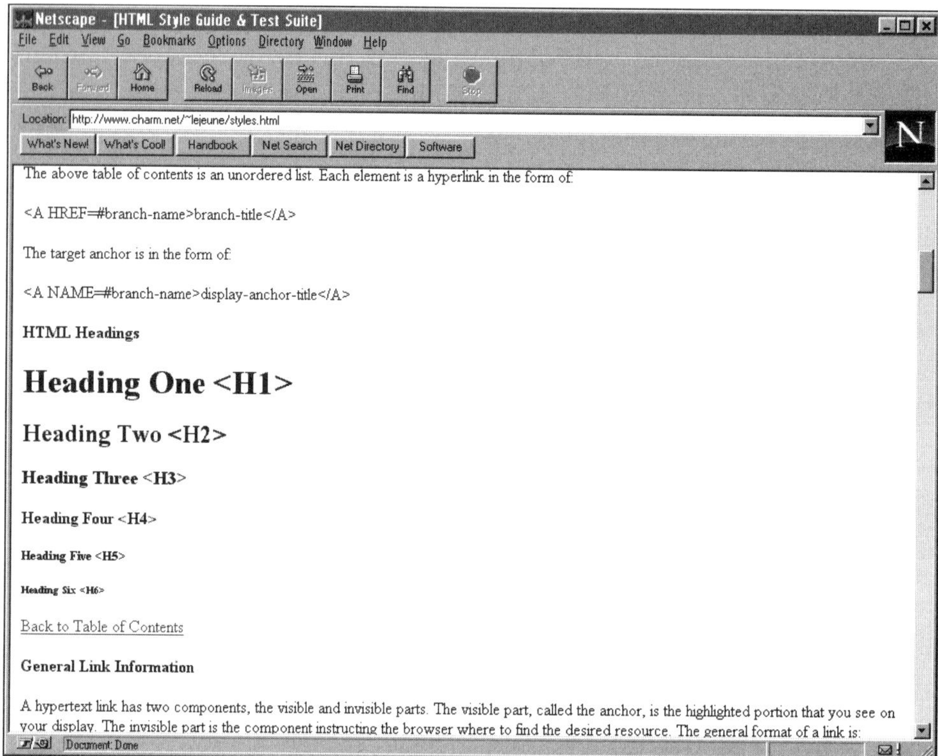

***Figure 15.6** Screen 2 of the style guide—HTML headings.*

symbol (<) and the code **>** represents greater than (>). Remember that all of the unique symbols that HTML supports are presented in the style guide. When using these codes, you must place a semicolon after the end of each code.

The remainder of the screen displays the six different heading formats. Note also that this HTML section contains an anchor with a reference to the **TOC** target that links the reader back to the table of contents.

Screens 3 and 4—Exploring the Basics of Links

We now come to our part of the guide that covers hypermedia links. There is more to say here so we'll easily fill up two pages. First, we start with screen 3. This screen features the text that describes general link information and techniques for defining links that reference other locations within the same HTML document. Figure 15.7 shows the actual browser window.

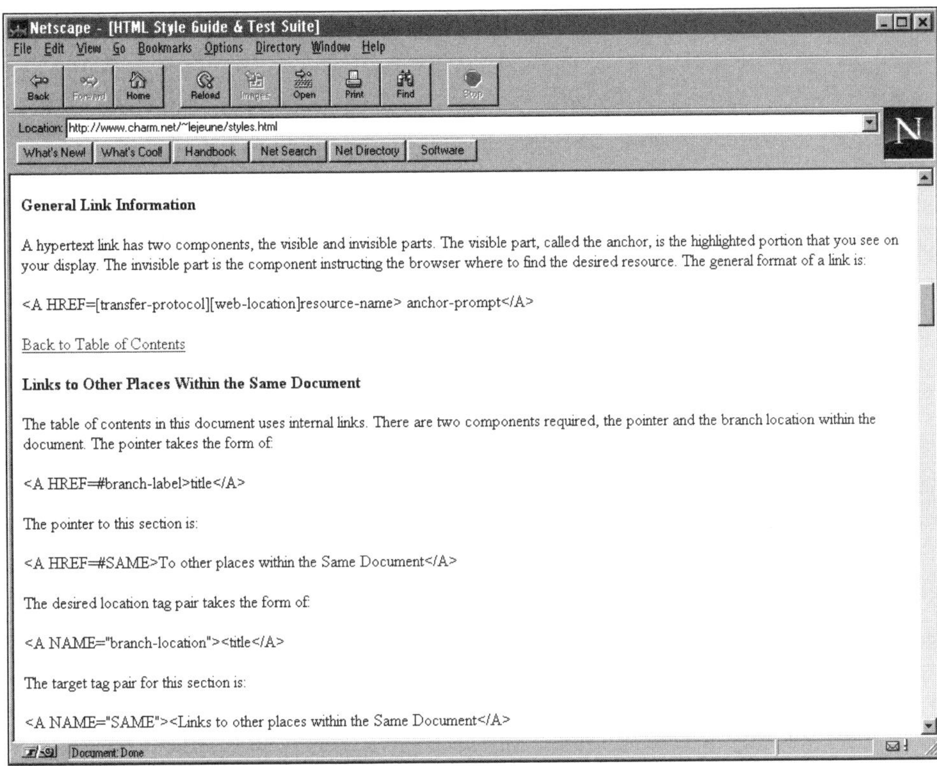

***Figure 15.7** Screen 3 of the style guide—exploring links.*

The HTML required to display this screen is:

```
<H4><A NAME="GENERAL">General Link Information</A></H4>

A hypertext link has two components, the visible and invisible
parts. The visible part, called the anchor, is the highlighted
portion that you see on your display. The invisible part is the
component instructing the browser where to find the desired resource.
The general format of a link is:
<P>
&lt;A HREF=[transfer-protocol][web-location]resource-name&gt;
anchor-prompt&lt;/A&gt;
<P>
<A HREF=#TOC>Back to Table of Contents</A>
<H4><A NAME="SAME">Links to Other Places Within the Same
  Document</A></H4>
<P>
The table of contents in this document uses internal links. There
are two components required, the pointer and the branch location
within the document. The pointer takes the form of:
<P>
```

```
&lt;A HREF=#branch-label&gt;title&lt;/A&gt;
<P>
The pointer to this section is:
<P>
&lt;A HREF=#SAME&gt;To other places within the Same Document&lt;/A&gt;
<P>
The desired location tag pair takes the form of:
<P>
&lt;A NAME=&quot;branch-location&quot;&gt;title&lt;/A&gt;
<P>
The target tag pair for this section is:
<P>
&lt;A NAME=&quot;SAME&quot;&gt;Links to other places within
the Same Document&lt;/A&gt;
<P>
<A HREF=#TOC>Back to Table of Contents</A>
```

The first paragraph of text, labeled with the anchor **NAME="GENERAL"**, describes the general information about defining hypertext links. The second paragraph, labeled with **NAME="SAME"**, illustrates the process of pointing to links within the same document. Notice that at the end of both paragraphs a **TOC** return link is provided to take the user back to the table of contents. The text for this link, "Back to Table of Contents," is underlined in the screen shown in Figure 15.7. Providing the user with an easy way to always access the top level menu is good style; your users will thank you if you design your Web pages this way.

Okay, on to screen 4. Figure 15.8 shows the second part of the hyperlinks reference. This time, we need to cover two topics: linking to other resources at the same Web site and linking to files at other Web sites. Here's the required HTML:

```
<H4><A NAME="OTHER">Links to Other Resources at the Same Web Site</A>
</H4>

<P>
If the desired resource is located at the same Web site and uses
the same protocol, all that is needed is the name of the resource.
This pointer takes the form:
<P>
&lt;A HREF=resource-name&gt;anchor-prompt&lt;/A&gt;
<P>
To illustrate, a file named SECOND.HTM that is located at the
same site and in the same directory as the document currently
being viewed would be fetched using the link:
<P>
&lt;A HREF=SECOND.HTM&gt;Click here to activate SECOND.HTM&lt;/A&gt;
<P>
```

```
<A HREF=#TOC>Back to Table of Contents</A>
<H4><A NAME="OUTSIDE">Hypermedia Links in Web Space</A></H4>

<P>
An external link points to a resource at another Web site. As
an example, my home page link is:
<P>
&lt;A HREF=HTTP://www.charm.net/~lejeune&gt;Urb's Home Page&lt;/A&gt;
<P>
It would appear on your screen as: <A HREF=HTTP://www.charm.net/
 ~lejeune>Urb's home page</A>
<P>
<A HREF=#TOC>Back to Table of Contents</A>
```

Notice that links are provided to take the reader to either the table of contents or my home page.

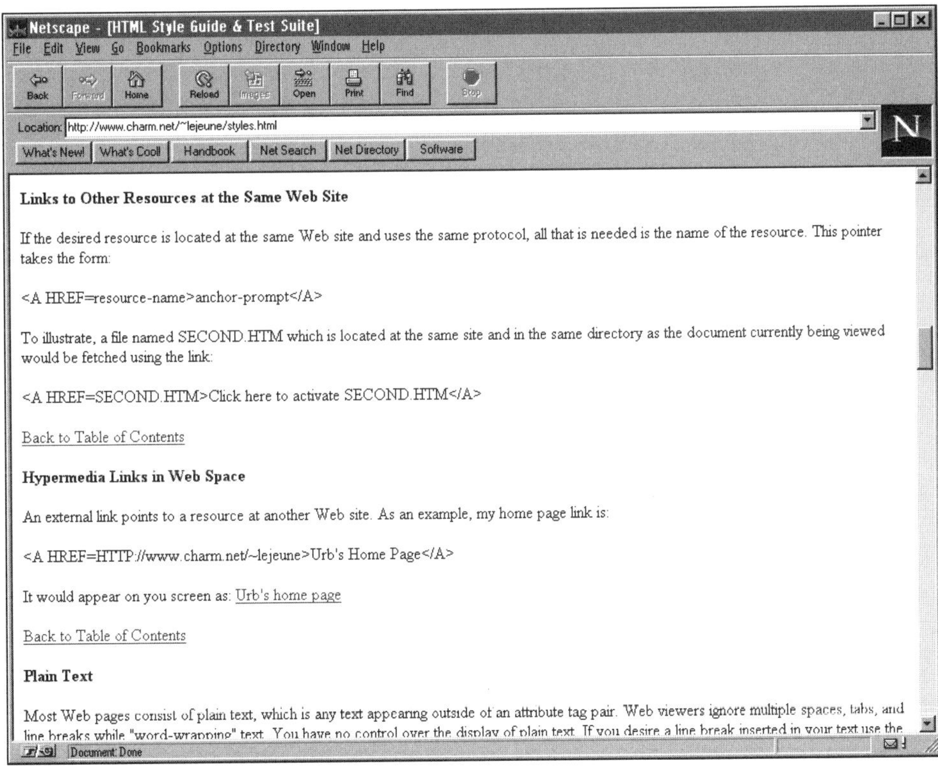

***Figure 15.8** Screen 4 of the style guide—more links.*

Screen 5—Using Text Formatting Styles

As we work our way through the HTML document, we come to the part of the guide that covers text styles. As Figure 15.9 shows, we cover both logical and physical text styles. If you look closely, you'll see that Netscape does not support all HTML text styles. The HTML for this section follows.

```
<H4><A NAME="PLAIN">Plain Text</A></H4>

<P>
Most Web pages consist of plain text, which is any text appearing
outside of an attribute tag pair. Web viewers ignore multiple
spaces, tabs, and line breaks while &quot;word-wrapping&quot;
text. You have no control over the display of plain text. If you
desire a line break inserted in your text use the &lt;BR&gt; tag.
To force a paragraph use the &lt;P&gt; tag.
<P>
Line one. &lt;BR&gt; Line two. &lt;P&gt; appears as: <BR>
Line one.<BR>
Line two.
<P>
If text is to be displayed with formatting retained, as an example
a program listing, use the &lt;PRE&gt; &lt;/PRE&gt; tag pair.
<P>
    Paragraphs are not indented, however, multiple blanks are
inserted using a series of &quot;&amp;#160;&quot; groupings. This
paragraph starts with two such groupings.
<H4><A NAME="LOGICAL">Logical Text Styles</A></H4>

<P>
This sentence is normal text. Each of the following styles is
enclosed between the tags indicating the style. <EM>Emphasized
Text</EM>
<P>
<STRONG>Strong Text</STRONG>
<P>
<CITE>Cited Text</CITE> line break is next.<BR>
<A NAME="PHYSICALL"> </A>
<H4>Physical Text Styles</H4>

<P>
<B>Bold Text</B>
<P>
<I>Italics Text</I>
<P>
<U>Underlined Text</U>
<P>
<TT>Typewriter Font</TT>
<P>
Horizontal Rule &lt;HR&gt; is next<HR>
```

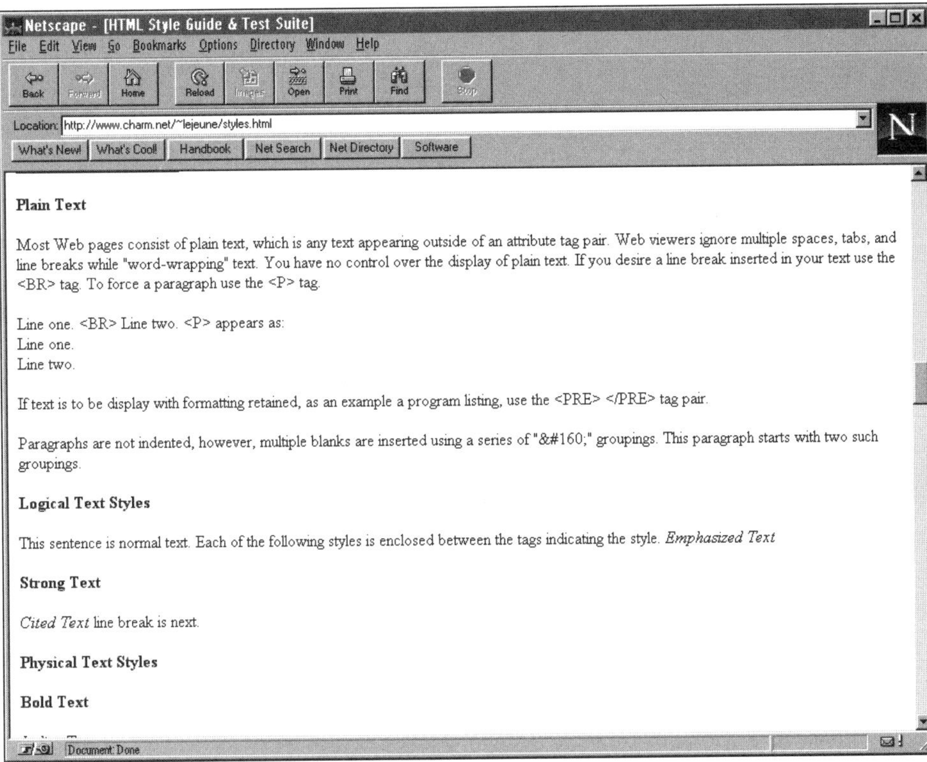

***Figure 15.9** Screen 5 of the style guide—text formatting.*

In Chapter 14 we presented all of the physical text style tags that HTML provides—**<B>**, **<I>**, and so on. In addition to these styles, HTML provides *logical* tags for character formatting. Logical styles are used to mark text according to its meaning. For example, if you were writing a sentence like this that referenced the name of a book

```
The Netscape and HTML EXplorer is a great read.
```

the name of the book is considered a citation. In this case, you could use a special HTML logical tag named **<CITE>** to mark the citation.

It turns out that many of the logical tags cause text to be displayed in one of the three physical styles: bold, italic, or underlined. For example, text marked with **<CITE>** will appear as italic text; text marked as **<STRONG>** will appear as bold text. I've included some of the more widely used logical tags in the style guide so you can see how they are used and how they change the appearance of displayed text. The complete set of logical tags is presented in Appendix A.

Blinking Text for Netscape Users

If you are a Netscape user, there is a logical style you just have to check out. Its tag is **<BLINK>**, and as you might guess, it makes text blink on the screen. This is a good way to really get a user's attention. To use this feature, simply format the text like this:

```
<BLINK>This is blinking text!</BLINK>
```

Don't forget to include the terminating tag. If you forget, all of your text will blink and your Web page will look like it belongs in Las Vegas!

Screens 6 and 7—Displaying Inline Graphics and Thumbnails

This is your chance to check out many of the inline graphics features we've been exploring in the first part of the chapter. Screen 6, shown in Figure 15.10, presents some of the different image display options supported by the **<IMG>** tag. This is your chance to see the different effects produced by the **ALIGN** modifier. For example, the text displayed with the first picture is positioned by using the statement **ALIGN=TOP** within the **<IMG>** tag.

The HTML that produces this screen is:

```
<H4><A NAME="GRAPHICS">Inline Graphics</A></H4>

<P>
An inline graphic is treated like a character, albeit a very large
one, by graphical WWW browsers. The format for displaying an inline
image is
<P>
&lt;IMG [ALT=&quot;alternative-text&quot;] [ALIGN=text-position]
SRC=url-of-graphic&gt;
<P>
Where &quot;alternative-text&quot; is the text that will be displayed,
in lieu of the image on a non-graphic browser such as Lynx.
<P>
The parameter for ALIGN= may be TOP, CENTER, or BOTTOM. This determines
where one line of text will be displayed within the same paragraph.
<P>
Align Top <IMG ALT="Netscape Image Goes Here" ALIGN=TOP SRC=big-net.gif>
Align Top
<P>
Align Middle <IMG ALT="Netscape Image Goes Here" ALIGN=MIDDLE SRC=big-
net.gif>
```

```
Align Middle
<P>
Align Bottom <IMG ALT="Netscape Image Goes Here" ALIGN=BOTTOM SRC=big-
net.gif>
Align Bottom
<P>
<A HREF=#TOC>Back to Table of Contents</A>
```

First, we set an anchor target “Inline Graphics” to reference this section from the hotlink in the table of contents. We also need to use some of the HTML special characters to display the full form of the **<IMG>** tag. Next comes the HTML to display the Netscape image in three different ways. In each variation, different text alignment options are used to show you the HTML required to combine text with images. Notice that the paragraph tag **<P>** is placed after the HTML instructions used to display each group of images and text. If we omitted this tag, the browser would try to display all three images on the same line. Always keep in mind that a graphic is treated like a single character, albeit a large one.

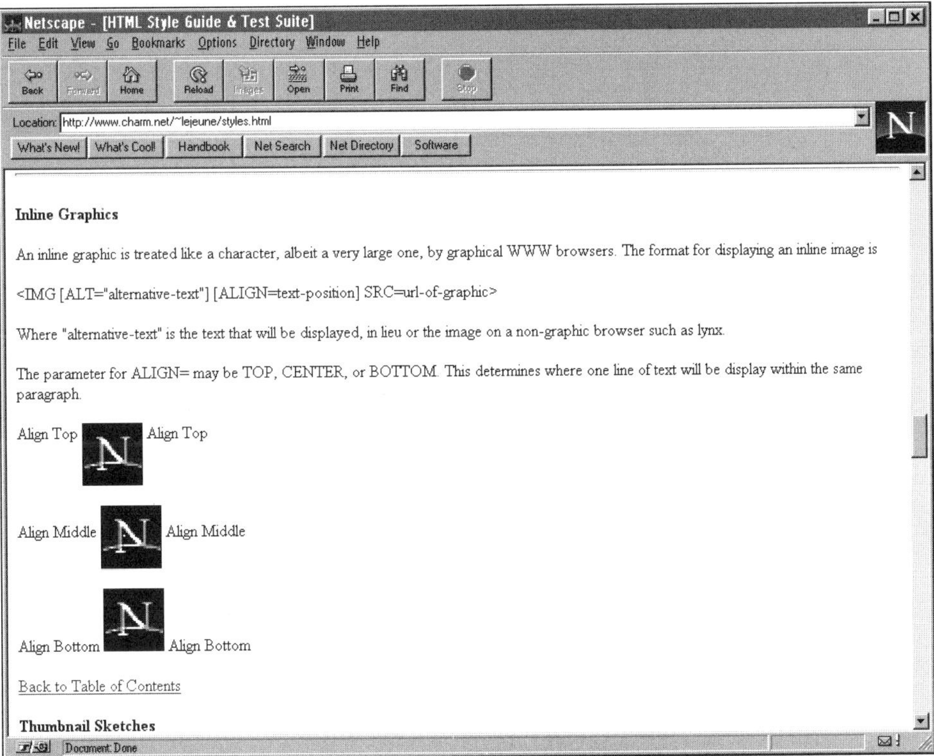

Figure 15.10 *Screen 6 of the style guide—inline images and text.*

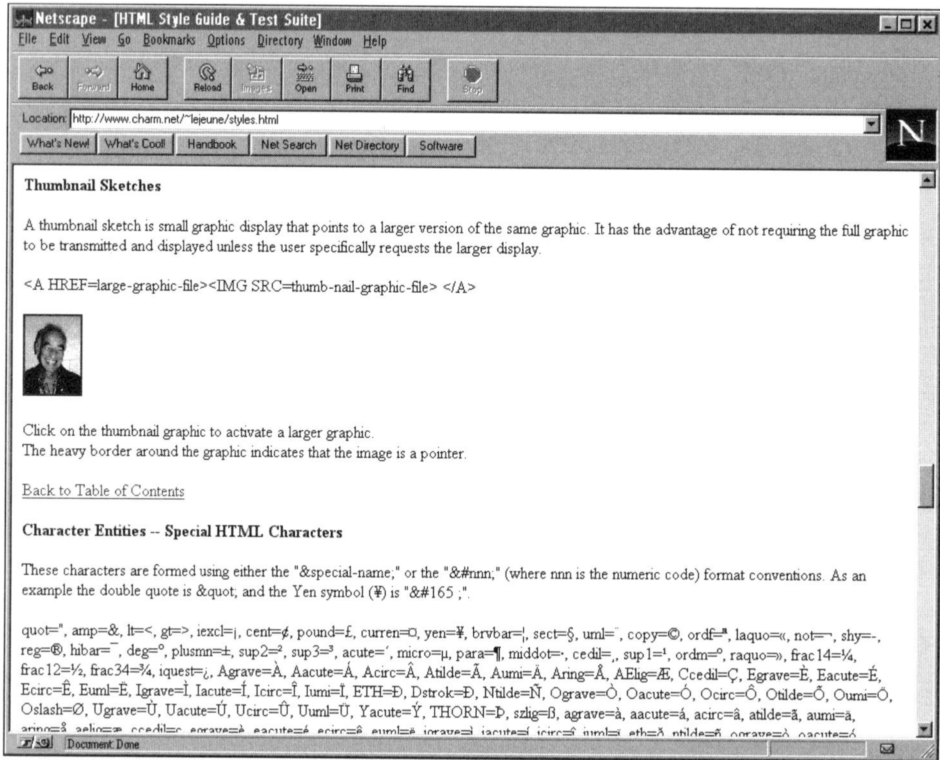

***Figure 15.11** Screen 7 of the style guide—thumbnails.*

Our next stop is thumbnails. Figure 15.11 shows the basics of how a thumbnail is defined using the anchor tag **<A>**. Notice that a heavy border is displayed around the image to indicate that it is a hotlink. When the users click on it, the file urb.gif will be transmitted to them for viewing. Here's the HTML for screen 7:

```
<H4><A NAME="THUMB">Thumbnail Sketches</A></H4>

<P>
A thumbnail sketch is small graphic display that points to a larger
version of the same graphic. It has the advantage of not requiring
the full graphic to be transmitted and displayed unless the user
specifically requests the larger display.
<P>
&lt;A HREF=large-graphic-file&gt;&lt;IMG SRC=thumb-nail-graphic-file&gt;
&lt;/A&gt;
<P>
<A href=urb.gif><IMG SRC=urbsmall.gif></A>
```

```
<P>
Click on the thumbnail graphic to activate a larger graphic.
<BR>
The heavy border around the graphic indicates that the image is
a pointer.
<P>
<A HREF=#TOC>Back to Table of Contents</A>
```

Screen 8—Inserting Special Characters

Screen 8 gives our viewers a chance to see all of the special characters that HTML supports. I found this to be a very helpful reference as I was creating other HTML documents. After all, it's very easy to forget the actual code for a special character like the copyright sign. Figure 15.12 shows the browser window with some of the symbols and their codes displayed. The HTML to display this table of special characters is actually quite simple (although I did have to type a lot of code to create the table!):

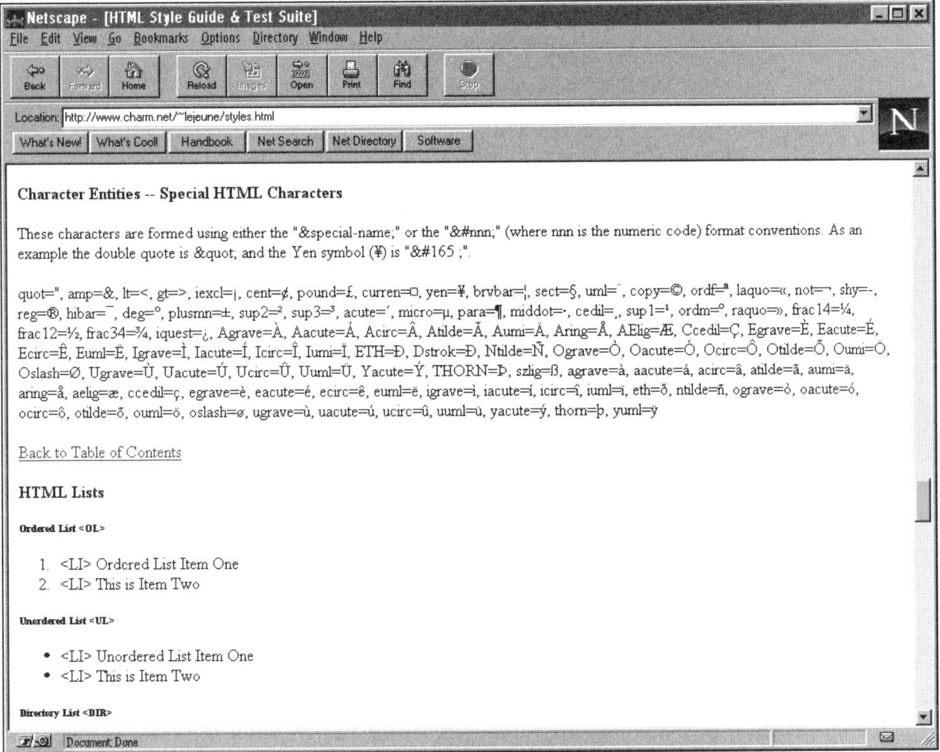

Figure 15.12 *Screen 8 of the style guide—special HTML characters.*

```
<P>
These characters are formed using either the &quot;&amp;special-name;&quot;
or the &quot;&amp;#nnn;&quot; (where nnn is the numeric code)
format conventions. As an example the double quote is &amp;quot;
and the Yen symbol (&#165;) is &quot;&amp;#165 ;&quot;.
<P>
quot=&quot;, amp=&amp;, lt=&lt;, gt=&gt;, iexcl=&#161;, cent=&#162;,
pound=&#163;, curren=&#164;, yen=&#165;, brvbar=&#166;, sect=&#167;,
uml=&#168;, copy=&#169;, ordf=&#170;, laquo=&#171;, not=&#172;,
shy=&#173;, reg=&#174;, hibar=&#175;, deg=&#176;, plusmn=&#177;,
sup2=&#178;, sup3=&#179;, acute=&#180;, micro=&#181;, para=&#182;,
middot=&#183;, cedil=&#184;, sup1=&#185;, ordm=&#186;, raquo=&#187;,
frac14=&#188;, frac12=&#189;, frac34=&#190;, iquest=&#191;, Agrave=&Agrave;,
Aacute=&Aacute;, Acirc=&Acirc;, Atilde=&Atilde;, Aumi=&Auml;,
Aring=&Aring;, AElig=&AElig;, Ccedil=&Ccedil;, Egrave=&Egrave;,
Eacute=&Eacute;, Ecirc=&Ecirc;, Euml=&Euml;, Igrave=&Igrave;,
Iacute=&Iacute;, Icirc=&Icirc;, Iumi=&Iuml;, ETH=&ETH;, Dstrok=&ETH;,
Ntilde=&Ntilde;, Ograve=&Ograve;, Oacute=&Oacute;, Ocirc=&Ocirc;,
Otilde=&Otilde;, Oumi=&Ouml;, Oslash=&Oslash;, Ugrave=&Ugrave;,
Uacute=&Uacute;, Ucirc=&Ucirc;, Uuml=&Uuml;, Yacute=&Yacute;,
THORN=&THORN;, szlig=&szlig;, agrave=&agrave;, aacute=&aacute;,
acirc=&acirc;, atilde=&atilde;, aumi=&auml;, aring=&aring;, aelig=&aelig;,
ccedil=&ccedil;, egrave=&egrave;, eacute=&eacute;, ecirc=&ecirc;,
euml=&euml;, igrave=&igrave;, iacute=&iacute;, icirc=&icirc;,
iuml=&iuml;, eth=&eth;, ntilde=&ntilde;, ograve=&ograve;, oacute=&oacute;,
ocirc=&ocirc;, otilde=&otilde;, ouml=&ouml;, oslash=&oslash;,
ugrave=&ugrave;, uacute=&uacute;, ucirc=&ucirc;, uuml=&uuml;,
yacute=&yacute;, thorn=&thorn;, yuml=&yuml;
<P>
    <A HREF=#TOC>Back to Table of Contents</A>
```

Screen 9—Everything You Wanted to Know about Lists

By now you probably know that lists are one of the most useful HTML constructs. And what could be better than a Web page that shows you the syntax for creating each of the list types supported by HTML? The complete HTML that creates the screen shown in Figure 15.13 follows:

```
<H4><A NAME="LISTS">HTML Lists</A></H4>

<H6>Ordered List &lt;OL&gt; </H6>

<OL>
<LI>&lt;LI&gt; Ordered List Item One
<LI>&lt;LI&gt; This is Item Two
</OL>

    <H6>Unordered List &lt;UL&gt;</H6>

<UL>
```

```
<LI>&lt;LI&gt; Unordered List Item One
<LI>&lt;LI&gt; This is Item Two
</UL>

<H6>Directory List &lt;DIR&gt;</H6>

<DIR>
<LI>&lt;LI&gt; Directory List Item One
<LI>&lt;LI&gt; This is Item Two
</DIR>

<H6>Definition List &lt;DL&gt;</H6>

<DL>
<DT>&lt;DT&gt; Definition List first entry to be defined
<DD>&lt;DD&gt; Definition of first entry
<DT>&lt;DT&gt; Second entry to be defined
<DD>&lt;DD&gt; Definition of second entry
</DL>

<H6>Two Unordered Lists &lt;UL&gt; Nested within an Ordered List
&lt;OL&gt;</H6>

<OL>
<LI>&lt;LI&gt; Major List Item One
<UL>
<LI>&lt;LI&gt; First Nested List Item One
<LI>&lt;LI&gt; First Nested List Item Two
</UL>

<LI>&lt;LI&gt; Major List Item Two
<UL>
<LI>Second Nested List Item One
<LI>&lt;LI&gt; Second Nested List Item Two
</UL>

</OL>

<H6>Menu List &lt;MENU&gt;</H6>

<MENU>
<LI>&lt;LI&gt; First Menu List Item
<LI>&lt;LI&gt; Second Menu List Item
</MENU>

<P>
<A HREF=#TOC>Back to Table of Contents</A>
```

Every type of list is coded here: ordered, unordered, directory, definition, and menu.

One feature we didn't explore in our HTML guide is the use of images with lists. You can easily combine inline graphics, especially if they are small images like

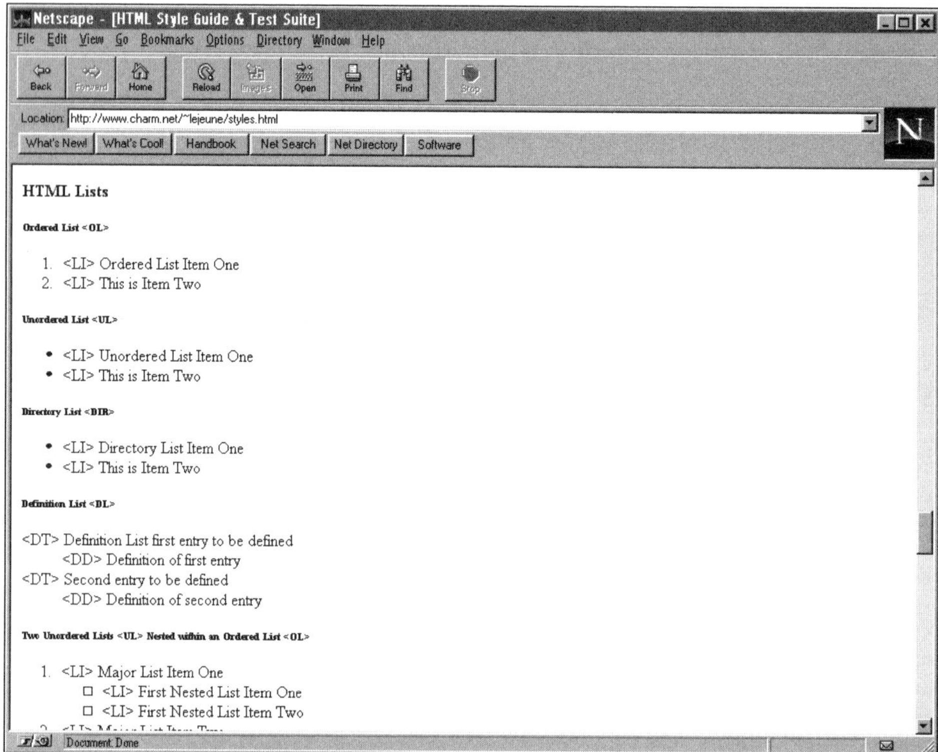

Figure 15.13 Screen 9 of the style guide—lists.

thumbnails, with list items. As an example, let's recode one of the menus shown in Figure 15.13. This time around, I'll add a thumbnail to the first unordered list item:

```
<H6>Unordered List &lt;UL&gt;</H6>
<UL>
  <LI>&lt;LI&gt;  Unordered List Item One <A href=urb.gif><IMG
  SRC=urbsmall.gif></A><P>
  <LI>&lt;LI&gt;  This is Item Two
</UL>
```

This is the same anchor definition used before to define a thumbnail. You might want to experiment with this feature on your own to see how useful it is.

Screens 10 and 11—Applying Netscape's Enhancements to HTML

If you are tired of standard font sizes and stationary text, you'll enjoy playing around with some of Netscape's HTML enhancements. Figure 15.14 shows

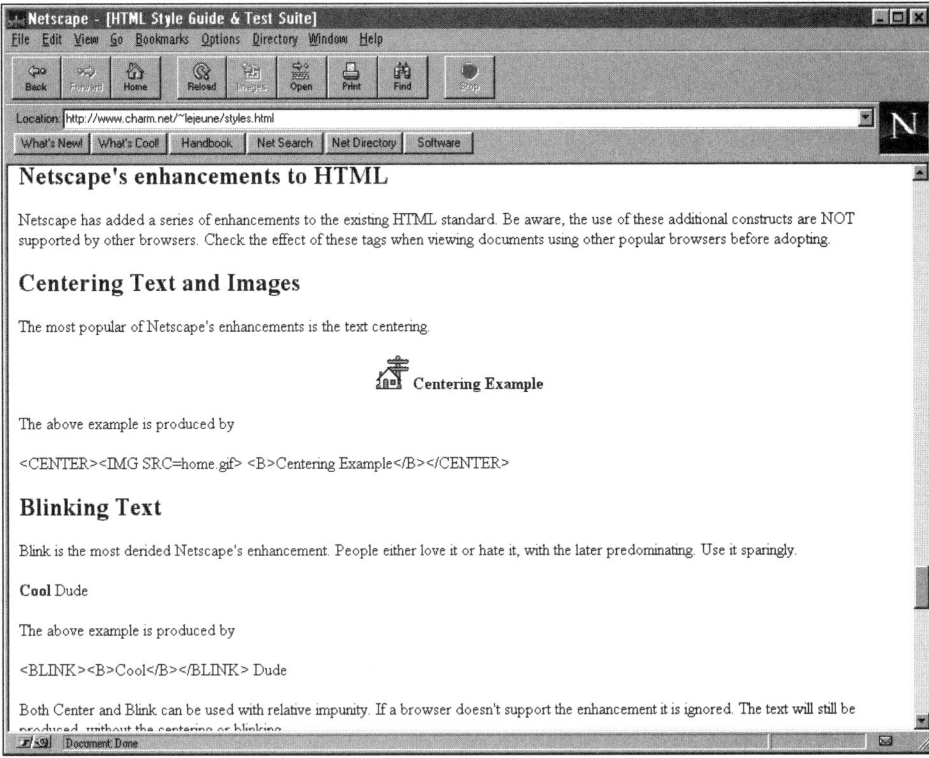

Figure 15.14 *Screen 10 of the style guide—Netscape's centering and blinking features.*

the first screen of some of the text-related enhancements that I've added to our style guide. The HTML to create this first screen of enhancements is:

```
<H2><A NAME="NETSCAPE">Netscape's enhancements to HTML</A></H2>

<P>
Netscape has added a series of enhancements to the existing HTML
standard. Be aware, the use of these additional constructs are
NOT supported by other browsers. Check the effect of these tags
when viewing documents using other popular browsers before adopting.
<H2><A NAME="CENTER">Centering Text and Images</A></H2>

<P>
The most popular of Netscape's enhancements is the text centering.
<P>
<CENTER><IMG SRC=home.gif> <B>Centering Example</B> </CENTER>
<P>
The above example is produced by
<P>
&lt;CENTER&gt;&lt;IMG SRC=home.gif&gt; &lt;B&gt;Centering Example&lt;
```

```
/B&gt;&lt;/CENTER&GT;
<H2><A NAME="BLINK">Blinking Text</A></H2>

<P>
Blink is the most derided Netscape's enhancement. People either
love it or hate it, with the later predominating. Use it sparingly.
<P>
<BLINK><B>Cool</B></BLINK> Dude
<P>
The above example is produced by
<P>
&lt;BLINK&gt;&lt;B&gt;Cool&lt;/B&gt;&lt;/BLINK&gt; Dude
<P>
Both Center and Blink can be used with relative impunity. If a
browser doesn't support the enhancement it is ignored. The text
will still be produced, without the centering or blinking.
<H2><A NAME="FONTS">Font Sizing</A></H2>
```

In addition to formatting your Web pages by centering text and graphics or displaying blinking text, you can change the size of your text on a Web page using another useful HTML extension. Figure 15.15 shows the next screen of

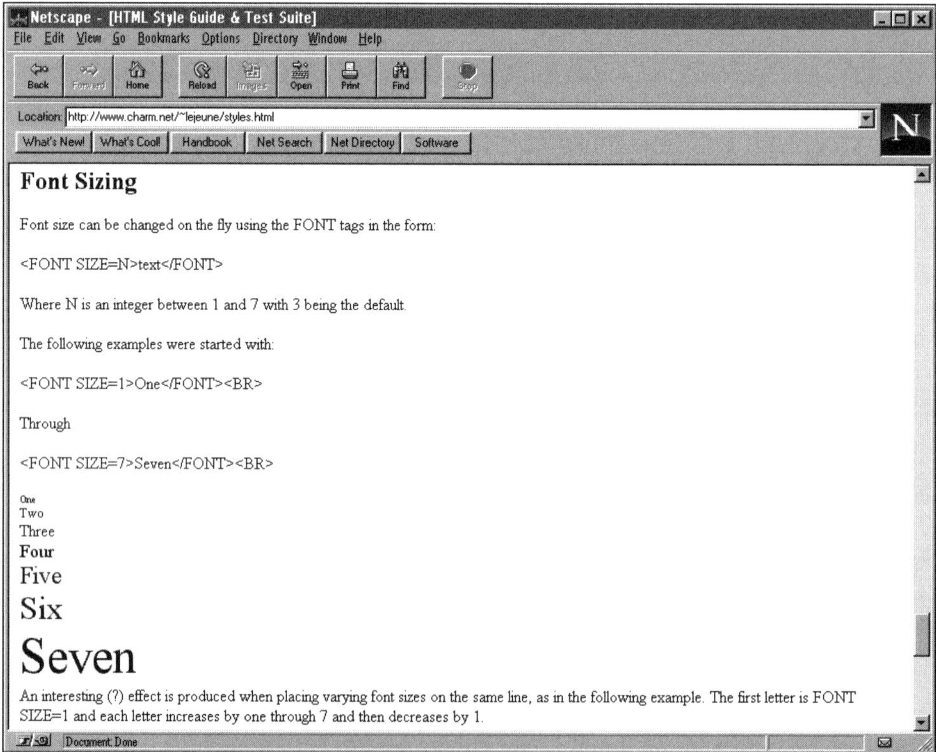

***Figure 15.15** Screen 11 of the style guide—font sizes.*

our style guide that shows off this new feature. Here's the HTML for specifying font sizes:

```
<P>
Font size can be changed on the fly using the FONT tags in the
form:
<P>
&ltFONT SIZE=N&gt;text&lt;/FONT&gt;
<P>
Where N is an integer between 1 and 7 with 3 being the default.
<P>
The following examples were started with:
<P>
&lt;FONT SIZE=1&gt;One&lt;/FONT&gt;&lt;BR&gt;
<P>
Through
<P>
&lt;FONT SIZE=7&gt;Seven&lt;/FONT&gt;&lt;BR&gt;
<P>
<FONT SIZE=1>One</FONT><BR>
<FONT SIZE=2>Two</FONT><BR>
<FONT SIZE=3>Three</FONT><BR>
<FONT SIZE=4>Four</FONT><BR>
<FONT SIZE=5>Five</FONT><BR>
<FONT SIZE=6>Six</FONT><BR>
<FONT SIZE=7>Seven</FONT><BR>
An interesting (?) effect is produced when placing varying font
sizes on the same line, as in the following example. The first
letter is FONT SIZE=1 and each letter increases by one through
7 and then decreases by 1.
<P>
<FONT SIZE=1>A</FONT><FONT SIZE=2>B</FONT><FONT SIZE=3>C</FONT>
<FONT SIZE=4>D</FONT><FONT SIZE=5>E</FONT><FONT SIZE=6>F</FONT>
<FONT SIZE=7>G</FONT> <FONT SIZE=6>H</FONT><FONT SIZE=5>I</FONT><FONT
SIZE=4>J</FONT>
<FONT SIZE=3>K</FONT><FONT SIZE=2>L</FONT><FONT SIZE=1>M</FONT>
<H2><A NAME="BASE_FONT">Base Font Sizing</A></H2>

<P>
Font size may also be changed using the BASEFONT tag &lt;BASEFONT
SIZE=N&gt;, where N in an integer in the range of 1 to 7 which
represent the range of font sizes. The sizing integers are identical
to the font sizes produced by the FONT SIZE pair. A major difference
is the absence of a closing tag. Once the font size is changed
it remains in effect until a new BASEFONT tag appears. If there
is an embedded FONT SIZE pair, the font size returns to the stated
BASEFONT size following the closing &lt;/FONT&gt; tag.
I would strongly suggest that you either don't use this enhancement
- since it tends to be at odds with conventional HTML matching
tag pair wisdom - or that you immediately enter a &lt;BASEFONT
SIZE=3&gt; as a pseudo closing tag which will set the font
size back to normal.
```

```
<P>
<BASEFONT SIZE=1> This line produced a &lt;BASEFONT
SIZE=1&gt; tag<BR>

&lt;FONT SIZE=4&gt;
<FONT SIZE=5>Embedded FONT SIZE=4 pair</FONT>&lt;/FONT&gt;<BR>
This line follows the embedded tag pair and is back to the BASEFONT
size of 1
<P>
<BASEFONT SIZE=3> <!- set font size back to normal ->The previous
line is: &lt;BASEFONT SIZE=3&gt; &lt;!- Set font
size back to normal -&gt;
<P>
<B>Stayed tuned. More Netscape HTML enhancements are on the way.</B>
<P>

<A HREF=#TOC>Back to Table of Contents</A>
```

As Figure 15.15 shows, seven font sizes are supported. The HTML tag for specifying a font size is:

```
<FONT SIZE=N>Text goes here</FONT>
```

where *N* must be a number from 1 to 7. The default font size setting is 3.

In addition to setting the font size, a tag is provided so that you can set the size used for all of your text in a document. This tag, formatted as **<BASEFONT SIZE=*N*>** serves as a global setting. Again, *N* must be a value from 1 to 7. Once this tag is encountered in a document, all of the text will be displayed using the specified setting. Of course, you can override the base font setting at any time by using the **<FONT> ... </FONT>** sizing tag pair.

Screen 12—Is There an Author in the House?

We've finally arrived at the end of our style guide. The reward is that I get to tell the world who created this document (see Figure 15.16). Here is the final section of HTML:

```
<P>
<A NAME="AUTHOR"> </A>

<A HREF=HTTP://www.charm.net/~lejeune/><IMG ALIGN=CENTER SRC=home.gif>
 Check out my home page. </A><P>

Document Last Updated May 28, 1995

<P>
```

```
    &copy; 1995 by:<BR>
    Urban A. LeJeune<BR>
    43 Willis Drive<BR>
    Tuckerton, NJ 08087<P>

    <B>Please mail any comments or suggestions about this document to:
    </B><BR>

    <A HREF="mailto:lejeune@acy.digex.net">
    <IMG ALIGN=CENTER SRC=mailbutt.gif>
    lejeune@acy.digex.net

    <IMG SRC=line.gif></A>
  </BODY>
</HTML>
```

The anchor target name that takes the reader to this section is AUTHOR. The **
** tags at the end of each address line caused a "hard" line break at that point, allowing you to format short text lines precisely as given. (The **<PRE>** tag pair is another way to do this.) Be careful not to put **
** at the end of

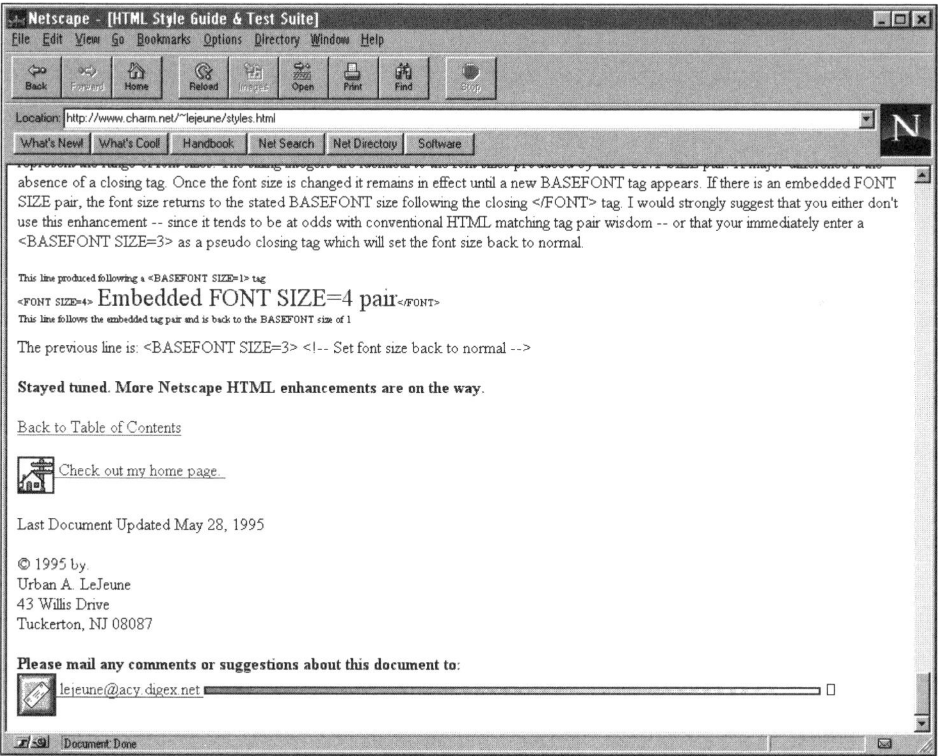

Figure 15.16 *Screen 12 of the style guide—addresses.*

too long a line; if the browser tries to wrap a line ending in **
**, what the user sees will be unpredictable at best.

The last section of the styles.htm file demonstrates a feature I haven't introduced yet—a "mailto" URL. The mailto protocol allows you to email a message while viewing a document. The last block of HTML contains the following instructions:

```
<B>Please mail any comments or suggestions about this document to:
</B><BR>

<A HREF="mailto:lejeune@acy.digex.net">
<IMG ALIGN=CENTER SRC=mailbutt.gif>
lejeune@acy.digex.net
```

If you would click on the "lejeune@acy.digex.net" anchor, you would be taken through a series of prompts that would conclude with email being sent to me. Unfortunately, older versions of Mosaic and several other Web browsers do not support the "mailto" URL. Netscape, on the other hand, will pop up a window so that a user can easily type the email message and then send it.

Finally, note that I've created an interesting effect by including an inline image as part of the **<ADDRESS>** section, as this is the last bit of HTML. The graphic is enclosed in a blue border indicating that it is part of the mailto anchor. This isn't exactly what you'd call very functional, but what the heck—we at least get to finish our project with style!

LET'S REVIEW

HTML provides support for five types of lists: ordered, unordered, menu, directory, and description. Each of these list types can be defined using special tags. For example, the tag pair **<UL>** ... **</UL>** defines an unordered list. Some of the list types can also be nested to create more functional lists.

A number of options are available for displaying images with the **<IMG>** tag, including displaying images with optional text descriptions and aligning images.

HTML documents are fun to create once you learn the basics of using the key HTML features. Appendix A provides a complete reference guide to all of the standard HTML features including forms. You should refer to this appendix whenever you need to look up the format of an HTML tag.

Web Publishing Tips and Techniques

If you'd like to add special features, such as colored or textured backgrounds or text that will wrap around your images and Web pages. This collection of FAQs and tips will show you how.

We've covered a lot of HTML ground in the previous three chapters; however, you still probably have a number of questions, especially if you've surfed the Web and seen some of the neat features you can add to your Web pages, such as custom rules, shaded backgrounds and colors, and text that flows around images.

Many features like these are possible because several extensions have been added to HTML. Some extensions are part of the HTML 3.0 specification and others have been introduced by Netscape. In this chapter, I'll show you how to do much more with HTML so that you can liven up your documents. I'll start with a set of useful HTML FAQs (Frequently Asked Questions) and then we'll look at some clever Web publishing tips.

In the final part of the chapter, I've put a tips and techniques guide of what's available on the Web to help you create and publish HTML documents, and also to show you how to design and create better Web pages. I'll present a few projects to show you how to apply some of the more useful tools.

HTML FAQS

Whenever I'm trying to master something new, I love to read useful FAQs and tips to jump-start the learning process. FAQs are great because they often cut right to the chase. And HTML and Web publishing are two important subjects that could really use a good set of FAQs and tips.

In this section I'll give you some answers that will help you write better HTML documents and add features to your Web pages—such as custom horizontal lines, resizable images, images without borders, and so on.

What happens if I use an HTML 3.0 extension that is not supported by a browser?
The HTML standards police will take your Web publishing license away. (You do have a license, don't you?)

Actually, nothing will happen. If you use a feature that isn't supported by a browser, the browser will just ignore it. For example, let's say you use the **<CENTER> ... </CENTER>** tag pair to center text in an HTML document. If someone is using an older version of Mosaic, the text will be displayed as left-justified.

If you are really concerned about including a feature that can't be viewed by all browsers, my advice is to avoid all of the HTML extensions. If you feel that Netscape is the best thing since the invention of hot showers and that everyone should be using it (or will be in the near future), go ahead and use the extensions.

Do I need to always use HTML tags such as <HTML>, <HEAD>, and <BODY> to create my HTML documents?
No. I've been using them in this book to help standardize the format for our HTML documents. These tags are provided to help you keep your HTML documents structured.

Should I be concerned that my HTML documents will become obsolete and won't work with newer Web browsers?
At the rate the Internet and World Wide Web are changing, I would be concerned. Is there anything you can do about this? Try not to worry too much. So far, every new browser or new version of an existing browser has been backward compatible. But to be safe, try to use HTML features that you know work with most browsers. Once a feature is in wide use, it's unlikely that it will go away.

Will desktop publishing programs like PageMaker or QuarkXPress output files in an HTML format?

Yes and no. Currently, these popular page-design programs don't create HTML documents. However, independent developers are adding extensions so that PageMaker or Quark files can be converted to HTML. For instance, a program (available now) called *Dave* will convert Mac PageMaker files to HTML. To find out why this program is named Dave or to retrieve it, here's where you should go:

```
http://www.bucknell.edu:80/bucknellian/dave/
```

How can I incorporate Acrobat PDF files into my Web pages?

Acrobat PDF files are Postscript files (which are generated by desktop publishing programs) that have been converted to a special format so that they can be read by the Acrobat electronic viewer. Web browsers don't currently read PDF files; however, you can easily set up the Acrobat Reader as a player or helper program with Netscape. Then, when you select a PDF file from a Web page, the file will automatically be displayed.

The Acrobat Reader can be freely distributed. You'll find a copy of this program on the companion CD-ROM in the directory \helpers\acrobat. For more information on how to set up player programs, see Chapter 4.

Can I include a comment in an HTML document?

You're in luck. HTML provides a special tag that allows comments to be inserted in your documents. When HTML documents are read by a browser like Netscape, the comments will *not* be displayed. To include a comment, here's the tag you use:

```
<!--Your comment text goes here-->
```

Don't forget to include the closing "- - >". If you leave this out, everything else in your document will be ignored. If this happens to you, don't call me at midnight to ask me where your document went.

How can I add a horizontal line to a Web page?

You're in luck again because HTML provides a standalone tag that performs this task. To display a horizontal line across a page, you use **<HR>**. For example,

```
This text is above the line<BR>
<HR>
This text is below the line
```

would display a horizontal line between the two lines of text.

How do I change the size and look of horizontal lines?
By default, a horizontal line is displayed as a thin shaded line across a page when you use the **<HR>** tag. The width of the displayed line is two pixels. If you are using a browser like Netscape that supports extended HTML features, you can change a line's thickness, width, and alignment, and turn off the shading.

So, how do I use this extended tag?
The **<HR>** tag provides special modifiers or settings that you can include. The actual format for this tag with all its bells and whistles is:

```
<HR SIZE=pixel-setting-for-thickness
    WIDTH=pixels-or-percent
    ALIGN=Left|Right|Center
    NOSHADE>
```

Let's look at some examples. To change the thickness of a line, you would use a tag like this:

```
<HR SIZE=5>
```

This displays a line that is five pixels thick. To change the width, you could use

```
<HR WIDTH=100>
```

or you could use this format:

```
<HR WIDTH=30%>
```

The first version displays the line as 100 pixels in width. The second version says "display the line by taking up 30 percent of the document window width." In either case, the line will be centered across the screen.

So, how can I change the alignment of the horizontal line?
Use one of these options:

```
<HR ALIGN=Left|Right|Center>
```

For example, this tag would display a horizontal line that is right-justified and 200 pixels in width:

```
<HR ALIGN=Right WIDTH=200>
```

How can I turn off the shading from a displayed horizontal line?
Another easy answer. Try this:

```
<HR NOSHADE>
```

Should I care whether users with slow Internet connections have to wait a long time to view my Web pages because they have a lot of graphics?
Imagine you are taking your family on vacation to Colorado and you get stuck behind a big fat motorhome. If you had to travel like this for a few hours on those famous steep and winding Colorado roads, you'd be mad as hell. It would probably ruin your vacation.

Thousands of people are still surfing the Web at very slow speeds If you don't care about these users, go ahead and be a road hog. But if you do, think about streamlining your Web pages.

Ok, but I'm too attached to my great images; is there anything I can do?
First, make sure that you save your GIF files using the lowest resolution possible. Instead of creating images with 2 million colors, try to use some images that will still look nice with only eight colors. You can use programs like Paint Shop Pro, included on the companion CD-ROM, to convert the resolution of your images and the number of colors used. Remember that an image can only be displayed at 72 dpi on the screen. Therefore, if you use an image that has a higher resolution than this, no one will be able to enjoy the higher resolution while viewing it on the screen.

If you are willing to make two versions of your bigger images, there is an extended HTML feature you can use to speed up the process of displaying images. See the next question.

I've seen Web pages with images that seem to display very quickly from low resolution to high resolution. How can I set up my images to be displayed like this?
Here's a neat trick that you can add to your Web pages if you're using Netscape. It's a great way to make readers of your Web pages feel they're getting a very quick response even when you are displaying large images.

This sample HTML tag shows how the feature works:

```
<IMG SRC=HIGHRES="slow.gif" LOWSRC="fast.gif">
```

As shown, the **<IMG>** tag supports two modifiers: **HIGHRES** and **LOWSRC**. The high resolution file is specified first and then the low resolution file is listed. When this command is processed, Netscape will first display the low resolution file. This tag speeds up the display process because Netscape can quickly determine how much room to leave for the image and then it can go about its business filling in the details.

Should I create Web pages that both Netscape users and text-based browser users can access and read?
Sure. Why leave anybody out? The best way to achieve this goal is to create both text- and graphics-based versions of your Web pages. Include an option on your home page that users can click on as soon as the page starts to appear so that they can access the text-based version.

Can I use an image that's not saved as a GIF file?
Many browsers only support GIF files, although some browsers, such as Netscape, do provide built-in support for JPEG images. If your image files are in another format such as TIF or PCX, you'll need to convert them to GIF so that all users can view them with their Web browsers. I like to use the Paint Shop Pro program to convert my images because it provides a "batch conversion" feature to automate the process of converting multiple files.

How do I remove a border from a linked image?
Suppose you have an image that you want to display as a clickable button or icon without a border. (Those big blue borders that Netscape displays can overpower a small icon.) To do so, use this version of the **<IMG>** tag:

```
<IMG BORDER=0 SRC="mybutton.gif">
```

The **BORDER** parameter specifies the line width of the border in pixels.

How do I place left-justified and right-justified images on the same line?
Suppose you're creating a catalog or brochure and you want to position pictures at the margins, with text in the middle. Fortunately, the **<IMG>** tag provides a parameter called **ALIGN** for controlling the alignment of an image. Here's how you can use this feature to sandwich text between two images:

```
<IMG ALIGN=LEFT SRC="leftp.gif"> <IMG ALIGN=RIGHT SRC="rightp.gif">
Text goes here!
<BR CLEAR=LEFT>
More Text here!
<BR CLEAR=ALL>
```

How can I display two images side by side, with about 4 to 5 spaces between them?
There are three ways that I know of. The first is easy: Use the special code for a space—** **. This example puts three spaces between two images:

```
<IMG SRC="image1.gif">     <IMG SRC="image2.gif">
```

The second method for doing this is to create a "spacing" image and display it between the two images. The third is to put the images in a table without borders. But keep in mind that only the latest versions of Netscape and Mosaic support tables. I'll show you how to create and use tables in Chapter 17.

How can I resize an image?
Again, the **<IMG>** tag comes to the rescue. Here's the format for this tag when using it to resize an image:

```
<IMG HEIGHT=pixels WIDTH=pixels SRC="filename">
```

As an example, this tag would display the image stored in pict.gif as 32x40 pixels:

```
<IMG HEIGHT=32 WIDTH=40 SRC="pict.gif">
```

You can specify a height and width that is either larger or smaller than the original image. When the image is displayed, it will be scaled to fit the dimensions you specify. The image will not be cropped. So, no matter what size you provide, you'll still see the entire image.

This tag provides a hidden advantage even if you don't need to resize an image. If you know the size of an image, you can specify its dimensions using the **HEIGHT** and **WIDTH** parameters and Netscape will be able to display your HTML document much faster. Let's look at an example. Assume that Netscape is reading the following HTML:

```
<IMG HEIGHT=100 WIDTH=100 SRC="pict1.gif">
<IMG HEIGHT=100 WIDTH=100 SRC="pict2.gif">
<BR>
Welcome to my home page.
<P>
<IMG HEIGHT=100 WIDTH=100 SRC="pict3.gif">
...
```

Each time Netscape encounters the **HEIGHT** and **WIDTH** parameters, it knows exactly how much space to leave for an image. This allows it to quickly put up a border (bounding box) for the image and then move on to create the remainder of the page. The details are then filled in later.

If you have a little extra time on your hands, you can determine the width and height of all your images, and then update your **<IMG>** tags so that your pages will display quicker. Your fellow Web surfers will thank you.

When I use the ALIGN=Middle with the <IMG> tag, my text isn't truly centered. How do I fix it?

Write to the people who invented HTML and complain. Actually, I think enough people have complained about this because they've added a new alignment feature called **Absmiddle**. Here's how it works:

```
<IMG ALIGN=Absmiddle SRC="pict.gif">
```

How do I change the size of my text (font size)?

Here's the basic format:

```
<FONT SIZE=size> text </FONT>
```

The *size* parameter can be a number from 1 to 7. The default font size is 3. Once the size has been changed with this tag, all of the text within the tag will be displayed using the specified size.

How can I include my Internet address on a Web page so that users can click on it and send me email?

This is easily accomplished using the *mailto* protocol. When you define a link using the **<A HREF>** tag, you include the mailto protocol instead of the typical http protocol that you'd use to link to a Web page. As an example, let's assume that your email address is johnsmith@surfstuff.com. Here's how you would define an anchor:

```
<A HREF="mailto:johnsmith@surfstuff.com"> Send me mail, please!</A>
```

When a user clicks on the link, "Send me mail, please," a message box will pop up so that a mail message can be entered.

How can I set up a link on a Web page so that a user can access an FTP area on a Web site?

This is another protocol variation. This time, instead of using http or mailto, you use FTP as the link protocol. Here's an example:

```
<A HREF=ftp://www.coriolis.com> Click here to download something special!</A>
```

How do I display a background image on a Web page?

This question is a good one, but it deserves a special section just to answer it. So, let's roll up our sleeves and explore backgrounds.

ADDING BACKGROUNDS AND COLORS

HTML 3.0 provides a feature for adding backgrounds to Web pages. The background attribute, as implemented by Netscape, allows your documents to override the background specified by a local browser. The attribute specifies a URL that, in turn, points to an image used as the document's background. Netscape supports additional enhancements so that you are even able to control the color of your backgrounds.

If you've never seen a Web page containing a background, check out the Coriolis Group Web page at:

```
http://www.coriolis.com
```

Figure 16.1 shows how Netscape will display this document. It's difficult to identify in black and white, but one small GIF image is tiled to fill the entire screen.

Figure 16.1, The Coriolis Group's home page, uses a background graphic. A simplified outline of the **<BODY>** portion of the Coriolis page that displays this background is:

```
<BODY BACKGROUND="gifs/vdm01.jpg">
     Remainder of Document
</BODY>
```

Netscape maintains an interesting Background Sampler that you can access by pointing your browser to:

```
http://home.netscape.com/assist/net_sites/bg/backgrounds.html
```

This collection includes more than 50 background GIFs. Figure 16.2 shows some available images, of which Netscape allows free use. There are two ways to use them:

- Download an image to your HTML server and reference it in your document.
- Leave the image at Netscape; reference the Netscape URL in your document.

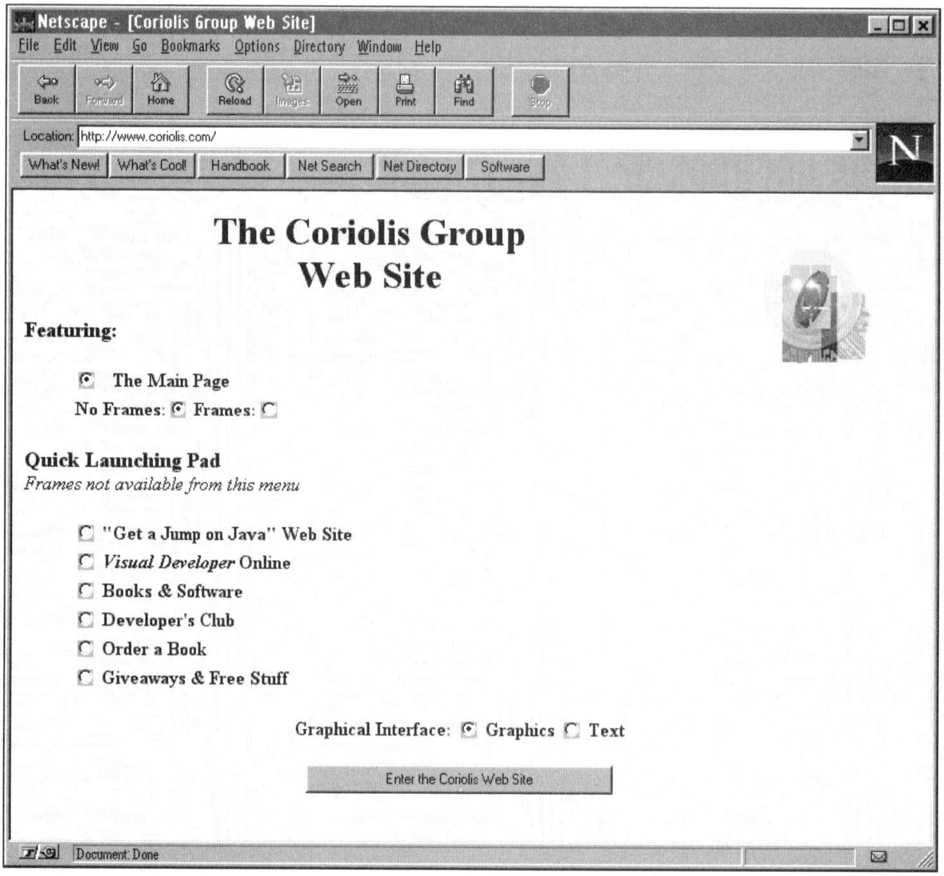

Figure 16.1 The Coriolis Group's Home Page.

Building a Document with a Background

In this project we'll actually build a document using a Netscape-provided GIF. We'll first download the image to our PC and reference the local copy. Then, we'll modify the document to fetch the image from Netscape.

First, connect to Netscape's Background Sampler at:

```
http://home.netscape.com/assist/net_sites/bg/backgrounds.html
```

Find a background you like. This could take a while (because the Web page loads slowly). The image I've selected is Netscape's 70s_marble.gif. I saved it as marble.gif in my Netscape directory. Next, I created a new file using HTML

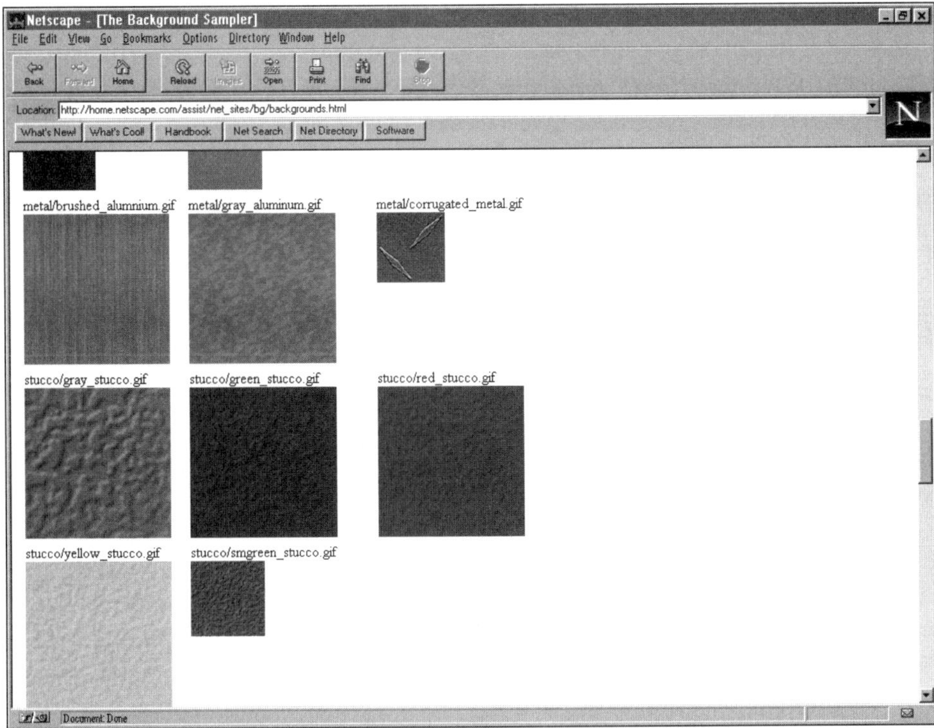

***Figure 16.2** Home of Netscape's background GIFs.*

Notepad. In the document's **<BODY>** tag I put:

```
<BODY BACKGROUND="marble.gif">
```

That's all there is to it. Figure 16.3 shows Netscape displaying the document. Unfortunately, the document's title and other text are barely visible. I'll show you how to fix this in a minute.

Let's modify marble.htm so the background image is fetched directly from Netscape. The sampler document uses this URL:

```
http://home.netscape.com/home/bg/fabric/gray_fabric.gif
```

The last part of the URL, /fabric/gray_fabric.gif, is the directory and file name for the image. So, the URL to use when fetching your choice is

```
http://home.netscape.com/home/bg/
```

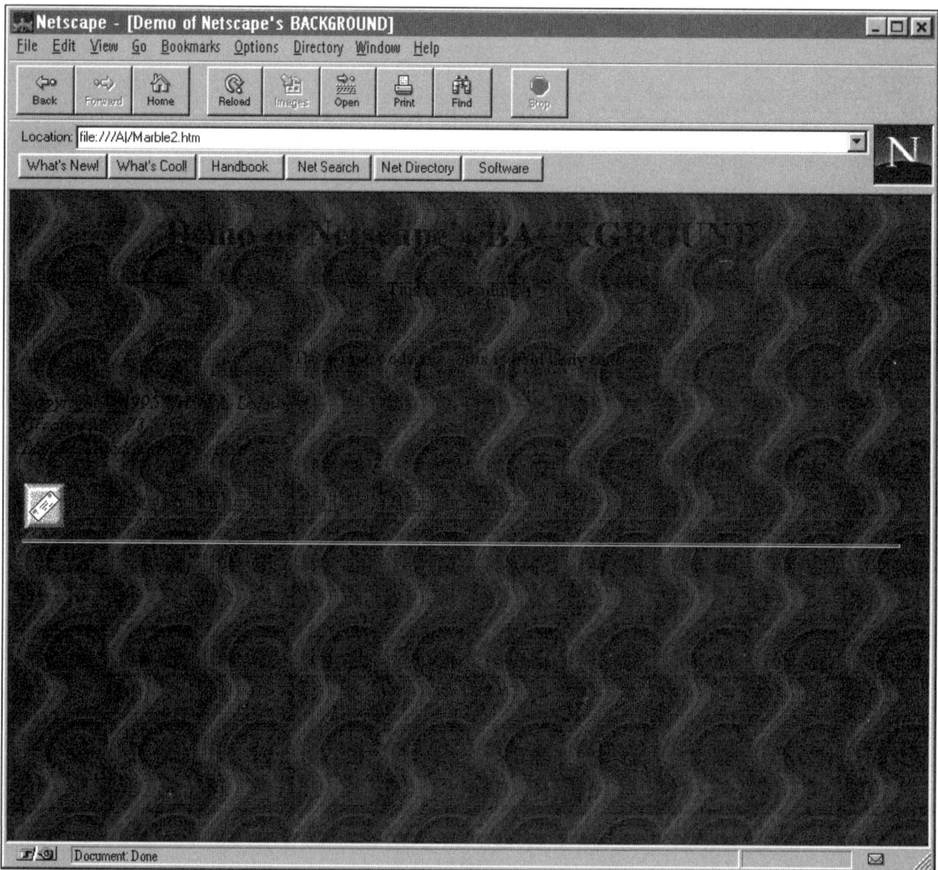

Figure 16.3 *Our first attempt at using a background.*

plus the directory and file name shown on the swatch background image collection. My choice was in the directory /marble and the file name was 70s_marble.gif. So, the new **<BODY>** tag in the modified marble.htm is:

```
<BODY BACKGROUND="http://home.netscape.com/home/bg/marble/70s_marble.gif">
```

You aren't limited to just using Netscape's choices of backgrounds. You can use any graphics file you want as a background for your Web page, but beware! If you use an image that is too large, it will take forever for your background to load. Make sure you use small GIF files, so they don't take up too much space.

Another area of backgrounds to look out for is how your chosen image will look blanketing the background of your page. Using a picture of your dog to put in the background may sound cute, but thousands of tiny dog images can make it hard for users to read what you have to say, and they will go elsewhere. As with everything else in Web publishing, keep it simple!

If you use a background image that does not contrast clearly with the black text normally displayed when viewing Web documents, you'll want to specify different text colors. Netscape to the rescue.

Changing Various Document Colors

The HTML 3.0 specification contains the **BACKGROUND** attribute, which is placed in the **<BODY>** tag. Several newly introduced attributes from Netscape can be used in the **<BODY>** tag. They all take the same general form, namely:

```
<BODY attribute="RGB-color">
```

One of the available attributes is **TEXT**. Could this be the answer to our contrast dilemma? You bet!

The RGB-color parameter shown in the syntax template is a triplet of color numbers. The numbers must be specified in hexadecimal. Don't panic—yet! Let's first look at the decimal equivalent. In the color palette, 0 is the lowest intensity and 255 is the highest intensity. The first number in the triplet series is the red specification, the second is green, and the third is blue. If we want to specify bright red, the specification would be 255, 0, 0. That is, give red the maximum intensity and don't muck it up with any green or blue. Conversely, all green would be 0, 255, 0 and drop-dead blue would be 0, 0, 255. The RGB triplet tells Netscape how to combine the three basic colors.

HTML Notepad's Built-in Color Sampler

Colors and colorization are tough for me conceptualize. Fortunately, HTML Notepad contains a great tool to simplify choosing a color for your page. Here's what to do:

1. First make sure your cursor is within the **<BODY>** brackets, directly after the word **BODY**. Then, to create a background color, execute the sequence Netscapisms | Background Color.

2. Now you can either click on one of the ready-made color boxes, or choose the Define Custom Colors button to expand the dialog box and expose the color palette.

3. You can now move the mouse around inside the color field to choose a color that you like. You can also move the arrow to the right of the rectangular color box to choose a preferred shade of that color. If you really like the color you've just created, you can click on the Add to Custom Colors button.

You can also manually enter the appropriate decimal number in each of the three boxes to view the represented color in the box marked Color | Solid. Use the palette to pick colors for your various **BACKGROUND** attributes.

Modifying the Color of Textual Information

In this project we'll take the HTML document created in the previous project and modify it. We'll change the displayed color of a document's normal text and also the color of the various links.

Selecting Text Color

As I mentioned earlier, the color parameter for the **TEXT** attribute must be specified in hexadecimal. Programmers sometimes use hex when it's more convenient to do so for computer representations. Hex is a base 16 numbering system. Each placeholder can have 16 different characters, as opposed to the decimal system's 10 (0 through 9). Hex character representation uses 0 through 9 in addition to A through F. Decimal 9 is hex 9, decimal 10 is hex A, 11 is hex B and so on. Decimal 15 is hex F, the last available character.

So, then what would decimal 16 be in hex? You use the same placeholder principle that you would use with decimal numbering. In decimal, if we count to 9 (the largest character) and want to add 1, we put 0 in the current placeholder and add 1 to the next-higher order place holder, giving us 10. Decimal 15 is hex F, so decimal 16 would be hex 10. In hex-speak, decimal 0 is 0 and decimal 255 is hex FF.

As Artie Johnson used to say on *Laugh In*, "Very interesting, but stupid." Requiring a non-programmer to enter hex numbers is another example of programmers forgetting about those of us in the real world. Having said that, we still need to use hex numbers, but HTML Notepad can do it for us.

Follow the same instructions as you would to choose a **BODY BACKGROUND**, but choose the Netscapisms | Text Color | Text sequence. We'll choose white as our text color, so click on the white box.

As is true with the **<BODY>** tag, **TEXT** allows multiple attributes. Let's modify marble.htm to include the following **<BODY>** tag.

```
<BODY BACKGROUND="marble.gif" TEXT="FFFFFF">
```

Figure 16.4 shows the effect this tag produces. The text went from non-readable to something my granddaughter Lauren describes as "cool." If for some reason the specified background image is not loaded, the other color attributes are ignored. This is really a good idea. If I had specified my background color preference as white (which I have) and displayed marble.htm, sans marble.gif, I would be looking at white text displayed on a white background—just a wee bit tough to read.

We still have a little problem with the display. The link text is blue (or whatever color the user specifies from within the Font and Colors preferences

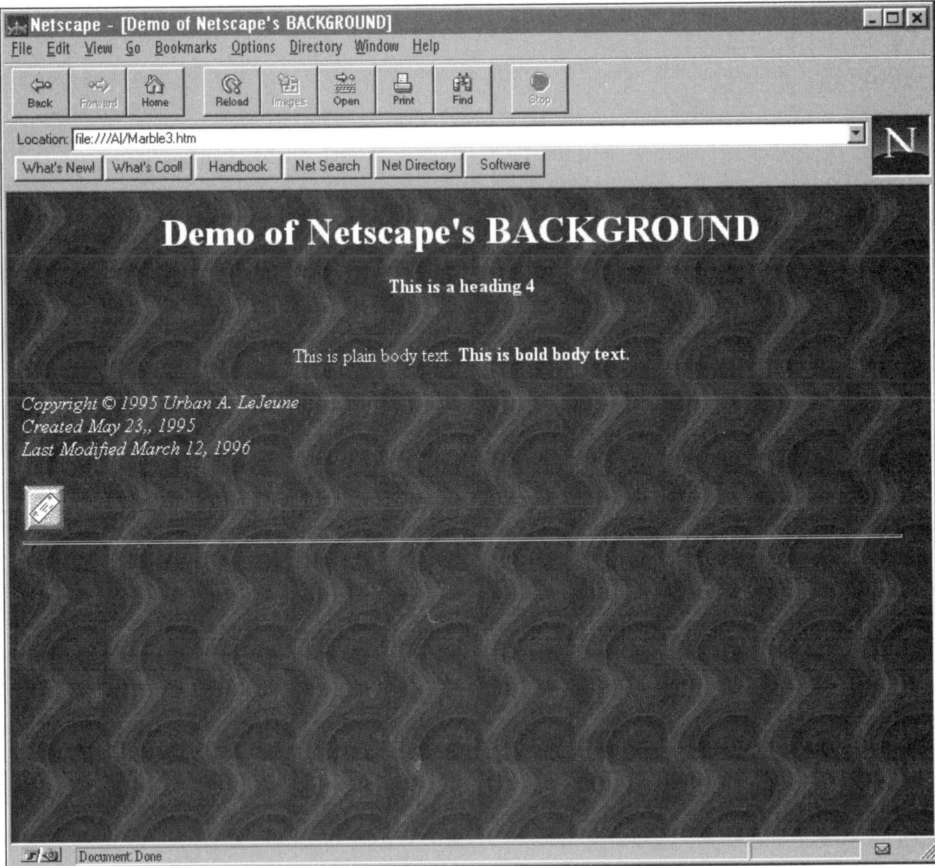

Figure 16.4 *Now our page is much easier to read.*

dialog box), which makes for difficult reading. There are three other optional link attributes—**LINK**, **VLINK**, and **ALINK**. **LINK** is used when displaying an unfollowed link, while **VLINK** is used when displaying an anchor that has previously been followed. **ALINK** is the color you see while you're actively clicking on a link.

To make the link display in white, Go back to Netscapism | Text Color, but this time choose Link instead of Text. add the following attribute by clicking on the white box again:

```
LINK="FFFFFF"
```

But now we have yet another problem with the display. White is fine for unvisited links, but after the link is made, the anchor displays in the user-specified color, which may represent a poor contrast. Red contrasts well with the marble display. So, add the following attribute to our growing list by choosing Vlink and clicking on the red box:

```
VLINK="FF0000"
```

Figure 16.5 demonstrates the results of our handiwork, showing the mailto anchor displayed in red. Take a closer look at the bottom of the screen in Figure 16.5. The mail button and everything displayed below the button has a border that's the same color as the mail link. I once forgot to include a closing **</A>** at the end of my mail link. Everything below that point was treated as part of the anchor. I really like the effect and now do it on purpose. Here's the code:

```
<A HREF="mailto:lejeune@acy.digex.net">
<IMG ALIGN=CENTER SRC=mailbutt.gif>
<B>Please send your comments about this page to</B>
<i>lejeune@acy.digex.net</i>
</A>
```

For consistency, let's add colorization for an active link. Yellow also contrasts well with the marble background. Yellow is 255, 255, 0 or FFFF00. Again, go into Netscapisms | Text Color and choose Alink. Then simply click on the yellow box. So, the active link attribute is:

```
ALINK="FFFF00"
```

Here's what we end up with:

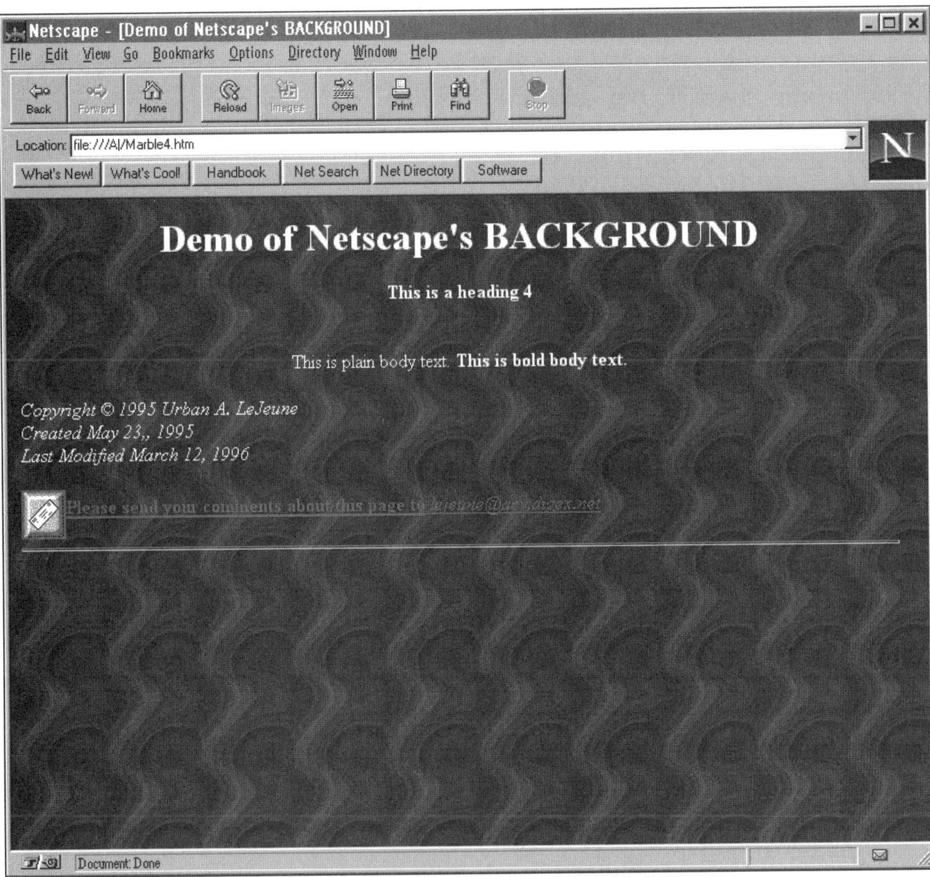

*Figure 16.5 Our sample page with a red **VLINK**.*

```
<!--
    The following BACKGROUND attributes use a marble background—
    displays normal text in white and displays unvisited anchors in white.
    Visited anchors are displayed in red  and  active links display in yellow.
-->
  <BODY BACKGROUND="marble.gif"
             TEXT="FFFFFF"  LINK="FFFFFF"  VLINK="FF0000"  ALINK="FFFF00">
```

Notice that HTML has a provision for comments. They are enclosed between the <!- - remarks - -> pair. I like to add a comment before any lines that might lead me to ask myself at a later date, "Why the heck did I do that?"

Solid Background Colors without Images

There are times when you simply want a plain, patternless background. This next attribute will override the user's background specification (made in the

Font and Color preferences dialog box). For instance, if you think your document would look better with a black background, you could use the background color (**BGCOLOR**) attribute to change the background color.

Let's once again modify marble.htm to make a negative display—white text displayed on a black background. The background color attribute is **BGCOLOR**. The modified **BODY** tag for our reverse image display would look like this:

```
<BODY BGCOLOR="000000" TEXT="FFFFFF" LINK="FFFFFF" VLINK="FFFFFF">
```

Figure 16.6 shows the result. It's interesting, but a little spooky. Try a blue background with white text, something I find soothing. The value for a simple blue background would be 0000FF.

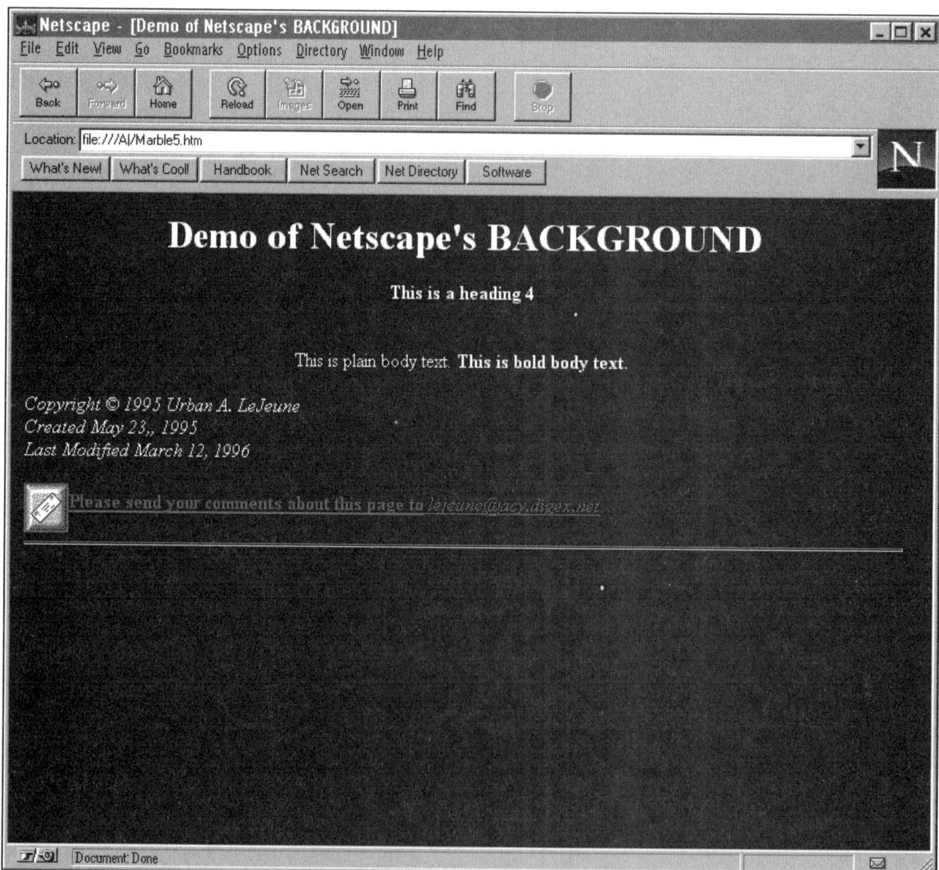

Figure 16.6 *Our new, spooky test page.*

Aesthetics aside, there's also a pragmatic reason to use **BGCOLOR**. Establishing a background image requires the fetching of an image from a second server connection. The second connection will slow down the loading of a document. In other words, none of your document will display until the image is loaded and decoded. When you use a background color, as opposed to a background image, everything is accomplished in one fetch. This speed issue is also a good reason to keep your background images small.

GREAT WEB PUBLISHING TIPS

Since you've probably been surfing the Web for a while, you must realize that it is bursting at the seams with great publishing resources, tips and techniques to help you create HTML documents and publish on the Web. If you know where to look, you can find useful information and tools to help you design pages, add great icons and images, design your own graphics, check your HTML documents for errors, convert documents created by other desktop publishing applications such as PageMaker to HTML, and much more.

In this section, I'll show you some of the better places to go to help you create better Web pages. But we won't just explore lists of resources. I'll also show you how to use resources and tools on the Web to perform a number of useful tasks, including:

- Creating custom graphics for your Web pages
- Spell checking your Web pages
- Checking your HTML documents for proper formatting

Creating Your Own Graphics

Wouldn't it be nice if you could design your own graphics as you were surfing the Web? Sure, you can find graphics you like and download them as GIF files, but a much more useful technique would be to build them on the fly while you're surfing the Web.

Patrick Hennessey has created what I think is one of the most innovative publishing/design tools I've seen on the Web. His creation, called the Interactive Graphics Renderer page, is located at:

```
http://www.eece.ksu.edu/IGR/
```

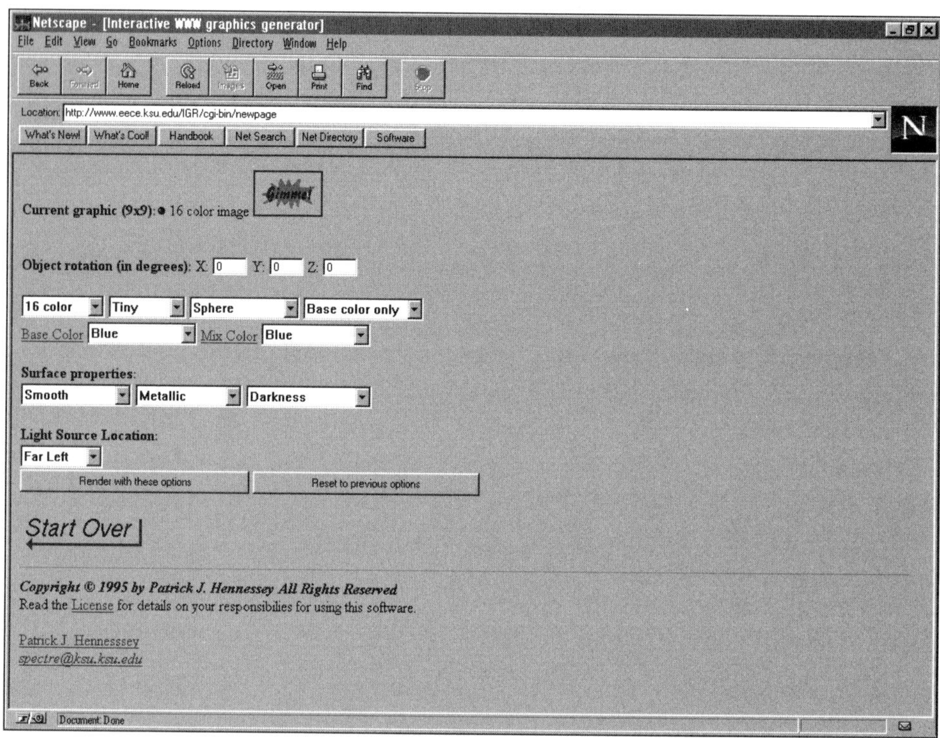

Figure 16.7 *The Interactive Graphics Renderer tool.*

When you get to his home page, click on the button that takes you to the Interactive Graphics Renderer tool. Figure 16.7 shows the form that you'll get.

To use this tool to build your own images, here are the steps to follow:

1. Select the settings for the image using the text boxes and option boxes. You can rotate your object, select a size and object type, change its colors and surface properties, and so on.
2. Click the "Render with these options" button to create the image. If it doesn't come out the way you want, just change some of the settings and create it again.
3. When you finish, click on the Gimme button and the GIF image you've created will be downloaded. I don't know anyone else on the Web who offers service like this!

Creating a Home Page

In Chapter 13, I presented our very own HomePage Creator that you can run from Windows to help you create your own home page. There is also another program you can download from the Web that offers this service. This program is called Web Wizard and you can locate it at:

```
http://www.halcyon.com/artamedia/webwizard
```

Web Wizard works a little differently than HomePage Creator; it interviews you for the information to put on your home page and then it generates an HTML document for you. Try it out. Everyone can always use an extra program to help generate a home page.

Checking a Web Page

If you are concerned about the accuracy of your HTML documents, there is a neat tool available on the Web you can use to check them. The tool is called Weblint; it reads an HTML document and checks for a number of possible errors in your documents, including:

- Incorrect structure
- Unsupported HTML tags
- Mismatched tags
- Obsolete tags

You can think of this tool as the HTML style enforcer. It will even complain if you use the word "here" as anchor text. I like to use Weblint to check whether an HTML document uses HTML tags that are not supported by most browsers.

Checking Coriolis Group's Home Page

Let's take Weblint for a test drive and have it check Coriolis Group's home page, which is at the following location:

```
http://www.coriolis.com
```

But first, to use Weblint, point Netscape to this site:

```
http://www.unipress.com/weblint/index.html#form
```

Figure 16.8 shows the Web page that is displayed. Next, enter the URL for the Coriolis Group home page, then scroll down and click the Check it... button. Weblint will then go to work and analyze the HTML document specified by the URL we entered.

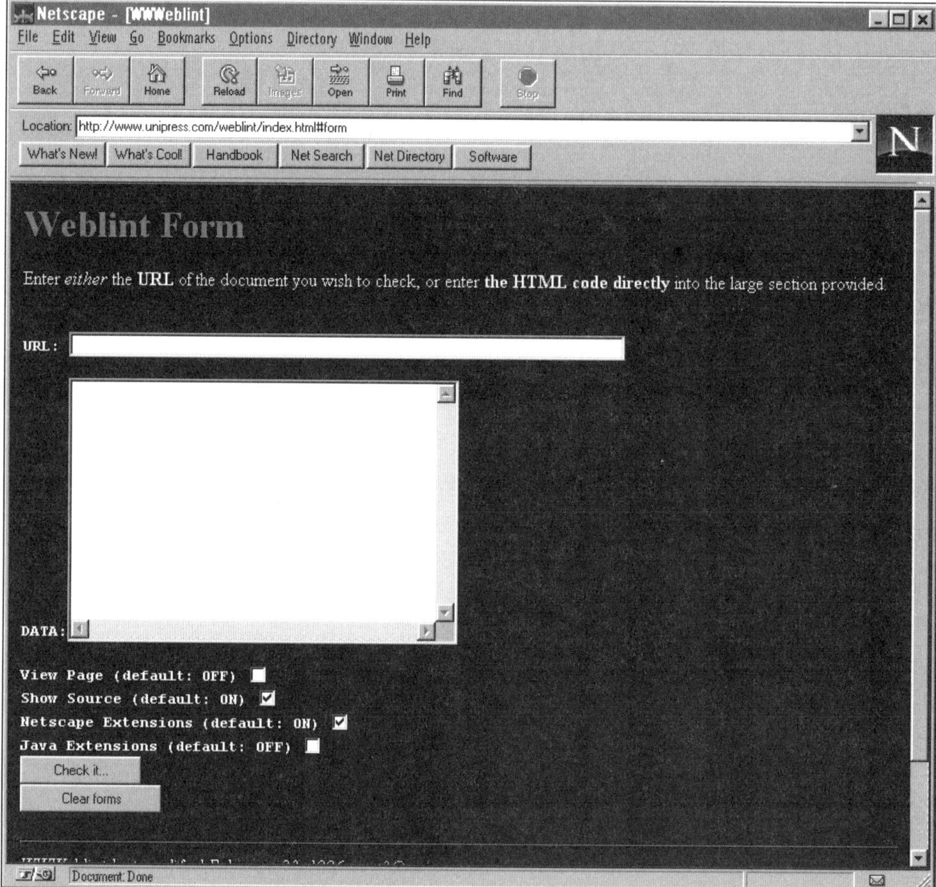

Figure 16.8 The Weblint HTML testing form.

Did this Web page pass? Sure. In fact, I would give them a B+. Figure 16.9 shows the results of the test. As you can see, Weblint is pretty picky. When it finishes checking an HTML document, it displays the errors or inconsistencies it finds, along with the HTML tags for the document. This is a nice feature because you can see exactly where and why errors have occurred. Try Weblint on one of your HTML pages.

If you are interested in this type of Web page verification, you can find another tool at this location:

```
http://www.webtechs.com/html-val-svc/
```

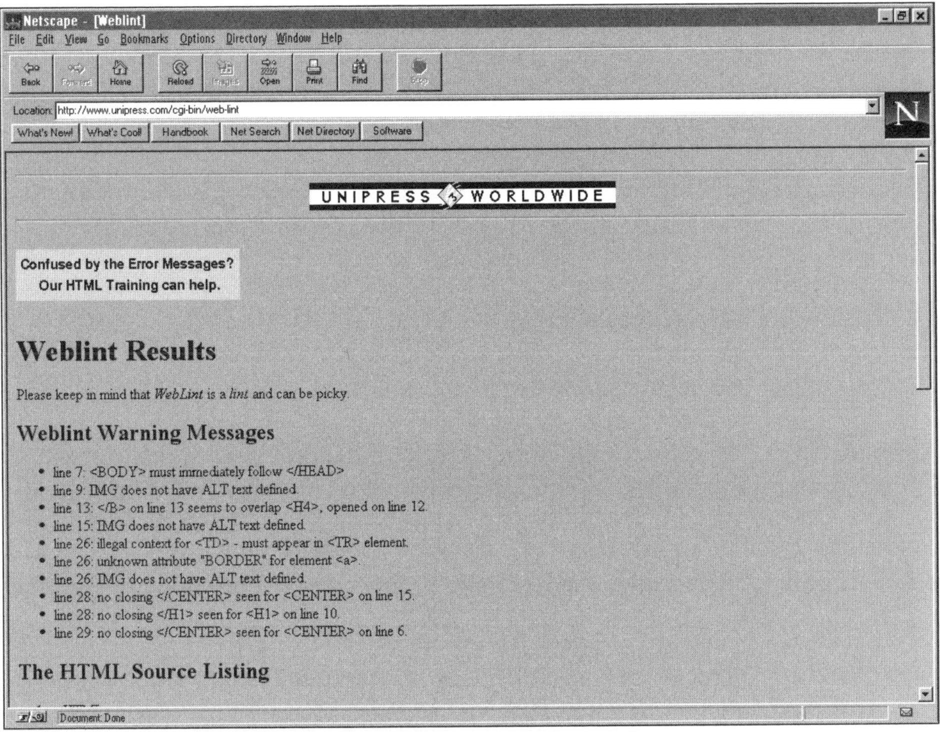

Figure 16.9 *The results of the Weblint test.*

Spelling Bee

If you're like me, you'll agree that one of the best inventions to come along in ages is the spellchecker. I couldn't live without mine. Unfortunately, most of the HTML editors available don't provide any spell checking features. So, you're likely to find a lot of Web pages out there in cyberspace that have a lot of typos. One solution to this problem is the automatic spell checker called WebSter's Dictionary that you can run right from the Web. To use this tool, go to:

```
http://www.eece.ksu.edu/~spectre/WebSter/spell.html
```

Once you are there, you can enter a URL for an HTML document and the program will produce a Web page showing all of the words that are misspelled. You might be wondering, how good is this tool? I haven't fully tested it but I did try testing it on itself. That is, I entered the URL for the WebSter's Dictionary HTML document and guess what happened? I got a list of misspelled words. Oh well, I guess the person who created this tool was so busy programming that he or she forgot to spell check the page!

LET'S REVIEW

The HTML 3.0 specifications make it possible to use a number of extensions from font sizing to backgrounds.

Netscape, starting with version 1.1N, has also implemented several enhancements. These include the ability to specify the color of the entire document area, as well as the color of link anchors.

The basic format for colorization is:

```
<BODY attribute="RGB-colors-in-hex">
```

Attributes are usable in combination. The HTML code (including Netscape's enhancements) used in the specification of colors are shown in Table 16.1

Colors are specified in the range of 0 through 255 (hex 0 through hex FF) with 0 being the lowest intensity and 255 the highest. Colors are specified in red-green-blue order. Bright red would be 255,0,0 or FF0000 in hex.

Different color effects may look different, or may not display at all, on different browsers, or even when using the same browser with different user-specified values. Don't assume that a person viewing your document will see what's identical to your screen.

Table 16.1 Body Enhancements

Opening Tag	Closing Tag	Description
<BODY>	</BODY>	No special color effects
<BODY BACKGROUND="URL">	</BODY>	Use the image stored at URL to construct background
<BODY BGCOLOR="RGB-in-Hex">	</BODY>	Solid background color display specified in Hex
<BODY TEXT="RGB-in-Hex">	</BODY>	Normal, non-link, text color display specified in Hex
<BODY LINK="RGB-in-Hex">	</BODY>	Link anchor display color specified in Hex
<BODY VLINK="RGB-in-Hex">	</BODY>	Visited link anchor display color specified in Hex
<BODY ALINK="RGB-in-Hex">	</BODY>	Active link anchor display color specified in Hex

Mastering Tables

Are you looking for a better way to display lots of data on your Web pages? Then look no further, because you're about to see how you can use tables to publish more information in less space.

"People," I was saying at a recent meeting of the South Jersey Internet User's Group, "can be divided into two groups—those who divide people into groups, and those who don't."

The dividers are those people—me for one—who prefer placing objects in neatly defined pigeon holes; we love spreadsheets and any extensively organized system. Conversely, the non-partitioners are those people who have been given the gift of creativity. These creative people, most of whom prefer Macs, disdain anything with a straight line while the left side of their brain cranks out another work of art. Somehow it just doesn't seem fair—we denizens of the neatly structured world truly admire the creative output of our gifted counterparts, while they routinely relegate our predictable, organized output to the trashbasket.

In this chapter I'm going to take up my role as divider as I present HTML tables. Both Netscape and Mosaic have implemented HTML table tags in their latest versions. This chapter will show you how to use the basic HTML 3.0 table tags as implemented by Netscape.

GETTING STARTED WITH TABLES

Tables are interesting critters. Many people prefer information presented in the two-dimensional linear format offered by tables. It's no accident that a spreadsheet program provided the catalyst for the desktop computer revolution—desktop revolting, some might say.

On the other hand, highly creative people aren't big fans of tabular displays of data. They prefer presentations with more pizzazz. Whatever your bag, the addition of tables to the creates display options previously unavailable for your Web documents.

As you will see, very creative things can be done with tables. In essence, each cell in a table is its own miniature HTML document. You can even create tables without borders and produce neat effects in your Web documents like text flowing around images—something not very easily done without tables.

HTML tables are easier seen than talked about. For this reason I have built a tutorial HTML document called tables.htm. The file is in the \urbstuff\html\tables directory on the companion CD-ROM. In the event you don't have a CD-ROM drive, I have also put the document "on the air" at:

```
http://www.charm.net/~lejeune/tables.html
```

I'll try to keep the "live" version up to date with any standards changes and added tutorial information. The online document will also have links to table information on the Web. In addition to tables.htm, the individual tutorial components are kept in a file of their own. This arrangement allows you to copy a specific table construction and use it as a starting point for your own table publishing projects.

All the tables presented in the tutorial, with the exception of the first one, will show the actual table, immediately followed by the HTML construction that produced the table.

Let the Tutorial Begin

First, we need to get a few simple conventions out of the way. Tag labels in the examples I present will be all uppercase. Anything within a table shown in either upper or mixed case is something you must construct.

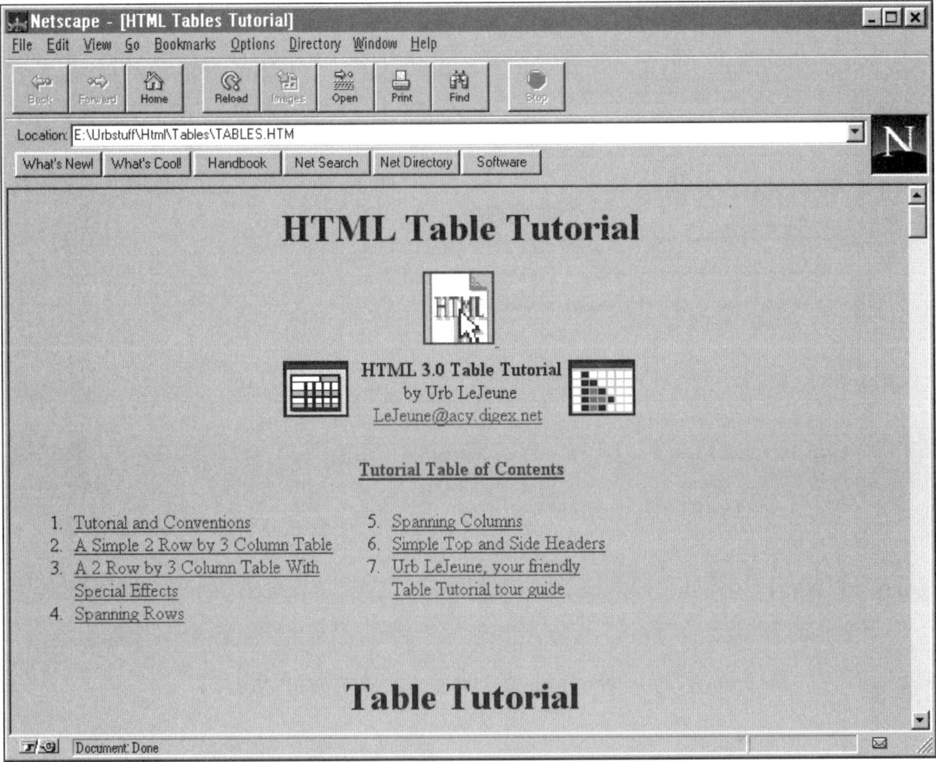

***Figure 17.1** The opening page of the Table Tutorial showing two interesting tables.*

Let's start our tutorial by looking at the results rather than the process. Figure 17.1 shows the first page of the table tutorial. Here we are looking at two tables. The upper table, which contains the three images, is a two row by three column table. The lower table is a one row by two column table. (The number list displayed is actually two lists that take advantage of Netscape's **START=** option.)

Another interesting use of a table is the BrowserWatch home page as shown in Figure 17.2. The URL for this site is:

```
http://www.browserwatch.com/
```

The basic HTML tags used to construct tables are shown in Figure 17.3. This example table is a whopping seven rows by three columns. The table also has a visible border. (The tables presented in Figure 17.1 did not use borders.) Netscape treats borders in tables a little differently depending upon the background color that is selected. As with almost all Web publishing activities, don't assume that what you see on the screen will be what someone else sees, even if they are also using Netscape.

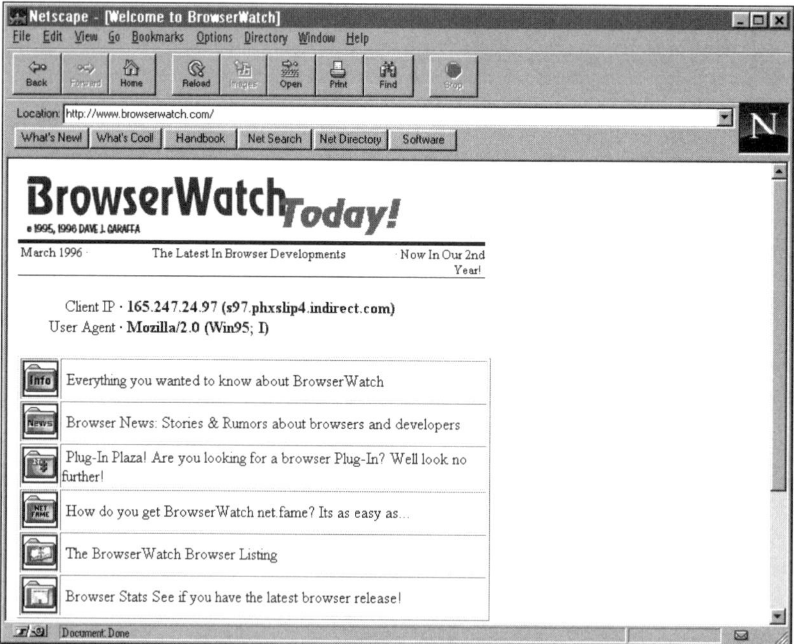

***Figure 17.2** The BrowserWatch home page showing a different type of table.*

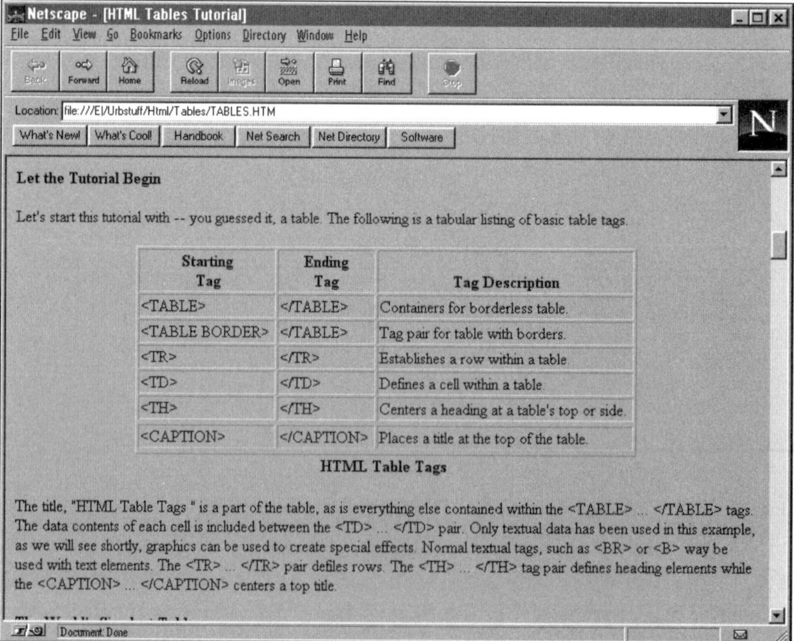

***Figure 17.3** HTML table tags in a bordered table.*

Summary of HTML Table Tags

Table 17.1 lists all of the main HTML tags that are used to create tables. As you explore the examples presented in this chapter, you'll want to refer back to this table to look up the function of a particular tag.

The World's Simplest Table

Conceptually, an empty table is the simplest table. However, an empty table is not very useful—it doesn't even look good! The simplest practical table would be a one row by one column structure. Here's an example:

```
<TABLE>
    <TD>Row One - Column One</TD>
</TABLE>
```

Each table is enclosed between the **<TABLE> ... </TABLE>** tag pair. A *cell* (table data) is enclosed between the **<TD> ... </TD>** tag pair. A non-empty table is assumed to have one row; therefore, the **<TR> ... </TR>** tag pairs (which are used to define a new row) may be eliminated for a one row table. There is never a designation for a column. The position of cells within a row determine the column location.

A table, by default, has no border. Typically, a table with a border is cosmetically more appealing than a borderless table. All bets are off however, if we want to use the capabilities of a table without tipping our hand that it is a table. The next table is the same as the 1x1 table shown above, but with a border:

```
<TABLE BORDER>
     <TD>Row One - Column One</TD>
</TABLE>
```

Table 17.1 *HTML Table Tags*

Starting Tag	Ending Tag	Tag Description
<TABLE>	</TABLE>	Container for a borderless table.
<TABLE BORDER>	</TABLE>	Tag pair for a table with borders.
<TR>	</TR>	Establishes a row within a table.
<TD>	</TD>	Defines a cell within a table.
<TH>	</TH>	Centers a heading at a table's top or side.
<CAPTION>	</CAPTION>	Places a title at the top of the table.

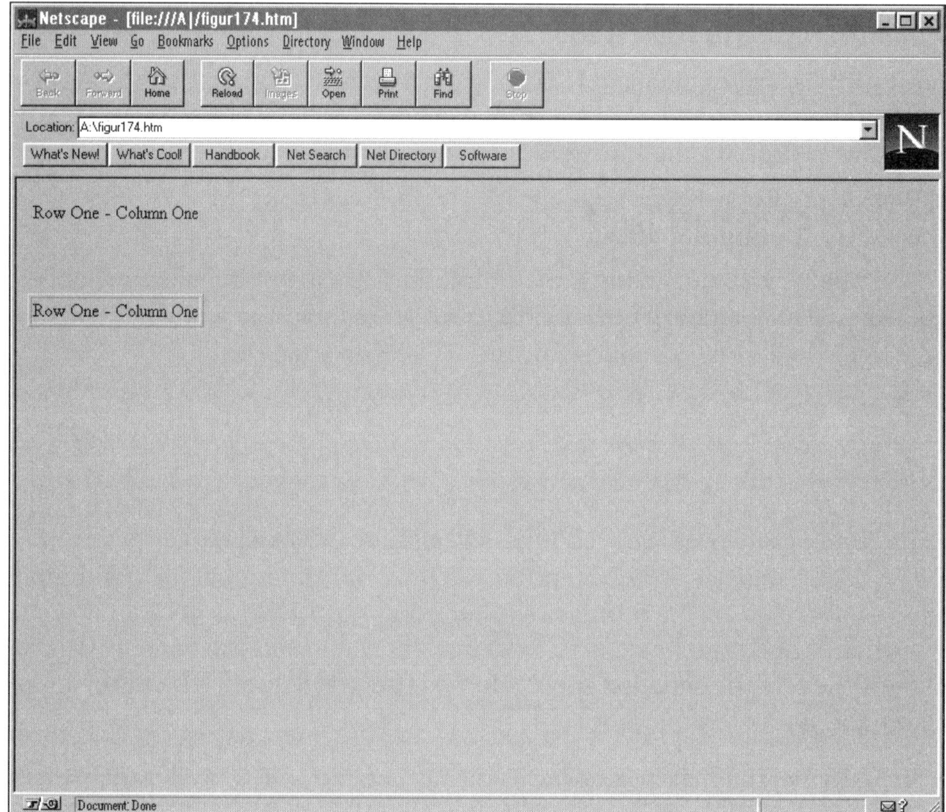

Figure 17.4 *Two 1x1 tables, the upper without a border and the lower with a border.*

The upper table in Figure 17.4 shows a borderless one row by one column table. The lower table demonstrates the effect of adding the **<TABLE BORDER>** tag.

Here's a basic shell for a one row by two column table:

```
<TABLE>
     <TD>Row One - Column One</TD><TD>Row One - Column Two</TD>
</TABLE>
```

Remember, your mileage with borders may vary. A table will have a different appearance if the background color changes, even if it is using the same document, browser, and computer.

Two-Dimensional Tables

A table row is defined using the **<TR> ... </TR>** tag pair. A two row by two column example would be:

```
<TABLE>
     <TR><TD>Row One - Column One</TD><TD>Row One - Column Two</TD></TR>
     <TR><TD>Row Two - Column One</TD><TD>Row Two - Column Two</TD></TR>
</TABLE>
```

Are you ready to get a little fancy? Let's take another look at the actual table before we write the HTML. Figure 17.5 shows two Not So "Plain Vanilla" Two Row by Three Column Tables. Both tables have captions and sizing and effect attributes, but otherwise they are the same.

A table may have an optional caption enclosed between, you guessed it, the **<CAPTION> ... </CAPTION>** tag pair. As we have seen with other Netscape HTML enhancements, tags may frequently contain attributes. The opening **<CAPTION>** tag may have an optional alignment tag. The formats are:

```
Opening Tag                  Closing Tag
<CAPTION>                    </CAPTION>
<CAPTION ALIGN=TOP|BOTTOM>   </CAPTION>
```

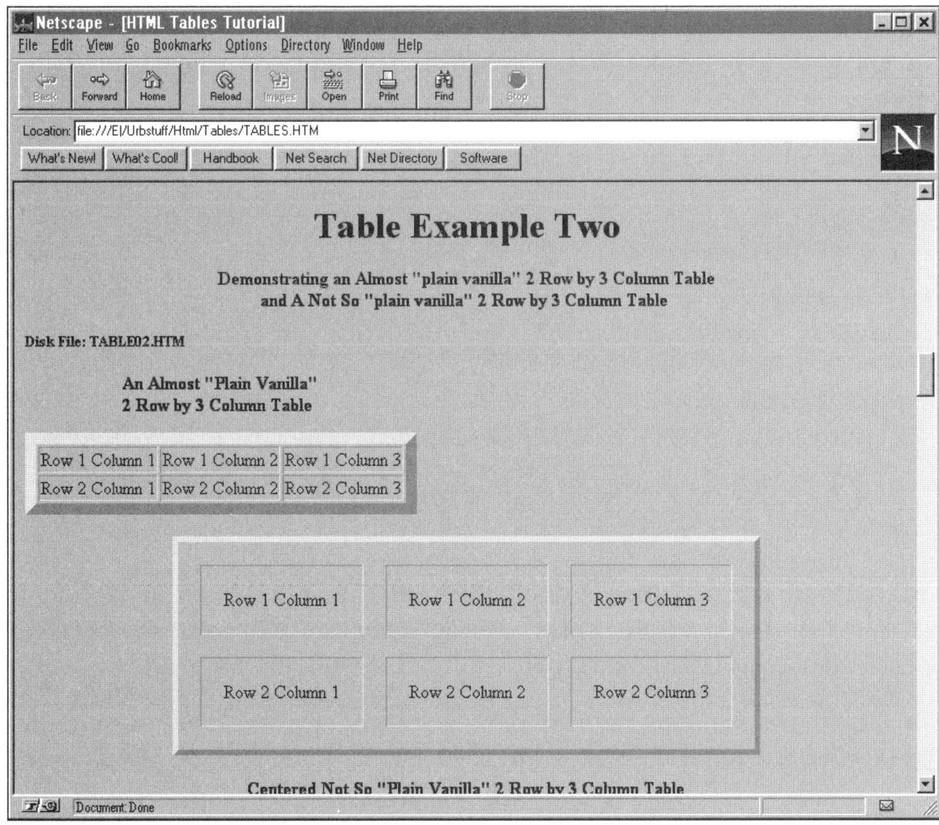

Figure 17.5 *Two identical tables showing the special effects created by sizing.*

If the **ALIGN=** option is used, it must immediately be followed by "**TOP**" or "**BOTTOM**". The default is **ALIGN=TOP**. I once wanted to move a caption from the top to the bottom of a table. I changed **TOP** to **BOTTOM** and the caption still showed up on the top of the table. About five microseconds before I was about to send a message to Netscape reporting a bug, I noticed that I had started the attribute with ALIGH. If a browser doesn't recognize an HTML tag or modifier, it ignores it. Since Netscape didn't recognize "ALIGH" it ignored the attribute; without the **ALIGN** attribute, **TOP** was meaningless.

The upper table in Figure 17.5 contains a **TOP** aligned caption while the lower caption is **BOTTOM** aligned. Both tables have enhanced **<TABLE>** tags. A listing of table tags may be found in Table 17.2.

The table attributes are combinable. To illustrate, this HTML

```
<TABLE BORDER=5 WIDTH=50%>
```

would create a table with a border size of 5 pixels and it would take 50 percent of the page width. If the natural size of the table exceeds any of the attribute sizes, the attributes are ignored.

The HTML producing the upper table in Figure 17.5 is shown here:

```
<TABLE BORDER=10>
      <CAPTION ALIGN=TOP>
         <B>An Almost;Plain Vanilla&quot;<BR> 2 Row by 3 Column Table</B>
      </CAPTION>
      <TR>
         <TD>Row 1 Column 1</TD> <TD>Row 1 Column 2</TD> <TD>Row 1 Column 3</TD>
      </TR>

      <TR>
         <TD>Row 2 Column 1</TD> <TD>Row 2 Column 2</TD> <TD>Row 2 Column 3</TD>
      </TR>
</TABLE>
```

Just as a refresher, unadorned double quotation marks are not useable in an HTML document since they have special meaning in HTML. The """ special character causes the display of the double quotation marks.

The table has a caption and a border size. The default border size is 1. The lower table in Figure 17.5 has a few bells and whistles. The HTML code is:

Table 17.2 Enhanced Table Tags

Opening Tag	Closing Tag	Description
<TABLE>	</TABLE>	No border or special effects
<TABLE BORDER>	</TABLE>	Default border size of 1
<TABLE BORDER=n>	</TABLE>	Where n is border size in pixels
<TABLE CELLPADDING=n>	</TABLE>	Where n is cell padding size in pixels
<TABLE CELLSPACING=n>	</TABLE>	Where n is cell spacing size in pixels
<TABLE WIDTH=n>	</TABLE>	Where n is table width in pixels
<TABLE WIDTH=%>	</TABLE>	Where % is table width as a percentage of page width

```
<CENTER>
 <TABLE BORDER=5 CELLSPACING=20 CELLPADDING=20>
      <CAPTION ALIGN=BOTTOM>
         <B>Centered Not So &quot;Plain Vanilla&quot; 2 Row by 3 Column
         Table<BR>
         BORDER=5 and CELLSPACING=20 and CELLPADDING=20</B>
      </CAPTION>
      <TR>
        <TD>Row 1 Column 1</TD> <TD>Row 1 Column 2</TD> <TD>Row 1 Column 3</TD>
      </TR>

      <TR>
        <TD>Row 2 Column 1</TD> <TD>Row 2 Column 2</TD> <TD>Row 2 Column 3</TD>
      </TR>
</TABLE>
</CENTER>
```

In addition to being centered, the table has **BORDER**, **CELLSPACING**, and **CELLPADDING** attributes. The **BORDER** attribute controls the size of the 3-D effect. The **CELLPADDING** controls the width of the cells while **CELLSPACING** controls the size between the cells both vertically and horizontally.

Text Formatting within Cells

Now we're getting to my favorite part of table construction: *cells*. Each cell within a table has a life of its own. A cell may contain anything you would normally find in the body section of an HTML document, including nothing or another table! Indeed, empty cells and nested tables produce interesting effects. A cell's content doesn't need to have any logical relationship with the contents of its neighboring cells.

Within a table, the widest cell in any column determines the width of the column. Likewise, the height of the highest cell determines the height of all the cells in the same row. The contents of a cell are left aligned and vertically centered. Netscape has added optional cell width and alignment attributes. More on these in a minute.

Let's take a look at our old reliable two by three table containing some HTML formatting. Figure 17.6 shows the table with all kinds of goodies. The text within the cells determines the size formatting. The center cell in the second row is empty, while the cell in the lower right corner contains an image. The code producing this gem is:

```
<TABLE BORDER>
     <TR>
        <TD><EM>This is Emphasis</EM></TD>
        <TD><H3>Heading 3</H3></TD>
        <TD>Unformatted text</TD>
     </TR>

     <TR>
        <TD><B>Bold<BR>with<BR>three lines</B></TD>
        <TD></TD> <!- This is a null cell ->
        <TD><IMG SRC="home.gif"></TD>
     </TR>
 </TABLE>
```

Surprisingly simple, isn't it? The content of a cell is alignable both vertically and horizontally. Table 17.3 shows more Netscape HTML table enhancements.

Both vertical and horizontal alignments, as well as width attributes are permitted within the same cell. Figure 17.7 shows the same table shown in Figure 17.6 with alignment and width attributes. The HTML for this table is:

```
<TABLE BORDER>
     <TR>
        <TD WIDTH=50%><EM>This is Emphasis</EM></TD>
        <TD><H3>Heading 3</H3></TD>
        <TD>Unformatted text</TD>
     </TR>

     <TR>
        <TD ALIGN=CENTER><B>Bold<BR>with<BR>three lines</B></TD>
        <TD></TD> <!- This is a null cell ->
        <TD ALIGN=RIGHT VALIGN=BOTTOM><IMG SRC=home.gif></TD>
     </TR>
</TABLE>
```

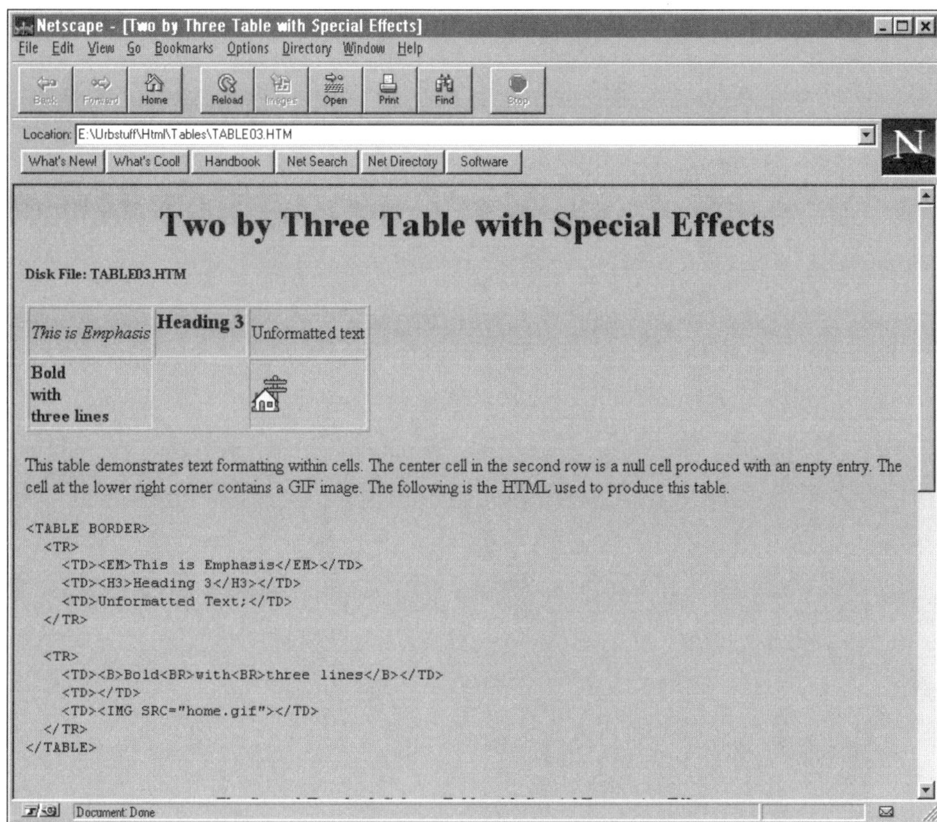

Figure 17.6 *A table containing special effects including an image and a blank cell.*

Table 17.3 *Table Cell Enhancements*

<table>
<tr><th>Opening Tag</th><th>Closing Tag</th><th>Description</th></tr>
<tr><td><TD></td><td></TD></td><td>No special effects</td></tr>
<tr><td><TD ALIGN=LEFT|RIGHT|CENTER></td><td></TD></td><td>Horizontal alignment within cell</td></tr>
<tr><td><TD VALIGN=TOP|MIDDLE|BOTTOM></td><td></TD></td><td>Vertical alignment within cell</td></tr>
<tr><td><TD WIDTH=n></td><td></TD></td><td>Where n is cell width in pixels</td></tr>
<tr><td><TD WIDTH=%></td><td></TD></td><td>Where % is percentage of table width</td></tr>
</table>

The cell in row one, column one has the **WIDTH** set to 50 percent of the total table size. The **WIDTH** attribute establishes the size of all cells in the same column. The text row two, column one is centered because of the **ALIGN=CENTER** attribute. The GIF in row two, column three is horizontally

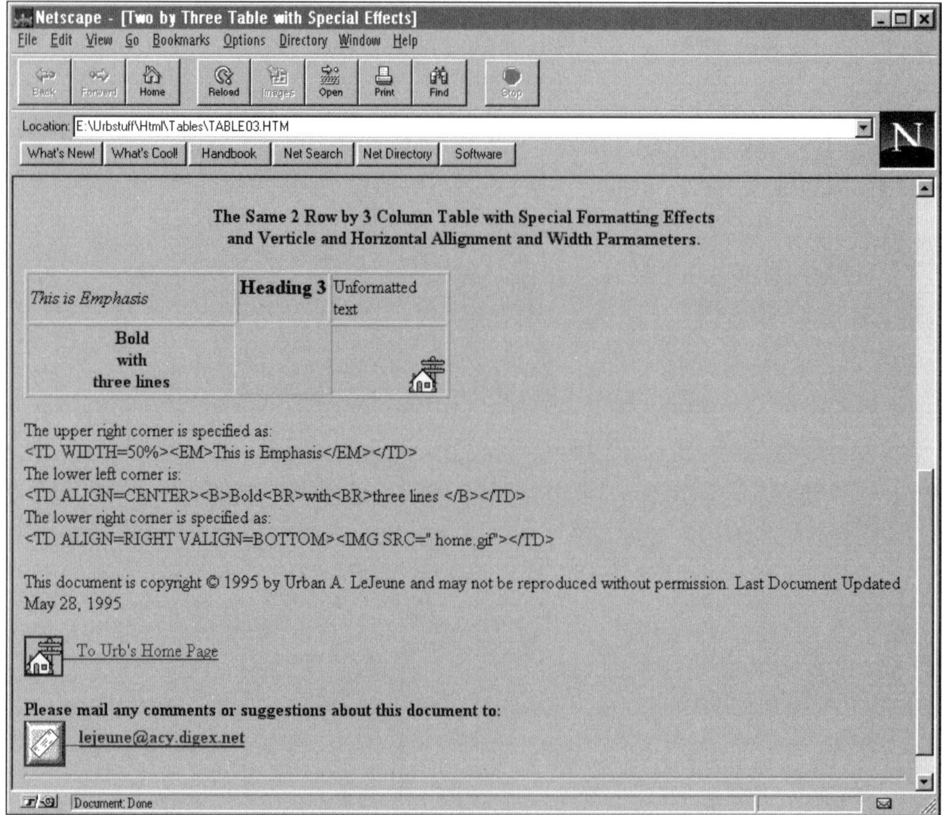

Figure 17.7 *Vertical and horizontal alignment applied to the table in Figure 17.6.*

aligned to the right and vertically aligned at the bottom of the cell because of the **ALIGN=RIGHT** and **VALIGN=BOTTOM** attributes.

Cell Spanning

All the tables we have created and viewed so far have been symmetrical. All rows contained the same number of cells, and all columns contained the same number of cells. This is certainly not a requirement. Both rows and columns may be spanned by connecting two or more cells through the use of the **ROWSPAN** and **COLSPAN** attributes. The syntax of these attributes is:

```
<TD COLSPAN=n>  </TD>   Where n is the number of columns to span
<TD ROWSPAN=n>  </TD>   Where n is the number of rows to span
```

Let's first look at some ROWSPANs. Figure 17.8 demonstrates the use of row spanning. The center column is just one big row because of the **ROWSPAN=3**

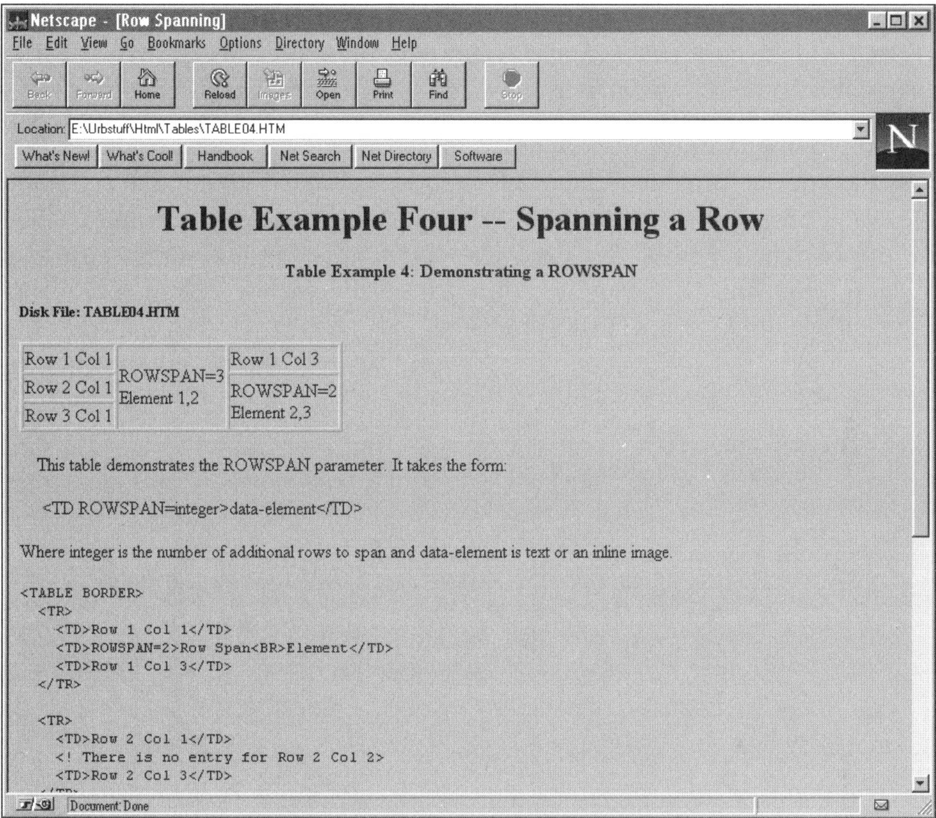

Figure 17.8 *The use of the* ***ROWSPAN*** *attribute to combine multiple rows.*

specification. The right column has the lower two rows connected using the **ROWSPAN=2** attribute. The required HTML for these effects is:

```
<TABLE BORDER>
    <TR>
       <TD>Row 1 Col 1</TD>
       <TD ROWSPAN=3>ROWSPAN=3<BR>Element 1,2</TD>
       <TD>Row 1 Col 3</TD>
    </TR>

    <TR>
       <TD>Row 2 Col 1</TD><TD ROWSPAN=2>ROWSPAN=2<BR>Element 2,3</TD>
    </TR>

    <TR>
       <TD>Row 3 Col 1</TD>
    </TR>
</TABLE>
```

Since the center cell of the first row specifies **ROWSPAN=3** there are no **<TD> ... </TD>** tags for the center column in the second and third rows. The phantom cells tend to be confusing when you're constructing the table.

Hold on to your hat, we're now going to get really fancy with column spanning and special formatting. Figure 17.9 shows a table with column spanning and some other formatting effects. Row two spans all three columns, while the upper-right corner spans two. The center row is interesting because it contains a link and GIF image which is part of the anchor. The anchor text is also center aligned. The HTML code is:

```
<TABLE BORDER>
    <TR>
        <TD>Row 1 Col 1</TD>
        <TD COLSPAN=2>COLSPAN=2<BR>Element 1,2</TD>
    </TR>

    <TR>
         <TD ALIGN=CENTER COLSPAN=3><A HREF=http://www.charm.net/~lejeune>
          <IMG ALIGN=CENTER SRC="home.gif">
           Urb's Home Page</A><BR> COLSPAN=3 - Element 2,1</TD>
    </TR>

    <TR>
       <TD>Row 3 Col 1</TD><TD>Row 3 Col 2</TD><TD>Row 3 Col 3</TD>
    </TR>
</TABLE>
```

The second row's starting table data tag has both a **COLSPAN=3** attribute and an **ALIGN=CENTER** attribute. The link reference

```
<A HREF=http://www.charm.net/~lejeune> <IMG ALIGN=CENTER SRC="home.gif">
```

contains both the address reference and an image. When an image is included in this fashion, it is bordered with the specified anchor color. Since the image is part of the anchor, clicking on it activates the link.

Top and Side Table Headings

A table heading is much like a cell element; the difference is that the content is centered and bolded. The table heading is enclosed between the **<TH> ... </TH>** tag pair. Table headings have much the same syntax as **<TD>** elements, as shown in Table 17.4.

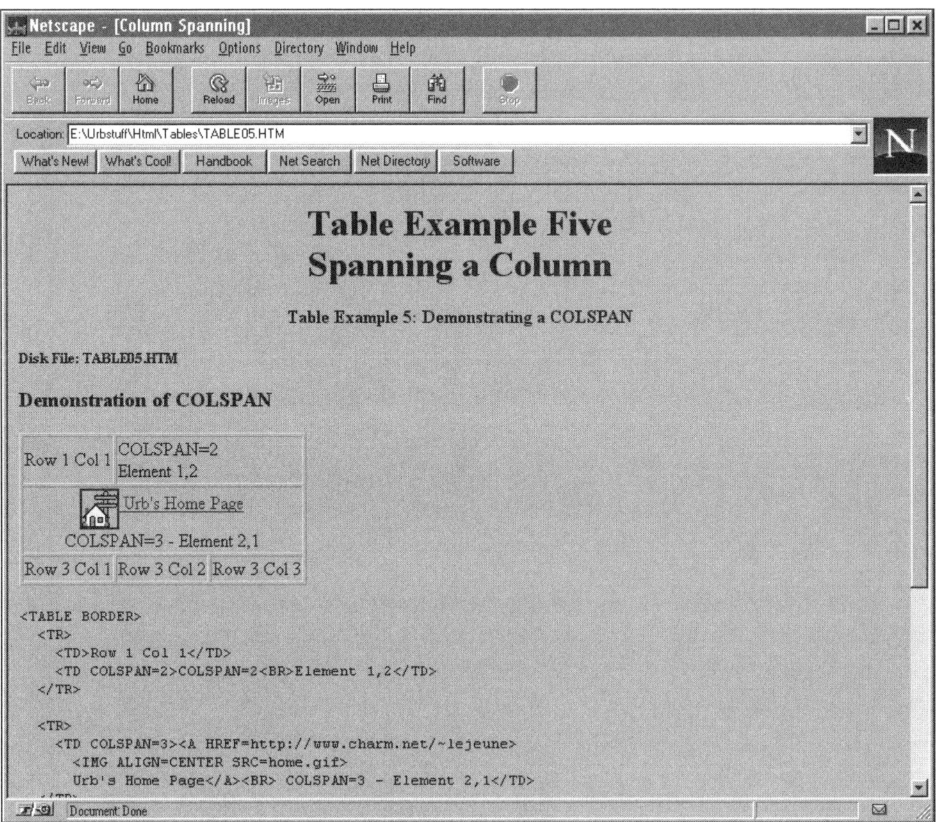

Figure 17.9 *An example of using COLSPAN to span three columns.*

Table 17.4 *Table Heading Codes*

<table>
<tr><th>Opening Tag</th><th>Closing Tag</th><th>Description</th></tr>
<tr><td><TH></td><td></TH></td><td>No special effects other than bold and centered</td></tr>
<tr><td><TH ALIGN=LEFT|RIGHT|CENTER></td><td></TH></td><td>Horizontal heading alignment within cell</td></tr>
<tr><td><TH VALIGN=TOP|MIDDLE|BOTTOM></td><td></TH></td><td>Vertical heading alignment within cell</td></tr>
<tr><td><TH WIDTH=n></td><td></TH></td><td>Where n is cell width in pixels</td></tr>
<tr><td><TH WIDTH=%></td><td></TH></td><td>Where % is percentage of table width</td></tr>
<tr><td><TH ROWSPAN=n></td><td></TH></td><td>Where n is heading span in number of rows</td></tr>
<tr><td><TH COLSPAN=n></td><td></TH></td><td>Where n is heading span in number of columns</td></tr>
</table>

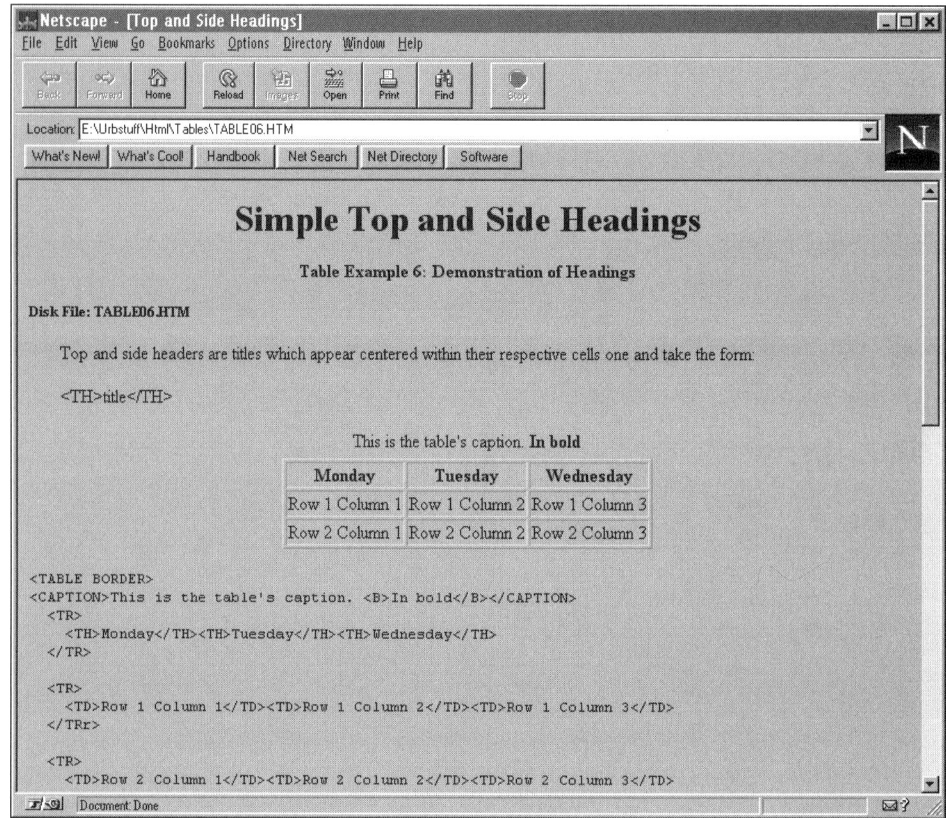

Figure 17.10 *The use of top headings in a simple table.*

Figure 17.10 demonstrates how the **<TH> ... </TH>** pair can be used to create column headings for our old reliable two by three table. The code is:

```
<TABLE BORDER>
    <CAPTION>This is the table's caption. <B>In bold</B></CAPTION>
    <TR>
    <TH>Monday</TH><TH>Tuesday</TH><TH>Wednesday</TH>
    </TR>

    <TR>
    <TD>Row 1 Column 1</TD><TD>Row 1 Column 2</TD><TD>Row 1 Column 3</TD>
    </TR>

    <TR>
    <TD>Row 2 Column 1</TD><TD>Row 2 Column 2</TD><TD>Row 2 Column 3</TD>
    </TR>
 </TABLE>
```

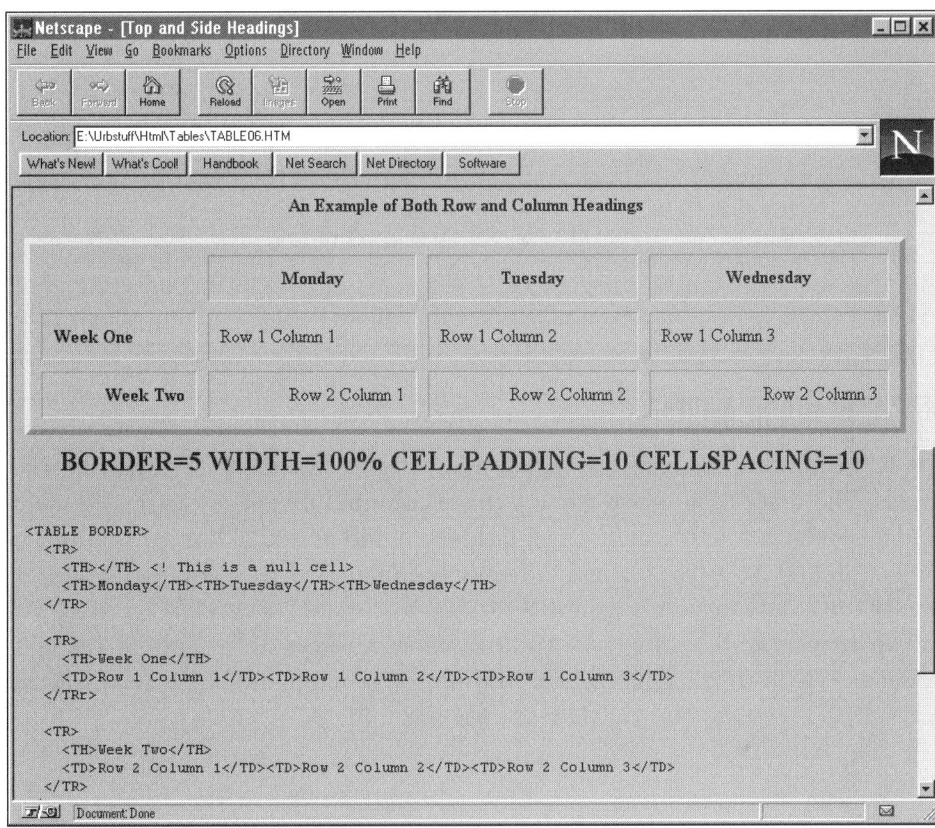

Figure 17.11 *A table that's full of effects.*

Figure 17.11 again shows off a variety of effects. The purpose of the formatting is illustration, not cosmetic purity. The entire row with the "Week One" heading is left aligned with the **<TR ALIGN=LEFT>** starting tag. The row titled "Week Two" is right aligned using the **<TR ALIGN=RIGHT>** starting tag. The caption demonstrates **BOTTOM** alignment and also the use of Netscape's **<FONT SIZE>** pair. The complete code is:

```
<CENTER>
 <TABLE BORDER=5 WIDTH=100% CELLPADDING=10 CELLSPACING=10>
    <CAPTION ALIGN=BOTTOM>
          <FONT SIZE=5>
            <B>BORDER=5 WIDTH=100% CELLPADDING=10 CELLSPACING=10</B>
          </FONT>
    </CAPTION>
    <TR>
         <TD></TD> <!— This is a null cell —>
         <TH>Monday</TH><TH>Tuesday</TH><TH>Wednesday</TH>
```

```
    </TR>
    <TR ALIGN=LEFT>
        <TH>Week One</TH>
        <TD>Row 1 Column 1</TD><TD>Row 1 Column 2</TD>
        <TD>Row 1 Column 3</TD>
    </TR>
    <TR ALIGN=RIGHT>
        <TH>Week Two</TH>
        <TD>Row 2 Column 1</TD><TD>Row 2 Column 2</TD>
        <TD>Row 2 Column 3</TD>
    </TR>
</TABLE>
</CENTER>
```

Practical Applications

The first figure in this chapter, Figure 17.1, shows two tables that use special effects. The first one is a one row by three column table. The outer cells each hold an image while the center cell holds text and an email link. No border is used so the effect is two horizontally aligned images with text between them. One of the most frequently asked questions by new HTML coders is, "How do I wrap text around an image?" Until now, it was possible only by using a Netscape HTML enhancement. Text wrapping is now possible with any browser that supports tables. The HTML code for this table is:

```
<TABLE>
     <TR>
         <TD><IMG SRC="table.gif"></A></TD>
         <TD>
            <B>HTML 3.0 Table Tutorial</B><BR>
            <CENTER> by Urb LeJeune<BR>
            <A HREF="mailto:LeJeune@acy.digex.net">LeJeune@acy.digex.net</A>
            </CENTER>
        </TD>
        <TD> <IMG SRC="table2.gif"></TD>
    </TR>
</TABLE>
```

The lower table in Figure 17.1 demonstrates another interesting construct. HTML lists frequently have large amounts of blank space since they often take less than half a page. This representation is a one row by two column table. Each column holds an ordered **<OL>** list. What makes it work is Netscape's enhancement of **<OL START=n>** where n is the number starting the list. The right ordered list starts with 5. The code for this table is:

```
<CENTER>
 <TABLE>
```

```
    <TR>
      <TD>
        <OL>
          <LI><A HREF=#TABLE01>
              Tutorial and Conventions</A>
          <LI><A HREF=#TABLE02>
              A Simple 2 Row by 3 Column Table</A>
          <LI><A HREF=#TABLE03>
              A 2 Row by 3 Column Table With<BR>
              Special Effects</A>
          <LI><A HREF=#TABLE04>
              Spanning Rows</A>
        </OL>
      </TD>

      <TD>
        <OL START=5>
          <LI><A HREF=#TABLE05>
            Spanning Columns</A>
          <LI><A HREF=#TABLE06>
            Simple Top and Side Headers</A>
          <LI><A HREF=#AUTHOR>
            Urb LeJeune, your friendly<BR>
            Table Tutorial tour guide</A>
           <BR><BR><BR>
        </OL>
      </TD>
    </TR>
</TABLE>
</CENTER>
```

LET'S REVIEW

Tables have traditionally been used to display tabular data. The ability to display a table without borders and the fact that each cell is essentially a miniature HTML document presents the opportunity to create interesting and useful effects.

The HTML code, including Netscape's enhancements, used in the construction of tables is shown in Table 17.5. Netscape's Atlas, a preview of a future Netscape version, is proposing some new options for tables. The most interesting change is the ability to specify different background colors within a table. The table can be a different color than the rest of the page, and even each cell within a table can be different. Think of the interesting effects you could have on your Web page! However, Atlas is, as this book went to press, still just an alpha program, and this tag is still in the experimental stage. But it's nice to dream.

Table 17.5 HTML Code Used in Tables

<table>
<tr><th>Opening Tag</th><th>Closing Tag</th><th>Description</th></tr>
<tr><td colspan="3">Table Definition</td></tr>
<tr><td><TABLE></td><td></TABLE></td><td>No border or special effects</td></tr>
<tr><td><TABLE BORDER></td><td></TABLE></td><td>Default border size of 1</td></tr>
<tr><td><TABLE BORDER=n></td><td></TABLE></td><td>Where n is border size in pixels</td></tr>
<tr><td><TABLE CELLPADDING=n></td><td></TABLE></td><td>Where n is cell padding size in pixels</td></tr>
<tr><td><TABLE CELLSPACING=n></td><td></TABLE></td><td>Where n is cell spacing size in pixels</td></tr>
<tr><td><TABLE WIDTH=n></td><td></TABLE></td><td>Where n is table width in pixels</td></tr>
<tr><td><TABLE WIDTH=%></td><td></TABLE></td><td>Where % is table width in % of page width</td></tr>
<tr><td colspan="3">Table Data</td></tr>
<tr><td><TD></td><td></TD></td><td>No special effects</td></tr>
<tr><td><TD ALIGN=LEFT|RIGHT|CENTER></td><td></TD></td><td>Horizontal alignment within cell</td></tr>
<tr><td><TD VALIGN=TOP|MIDDLE|BOTTOM></td><td></TD></td><td>Vertical alignment within cell</td></tr>
<tr><td><TD WIDTH=n></td><td></TD></td><td>Where n is cell width in pixels</td></tr>
<tr><td><TD WIDTH=%></td><td></TD></td><td>Where % is percentage of table</td></tr>
<tr><td><TD COLSPAN=n></td><td></TD></td><td>Where n is the number of columns to span</td></tr>
<tr><td><TD ROWSPAN=n></td><td></TD></td><td>Where n is the number of rows to span</td></tr>
<tr><td colspan="3">Table Heading</td></tr>
<tr><td><TH></td><td></TH></td><td>No special effects other than bold and centered</td></tr>
<tr><td><TH ALIGN=LEFT|RIGHT|CENTER></td><td></TH></td><td>Horizontal heading alignment within cell</td></tr>
<tr><td><TH VALIGN=TOP|MIDDLE|BOTTOM></td><td></TH></td><td>Vertical heading alignment within cell</td></tr>
<tr><td><TH WIDTH=n></td><td></TH></td><td>Where n is cell width in pixels</td></tr>
<tr><td><TH WIDTH=%></td><td></TH></td><td>Where % is percentage of table</td></tr>
<tr><td><TH ROWSPAN=n></td><td></TH></td><td>Where n is heading span in number of rows</td></tr>
<tr><td><TH COLSPAN=n></td><td></TH></td><td>Where n is heading span in number of columns</td></tr>
<tr><td colspan="3">Caption</td></tr>
<tr><td><CAPTION></td><td></CAPTION></td><td>Caption with no special effects</td></tr>
<tr><td><CAPTION ALIGN=TOP|BOTTOM></td><td></CAPTION></td><td>Caption above or below the table</td></tr>
</table>

Different table effects may not look the same, or may not display at all, on a different browser, or even using the same browser with a different user-specified background color. Don't assume that the viewer of your document will see the same screen that you see.

Interesting Online Uses of Tables

Here are some Web pages you can check out:

Browser Watch by Dave J. Garaffa
`http://www.browserwatch.com`

Colors and their HEX equivalents. An interesting use of a table.
`http://www.ohiou.edu/~rbarrett/webaholics/ver2/colors.html`

ESPNet SportZone. One giant table.
`http://espnet.sportzone.com`

Discovery Online. Uses varied COLSPANs and ROWSPANs.
`http://www.discovery.com`

Online References

HyperText Markup Language Specification Version 3.0 Cover Page
`http://www.hpl.hp.co.uk/people/dsr/html/CoverPage.html`

Netscape Extensions
`http://webreference.com/html3andns`

Online HTML Training Course
`http://www.usask.ca/dcs/courses/cai/html/`

Yahoo HTML Listings
`http://www.yahoo.com/Computers/World_Wide_Web/HTML/`

Yale WWW style manual
`http://info.med.yale.edu/caim/StyleManual_Top.HTML`

Unlocking the Mysteries of CGI

The world of truly interactive Web pages is waiting for you. All you need to know is a little about Common Gateway Interface (CGI) scripting.

My editor jokingly calls us Webheads. My wife lovingly calls us Webaholics. I prefer something less pejorative, like slightly dysfunctional Web reclusives. Whatever the title, we've arrived at this lofty station in life by passing through three highly distinguishable phases on our way toward becoming a certified Web maniac: surfer, author/publisher, and programmer.

After operating as a Web surfer for a while, you'll know you're ready to move on when you have voluntarily visited ten different governmental home pages looking for design ideas. Another obvious sign is when you visit URouLette and the same site comes up for the third time. URouLette is a page at the University of Kansas that brings up a random site from a massive database each time you visit. The URL is:

```
http://www.uroulette.com:8000
```

The second phase (Web authoring) begins innocently enough when you decide that you want to publish your own home page. Of course, before you know it, you'll become a web publishing mogul and your home page directory will contain hundreds of html or htm documents. But the real fun (and obsession) begins when you start becoming interested in the Common Gateway Interface (CGI) and start writing your own scripts.

In this chapter I'll show you the basics of how to write CGI scripts. These scripts are very useful because they allow you to make your Web pages much more dynamic. With them, your users will be able to search for information, fill out forms, and send you feedback, and you can send custom messages back to your users. We'll start by discussing what CGI scripts are and how they work. Then, we'll create a few of our own. If you get the scripting bug, you can take the sample scripts presented and modify them to create your own custom scripts. In the next chapter we'll go one step further and look at how scripts work with HTML forms.

MEET JON, THIS CHAPTER'S CO-AUTHOR

One of my favorite discussion lists is html-list@netcentral.net. (The subscription details for this list are presented at the end of this chapter.) As the name implies, this group discusses HTML issues such as standards, problems, and tools. Jon Lewis (jlewis@inorganic5.chem.ufl.edu) is a major contributor to the list. He also runs a Web server at the University of Florida (http://inorganic5.chem.ufl.edu). Jon is a walking depository of information about HTML, servers, and—you guessed it—CGI. After several email discussions with Jon, I convinced him that if he helped with this chapter, he would become instantly famous. After a little arm-twisting, he agreed. Am I a smooth-talking Yankee, or are graduate students just gullible? We ultimately decided to co-author this chapter and the next one by splitting the work equally. I did all the easy parts and Jon did all the difficult parts—as I said, 50/50.

WHAT IS A SCRIPT?

Your first question might be, what are Common Gateway Interface scripts? The vast majority of documents you have retrieved on the Web are purely passive. You retrieve them and they arrive just as their authors wrote them, weeks or even months before. Your home page is one example. You create a document with an .html extension (.htm if you're on a DOS server) and everyone in the world visiting your home page sees pretty much the same thing.

Web browsers read the HTML codes stored in the document and display appropriate text and graphics. When you are accessing an HTML document, all you can do is view what is displayed and select links to view additional information. HTML by itself provides no direct way for you to receive customized information or to send information back to a Web server.

A script, on the other hand, is an executable file of some type. It serves as the dynamic communication link between a Web server computer and a computer that is running a Web browser like Netscape. The purpose of a script is illustrated in Figure 18.1. As you can see, a script gathers information from a user, sends the information to a host computer and performs specialized commands, and then sends the results back to the user. In a nutshell, these are the general operations that a basic computer program performs. When a script needs to communicate with a user, it generates custom HTML documents "on the fly" and sends them down to the user's Web browser.

Now that you know that CGI scripts are your two-way link to the outside world, your next question might be, what are scripts used for? Let's look at an example. Assume you have a database on your computer of the best bird watching sites in your part of the country. You could create a script so that Web surfers who come to your Web site could access your database using a simple fill-in-the-blanks form. They could query for information, such as where is the best place to look for cardinals or brown towhees, and the results could be displayed—complete with nice pictures of the requested bird species. Of course, gathering and processing information is just one type of operation that can be programmed with CGI scripts. You can also use them to process forms, display information like the date and time, or keep track of the number of people who come to visit your home page.

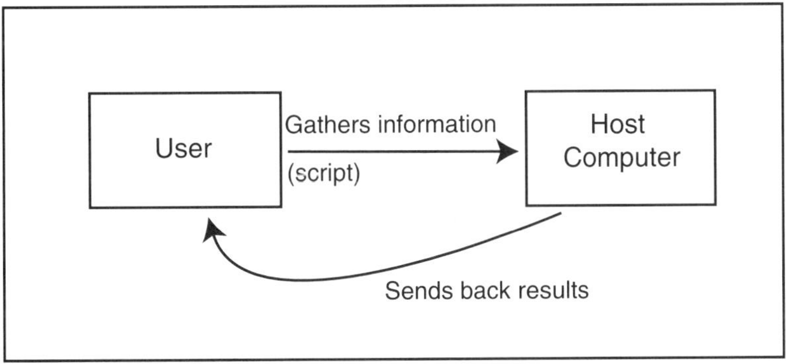

Figure 18.1 *How CGI scripts work.*

How Can You Tell When Scripts Are Used?

When you are accessing a Web site that uses CGI scripts, you can sometimes tell that a script is being executed when you see the words "cgi-bin" in a URL as you are accessing a specific document. This isn't always the case—but it's an important hint. A better clue is the presence of any "control" on an HTML form—a push button, an edit box, a group of check boxes or radio buttons—anything that can be used to enter data into the HTML document and thus "talk back" to the Web server. Other clues are the presence of customized information in an HTML document—the current time or date, or some other data that seems specific to you or your location.

How Are Scripts Executed?

When the URL of an HTML document with an associated CGI script is selected by clicking on a link in a Web page, the script (which is named in the HTML file) is located on the server computer and then launched for execution. The script will take input from the browser (if it needs any) and perform a specific action, such as searching a database or performing some calculation. It may then respond to the user by issuing customized, script-generated HTML to the user's Web browser.

Do You Need to Use a Programming Language to Create Scripts?

Yes and no. The real answer to this question depends on what you consider a programming language. If you have never written a computer program before, or used or written batch files such as DOS bat files, you might be feeling a little put off by all of this talk about scripting, programming, and writing batch commands. But don't panic yet. The basics of script writing are easy to master. In fact, you're halfway there if you already know HTML, because you know how to compose commands to display output in a Web browser.

The best part about CGI scripts is that they can be written using a number of different languages and techniques. The actual executable script on a Web site may be a Unix script file, which functions much like a DOS batch file. It contains relatively simple Unix commands. This type of CGI script may also be an executable program produced by a programming language. One widely used language for doing this is called Perl. Fairly complicated scripts are frequently written in the C programming language. (Don't worry—we won't be programming in C in this book!)

Don't make the mistake of assuming that CGI itself is a programming language. It's actually just a set of conventions or protocol for setting up two-way communication between a computer running a Web browser and a computer running a server. The script itself may be written in a traditional programming language like C, C++, or Pascal, or the script may be written in a higher-level "shell" language. In this book, I'll be using the Unix bourne shell called "sh" to write scripts. This is a good place to start because most Web servers run on Unix machines and this Unix shell language is easy to learn. If you are writing scripts for a server that runs on another type of computer such as a PC, you should easily be able to convert the scripts presented.

What Do You Need to Run Scripts?

The only thing you'll need to run the scripts you write is access to a Web server. You can write your scripts on your own PC and download them to your server, or you can log onto your server and create your scripts there. If you are running your own server, you're all set.

When you copy a script file to the server you are using, you must make sure that you put it in a directory where it can be located. You'll need to make sure that your server is configured to accept script requests from Web browsers. If you are not sure how to do this, you'll need to talk to the person in charge of running your Web server. Most servers set aside a subdirectory named /cgi-bin for storing script files. When a user performs an action with a Web browser, such as clicking on a hyperlink or selecting a form button, the corresponding script is located and executed.

What's the Best Way to Learn How to Create Scripts?

The first phase of scripting involves creating a simple but customized HTML document, such as one to display the current date to the user. The script's simple job is to merge "boilerplate" HTML lines with customized text and send the generated HTML document to the user.

The second phase gets a little more mystical. It involves setting up the interaction between the script and the user. The script initially prompts the user for some information and does something with the information. Then, it sends the results back to the user. As an example, I could ask you for an e-mail address and subsequently display the resulting "finger" information. We might also ask a user for a file name, then perform an Archie search and subsequently display the results. The trick here is to have the same script do both parts of the transaction. It must first ask for information and then the same script must respond to the information in some fashion.

These more sophisticated scripts set up and process HTML forms, which can be used to process more than one piece of information at a time. Handy features such as radio buttons and check boxes may be included on forms, increasing the user-friendliness. We'll take a closer look at forms in the next chapter.

Unlike HTML files, which you can view with Netscape, scripts are usually tucked away in special directories on Web servers, and they typically can't be accessed from outside the server system. If you're friendly with the person who runs your Web server, you might ask him or her to show you some scripts that others have written.

As you are surfing the Web, you might want to keep a close eye out for Web sites that use CGI scripts. Although you won't be able to look at the actual scripts, it will give you more insight into the types of operations that can be performed with scripts. As an example, if you are using a Web page such as WebCrawler (http://www.webcrawler.com) and you click on the Search button, a script named WebQuery will execute. This process is illustrated in Figure 18.2. Notice that the Location: text box contains a URL that references the script:

```
http://www.webcrawler.com/cgi-bin/WebQuery
```

The giveaway is the part of the URL that contains /cgi-bin/WebQuery.

The first script we'll build in this chapter will display the current date and time on the user's screen. Whenever the user immediately reloads our URL, a new time will be delivered. (A new date may even be displayed, if they are literally burning the midnight oil.) This script will get you started. If you are feeling really brave, you'll want to modify it to add other features.

Do You Need to Become a Unix Expert?

I've tried to shield you from dreaded Unix commands up until now. Unfortunately, we can't put it off any longer. Since some readers may already know Unix, I'll skip the basic Unix introductions in this chapter. But don't despair if you are not one of the chosen few, because Appendix C provides a Unix survivor's guide. As the name implies, it's a gentle introduction to Unix and it covers much of what you need to know so you can get started down the path of CGI scripting. Unless you're a Unix whiz, you might want to at least skim this appendix.

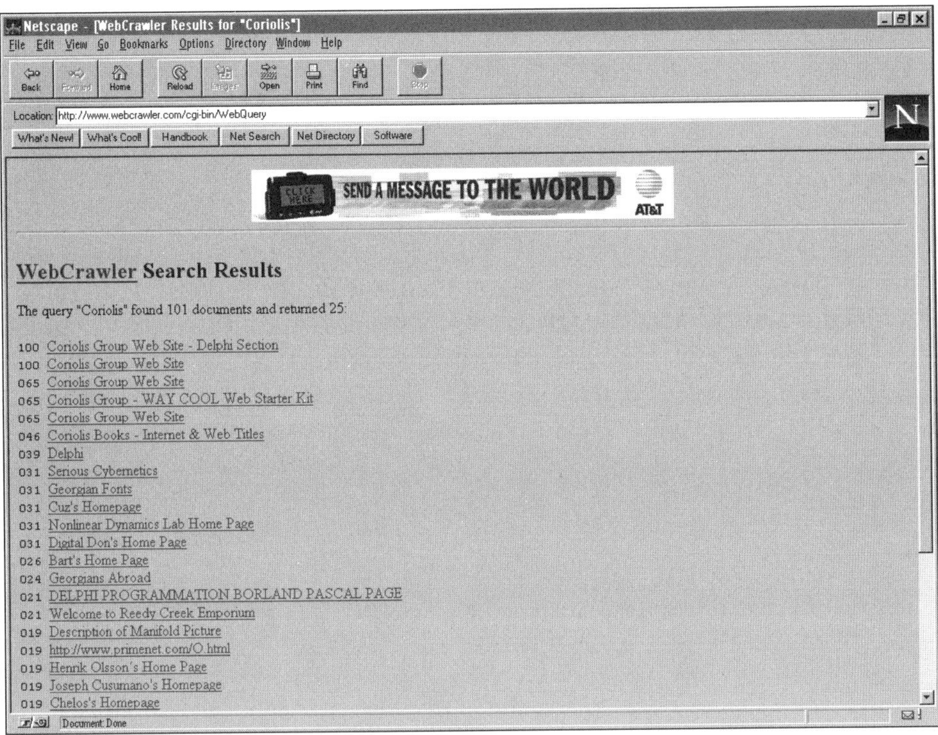

Figure 18.2 *The results of a CGI script in WebCrawler.*

What Time Is It in Tuckerton?

In this project we'll develop a CGI script that will return your Web server's local time and date when queried by a remote browser. Once you know how to create a functional script, you'll be surprised how easy it is to expand.

To create our first script, we'll work backwards starting with something we already know how to do—HTML coding. We'll set up a simple HTML document and then convert it into a CGI script using Unix shell commands. Once the script is finished and loaded on your Web server, you can link one of your Web pages to it by setting up a simple link.

The first step for creating our script is to build a file representing a minimal HTML document structure. Although most Web browsers will recognize a document without **<HTML>**, **<HEAD>**, and **<BODY>** tag pairs, let's conform to the standard and get into the habit of producing *good* HTML—as opposed to HTML that simply works. Open your favorite editor and enter:

```
<HTML>
   <HEAD>
   </HEAD>

   <BODY>
   </BODY>
</HTML>
```

You might even want to use the HTML Notepad editor provided on the companion CD-ROM, which will help you to automate the work of entering the HTML tags. Let's now add a few components to make this HTML document more specific for our local date and time example:

```
<HTML>
   <HEAD>
     <TITLE>Welcome to Tuckerton, New Jersey</TITLE>
   </HEAD>

   <BODY>
      <H1>Welcome to Tuckerton, New Jersey</H1>
      <H4>The local time and date near Atlantic City is</H4>
      The local date and time will go here.
      <HR>
   </BODY>
</HTML>
```

To get a little more creative, we could also add a little Netscape centering. The centering feature is one of the few Netscape HTML enhancements we can use with impunity. If a visitor's browser doesn't support centering, the output is left justified as if the center tags weren't even there. Here's the final (for a while, at least) version of the body section:

```
<BODY>
   <CENTER>
     <H1>Welcome to Tuckerton, New Jersey</H1>
     <H4>The local time and date near Atlantic City is</H4>
     The local date and time will go here
     <HR>
   </CENTER>
</BODY>
```

In a Unix environment, you'll want to save this file as mytime.html. (If you're working on a PC, give the file an .htm extension for now. If you later need to copy the file to a Unix server, you may need to change the extension to .html when you copy the file.)

Next, let's test the file. Fire up your Web browser, and open the HTML file. When you're satisfied the file works as planned, you'll be ready for step two—turning the file into a real script.

I like to use the extension .sh to name my script files. Copy mytime.htm or mytime.html to mytime.sh so you can transform it into a Unix executable script. The copy command for Unix is:

```
unix% cp mytime.html mytime.sh
```

By storing all of my Unix script files with the "sh" extension, I can perform directory listings like

```
unix% ls -la *.sh
```

and easily view all of my script files.

Creating the Script

What we must do now is modify the newly created mytime.sh file to become an executable script. This involves creating an executable program of some sort that issues the text that makes up your HTML file, line by line. When executed, the script will produce an HTML document on the fly and send it down to the user's browser. The HTML output will be the same as the output from the original file. We can test the script by capturing its output to a file so that it can be checked before putting the script on a Web server.

A script is a series of lines, each of which is an executable statement. Technically, more than one statement can appear on a line, but let's keep life simple. A Unix script, as with a DOS batch file, executes when its name is entered as a command.

The file we've created so far simply contains HTML tags, which unfortunately are not executable statements. There are two different ways we can covert the HTML so that it can be executed as a script which produces output. The first method involves using the DOS-like **echo** command. Here's an example:

```
echo "<HTML>"
```

This statement is now a valid Unix command, which will output **<HTML>** as text. To preserve indentation in the output, you can use leading spaces, such as:

```
echo "  <HEAD>"
```

I'll show you the second method (which Jon prefers) for building scripts from HTML files shortly.

Using the **echo** statement, we can easily convert our complete HTML file into an executable script:

```
echo "<HTML>"
echo "   <HEAD>"
echo "     <TITLE>Welcome to Tuckerton, New Jersey</TITLE>"
echo "   </HEAD>"
echo "   <BODY>"
echo "     <CENTER>"
echo "        <H1>Welcome to Tuckerton, New Jersey</H1>"
echo "        <H4>The local time and date near Atlantic City, New Jersey is</
H4>"
echo "        The local date and time will go here."
echo "        <HR>"
echo "      </CENTER>"
echo "   </BODY>"
echo "</HTML>"
```

Notice how the double quotation marks are used to preserve formatting.

Now that we have a file in script form, the next step is to make it executable. We'll use the Unix change mode command, **chmod**, to make the transition. Here's the command that should be executed to convert mytime.sh to an executable script:

```
unix% chmod 700 mytime.sh
```

Here I'm using the prompt "unix%" to indicate a Unix command line. This prompt will certainly be different on your system. The **chmod** command simply converts the file attributes of the mytime.sh file so that Unix will treat it as an executable file. Without doing that, it's simply text.

Now we're ready to take our script for a spin. Enter this command at the Unix command line:

```
unix% mytime.sh
```

You'll then see this output:

```
unix% mytime.sh
<HTML>
  <HEAD>

    <TITLE>Welcome to Tuckerton, New Jersey</TITLE>

  </HEAD>
  <BODY>
    <CENTER>
```

```
    <H1>Welcome to Tuckerton, New Jersey</H1>
    <H4>The local time and date near Atlantic City is</H4>
     The local time and date will go here.
    </CENTER>
    <HR>
  </BODY>
</HTML>
unix%
```

We now have a program that emits HTML. We're looking good! Let's now make this script display the current time and date. We can use the Unix **date** command to do exactly that. (Remember, the purpose of a script is to execute Unix commands.) Change the line containing:

```
echo "     local time and date will go here."
```

to:

```
/bin/date
```

Notice that we are also specifying the path (/bin/) where the **date** program is located. It's a good idea in Unix (or DOS for that matter) to include a path to the desired executable file. (More on this shortly.)

Since the **echo** command directs its output to the terminal, let's redirect the output from our script to a file using the ">" redirection command. And now, here's the acid test:

```
unix% mytime.sh > temp.html
```

This command looks a little strange but it's actually easy to understand. It simply executes the script mytime.sh and redirects its output to a file named temp.html. But here's a general word of caution about using the Unix ">" redirection symbol. If the file on the right side of the ">" already exists, it's history when you execute the command. If the file doesn't exist, it's created.

If you are using a Unix system that has the Lynx program available, you can test your script in text-mode by entering this command at the Unix command line:

```
unix% lynx temp.html
```

This command passes the newly created output of our script to Lynx. The result, which will appear on the screen, should be:

```
Welcome to Tuckerton, New Jersey

                      WELCOME TO TUCKERTON, NEW JERSEY

    The local time and date near Atlantic City is

   Fri Mar 15 09:27:29 GMT 1996
```

We made it! You might want to take a look at the contents of temp.html. The Unix **more** command displays on the screen, one screenful at a time. Enter:

```
unix% more temp.html
```

To finish, you'll want to add the following five lines at the top of your script:

```
#!/bin/sh
# Script mytime.sh - displaying local time and date - was written by Urb
#  LeJeune, lejeune@acy.digex.net
echo Content-type: text/html
echo
```

The first line is an incantation telling Unix which script to run rather than any script just hanging around doing nothing. The script "sh" is conceptually somewhat like the DOS program command.com, in that both are command interpreters. The Unix script interpreter is usually called a *shell*, hence the term "shell account." Unix installations typically support a variety of shell scripts so the first line

```
#!/bin/sh
```

explicitly states *which* shell should be executed. The default shell on systems may vary, and explicit statements like this guarantee uniformity of command response when your script runs. This is very important because there are many syntactical differences in scripting languages.

The second line is a comment attesting to your authorship and script purpose. In Unix the "#" symbol starts a comment. Everything between a "#" and the end of the line is considered a comment and is not executable. The "#" tells Unix to ignore anything following the symbol. It's a good idea to use comments so others can understand your logic.

The fourth line, starting with **echo,** is a message the server sends to the browser, stating the sort of creature to expect—in this case an HTML document. A browser typically knows what to expect based upon the file extension specified in the

URL. For example, index.html tells the server the name of the document to return, and it also tells the browser to expect an HTML formatted document.

There is a snag with scripts, however. When a script creates a dynamic HTML document on the fly, there is no file extension to guide the browser. The first thing our dynamic HTML document must send to the browser is "Content-type: text/html" (followed by a mandatory blank line) indicating that an HTML or text document will be arriving shortly. The fifth line in the script, which contains only the command **echo**, is necessary to produce the mandatory blank line following the "Content-type: text/html" statement. Simply leaving a blank line in the script file won't do it!

Here is the script mytime.sh in its final form:

```
#!/bin/sh
# Script mytime.sh - displaying local time and date - was written by Urb
#  LeJeune, lejeune@acy.digex.net
echo "Content-type: text/html"
echo
echo "<HTML>"
echo "  <HEAD>"
echo "    <TITLE>Welcome to Tuckerton, New Jersey</TITLE>"
echo "  </HEAD>"
echo "  <BODY>"
echo "    <CENTER>"
echo "    <H1>Welcome to Tuckerton, New Jersey</H1>"
echo "    <H4>The local time and date near Atlantic City is</H4>"
TZ=EST5EST /bin/date
echo "    </CENTER>"
echo "    <HR>"
echo "  </BODY>"
echo "</HTML>"
```

There's still one line in this file that needs a little explanation:

```
TZ=EST5EST /bin/date
```

When executed, our previous script produced output in Greenwich Mean Time (GMT). The prefix "TZ–EST5EST" is required to produce an output in Eastern Standard Time (EST). You may or may not need it. Try /bin/date, without the prefix first. If you're not in the EST zone, check with your system administrator for the correct syntax.

Figure 18.3 shows how Netscape displays a Web page that uses our script. What distinguishes this document from many other Web documents is that the time and date will be different each time the URL is accessed.

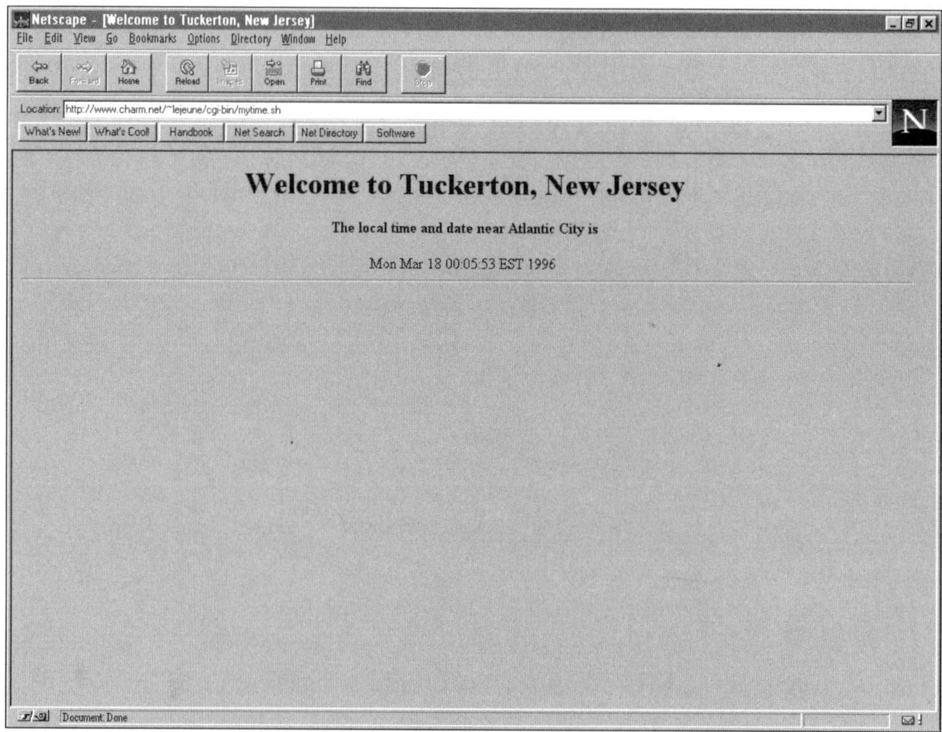

Figure 18.3 *Netscape's display of our first CGI script.*

Using the Script

Where you put the script, if indeed you can use scripts at all, depends upon your Internet provider. Check with them for details. As I mentioned before, the script will almost always go in a subdirectory called /cgi-bin.

To use the script with a Web page, I include an anchor, such as the following:

```
<A HREF="http://charm.net/~lejeune/cgi-bin/mytime.sh">Show me the date and
  time</A>
```

When a user clicks on the hyperlink, "Show me the date and time," the script that is stored on my server executes. Typically, when you click on a link, an HTML file is loaded. But in this case, the link accesses the /cgi-bin subdirectory where my scripts are stored and it runs mytime.sh. The script itself returns a set of HTML commands that are displayed in Netscape.

Now you see how easy it is to use CGI scripts to communicate with a Web server. We've already seen the Web page created by this script in Figure 18.3.

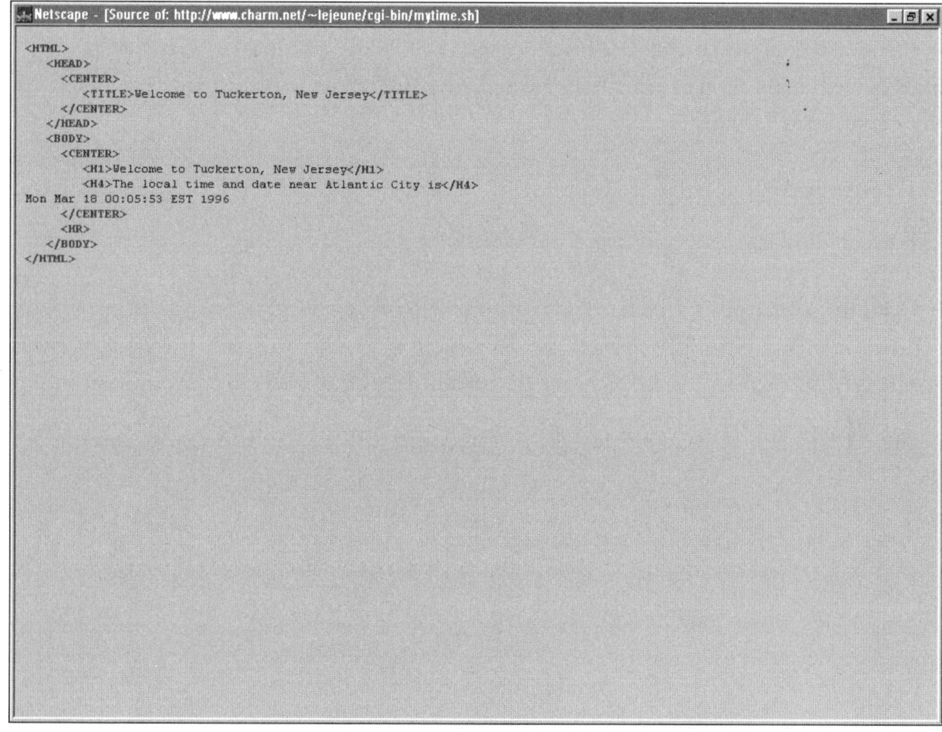


```
<HTML>
  <HEAD>
    <CENTER>
      <TITLE>Welcome to Tuckerton, New Jersey</TITLE>
    </CENTER>
  </HEAD>
  <BODY>
    <CENTER>
      <H1>Welcome to Tuckerton, New Jersey</H1>
      <H4>The local time and date near Atlantic City is</H4>
Mon Mar 18 00:05:53 EST 1996
    </CENTER>
    <HR>
  </BODY>
</HTML>
```

***Figure 18.4** The Document Source for our first CGI script.*

If you execute Netscape's sequence View | Source, the HTML that is received by Netscape is displayed as shown in Figure 18.4.

What Time Is It in Tuckerton? Part 2

In this project we'll develop a CGI script that improves upon the script created in the first project. We'll use a different method of building the script and we'll also get fancier with some time and date formatting.

We'll name the new script that we create mytime2.sh. We'll actually be building this script in a few parts. The first part will contain the main text for the Web page that is produced by the script. Then, we'll use a special form of the Unix **date** command to display the date and time in a unique format. Finally, the last part of the script will contain the closing HTML tags for the script.

If you recall from the previous script project, we needed to use a number of **echo** commands to transmit HTML lines from a Web server (where the script is running) to a Web browser. Fortunately, Unix provides a command we can use to get rid of all of those **echo** commands. This command **cat**, for concatenate, allows us to join multiple text lines into one long string. Here's how this command is used:

```
cat<<user-supplied-label

user-supplied-label
```

Essentially, **cat** tells Unix to treat everything between the two statements as multi-line input. The labels may be anything you choose, but they must both be the same. Again, it's important to remember that Unix is case sensitive.

In the first part of the mytime2.sh script, here's how the **cat** command is set up:

```
# Script mytime2.sh by Urb LeJeune lejeune@acy.digex.net and
# Jon Lewis, jlewis@inorganic5.chem.ufl.edu. Demonstrates formatted date
cat << Part1
Content-type: text/html

<HTML>
   <HEAD>

         <TITLE>Welcome to Tuckerton, New Jersey</TITLE>

   </HEAD>
   <BODY>
       <CENTER>
         <H1>Welcome to Tuckerton, New Jersey</H1>

         <H4>The local time and date near Atlantic City is</H4>
Part1
```

Here we start out with two comment lines. Next, comes the **cat** command. Notice that the label used to group the text is "Part1". Note also the blank line following the "Content-type: text/html" line. A Web browser will not handle the document properly unless there is a blank line following the "Content-type" line. (The blank line indicates to the browser that the "Content-type" header ends and that the content itself follows.) That's all there is to the first part of this script. Let's now add the **date** command.

The Unix **date** command has a variety of formatting switches. Formatted date output is indicated by an argument enclosed within double quotes. Date formatting begins with a "+", followed by the information telling the command what information to display and how to display it. The format specifications use the percent sign "%". A few of the more common ones are seen in Table 18.1.

Table 18.1 Formatting Switches for the Unix date Command

Description	Switch	What's Displayed
Year	y	96
	Y	1996
Month	m	12
	b	Dec
	B	December
Day	a	Mon
	A	Monday
Day of Month	d	18
Hour	I	00 to 12
	H	00 to 23
Minute	M	23
Second	S	58
AM/PM	P	pm
Time	t	12:45:48
Day of Year	j	145

Let's use a few of these formatting codes to display the date and time. Here are the commands needed to do this work:

```
TZ=EST5EST /bin/date "+The time in Tuckerton is %I:%M %p %Z or %H:%M if \
  you like 24 hour time."
echo "<BR><BR>"
TZ=EST5EST /bin/date "+Today is %A: %B %d, which is day %j of %Y"
```

Produce Your Own Manual

You can get documentation for any Unix command available on your server computer by entering this command:

```
unix% man <command-name>
```

This command produces a manual for the specified parameter. Here's an example of how you can view the manual for the **date** command:

```
unix% man date
```

To create your own copy of the manual, use the Unix redirection symbol ">", as shown:

```
unix% man date > date.man
```

This produces a file named date.man to store the output of the **man date** command.

We're now ready to finish the last part of our script. Here's all we need:

```
cat << Part2
   </CENTER>
    <HR>
</BODY>
</HTML>
Part2
```

The output from this script is shown in Figure 18.5.

Let's Get Fancy

To update our script we'll want to add a little pizzazz. Let's display a few GIFs and add some gingerbread to the bottom of the document. As mentioned

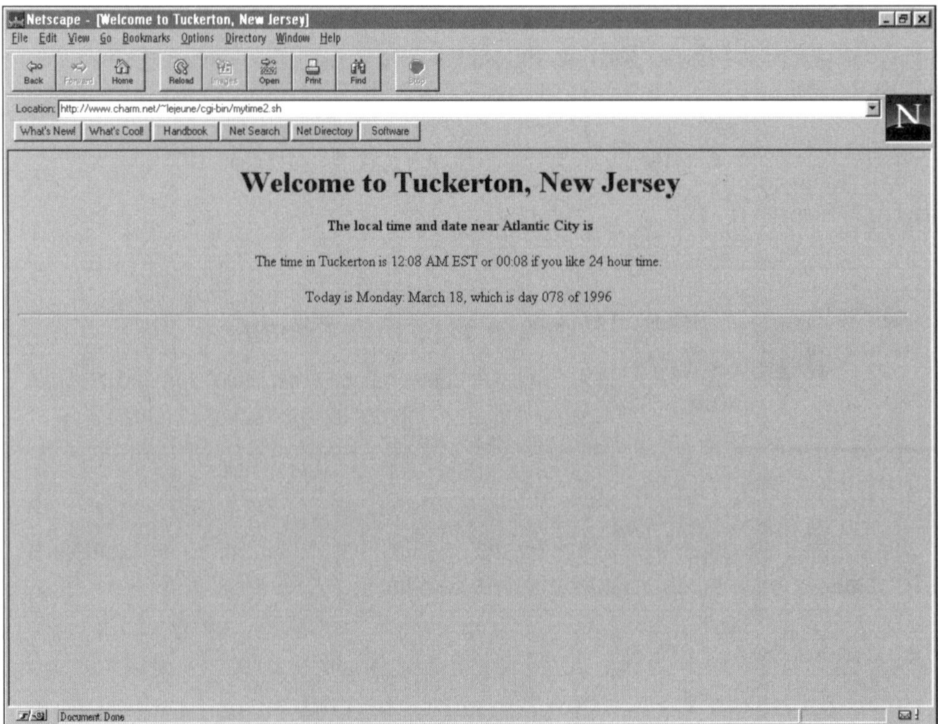

Figure 18.5 The output from the CGI script mytime2.sh.

earlier, most CGI scripts are placed in a Unix subdirectory called /cgi-bin. Most of the time this directory is directly subordinate to the directory holding the conventional HTML documents. Let's assume this is the case.

When referencing URLs within a document, it is highly desirable to preserve relative addressing. On my provider's machine, HTML documents for use by a Web server are placed in a directory called public_html. The use of a directory named public_html is rapidly becoming a standard. The URL

```
http://www.charm.net/~lejeune/cgi-bin/mytime2.sh
```

indicates several things. First, "~lejeune" is a *symbolic link*. This link is shorthand for a much longer path name. In addition to brevity, symbolic links permit changing paths, or even servers, without the outside world being aware that a change has been made. Again in my specific—although common—case, the symbolic path terminates in a directory named public_html. The subdirectory /cgi-bin is therefore a child of directory public_html. Most administrators managing Web servers only allow executable files in the directory /cgi-bin. If we want our script to include a reference to a graphics file such as a GIF, we must "point" to another directory. To illustrate, assume directory public_html holds a graphic called home.gif. In Unixspeak (as well as DOS) a parent directory may symbolically be referenced by "..". Our pseudo document may therefore include a graphics link to home.gif in the following form:

```
<IMG SRC="../home.gif">
```

This is functionally the same thing as saying:

```
<IMG SRC="/public_html/home.gif">
```

The advantage of this notation is portability. If I were to move to another provider having a directory structure of

```
/html/cgi-bin
```

the first notation would still work, but the second would not.

Here's the complete listing of our new fancy-shmantzy Tuckerton time script:

```
#!/bin/sh
# Script mytime2.sh by Urb LeJeune lejeune@acy.digex.net
# Jon Lewis, jlewis@inorganic5.chem.ufl.edu. Demonstrating
# Date formatting and relative graphics referencing
```

```
cat << Part1
Content-type: text/html

<HTML>
  <HEAD>

        <TITLE>Welcome to Tuckerton, New Jersey</TITLE>

  </HEAD>
  <BODY>
      <CENTER>
      <H1>Welcome to Tuckerton, New Jersey</H1>
      <H4>The local time and date near Atlantic City is</H4>
Part1

TZ=EST5EST /bin/date "+The time in Tuckerton is %I:%M %p %Z or %H:%M if \
you like 24 hour time."
echo "     <BR><BR>"
TZ=EST5EST /bin/date "+Today is %A: %B %d, which is day %j of %Y"

cat << Part2

     <P>
       <A HREF="../index.html">
         <IMG ALIGN=CENTER SRC="../home.gif">
           Visit my home page</A>

       <A HREF="../urb-book.html">
         <IMG ALIGN=CENTER SRC="../up-arrow.gif">
         The Netscape EXplorer Main Page</A><BR>

       Created by Urb LeJeune
       <A HREF="mailto:lejeune@acy.digex.net">
         <IMG ALIGN=CENTER SRC="../mailbutt.gif"> lejeune@acy.digex.net<P>

         <IMG SRC="../line.gif">
       </A>
     </CENTER>
   </BODY>
</HTML>
Part2
```

The URL that executes this script is:

```
http://www.charm.net/~lejeune/cgi-bin/mytime3.sh
```

The output of this script is shown in Figure 18.6.

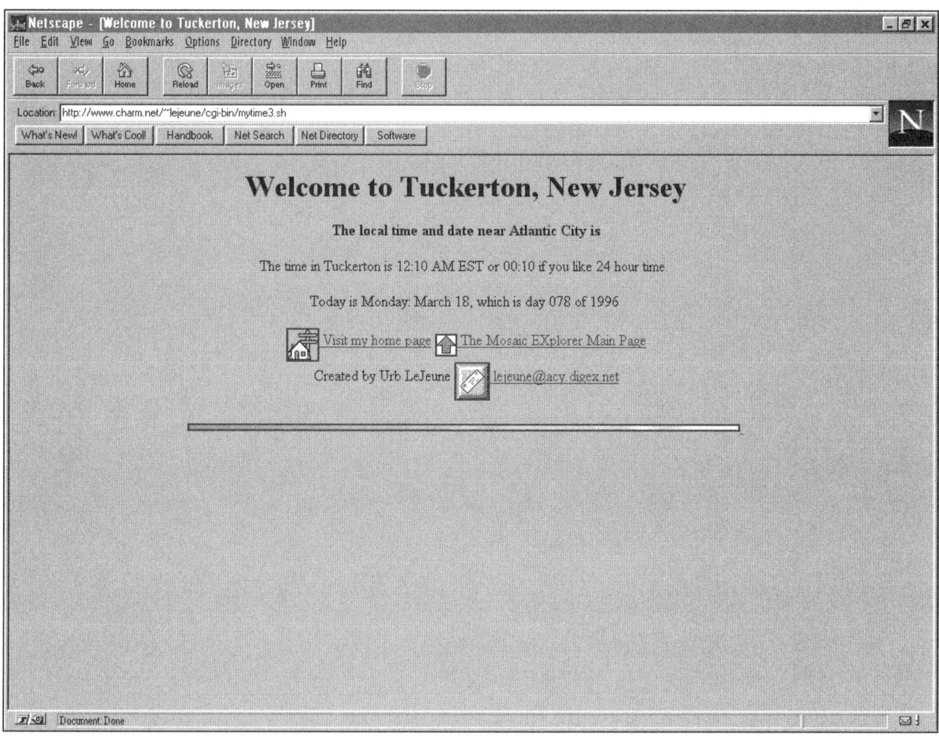

Figure 18.6 The output produced when executing the script mytime3.sh.

A PEEK AT OTHER LANGUAGES

As scripts get more complicated they frequently are written in a scripting language called Perl or in the C programming language. Perl is somewhat like a hybrid between a Unix shell language and the C language. When learning any programming language, a student's first program is usually an ultra-simple one producing as output "Hello World." To give just a little taste of programming, here is a Perl "Hello World" script:

```
#!/usr/bin/perl
# Script hello.pl is a demonstration "hello world" program by
# Urb LeJeune, lejeune@acy.digex.net.
print "Content-type: text/plain\n\n";
print
print "Hello, world!\n";
print "My name is Urb LeJeune\n";
print "My email address is lejeune@acy.digex.net\n";
```

Again note the empty print statement to produce the requisite blank line after the "Content-type" header.

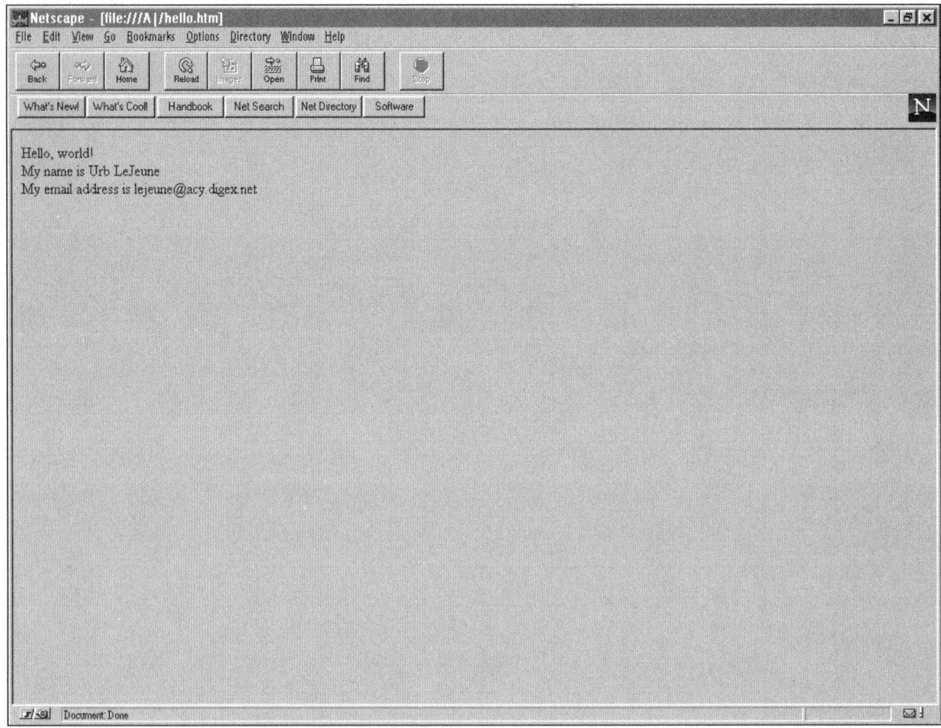

Figure 18.7 *The world's most useless program*

Figure 18.7 demonstrates the output from one of the world's most useless programs.

LET'S REVIEW

The Common Gateway Interface (CGI) is a standard that allows executable files to run as "custom extensions" of a Web server. These executable files are called CGI scripts. They can (as demonstrated in this chapter) create customized HTML content and (to be demonstrated in the next chapter) allow information to be sent to a Web server via HTML forms.

The simplest kind of CGI script is an executable program of some sort that creates lines of text formatted as HTML. This output is sent by the server to the Web browser as a dynamic HTML document created "on the fly." Ordinary, static HTML documents, by contrast, are created once and never change, and are always the same when downloaded.

A CGI script is an executable program written in any language capable of reading from standard input, writing to standard output, and accessing environment variables. Under Unix, most scripts are written in a scripting language such as Perl, although some more advanced scripts are written in C.

More advanced CGI scripts allow two-way communication between the browser and server. The output of a script may vary depending upon the input supplied by the user. This topic will be covered in the next chapter.

If you're starting to get into more exotic HTML, you might want to give the discussion list html-list a try. To subscribe, send a message to

```
listserv@netcentral.net
```

and in the body of the message put:

```
sub html-list <your-first-name> <your-last-name>
```

Well, there you have it. You're on your way to becoming a CGI junkie. Be forewarned, if you proceed into the next chapter and look at interactive scripting, there is no turning back.

ONLINE RESOURCES

CGI Programmer's Reference
`http://www.best.com/~hedlund/cgi-faq/cgi-faq.txt`

Common Gateway Interface
`http://hoohoo.ncsa.uiuc.edu/cgi`

Introduction to CGI Programming - A Tutorial
`http://ute.usi.utah.edu/bin/cgi-programming/counter.pl/cgi-programming/index.html`

Publishing with Forms

In the next leg of our Web publishing exploration, we'll look at techniques for using HTML forms and document queries to make our Web pages more attractive.

In the previous chapter we explored CGI (Common Gateway Interface). We learned that CGI is used to communicate between a client and a server to perform all kinds of tasks, such as searching databases, performing calculations, and displaying such information as the current date and time. Although gateway scripts are extremely useful, they can't do everything by themselves. To really extend the power of scripts, we need a better way to get information from a Web page to a Web server and back again. That's where HTML document queries and forms come in.

In this chapter we'll explore the basics of using HTML to create document queries and forms. We'll also look at how we can write some basic scripts to process HTML forms. If you've never used forms in your Web pages, you'll be surprised at how flexible and powerful the key HTML tags, such as **<FORM>** and **<INPUT>**, are.

Instead of jumping in and showing you how to compose forms using HTML tags, I'll first present the basics of document query techniques so that you can see the process involved in having interactive Web pages communicate with Web servers. Then, we'll start to build an HTML document that uses different form components—including text boxes, radio buttons, checkboxes, and menus. If you want to continue further by using other powerful form features, be sure to read Appendix A.

GETTING INPUT

To make the Web pages you publish more interactive, you'll need a way to get information from your users. For example, let's assume you want to publish a catalog featuring the products your company sells. To make this catalog a true sales-getter, you'll want to have an online order form that users can fill out. You can even provide a questionnaire to obtain important information about your customers. With HTML forms, gathering this kind of information is possible with only a little effort.

Without the ability to get input from users, your Web pages would be very limited. Sure, you could display information and provide links to hot Web sites, but you wouldn't be able to engage in two-way communication with your users. Fortunately, techniques for getting input from a user on the Web have been around for a while, even before features like graphical forms and buttons were implemented in HTML. Some of the earliest browsers were designed to be interactive. A user could enter a keyword, the keyword would then be sent to a Web server, and the server would search a database and return the result, nicely formatted. The original HTML specification provided a feature that sent a single piece of user-supplied information to a server. After this, the demand for more interactive communication grew so quickly that the HTML 2.0 specification provided the basis for reasonably complex interactive forms.

So, how does the communication system between a Web browser and a Web server operate? In a nutshell, this interactivity involves a five-step process:

1. The Web server script requests information from the user.
2. The user's Web browser supplies the requested information (input).
3. The server script processes the user-supplied information.
4. The server script returns the information (output) as a (hopefully) nicely formatted document.
5. The user tells everyone about the script writer's cleverness.

Okay, so it's really a four-step process. Of course, the CGI script is the glue that makes the communication process possible. As we learned in the previous chapter, a script is an executable set of computer instructions that can be written in many different languages, including Perl or the workhorse of all languages, C. But our mission in this chapter isn't to cover everything there is to know about scripting with CGI. (That would take a rather large book.) Instead, we'll focus on the interactive portion of the information exchange concept, with enough scripting thrown in to give you some examples that will get you started publishing more interactive Web pages.

DOCUMENT- AND FORM-BASED QUERIES

I'll be using the word "query" a lot in this chapter, so let's come up with a good definition: A query is essentially a request for information. When you run your favorite database program and it displays a field asking you to enter a specific piece of information, such as a customer's phone number or social security number, you are being queried by the program.

The interactive Web pages that you create can communicate information to Web servers in one of two ways: by document-based queries or form-based queries. The query used is actually performed by a CGI script; however, HTML does the work of setting up the query. Document-based queries have been around since the first version of HTML was unleashed. Form-based queries arrived with HTML 2.0 and have continued to move into center stage with HTML 3.0. The best way to understand the differences between these two types of queries is to look at an example.

A document-based query uses a special tag named **<ISINDEX>**. This tag is placed in the **<HEAD>** section of an HTML document. When the **<ISINDEX>** tag is encountered by a Web browser, some type of input prompt is displayed so that the user can enter information. A script for a document-based query generates HTML that looks something like this:

```
<HTML>
  <HEAD>
    <TITLE>Document Based Forms Demo</TITLE>
    <ISINDEX>
  </HEAD>
  <BODY>
    <H1>Document Based Forms Demo</H1>
        Your Body Text Goes Here
  </BODY>
</HTML>
```

Figure 19.1 shows what this document looks like when it is displayed by Netscape. As you can see, it is a really simple query. When Netscape reads the **<ISINDEX>** tag, it displays a text box. The big drawback with a query like this: You can't select your own prompt. Another disadvantage is that you can't ask for more than one piece of information from the user. And there's yet another limitation: You can't place the text box that queries for information in a specific location relative to the remainder of the document. What you see in Figure 19.1 is all you get.

Anything this simple turns out to be rather inflexible. Form-based queries, on the other hand, allow you to support a substantial amount of interactive features. If you've seen any of the forms that have been included on Web pages during your surfing explorations, you know that form-based queries look much more interesting than the simple document-based query we just looked at. With forms, you can include text boxes, pop-up selection boxes, buttons, scrolling text windows, radio buttons, and a few other elements. And the best part is that you can place these objects wherever you want on your Web pages. This type of flexibility opens up a lot of publishing possibilities. Forms capabilities have even led to businesspeople staying up nights contemplating the kinds of businesses they can set up and the money that will pour in from their interactive, online ordering systems.

Until recently, lack of security has been a real deal breaker, putting a damper on the commercialization of the Internet. In theory, almost anyone can publish a set

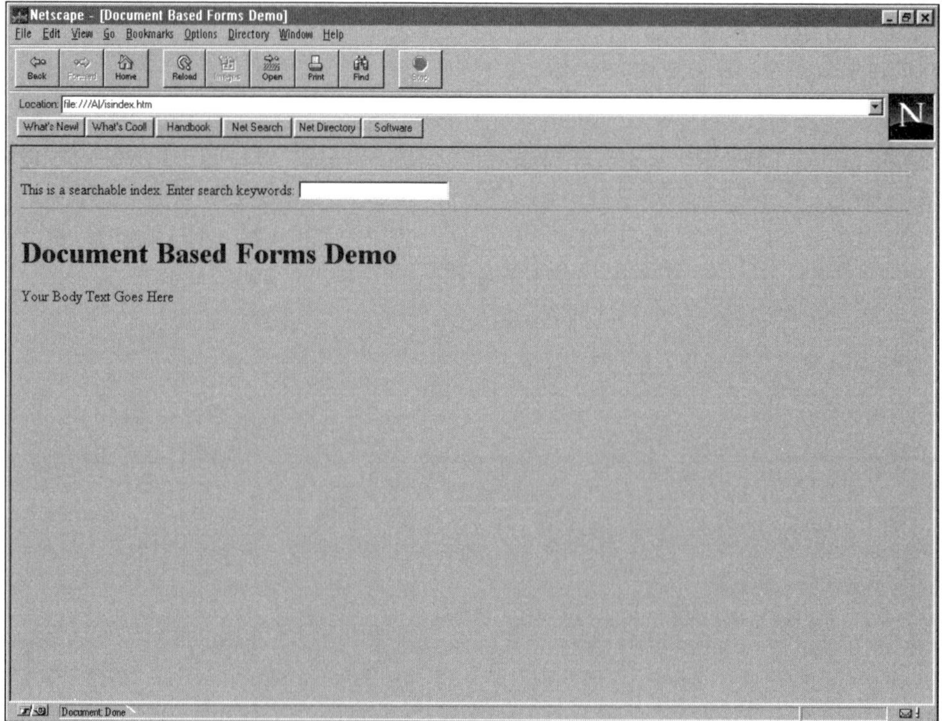

Figure 19.1 *The world's simplest document-based query.*

of Web pages that provides interactive forms to capture sensitive information, such as credit card or bank account numbers. Unfortunately, it's easy for unauthorized "information scoopers" to get at this data as it is being sent, especially if they are dedicated hackers. Secure Web servers, such as those supplied by Netscape, should make commercial use of the Web a reality. Experienced forms designers and CGI script writers may soon be in be high demand and short supply. So, read this chapter closely, do your homework, and get your résumé out.

USING DOCUMENT-BASED QUERIES

Before we roll up our sleeves and start creating powerful forms, let's take a closer look at document-based queries. This will give you some techniques to help you better understand how communication links are established between Web pages and Web servers. Since the HTML part of document-based queries is really simple, we'll spend our time in this section discussing the role that CGI scripts play in processing simple queries. Here are the questions we'll answer:

- How does one script perform two jobs?
- How does a script receive its parameters?
- How are parameters used to perform different tasks?
- How are HTML documents sent?

Once you know how to set up communication links between a Web browser and a server, all you'll need to learn to create forms for Web pages are the basic HTML tags required for displaying and processing forms.

Performing Two Jobs with a CGI Script

A little sleight of hand occurs when a document-based query is processed. First, your browser sends a request and back comes a simple page with a single field that needs data. You enter the data and click on Submit, or in some cases you press Enter. Then, the information gets sent to the server and the same script executes, but this time the response is a formatted reply. What's going on here? How can the script know what to do each time it is called?

The script performs double duty by sensing the nature of the request. (Actually, the script only knows if the first request it receives is in fact the first one.) The difference between the requests is the presence (or absence) of the user-supplied data. In the world of computer programming, the supplied information is called a *parameter* or an *argument*. I prefer the term parameter; however, you will see both terms used in scripting literature.

You've actually used parameters many times without realizing it. When you enter DIR (or dir) at the DOS command-line prompt, DOS supplies you with a directory listing of all file names and all file types in the current directory path. You receive a display of all files because the default parameter is *.*. (A default is what happens if you don't specify something else.) When you enter the command

```
C:\> DIR *.BAT/P
```

DOS gives you a listing of all file names with a BAT extension (*.BAT) and it stops when the screen fills up, because you included the /P (for page) switch parameter. The output of the DIR command changes depending on the parameters you provide. Several different DIR commands each would produce different results; the same is true for CGI scripts that use parameters. Now you know the secret.

Creating a Document-Based Script

For this project we'll create a simple script to process a document-based query. The query will ask the user to input a string. The script then echoes the user's response. The trip we need to make goes like this:

1. From browser to server: request the URL
2. From server to browser: supply the simple form (document query)
3. From browser back to server: return the completed form
4. From server back to browser: process the supplied information and send a response

A script's ability to recognize whether a request is a "first request" requires a little programming logic. So, put your programming hat on. The logic that makes this black magic work looks something like this:

```
if this is the first time
  then
     send the user a simple fill-out form (document-based query)
  else
     process the passed parameter(s)
     create and send a report
end if
```

Let's write an actual Unix script to perform the if-then-else logic, complete with feedback results.

```
#!/bin/sh

if [  $#  =  0  ]
  then # There is no passed parameter
    echo "There are no passed parameters."
  else  # There is a passed parameter
    echo "Whoopie! There is at least one passed parameter."
fi # end if
```

(If Unix scripts still make you feel nervous, spend a few minutes reading Appendix B.) The first line in our script is an incantation that tells Unix to execute the script using the sh shell. The syntax for the Unix **if** construct requires that we start with the keyword **if** and end with the keyword **fi** (which is "**if**" spelled backwards, of course). These Unix people are just too cute for words.

The **[$# = 0]** test looks scary. Actually, though, it simply asks if the number of passed parameters (**$#**) is equal to zero. Any number of statements may follow the required **then** keyword. The statements to be executed if our test is true must be enclosed between the **then** keyword and either the **else** or **fi**. The keyword **else** is optional, but if used, any number of statements may be embedded between the **else** and the **fi**. Anything between a **#** character and the end of the line is treated as a comment for humans and ignored by Unix. Try the above script to get the hang of it.

Parameter Magic

Let's now create a real script to see how a parameter can be passed. The script we'll use is named isindex.sh. (The complete script is shown at the end of this section.) What does the script do? When it starts, it displays an HTML document like the one shown in Figure 19.2. At first glance, you'll notice that the script looks like one we created in the previous chapter. The Web page displays a greeting, along with the current date and time. But the difference with this script is that a text box is displayed so that you can enter some information. If you look at the script, you'll see that the **<ISINDEX>** tag is included in the **<HEAD>** section of the HTML document generated by the script:

```
<HTML>
  <HEAD>
    <CENTER>
        <TITLE>Welcome to Tuckerton, New Jersey</TITLE>
    </CENTER>
    <ISINDEX>
  </HEAD>
```

The second part of the script performs some parameter magic. When the script is called with a parameter, a different HTML document will be displayed. We'll

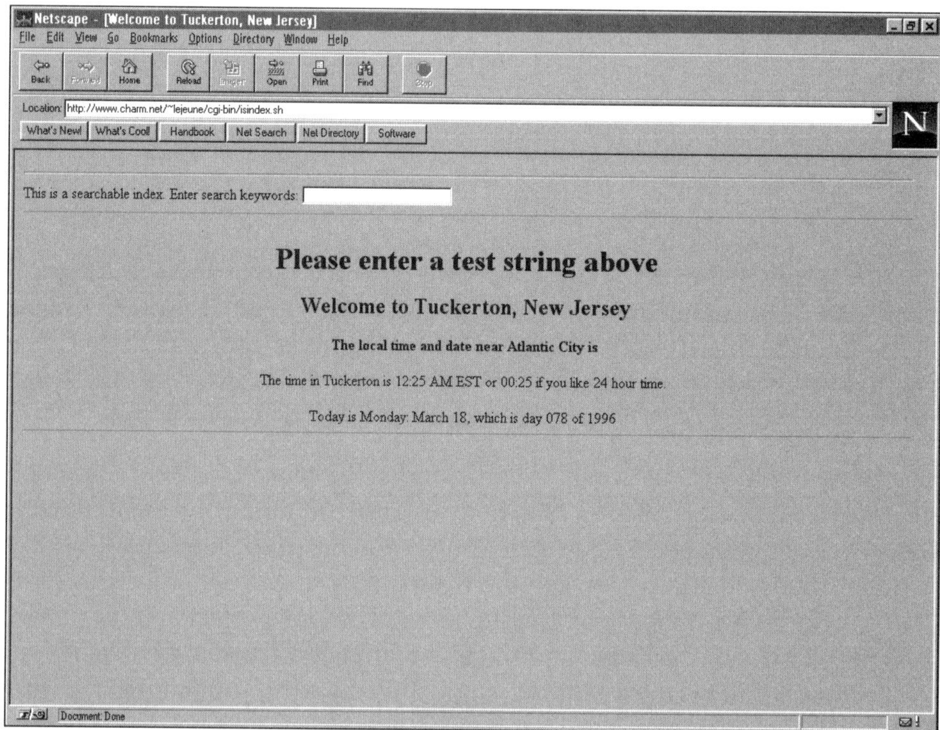

***Figure 19.2** The document returned when "isindex.sh" was executed for the first time.*

see what the second page looks like in a moment, but first let's see how the script is used.

As we learned in the previous chapter, executable scripts are almost always placed in a directory called /cgi-bin. The URL I use to activate the script on my Charm Net account would therefore be:

```
http://www.charm.net/~lejeune/cgi-bin/isindex.sh
```

When this URL is entered, the browser tells the Web server at www.charm.net to execute the script isindex.sh without any parameters. The script in turn generates an HTML document and sends it back to the browser. (This is the page shown in Figure 19.2.) The document requests the user to enter a string in the text box at the top. If I enter "hello" the browser takes this string and appends it to the URL following a "?". The browser then sends the newly formulated URL back to the server. This time the URL will look like:

```
http://www.charm.net/~lejeune/cgi-bin/isindex.sh?hello
```

As you might have guessed, "hello" is the parameter for the isindex.sh script. The server then removes the URL component following the "?" and passes it to the script. The script can access the first parameter as **$1**, the second as **$2**, and so on. The script, using the if-then-else logic we explored in the previous section, gets the parameter to produce a second document.

Figure 19.3 displays the returned document. Notice the URL in the Location: box. The complete script for this act of magic is shown next. I've included the complete script file on the companion CD-ROM as isindex.sh. To use it, just copy it to your Web server and place it in a directory that you can access. Then, run Netscape and enter the URL and name of the script, just as I did earlier.

```
#!/bin/sh
# Script isindex.sh by Urb LeJeune lejeune@acy.digex.net

if [ $# = 0 ]
  then # There is no passed parameter

cat << Part1
```

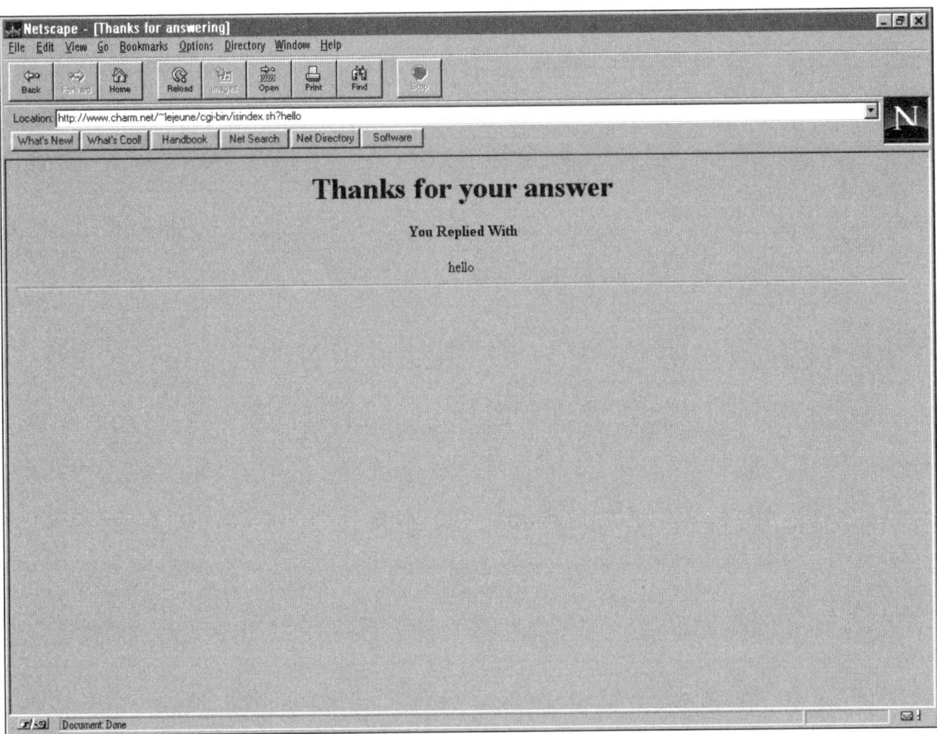

Figure 19.3 The document returned when isindex.sh was executed with a parameter.

```
Content-type: text/html

<HTML>
  <HEAD>
    <CENTER>
        <TITLE>Welcome to Tuckerton, New Jersey</TITLE>
    </CENTER>
    <ISINDEX>
  </HEAD>
<BODY>
    <CENTER>
        <H1>Please enter a test string above</H1>
        <H2>Welcome to Tuckerton, New Jersey</H2>
        <H4>The local time and date near Atlantic City is</H4>
Part1

TZ=EST5EST /bin/date "+The time in Tuckerton is %I:%M %p %Z or %H:%M if \
   you like 24 hour time."
echo "<BR><BR>"
TZ=EST5EST /bin/date "+Today is %A: %B %d, which is day %j of %Y"

cat << Part2
   </CENTER>
    <HR>
</BODY>
</HTML>
Part2

else # There is a passed parameter
    # Create a document
cat << Part3
Content-type: text/html

<HTML>
<HEAD>
  <CENTER>
        <TITLE>Thanks for answering</TITLE>
    </CENTER>
  </HEAD>
<BODY>
    <CENTER>
        <H1>Thanks for your answer</H1>
        <H4>You Replied With</H4>
$1

   </CENTER>
    <HR>
</BODY>
</HTML>
Part3
fi # end if
```

The **$1** about three-quarters of the way down in the listing references the first passed parameter. When the executing script encounters the **$1**, it expands the parameter and displays the value it contains. If any part of the isindex.sh script doesn't make sense, you may want to review the CGI chapter.

Supporting Multiple Options

A script may first request information. Next, it may do different things depending upon the parameters that are sent. Let's assume your first form requests the user to enter "m" for male or "f" for female. Different HTML documents could be returned by the script, based upon the user's gender answer. Here's an example of how this type of system could be set up:

```
#!/bin/sh
if [  $#  =  0  ]
  then # There is no passed parameter
     send form requesting information
  else  # There is a passed parameter
     if [  $1 = "m" ]
         then #  It's a male reply
           send male-related document
    else # There is a passed parameter but not "m"
      if [ $1 = "f" ]
        then # It's a female reply
          send female-related document
    else # Invalid reply
        send error message and request "m" or "f" again
fi # end if
```

First, the script checks to see if a parameter has been sent. If one hasn't, the basic document-based query is sent to ask the user to enter a gender. The first **else** statement checks to see if an "m" response has been entered. In this case, the male-specific document would be sent to the user's browser. The second **else** statement looks for an "f" response and sends the female-specific document. Finally, notice that a third **else** statement handles an error condition. This is good practice, especially if you think your users might enter an incorrect response and you want to tell them what they've done wrong.

Sending Actual HTML Documents

In the above example, I showed how an actual prewritten HTML document could be sent by a script instead of having the script create the document on the fly. The syntax for doing this is:

```
Location: URL
required blank line
```

The **Location** line replaces the normal script output. When you use **Location**, you don't need to use Content-type (nor *can* you use it). The URL may be actual or relative. Let's assume we have two documents named male.html and female.html. They reside in the directory just above the /cgi-bin directory. The script shown above could then be written as:

```
#!/bin/sh
if [  $#  =  0  ]
  then # There is no passed parameter
     send form requesting information
  else  # There is a passed parameter
     if [  $1 = "m" ]
         then #  It's a male reply
           echo Location: ../male.html    # return male.html
           echo                                    #  required blank line
   else # There is a passed parameter but not "m"
      if [ $1 = "f" ]
        then # It's a female reply
           echo Location: ../female.html    # return female.html
           echo                                    #  required blank line
   else # Invalid reply
        send error message and request "m" or "f" again
fi # end if
```

The ".." instructs Unix (and DOS) to look one directory above the current directory. I've left the error processing for you to complete, as an exercise. (This is frequently an author's euphemism for "I don't feel like doing it.")

FORM-BASED QUERIES

Now we're ready to move ahead to the good stuff. The document-based queries we've been exploring are not only limited but are also cumbersome to develop and write. Form-based queries, on the other hand, use prewritten HTML documents to request information from the user. CGI scripts only come into play when the server receives the user-supplied information.

Keep in mind that forms are a recent innovation and not all browsers support them. If you want to create interactive documents that will work with all browsers, you'll need to use the document-based query technique we introduced earlier.

Testing Your Forms

The NCSA folks have provided two test servers to help you develop and test your forms. The server for testing forms using the POST method is:

```
http://hoohoo.ncsa.uiuc.edu/htbin-post/post-query
```

The server for testing forms using the GET method is:

```
http://hoohoo.ncsa.uiuc.edu/htbin/query
```

Creating Form-Based Queries

In this project we'll take the HTML document created in the previous project and modify it so that it uses HTML-generated forms. For a little fun, we'll change the displayed color of the document's normal text and also the color of the various links.

There is a lot to learn, and many obstacles to overcome before you can truly master forms. But creating forms is fun and rewarding once you get the hang of it. To get good at creating your own forms, you'll need to master these three different skills:

- Creating form components using HTML tags.
- Decoding the input the user replies to your forms.
- Creating scripts that process the user input.

In this section we'll concentrate only on the first skill, building HTML query forms. NCSA has provided test servers that will take the output from a completed form and echo the results. Even if you do not have access to a server, you can create interactive forms using an NCSA test server. Once you have fully tested your Web documents that use forms, you can write the scripts you need to perform the necessary tasks on the server side.

Creating Forms with HTML

The general format of an HTML document that uses forms is:

```
<HTML>
    <HEAD>
        Normal heading stuff
    </HEAD>
    <BODY>
        Normal body stuff
        <FORM  form-specifications, normal text, and regular HTML formatting
           tags  </FORM>
        More normal body stuff
    </BODY>
</HTML>
```

The tag pair **<FORM> ... </FORM>** does the work of setting up a form. Within these tags, other form-related tags are placed—as you'll see shortly—to define the components of the form. A form-based query must have at least one input field. The input field can be a text box, radio buttons, drop-down menus, or check boxes. The components used in a form (text, input boxes, selection buttons, and so on) can be arranged in any combination. You can also use as many of these components as you like. Of course, if you clutter up your forms with too many options, they might become hard to use. As you gain more experience creating forms, you'll want to use such features as large text boxes with scroll bars, password fields, and even image maps.

Let's construct a simple form that uses a text box as the input field. We'll look at the important sections, then we'll build the whole enchilada. Here's the first part of our HTML document:

```
<HTML>
  <HEAD>
    <TITLE>Form Example One</TITLE>
  </HEAD>

  <BODY>
     <H1>One Text Box Form</H1>

     <H2>An example of a simple fill-out form using a text box</H2>
     <H4>The forms portion is enclosed between the two &lt;HR&gt;.
     <HR>
```

Everything in this listing should be familiar HTML stuff at this stage. Next, we need to set up the form:

```
<FORM METHOD="POST"
      ACTION="http://hoohoo.ncsa.uiuc.edu/htbin-post/post-query">
```

This is the start of the **<FORM>** section. Each form *must* have a **METHOD** attribute and an **ACTION** attribute. The **METHOD**, which can be either **POST** or **GET**, tells the script that processes the form how to handle the information the user provides when filling out the form. The **POST** setting tells the script that information is being sent to the server. The **GET** setting tells the script that information is being requested. The parameter for the **ACTION** attribute is a URL. It points to a program that decodes and processes the information. In this case, I'm using a script at NCSA called post-query to process the form.

Are you ready for the next step? To make the form useful, we need to have a way to get some input:

```
Input your name here: <INPUT TYPE ="text" NAME="USER-NAME">
Note that it has no default value. <P>
```

The **<INPUT>** tag is the component used to indicate that some type of input object should be displayed. In our case, we'll be displaying a text box. Two things are at work here. First, the **<INPUT>** includes the **TYPE** parameter to indicate the type of input item that is being created—a text box. Second, the **NAME** parameter assigns a name to the input field. You can supply any name that you like.

Next, we need a way to send form data to the server:

```
To submit the query, click on this button
<INPUT TYPE="submit"
       VALUE="Submit Query"> and you're done.<P>
```

We use another **<INPUT>** tag to define an additional **<FORM>** component. But this time, we are creating a submit button. The **VALUE** parameter is used to specify an initial value for the input item—in this case, the submit button. The following closing tags and the second **<HR>** finish our document.

```
        Since there is only one field you can press Enter to submit.</H4>
    </FORM>
    <HR>
  </BODY>
</HTML>
```

One underlying concept in creating forms is something called name/value pairs. Each form component (text box, radio button, and so on) has a name assigned by the document's author. The name part is assigned a value when the user enters data. You can think of the name part as a placeholder (the slot) and the value part as the piece of information stored in the slot. If you have any programming experience, you can think of the name as the variable and the value as the variable's content. If you worked for the post office, you could think of the name as a mailbox and the value as the letter you need to stuff in the mailbox.

Figure 19.4 shows how Netscape displays our HTML document with our first form. If you enter "Urb LeJeune" in the requested field and click the Submit Query button, you'll get the NCSA server's reply, shown in Figure 19.5 The complete listing for forms1.htm is displayed next. Look at the output in Figure 19.4 and try to figure out what's happening. The file forms1.htm is also on the companion CD-ROM for you to experiment with.

```
<HTML>
  <HEAD>
    <TITLE>Form Example One</TITLE>
  </HEAD>

  <BODY>
     <H1>One Text Box Form</H1>
```

```
    <H2>An example of a simple fill-out form using a text box</H2>
    <H4>The forms portion is enclosed between the two &lt;HR&gt;.
    <HR>
    <FORM METHOD="POST"
              ACTION="http://hoohoo.ncsa.uiuc.edu/htbin-post/post-query">

        Input your name here: <INPUT TYPE="text" NAME="USER-NAME">
        Note that it has no default value. <P>

       To submit the query, click on this button
       <INPUT TYPE="submit"
                 VALUE="Submit Query"> and you're done.<P>
        Since there is only one field you can press Enter to submit.</H4>

    </FORM>
    <HR>
  </BODY>
</HTML>
```

How Do Forms Work?

In true explorer fashion, we've built a form without understanding how it actually works, so let's review what we've done. **<FORM>** tags are paired, so

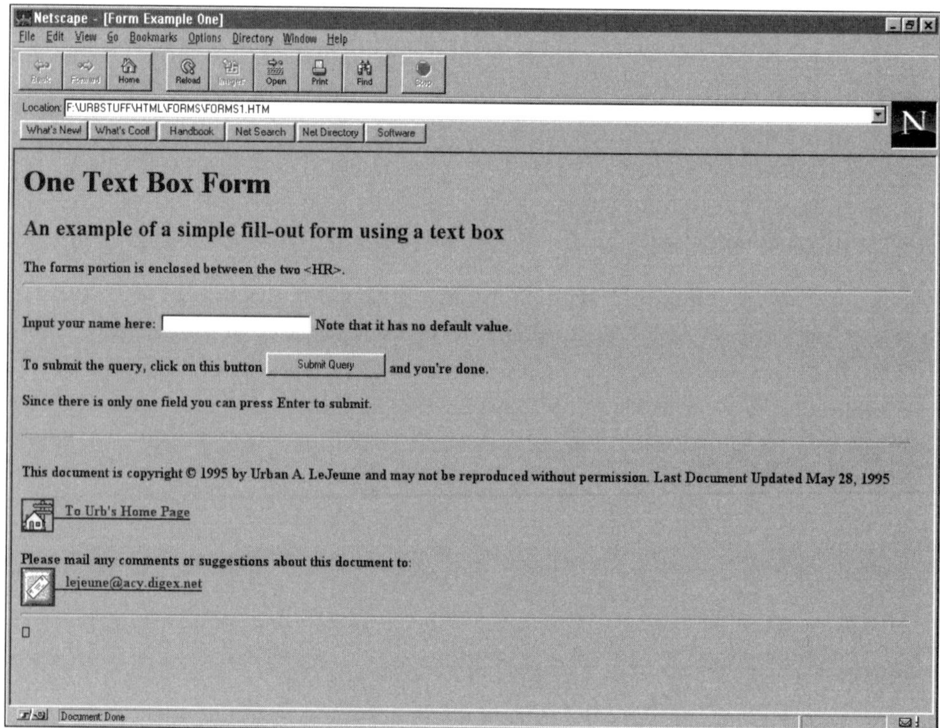

Figure 19.4 An example of a one text box form-based query.

there is always a closing **</FORM>** tag. All of the other form-related tags must be placed within this pair. Any HTML document syntax may come before or after the **<FORM> ... </FORM>** pair. A form's opening tag, **<FORM>,** requires at least two components, the **METHOD** and **ACTION** attributes. The **ACTION** attribute, which is a URL, points to the script that is called when the user submits the form. In our previous example (and the other examples in this chapter), we use the script available at the NCSA server.

The **METHOD** attribute has one of two possible parameters—namely, **POST** or **GET**. Let me cop out of a big technical discussion and say NCSA and CERN both recommend the **POST** method. In addition, most form-based queries use **POST**. Explaining why this is so would muddy the waters at this point. The major negative when using the **POST** method is the truncation of user-supplied information that will occur if the size of the information passed is large.

The first component in a form-based document is typically:

```
<FORM METHOD="POST|GET" ACTION="URL">
```

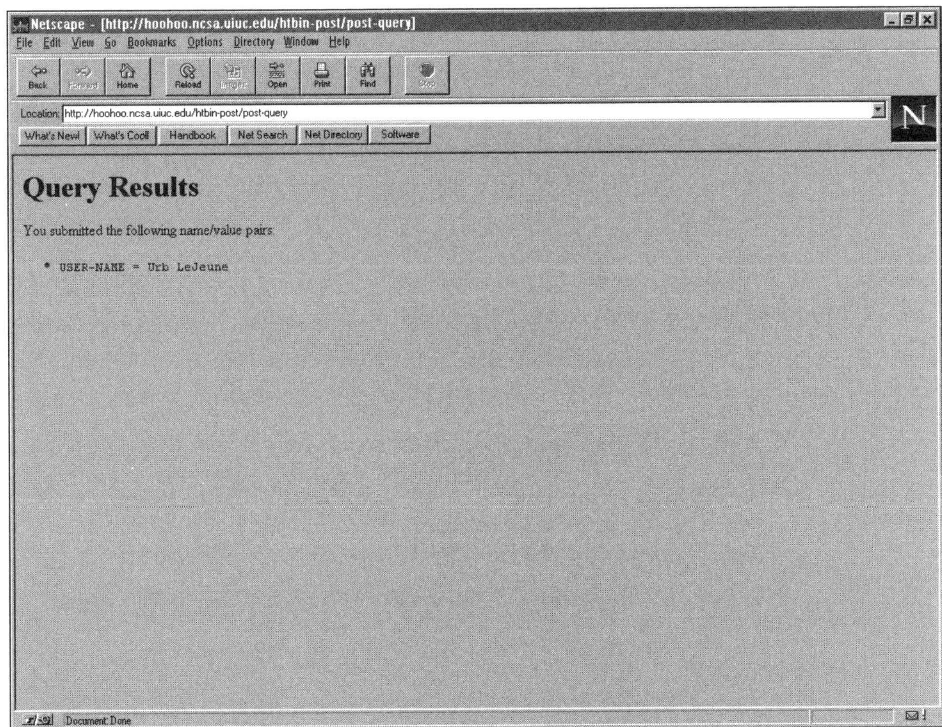

Figure 19.5 *The NCSA server's response to the submission of the form shown in Figure 19.4.*

Normal text—including the prompt—and HTML formatting tags would most likely be the first form component. The next form construct would normally be:

```
<INPUT NAME="assigned-name" TYPE="TEXT|RADIO|CHECKBOX|SUBMIT|PASSWORD|RESET">
```

If the **TYPE** attribute is omitted, **TEXT** is assumed. The **INPUT** attribute may also have a **VALUE** parameter. The value parameter is the starting value in a text box or the prompt on the submit button. In this example,

```
<INPUT TYPE="submit" VALUE="Submit Query">
```

indicates the type is a submit button and the text on the button, the **VALUE**, is Submit Query.

Now that we have a simple input form under control, let's add a second input field. I copied forms1.htm to forms2.htm before making any modifications, so you can look at the individual documents on the CD-ROM. I also made a few cosmetic changes to titles and such. The input fields for the new form are created with the following HTML:

```
Input your first name here: <INPUT NAME="FIRST-NAME"><P>
Input your last name here: <INPUT NAME="LAST-NAME"><P>
```

Notice the **<P>** tags. If they weren't there, the input fields would be displayed on one line. Figure 19.6 shows the form with the two new input fields, while Figure 19.7 displays the results of submitting Urb as a first name and LeJeune as a last name. We could expand this form by adding as many additional input fields as needed.

The complete listing of forms2.htm is shown here:

```
<HTML>
  <HEAD>
    <TITLE>Form Example Two</TITLE>
  </HEAD>

  <BODY>
      <H1>Two Text Box Form</H1>

      <H2>An example of a fill-out form using two text boxes</H2>
      <H4>The forms portion is enclosed between the two &lt;HR&gt;.
      <HR>
      <FORM METHOD="POST"
                 ACTION="http://hoohoo.ncsa.uiuc.edu/htbin-post/post-query">

          Input your first name here: <INPUT NAME="FIRST-NAME"><P>
```

```
        Input your last name here: <INPUT NAME="LAST-NAME"><P>

       To submit the query, click on this button
       <INPUT TYPE="submit"
                VALUE="Submit Query"> and you're done.<P>
        Since there is more than one field you CANNOT press Enter to submit.</
H4>

     </FORM>
     <HR>
  </BODY>
</HTML>
```

Using Default Values with Text Boxes

Let's explore one more variation on the theme of text boxes. The next HTML document we'll create, forms3.htm, creates a text box that contains a default value. The **INPUT** attribute in this example uses a **VALUE** parameter. The text "Netscape" will initially appear in the text box when the document displays. If the user changes the value of a field having a default value and subsequently clicks

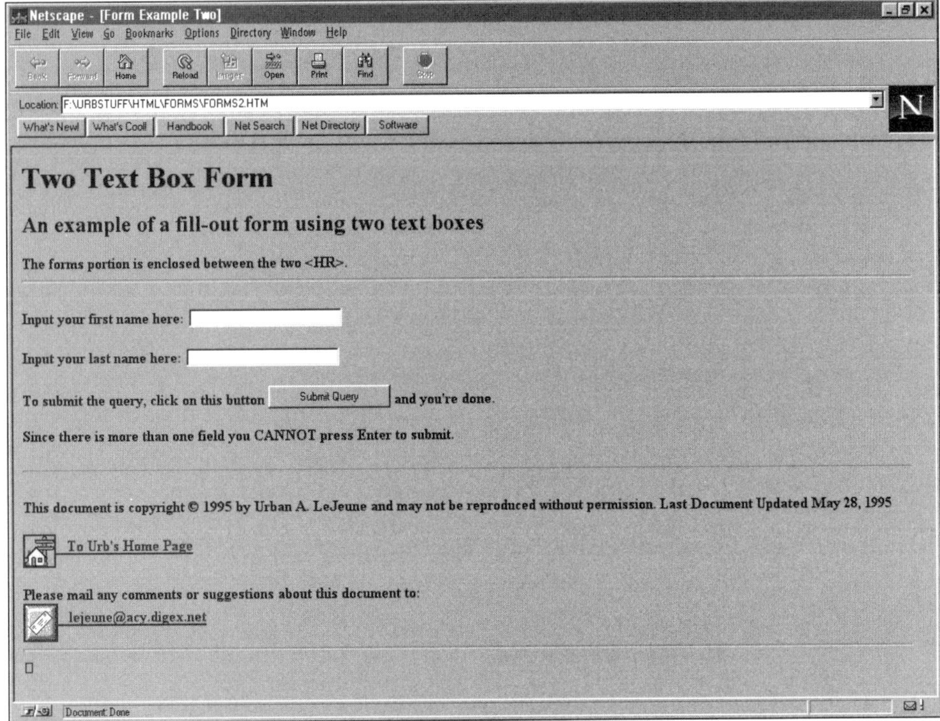

Figure 19.6 An example of a two text box form-based query.

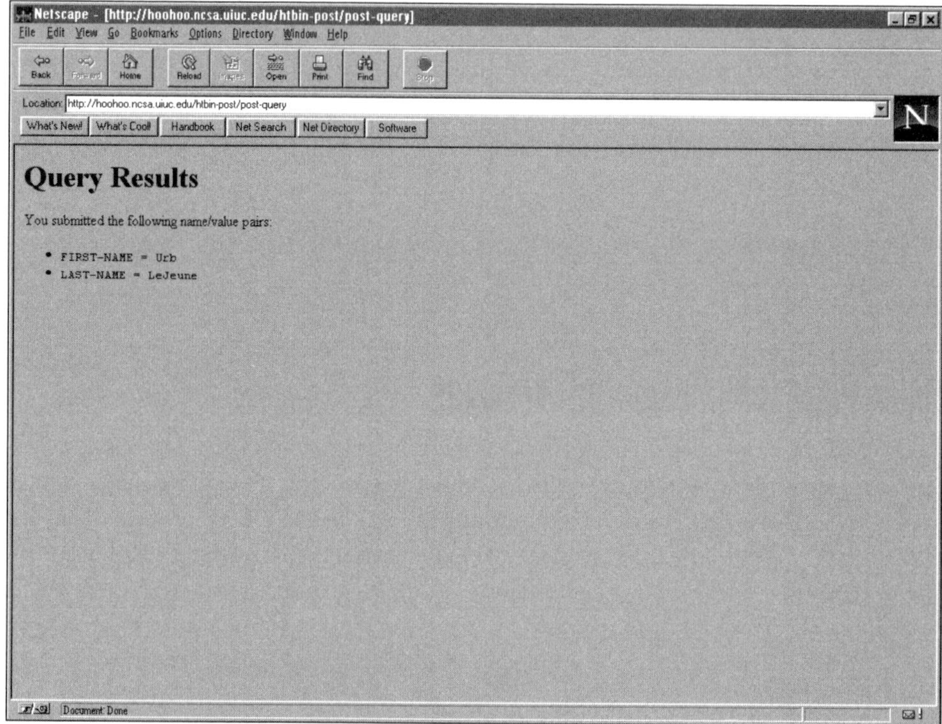

Figure 19.7 The NCSA server's response to the submission of the form shown in Figure 19.6.

on the Reset button (if present), the original value will reappear in the text box. The HTML instructions that set up the input field with a default value are:

```
What is your favorite Web Browser?
<INPUT NAME="Browser-Preference" VALUE="Netscape">
Notice default value<P>
```

Figure 19.8 and Figure 19.9 again show the form submission and server response pair. In this case "Netscape" was not typed into the browser question shown in Figure 19.8.

Here's the complete listing for forms3.htm:

```
<HTML>
  <HEAD>
    <TITLE>Form Example Three</TITLE>
  </HEAD>

  <BODY>
    <H1>Text Boxes With a Default</H1>
```

```
    <H2>Text Boxes With a Default</H2>
    <H4>The forms portion is enclosed between the two &lt;HR&gt;.
    <HR>
    <FORM METHOD="POST"
             ACTION="http://hoohoo.ncsa.uiuc.edu/htbin-post/post-query">

        Input your first name here: <INPUT NAME="FIRST-NAME"><P>
        Input your last name here: <INPUT NAME="LAST-NAME"><P>
        What is your favorite Web Browser?
        <INPUT NAME="Browser-Preference" VALUE="Netscape">
        Notice default value<P>

       To submit the query, click on this button
       <INPUT TYPE="submit"
                VALUE="Submit Query"> and you're done.<P>
        Since there is more than one field you CANNOT press Enter to submit.

    </FORM>
    <HR>
  </BODY>
</HTML>
```

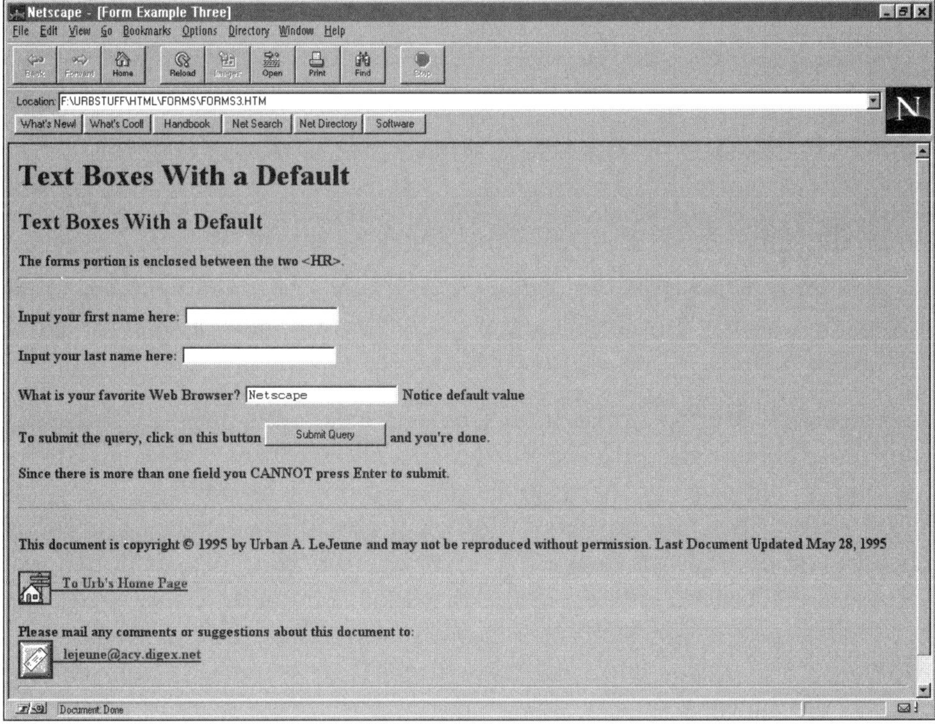

Figure 19.8 *An example of a three text box form-based query with "Netscape" being a default value.*

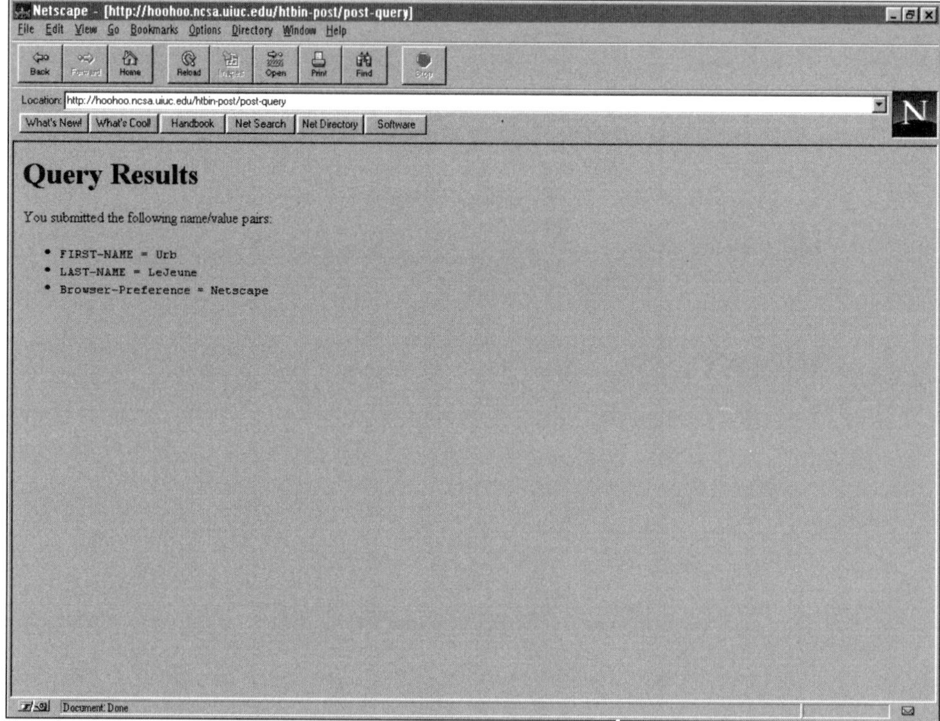

Figure 19.9 *The NCSA server's response to the submission of the form shown in Figure 19.8.*

Radio Buttons

In addition to text boxes, we can use other types of components to obtain information from a user. Let's look at the different options available, starting with radio buttons.

Any type of Windows application you use these days provides radio buttons (sometimes called option buttons) to allow a user to select different options. When a group of related radio buttons is displayed, a user can select only one of the buttons in the group. In this respect, radio button choices are mutually exclusive. To see how radio buttons are defined, let's change the form we created in the previous section and add a group of radio buttons that query the user about sex. Often, a list construct is used to set up radio button choices. Here's the HTML we need to compose our set of radio buttons:

```
What is your sex?<BR>
<DL>
```

```
     <DD><INPUT TYPE="radio" NAME="SEX" VALUE="Female" CHECKED> Female
     <DD><INPUT TYPE="radio" NAME="SEX" VALUE="Male"> Male
     <DD><INPUT TYPE="radio" NAME="SEX" VALUE="Not-Sure"> Unknown
</DL>
```

The **TYPE** parameter is set to **radio**. All of the associated choices must have the same name (**SEX** in this example). The browser sends the **VALUE** parameter to the server if the user checked the corresponding selection. The item listed with the **CHECKED** option indicates the radio button that will be selected by default when the document is displayed. One, and only one, item in the list of choices can be **CHECKED** and one *must* be **CHECKED**. The last item, outside the closing > specifies the text that is displayed with the radio button. Using a list to display radio buttons is certainly not mandatory, but is very convenient. Figure 19.10 and Figure 19.11 once more show the execution of the document and NCSA's reply.

The complete HTML document that uses the radio buttons is named forms4.htm.

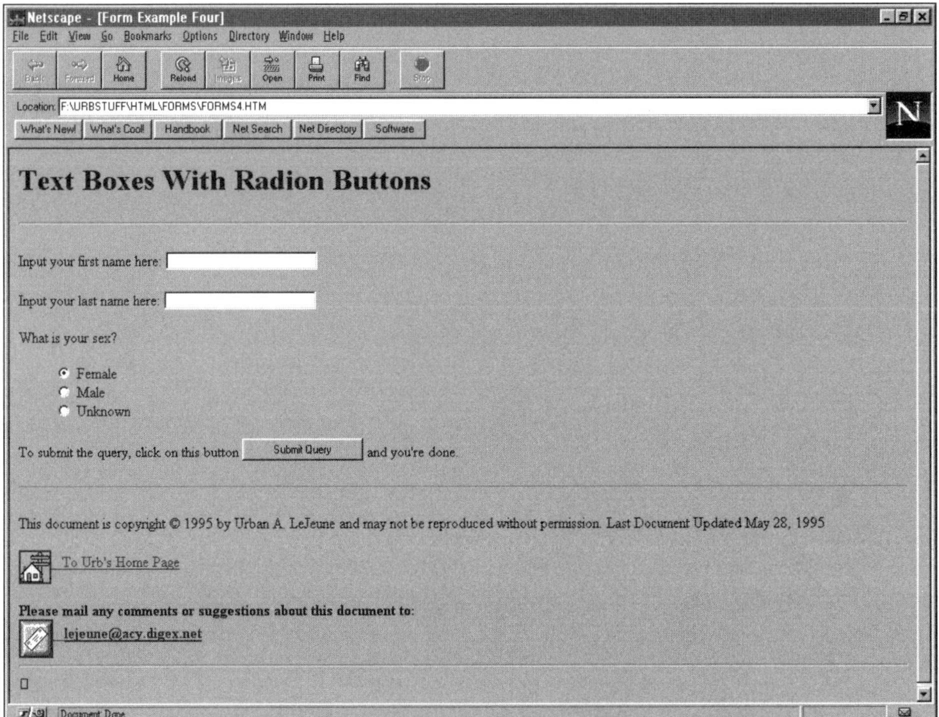

Figure 19.10 *A two text box form-based query, also using radio buttons.*

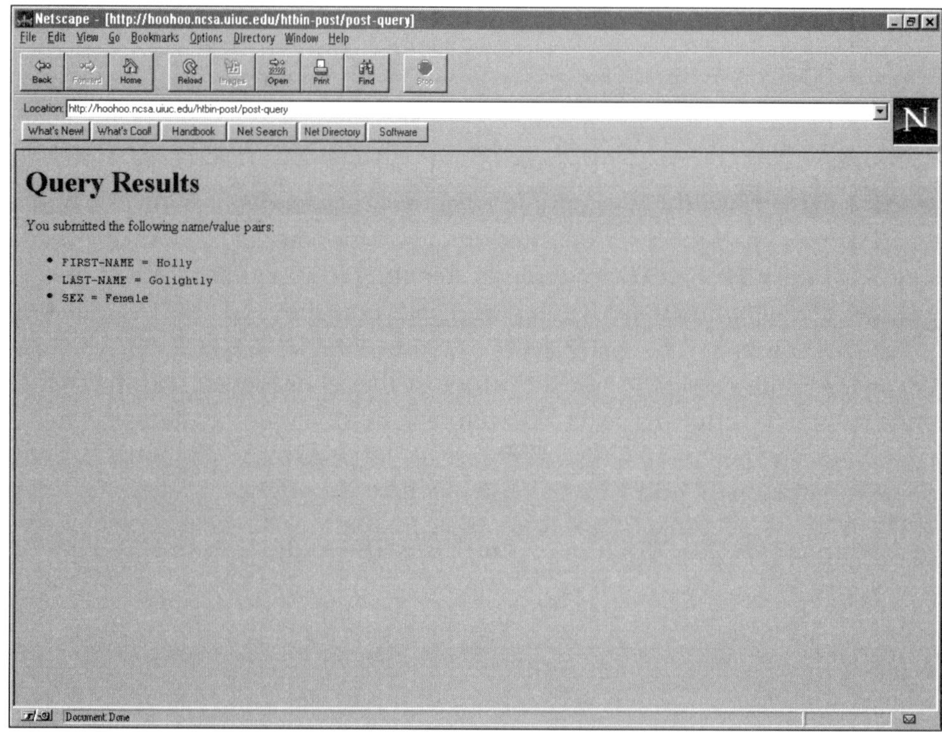

Figure 19.11 *The NCSA server's response to the submission of the form shown in Figure 19.10.*

```
  <HTML>
  <HEAD>
    <TITLE>Form Example Four</TITLE>
  </HEAD>
  <BODY>
     <H1>Text Boxes With Radio Buttons</H1>
     <HR>
     <FORM METHOD="POST"
                  ACTION="http://hoohoo.ncsa.uiuc.edu/htbin-post/post-query">
         Input your first name here: <INPUT NAME="FIRST-NAME"><P>
         Input your last name here: <INPUT NAME="LAST-NAME"><P>
         What is your sex?<BR>
      <DL>
         <DD><INPUT TYPE="radio" NAME="SEX" VALUE="Female" CHECKED> Female
         <DD><INPUT TYPE="radio" NAME="SEX" VALUE="Male"> Male
         <DD><INPUT TYPE="radio" NAME="SEX" VALUE="Not-Sure"> Unknown
       </DL>
        To submit the query, click on this button
        <INPUT TYPE="submit"
                     VALUE="Submit Query"> and you're done.<P>
     </FORM>
     <HR>
  </BODY>
</HTML>
```

Checkboxes

Checkboxes are similar to radio buttons except they are not mutually exclusive. No checkboxes need be selected and any number may be selected. Let's add a few checkboxes to our existing form to see how easy they are to create:

```
<INPUT TYPE="checkbox" NAME="Browser1"
       VALUE="Netscape" CHECKED> Netscape
<INPUT TYPE="checkbox" NAME="Browser2"
       VALUE="Mosaic"> Mosaic
<INPUT TYPE="checkbox" NAME="Browser3"
        VALUE="Cello"> Cello
...

<INPUT TYPE="checkbox" NAME="Browser8"
         VALUE="CompuServ"> CompuServe
<INPUT TYPE="checkbox" NAME="Browser9"
         VALUE="NetCom"> NetCom
<INPUT TYPE="checkbox" NAME="Browser10"
         VALUE="Others"> Others
```

The **TYPE** parameter in this case is set to **checkbox**. Each input item must have a different name. Notice that the prompt or label for the checkbox appears outside the closing tag. When a group of checkboxes is defined, you don't need to specify a default item, but I did in this example. The **CHECKED** parameter is included with the first **<INPUT>** tag so that this checkbox will automatically be selected (checked) when the form is first displayed. Because multiple checkboxes in a group can be selected, we could use the **CHECKED** parameter with any of the other **<INPUT>** tags defined here as well.

Adding Formatting Features

Now that we have a handle on text boxes, radio buttons, and checkboxes, let's add some more interesting formatting features to the document that uses the form we've been constructing. The file name for the new version will be forms5.htm.

To get a better idea of where we are headed, take a peek at Figure 19.12. Unfortunately, what doesn't show up in the black and white screen shot is the nice light blue background. The HTML instruction used to produce this effect is:

```
<BODY BGCOLOR="7FFFFF">
```

I'll also use text formatting—the **<B> ... </B>** tag pair—to highlight our checkboxes. In addition, I've increased the font size of the checkboxes by using the **SIZE=+1** parameter. I've also placed the checkboxes in a table containing one row and two columns. The first column contains an ordered list **<OL>** while the second column also contains an ordered list, starting with 6. This is probably not a good

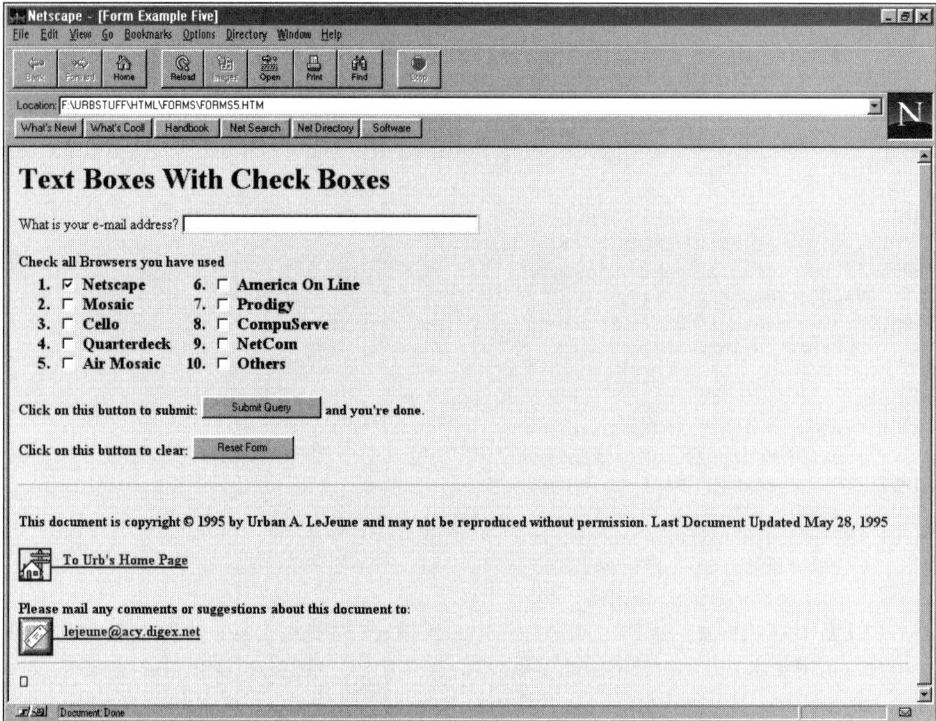

Figure 19.12 *A query form demonstrating checkboxes replete with special effects.*

idea, since only Netscape supports the **START=** attribute for an ordered list. However, let's have some fun while we try out some of the more interesting Netscape enhancements. The skeletal syntax for all this gingerbread is:

```
<TABLE>
       <TR>
          <B>
          <TD>
              <OL>
                  <FONT SIZE=+1><B>
                   <LI><INPUT TYPE="checkbox" NAME="Browser1"
                        VALUE="Netscape" CHECKED>

...

                 </FONT></B>
              </OL>
           </TD>
           <TD>
              <OL START=6>
                  <FONT SIZE=+1><B>
                  <LI><INPUT TYPE="checkbox" NAME="Browser6"
                       VALUE="America On Line">
...
```

```
                    </FONT></B>
                </OL>
            </TD>
        </TR>
</TABLE>
```

Notice that the Netscape item is **CHECKED**, meaning it is preselected. The default size for a text box is 20 characters. More text may be entered, but only 20 characters will be listed. You can change the size by using the **SIZE** parameter. Here's how we've used this feature in our new form:

```
<INPUT NAME="E-MAIL" SIZE=40><P>
```

Our form also has a reset button created by this tag:

```
Click on this button to clear:
<INPUT TYPE="reset" Value="Reset Form">
```

Figure 19.12 displays the form in all its glory. The NCSA response in shown in Figure 19.13.

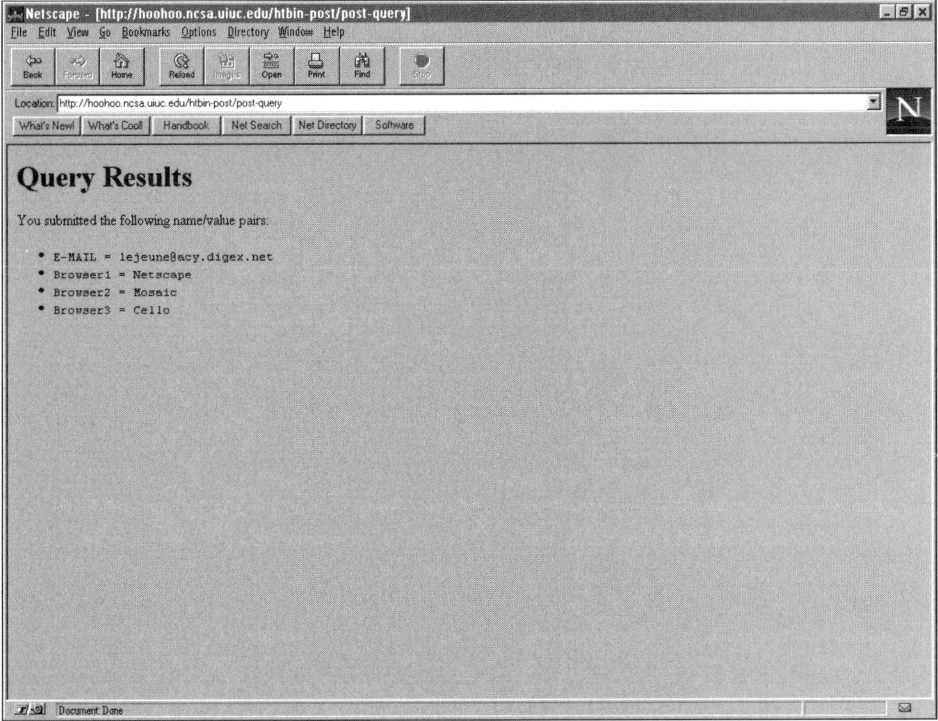

Figure 19.13 *The NCSA server's response to the submission of the form shown in Figure 19.12.*

The complete listing for forms5.htm follows.

```
<HTML>
   <HEAD>
     <TITLE>Form Example Five</TITLE>
   </HEAD>
   <BODY BGCOLOR="7FFFFF">
      <H1>Text Boxes With Check Boxes</H1>
      <FORM METHOD="POST"
                  ACTION="http://hoohoo.ncsa.uiuc.edu/htbin-post/post-query">
          What is your e-mail address?
         <INPUT NAME="E-MAIL" SIZE=40><P>
         <B>Check all Browsers you have used</B><BR>
    <TABLE>
       <TR>
          <B>
          <TD>
              <OL>
                  <FONT SIZE=+1><B>
                   <LI><INPUT TYPE="checkbox" NAME="Browser1"
                        VALUE="Netscape" CHECKED>
                        Netscape
                   <LI><INPUT TYPE="checkbox" NAME="Browser2"
                        VALUE="Mosaic"> Mosaic
                   <LI><INPUT TYPE="checkbox" NAME="Browser3"
                         VALUE="Cello"> Cello
                   <LI><INPUT TYPE="checkbox" NAME="Browser4"
                        VALUE="Quarterdeck"> Quarterdeck
                   <LI><INPUT TYPE="checkbox" NAME="Browser5"
                        VALUE="Air Mosaic"> Air Mosaic
                   </FONT></B>
              </OL>
           </TD>
           <TD>
              <OL START=6>
                  <FONT SIZE=+1><B>
                  <LI><INPUT TYPE="checkbox" NAME="Browser6"
                       VALUE="AOL"> America Online
                  <LI><INPUT TYPE="checkbox" NAME="Browser7"
                        VALUE="Prodigy"> Prodigy
                  <LI><INPUT TYPE="checkbox" NAME="Browser8"
                        VALUE="CompuServ"> CompuServe
                  <LI><INPUT TYPE="checkbox" NAME="Browser9"
                        VALUE="NetCom"> NetCom
                  <LI><INPUT TYPE="checkbox" NAME="Browser10"
                        VALUE="Others"> Others
                  </FONT></B>
              </OL>
          </TD>
        </TR>
     </TABLE>
        Click on this button to submit:
        <INPUT TYPE="submit"
                     VALUE="Submit Query"> and you're done.<P>
        Click on this button to clear:
```

```
        <INPUT TYPE="reset" Value="Reset Form">

    </FORM>
    <HR>
  </BODY>
</HTML>
```

Drop-Down Menus

Last on our forms hit parade is drop-down menus. A drop-down menu, created using the **<SELECT>** tag, is conceptually much like a radio button. Only one choice can be made from a list of displayed items. The basic format for this tag is:

```
<SELECT> NAME="name"
         SIZE=number
         MULTIPLE> text or option list </SELECT>
```

The **SIZE** and **MULTIPLE** parameters are optional. If **MULTIPLE** is provided, the menu will allow the user to select more than one option. The individual items in a menu are defined using the **<OPTION>** tag. To see how this is done, let's look at the HTML required to define the actual menu used in the previous version of the HTML form presented in this chapter:

```
<B>Select your highest level of education:</B>
<SELECT NAME="Education">
       <OPTION>Less than 8 years
       <OPTION>Grammar School
       <OPTION>High School
       <OPTION>Some College
       <OPTION>College Graduate
       <OPTION>Master Degree
       <OPTION>Earned Doctorate
</SELECT><P>
```

The first option item is the default. The prompt will appear in the box when the form is first displayed. If there is an **<OPTION>** tag with no prompt, the starting value would be null and the selection box would be empty. The **<OPTION>** tag may also contain a **VALUE** attribute, in the form:

```
<OPTION VALUE="My Choice">
```

If used, the **VALUE** parameter is sent to the server when the item is selected. If **VALUE** isn't used, the prompt becomes the value and is sent to the server. Use caution on the placement of the drop menus. Make sure the menu, when dropped, doesn't exceed the screen size for a variety of different browsers and terminals.

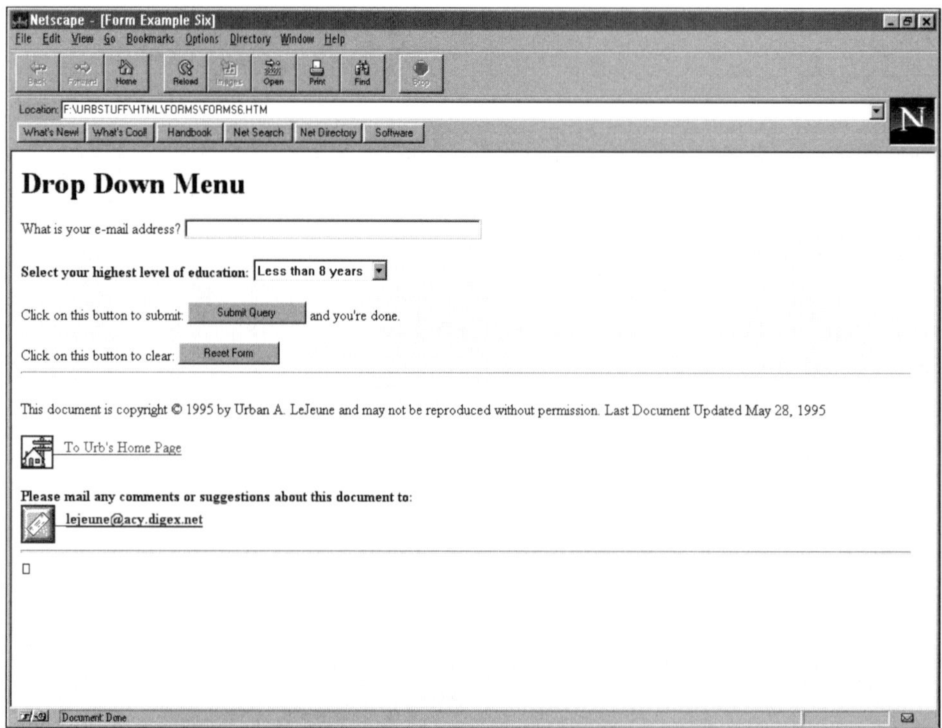

Figure 19.14 An example of a drop-down menu used in a form.

Figure 19.14 displays a form employing the drop menu, while Figure 19.15 shows NCSA's reply to the entries shown in Figure 19.14.

The complete HTML file for the final version of our example document is forms6.htm. Here it is:

```
<HTML>
   <HEAD>
     <TITLE>Form Example Six</TITLE>
   </HEAD>
   <BODY BGCOLOR="FFFF00">
      <H1>Drop Down Menu</H1>
      <FORM METHOD="POST"
                 ACTION="http://hoohoo.ncsa.uiuc.edu/htbin-post/post-query">
          What is your e-mail address?
         <INPUT NAME="E-MAIL" SIZE=40><P>
         <B>Select your highest level of education:</B>
         <SELECT NAME="Education">
                 <OPTION>Less than 8 years
                 <OPTION>Grammar School
                 <OPTION>High School
```

```
            <OPTION>Some College
            <OPTION>College Graduate
            <OPTION>Master Degree
            <OPTION>Earned Doctorate
      </SELECT><P>
     Click on this button to submit:
     <INPUT TYPE="submit"
                  VALUE="Submit Query"> and you're done.<P>
     Click on this button to clear:
        <INPUT TYPE="reset" Value="Reset Form"
      </FORM>
    <HR>
  </BODY>
</HTML>
```

Decoding Name/Value Pairs

If you plan to get serious about forms, you'll need to decode the name/value pairs supplied by the browser. Thankfully, robust scripts to accomplish this task are available. A commonly used parser is the one supplied with the CERN HTTPD server. It's called cgipars and may be available on your system

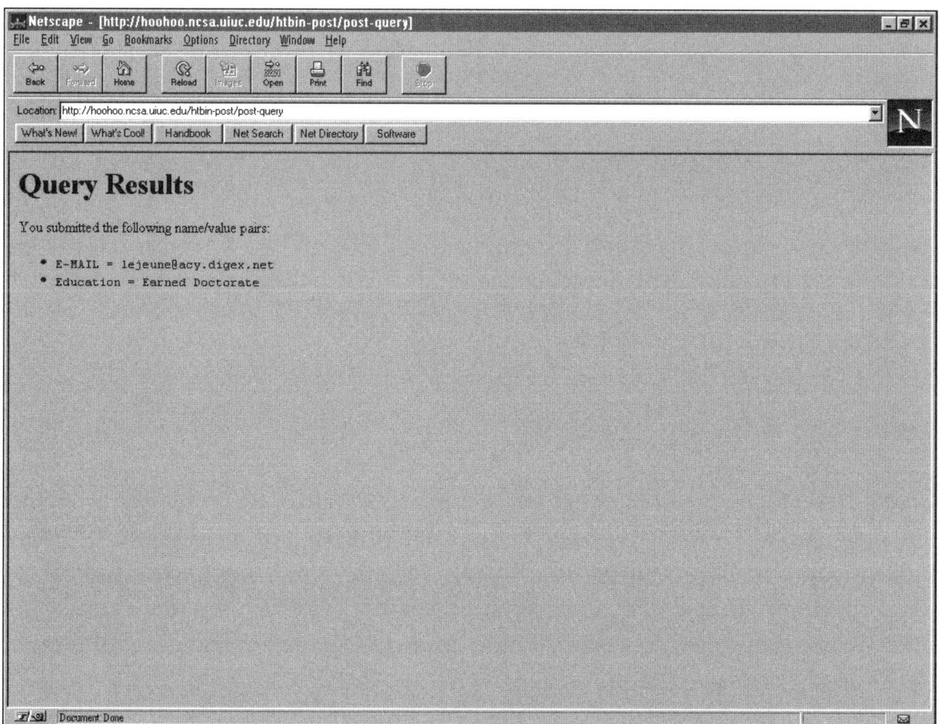

Figure 19.15 NCSA's Query Results display.

in the /usr/local/bin/cgiparse directory. NCSA also makes C source code available to parse the name/value pairs. Their FTP URL is:

```
ftp://ftp.ncsa.uiuc.edu/Web/httpd/Unix/ncsa_httpd/cgi/cgi-src/
```

There are many CGI scripts available on the Web simply for the asking, or downloading. Visit some of the sites listed in the resource guide that follows. Existing scripts serve two purposes—they prevent you from reinventing the wheel if you can find a script that come close to doing what you want it to do, and they are great learning vehicles.

It is always a good idea to check on script availability with your Internet service provider or system administrator. You may have to look no further.

LET'S REVIEW

Form-based queries became a reality with HTML 2.0. However, care must be taken when using forms since some browsers may not support them.

Document-based queries have been with us since the beginning of HTML. Only one input field is supplied with a document-based query. The tag **<ISINDEX>** must appear in the **<HEAD>** section of a document-based query. A script must be used to generate the input form and to format a report based upon the user's input.

Forms-based queries are much more flexible and much easier to write and test. The document supplied to the user is actually a conventional HTML document with a **<FORM>** section.

The basic format for creating a form is:

```
<FORM METHOD="POST|GET" ACTION="URL">
</FORM>
```

A form-based query must have at least one input field. The input fields can be text entry boxes, radio buttons, drop-down menus, or checkboxes. These components can be arranged in any combination and you can use any number of them. You can also use more advanced features, such as large text boxes with scroll bars, password fields, and image maps. The general format of a forms-related document is:

```
<HTML>
    <HEAD>
```

```
    Normal heading stuff
</HEAD>
<BODY>
    Normal body stuff
    <FORM  form-specifications, normal text, and regular HTML formatting
       tags  </FORM>
    More normal body stuff
</BODY>
```

Once a user completes a form—by clicking on the submit button—name/value pairs are sent to a server. Public domain scripts are available to decode these pairs.

Resources

The following may be helpful when exploring the construction of forms.

CGI-Forms Tutorial
http://www.catt.ncsu.edu/~bex/tutor/index.html

Advanced Development Tools: HTML Tables, Forms, and CGI
www.stars.com/seminars

CyberWeb's Virtual Library
http://WWW.Stars.com/Vlib

W3 Browse at NASA—Super Examples
http://guinan.gsfc.nasa.gov/cgi-bin/W3Browse/w3browse.pl

Web Developer's Virtual Library—This is a gold mine!
http://WWW.Stars.com/

Decoding Forms with CGI
http://hoohoo.ncsa.uiuc.edu/cgi/forms.html

WWW FAQ in HTML
http://www.boutell.com/faq

Yahoo CGI List
http://www.yahoo.com/Computers/World_Wide_Web/CGI__Common_Gateway_Interface

Working with Frames

The new Netscape opens up all kinds of new design possibilities for your Web pages. Here's one that will change the entire look of your pages—frames.

Once you begin working with frames you'll learn that a little really does go a long way. With the addition of a few simple tags and attributes, you can dynamically transform your Web pages in a multitude of ways including adding much better navigational aids.

The challenge, though, is far greater than mastering the few simple tags introduced with frames. The real challenge is learning how to use frames effectively while managing the changes frames cause in your Web site's file structure. There are also a host of design questions that arise when you start using frames, which I'll cover in this chapter.

Navigating with Frames

When you first start looking at Web pages that use frames, such as the one shown in Figure 20.1, you'll probably have a hard time navigating around them. That's because frame pages contain an entirely different structure than standard Web pages. You can't just use the Forward and Back buttons at the top of

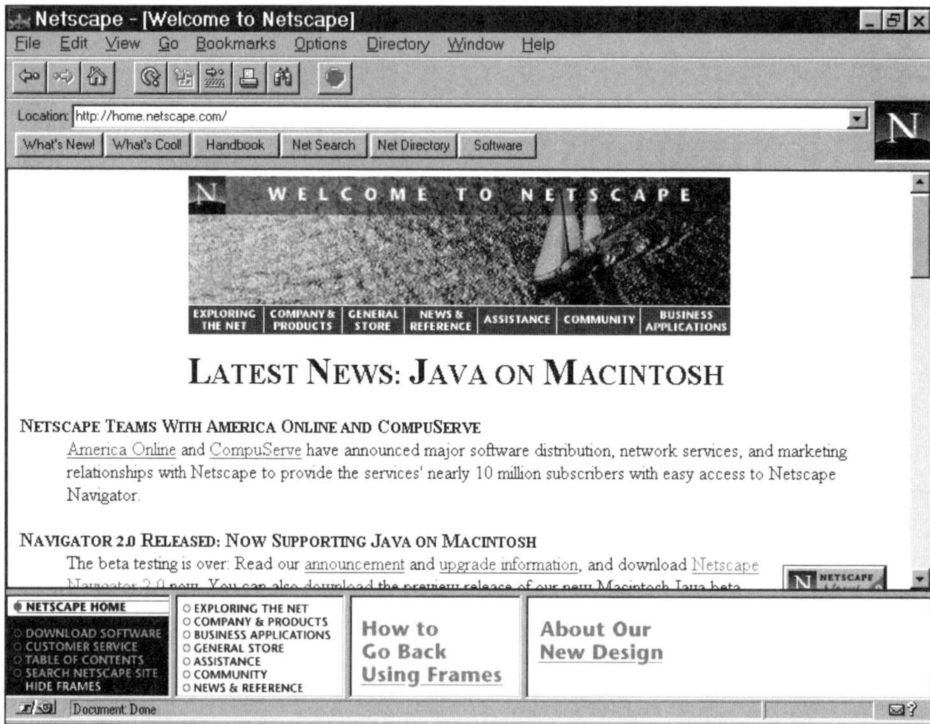

Figure 20.1 *Netscape's home page provides a good example of what frames look like.*

the browser to get around. If you want to get back to a page you just looked at, and you use the Back button, you'll probably end up back at a main menu.

When navigating in frames, remember to use your right mouse button. When you click on it, it will give you a choice of going Back in Frame or Forward in Frame. The reason behind these different commands will become more clear as we explain the structure and design of frames.

A proposed new version of Netscape, currently called Atlas, will help to simplify navigation with frames. Atlas will restore the ability to use the Back button in frames, so when you click on Back within a frame, it will take you back to the last frame, instead of the last whole page. Hopefully, this will be included in the forthcoming Netscape release. It should make frames a lot easier to use, and therefore more popular.

Frame Structure

One of the most important things to learn about frames is how they will change the file structure of your Web page. Previously, one screen was made up of one HTML file. Now, with frames, you will use multiple HTML files to construct one screen. Web page design with frames requires more HTML files because a separate HTML file is required for each frame you have on your screen. You also need to include one "frame file" that acts as an overall structure file for your Web page. The basic formula for creating frames is:

```
Number of HTML files needed for a "frame-aware" site = Number of frames + 1
```

As soon as you start working with frames you'll be introduced to an element of Web site file management that you haven't seen before. Therefore, you need to be sure to use a good filenaming system and directory structure to keep track of all the different files you'll be constructing.

Understanding the Frame Construction Process

Let's start by exploring the simplest form of a frame setup—a two frame Web page. The most important and basic HTML tag you need to know is:

```
<FRAMESET>...</FRAMESET>
```

When you define a set of frames, you enclose your frame code inside the **<FRAMESET>** tags. The **<FRAMESET>** tag replaces the normal **<BODY>** tag and helps to alert Netscape that the file is a frame file that will set up the overall layout of the screen. Within the **<FRAMESET>** tag you can only have other nested **<FRAMESET>** tags, **<FRAME>** tags, or the **<NOFRAMES>** tag.

Let's cover the attributes you can add to the **<FRAMESET>** tag:

```
<FRAMESET ROWS="row info, row info, row info...">
```

The **ROWS** attribute uses a comma-separated list of values, either specific pixel values, percentages of the screen (1 to 100), or a relative scaling value. The scaling value is used to divide a section of the screen into separate frames divided into rows. The number of rows is limited only by the screen resolution and your own design needs. If you leave out the **ROWS** attribute, Netscape assumes that you're dealing with a single row and it will automatically size the row to fit.

A value list can have three distinct looks; here are some examples:

```
<FRAMESET ROWS="120,120,120">
```

This tag creates three frames, all divided into rows that are exactly 120 pixels in height. Of course, this is not the best way to use frames, because Netscape users may resize their browser or use it in such different resolutions that you could be giving them very undesirable results. Where I find it most useful is in defining frames that might house graphics that I want to fit perfectly within a frame. This requires really good planning though, so don't just jump in head first when using pixel resolution values.

The following tag would create three frames, all divided into rows that divide the available screen space using the percentages provided:

```
<FRAMESET ROWS="20%, 50%, 30%">
```

Using the next tag you can create what Netscape calls a "relative-sized" frame. This is a request to give a frame all the remaining space without regard to percentages or values. In this example I've created two rows which will evenly divide the remaining space.

```
<FRAMESET ROWS="*, *">
```

You can also introduce a value before the *, such as **<FRAMESET ROWS**="3*,*"> which will create a relative frame setup giving one frame 3/4 of the screen and the other frame 1/4. If you used a tag like, **<FRAMESET ROWS**="3*,*,*"> you would be assigning one frame 3/5 of the space and the other two would evenly divide up the remainder at 1/5 each.

Finally, you might combine the fixed pixel setup with a relative frame setup by using a tag like this:

```
<FRAMESET ROWS="50,*,*,50">
```

This tag assigns top and bottom frame rows 50 pixels in height and then divides up the remaining space evenly between two additional frames.

Relative framing works really well when you're creating nested **FRAMESET**s to create fancy displays that include **ROW** and **COL** setups, which I'll show you a little later:

```
COLS="col info, col info..."
```

The **COLS** attribute works just like the **ROWS** attribute, but divides the frames up vertically instead of horizontally.

Nesting FRAMESETs

To divide the screen into both rows and columns, we can nest **<FRAMESET>** tags, alternating between rows and columns until the overall screen looks the way you want. Here's a simple example:

```
<HTML>
   <HEAD>
        <TITLE>
            A Frames Example
        </TITLE>
   </HEAD>
     <FRAMESET ROWS=*,*>
           <FRAME SRC="title.htm" NAME="title">
      <FRAMESET COLS=*,*>
           <FRAME SRC="part1.htm" NAME="part1">
           <FRAME SRC="part2.htm" NAME="part2">
   </FRAMESET>
   </FRAMESET>
</HTML>
```

There is actually a second way to create nested frames. First, you create multiple frame files and then you can reference them in the master frame file. As an example, consider the frame layout shown in Figure 20.2. Let's write the HTML code to build this nested frame setup.

First, create a file which breaks up a window into two rows, the top being 2/3 and the bottom being 1/3. For the first frame, reference a source file called top.htm, which is really another frame file. For the second frame, reference a source file called bottom.htm, which is also another frame file. Finally, write

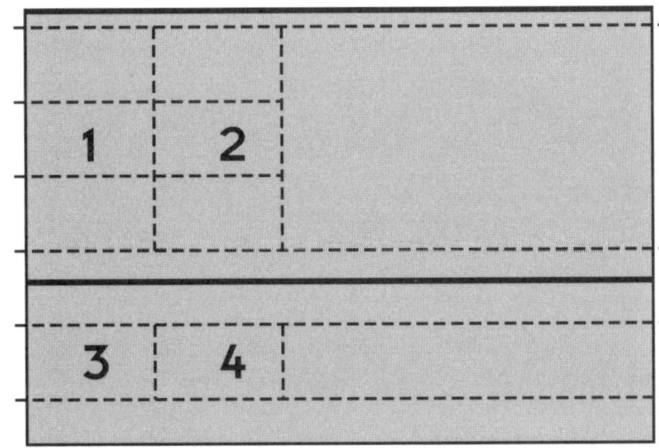

Figure 20.2 *Creating a Web page with a nested frame setup.*

frame files for top.htm and bottom.htm that split each frame into columns of 2/3 and 1/3. Here's the code:

Source file for master.htm.

```
<HTML>
   <HEAD>
        <TITLE>
           The Master Frames Document
        </TITLE>
   </HEAD>
   <FRAMESET ROWS=2*,*>
       <FRAME SRC="top.htm" NAME="top">
       <FRAME SRC="bottom.htm" NAME="bottom">
   </FRAMESET>
</HTML>
```

Source file for top.htm.

```
<HTML>
   <HEAD>
        <TITLE>
           The Top Frame
        </TITLE>
   </HEAD>
   <FRAMESET COLS=2*,*>
       <FRAME SRC="main.htm" NAME="main">
       <FRAME SRC="guide.htm" NAME="guide">
   </FRAMESET>
</HTML>
```

Source file for bottom.htm.

```
<HTML>
   <HEAD>
        <TITLE>
           The Bottom Frame
        </TITLE>
   </HEAD>
   <FRAMESET COLS=2*,*>
       <FRAME SRC="banner.htm" NAME="banner">
       <FRAME SRC="jumpspot.htm" NAME="jumpspot">
   </FRAMESET>
</HTML>
```

Using the FRAME Tag

After we've used **<FRAMESET>** to define the overall outline of the frame layout we need to work on the specific characteristics of each frame. This is done by using the **<FRAME>** tag. The following statement lists all the possible attributes of the **<FRAME>** tag:

```
<FRAME SRC="url" NAME="window_name" MARGINWIDTH=value MARGINHEIGHT=value
SCROLLING="YES|NO|AUTO" NORESIZE>
```

Because of the complexity of this tag, let's dissect it and take a close look at each component.

SRC

First, the **<FRAME>** tag specifies a source URL (**SRC=**), which tells Netscape which HTML file or picture to load into the frame. For example, **<FRAME SRC**="/aboutme.html"> would load the aboutme.html file into the specific frame. If you fail to initially define a source, the frame is displayed as blank space.

NAME

After the **SRC** has been specified, you'll want to give the frame an internal name, so you can refer to the frame later in your HTML code. **NAME** is an optional attribute, but one that makes a lot of sense to use, since all windows are unnamed by default and thus can't be targeted by your references. When naming frames make sure they begin with an alphanumeric character. For example, **<FRAME SRC**="/aboutme.html" **NAME**="ABOUT"> labels the particular frame "ABOUT". Later we'll be using **<FRAME NAME=>** to load new URLs into a specific frame using a **TARGET** attribute that you add to the normal **<A HREF>** tag.

MARGINWIDTH and MARGINHEIGHT

These two attributes define how much of a border you want between the displayed document and the actual borders of the frame. This value is specified in pixels and can range from 0 to completely fill the frame, or can be large enough to create a sizable offset from the frame. These settings are optional. If you don't use them, Netscape will set the appropriate margin width automatically. Be sure you don't over-assign the border, because this situation will produce a blank frame.

SCROLLING

When you define a frame you can choose to have it scroll or not scroll. The default setting is **AUTO**, which allows the browser to scroll if the document loaded to that frame is bigger than the frame size allows. If you set the scrolling attribute to **YES**, the scroll bar will always be there. If you assign it **NO**, it won't show up. I use the **SCROLLING**="NO" attribute for frames that I want to house graphics, so I don't get a scroll bar just because the graphic is 1 pixel bigger than the frame.

NORESIZE

Adding **NORESIZE** to the **FRAME** tag denies the user the ability to resize the frame. The default setting allows the user to resize a frame, and if you have a delicately layed out display, resizing can wreak havoc on it. Many times I use **NORESIZE** for frames dealing with graphics (such as a banner across the top of the screen).

Using the NOFRAMES Tag

Any HTML code inserted between the following tags

```
<NOFRAMES>...</NOFRAMES>
```

is activated by browsers that don't support frames. It's a good idea to keep people without frames-capable browsers involved in your site. Even if you simply use the following:

```
<NOFRAMES>
In order to properly view this site you need a frames capable browser like
NETSCAPE 2.0.
</NOFRAMES>
```

PUTTING A FRAME PROJECT TOGETHER

Now that we've covered the key aspects of frame syntax let's do a complete example of a really fancy frame file. We'll use nested frames, but we'll implement them in one frame file:

```
<HTML>
   <HEAD>
        <TITLE>
           A Fancy Frame File
        </TITLE>
   </HEAD>
   <FRAMESET ROWS=2*,*>
      <FRAMESET COLS=3*,4*>
          <FRAME SRC="TOC.HTM">
          <FRAME SRC="MAINBODY.HTM">
      </FRAMESET>
   <NOFRAMES>
      In order to properly view this site you need a frames capable browser like
Netscape 2.0.
```

```
</NOFRAMES>
    <FRAMESET COLS=*,*,*>
        <FRAME SRC="Picture5.gif" SCROLLING=NO NORESIZE MARGINWIDTH=1
MARGINHEIGHT=1>
        <FRAME SRC="Picture4.gif" SCROLLING=NO NORESIZE MARGINWIDTH=1
MARGINHEIGHT=1>
        <FRAME SRC="Picture3.gif" SCROLLING=NO NORESIZE MARGINWIDTH=1
MARGINHEIGHT=1>
    </FRAMESET>
</FRAMESET>
```

In this example I created a really big frame that I will use to display the main body of my site. Then I created a separate column that will serve as a table of contents for that frame. Finally, using a nested **<FRAMESET>** tag, I created three evenly divided frames along the bottom to display some simple graphics (perhaps advertisements or links to other sites).

Note how I make good use of all the attributes the **<FRAME>** tag offers to define how I expect each specific frame to behave. Figure 20.3 shows the final product after I married it to some HTML files that display graphics and text.

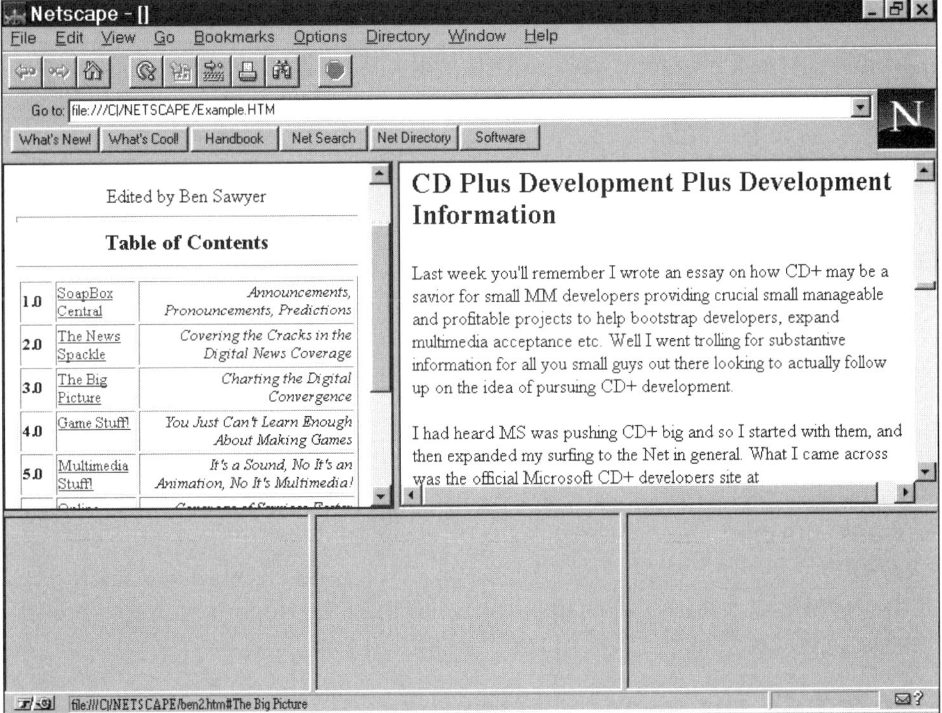

Figure 20.3 *The final product of our frame file.*

By now you're probably busily doodling away, creating all sorts of fanciful frame layouts. Let's move on and learn exactly how to manage links and other aspects that come into play when we go from a single browser window to one that uses any number of frames to create a dynamic site.

LINKING SYNTAX

We've covered how to set up some simple frame files, now comes the next step, reapplying all that we know about linking and URLs to a frame setting. This is really not a hard process; what is confusing isn't the syntax of the linking, but the shift to using more anchor-style tags and using a new attribute called **TARGET**.

Prior to frames, when a browser clicked on a hyperlink, Netscape responded by loading a new document into a window, or an entirely new browser was launched, giving you two complete windows. With frames, a click on the screen might load a new document, but instead of loading it into the whole browser window or launching a new window, it will update a section of the screen by loading the new document or graphic into a specific frame.

As you'll see in a moment, you can control how links activate frame updates in two different ways: *file specific* and *by using the **TARGET** attribute.*

File Specific

You can assign a document to be sent with the optional HTTP header "Window-target:[window_name]", and that document will always load into the named window. What this does is force the document to load in the specified windows and if the windows don't exist, Netscape will launch a new window and load the document there.

Using the TARGET Attribute

A document can be accessed via a targeted link. This requires the use of the **TARGET** attribute in conjunction with several key linking tags like the **<A HREF=**"filename"**></A>** tag. This approach requires you to make good use of the **NAME** attribute so Netscape knows to load the document into a specific frame.

MASTERING THE TARGET ATTRIBUTE

The **TARGET** attribute is the main resource Netscape offers to direct exactly which frame is updated by a specific user action. Remember how I said that even though **NAME** was an optional attribute, it's best to use it all the time? Well if you've been doing that, the **TARGET** attribute will use those names to tell Netscape which frame to update. **TARGET** uses the following basic syntax:

```
TARGET="window_name"
```

TARGET can be used in conjunction with several tags including the **<A>** and **<BASE>** tags.

TARGET with an <A> Tag

By now you're familiar with the basic anchor tag **<A HREF**="filename"**></A>**. Adding the **TARGET** attribute to this tag directs the hyperlink to load the document into a specific frame. Here's an example:

```
<A HREF="myhtml.html" TARGET="mywindow">update my window.</A>
```

TARGET in the <BASE> Tag

Let's assume you want to create a universal target. Thus, you'll want every link to load a URL into a specific frame without having to constantly give the target. In this case, you can use the **<BASE>** tag and establish your own default target that is only overridden by other specified targets. Here's an example:

```
<BASE TARGET="pictureframe">
```

This approach provides a good way to set up a list of pictures in one frame by using the **BASE** tag to tell Netscape to display any of the **<A HREF=** "/picture.gif"> links in a frame reserved for displaying them.

TARGET in the <FORM> Tag

When you activate a form using the **<FORM ACTION>** tag you can add **TARGET** to it to tell Netscape which frame gets the result from the submitted form:

```
<FORM ACTION="/process.cgi" TARGET="verification_window">
```

TARGET Magic

All **TARGET** names need to begin with an alphanumeric character to be valid, the only exception is for a series of constant **TARGET** names that Netscape calls "magic **TARGET** names."

All of these begin with an underscore (_) character. Other than magic **TARGET**s, all other **TARGET** names with non-alphanumeric beginnings will be ignored. Here is the breakdown and characteristics of each magic **TARGET**.

```
TARGET="_blank"
```

This target will cause the link to always be loaded in a new blank window.

```
TARGET="_self"
```

This target causes the link to always load in the same window the anchor was clicked in. You can use this when you want to override a **<BASE TARGET**="window_name"> tag that is referencing another frame when you want to update the current frame.

```
TARGET="_parent"
```

This target makes the link load in the immediate **<FRAMESET>** parent of this document. This defaults to acting like "_self" if the document has no parent.

```
TARGET="_top"
```

This target makes the link load in the full body of the window. This defaults to acting like "_self" if the document is already at the top. When you've got lots of frames that are nested in a delicate display, you can use this to return to the full window.

A Quick Linking Tutorial

Now that we've covered how to set up some simple frame files we're ready for the next step—applying everything that we've learned about linking and URLs to a frame setting.

A frame setting usually uses anchor-style tags, so my example is going to center around them. By using anchor-style tags we're able to allow the user to quickly jump through that document. This approach, shown in Figure 20.4, is used in a very common application using two frames, one for a main body document and the other to serve as a table of contents.

First, I'll show you the code for the frame file itself:

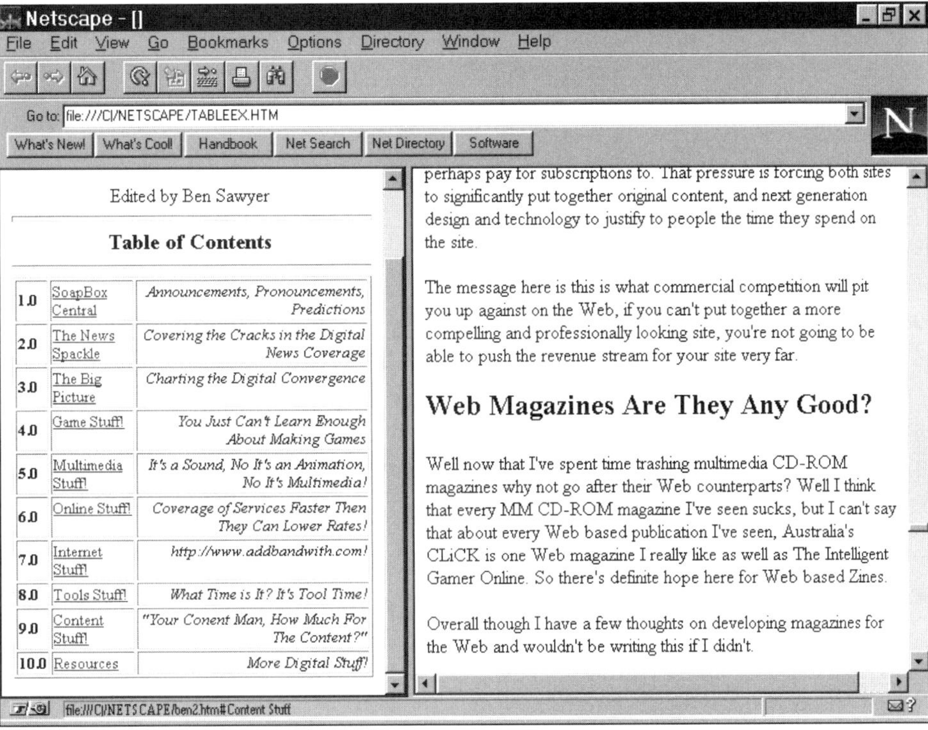

Figure 20.4 *A simple two frame document.*

```
<HTML>
   <HEAD>
        <TITLE>
            This Is a Simple Table of Contents Setup Using Frames
        </TITLE>
   </HEAD>
   <FRAMESET COLS="35%,65%">
       <FRAME SRC="TOC.HTM" NAME="TOC">
       <FRAME SRC="MAINBODY.HTM" NAME="MAIN BODY">
   </FRAMESET>
</HTML>
```

In the main body section we want to work through the key headings and place anchor tags in the file because the table of contents frame is going to help the user jump around the site:

```
<HTML>
   <HEAD>
        <TITLE>
            This Is a Simple Template for the Main body
        </TITLE>
```

```
    </HEAD>
    <BODY>
       <A NAME="Heading1">Heading One.</A>
          [BODY TEXT]
       <A NAME="Heading2">Heading Two.</A>
          [MORE BODY TEXT]
       <A NAME="Heading3">Heading Three.</A>
          [EVEN MORE BODY TEXT]
    </BODY>
</HTML>
```

Once we've set up the main body it's time to set up the table of contents HTML file. This is nothing more than a regular HTML file that references the file we want as well as the specific anchor we want to go to in that file. Before frames were introduced, most people used a technique of referencing an entirely new file or an anchor within the loaded file. With frames, you can reference both at the same time, and it's one of the little wrinkles of working with frames.

Let's look at some HTML instructions for creating a simple table of contents:

```
<HTML>
   <HEAD>
        <TITLE>
            This Is a Simple Table of Contents Using Frames.
        </TITLE>
   </HEAD>
   <BODY>
      <A HREF="/mainbody.html#Heading1" TARGET="MainBody">Heading One.</A></P>
      <A HREF="/mainbody.html#Heading2" TARGET="MainBody">Heading Two.</A></P>
      <A HREF="/mainbody.html#Heading3" TARGET="MainBody">Heading Three.</A></P>
   </BODY>
</HTML>
```

The **TARGET** tag is the key to referencing the frame you want. By creating your names in the beginning, you will be able to easily zip through your link coding.

DESIGNING WITH FRAMES

Remember when I said that the challenge in using frames is not in mastering the frame tags but in how you choose to use them? Well after we've covered a number of the design factors involved in using frames you'll have enough information to make the best use of them in your Web pages. I've organized a few key thoughts that you need to keep in mind when working with frames.

Optimizing Frame Layout

When I first started working with frames I created about a dozen different frame files, each with a different layout scheme. I've included those on the CD-ROM for you. What I was doing was seeing exactly how I could optimally use frames. Many of my first attempts had so many frames that it overwhelmed the site, so instead I began experimenting to figure out how could I create nice 6 or 7 frame layouts. I started by designing a few two frame sites, then a few three frame sites, and four frame, and so on.

I suggest you do the same. Take an hour to just create useful frame layouts, and then experiment with different resolutions and window sizes, as they can be key design issues.

The Resolution Matters

One thing to be aware of is that all people don't run Netscape in the same resolution or at the same window size. Be careful to test your frame setups at different resolutions. When I first started working with frames, I was designing in 1024×768, full screen. When I browsed at 800×600 the entire setup looked awful. Be careful to check at least 640×480, 800×600, and 1024×768 resolutions when designing with frames.

Window Size Matters

I don't always run Netscape at full window size. This also can affect the use of frames. If you design your frames using absolute pixel size you won't get the dynamic resizing results that you might want to offer people who don't always run their browser in full screen mode. In addition, the window size works just like resolution—the smaller the size the user makes his or her window the more it potentially messes up your gorgeous layout. After you've started constructing with frames and tested resolutions, be sure to resize windows below 640×480, or at wacky sizes like 600×1024, and see if that hurts the frame layout.

Test Your Graphics Carefully

When you work with frames you'll soon find that the available real estate for graphics starts shrinking fast. Make sure to double-check your graphics and their sizes to ensure that when they're used with frames they work well.

Test Constantly

Frames, as you've probably already guessed, take a lot of testing as you build your site, so make sure to test frequently. If you don't you may find yourself redoing all kinds of graphics and URL link codes at the end of your project.

Create <NOFRAMES> Sites Too

I know, the world should keep up with you, but it doesn't. Understand that people using all kinds of browsers may want to access your site and using the **<NOFRAMES>** syntax will at least warn them about your site's frames. You can go even further and create a simple greeting window which offers the user a frames or no-frames approach, just like some sites have a heavy graphics version and one that's light or free of graphics.

Beware of New Users

If your site attracts many new users or has been a no-frame site for a long time, understand that navigating with frames is very different and somewhat confusing for new users. While in the long run frames make it easier to navigate a well designed site, you might want to introduce frames slowly, over a period of time, to allow your users to get comfortable with them. Everyone will take frames for granted soon enough, but even for some veteran surfers, frames are an entirely new navigational feature.

LET'S REVIEW

We've covered quite a bit of ground in this chapter, but by now you can see that what I said at the beginning is true: With just a simple addition of a few tags and new attributes you can dynamically transform your Web pages in a multitude of ways.

Take this simple challenge: Surf to a few sites like Netscape's own home page (http://home.netscape.com) or CMP's TechWeb (http://www.techweb.com) and see for yourself. Both make excellent use of frames and offer a no-frames version. The difference between their frame and non-frame versions is so dramatic that they make the Net look like an entirely different world.

As you learn more about using frames I think you'll say the same thing. Frames provide the ability to create more informative sites and more professional displays, and therefore increase the flow of information from the Internet, which, after all, is what we're all looking for.

A Crash Course in JavaScript

Netscape's answer to adding dynamic interactive features to Web pages is JavaScript—a full-featured scripting language that is designed for power and ease of use.

Perhaps the most powerful addition to the new Netscape Navigator is JavaScript. Because of its simplicity and its availability to millions of Netscape users, JavaScript is rapidly becoming the language most Web page authors are using to add more interactivity to their Web pages.

Originally, JavaScript was named LiveScript by Netscape, whose initial goal was to create a simple scripting language that would allow Netscape users to customize their browser and create more interactive Web pages. Soon after, Sun Microsystems announced their flagship Java programming language, and interest in Java grew so quickly that Netscape decided to work closely with Sun and turn LiveScript into JavaScript. But as you'll soon discover in this chapter, JavaScript is *not* Java. The two languages share a similar syntax, but they are used to handle different types of tasks. JavaScript is designed for light Web duties, where a more hefty language like Java really isn't needed. With JavaScript you can process simple user actions (events), control how forms are processed, and add much more flexibility in the way HTML documents are displayed. In a sense, you can use JavaScript to turn Netscape into your own custom browser.

In this chapter we'll cover the basics of JavaScript so that you can add useful scripts to your HTML pages. As you'll see, there are a lot of simple things you can do with JavaScript that will completely change the look of your Web pages. We'll start by explaining what JavaScript is and why it was created. This will help you better understand how JavaScript differs from Java. Next, I'll show you how JavaScript works and what you can do with it. Then I'll try to cover some basics of scripting with JavaScript, including the underlying object model that JavaScript is based on. Keep in mind that this chapter is designed to be a crash course, so we'll move along as quickly as we can. In Appendix B, you'll find a useful, hands-on reference guide to the core of the JavaScript language.

THE ART OF SCRIPTING

When you approach a new language like JavaScript, the most important thing to understand is that it is not a traditional programming language—it is a *scripting* language. Programming languages are used to write complete programs that are compiled by special programs called *compilers* so that they can be run on a computer. Some common programming languages that you may have heard about or may be familiar with include Pascal, C, C++, and Java. Programs that you write with traditional languages like these are often written to handle big projects such as Web browsers, tax programs, word processors, database systems, and so on.

But the world of using computers and programming involves much more than big applications. Often, we have small problems to solve and big complex programming languages turn out to be overkill. For example, assume you are using a spreadsheet and you want to display in bold each cell that contains a dollar value. You could do this manually by highlighting each cell and selecting a menu option to display text in bold. If you were working on a large spreadsheet and up against a tight deadline, this approach would be very frustrating. Instead of performing the task manually, you could write a macro (which is really another name for a script), and have the task performed for you automatically. This, in a nutshell, is the benefit of scripts—they help you automate simple processes that you typically do by hand.

For years, many software applications like telecommunications programs, multimedia development tools, and so on, have provided scripting languages to help users better use the programs. Perhaps the most popular and successful scripting language of all time was HyperTalk—the language provided with Apple's innovative HyperCard software.

Why the Java Connection?

Soon after Netscape announced that their new Netscape browser would provide a scripting language adapted from Java, many developers and browser users wondered if this approach would best serve the needs of Netscape users. As it turns out, Java is based on a powerful object-oriented system that makes it well suited for using as the basis of a scripting language.

The two ways that you can add greater interactivity to your Web pages involve either embedding Java applets written in the Java language in your Web pages or using JavaScript to embed Java code directly into your pages. Since programming with the Java language is complex and would require an entire book, we won't cover it here. (But if you want to see how Java applets are added to Web pages, make sure you read Chapter 22.)

Most developers who use both Java and JavaScript describe JavaScript as a "stripped-down" version of Java. JavaScript instructions are placed directly in an HTML file using the **<SCRIPT> ... </SCRIPT>** tag pair. Here's a simple example:

```
<SCRIPT>
document.write("This message is displayed by a simple script")
</SCRIPT>
```

Now, compare this to a Java program which looks like something from another planet:

```
// Filename: Atom_ant.java
public class Atom_ant {
   public static void main (String args[]) {
      System.out.println("This message is displayed by a simple Java program ");
   }
}
```

The big difference between the two approaches is that the JavaScript code is interpreted by the Netscape browser and the Java program must be compiled and then run by a software program capable of running compiled Java code. If you have some programming experience with C++, you'll notice right off that the Java code looks similar to C++ syntax. Fortunately, to write useful JavaScripts you don't need to be an experienced programmer, because the JavaScript language is much simpler.

What Can You Do with JavaScript?

The main reason JavaScript was developed for Netscape was to allow Web page designers to extend the power of HTML documents in ways that would not be possible without a scripting language. Here's a list of the kinds of features you can incorporate into your Web pages:

- Display Web pages and links in different colors
- Validate data that users enter into forms used with Web pages
- Add and process custom interface objects like buttons, dialog boxes, text fields, checkboxes, and so on
- Perform all kinds of calculations and display the results

In addition to controlling how Web pages are displayed, you can use JavaScript to process events that occur while a user is accessing your Web pages. For example, when a user clicks on a link, Netscape determines the URL of the link and automatically loads a new Web page. With JavaScript you can "catch" an event like this and perform your own custom action.

CREATING OUR FIRST SCRIPT

Once you master the essentials of creating Web pages with HTML, you'll find that learning JavaScript is the next logical step. In fact, you probably have a list a mile long of features that you would like to add to your Web pages but you haven't been able to because of the limitations of HTML. As you start to write scripts, keep in mind that writing JavaScript code is very different than writing HTML tags. HTML is a *markup* language, not a *programming* language. When you write a tag like this

```
<CENTER>Center this text</CENTER>
```

you are specifying formatting operations. When you use JavaScript, on the other hand, you are writing instructions that are interpreted, which in turn cause actions or calculations to be performed.

Enough introduction already, let's write our first script and put it to work. Then, we'll explain the JavaScript language in a little more detail. Our first script uses a few JavaScript features to multiply two numbers together and display the results on a Web page. Here's everything you need:

```
<HTML>
<HEAD>
<TITLE>First JavaScript Example</TITLE>
```

```
<SCRIPT LANGUAGE="JavaScript">

<!-- Beginning of JavaScript Example ----

   function compute(i,j)
   {
        document.writeln
        document.write("The total is " + i*j)
        document.writeln
   }

// -- End of JavaScript code ---->

</SCRIPT>
</HEAD>
<BODY>
  <H1> Displays the total of two numbers </H1>
  <H3>
  <SCRIPT>
    <!-- Call the compute() function
   compute(10,5)
    // -->
  </SCRIPT>
   That's all folks!
</BODY>
</HTML>
```

To see this script in action, type all of the instructions shown here and save them in an HTML file. I've called mine Jstest.htm. Then, load the HTML file into Netscape. You should see the results shown in Figure 21.1.

First notice that everything is included between the **<HTML> ... </HTML>** tag pairs. The JavaScript code is included within the HTML instructions. The magic tag pair that tells Netscape that JavaScript code is being used is **<SCRIPT> ... </SCRIPT>**. In our case, we use the following format for the first **<SCRIPT>** tag:

```
<SCRIPT LANGUAGE="JavaScript">
```

In this case I am using the optional **LANGUAGE=** attribute, which tells Netscape which scripting language is being used. By default, Netscape assumes that all scripting code is JavaScript, so this attribute does not need to be included.

The first part of our HTML instructions defines a script that is a function that multiplies two number together. The name of the function is **compute()** and it allows two values to be passed to it. The function first prints two blank lines and then it outputs a message that looks something like this:

```
The total is 50
```

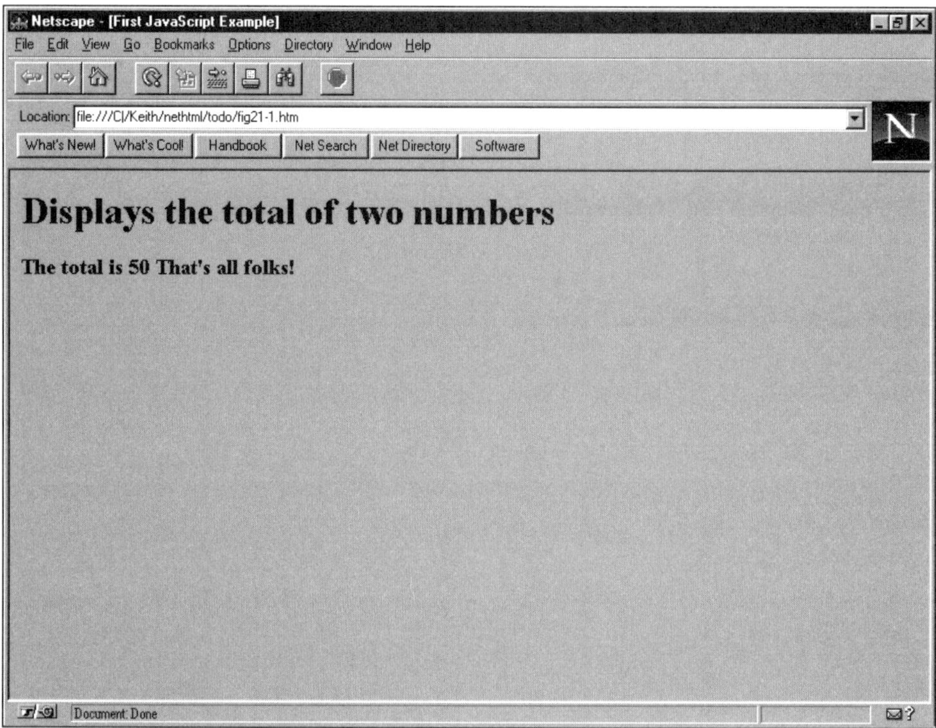

Figure 21.1 Running our first JavaScript example.

If you jump ahead for a moment you'll see that the body of our HTML file contains JavaScript instructions that look like this:

```
<SCRIPT>
   compute(10,5)
</SCRIPT>
```

This script "calls" the **compute()** function defined in the heading section of the HTML document and sends the values 10 and 5. In case you haven't realized it already, the secret ingredient that makes our JavaScript example work is objects. I'll explain the concept of objects in a little more detail in the next section, but for now you just need to know that an object can be a number of things including a window, frame, URL, document, form, button, and so on. Much of the JavaScript code you'll be writing involves manipulating objects in one way or another. For example, in our first script, I've used the built-in object called **document** that JavaScript provides for working with documents. Here's one example of how this object is used in our script:

```
document.write("The total is " + i*j)
```

In this case, the **document** object is used to call the **write()** method, which in turn writes a line of text to our HTML document. As you'll learn in this chapter, JavaScript provides a number of built-in objects and functions to help you write more useful scripts.

One of the keys to writing successful scripts is understanding both how HTML documents are processed by Netscape and where JavaScript code should be placed. If you look closely at our first script you'll see that the code that defines the **compute()** function is placed within the **<HEAD> ... </HEAD>** tags. When Netscape loads the HTML file, it will *not* try to execute the function definitions placed within these tags. If you look at the section of the HTML file between the **<BODY> ... </BODY>** tags, you'll find the actual JavaScript code that calls the **compute()** function.

Bulletproofing Your HTML Documents

The one disadvantage of adding JavaScripts to your HTML documents is that not all Web browsers can read and interpret JavaScript code. Fortunately, most Web surfers use Netscape, but you can't always count on everyone who comes to your Web site running the latest JavaScript-supported version. If someone tries to read an HTML file with a script-unaware browser, he or she might get a few surprises. In theory, Web browsers are suppose to ignore tags they don't support, such as **<SCRIPT> ... </SCRIPT>**. But if I were you, I wouldn't count on this.

To help you bulletproof your documents that use scripts, you can use the HTML comment feature, with a slight twist. In its basic format, comments are added to HTML documents as follows:

```
<B>Display this text in bold</B>
<!-- This is the start of a comment
<B>This text won't be displayed</B>
This is the end of the comment -->
<I>Display this text in italic</I>
```

The characters "<!--" tell a Web browser that the text that follows should be ignored until the "end of the comment" characters "-->" are encountered. This basic syntax can be used to enclose JavaScript statements so that Web browsers that don't understand JavaScript will ignore the unsupported commands. The trick is to place the // characters before the comment closure. This tells Netscape to still process the text that follows the **<SCRIPT>** tag as JavaScript code, but other browsers will skip over the instructions, because they will interpret the instructions as comments. The double slashes (//) are required to keep Netscape from interpreting the comment closing characters (-->) as JavaScript code. Here's an example of how this feature is used:

```
<SCRIPT LANGUAGE="JavaScript">

<!-- Beginning of JavaScript code ----
  document.write("Hello there")
//-->

</SCRIPT>
```

In reality, the HTML comment characters are ignored by a JavaScript-supported browser when they are used within the **<SCRIPT> ... </SCRIPT>** tags. Any text that is encountered within these tags is treated as JavaScript code. The only exception is the **//** characters, which indicate that a line of text should be treated as a comment in JavaScript.

JAVASCRIPT ESSENTIALS

Now that we've written our first script and quickly looked at how JavaScript instructions are placed in HTML files using the **<SCRIPT> ... </SCRIPT>** tag pair, let's move on and look at some of the key concepts behind the JavaScript language. The key to understanding JavaScript is quickly coming up to speed with the basic language elements, such as assignment statements and looping statements, and the four very special components of the JavaScript language: *objects*, *properties*, *methods*, and *events*.

The Basic JavaScript Language Statements

As I've mentioned already, JavaScript's syntax borrows a bit from the C/C++ languages. If you don't have any experience programming in either of these languages, you might find the syntax a little confusing at first. But once you get a few scripts under your belt, you'll quickly get the hang of things.

The basic elements of all programming languages are statements. These are the instructions you write to perform actions, make decisions, declare variables, assign values to variables, and so on. The basic statements you can write in JavaScript include:

Variable Declaration Statements

These types of statements are used to declare variables that you use in your scripts. You can think of a variable as a simple container that holds values that will later be used in a calculation. Here is an example of how a variable is declared:

```
var i = 10
```

In this case, **i** is declared as a variable and then it is assigned a value of 10. The variable can then be used in other JavaScript statements. Because JavaScript is a "loosely typed" language, you don't have to declare the type that will be assigned to a variable up front. You can assign a numeric value, a logical value (True or False), a string, or a null value. Later in this chapter I'll show you how to use variables with your scripts, and in Appendix B I'll provide detailed guidelines for naming, declaring, and using variables.

Assignment Statements

These types of statements are used to assign values to properties and are variables that are predefined by JavaScript or have values that you declare in your scripts. Here is an example:

```
i = i * 20
```

In this case, **i** is assigned the results of the expression **i * 20**. Since we previously defined **i** as a variable and assigned it an initial value of 10, the results of this expression would be 200. This is the new value that is assigned to **i** in this assignment statement.

Conditional Statements

These are statements that are used to choose between two or more courses of action. Conditional statements allow programs to make logical decisions and then branch depending on the outcome of the decision. The basic conditional statement used in JavaScript is the if-then statement, as shown in this example:

```
if (i < min || i > max)
{
document.write("the variable is out of range")
}
```

Here, the variable **i** is compared with the variables **min** and **max** to see if it is less than or greater than, respectively. If it is, the statement **document.write("the variable is out of range")** is executed.

Looping Statements

These are statements used to repeat actions. They are great for things like performing mathematical operations, reading and processing data from forms, and so on. Here's an example:

```
for (var i = 0; i < max; I++ )
{
document.write("the value of i is " + i)
}
```

In this case, the loop repeats until the variable **i** is equal to the value stored in **max**. Each time the loop repeats, the value of **i** is displayed.

Function Definitions

As I demonstrated in our first script, JavaScript allows us to define our own functions for performing specialized tasks. Usually, you create functions for operations that you plan on performing over and over. To refresh your memory, here's the function we defined earlier:

```
function compute(i,j)
{
     document.writeln
     document.write("The total is " + i*j)
     document.writeln
}
```

When a function like this is defined, it is not actually executed; that comes later when the function is "called." In a sense, a function definition serves as a placeholder for instructions you wish to use later.

Function Calls

Function calls tell JavaScript to execute the instructions listed. For example, when a statement like this is encountered:

```
compute(10,5)
```

Each line of instruction in the **compute()** is executed one at a time.

Understanding Functions

We'll be using functions a lot in the examples we write in this chapter, so let's take a moment to make sure we understand the fundamentals of functions. Functions are self-contained blocks of code that are called upon either by JavaScript code or by various events triggered by actions in the browser or on forms in the browser. Functions can optionally accept and return values as well. Functions are different than simple JavaScript instructions because they begin with the word **function**. Using this keyword defines a set of scripting instructions that sit in the background until the function name is called by an event, a script, or another function. To write a function in JavaScript is simple. Some functions may take a while to write, but the overall structure of a function is very basic.

A function in JavaScript is made up of a specific function keyword followed by the name of the function and a parameter list in parentheses, which details all the variables that the function requires to work.

Let's quickly look at a simple function to understand the basics of writing our own:

```
function askuser_age (username)
{
stringtoprint=username+" What is your age?"
document.write("<B>"+stringtoprint+"</B>")
}
```

This function takes a string value, in this case the name of the user, and then displays the question asking the user his or her age using the **write()** method. Remember, just because you've written a function doesn't mean it runs. You have to call upon it for it to actually execute. The function I've written is a simple function with one parameter. You can actually have lots of parameters, and they can be numbers, strings, and even complex objects.

Functions are usually defined within the **<HEAD> ... </HEAD>** tag pair of an HTML document. You can define as many functions as you like, as long as each function has a different name. By placing your function definitions within the heading section, you can ensure that they can be called by any script, form, or event used in the body section of an HTML document. Since the **<HEAD>** section always is processed before the **<BODY>** section, you'll be certain that Netscape knows about your functions before you try to use them. Even though a function can only be defined once, you can call it as many times as you want.

Here's a simple function that adds up three numbers and returns an answer:

```
<HTML>
<HEAD>
<TITLE>Java Function Example</TITLE>
<SCRIPT LANGUAGE="JavaScript">

<!-- Beginning of JavaScript code ----
```

```
   function compute(obj)
   {
   var a=parseFloat(obj.Number1.value)
   var b=parseFloat(obj.Number2.value)
   var c=parseFloat(obj.Number3.value)
   obj.Answer.value=a+b+c
   }

// -- End of JavaScript code ---->

</SCRIPT>
</HEAD>
<BODY>
<FORM NAME="MYFORM">

Number 1:<INPUT TYPE=text NAME="Number1" SIZE=20 ><P>
Number 2:<INPUT TYPE=text NAME="Number2" SIZE=20 ><P>
Number 3:<INPUT TYPE=text NAME="Number3" SIZE=20 ><P>

<INPUT TYPE="button" VALUE="Click Me" onClick="compute(this.form)"><P>
Answer:<INPUT TYPE=text NAME="Answer" SIZE=20 ><P>
</FORM>

</BODY>
</HTML>
```

The Web page created by this example is shown in Figure 21.2. In this example, I am introducing a useful feature we haven't seen yet—I've combined JavaScript code with an HTML form. The form is used to gather data from the user and the JavaScript code is used to process the data. This is a common use of applying JavaScript code.

Notice again that the function is defined in the heading section of the HTML document. But this time, the body of the document does not contain an explicit call to the **compute()** function. The call to this function is hidden in the HTML code that defines the form. Here is the specific line of code:

```
<INPUT TYPE="button" VALUE="Click Me" onClick="compute(this.form)"><P>
```

When the user clicks on the "Click Me" button, the **compute()** function will be called. It will pass the information gathered from the form—the three numbers that the user types in. The **compute()** function will then process these numbers, add them together, and return the sum of the numbers. The result is returned using a statement that might look a little unusual to you at the moment:

```
obj.Answer.value=a+b+c
```

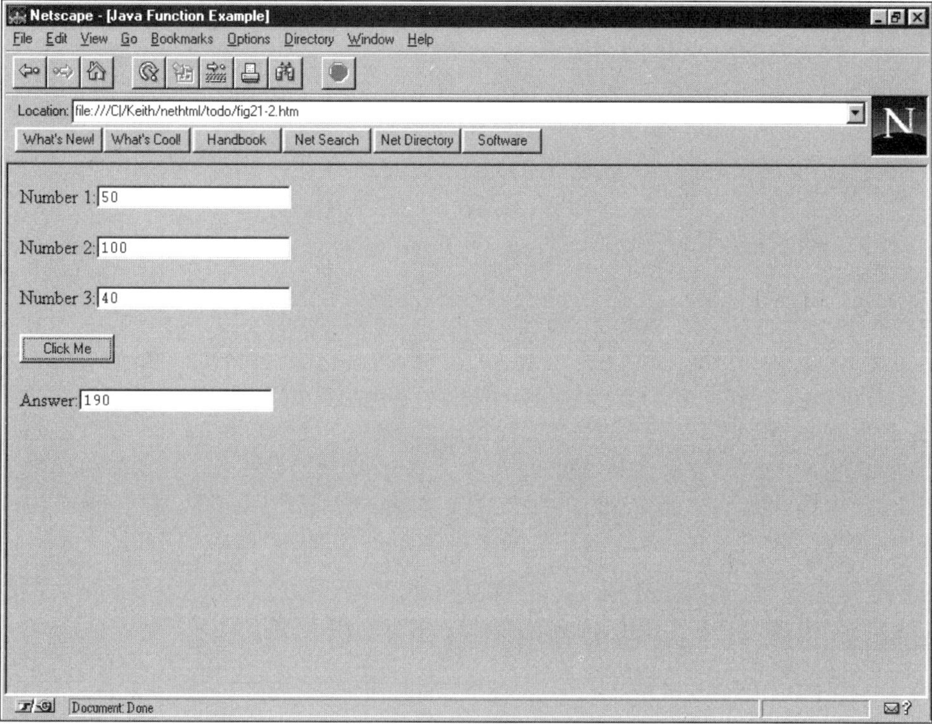

***Figure 21.2** Using a function to calculate values input from a form.*

Here, the first component, **obj**, is an object that references the form. **Answer** is the component that is used to access **value**, which is the property that stores the result of the function. By placing the result of the function in this property, the HTML code can later access it and display the result:

```
Answer:<INPUT TYPE=text NAME="Answer" SIZE=20 ><P>
```

We just explored one way in which functions can be used to process data input from a form and return a result that can later be used within the form. And if you recall from the first script we wrote in this chapter, functions can be directly called from the body of an HTML document. You can also write functions that return a value by using the **return** statement. Here's an example:

```
function compute(a,b,c)
{
   return (a+b+c)
}
```

You could then call this function in the body section of an HTML document by using a statement like this:

```
document.write("The result is " + compute(1,2,3))
```

A Function or a Method

When you first start to program with JavaScript you'll notice that the terms *function* and *method* are often used interchangeably. The term method comes from languages like Smalltalk, C++, and Java, which are object-oriented in nature. Because JavaScript is also object-based, functions are often called methods. The basic idea is that methods are used to define the behavior of objects. For example, the **document** object provides a method named **write()** which determines how document objects should display text on the screen. As I begin to introduce the object-oriented features of JavaScript, I'll start to use the method terminology to refer to functions that have been defined for objects.

General Rules to Follow in Writing JavaScript Statements

As you begin to write basic JavaScript statements, there are some general rules that you must follow so that your statements won't be rejected by Netscape:

JavaScript is case sensitive. When you refer to built-in objects, properties, and methods (or ones that you define), you must use the proper case. For example, to reference the **document** object, you must use a statement like **document.write("hello")** and not **Document.write("hello")**.

Grouping statements. JavaScript statements should be placed one per line. If you put multiple statements on a single line, each statement must be separated by a semicolon as shown here:

```
document.write("hello"); document.write("<P>")
```

Some statements are grouped together as part of a *block of statements* and in this case the curly braces are used to specify the beginning of a block ({) and the end (}). Here's an example:

```
If (i < min || i > max) {
  document.write("the variable is out of range")
  document.write("the value of i is" + i)
}
```

If you have statements that won't fit on a single line, you must use the underscore character (_) as a continuation indicator:

```
if (i < min || i > max_
  Num) document.write("the variable is out of range")
```

Proper comment syntax. JavaScript supports two types of comments: single line comments that begin with the // characters and multi-line comments that begin with the characters /* and end with the characters */. Here's an example of each style:

```
// This is a single line comment

/* this is a very very very very very very long comment that
   takes up multiple lines */
```

In each case, the text after the comment start symbols is ignored.

Using dot notation. JavaScript uses *dot notation* to separate objects and identifiers from properties and function (method) names. For example, in the following statement the dot notation is used to assign a value to the background color property (**bgColor**) of the **document** object:

```
document.bgColor="yellow"
```

JavaScript Objects

As we learned in our first script, objects are the basic JavaScript building blocks. There are two types of objects you will encounter in JavaScript. The first are *built-in* objects provided by Netscape Navigator and the JavaScript language. Some of the standard objects include:

- navigator
- window
- document
- form
- button
- checkbox

We'll look at some of these useful objects a little later in this chapter. The second type of objects are *custom objects* you create using JavaScript code. For example, if you were processing strings of text in a script you could create a string object called *personname*.

Objects have *properties* that describe them. For example, the **document** object I introduced earlier has a **fontcolor** property that tells Netscape what the color of the document's text is. Objects also have *methods*, which specify the commands they can perform. For example, the **document** object has a method named **write()** which allows you to print text or HTML code to a document. Up until now we've be calling these types of routines functions, but the object-oriented terminology is methods. Finally, objects can trigger *events* that you can write responses for. An event is an action that occurs, such as a mouse click, or a window activity like scrolling. As an example, JavaScript provides a built-in **button** object that has an event called **OnClick** which is triggered whenever the user clicks on a button in a Web page.

You can think of objects as types of matter in the JavaScript universe. *Properties* decide what the matter looks like and how it behaves, *methods* are the actions that objects can perform, and *events* are the actions that trigger methods to be called.

Properties

Objects can have properties or characteristics that you can set. For instance, when writing a **document** object you might have a property for it like **bgcolor** (background color). When you set this property, the background color of the document in the browser changes. Just as you can create your own objects, you can also create your own properties for those objects. Because of the large assortment of properties that are available, some JavaScript users like to call Java a properties-based language. The complete set of JavaScript properties are listed in Appendix B. You'll find a description of each property along with the name of the object the property is assigned to.

Methods

Methods are a fancy type of function that work specifically with an object. In JavaScript certain objects allow you to do certain things via methods. For example, you can use a statement like this to have the **document** object call the **write()** method to display specified text on the screen:

```
document.write("Here's a test message")
```

Some methods such as **write()** are built into JavaScript, but you can also create your own by using the function notation that we presented earlier when we wrote our first script. Later in this chapter, I'll show you how to create your own objects and custom methods.

Events

Events are actions that take place in Netscape. For example, you might click on a button or type in some text, which in turn causes an event to occur. Events are the primary launching pad of JavaScript routines. Learning what the different events are and then thinking up programming responses to them is a key part of learning JavaScript.

JavaScript events take place mostly in the forms portion of your HTML code. Appendix B provides a description of the key events that are supported by JavaScript.

JAVASCRIPT OBJECTS AND HTML

To use JavaScript properly, it is important to have a basic understanding of how Netscape processes HTML tags and performs layout tasks. This involves transforming the plain text directives of HTML into a graphical display on your computer. Generally speaking, layout happens sequentially, that is, Netscape starts with the <**HEAD**> tag in an HTML document, then goes to the top of the <**BODY**> and works its way down, figuring out how to output information to the screen as it goes.

Because of this "top-down" processing system, JavaScript only knows about HTML that it has encountered. For example, suppose you define a form with a couple of text input elements:

```
<FORM NAME="statform">
<input type = "text" name = "username" size = 20>
<input type = "text" name = "userage" size = 3>
```

These form elements are represented to Netscape as JavaScript objects, including **document.statform.username** and **document.statform.userage**. Once these objects have been encountered, you can use them anywhere after the form is defined. For example, you could display the value of these objects in a script after the form definition:

```
<SCRIPT>
document.write(document.statform.username.value)
document.write(document.statform.userage.value)
</SCRIPT>
```

However, if you tried to do this before the form definition, you would get an error, since the objects don't exist yet according to Netscape. Likewise, once layout has occurred, setting a property value does not affect its value or its appearance. For example, suppose you have a document title defined:

```
<TITLE>My JavaScript Page</TITLE>
```

This is reflected in JavaScript as the value of the property **document.title**. Once Netscape has displayed this in layout (in this case, in the title bar of the Navigator window), you cannot change the value in JavaScript. Therefore, if you have the following script later in your HTML document

```
document.title = "The New Improved JavaScript Page"
```

it will not change the value of **document.title** nor affect the appearance of the page, nor will it generate an error.

UNDERSTANDING THE OBJECT HIERARCHY

To fully understand how to use objects with JavaScript, you'll need to know the organization of JavaScript's object model. Fortunately, the object model is based on a simple hierarchy that reflects the basic structure of how Netscape works and how HTML documents are processed. Windows contain all other objects, including documents, which in turn contain forms, links, and anchors. Understanding which objects spawn other objects helps you to properly address these objects in your JavaScript code. Figure 21.3 shows the basic hierarchy, as laid out by Netscape.

To refer to specific properties of these objects, you must specify the object name and all its ancestors. Both objects and their properties are referenced using the dot notation I introduced earlier. For example, this statement references the **alinkColor** property for the **document** object:

```
document.alinkColor
```

Now, if you have a textbox named **RESULT** on a form named **MyForm** in the current document and you want to set its value, you would need to use a statement like this:

```
document.MyForm.RESULT.value="Hello World!"
```

In this case, the starting object is **document**. Next comes the form object, **MyForm**, followed by the textbox object named **RESULT**. Referencing a form named MyForm in a document in a window named MyWindow is done using a syntax like this:

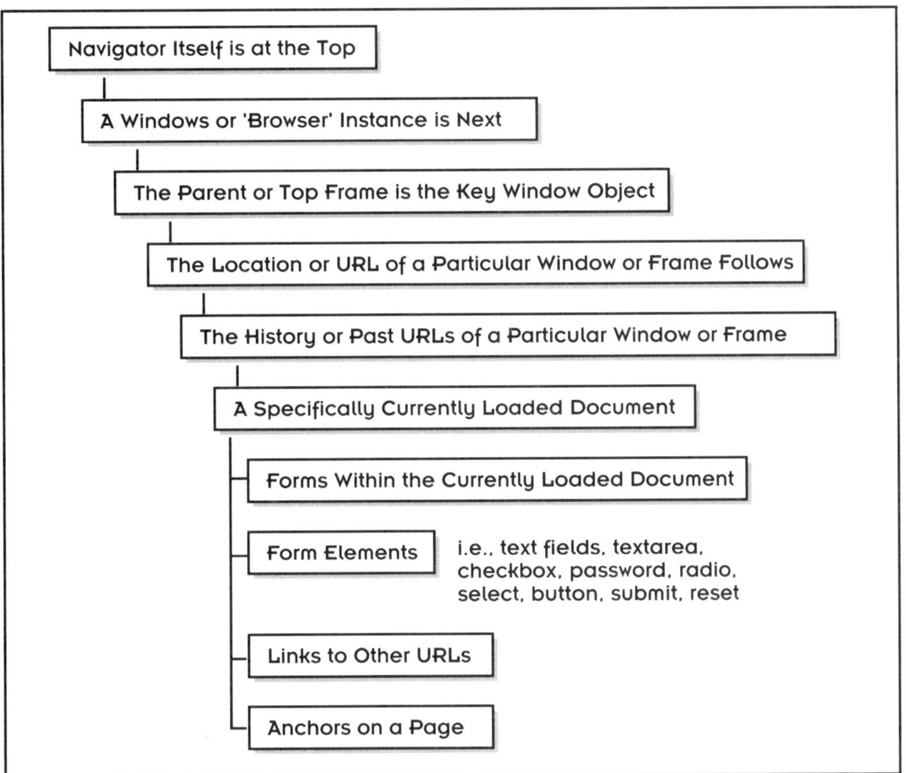

Figure 21.3 *The basic hierarchy of the JavaScript object model.*

```
MyWindow.document.MyForm
```

Make sure you keep the hierarchy intact, otherwise your code won't work. As you look over the example code throughout this chapter, note how I address objects using this scheme.

A Quick Look at the JavaScript Objects

The reason why objects work so well with Netscape is because Netscape is designed from the ground up with objects in mind. Whenever you perform a basic operation, like loading an HTML page, it involves the use of a number of objects, such as at least one window object to display the page, a location object to display the current URL, a history object to keep track of the previously visited URLs, and at least one document object.

As you've seen by looking at Figure 21.3, the top level object is the **Navigator** object. This object isn't that useful to us because it only supports a few properties for allowing us to determine information like the name, version, and code name of the browser application. We won't be writing any scripts in this chapter that use the **Navigator** object, but the properties supported by it are presented in Appendix B.

Working our way down the chain of command in the object hierarchy, we come to the **window** object. This object serves as the base reference point for the document it contains, as well as for the URL, history of previously visited URLs, and so on. The organization looks like this:

window: The top-level client-side object; contains properties that apply to the entire window.

child windows: Windows created by frames.

location: The object that provides properties pertaining to the current URL.

history: The object that provides properties pertaining to past URLs the user has visited.

document: The object that provides properties pertaining to the content in the currently browsed file, such as title, background color, and current active form items.

In writing JavaScript code, you typically do not need to reference a **window** object, since all **document** objects are, by default, contained within a **window** object. (If this sounds a little confusing, just remember that all HTML documents are displayed within a window.) This means that when you write a statement like this

```
document.write("Display this simple message")
```

you are really stating:

```
window.document.write("Display this simple message")
```

To continue our exploration of JavaScript objects, let's spend a little more time looking at the basic features of **window**, **document**, and **form** objects.

Introducing the window Object

Windows are important objects because they serve as the parents for all other objects in Netscape. In addition, you can use new **window** objects to create new displays and pop-up dialog buttons for your JavaScript programs.

A **window** object can be controlled by accessing and setting properties, of which there are seven. These properties are described in more detail in

Appendix B. In general, you'll find useful properties for determining how windows should be displayed and organized. Some examples include a status property that enables you to create messages in the status bar that's at the bottom of all client windows. You might already have seen JavaScript programs that use this feature to scroll messages across the bottom of the screen.

Another useful property called **frames** allows you to set and access all of the frames used in a frameset. The frames are stored in a frames array, which contains an entry for each child frame in a window. For example, if a window contains three child frames, these frames are referenced as **window.frames[0]**, **window.frames[1]**, and **window.frames[2]**.

The methods provided for processing **window** objects are listed in Table 21.1. Three of them are used for displaying dialog boxes, two are used for opening and closing windows, and the other two are provided for controlling the timing of actions.

Table 21.1 *The Methods Provided for Processing the window Object*

Method	Explanation	Syntax
alert()	Creates an Alert dialog box with the string message.	window.alert("String")
close()	Closes the referred to window.	window.close()
confirm()	Creates a Confirm dialog box with OK and Cancel buttons plus the current message.	window.confirm("String")
open()	Opens a new window.	window.open("URL", "windowName", ["windowFeatures"])
prompt()	Creates a Prompt dialog box showing a message. Gives user a box to reply. inputDefault may be used to give a suggested answer.	window.prompt(String, [inputDefault])
setTimeout()	This command will execute the JavaScript code contained in the string in whatever number of milliseconds defined in msec.	window.setTimeout ("String",msec)
clearTimeout()	This command will clear the current setTimeout command. timeoutID is a variable that uniquely identifies the setTimeout command you want to stop.	window.cleartime (timeoutID)

Using the document Object

The **document** object is used so often because the majority of JavaScript code is written to respond to activities that take place in the current document. As you may have seen from some of the demonstration code that I've been using, the document object is often used in conjunction with the **write()** and **writeln()** methods to generate HTML code on the fly. The **document** object also provides useful **onLoad()** and **onUnload()** event handlers to perform functions when a user first loads and exits a page.

When you work with the **document** object, you will have a range of additional objects and properties to consider. As I stated above, almost everything that is a unique aspect of the current document is an object waiting to be used. That means that if you have a form with a set of buttons and text boxes on it, the form, the buttons, and the text boxes are all objects contained within the document.

Let's start by looking at some HTML that shows different document attributes:

```
<HTML>
<HEAD>
<TITLE>Java Function Example</TITLE>
<SCRIPT LANGUAGE="JavaScript">

<!-- Beginning of JavaScript Applet ————————


mystring="This is a test of string methods! <P>"
document.write("Here is a simple test of various string methods.<P>")
document.write("For purposes of this test mystring=This is a test of string
methods!<P><HR><P>")

document.write("document.write(mystring.big())=")
document.write(mystring.big())

document.write("document.write(mystring.blink())=")
document.write(mystring.blink())

document.write("document.write(mystring.bold()))=")
document.write(mystring.bold())

document.write("document.write(mystring.charAt(3))=")
document.write(mystring.charAt(3))

document.write("document.write(mystring.fixed())=")
document.write(mystring.fixed())

document.write("document.write(mystring.fontcolor('Aqua'))=")
document.write(mystring.fontcolor("Aqua"))
```

```
document.write("document.write(mystring.big())=")
document.write(mystring.big())

document.write("document.write(mystring.italics())=")
document.write(mystring.italics())

document.write("document.write(mystring.lastIndexOf('test'))=")
document.write(mystring.lastIndexOf("test")+"<P>")

document.write("document.write(mystring.link('http://www.coriolis.com'))=")
document.write(mystring.link("http://www.coriolis.com"))

document.write("document.write(mystring.small())=")
document.write(mystring.small())

document.write("document.write(mystring.strike())=")
document.write(mystring.strike())

document.write("document.write(mystring.sub())=")
document.write(mystring.sub())

document.write("document.write(mystring.sup())=")
document.write(mystring.sup())

document.write("document.write(mystring.toLowerCase())=")
document.write(mystring.toLowerCase())

document.write("document.write(mystring.toUpperCase())=")
document.write(mystring.toUpperCase())


// -- End of JavaScript code ---->

</SCRIPT>
</HEAD>
<BODY>


</BODY>
</HTML>
```

When Netscape processes this HTML code, it soon encounters the **<BODY>** tag. And guess what this tag does? It tells Netscape to create a **document** object. Any JavaScript instructions placed within the **<SCRIPT> ... </SCRIPT>** tags that reference the **document** object will by default access the window the document is displayed in.

After the HTML creates a simple form it uses a few lines of JavaScript code to interact with the buttons and the text boxes. For this example, notice the process I use to reference the various objects in the document in the JavaScript code. The sequence of **document.testform.button** is dictated by Navigator's object hierarchy, which I introduced earlier.

A Note about document Objects

The properties provided for **document** objects are largely content-dependent. That is, they are created based on the content that you put in the document. For example, a **document** object includes a property for each form and each anchor used in the document.

Netscape always uses just one **document** object for an HTML file, and this object serves as the base level for all of the form, link, and anchor objects used in the page. To help you process **document** objects, Netscape provides 13 properties and 5 methods. The properties are presented in Appendix B and the methods are listed in Table 21.2. The three main types of activities you can control with the properties include setting and accessing document colors, setting and accessing document status information (title, last modified, and so on), and setting and accessing content-related information, such as forms, links, and anchors.

The form Object

Any time you create a form using the **<FORM> ... </FORM>** HTML tags a **form** object is created by Netscape. The name of the form is assigned using the **<FORM NAME="newform">** option. By doing so, you create a JavaScript object named **newform** that you can easily reference in your JavaScript code.

When you have more than one form, you can refer to them either by name or in an array format using the syntax **document.forms[0]**, **document.forms[1]**, and so on. Each number refers to a different form in a document with 0 being the topmost form and so on down the line until you get to the last form on the page. JavaScript works with all elements in each form in a similar fashion.

JavaScript provides five properties for **form** objects, but only one method—**submit()**. The properties are provided to help you process forms and determine how form components, such as checkboxes, radio buttons, and so on, should be handled. The **submit()** method performs the same operation as the one performed when the user clicks on a Submit button on a form—it transmits the form's contents to a server so that the form can be processed.

Table 21.2 The Methods Provided for Processing document Objects

Method	Explanation	Syntax
clear()	Clears the current document.	document.clear()
close()	Closes the document.	document.close()
open()	Opens the referred to mimeType in the document.	document.open (["mimeType"])
write()	Writes a string or text to the document.	document.write("string")
writeln()	Writes a string or text to the document.	document.writeln("string")

USING OTHER BUILT-IN JAVASCRIPT OBJECTS

JavaScript itself has other lower-level built-in objects, like buttons and checkboxes, that you can use in your HTML documents. The ones that I found most useful are the **string**, **Math**, and **Date** objects. Learning to work with these built-in objects and their methods is a key part of working with JavaScript.

The string Object

Whenever you create a string variable in JavaScript it becomes a **string** object. You can manipulate the contents of the **string** object using various methods and properties that work directly on and with string values in JavaScript. Table 21.3 presents the complete set of **string** methods and the properties are provided in Appendix B.

The Math Object

The **Math** object is a built-in special JavaScript object that gives you access to various special properties and methods for mathematical operations. For example, you can use the PI property of the math object to calculate the circumference of a circle using the following simple code:

```
diameter=5
circumfrence=diameter*Math.PI
```

Table 21.4 presents the various **Math** object methods that you can use in your code.

Let's write some JavaScript code to help you see how some of the math methods are used:

Table 21.3 The Methods Provided for Processing string Objects

Method	Explanation	Syntax
anchor()	This is used to create an anchor. The text in mystring is the text you want highlighted (the user to see) in the document.	document.write(mystring. anchor("contents_anchor"))
big()	Causes string to appear as big text.	document.write(mystring.big())
blink()	Causes string to appear as blinking text.	document.write(mystring.blink())
bold()	Causes string to appear as bold text.	document.write(mystring.bold())
charAt()	Retrieves the character at a specified position in a string.	document.write(mystring. charAt(3))
fixed()	Causes a string to be displayed in fixed-pitch font.	document.write(mystring.fixed())
fontcolor()	Causes string to appear in the color specified.	document.write(mystring. fontcolor(color))
fontsize()	Causes string to appear in the specified font size.	document.write(fontsize (3)
indexOf()	Looks for the first instance of searchValue (a string) in your current string. The string is searched forwards. fromIndex is a number that denotes where to start from and if omitted the search starts from the first character in the string.	document.write(mystring. IndexOf(searchValue, [fromIndex]))
italics()	Causes string to appear as italic text.	document.write(mystring. italics())
lastIndexOf()	Looks for the last instance of searchValue (a string) in your current string. The string is searched backwards. fromIndex is a number that denotes where to start from and if omitted the search starts from the last character in the string.	document.write(mystring. lastIndexOf(searchValue, [fromIndex]))
link()	This is used to create a link to text you might write to the document. URL is a string denoting the specific URL and the text in mystring is the text you want the user to see in the document.	document.write(mystring. link(URL))
small()	Causes string to appear as small text.	document.write(mystring.small())

Continued

Table 21.3 The Methods Provided for Processing string Objects (Continued)

Method	Explanation	Syntax
strike()	Causes string to appear as striked text.	document.write(mystring.strike())
sub()	Causes string to appear as subscript text.	document.write(mystring.sub())
subString()	This method is used to refer to only a portion of a string. indexA and indexB are two numbers, 0 to stringlength-1, which denote the specific section of the string to refer to.	Subsetstring=mystring.subString(indexA, indexB)
sup()	Causes string to appear as superscript text.	document.write(mystring.sup())
toLowerCase()	Causes string to be converted to lowercase text.	document.write(mystring.toLowerCase())
toUpperCase()	Causes string to be converted to uppercase text.	document.write(mystring.toUpperCase())

Table 21.4 The Methods Provided for Processing Math Objects

Method	Explanation	Syntax
abs()	Returns the absolute value of a number.	Math.abs(number)
acos()	Returns the arc cosine (in radians) of a number.	Math.acos(number)
asin()	Returns the arc sine (in radians) of a number.	Math.asin(number)
atan()	Returns the arc tangent (in radians) of a number.	Math.atan(number)
ceil()	Returns the least integer greater than or equal to a number.	Math.ceil(number)
cos()	Returns the cosine of a number.	Math.cos(number)
exp()	Returns enumber, where number is the argument, and e is Euler's constant, the base of the natural logarithms.	Math.exp(number)
floor()	Returns the greatest integer less than or equal to a number.	Math.floor(number)
log()	Returns the natural logarithm (base e) of a number.	Math.log(number)
max()	Returns the greater of two numbers.	Math.max(number1, number2)
min()	Returns the lesser of two numbers.	Math.min(number1, number2)

Continued

Table 21.4 *The Methods Provided for Processing Math Objects (Continued)*

Method	Explanation	Syntax
pow()	Returns base to the exponent power, that is, base exponent.	Math.pow(number)
random()	Returns a pseudo-random number between zero and one. This method is available on Unix platforms only.	Math.random()
round()	Returns the value of a number rounded to the nearest integer.	Math.round (number)
sin()	Returns the sine of a number.	Math.sin(number)
sqrt()	Returns the square root of a number.	Math.sqrt(number)
tan()	Returns the tangent of a number.	Math.tan(number)

```
<HTML>
<HEAD>
<TITLE>Java Function Example</TITLE>
</HEAD>
<BODY>
<SCRIPT LANGUAGE="JavaScript">

<-- Beginning of JavaScript code ----

var number1=-12
var number2=36
var number3=5.7845
var number4=140

document.write("The absolute value of "+number1+" is:"+Math.abs(number1)+"<P>")
document.write("The arc cosine of "+number4+" is:"+Math.acos(number4)+"<P>")
document.write("The arc sine of "+number4+" is:"+Math.asin(number4)+"<P>")
document.write("The arc tangent of "+number4+" is:"+Math.atan(number4)+"<P>")
document.write("The least integer greater than "+number3+"
is:"+Math.ceil(number3)+"<P>")

document.write("The cosine of "+number4+" is:"+Math.cos(number4)+"<P>")
document.write("The Euler's constant of "+number4+"
is:"+Math.exp(number4)+"<P>")
document.write("The Least inbteger lesser than "+number3+"
is:"+Math.floor(number3)+"<P>")
document.write("The natural logarithm of "+number2+"
is:"+Math.log(number2)+"<P>")

document.write("The larger value of "+number1+" & "+number3+"
is:"+Math.max(number1,number3)+"<P>")
document.write("The lesser value of "+number1+" & "+number3+"
is:"+Math.min(number1,number3)+"<P>")

document.write("The rounded value of "+number3+" is:"+Math.round(number3)+"<P>")
document.write("The sine of "+number4+" is:"+Math.sin(number4)+"<P>")
```

```
document.write("The square root of "+number2+" is:"+Math.sqrt(number2)+"<P>")
document.write("The tangent value of "+number4+" is:"+Math.tan(number4)+"<P>")

// -- End of JavaScript code ———— -->

</SCRIPT>
</BODY>

</HTML>
```

The Web page created by this JavaScript code is shown in Figure 21.4. Notice that it displays the results of a number of calculations. Our script starts by declaring four variables; three of the variables are assigned integer values and the other variable is assigned a floating point value. Because JavaScript is a loosely typed language, we can write expressions that perform calculations using both integer and floating point values. For example, in this statement we determine if one of the variables that stores an integer value is larger than the variable that stores the floating point value:

```
document.write("The larger value of "+number1+" & "+number3+"
is:"+Math.max(number1,number3)+"<P>")
```

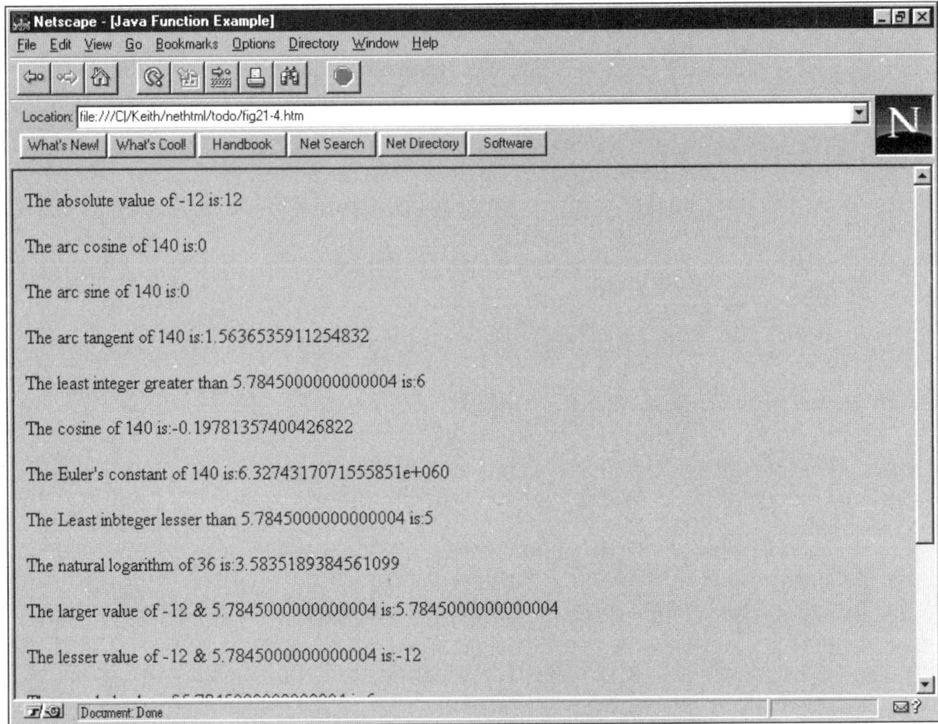

Figure 21.4 *A Web page that uses various methods from the **Math** object.*

The Date Object

Dates are very important in JavaScript and the Web in general. That's why JavaScript has a **Date** object. This object and its associated methods (the Date object has no properties) gives you an enormous range of flexibility and power when working with dates in JavaScript.

JavaScript handles dates very similarly to Java. The two languages have many of the same Date methods, and both languages store dates as the number of milliseconds since January 1, 1970 00:00:00.

You create a date object in JavaScript by initiating a variable using various **Date()** methods such as:

```
DateToday=new Date()
```

This simple statement sets the variable **DateToday** to the current date on the local server the document resides on. The **Date()** object can also take values which it assigns to a variable. For example:

```
MyBirthDate=new Date("June 25, 1971")
```

This simple statement sets the variable MyBirthDate equal to the date in the quotes. The example used a string method in the form of "Month day, year hours:minutes:seconds".

Note: If you omit hours, minutes, or seconds, the value will be set to zero.

You can also use a series of integer values in the order of year, month, day, hour, minute, seconds. For example, the same statement from above using this syntax would look like:

```
MyBirthDate=new Date(71,5,25).
```

Note: My birthday is actually in June, so why did I write 5 in the month part of the above statement? Because for months, the date object uses 0 for January, so every month is one number less than you normally would think. It does the same with hours (0-23) and days (0-6 for days of the week), but not with years or days of the month. Don't ask me why it works this way.

For the methods shown in Table 21.5, assume that the object "mybirthday" is set with the following command:

```
mybirthday=new Date("June 25, 1971 13:15:00")
```

Table 21.5 *The Methods Provided for Processing Date Objects*

Method	Explanation	Syntax
getDate()	Returns the day of the month for the specified date.	birthday= mybirthday.getDate()
getDay()	Returns the day of the week for the specified date.	Birthweekday= mybirthday.getDay()
getHours()	Returns the hour for the specified date.	birthhour= mybirthday.getHours()
getMinutes()	Returns the minutes for the specified date.	Birthminutes= mybirthday. getMinutes()
getMonth()	Returns the month for the specified date.	birthmonth= mybirthday.getMonth()
getSeconds()	Returns the seconds for the current time.	Birthseconds= mybirthday. getSeconds()
getTime()	Returns the numeric value corresponding to the time for the specified date.	birthtime= mybirthday.getTime()
getTimeZoneOffset()	Returns the time zone offset in minutes for the current locale.	birthoffset= mybirthday. getTimeZoneOffset()
getYear()	Returns the year in the specified date.	birthyear= mybirthday.getYear()
parse()	Returns the number of milliseconds in a date string since January 1, 1970 00:00:00, local time.	timesince= parse(mybirthday)
setDate()	Sets the day of the month for a specified date.	mybirthday.setDate(25)
setHours()	Sets the hours for a specified date.	mybirthday. setHours(13)
setMinutes()	Sets the minutes for a specified date.	mybirthday. setMinutes(15)
setMonth()	Sets the month for a specified date.	mybirthday.setMonth(6)
setSeconds()	Sets the seconds for a specified date.	mybirthday. setSeconds (00)
setTime()	Sets the value of a date object by giving it a number representing the milliseconds since January 1, 1970 00:00:00, local time.	mybirthday. setTime(msec)

Continued

Table 21.5 The Methods Provided for Processing Date Objects (Continued)

Method	Explanation	Syntax
setYear()	Sets the year for a specified date.	mybirthday. setYear(1971)
toGMTString()	Converts a date to a string, using the Internet GMT conventions.	birthGMT=mybirthday. toGMTString()
toLocaleString()	Converts a date to a string, using the current birth locale's conventions.	Locale=mybirthday. toLocaleString()
UTC ()	Returns the number of milliseconds in a date birth object since January 1, 1970 00:00:00, Universal Coordinated Time (GMT).	millisecondsfrom1970 =mybirthday.UTC()

Note that for some circumstances, such as the **toGMTString()** method, Daylight savings time can change the result. In addition, don't forget about Leap Year when doing calculations.

USING BUILT-IN FUNCTIONS

JavaScript has several "top-level" functions built into the language. They are listed in Table 21.6.

Let's cover a few of these in detail because they're really useful.

The eval() Function

The built-in function **eval()** takes a string as its argument. The string can be any string representing a JavaScript expression, statement, or sequence of

Table 21.6 The Built-in JavaScript Functions

Function	Description	Example
escape()	Returns the ASCII encoding of a string in the ISO Latin-1 Character Set.	escape("string")
eval()	Evaluates JavaScript expressions or statements.	eval(string)
isNaN()	Determines if a value passed is a valid number or not.	isNaN(value)
parseFloat()	Converts a floating point number represented as a string to a numeric value.	parseFloat(string)
parseInt()	Converts an integer represented as a string to a numeric value.	parseInt(string [,radix])
unescape()	Returns the ASCII string for the specified value.	unescape("string")

statements. The expression can include variables and properties of existing objects. If the argument represents an expression, **eval()** evaluates the expression. If the argument represents one or more JavaScript statements, **eval()** performs the statements.

This function is useful for evaluating a string representing an arithmetic expression. For example, input from a form element is always a string, but you can use **eval()** to convert this data to a numerical value so that it can be processed.

Here's a simple JavaScript example, which shows you how to use the **eval()** function:

```
<HTML>
<HEAD>
<TITLE>Java Function Example</TITLE>
<SCRIPT LANGUAGE="JavaScript">

<!-- Beginning of JavaScript code ----

expression="1+2+3+4+((5*6)+2)/8"
answer=eval(expression)
document.write("The answer to: "+expression+" is... "+answer)

// -- End of JavaScript code ---->

</SCRIPT>
</HEAD>

<BODY>
</BODY>

</HTML>
```

This JavaScript program lets you try your own expressions:

```
<SCRIPT>
  function compute(obj) {
    obj.result.value = eval(obj.expr.value)
  }
</SCRIPT>

<FORM NAME="evalform">
  Enter an expression: <INPUT TYPE=text NAME="expr" SIZE=20 ><BR>
  Result: <INPUT TYPE=text NAME="result" SIZE=20 ><BR>

<INPUT TYPE="button" VALUE="Click Me" onClick="compute(this.form)">

</FORM>
```

The parseInt() and parseFloat() Functions

These two built-in functions return a numeric value when given a string as an argument. **parseFloat()** takes a string as an argument and tries to return a floating point number. If it comes across anything other than a valid floating point number (0-9 or a decimal point or a + or - sign) it stops and gives you what it got up to that point. For example, if you have a string "1.0424xxx043" it returns 1.0424 and stops. If it finds a character at the beginning that it can't recognize, it returns NaN, which means it's an invalid number.

parseInt() operates like **parseFloat()** except that it processes integer strings. It also can work with different bases which you denote in the optional (radix) value when executing the function. Supported bases are 10 for decimal, 8 for octal, 16 for hexadecimal, and so on. **parseInt()** also treats unrecognized characters in the same way as **parseFloat()**.

CREATING CUSTOM JAVASCRIPT OBJECTS

So far we've only covered the basics of object-oriented programming with JavaScript. We've also only explored the built-in objects that JavaScript provides, the majority of which are visual in nature. Objects like the browser window, buttons on a form, and frames are all visible objects that you can easily understand because you can see them.

However, JavaScript objects don't stop there; in fact that's just the beginning. JavaScript gives us the ability to construct our own objects, called *variable objects*. In addition, we can create our own special functions for those objects which are called *custom methods*. Understanding the basics of how custom objects and methods are created will help you get on the road to writing much more useful and powerful scripts.

Creating your own object is as simple as defining a variable; you simply think up an object structure and then assign it a value. For example, here is an object named **book** I came up with for a program:

```
book.name="Netscape and HTML Explorer"
book.series="Explorer"
book.topic="Internet"
```

In this case I have also created properties for this new object and assigned the properties values. Once the properties have been initialized, they can be used in a script. Let's expand on this example and create a script that lets the user enter values into a form and then the values are assigned to our custom object. Once they are assigned they will be displayed back to the user in a text box. This is a useful example because it shows how custom objects are useful for processing Web pages that contain forms:

```
<HTML>
<HEAD>
<TITLE>Java Function Example</TITLE>
<SCRIPT LANGUAGE="JavaScript">

<!-- Beginning of JavaScript code ----
// Assigns a new book object its values
function assignbook(form)
{
mybook=new book(form.name.value,form.series.value,form.topic.value)
}

// Creates a new book object
function book(name, series, topic)
{
  this.name = name
  this.series = series
  this.topic = topic
}

// Display the values stored in the book object
function showbook(form)
{
form.RESULT.value="Name:"+mybook.name+"  |Series:"+mybook.series+"_
|Topic:"+mybook.topic
}

// -- End of JavaScript code ----
</SCRIPT>
</HEAD>

<BODY>
<FORM NAME="MyForm">

Input Book Name:<INPUT TYPE=Text NAME="book" SIZE=20><BR>
Input Book Series:<INPUT TYPE=Text NAME="series" SIZE=20><BR>
Input Book Topic:<INPUT TYPE=Text NAME="topic" SIZE=20><BR>
<HR>
Click Here to Create Object
<INPUT TYPE="button" VALUE="Object Creation" onClick="assignbook(this.form)"><P>
<INPUT TYPE=TEXT NAME="RESULT" SIZE=50,5>
<INPUT TYPE="button" VALUE="Object Print" onClick="showbook(this.form)"><P>
</FORM>

</BODY>

</HTML>
```

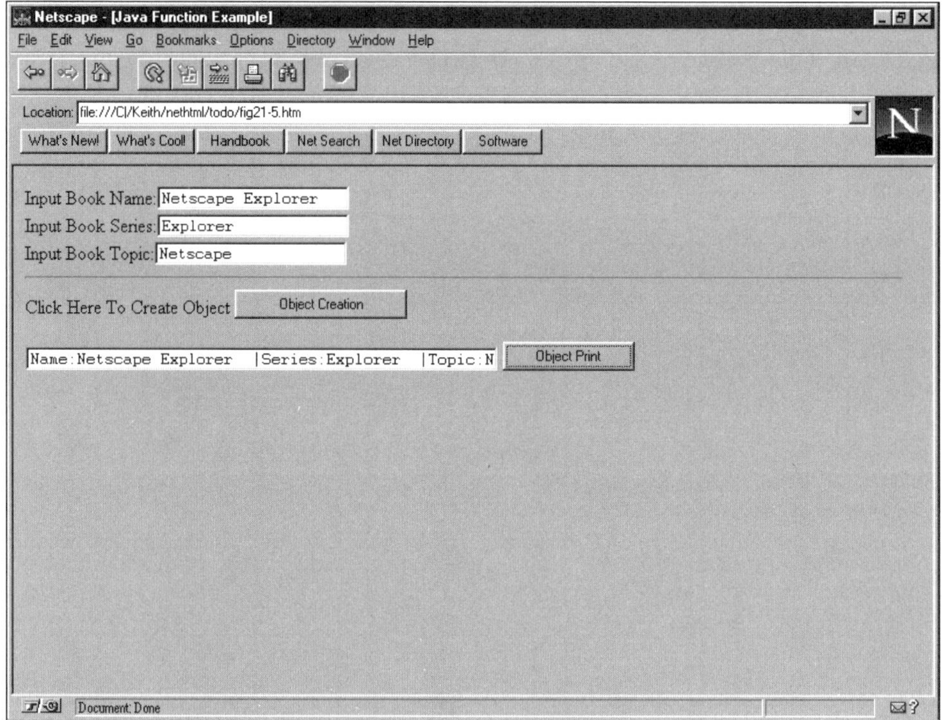

Figure 21.5 *The JavaScript example that uses a form and a custom object.*

When you load this HTML file, you should see a Web page like the one shown in Figure 21.5. Notice the form that is displayed.

Let's look at what the code does. The **<HEAD>** section defines three JavaScript functions or methods: **assignbook()**, **book()**, and **showbook()**. These methods are called later when the form is processed. The first method assigns a basic object of book and then creates the properties for it: **name**, **series**, and **topic**. Notice that the **assignbook()** method calls the **book()** method to actually create the new **book** object and assign values to the three properties. The **assignbook()** method assists in moving the values from the input boxes of the form to the newly created object named **mybook**.

To actually create a real instance of this object I call the function by assigning a name to the object I'm really creating, in this case the book object **mybook**. I use the "new" keyword before calling the function to denote I am creating a new *instance* of the object. Then I retrieve the object using the **showbook()** method, which displays it in the text at the bottom of the page.

In the **<BODY>** section of the HTML file you'll find the instructions for creating the form. Notice that three input fields are defined for the form, which have the same names as the properties defined for the **book** object: **name**, **series**, and **topic**. The actual HTML instruction that causes the **assignbook()** method to be called and thus, gets the ball rolling is:

```
<INPUT TYPE="button" VALUE="Object Creation" onClick="assignbook(this.form)"><P>
```

Here the **onClick** action is assigned the **assignbook()** method. This causes the method to be called when the user clicks the "Object Creation" button on the form. The parameter that is passed to the method is a reference to the current form. At the moment, the keyword "this" may look a little foreign to you, but I'll explain what it does in a moment.

The method that displays the data that the user enters into the form, **showbook()**, is also triggered by having the user click on a button. In this case, the button defined for this action is "Object Print":

```
<INPUT TYPE="button" VALUE="Object Print" onClick="showbook(this.form)"><P>
```

Again, notice how the method is assigned to the **onClick** action.

Although our script is fairly simple, it illustrates how custom objects can serve as the link between data entered in forms and procedures that can be performed on the data. For example, you could check each data element entered into a form and display a message if the data was not entered correctly. This gives you much more control over the data processing capabilities available with CGI scripts. The more you work with custom objects, the more you'll find that you can create very complex objects which might contain arrays and other objects within them.

Understanding the "this" Keyword

Pay attention very carefully here—if you come away with a better understanding of any part of JavaScript from this chapter, it will be about a special keyword, **this**, which is used a lot in JavaScript code. Without a good understanding of the **this** keyword, you'll easily be lost when you try programming in JavaScript or reading scripts written by other Web page developers.

The **this** keyword is essentially used to refer to the current object in play. It's a useful features because it allows you to create much more general purpose methods, which in turn saves you from having to write a lot of JavaScript code. For example, assume you wanted to check 20 text boxes to see if each text box contained the proper information before executing any more code. With the **this** keyword, you could write a method which, when called upon, checks the currently active textbox.

Before I confuse you further, look at this code:

```
<HTML>
<HEAD>
<TITLE>Java Function Example</TITLE>
<SCRIPT LANGUAGE="JavaScript">

<!-- Beginning of JavaScript code ----

function checkme(input)
{
   score=eval(input.value)
   if (score>5) {
   score=5
   }
   if(score<1) {
   score=1
   }
   input.value=score
}

// -- End of JavaScript code ---->
</SCRIPT>
</HEAD>

<FORM NAME="Myform">

On a Scale of 1-5  How Good Is This Page Overall?:<INPUT TYPE=text NAME="Answer"
SIZE=20 onChange=checkme(this)><P>

On a Scale of 1-5  How Are the Graphics on This Page?:<INPUT TYPE=text
NAME="Answer" SIZE=20 onChange=checkme(this)><P>

On a Scale of 1-5  How Are the Links on This Page?:<INPUT TYPE=text
NAME="Answer" SIZE=20 onChange=checkme(this)><P>

On a Scale of 1-5  How Good Is the Content on This Page?:<INPUT TYPE=text
NAME="Answer" SIZE=20 onChange=checkme(this)><P>

On a Scale of 1-5  How Neat Is the JavaScript on This Page?:<INPUT TYPE=text
NAME="Answer" SIZE=20 onChange=checkme(this)><P>

</FORM>
<BODY>
</BODY>

</HTML>
```

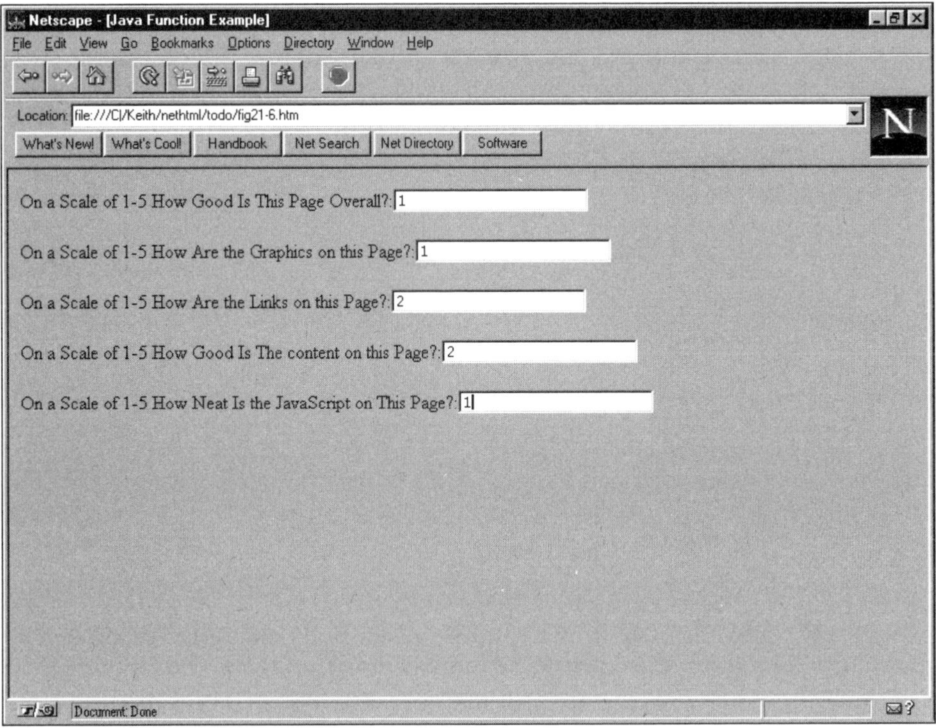

Figure 21.6 *A JavaScript example that uses the "this" keyword.*

The Web page created by this code is shown in Figure 21.6. The function **checkme()** is written to check all of the text boxes to see if each one contained a value in the range 1-5. What I did was substitute the **this** keyword wherever I wanted to refer to a specific text box object. By using **this**, the code works on the current object that called upon it. So instead of writing 20 specific routines, each identical except for the object reference, I can use **this** and write one piece of code. Pretty neat, huh?

Defining Your Own Methods

Just as you can define your own objects, you can define your own methods. A method is simply a type of function that you attach to a specific object you've created. To do this, simply make a reference in your object definition to a specific function name which has been previously defined using the standard function definition syntax.

The general syntax for assigning a custom method to an object is:

```
object.methodname = function_name
```

where *function_name* is the actual name of a function that has been defined. The *function_name* and *method_name* can be the same. Once the function name is assigned to an object, you can call the new method in much the same way you call the built-in methods already present in JavaScript:

```
object.methodname(params)
```

Let's return to our earlier example where we created a custom object named **book**. We'll rewrite one of the functions used so that a custom method is assigned to the **book** object:

```
function book(name, series, topic)
{
   this.name = name
   this.series = series
   this.topic = topic
   this.showbook=showbook
}
```

Now **showbook()** is a method that can be accessed using a **book** object. Instead of calling the **showbook()** function directly, as we did in the previous example, we'll execute it as a method. To refresh your memory, we previously called the function using this HTML code:

```
<INPUT TYPE="button" VALUE="Object Print" onClick="showbook(this.form)"><P>
```

Now with the newly setup **showbook()** method, we can call it like this:

```
<INPUT TYPE="button" VALUE="Object Print"
onClick="mybook.showbook(this.form)"><P>
```

Creating your own methods is perhaps one of the most challenging parts of mastering JavaScript. Coupled with what we learned about the creation of our own objects, we've actually learned the basics of an incredibly advanced method of programming!

MORE ABOUT EVENTS

JavaScript applications are largely event-driven. Events are actions that occur, usually as a result of something the user does. For example, a button click is an event. There is a specific set of events that Netscape recognizes. Once you understand events, you can define event handlers—scripts that are automatically executed when an event occurs.

Event handlers are embedded in documents as attributes of HTML tags. You then assign JavaScript code for them to execute. The basic outline of a JavaScript handler is as follows:

```
<TAG eventHandler="JavaScript Code">
```

The *TAG* is any HTML tag and *eventHandler* is the name of the event you define.

Let's say there's a button on your page that will be pushed. Suppose you have created a JavaScript function called **compute()**. You can get Netscape to execute this function when the user clicks on a button by assigning the function call to the button's **onClick** event handler. Here's an example:

```
<INPUT TYPE="button" VALUE="Calculate" onClick="compute(this.form)">
```

You can put any JavaScript statement inside the quotes following **onClick**. These statements get executed when the user clicks on the button. If you want to include more than one statement, you must separate the statements with a semicolon.

In general, it is a good idea to define functions for your event handlers because you can use the same function for many different items. It also makes your code easier to read.

Events apply to HTML tags as follows:

Focus, Blur, Change events:	text fields, textareas, and selections
Click events:	buttons, radio buttons, checkboxes, submit buttons, reset buttons, links
Select events:	text fields, textareas
MouseOver event:	links

If an event applies to an HTML tag, you can define an event handler for it. In general, an event handler has the name of the event, preceded by "on". For example, the event handler for the Focus event is **onFocus**. Many objects also have methods that emulate events. For example, buttons have a **click()** method that emulates the button being clicked.

Note: The event-emulation methods do not trigger event handlers. So, for example, the **click()** method does not trigger an **onClick** event handler. However, you can always call an event handler directly (for example, you can call **onClick** explicitly in a script).

Table 21.7 *The Key Netscape Events and Event Handlers*

Event	Occurs when...	Event Handler
Blur	User removes input focus from form element.	onBlur
Click	User clicks on form element or link.	onClick
Change	User changes text, textarea, or selects element.	onChange
Focus	User gives form element input focus.	onFocus
Load	User loads an HTML document in Netscape.	onLoad
MouseOver	User moves mouse pointer over a link or anchor.	onMouseOver
Select	User selects form element's input field.	onSelect
Submit	User submits a form.	onSubmit
Unload	User exits the page.	onUnload

Table 21.7 lists some of the key events that occur when Web pages are processed with Netscape. For each event, I've listed the action that triggers the event and the name of the event handler that can be accessed using JavaScript code.

```
<HTML>
<HEAD>
<TITLE>Java Event Example</TITLE>
<SCRIPT LANGUAGE="JavaScript">

<!-- Beginning of JavaScript code ----

function compute(form)
{
form.TEXT1.value="Clicked!"
}

function changed(obj)
{
obj.value="Can't Change Me!"
}

function blurry(obj)
{
obj.value=obj.value+"Blurred!"
}

function FocusOn(obj)
{
obj.value="Hi!"
}
// -- End of JavaScript code ---->

</SCRIPT>
</HEAD>
```

```
<FORM NAME="EventForm">

<FONT SIZE=4>Test of Click Event<HR></FONT>
<INPUT TYPE="button" VALUE="Test Click Here" onClick="compute(this.form)">
<INPUT TYPE=INPUT NAME="TEXT1" SIZE=20 onChange=""><HR><BR><BR>

<FONT SIZE=4>Test of Change Event<HR></FONT>
Try To Change Text! <INPUT TYPE=INPUT NAME="TEXT2" SIZE=20
onChange="changed(this)">
<HR><BR><BR>

<FONT SIZE=4>Test of Blur Event<HR></FONT>
Try To Change Text!<INPUT TYPE=INPUT NAME="TEXT3" SIZE=20 onBlur="blurry(this)">
<HR><BR><BR>

<FONT SIZE=4>Test of Focus Event<HR></FONT>
Enter Here:<INPUT TYPE=INPUT NAME="TEXT3" SIZE=20 onFocus="FocusOn(this)">
<HR><BR><BR>

<FONT SIZE=4>Test of onMouseOver Event<HR></FONT>
<A HREF="http://home.netscape.com/"
   onMouseOver="window.status='Click Here To Go To NetScape Home Page!';return
true">
Netscape Here!</A>

</FORM>

<BODY onLoad="window.alert('This Window Alert Represents a Test of the onLoad
Event!')">

</BODY>

</HTML>
```

The Web page created by loading this document is shown in Figure 21.7. When the document first loads, the **onLoad** event handler instructs Netscape to display an alert window. A form is also displayed that traps some of the typical event handlers associated with forms including **onClick**, **onChange**, **onFocus**, **onBlur**, and **onMouseOver**. When each of these corresponding events occur, different JavaScript functions are called to display appropriate messages. For example, when you click on the first button, the **onClick** event handler instructs Netscape to call the **compute()** function, which in turn displays the message "Clicked". The new event handler is set up in the **<FORM>** section of the HTML document, using a statement like this:

```
<INPUT TYPE="button" VALUE="Test Click Here" onClick="compute(this.form)">
```

Here, notice how the **onClick** event handler is assigned to the **compute()** function. The parameter that is passed is a reference to the current form the button is assigned to.

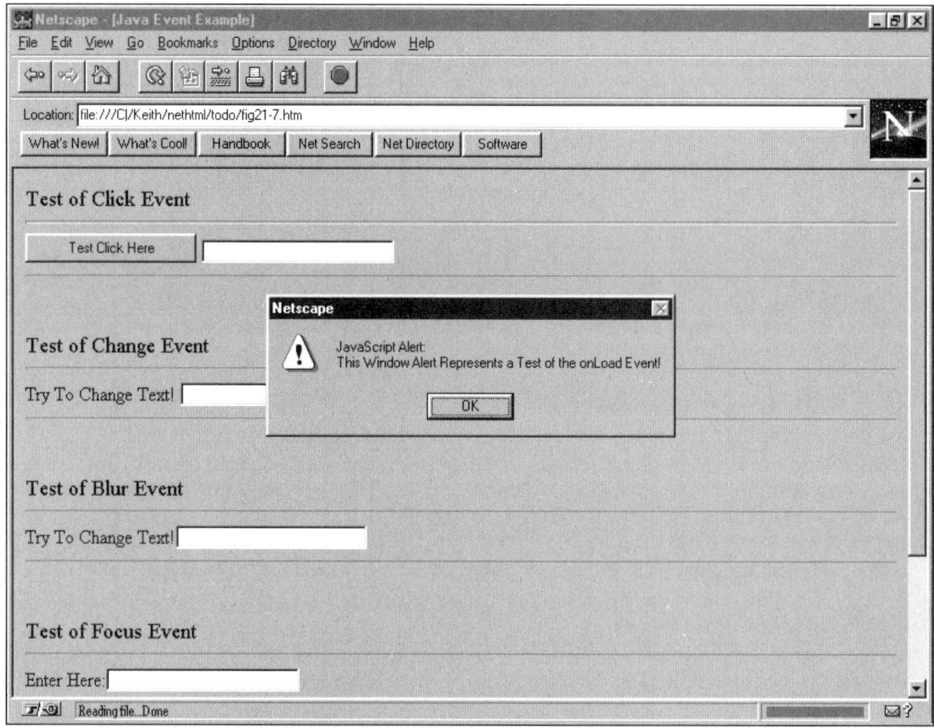

Figure 21.7 *Using JavaScript to process events that occur in forms.*

To fully understand how each of the event handlers are set up, you should type in the HTML code in a file, load in the file, and interact with the form that is displayed.

CREATING SOME SAMPLE PROGRAMS

Now that we've covered the core of the JavaScript language, let's have some fun and create a few interesting projects. First, we'll build a simple calculator that can be incorporated into a Web page using JavaScript and HTML forms. Then we'll create a JavaScript function that displays a scrolling banner on a Web page. Both of these projects will use many of the features we introduced during this chapter, including built-in objects, functions, properties, and events.

A Calculator Project

Everyone needs a basic calculator, right? After all, without a calculator you won't be able to determine how much money you can afford to spend when you get your next raise. Here's a complete HTML file that contains JavaScript code to implement a fully working calculator.

```
<HTML>
<HEAD>
<TITLE>Java Function Example</TITLE>
<SCRIPT LANGUAGE="JavaScript">

<!-- Beginning of JavaScript code ----

oldnum=0  // Initialize the calculator total to 0

// Store a number that has been selected
function newnumber(form,num)
{
   // Convert the number to a numeric value
   num=eval(num)
   form.Answer.value=form.Answer.value+num
}

// Convert the number to a decimal value
function decimal(form)
{
   newnum=form.Answer.value
   newnum=newnum+"."
   form.Answer.value=newnum
}

// Determine which operator button has been pressed
function operator(form,buttonpressed)
{
   oldnum=eval(form.Answer.value)
   form.Answer.value=""

   if(buttonpressed==" +  ")
   {operation=1}

   if(buttonpressed=="  -  ")
   {operation=2}

   if(buttonpressed==" x  ")
   {operation=3}

   if(buttonpressed=="  /  ")
   {operation=4}
}

function equals(form)
{
   num=eval(form.Answer.value)

   if(operation==1)   // addition
   {
   newnum=num+oldnum
```

```
    form.Answer.value=newnum
    }

    if(operation==2)   // subtraction
    {
    newnum=oldnum-num
    form.Answer.value=newnum
    }

    if(operation==3)   // multiplication
    {
    newnum=num*oldnum
    form.Answer.value=newnum
    }

    if(operation==4)  // division
    {
    newnum=oldnum/num
    form.Answer.value=newnum
    }
}

// -- End of JavaScript code ---->

</SCRIPT>
</HEAD>
<FORM NAME="Myform">
<FONT SIZE=6>Calculator Example</FONT><BR>
<HR SIZE=5 ALIGN=LEFT>
<P>
<INPUT TYPE=text NAME="Answer" SIZE=12><BR>
<HR SIZE=2 WIDTH=105 ALIGN=LEFT>
<INPUT TYPE="button" VALUE=" 7 " onClick="newnumber(this.form,this.value)">
<INPUT TYPE="button" VALUE=" 8 " onClick="newnumber(this.form,this.value)">
<INPUT TYPE="button" VALUE=" 9 " onClick="newnumber(this.form,this.value)">
<INPUT TYPE="button" VALUE=" / " onClick="operator(this.form,this.value)">
<BR>

<INPUT TYPE="button" VALUE=" 4 " onClick="newnumber(this.form,this.value)">
<INPUT TYPE="button" VALUE=" 5 " onClick="newnumber(this.form,this.value)">
<INPUT TYPE="button" VALUE=" 6 " onClick="newnumber(this.form,this.value)">
<INPUT TYPE="button" VALUE=" x " onClick="operator(this.form,this.value)">
<BR>

<INPUT TYPE="button" VALUE=" 1 " onClick="newnumber(this.form,this.value)">
<INPUT TYPE="button" VALUE=" 2 " onClick="newnumber(this.form,this.value)">
<INPUT TYPE="button" VALUE=" 3 " onClick="newnumber(this.form,this.value)">
<INPUT TYPE="button" VALUE=" - " onClick="operator(this.form,this.value)">
<BR>

<INPUT TYPE="button" VALUE=" 0  " onClick="newnumber(this.form,this.value)">
<INPUT TYPE="button" VALUE=" .  " onClick="decimal(this.form)">
<INPUT TYPE="button" VALUE=" +  " onClick="operator(this.form,this.value)">
<BR>
```

```
<INPUT TYPE="button" VALUE=" =  " onClick="equals(this.form)">

</FORM>
<BODY>
</BODY>

</HTML>
```

The calculator created by this HTML document is shown in Figure 21.8. Notice that the interface to the calculator is set up as a form with buttons to represent the digits 0 through 9, the decimal point, and buttons to perform simple operations like addition, subtraction, multiplication, and division. With this interface you can enter values by clicking buttons and then click on a desired operator button (-, +, *, /) to select an operation. A new total is produced by clicking the "=" button.

The body section of the HTML document contains the HTML code for the form that is displayed. When different buttons are pressed, an appropriate JavaScript function is called. For example, the HTML instruction that processes the * button is

```
<INPUT TYPE="button" VALUE=" x  " onClick="operator(this.form,this.value)">
```

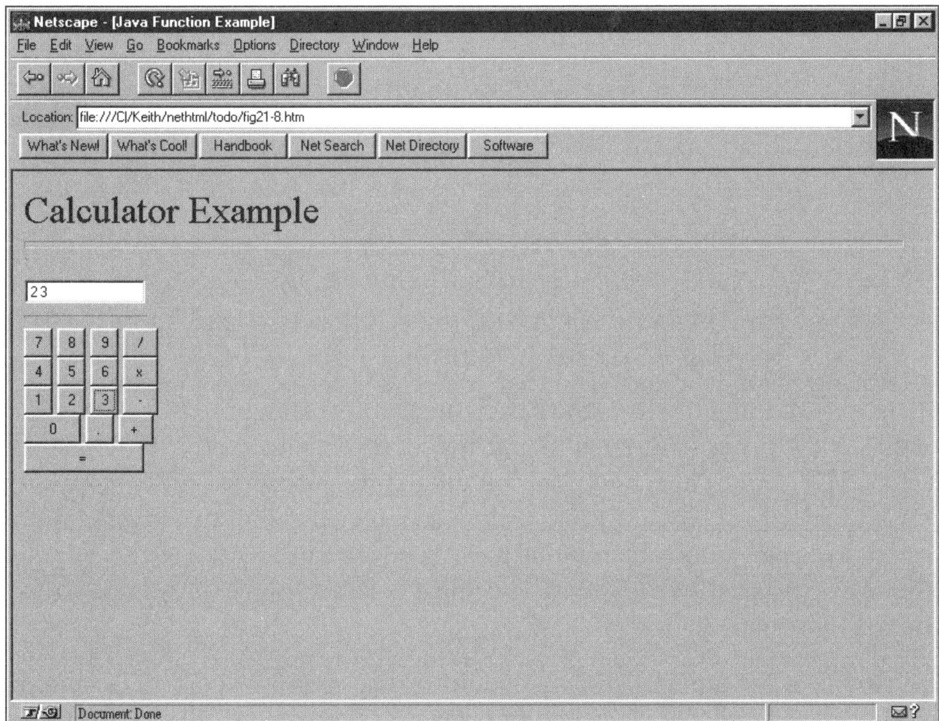

Figure 21.8 *The calculator program created using HTML forms and JavaScript.*

As indicated, when this button is pressed the **operator()** function is called with a reference to the current form and the "value" of the button being passed as parameters. This approach allows us to use a single function for processing all of the operator buttons (+, -, *, /).

If you examine the JavaScript code in the **operator()** function, you'll find if-then statements that look like this:

```
if(buttonpressed==" +  ")
   {operation=1}

if(buttonpressed=="  -  ")
   {operation=2}
```

The **operation** variable keeps track of which operator the user has selected, so that when the "=" button is clicked, the appropriate operation can be performed. The main processing function is **equals()**, which is called whenever the user clicks the "=" button. This function simply determines which operation should be used (based on the operator button the user previously selected), performs the appropriate calculation, and stores the result so that it can be displayed by the form. For example, here is the code used to add two numbers together:

```
if(operation==1)   // addition
   {
    newnum=num+oldnum
    form.Answer.value=newnum
   }
```

The key variable that makes the calculator work properly is **oldnum**. This variable keeps track of the previous calculation performed by the calculator. When a user selects a new number and a new operator, the previous value produced by the calculator is retrieved by using **oldnum** and a new total is computed.

Because of the modular design of the calculator, you could easily add more mathematical operations, such as trig functions, square root, and so on. All you would need to do is add more buttons to the form, using HTML instructions. Then, you could add more if-then statements to the **operator()** function to determine which operations have been selected by the user. The only other step required would be to add the necessary processing code to the **equals()** function.

Even if you aren't especially interested in writing your own custom calculator, this example should convince you of JavaScript's flexibility and usefulness for processing HTML forms. When you need to add additional features to your Web pages, you can easily write or expand existing JavaScript functions, and away you go!

A Scrolling Banner

One of the first Java programs that most programmers cut their teeth on is a Java applet that scrolls text across the screen. Well, you can perform similar text animation tasks using just JavaScript. In our final example, we'll create a script that scrolls a text message across the status bar displayed at the bottom of a window. In order to accomplish this task, we'll use a predefined property of the window object named **status**. Here is the complete HTML file. Notice that only a single JavaScript function named **scrollmessage()** is needed:

```
<HTML><HEAD>
<TITLE>Scrolling StatusBar Example</TITLE>
<SCRIPT LANGUAGE="JavaScript">

<!-- Beginning of JavaScript code ---->

function scrollmessage(spaces)
{
   message  = "This Message Will Scroll Across The Status Bar At the Bottom of A_
Window"

   spaceholder = " "
   counter   = 1

   // Outside of the scrolling range
   if (spaces > 100)
   {
      spaces–
      STcommand="scrollmessage(" + spaces + ")"

      timerTwo=window.setTimeout(STcommand,10)
   }

   // Still in a scrolling range
   else if (spaces <= 100 && spaces > 0)
   {
      for (counter=0 ; counter < spaces ; counter++)
         {spaceholder+=" "}

    spaceholder+=message
    spaces–
    STcommand="scrollmessage(" + spaces + ")"
    window.status=spaceholder

    timerTwo=window.setTimeout(STcommand,10)
```

```
   }

   else if (spaces <= 0)
   {
      if (-spaces < message.length)
      {
         spaceholder+=message.substring(-spaces,message.length)
         spaces—
         STcommand="scrollmessage(" + spaces + ")"
         window.status=spaceholder
         timerTwo=window.setTimeout(STcommand,10)
      }

      else {
         window.status=" "

         timerTwo=window.setTimeout("scrollmessage(100)",10)
      }
   }
}
// -- End of JavaScript code ---->

</SCRIPT>
</HEAD>
<BODY onLoad="timerONE=window.setTimeout('scrollmessage(50)',50)">
<center><Blink>Note:Moving the mouse scrolls the message faster!</Blink><center>
</BODY>

</HTML>
```

The best way to understand what is going with this example is to jump to the body section of the HTML code. When the HTML document containing this code is loaded, the load event occurs and the **onLoad** event handler is triggered. In our case, we've assigned this event handler to call our predefined **scrollmessage()** function. The trick is in the way we've made this assignment:

```
onLoad="timerONE=window.setTimeout('scrollmessage(50)',50)"
```

We've written some tricky JavaScript code in this chapter but I'm sure you haven't seen anything quite like this yet. As it turns out, the built-in, high-level **window** object (which the current **document** object is contained in) provides a handy method for controlling the timing of actions called **setTimeout()**. The syntax for using this method is

```
timerID = window.setTimeout('action to be taken', delay)
```

This method counts down for the specified delay and then it kicks off the action that is provided. The *timerID* is assigned a value for keeping track of the timer. In our example, the action we want to initiate is to call the

scrollmessage() function and the delay is defined as 50 milliseconds. (A millisecond is 1/1000 of a second.)

The **scrollmessage()** function itself performs its magic by using a counter to keep track of the position of the text string that is scrolled. The code is a little tricky, so let's dissect some of it to see what is going on behind the scenes. Here is the section of code that executes when the parameter passed to the function is in the range from 0 to 100:

```
else if (spaces <= 100 && spaces > 0)
   {
      for (counter=0 ; counter < spaces ; counter++)
         {spaceholder+=" "}  // Add in corresponding blank spaces

    spaceholder+=message   // Add spaces in front of message
    spaces-
    STcommand="scrollmessage(" + spaces + ")"  // Set up another call to
                                               // scrollmessage()
    window.status=spaceholder

    timerTwo=window.setTimeout(STcommand,10)
   }
```

Because we need to give the text the appearance that it is scrolling, we need to pad the message with a set of blank spaces. The number of blank spaces added corresponds with the value contained in the variable **spaces**. The job of the **for** loop is to repeat until the appropriate number of spaces have been added. The next task involves writing the message string to the current window's status bar area by assigning the string to the **status** property. This property always contains the string currently displayed in the window's status area.

Once this is done, something interesting happens—something you don't see in your typical JavaScript program. The **scrollmessage()** function, in a sense, calls itself! In the world of programming this technique is called *recursion*. What happens is that another **setTimeout()** method is activated to kick off another call to **scrollmessage()**. But when our scrolling function is called again, the spacing parameter is reduced by one. So what happens is that **scrollmessage()** continues to call itself, each time decreasing the amount of blank spaces that are added to the scrolling message. This kind of programming can make your head spin!

SCRIPTING: THE POSSIBILITIES ARE ENDLESS...

The sample programs we just created are relatively basic—even the scrolling banner is done with less than 50 lines of JavaScript code. However, now that you know the basics, you can go to work and create scripts that go well beyond our examples and add all kinds of cool interactive elements to your Web pages. I've seen complete games and intense applications written with just JavaScript.

Certainly JavaScript leaves a lot of power and capability out of the language (that's really where other languages like Java come in) but there is still enough power in JavaScript to fuel endless hours of your imagination and programming skill.

Developing Your JavaScript Skills

Keep in mind that I haven't covered all of the JavaScript objects, methods, and events in this chapter. I've only scratched the surface of how you can create your own objects and methods. I also haven't showed you how you can use JavaScript and frames together for creating unbelievably dynamic Web pages. I decided to keep our scripts as simple as possible but still provide you with a number of JavaScript programming tips and techniques.

So don't stop learning about JavaScript after you read this chapter. I'll list some resources at the end of the chapter that will show you more about JavaScript than I could possibly do in this chapter. (Even Netscape offers a 150+ page reference guide!)

Additionally, take time to play with the source code sprinkled throughout the chapter. There's a lot more to learn from it. I would recommend typing it all in by hand, instead of copying it, to get a really good feel for the syntax of JavaScript. Practice your skills by renaming the variables and the names of objects like the textboxes and then see if you can make the necessary changes elsewhere in the code. That's how I learned a lot about JavaScript when I first started.

I also try to learn each command individually by writing a simple JavaScript app that demonstrates that specific command in action. Throughout this chapter I've provided you with larger apps that show many features at once, but take the time to go through a comprehensive reference to JavaScript (such as the online one from Netscape) and learn to individually master each part. To help you better navigate your way around the vast sea of JavaScript objects, properties, and methods, I've also provided a reference guide in Appendix B.

Even the Simplest Stuff Works Well

It's important to understand that even a simple JavaScript program can do a lot. You don't have to write a complex program to have your Web site take advantage of JavaScript. That's why even a small understanding is useful. Don't cast aside JavaScript just because you don't understand everything here or elsewhere about JavaScript. Mastering a language like JavaScript takes time, and as you learn more you can have fun adding simple JavaScript examples to your Web site!

Where to Learn More about JavaScript

After you've finished this chapter, fire up Netscape, surf to the URLs listed below, and download and consume the various text files and sample JavaScript code they offer you. A few more days pouring over this material should make you a JavaScript expert in no time!

Netscape's Official JavaScript Reference Guide

`http://home.netscape.com/eng/mozilla/2.0/handbook/javascript/index.html`

I started here, and you should, too. Netscape created JavaScript and they have an extensive set of documentation, including a good reference guide to the language that's available for downloading.

Tecfa's JavaScript Manual

`http://tecfa.unige.ch/guides/java/tecfaman/java-1.html`

This university site offers a nice tutorial of JavaScript.

JavaScript 411

`http://www.freqgrafx.com/411/`

This site has the JavaScript FAQ, a tutorial, and much much more. If you're going to work with and learn JavaScript, bookmark this site today!

JavaScript 411's Snippet Page

`http://www.freqgrafx.com/411/library.html`

This is a great source for advanced JavaScript code that deals with all sorts of neat things you wish you knew how to do with JavaScript!

Example Site

`http://www.cis.syr.edu/~bhu/javascript.d/`

This site has links to a number of good example JavaScript programs, including a Converter: Temperature, Bgcolor and View History, A Meric Converter, Mutiple-Unit Converter, Calendar Greeting, Tax Form, and a Loan Interest Calculator.

Another Example Site

http://168.29.224.15:8001/~dfelteau/javascript.html

A nice site with several good examples, including a Calculator example.

THE FUTURE OF SCRIPTING

As more and more people become familiar with scripting languages like JavaScript, the Web will become a far more dynamic medium than it has already become. Now not only will you surf over to a page to read someone's text and view their nice looking layout, but you'll also be able to benefit from the interactive programs they provide. You might go to your bank's page and quickly see how much interest you'll earn on your money in their various CD offerings. Or you might go to a page created by a local store and add up the various things you might want to purchase prior to shopping there.

In the near future, the Web won't be about distributing just information via HTML, but entire interactive applications available directly on the pages for you to use. With this approach, the Web becomes a global resource of programs ready to help you with as many different needs as programmers can dream up. So what are you waiting for? Learn more about JavaScript and create cool JavaScript programs for your browsers to utilize!

Java Applets

Java applets can add interesting effects to your Web page. And you don't even have to program them yourself!

Perhaps the coolest addition to Netscape is Java. With Java, Netscape users can experience programs distributed over the Web that are like the full-fledged applications you use every day on your computer. Java is a very powerful language that is made even more powerful because programs written on it can run on any computer that has a Java-compatible program or browser. Java applets are the hottest Web page enhancements on the Internet. Figures 22.1 and 22.2 show how varied the uses of Java can be.

So what are Java applets? How do you use them? Where can the be found? What do they do? I'll try to answer these questions and more in this chapter. One thing I won't be answering is how to program in Java. As I said, Java is a very powerful language, and trying to teach someone how to program in it in less than 20 pages is impossible. So I'll simply concentrate on how to use existing Java applets in your Web site.

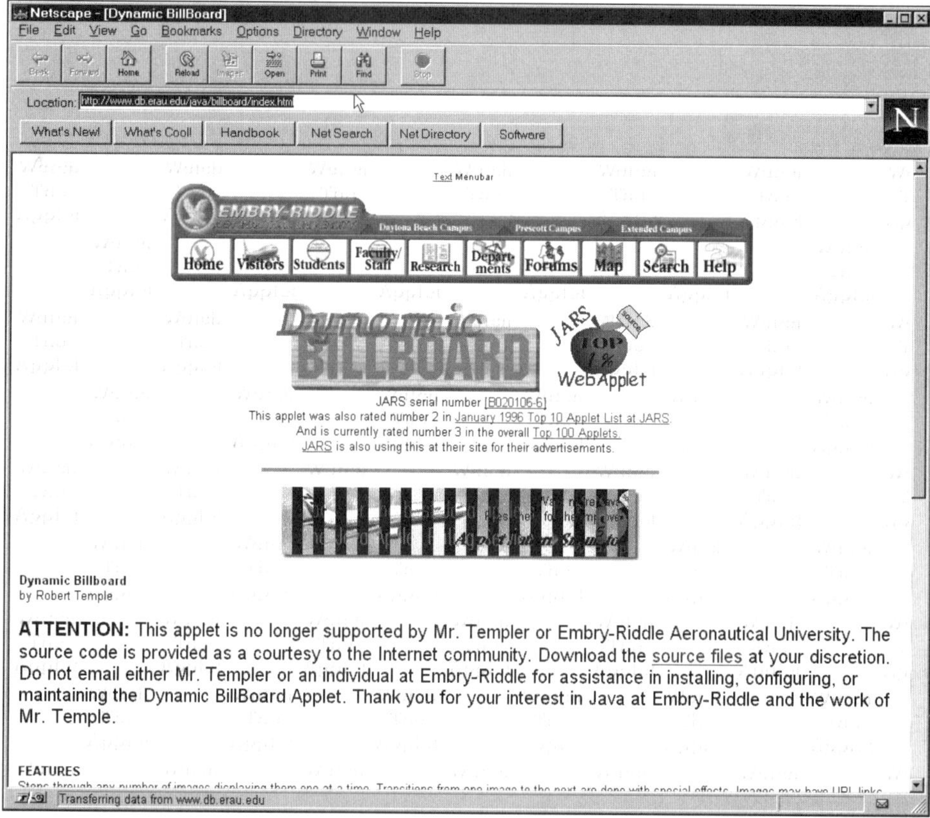

***Figure 22.1** Embry-Riddle Aeronautical University's page-turning billboard applet.*

WHAT EXACTLY IS JAVA?

Java is a language based on the principles put forth in C++, but which is designed specifically for secure two-way, real time interaction over networks—especially the Internet. It's also designed to be capable of running on any platform that supports Java. Thus, unlike C++, there is absolutely no need to port or recompile your Java code for other machine types. Write once, compile it once, and run it on as many different machines as you want. It is this functionality that is giving Java its widespread fame and use.

Java was invented by Sun Microsystems, the workstation maker that supplies many of the servers that run the Internet. They originally were creating a language to work for major interactive television systems, but when it appeared the market for ITV was not materializing, and the Internet started

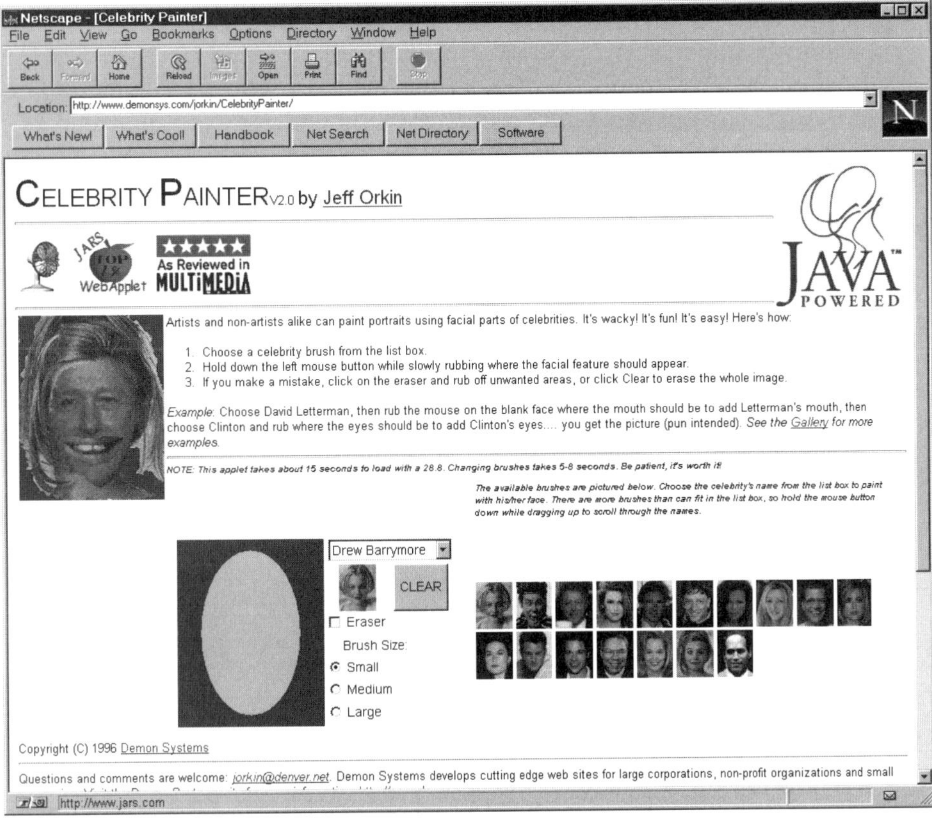

Figure 22.2 *An interactive and interesting use for Java.*

growing in popularity, Sun shifted gears and turned toward the Internet and Java was born!

Until now, Web developers were pretty much stuck with HTML and a few special plug-in products to help them create their Web pages. But now we have Java, which allows us to create almost anything our hearts desire and integrate it into our Web pages. No longer are Web sites vehicles for distributing only cool-looking text and downloadable programs—the Web is now alive, and the secret behind that new life is Java.

WHAT IS A JAVA APPLET?

An applet is a compiled Java program. First programmers write out a Java program. Once they're done, they compile that program into the specific applets that actually run on your machine. Java programs are called applets because they're meant to be short and sweet, not full-blown applications, hence Applets.

This doesn't mean Java isn't powerful—one could create a very large and complex application in Java. However Java is meant to go over the Internet, and the larger your program, the longer it takes to download. If anything, the use of the term applet is a good reminder to us all that download time still rules the day on the Internet—so keep it short and sweet.

What Does Java Look Like?

I'm glad you asked. While we're using this chapter to talk mostly about how to use the finished product—a compiled Java applet in our Web pages—it's always good to have an understanding of what's under the hood.

```
HTML Source:

<applet code=Animator.class width=55 height=70>
<param name=imagesource value="images">
<param name=endimage value=10>
<param name=soundsource value="audio">
<param name=soundtrack value=spacemusic.au>
<param name=sounds value="1.au|2.au|3.au|4.au|5.au|6.au|7.au|8.au|9.au|0.au">
<param name=pause value=200>
</applet>

Notes:

<APP CLASS="Animator"
     IMAGESOURCE="aDirectory"       - the directory that has the animation
                                      frames (a series of pictures in GIF
                                      format, named T1.gif, T2.gif, ...)
     STARTUP="aFile"                - an image to display at load time
     BACKGROUND="aFile"             - an image to paint the frames against
     STARTIMAGE="aNumber"           - number of the starting frame (1..n)
     ENDIMAGE="aNumber"             - number of the end frame (1..n)
     PAUSE="100"                    - milliseconds to pause between images
                                      default - can be overriden by PAUSES)
     PAUSES="300|200||400|200||100" - millisecond delay per frame.  Blank
                                      uses default PAUSE value
     REPEAT="true"                  - repeat the sequence?
     POSITIONS="100@200||200@100||200@200|100@100|105@105"
                                    - positions (X@Y) for each frame.  Blank
                                      means use previous frame"s position
     IMAGES="3|3|2|1|2|3|17"        - explicit order for frames - see below
     SOUNDSOURCE="aDirectory"       - the directory that has the audio files
     SOUNDTRACK="aFile"             - an audio file to play throughout
     SOUNDS="aFile.au||||bFile.au"  - audio files keyed to individual frames
>

You can specify either an IMAGES list or a STARTIMAGE/ENDIMAGE range, but not
both. The IMAGES list is a string of frame numbers in the order in which you
wish them to display, separated by vertical bars. STARTIMAGE and ENDIMAGE let
you specify a range of images. Specifying an ENDIMAGE that is numerically less
```

```
than the STARTIMAGE will display the images in reverse order. Both parameters
have default values of 1, so specifying only STARTIMAGE="15" means "play the
frames in reverse order from 15 to 1." Saying only ENDIMAGE="13" means "play the
frames from 1 to 13." Of course, you can use both STARTIMAGE and ENDIMAGE
together.
```

Pretty scary, huh? If you've ever worked with C++ code, or at least seen it, you can see that Java shares a lot of similarity to C++. If you're intrigued to the point of wanting to write your own Java applets, I've prepared some information at the end of this chapter to help you to learn Java. Figure 22.3 shows a Java applet in action.

HOW DO I USE JAVA APPLETS IN MY WEB SITE?

Let's cut to the chase—what we want to know is how to take the numerous Java applets available commercially, as shareware and public domain, and reuse them for our own Web sites. The basic process of embedding applets or

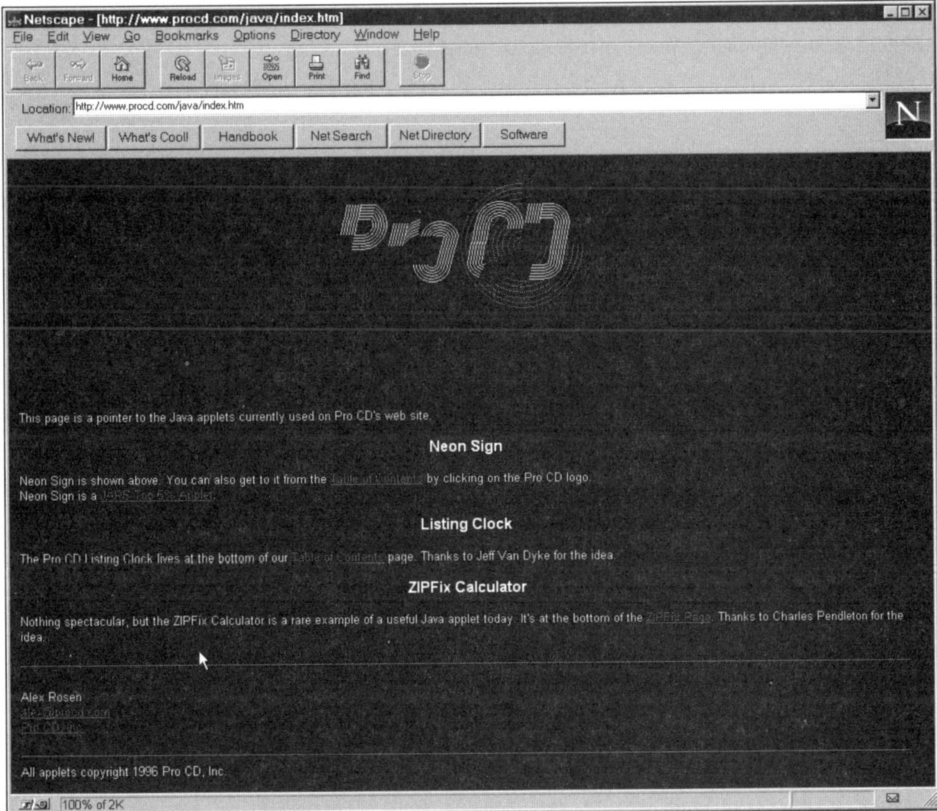

Figure 22.3 A "neon sign" applet.

programs into your site is done via the **<APPLET> ... </APPLET>** tags, which describe to Netscape exactly how to run the applet.

Many Java applets require you to send them some type of parameters. A parameter is some sort of value that it needs to run. For example, say I wrote a Java applet that displayed bouncing balls on the screen. I might require two parameters, one for the number of balls to bounce and one that decided on the colors for the balls. Without those I couldn't run the program. In addition, by using parameters I allow the users of my applet to be the decisionmakers behind the number and colors of the bouncing balls. That provides flexibility which makes the applet even cooler. To pass parameters to our applets we use the **<PARAM>** tag, which we place between the **<APPLET> ... </APPLET>** tags.

A lot of Java applets require parameters to be set in order to execute. In addition, you also want to set the size of the overall Java container for the page. The container defines the size of the applet on your page. You can set the size of the container in the applet tag. Let's take a look at a fictional HTML sequence for embedding the bouncing balls program I described above:

```
<APPLET CODE="Bounce.class" Width=320 HEIGHT=200>
   <PARAM NAME="balls" Value="10">
   <PARAM NAME="color" Value="Red">
</APPLET>
```

Not too difficult is it? First we give the name of the program to run, in this case the Bounce.class applet, and then we set the Java container size to 320x200. After that we passed two parameters to the applet, balls=10 and color=Red, which the applet would use to run a bouncing ball program that included ten red balls.

There are a slew of other options that go with the **<APPLET> ... </APPLET>** tag. The tag below lists all the possible attributes.

```
<APPLET CODEBASE="path"
        CODE="java class"
        ALT="text"
        NAME="text"
        WIDTH="value"
        HEIGHT="value"

ALIGN="left|right|top|texttop|middle|absmiddle|baseline|bottom|absbottom"
        VSPACE=value HSPACE=value>
```

I've gone into each of the attributes in more detail below.

```
<APPLET CODEBASE="path">
```

The **CODEBASE** attribute is used to redirect Netscape to a different URL as the source for an applet. If this attribute isn't used then the default URL is the same as the document. That isn't always a good thing, as some servers may demand you use a central Java applet repository (much like they do for CGI scripts).

When you define the **CODEBASE** attribute, all relative entities for that Java applet will also be drawn from that URL. So any images, audio files, etc. need to reside at that URL as well.

```
<APPLET CODE="java class">
```

A required attribute, this is the actual name of the Java applet that you want to run.

```
<APPLET ALT="text">
```

This optional attribute tells Netscape the text it should display if it doesn't run the Java applet. This is similar to the **<IMAGE ALT>** tag used to display alternate text for images.

```
<APPLET NAME="text">
```

Another optional attribute, the name attribute defines an internal name for the applet so other things such as JavaScript or other Java applets can communicate with it.

```
<APPLET WIDTH=value HEIGHT=value>
```

This is a required attribute that defines the width and height (in pixels) of the container for the applet.

```
<APPLET ALIGN=left|right|top|texttop|middle|absmiddle|baseline|bottom|absbottom>
```

An optional tag that works just like the similar attribute for the **<IMAGE>** tag. This attribute decides the alignment for the applet on your page.

```
<APPLET VSPACE=value HSPACE=value>
```

This optional attribute specifies an offset from the container frame that Netscape should provide for the Java applet area on a page. It works just like the **VSPACE** and **HSPACE** attributes used for an **<IMAGE>** tag.

<PARAM>

As I stated above, you pass values to an applet via the **<PARAM>** tag. Let's formally run through the attributes of this tag.

```
<PARAM NAME="name">
```

The **NAME** attribute is the actual name of the parameter to pass into the Java applet.

```
<PARAM VALUE="value">
```

Once the name is given you follow it up with the **VALUE** attribute, which specifies the value of the named parameter for the Java applet.

Bugs in the Java?

There are a number of problems coming to the surface with Java, but these are to be expected with any new programming language. One of the biggest problems is that Java is a 32-bit application; therefore Netscape for Windows 3.1 does not run Java. You need to have at least Windows 95 or Windows NT installed on your computer to run a Java-compliant version of Netscape.

Most of the problems with Java, aside from Beta browsers, bad installations, and machine-based problems, actually can be traced to the compiled applets themselves. Overall, though, Java and Netscape are becoming increasingly bug and error free. As people get better at programming in Java, the number of poorly-designed applets should decrease.

In the end, it's up to you to test your Java applets to make sure they work as advertised. Most will—I'm not trying to scare you off. Just understand that a Java applet is the result of a lot of programming and software power, and that means you need to treat it carefully to use it properly.

Where to Get Java Applets

Every day more and more applets hit the Web, and that means you have an incredibly fast-growing assortment of cool Java applets you can use. Remember, Java applets are like anything else—they're owned by the programmer, not you. While many of the applets that exist are freely available for you to use, *read the fine print!* You may find out that there are restrictions in using a programmer's applet without credit, cash, or some other form of acknowledgment.

Now that I've gotten that out of the way, here are some of the best places to go fishing for Java applets.

The Gamelan ("Gah'-meh-lonn") Registry
http://www.gamelan.com

By far the best place on the Web to go for ready-made Java applets is the Gamelan Registry—the number one outpost for Java applets. There are pointers here to most of the major Java applets available. You could spend hours exploring it all.

Sun Microsystems Javasoft
http://www.javasoft.com

Looking for information on Java applets? Why not go to the horse's mouth and visit Sun's Javasoft subsidiary.

Where to Find Out How to Insert a Java Applet in Your Page

I suggest you use the Gamelan directory to find your applets. The Gamelan site is shown in Figure 22.4. From there, most of the applets you want are easy to download. There's no standard practice that's evolved for giving you the rules for placing the Java applet on your site, but most of them put the instructions on their site. Make sure you read the sites carefully.

Many times you'll use the **CODEBASE** attribute to link to the direct page and URL where the original applet is stored, using the **PARAM** instructions given by the author (many provide an exact instance to simply cut and paste into your HTML file). Other times you can download the applet and use it locally—some even offer the original source.

I Want to Write My Own Java Programs!

Wow! You are the adventurous type now, aren't you? Writing Java applets is actually not as hard as I make it sound, it's like most software development—simple programs are simple to program and something more advanced takes a lot of work. However, if you have no programming background, I wouldn't recommend just diving in.

However, the quantity and quality of Java tutorials available for free over the Web are very, very good. One reason is because Java is a one-size-fits-all language. Thus, there's no need for a separate programming tutorial for Java

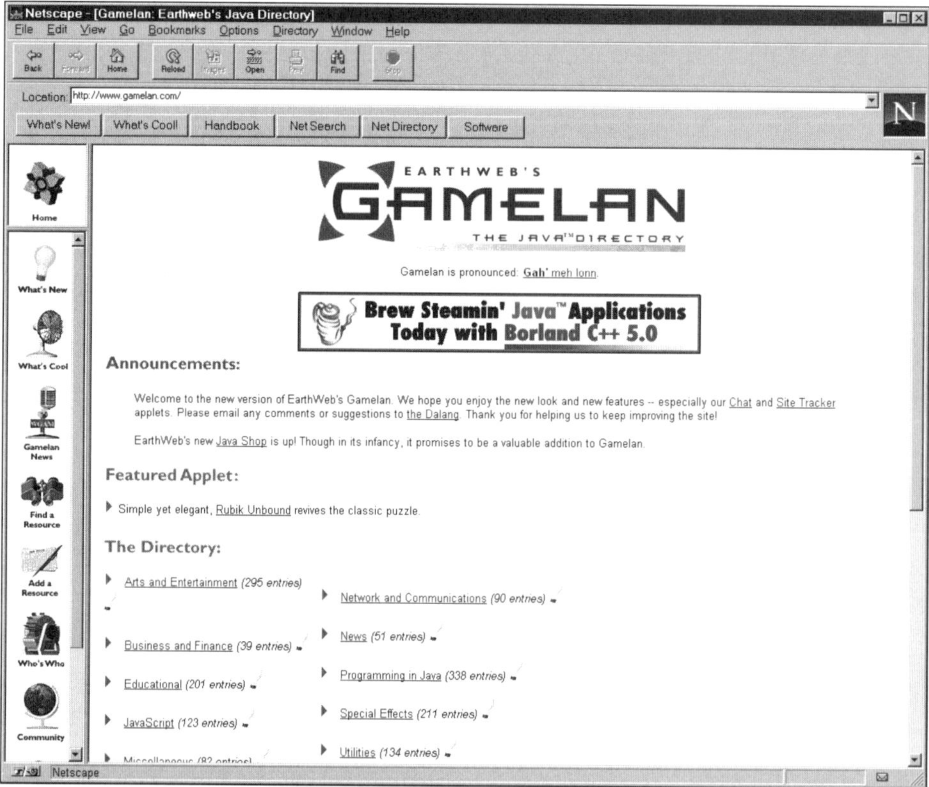

Figure 22.4 The Gamelan site is one of the best sources for applets.

for Windows, Java for the Mac, Java for Linux, and so on. While there might be some peculiarities as far as installation, there isn't any difference in the syntax or libraries you use, so there's no need to track down tons of processor- or machine-specific tutorials.

Here are my favorite places to go to learn about Java programming, as well as some recommended reading.

Digital Espresso
http://www.io.org/~mentor/DigitalEspresso.html

This is an extremely well-done magazine about Java done directly on the Web. Search the current and past issues for tons of information on Java, and especially Java Development.

Trail Map: A Java Tutorial
http://www.java.sun/tutorial/

This is a well-done tutorial that is housed directly on Sun's main Java information and software site.

Brewing Java: A Tutorial
http://moonbase.wwc.edu/homepages/cs_dept/Java/tutorial.alt/javatutorial.html

Created by Elliot Rusty Harold, this is one of the better tutorials on Java—in fact, I personally recommend it. It's packed with good and easy-to-understand writing. It's well-traveled and can be gotten at numerous sites on the Web. For the most up-to-date version check your best search engine and look at the dates and size of the file. I found the above site to be a quick load.

JavaWorld Magazine
http://www.javaworld.com

Where there's smoke there's fire, and where there's a hot new technology there's always the requisite theme magazine not far behind. JavaWorld is a major magazine devoted to Java and Java development. They have an extensive series of tutorials available at: http://www.javaworld.com/common/jw.nuts.toc.html. Check this site out!

The AWT Tutorial
http://ugweb.cs.ualberta.ca/~nelson/java/AWT.Tutorial.html

This is a great fundamental Java tutorial site. The AWT tutorial goes step by step through the creation of a Java applet.

LET'S REVIEW

Even though Java applets are the newest programming kid on the block, they don't require a lot of programming knowledge to use. You don't have to write your own applets, simply go to one of the Java sites mentioned above to find exactly what you're looking for to spice up your Web pages.

Netscape Gold

Netscape has gotten into the act with its own HTML editor, Netscape Gold. What makes it different from all the rest?

Navigator Gold is a special version of Netscape Navigator that has a built in Web editor. Other than its Web publishing ability, Navigator Gold is exactly like Netscape Navigator. Navigator Gold does not have any additional browsing features, so if you don't have Gold and aren't going to edit your own pages, don't worry—you're not missing anything.

However, if you're not content to just consume other people's content, Navigator Gold is a useful tool. With it, and a few other key applications, you can be producing your own cool looking Web pages in no time. In this chapter, I'll show you all the ins and outs of Navigator Gold.

Is Navigator Gold One of the Best Editors?

In a short answer—maybe. For Web pros it's a little lacking—there are higher-end products like Adobe's PageMill and Microsoft's FrontPage that are far more powerful than Navigator Gold. However, for the beginner and the part-time Web enthusiast, Navigator Gold is an excellent editor.

What makes Navigator Gold a better-than-average editor is its WYSIWYG (What You See Is What You Get) display and editing and its tight integration with Netscape Navigator. In addition, it has some very easy-to-use features, and unless you're doing complicated page displays using tables, forms, and frames, it's really easy to whip up some good Web pages with Navigator Gold.

The problem that some people have with Navigator Gold is that they were expecting more from the number one browser company. However, the majority of negative reviews are from professional Web page creators. It's important to ask yourself what level of Web creation you're planning to do. If you're doing major Web page creating, then you won't need Navigator Gold. If you're just creating a home page, you'll probably love it.

Netscape Navigator Gold is a very good editor for about 80 percent of Web page creators, and for the rest—well, it's a nice touch-up tool. Either way, let's play with it more and find out exactly what this program can do.

THE MAIN SCREEN

The main Navigator Gold Screen looks a little like Microsoft Word, but with bigger icons and a distinct red bar between the menu/toolbar section of the screen and the actual HTML document, as shown in Figure 23.1.

Looks pretty simple, doesn't it? Well it is! The tool bars at the top control a lot of the basic text formatting. It's easy to lay out a document with just a few simple point and clicks.

Toolbars

The first toolbar controls most of the key formatting options for documents. Figure 23.2 shows what the first toolbar looks like.

The following list explains what each button does.

A- This button decreases the font size by one increment.

A+ This button increases the font size by one increment.

+0 This drop-down list also controls the font size.

A This button bolds the text.

A This button italicizes the text.

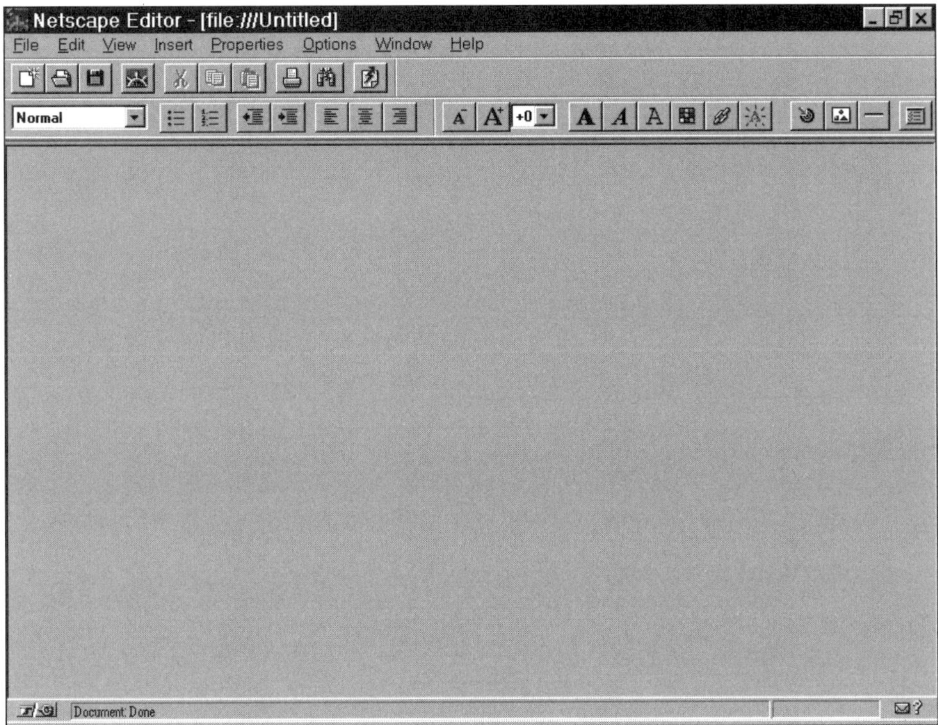

Figure 23.1 *The main screen of Netscape Navigator Gold.*

Figure 23.2 *The first toolbar on the main screen.*

Want a fixed space font? Click on this button.

Want to use all sorts of different colors? Click this button to bring up the color dialog box.

This button activates the links dialog box.

Use this button to remove all the formatting.

Click on this button to activate the anchor control.

Need an image? Press here to insert and add images.

To insert a line in your document click here.

This button activates the object properties dialog box.

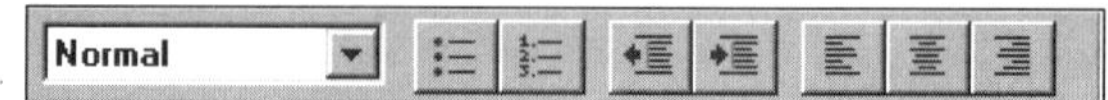

Figure 23.3 *The second Netscape Gold toolbar.*

The next major tool bar is for editing controls the styles, bulleted lists, and alignment of items. See Figure 23.3.

Let's detail each one.

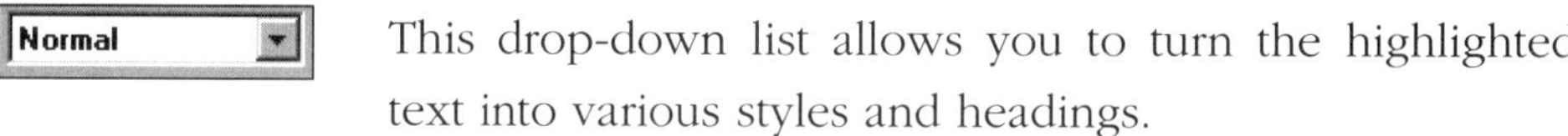

This drop-down list allows you to turn the highlighted text into various styles and headings.

This button creates a bulleted list from highlighted text or starts a new list.

This button creates a numbered list from highlighted text or starts a new list.

To move text back toward the left margin from previous indentations click this button.

This button indents paragraphs incrementally when clicked.

Flush text to the left.

To center text use this button.

Flush text to the right.

Finally we get to the third toolbar. When we finally finish our new creation, we still need to save, load, view, print, and definitely publish it. That can all be easily done right from Navigator Gold, because there's a simple tool bar available to execute all of those commands. That toolbar is shown in Figure 23.4.

Each button in the toolbar is described below.

This button loads a new Navigator Gold editor.

This button opens an existing document.

Figure 23.4 *The third and final toolbar.*

This button saves the current document.

This button saves the current document, brings up the Navigator browser, and loads the current document for viewing.

This button cuts highlighted items and text to the clipboard.

This button copies highlighted items and text to the clipboard.

This button pastes items in the clipboard to the current insertion point in the document.

This button prints the current document.

This button initiates the Find text box.

This button initiates the publishing dialog control.

All of these easy-to-use buttons are what makes Navigator Gold so great for beginners who up until now might have been using a simple shareware editor. It's really easy to use, and with the WYSIWYG editing capabilities you can see exactly what the results are without having to test it over and over again. A number of other editors have this capability, but most beginners don't want to spend a fortune for them, and the ones I've seen on the low end (i.e., less than $75) don't work as well as Gold.

MORE NAVIGATOR GOLD

Of course Navigator Gold is far more than a glorified text editor. It does more than that—you can insert pictures and customize them, and you can create links, anchors, and lines. You can also integrate it with your favorite text or HTML editor for raw HTML coding. You can even configure it to work with your favorite imaging or paint package.

Let's look more in depth at Navigator Gold by learning how to configure it using the Editor Preferences dialog box shown in Figure 23.5.

This box is the first area in which you set your Navigator Gold preferences. Here you're greeted with a dialog box with three tabs. The first tab sets general preferences for your editor, such as:

Author name: This is pretty self explanatory—put your name here.

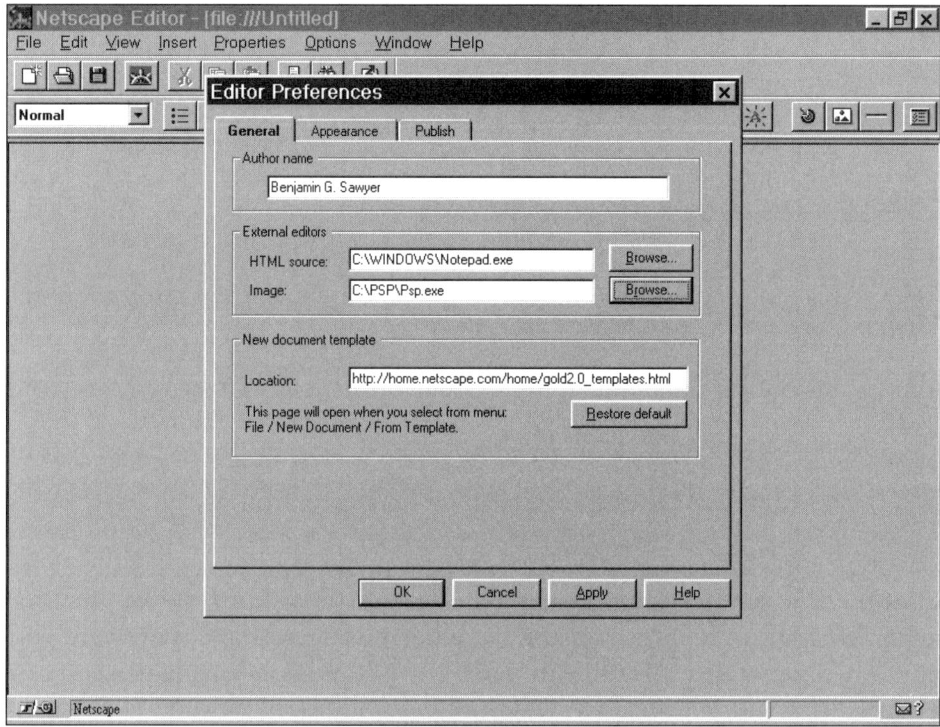

Figure 23.5 The Editor Preferences General dialog box.

External editors: In these two fields you can define an HTML source editor (I used notepad here but you might use HotDog or HTML Notepad) and an Image editor (I chose Paint Shop Pro, a popular shareware product).

It's good to set these two items in the beginning, since Navigator Gold is best used in conjunction with a good text editor for JavaScript code and frame code. In addition, you'll work with a lot of images and you'll often find yourself needing to touch them up, resize them, or image process them.

Document template: Say you have a favorite HTML setup that you always work with when starting a new Web page. If you put the filename here, when Navigator Gold starts a new document, it'll be your starting point.

The second dialog tab, the Appearances tab shown in Figure 23.6, is devoted to the color and background scheme you choose to use for your documents. In this example I've chosen a custom color setup to show the full use of the preferences settings. You can also choose to use the browser setting, which is the default setting.

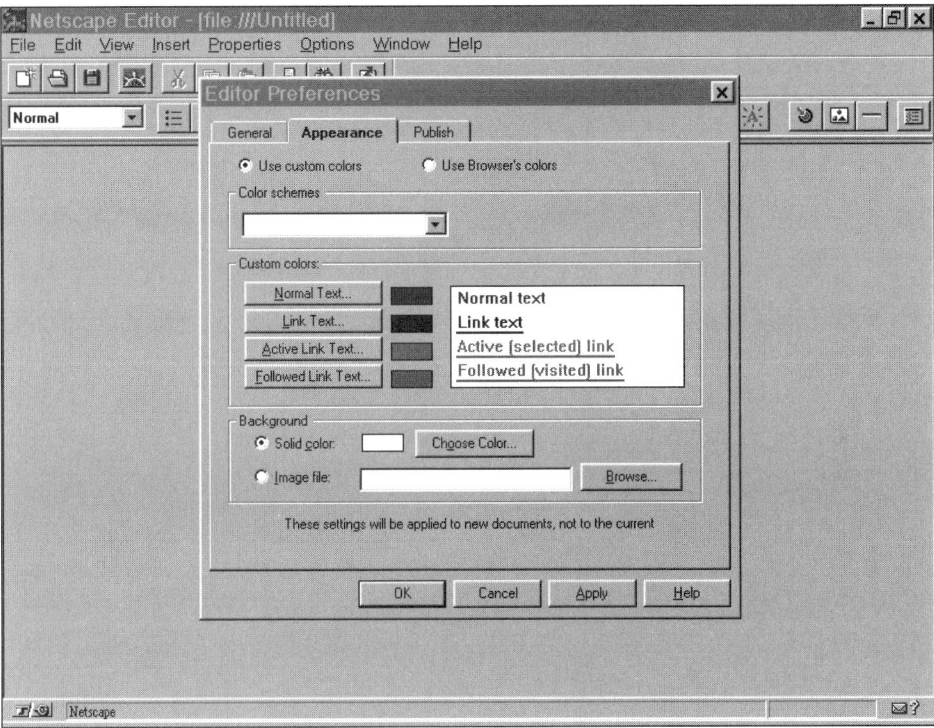

Figure 23.6 *The Editor Preferences Appearance tab.*

In the custom colors section you can click on each of the buttons to bring up a color selection box, so you can set the color of the four types of text that appear in Netscape. Figure 23.6 shows the default colors, but remember, you can override these.

The Background portion of this box gives you two basic choices—either a solid color or an image file. Click on the Choose Color button to pick a solid color. To choose an image, click on the Browse button to pull up a standard Windows file menu.

Note the comment at the bottom of this tab: "These setting will be applied to new documents, not to the current." Make sure you don't try to change color schemes in the middle of your document, because they won't apply to any current documents. At least they warned you.

Publishing Options

Navigator Gold lets you configure information about the location of your site. This is important for some Web page creators that will use Navigator Gold to upload their Web creations directly to their service provider. Most providers

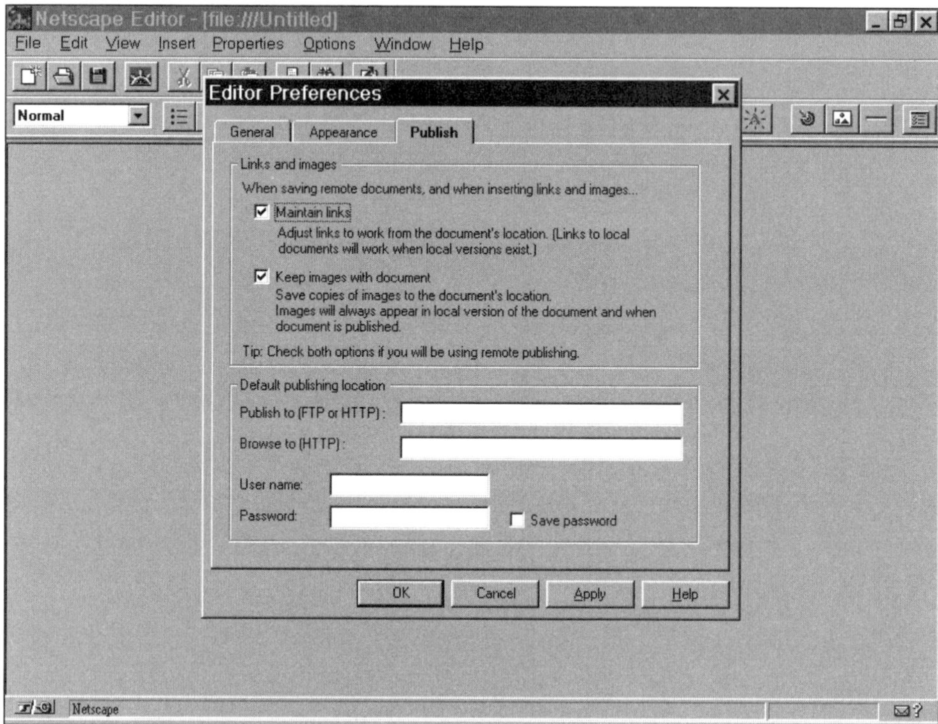

***Figure 23.7** The Publish tab of the Editor Preferences box.*

have different schemes as to how you're supposed to configure and upload pages, so make sure you check with your service provider. Many, if not all, service providers should be familiar with Netscape Navigator Gold so you might even ask them "How can I configure Gold to automatically upload my pages to you?" Figure 23.7 shows the Publish tab of the Editor Preferences box.

Here are the basics of this box:

Links and images: The first box, Maintain links, tells Navigator to maintain the links to a document that you pull directly from the Web. If you want to edit live documents from the Web and then re-upload them, it's important to make sure this box is checked.

The second box is important if you use a lot of images in your document. The Keep images with document checkbox tells Netscape to help you by making sure that all the images you pull from various directories are stored in one place. This makes it really easy to upload everything once you're done. I love it because I've got ten different directories that I store different images in, and now I don't have to do any of the maintenance on them as a result of Navigator Gold's work.

Default publishing location: This part of the Editor Preferences box provides the ability to have Netscape Navigator control the uploading of documents to your Web server. Essentially, you type in the ftp or http address of the publishing section of your server, as well as your user name and password (check "remember" so you don't have to enter this over and over). Then add your browsing http address and when you publish your page, it will contact that site and upload the document items as needed. Again, I strongly suggest you talk with your service provider or site administrator before doing this.

Inserting Lines and Pictures

The **<IMAGE>** tag in HTML contains a lot of options that can be confusing. That's easily solved by Netscape Navigator, because everything you want to do with an image in HTML is in one simple dialog box. The Properties box, shown in Figure 23.8, brought up by pressing the image button, greets you with everything you need to put pictures on your Web site.

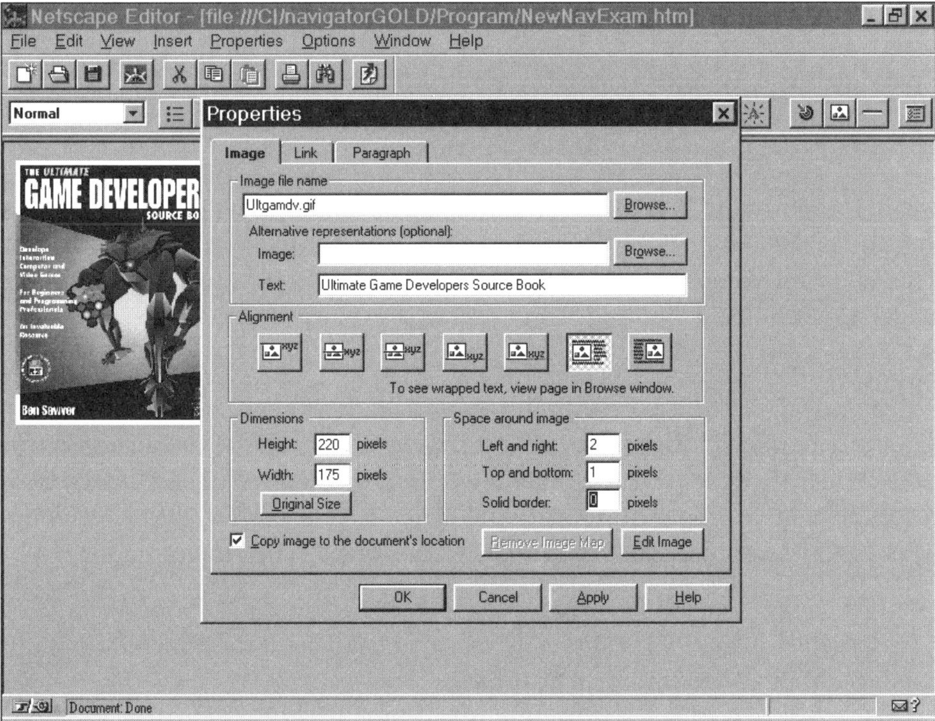

Figure 23.8 The Properties Image tab.

Pictures

Image file name: Here you insert the filename you want to display in the final loading of the document. You can click on the Browse button if you're not sure of the exact filename.

Alternative representations: Netscape supports the ability to first load a simple low resolution image while it loads your final higher resolution image on top of it. Simply click on the Browse button to find the URL you want. You can also insert alternative text into your document, so those who can't or don't want to see images know what is there. Simply type the text you want into the box.

Alignment: Here you can select from a number of sample buttons that allow you to choose how you want the graphics positioned relative to the text around it. Note: In order to see the specific request in action you have to view the page in the browser portion of Navigator Gold.

Dimensions: You can use this to enter the specific dimensions of an image. Remember, just because an image is originally 100x200 doesn't preclude you from telling Netscape to resize it to 50x50 or 150x200. To undo any custom scaling just click on the Original Size button to revert back to the original dimensions.

Space around image: Here you control the border and white space that surround an image. The border is done in black and the measurements for it and for the white space are in pixel widths.

Copy image: When this checkbox is checked Netscape will compile the image and place it in the same directory as the document currently being edited. This is useful when you're trying to centrally locate all of your content for easier uploading.

Lines

Adding a horizontal line to your Web page with Navigator Gold couldn't be easier. First, click on the horizontal line button on the toolbar. Navigator Gold responds with a simple horizontal line. Then if you want to add special options to it, just double-click on the line you want to customize.

Double-clicking on the line brings up the Horizontal Line Properties dialog box shown in Figure 23.9. There you are greeted with the four key options used to define a custom horizontal line.

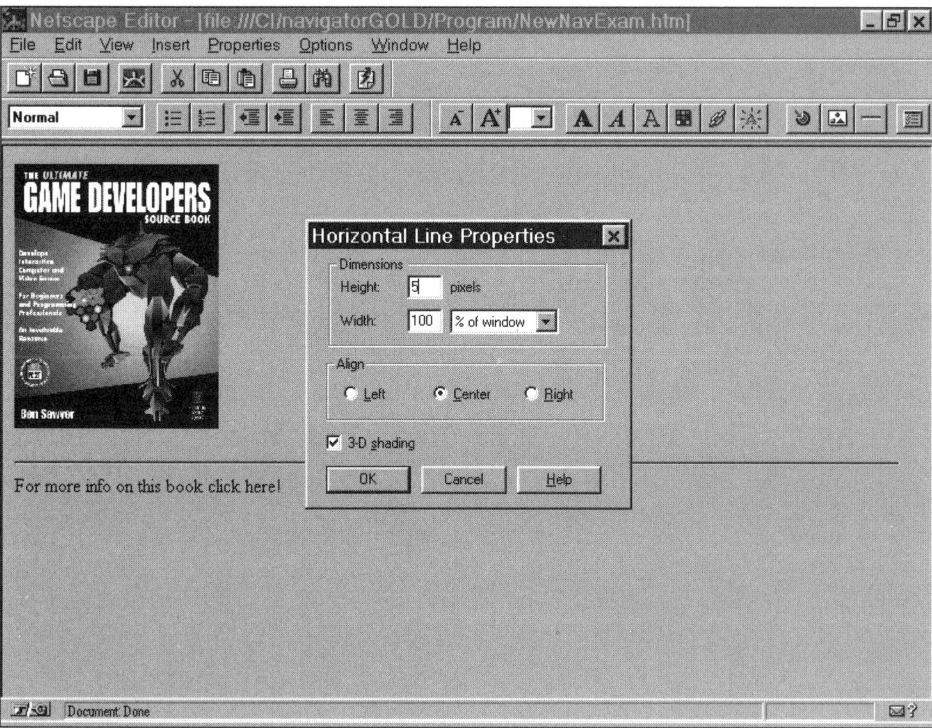

Figure 23.9 *The Horizontal Line Properties dialog box.*

Dimensions: You can define both the height and width of the line. Height is the number of pixels you want the line to have from top to bottom. The Width can either be set to a specific number of pixels, or a percentage of the window. The default is set to a percentage. Clicking on the list box next to the width amount box allows you to switch easily between a specific pixel setting or a percentage of the Window.

Align: The align box allows you to align the horizontal line to the left, center, or right of the window—of course for the right or left to be useful, the line has to be smaller than the window.

3-D shading: Finally, if you want 3-D shading (which is the default) then make sure this checkbox is clicked.

Setting Character Properties

The buttons on the toolbar control virtually every aspect of formatting text with Navigator Gold. However, there is another way to format—by using the

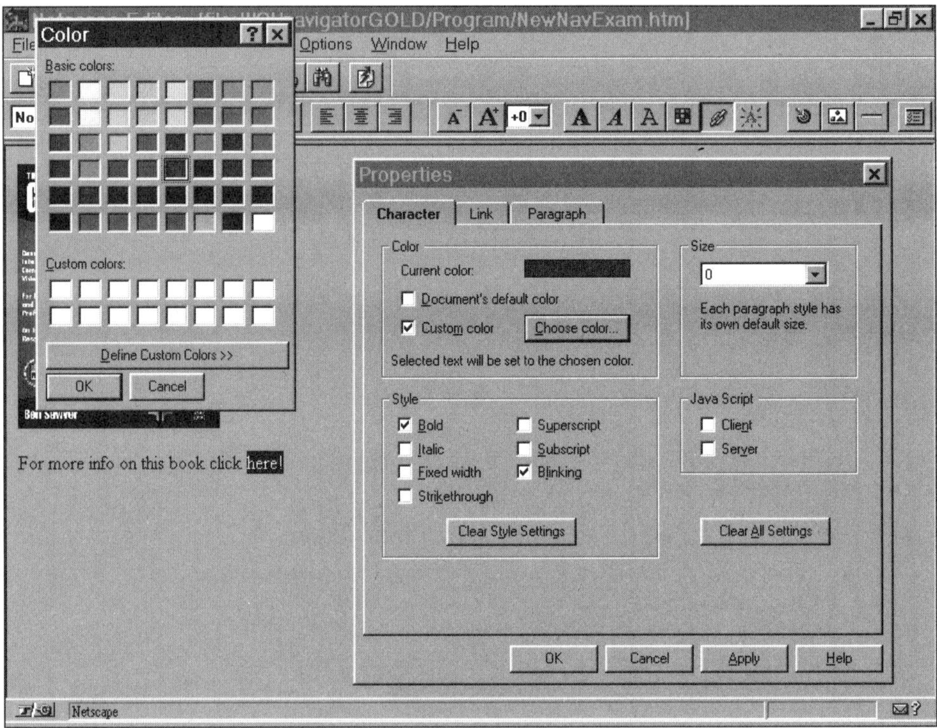

Figure 23.10 The Character Properties dialog box.

Character Properties dialog box. First highlight some text and then click on the Properties button on the toolbar (it's to the right of the horizontal line button). Doing that brings up the dialog box shown in Figure 23.10.

In this example I've shown both the Character tab and the Color dialog box, which is triggered when choosing a custom color for the highlighted text. This box can handle all of your character formatting needs. Each section is listed below.

Color: This box shows the current color of the text and lets you decide whether to use the document's default color or a custom color. When you choose a custom color, the Color dialog box shown in Figure 23.10 is displayed. Your selected text will be set to whatever color you choose.

Size: To the right of the Color section is the Size section, where you'll find a drop-down list similar to the list found on Navigator Gold's toolbar. You can choose from -2 to +4, with 0 being the default font size.

Style: Directly below the Color section is the Style section. Here you have a series of seven checkboxes that define the specific style the selected text will have. Click on the Clear Style Settings to remove all the styles and start over.

JavaScript: Here you can define the text as JavaScript code.

Clear All Settings: Clicked too much? Click here to clear all the features of the highlighted text and start over from scratch.

Anchors and Links

Anchors and links are quite simple to create in Navigator Gold. Typically, I find linking to be a lot of work—especially when I have a document with lots of links. However, with some simple and flexible dialog boxes, Navigator Gold gives you as pain-free a process as possible.

To create a link, first highlight the image or text you want to turn into a link. In my example I've created a link to my image. Once you've highlighted it, press on the link icon on the toolbar and you'll be presented with the Link Properties dialog box shown in Figure 23.11.

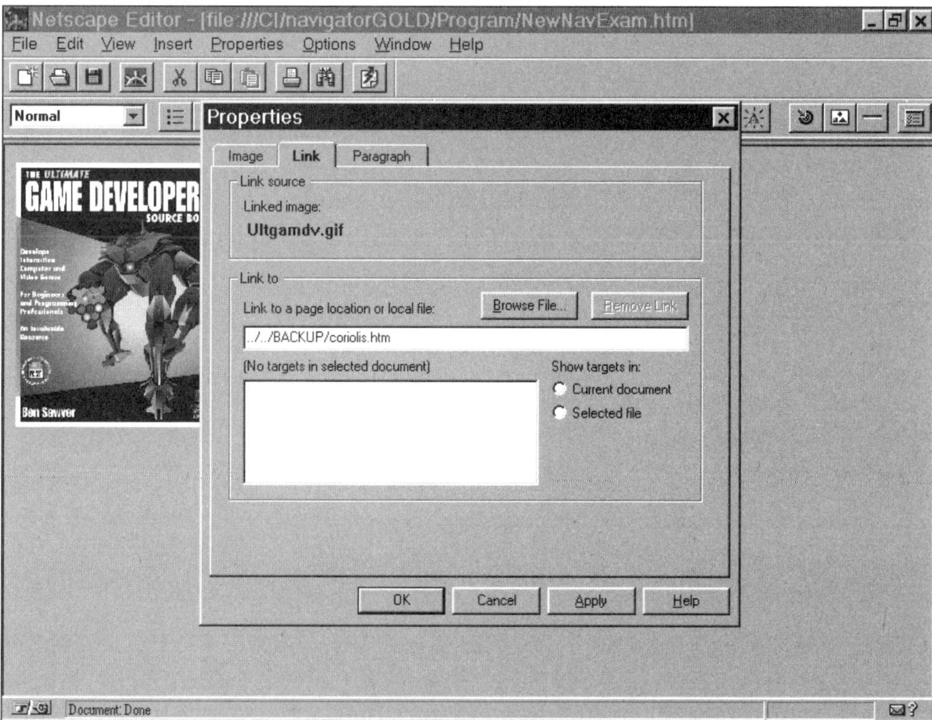

Figure 23.11 The Link Properties dialog box.

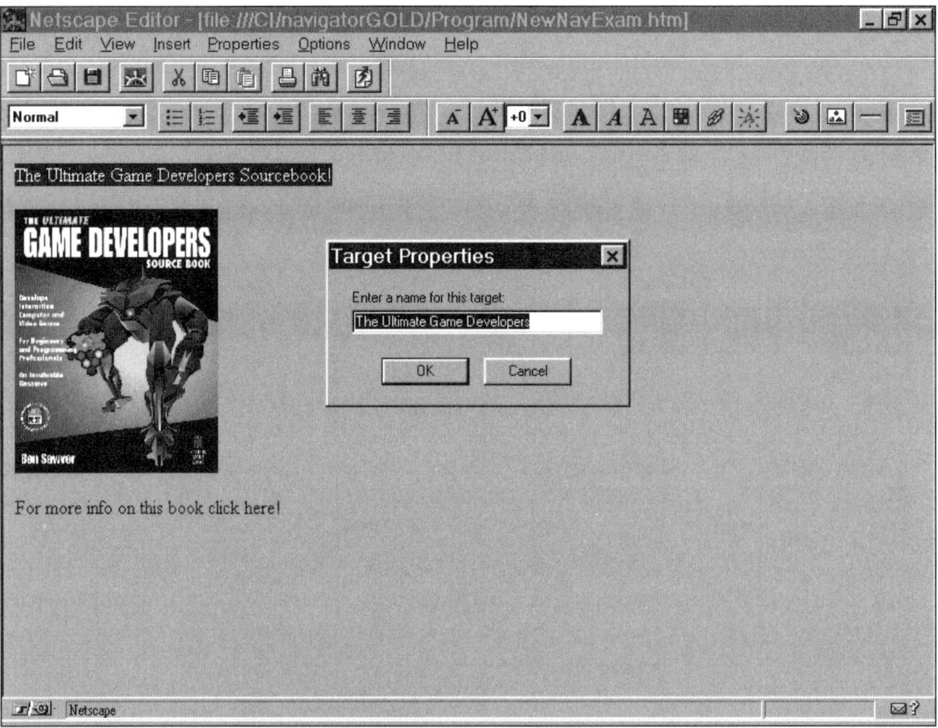

***Figure 23.12** The Target Properties dialog box.*

Link to: To define a link you can either type a file name or URL directly into the filename box, or you can use the Browse box to select a local file (as I've done in the example picture). Just below the filename box is a list of anchors you may have defined in the current document or the selected file. You can click on those as well. What you can't do is create links to other documents without typing it in the box directly. However, you can open your bookmark file and drag-and-drop in links from that database of URLs.

To make an anchor just place the cursor over or next to the text you want the anchor to reside at and hit the Anchor button (to the left of the picture button). The Target Properties dialog box shown in Figure 23.12 will appear on your screen. You can then give alternate text to your anchor, and then hit OK. Voilà! You now have an anchor.

Anchors are useful and often are not used enough. It's so simple to make an anchor with Navigator Gold it would be a crime not to have lots of good anchors in your document. Even if you're not going to use them yourself, you might consider putting in some key anchors for other people to use if they want to link to a specific portion of a page in your site.

OTHER EDITING FUNCTIONS

There are a few more editing features to cover, including a few menu items, the final toolbar, and the actual editor, so let's start with some of the editing functions that are only available from the menus. Hidden away in the menus of Navigator Gold are some gems you will use from time to time during your Web page editing endeavors. There are three specific menus that hold items we want to investigate: the View, Insert, and Properties menus.

View Menu

The first menu item you will find yourself using quite a bit is the View menu shown in Figure 23.13.

Among the many useful features in this menu are:

View Document Source: This brings up a window in Navigator Gold that shows you the raw HTML source code to your document, just like when you use the same item in Navigator. The source is not editable, but can be cut and pasted into another document.

Edit Document Source: If you've named an HTML editor in the Editor Preferences section, selecting this menu item will automatically place the document currently being edited into that editor. This is useful for quickly switching back and forth between Navigator Gold and your favorite HTML source editor.

Document Info: This feature brings up a window that is similar to an outline of the currently edited document. It doesn't list source or text, but it does show a listing of all the major components, like images. Clicking on each outline item brings up a brief summary of the item. Figure 23.14 shows what the Document Info window looks like.

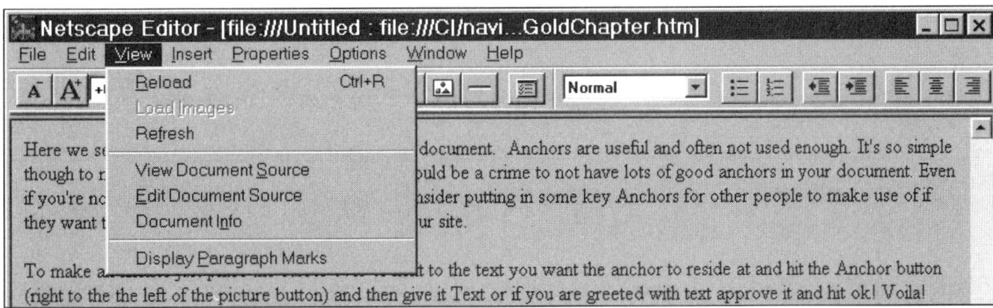

Figure 23.13 The View menu.

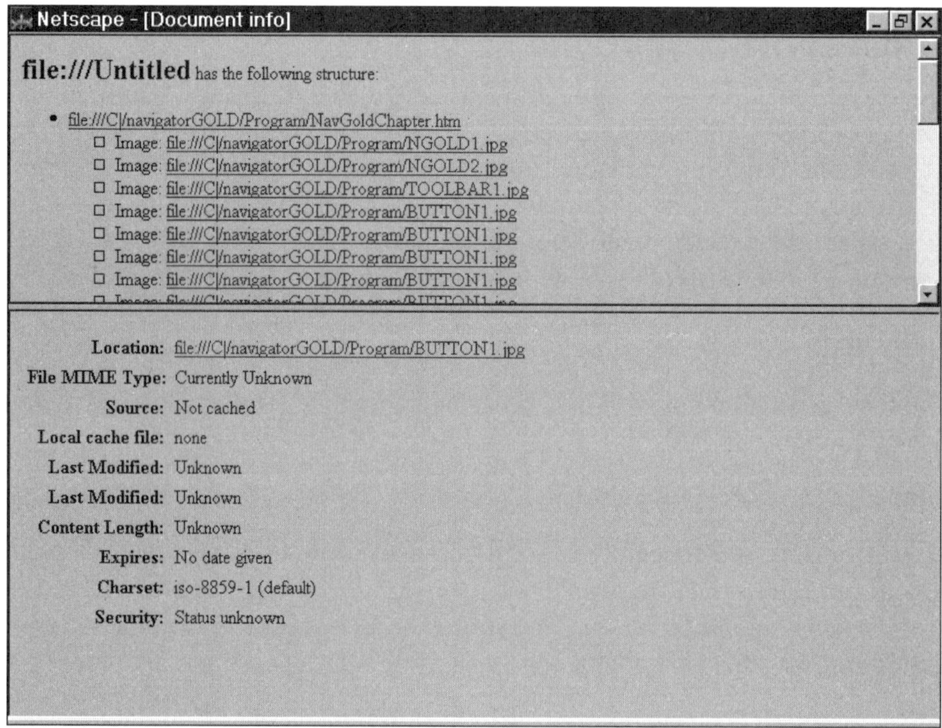

***Figure 23.14** The Document info window.*

The top half of the screen is devoted to the outline of items (in this case just images) and the bottom half shows info such as MIME type, Source, Local cache, and so on. Clicking on the location item will bring up the item to be viewed in the bottom window. So if I want to see the picture of BUTTON1.jpg, I would click on that link.

Paragraph Marks: This item turns Paragraph Marks on and off, which is useful for locating the ends of actual paragraphs. Paragraph marks appear in the document as simple black rectangles.

Insert Menu

The next menu to look at is the Insert menu, as it contains some other important features, especially concerning spacing in your HTML documents. The Insert menu is shown in Figure 23.15.

The first four items in this menu, Link...,Target(Named Anchor)..., Image..., and Horizontal Line... are all also available via the toolbars, so there's no need to discuss them again. However, the bottom four are new.

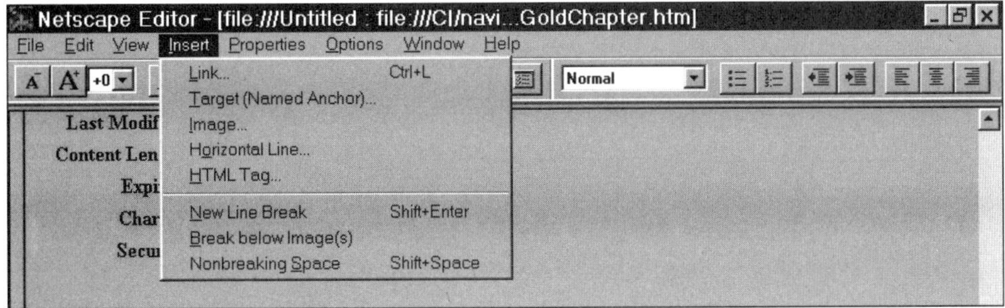

***Figure 23.15** The Insert menu.*

HTML Tag: This menu item brings up a dialog box which allows you to insert any HTML tag into your document. Navigator Gold does a lot of the basics of HTML for you, but there are still a slew of tags, for example any of the FORM oriented tags like **<FORM>, <INPUT TYPE>, <TEXTAREA>,** etc., that are not readily available. I prefer to use an HTML source editor for most of that work, but if you're doing some quick things, this is an easy way to insert a few tags without leaving the Navigator Gold editor. The HTML Tag dialog box is shown in Figure 23.16.

Basically, you just input the tag you want and click OK. You can click Verify to have Navigator Gold check to make sure the Tag is OK. However, it's not a very complex test, so don't rely on it for more than making sure you've opened and closed the tag correctly.

Tags in your Navigator Gold document show up as little yellow tags. Dragging the mouse over the tag makes the tag show up in the status bar.

New Line Break: Also available by pressing Shift+Enter, this is the equivalent of using the **
** tag in your HTML source.

Break below Image(s): This is the equivalent of the HTML code:

```
<br clear=both><p>
```

Nonbreaking Space: Also available by pressing Shift+Space, this is very useful for inserting more than one space between elements or text in your HTML document. For example, if you wanted to have

look at the extra space between these words!

you would use this feature.

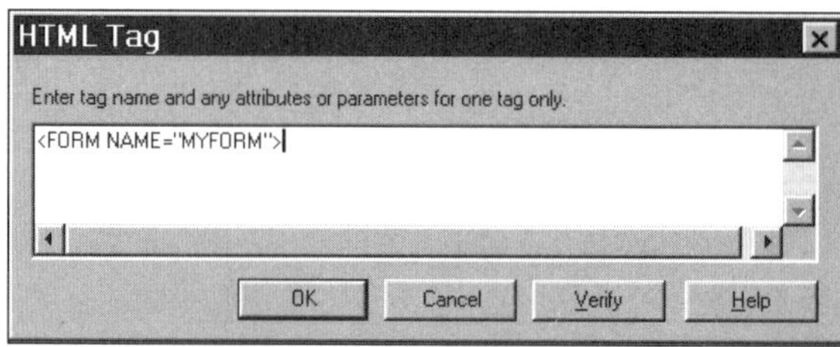

Figure 23.16 *The HTML Tag dialog box.*

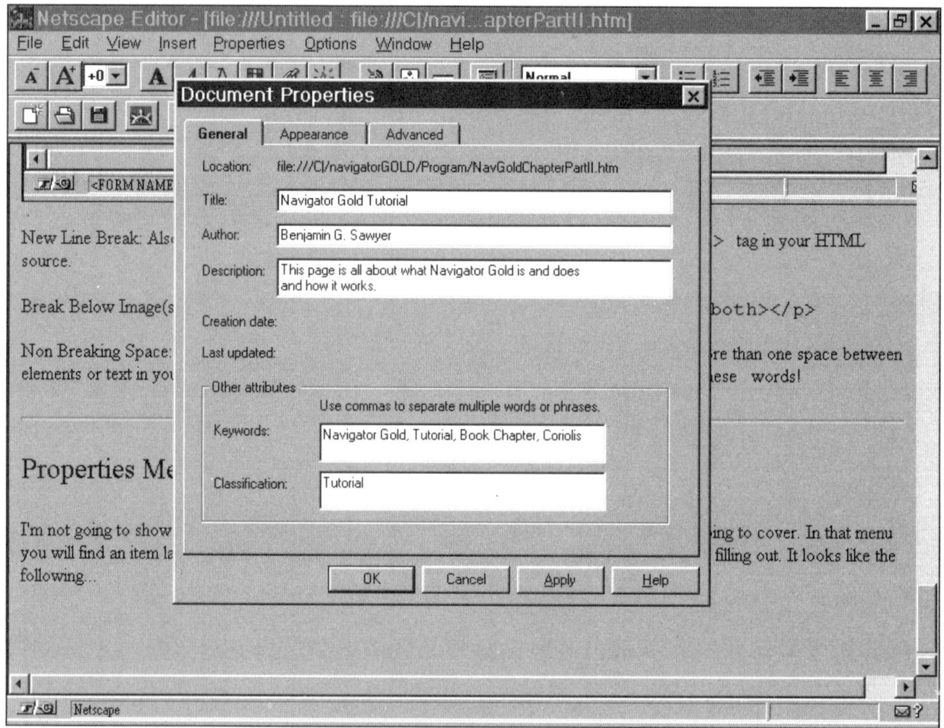

Figure 23.17 *The Document Properties summary box.*

Properties Menu

In the Properties menu you will find an item labeled Document..., as shown in Figure 23.17. Selecting Document... brings up a document summary box worth filling out.

This dialog box allows you to set a number of interesting aspects of your document. Let's run through them all:

Location: This part of the dialog box shows you the current location of the document currently being edited.

Title: Use this to set the Title of the document as it will appear in the top bar of the Navigator window.

Author: Place your name here. It defaults to the name you set earlier in the Editor Preferences part of Navigator Gold.

Description: Type in a description of the document.

Creation date: Shows the original creation date of the document, which is the first day you saved the document.

Last updated: Shows the date when the latest changes were made and saved.

Other attributes: This part of the dialog control is really nice. It allows you to put in text that Navigator Gold sets into your document to be scanned by many of the indexing services like Yahoo!. Here you can set up the words, phrases, and classification of your Web page to help them better index your work.

Keywords: Enter any keywords or phrases you want to be considered for your document. Separate phrases and words by commas.

Classification: Again, enter in additional classification keywords for your document that will be used by servers and search engines.

The Other Tabs: **Appearance** and **Advanced**

Notice there are two other tabs and dialogs associated with the Document Properties section of Navigator Gold. The Appearance section was covered earlier under Editor Preferences and works the same way, but affects only the specific document you're working on. The Advanced section concerns labeling the document for advanced Meta Tags and Netscape Variables, and I'm not going to discuss that here because it's not needed by most people. In addition, your service provider or Web site administrator should be able to discuss these items with you.

More about Publishing

One of the best items that Navigator Gold offers is its automated publishing feature. You can have Navigator dial up the site that receives your Web pages and upload all the elements from your page directly into the folder that holds them. You do this by simply pressing the publishing dialog control.

However, as I said earlier, before you begin using this feature make sure you talk with your service provider or site administrator. Some sites have very specific rules that govern how, where, and when pages should be uploaded to their server. If you have already discussed this with them and have gotten the basic information you need, here's the breakdown of how you can use the Automated Publishing feature.

1. First make sure you have finished and tested your document to your satisfaction. Once that's done press the publish button for the dialog control to come up. (I like to connect to the Internet first.)

2. Fill out the dialog box. Local Files shows you the directory you're primarily working from. You can select whether you want Navigator Gold to upload the entire directory (useful if there are other items in the directory that you want available from the page), or just the images referenced in the document. You can also optionally select those files so if you edit a document with 20 images, but 19 are already on the server, you can select the one you want.

3. Fill in the information concerning exactly where to upload the document, including the user name and password you acquired from your service provider or Web site administrator. Note: If you filled this out in the Editor Preferences section described earlier, it should be here waiting for you.

4. Once done click on OK and Navigator Gold will contact the site and transfer the information.

PAGE WIZARDS AND TEMPLATES

Navigator Gold allows you to edit with templates and page wizards. Whenever you start a new document, you're given the option of starting with a Page Wizard, Template, or Blank document. Ninety-five percent of the time it makes sense to start with a blank document, but in the interest of this chapter, I thought I'd show you page wizards and templates in action.

Page Wizard

You need to be connected to the Internet to use this feature. Once connected, choose to start a new document, and Netscape will switch from the Gold window to the browser window, and then load up the Page Wizard section on Netscape's own home page. This three-frame Web page leads you through the creation of a document which you can then save and re-edit or upload using Gold. It's quite self-explanatory and demonstrates how the Web can be used in an integrated manner with local software on your computer. Try it sometime—it's a fun five-minute process.

Templates

Templates are ready-to-use examples that Netscape has made available to you. Many are of things typical Web users might be doing with Navigator Gold, like making a home page for themselves or their small business, selling a home, and more.

To create a document from a template, first connect to the Internet and then choose to make a new document from a template. Netscape Navigator Gold will go into browser mode and surf over to Netscape's Template page. There you can select a template and when it's loaded choose the edit button and save it locally to your hard drive. You can then load and change the template to suit your specific needs.

Figure 23.18 shows a template being captured for later use.

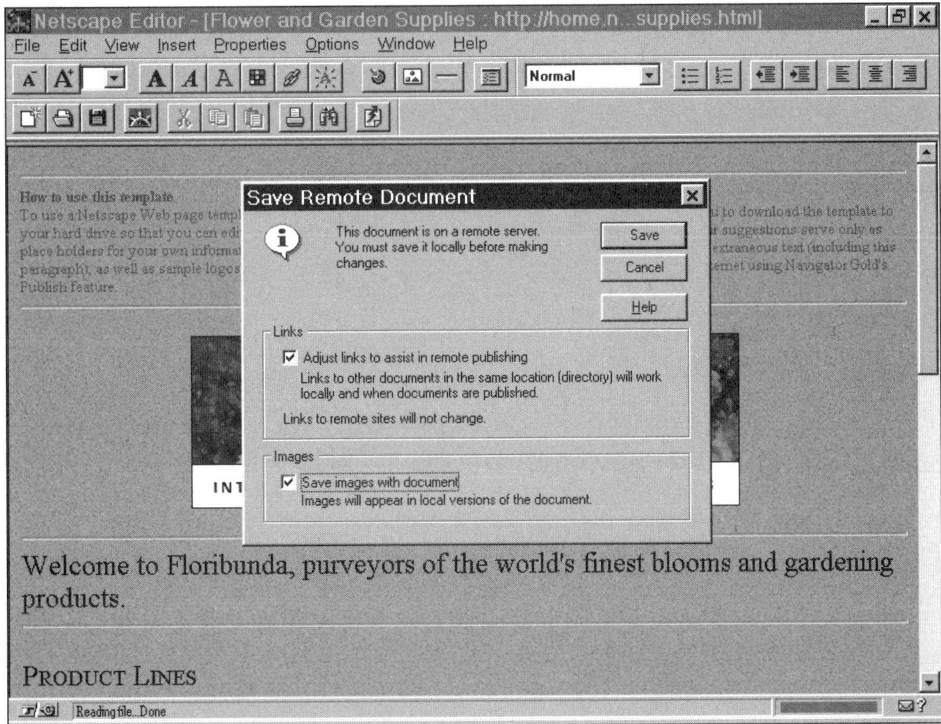

Figure 23.18 *A template being captured from Netscape's Template page.*

Press the save key and you can start editing over the original with your specific information. There are more than ten templates available, and certainly more to come.

THE NAVIGATOR GOLD TOOLBOX

Netscape has a specific section of their home page called Navigator Gold Toolbox that gives you access to resources like the templates and wizards described above. In addition, you can find artwork, JavaScript code, and more to help you use Navigator Gold to make really great looking Web sites.

Netscape's Navigator Gold Toolbox is located at:

```
http://home.netscape.com/assist/net_sites/starter/samples/index.html
```

NIT-PICKING NAVIGATOR GOLD

Ok, so what's missing from Navigator Gold? It's easy to use, has lots of good features, and contains an excellent WYSIWYG display; what more could someone ask for? Well, tables for one and form editing for another. For more advanced Web editors, forms and tables are key features they use almost every time they create a document.

Additionally, Navigator Gold doesn't spell check, which means you still need to run your text through a local word processor. Overall, Navigator Gold is best thought of not as an HTML editor, but a Web Processor—it's so similar to a Word Processor in style and function that when I was using it, a friend who isn't a Webhead yet thought I was using a word processor.

GO FOR THE GOLD?

The real question for many of you is should you go for the Navigator Gold. I have a great appreciation for what Navigator Gold does—fast, easy, and visual Web page editing. But for me, I need, in the words of Tim Allen, "More Power!" While I still plan on using Gold for most of my light Web editing features, I'll be doing a lot of raw text editing of my files, as well as using a major top-of-the-line package.

But you're not me and aside from the lack of forms and tables, Navigator Gold should do almost everything most beginning Web enthusiasts could possibly want. If you're impressed with how easy it is to use then go ahead and go for the Gold.

Appendix A: Writing Great HTML

Underneath the slick point-and-click user interface of a Web browser such as Netscape or Mosaic lies an ASCII "markup language" that can easily be composed and edited with any Windows or DOS editor.

As you probably know, the language used by the Web is called *HTML*, which stands for *HyperText Markup Language*. The *hypertext* part means that a Web page can contain references to other Web pages or to various Net resources such as Gophers and FTP sites. The *markup* part comes from the days when book and magazine publishing people made special marks on their authors' manuscripts to tell typesetters how to format the text. This process was called *markup*, and the term was adopted when people started inserting formatting instructions into their computer files.

Although we covered many of the basic features of creating Web pages with HTML in Part 2 of this book, this appendix provides a useful guide to most of the HTML features supported by leading Web browsers such as Netscape and Mosaic. As you spend more time creating Web pages, you'll find that this appendix will help you use the HTML tags.

HTML—The Language of the Web

HTML commands are enclosed in angle brackets, like <this>. Most commands come in pairs that mark the beginning and end of a part of text. The end command is often a repetition of the start command, except that it includes a forward slash between the opening bracket and the command name. For example, the title of an HTML document called "Habanero-Mango Chutney" would look like this:

```
<TITLE>Habanero-Mango Chutney</TITLE>
```

Similarly, a word or phrase that Netscape shows in **bold** type, would look like this:

```
<B>bold</B> type.
```

USING AN HTML EDITOR

Many people prefer using an HTML editor over a word processor like Microsoft Word or a simple text editor like Windows Notepad. In fact, we've included some handy HTML editors on the companion CD-ROM, including HTML Notepad and HTML Editor. It is easier to *start* writing HTML with an HTML editor than with a basic text editor because most HTML editors typically offer some sort of menu of tags. This can help you get acquainted with the HTML tag set.

The other advantage of an HTML editor is that when it inserts tags for you, it inserts both the start and the end tags. This feature greatly reduces the chance that your whole document will end up in the **<H1>** (first level header) style, or that a bold word will become three bold paragraphs.

You Still Have to Read HTML

No matter how you create HTML documents, you'll still need to learn how to read them. While an HTML editor may make it easier to insert tags such as **<B>** and **<OL>**, it can't help you decipher a document once it's created. Because an HTML editor lets you start writing without knowing all that much HTML, you might find yourself in a position where you can't even read your own work!

HTML BASICS

All HTML files consist of a mixture of text to be displayed and HTML tags that describe how the text should be displayed. Normally, extra *whitespace* (spaces, tabs, and line breaks) is ignored, and text is displayed with a single space between each word. Text is always wrapped to fit within a browser's window in the reader's choice of fonts. Line breaks in the HTML source are treated as any other whitespace, and must be specified with a *line break* tag, **
,** or a *paragraph break,* **<P>,** tag.

Tags are always set off from the surrounding text by *angle brackets,* or the less-than and greater-than signs. Most tags come in "begin" and "end" pairs:

for example, **<I>** ... **</I>**. The end tag includes a slash between the opening bracket and the tag name. There are a few tags that require only a start tag; I'll take particular care to point out these tags as they come up.

HTML is *case insensitive*: **<HTML>** is the same as **<html>** or **<hTmL>**. However, many Web servers run on Unix systems, which *are* case sensitive. This will never affect HTML interpretation, but will affect your hyperlinks: My.gif is not the same file as my.gif or MY.GIF.

Some begin tags can take *parameters*, which come between the tag name and the closing bracket like this: **<DL COMPACT>**. Others, like description lists, have optional parameters that will alter their appearance, if your reader's browser supports that option. Still others, such as anchors and images, require certain parameters and can also take optional parameters.

THE STRUCTURE OF AN HTML DOCUMENT

All HTML documents have a certain standard structure, but Netscape and most other Web browsers will treat any file that ends in .HTML—.HTM on PCs—as an HTML file, even if it contains *no* HTML tags. All HTML text and tags should be contained within this tag pair:

```
<HTML> ... </HTML>
```

<HEAD> ... </HEAD> Tag

All HTML documents are divided into a *header* that contains the title and other information about the document, and a *body* that contains the actual document text.

While you should not place display text outside the body section, this is currently optional since Netscape will format and display any text that's not in a tag. Also, while you can get away with not using the **<HEAD>** tag pair, it's strongly recommended.

<BODY> ... </BODY> Tag

The body of the document should contain the actual contents of the Web page. The tags that appear within the body do not separate the document into sections. Rather, they're either special parts of the text, like images or forms, or they're tags that *say something* about the text they enclose, like character attributes or paragraph styles.

Headings and Paragraphs

In some ways, HTML text is a series of paragraphs. Within a paragraph, the text will be wrapped to fit upon the reader's screen. In most cases, any line breaks that appear in the source file are totally ignored.

Paragraphs are separated either by an explicit paragraph break tag, **<P>**, a line break **
**, or by paragraph style commands. The paragraph style determines both the font used for the paragraph and any special indenting. Paragraph styles include several levels of section headers, five types of lists, three different "block formats," and the normal, or default paragraph style. Any text outside of an explicit paragraph style command will be displayed in the normal style.

<ADDRESS> ... </ADDRESS> Tag

The last part of the document body should be an **<ADDRESS>** tag pair, which contains information about the author and, often, the document's copyright date and revision history. While the address block is not a required part of the document in the same way that the header or the body is, official style guides urge that all documents have one. In current practice, while many documents don't use one of the **<HTML>**, **<HEAD>**, or **<BODY>** tag pairs, almost all documents have address blocks—perhaps because the address block is visible.

The format for using the **<ADDRESS>** tag is as follows:

```
<ADDRESS>Address text goes here</ADDRESS>
```

Comments

Comments can be placed in your HTML documents using a special tag as shown:

```
<!--Comment text goes here-->
```

Everything between the "<>" will be ignored by a browser when the document is displayed. Be sure to use the exclamation point!

HEADER ELEMENTS

The elements used in the header of an HTML document include a title section and internal indexing information.

<TITLE> ... </TITLE> Tag

Every document should have a title. The manner in which a title is displayed varies from system to system and browser to browser. The title could be displayed as a window title, or it may appear in a pane within the window. The title should be short—64 characters or less—and should contain just text.

The title should appear in the header section, marked off with a **<TITLE>** tag pair; for example, **<TITLE>**Lime-Jerked Chicken**</TITLE>**. Netscape is actually such an "easy-going" browser that the title can appear anywhere in the document, even after the **</HTML>** tag, but future browsers might not be quite so clever and accommodating. Including a title is important because many Web search engines will use the title to locate a document.

The format for using the **<TITLE>** tag is as follows:

```
<TITLE>Title text goes here</TITLE>
```

Other <HEAD> Elements

There are a few HTML optional elements that may only appear in the document's header (**<HEAD>** tag pair). The header elements that browsers use are the **<BASE>**, **<META>**, and **<ISINDEX>** tags. Both are *empty* or *solitary* tags that do not have a closing **</...>** tag and thus do not enclose any text.

The **BASE** tag contains the current document's URL, or *Uniform Resource Locator;* browsers can use it to find "local URLs." For more on **BASE** tags, see *Using URLs.*

The **META** tag specifies a specific act to be performed by the browser. For instance, a **META** tag can specify when the page expires, or can have the browser refresh the page every few seconds.

The **ISINDEX** tag tells browsers that this document is an index document, which means that the server can support keyword searches based on the document's URL. Searches are passed back to the Web server by concatenating a question mark and one or more keywords to the document URL and then requesting this extended URL. This is very similar to one of the ways that forms data is returned. (See the section *Form Action and Method Attributes* for more information.)

Other header elements are provided, such as **<NEXTID>** and **<LINK>**, which are included in HTML for the benefit of editing and cataloging software. They have no visible effect; browsers simply ignore them.

NORMAL TEXT

Most Web pages are composed of plain, or *normal*, text. Any text not appearing between format tag pairs is displayed as normal text.

Normal text, like every other type of paragraph style except the *preformatted* style, is wrapped at display time to fit in the reader's window. A larger or smaller font or window size will result in a totally different number of words on each line, so don't try to change the wording of a sentence to make the line breaks come at appropriate places. You'll be in for a big surprise!

 Tag

If line breaks *are* important, as in postal addresses or poetry, you can use the **
** command to insert a line break. Subsequent text will appear one line down, on the left margin.

The general format for this tag is:

```
<BR [CLEAR=Left|Right]>
```

The section listed between the "[]" is optional. This is a feature introduced as an HTML enhancement and supported by newer versions of Netscape.

Let's look at an example of how **
** is used. To keep

```
Coriolis Group Books
7339 East Acoma Drive, Suite 7
Scottsdale, Arizona 85260-6912
```

from coming out as

```
Coriolis Group Books 7339 East Acoma Drive, Suite 7 Scottsdale, Arizona
85260-6912
```

you would write:

```
Coriolis Group Books<BR>
7339 East Acoma Drive, Suite 7<BR>
Scottsdale, Arizona 85260-6912<BR>
```

The extended form of the **
** tag allows you to control how text is wrapped. The **CLEAR** argument allows text to be broken so that it can flow around an image to the right or to the left. For example, this tag shows how text can be broken to flow to the left:

```
This text will be broken here.<BR CLEAR=Left>
This line will flow around to the right of an image that can be displayed with
the IMG tag.
```

<NOBR> Tag

This tag stands for **NO BR**eak. This is another HTML extension supported by Netscape. To keep text from breaking, you can include the **<NOBR>** tag at the beginning of the text you want to keep together.

<WBR> Tag

This tag stands for **W**ord **BR**eak. If you use the **<NOBR>** tag to define a section of text without breaks, you can force a line break at any location by inserting the **<WBR>** tag followed by the **
** tag.

<P> Tag

The **
** command causes a line break within a paragraph, but more often we want to separate one paragraph from another. We can do this by ending each paragraph with a **<P>** command. Paragraph breaks may be shown with an extra line or half line of spacing, a leading indent, or both. A **</P>** command exists, but it's optional and rarely used.

Logical and Physical Attributes

Character attribute tags let you emphasize words or phrases within a paragraph. HTML supports two different types of character attributes: *physical* and *logical*. Physical attributes include the familiar bold, italic, and underline, as well as a *tty* attribute for monospaced text.

Logical attributes are different. Logical attributes let you describe what sort of emphasis you want to put on a word or phrase, but leave the actual formatting up to the browser. That is, where a word marked with a physical attribute like **<B>**bold**</B>** will always appear in **bold** type, an **<EM>**emphasized **</EM>** word may be *italicized*, underlined, **bolded**, or displayed in color.

Web style guides suggest that you use logical attributes whenever you can, but there's a slight problem: Some current browsers only support some physical attributes, and few or no logical attributes. Since Web browsers simply ignore any HTML tag that they don't "understand," you run the risk that your readers will not see any formatting at all if you use logical tags!

The standard format for using any of the physical attributes tags is as follows:

```
<tag>text goes here</tag>
```

You can nest attributes, although the results will vary from browser to browser. For example, some browsers can display ***bold italic*** text, while others will only display the innermost attribute. (That is, **<B><I>**bold italic**</I></B>** may show up as *bold italic.*) If you use nested attributes, be sure to place the end tags in reverse order of the start tags; don't write something like **<B><I>**bold italic**</B></I>**! This may work with some Web browsers but it may cause problems with others.

<BLINK> ... </BLINK>

This is an enhanced tag supported by Netscape. Text placed between this pair will blink on the screen. This feature is useful for getting someone's attention but if you use it too much, it could get rather annoying. The format for this tag is:

```
<BLINK>This text will blink</BLINK>
```

<CENTER> ... </CENTER>

This HTML enhancement makes some Web page authors feel like they've died and gone to heaven. Any text (or images) placed between this pair is centered between the left and right margins of a page. The format for this tag is:

```
<CENTER>This text will be centered between the left and right margins</CENTER>
```

<FONT> ... </FONT>

This HTML enhancement allows you to control the sizes of the fonts displayed in your documents. The format for this tag is:

```
<FONT SIZE=font-size>text goes here</FONT>
```

where *font-size* must be a number from 1 to 7. A size of 1 produces the smallest font. The default font size is 3. Once the font size has been changed, it will remain in effect until the font size is changed by using another tag.

<BASEFONT>

To give you even greater control over font sizing, you can use the **<BASEFONT>** tag to set the base font for all text displayed in a document. The format for this tag is:

```
<BASEFONT SIZE=font-size>
```

Again, *font-size* must be a number from 1 to 7. A size of 1 produces the smallest font. The default font size is 3. Once the base font size has been defined, you can display text in larger or smaller fonts using the "+" or "-" sign with the **<FONT>** tag. Here's an example of how this works:

Table A.1 List of Physical Attributes

Attribute	Tag	Sample	Effect
Bold	<B>	Some <B>bold</B> text	Some **bold** text
Italic	<I>	Some <I>italicized</I> text	Some *italicized* text
Underline	<U>	Some <U>underlined</U> text	Some underlined text
TTY	<TT>	Some <TT>monospaced (tty)</TT> text	Some `monospaced (tty)` text

Table A.2 List of Logical Attributes

Attribute	Tag	Use or Interpretation	Typical Rendering
Citation	<CITE>	Titles of books and films	Italic
Code	<CODE>	Source code fragments	Monospaced
Definition	<DFN>	A word being defined	Italic
Emphasis	<EM>	Emphasize a word or phrase	Italic
PRE	<PRE>	Used for tables and text	Preformatted text
Keyboard	<KBD>	Something the user should type, word-for-word	Bold monospaced
Sample	<SAMP>	Computer status messages	Monospaced
Strong	<STRONG>	Strong emphasis	Bold
Variable	<VAR>	A description of something the user should type, like <filename>	Italic

```
<BASEFONT SIZE=4>
This text will be displayed as size 4 text.
<FONT SIZE=+2>
This text will be displayed as size 6.
</FONT>
This text will return to the base font size—size 4.
```

HEADINGS

HTML provides six levels of section headers, **<H1>** through **<H6>**. While these are typically short phrases that fit on a line or two, the various headers are actually full-fledged paragraph types. They can even contain line and paragraph break commands.

You are not required to use a **<H1>** before you use a **<H2>**, or to make sure that a **<H4>** follows a **<H3>** or another **<H4>**.

Standard format for using one of the six heading tags is illustrated by this sample:

```
<H1>Text Goes Here</H1>
```

LISTS

HTML supports five different list types. All five types can be thought of as a sort of paragraph type. The first four list types share a common syntax, and differ only in how they format their list elements. The fifth type, the "description" list, is unique in that each list element has two parts—a tag and a description of the tag.

All five list types display an element marker—whether it be a number, a bullet, or a few words—on the left margin. The marker is followed by the actual list elements, which appear indented. List elements do not have to fit on a single line or consist of a single paragraph—they may contain **<P>** and **
** tags.

Lists can be nested, but the appearance of a nested list depends on the browser. For example, some browsers use different bullets for inner lists than for outer lists, and some browsers do not indent nested lists. However, Netscape and Lynx, which are the most common graphical and text mode browsers, *do* indent nested lists; the tags of a nested list align with the elements of the outer list, and the elements of the nested list are further indented. For example:

- This is the first element of the main bulleted list.
  - ♦ This is the first element of a nested list.
  - ♦ This is the second element of the nested list.
- This is the second element of the main bulleted list.

The four list types that provide simple list elements use the *list item* tag, **<LI>**, to mark the start of each list element. The **<LI>** tag always appears at the *start* of a list element, not at the end.

Thus, all simple lists look something like this:

```
<ListType>

<LI>
There isn't really any ListType list, however the OL, UL, DIR, and
MENU lists all follow this format.
```

```
<LI>
Since whitespace is ignored, you can keep your source legible by
putting blank lines between your list elements. Sometimes, I like to put the
&lt;li&gt; tags on their own lines, too.

<LI>
(If I hadn't used the ampersand quotes in the previous list element,
the "&lt;li&gt;" would have been interpreted as the start of a new
list element.)

</ListType>
```

Numbered List

In HTML, numbered lists are referred to as *ordered lists*. The list type tag is **<OL>**. Numbered lists can be nested, but some browsers get confused by the close of a nested list, and start numbering the subsequent elements of the outer list from 1.

Bulleted List

If a numbered list is an ordered list, what could an unnumbered, bulleted list be but an *unordered list?* The tag for an unordered (bulleted) list is **<UL>**. While bulleted lists can be nested, you should keep in mind that the list nesting *may* not be visible: Some browsers indent nested lists; some don't. Some use multiple bullet types; others don't.

Netscape List Extensions

Netscape has added a useful feature called **TYPE** that can be included with unordered and ordered lists. This feature allows you to specify the type of bullet or number that you use for the different levels of indentation in a list.

Unordered List with Extensions

When Netscape displays the different levels of indentation in an unordered list, it uses a solid disc (level 1) followed by a bullet (level 2) followed by a square (level 3). You can use the **TYPE** feature with the **<UL>** tag to override this sequence of bullets. Here's the format:

```
<UL TYPE=Disc|Circle|Square>
```

For example, here's a list defined to use circles as the bullet symbol:

```
<UL TYPE=Circle>
<LI>This is item 1
```

```
<LI>This is item 2
<LI>This is item 3
</UL>
```

Ordered List with Extensions

When Netscape displays ordered (numbered) lists, it numbers each list item using a numeric sequence—1, 2, 3, and so on. You can change this setting by using the **TYPE** modifier with the **<OL>** tag. Here's how this feature is used with numbered lists:

```
<OL TYPE=A|a|I|i|1>
```

where **TYPE** can be assigned to any one of these values:

A	Mark list items with capital letters
a	Mark list items with lowercase letters
I	Mark list items with large roman numerals
i	Mark list items with small roman numerals
1	Mark list items with numbers (default)

Wait, there's more. You can also start numbering list items with a number other than 1. To do this, you use the **START** modifier as shown:

```
<OL START=starting-number>
```

where *starting-number* specifies the first number used. You can use the feature with the **TYPE** tag. For example, the tag

```
<OL TYPE=I START=4>
```

would start the numbered list with the roman numeral IV.

Using Modifiers with List Elements

In addition to supporting the **TYPE** modifier with the **<UL>** and **<OL>** tags, Netscape allows you to use this modifier with the **<LI>** tag to define list elements for ordered and unordered lists. Here's an example of how it can be used with an unordered list:

```
<H2>Useful Publishing Resources</H2>
<UL TYPE=Disc>
<LI>HTML Tips
<LI>Web Page Samples
<LI TYPE=Square>Images
<LI TYPE=Disc>Templates
</UL>
```

In this case, all of the list items will be displayed with a disc symbol as the bullet except the third item, "Images," which will be displayed with a square bullet.

The **TYPE** modifier can be assigned the same values as those used to define lists with the **<UL>** and **<OL>** tags. Once it is used to define a style for a list item, all subsequent items in the list will be changed unless another **TYPE** modifier is used.

If you are defining **<LI>** list elements for ordered lists **<OL>**, you can also use a new modifier named **VALUE** to change the numeric value of a list item. Here's an example:

```
<H2>Useful Publishing Resources</H2>
<OL>
<LI>HTML Tips
<LI>Web Page Samples
<LI VALUE=4>Images
<LI>Templates
</OL>
```

In this list, the third item would be assigned the number 4 and the fourth item would be assigned the number 5.

Directory and Menu Lists

The directory and menu lists are special types of unordered lists. The menu list, **<MENU>**, is meant to be visually more compact than a standard unordered list: Menu list items should all fit on a single line. The directory list, **<DIR>**, is supposed to be even more compact: All list items should be less than 20 characters long, so that the list can be displayed in three (or more) columns.

I'm not sure if I've ever actually seen these lists in use, and their implementation is still spotty: Current versions of Netscape do not create multiple columns for a **<DIR>** list, and while they let you choose a directory list font and a menu list font, they do not actually use these fonts.

Description List

The description list, or **<DL>**, does not use the **<LI>** tag the way other lists do. Each description list element has two parts, a *tag* and its *description*. Each tag begins with a **<DT>** tag, and each description with a **<DD>** tag. These appear at the start of the list element, and are *not* paired with **</DT>** or **</DD>** tags.

The description list looks a lot like any other list, except that instead of a bullet or a number, the list tag consists of your text. Description lists are *intended* to be used for creating formats like a glossary entry, where a short tag is followed by an indented definition, but the format is fairly flexible. For example, a long tag will wrap, just like any other paragraph, although it should not contain line or paragraph breaks. (Netscape will indent any **<DT>** text after a line or paragraph, as if it were the **<DD>** text.) Further, you needn't actually supply any tag text: **<DT><DD>** will produce an indented paragraph.

Compact and Standard Lists

Normally, a description list puts the tags on one line, and starts the indented descriptions on the next:

```
Tag 1
Description 1.
Tag 2
Description 2.
```

If you'd like a tighter look, you can use a **<DL COMPACT>**. If the tags are very short, some browsers will start the descriptions on the same line as the tags:

```
Tag 1  Description 1
Tag 2  Description 2
```

However, most browsers do not support the compact attribute, and will simply ignore it. For example, with current versions of Windows Netscape, a **<DL COMPACT>** will always look like a **<DL>**, even if the tags are very short.

INLINE IMAGES

Using only text attributes, section headers, and lists, you can build attractive looking documents. The next step is to add pictures.

<IMG> Tag

The **<IMG>** tag is a very useful HTML feature. It lets you insert *inline images* into your text. This tag is rather different from the tags we've seen so far. Not only is it an empty tag that always appears alone, it has a number of *parameters* between the opening **<IMG** and the closing >. Some of the parameters include the image file name and some optional modifiers. The basic format for this tag is:

```
<IMG SRC="URL" ALT="text"
     ALIGN=top|middle|bottom
     ISMAP>
```

Since HTML 3.0 has emerged and additional Netscape extensions have been added, this tag has expanded more than any other HTML feature. Here is the complete format for the latest and greatest version of the **<IMG>** tag:

```
<IMG SRC="URL" ALT="text"
     ALIGN=left|right|top|texttop|middle|absmiddle|
          baseline|bottom|absbottom
     WIDTH=pixels
     HEIGHT=pixels
     BORDER=pixels
     VSPACE=pixels
     HSPACE=pixels
     ISMAP>
```

The extended version allows you to specify the size of an image, better control image and text alignment, and specify the size of an image's border.

Every **<IMG>** tag *must* have a **SRC=** parameter. This specifies a *URL*, or Uniform Resource Locator, which points to a GIF or JPEG bitmap file. When the bitmap file is in the same directory as the HTML document, the file name is an adequate URL. For example, **<IMG SRC=**MySmilingFace.gif**>** would insert a picture of my smiling face.

Some people turn off inline images because they have a slow connection to the Web. This replaces all images, no matter what size, with a standard graphic. This isn't so bad if the picture is incidental to your text, but if you've used small inline images as "bullets" in a list or as section dividers, the placeholder graphic will usually make your page look rather strange. Some people avoid using graphics as structural elements for this reason; others simply don't worry about people with slow connections; still others include a note at the top of the page saying that all the images on the page are small, and inviting people with inline images off to turn them on and reload the page.

Keep in mind that some people use text-only browsers, like Lynx, to navigate the Web. If you include a short description of your image with the **ALT=** parameter, text-only browsers can show *something* in place of your graphic. For example, **<IMG SRC=**MySmilingFace.gif **ALT=**"A picture of the author"**>**.

Since the **ALT** parameter has spaces in it, we have to put it within quotation marks. In general, you can put any parameter value in quotation marks, but you only need to do so if it includes spaces.

Mixing Images and Text

You can mix text and images within a paragraph; an image does not constitute a paragraph break. However, Web browsers like earlier versions of Netscape did *not* wrap paragraphs around images; they displayed a single line of text to the left or right of an image. Normally, any text in the same paragraph as an image would be lined up with the bottom of the image, and would wrap normally below the image. This works well if the text is essentially a caption for the image, or if the image is a decoration at the start of a paragraph. However, when the image is a part of a header, you may want the text to be centered vertically in the image, or to be lined up with the top of the image. In these cases, you can use the optional **ALIGN=** parameter to specify **ALIGN=top**, **ALIGN=middle**, or **ALIGN=bottom**.

Using "Floating" Images

With the extended version of the **<IMG>** tag, you can now create "floating" images that will align to the left or right margin of a Web page. Text that is displayed following the image will either wrap around the right-hand or left-hand side of the image. Here's an example of how an image can be displayed at the left margin with text that wraps to the right of the image:

```
<IMG SRC="limage.gif" ALIGN=left>
This text will be displayed to the right of the image
```

Specifying Spacing for Floating Images

When you use floating images with wrap-around text, you can specify the spacing between the text and the image by using the **VSPACE** and **HSPACE** modifiers. **VSPACE** defines the amount of spacing in units of pixels between the top and bottom of the image and the text that is displayed. **HSPACE** defines the spacing between the left or right edge of the image and the text that wraps.

Sizing Images

Another useful feature that has been added to the **<IMG>** tag is image sizing. The **WIDTH** and **HEIGHT** modifiers are used to specify the width and height of an image in pixels. Here's an example:

```
<IMG SRC="logo.gif" WIDTH=250 HEIGHT=310>
```

When a browser like Netscape displays an image, it needs to determine the size of the image before it can display a placeholder or *bounding box* for the image. If you include the image's size using **WIDTH** and **HEIGHT**, a Web page can be built much faster. If the values you specify for **WIDTH** and **HEIGHT** differ from the image's actual width and height, the image will be scaled to fit.

Using Multiple Images per Line

Since an image is treated like a single (rather large) character, you can have more than one image on a single line. In fact, you can have as many images on a line as will fit in your reader's window! If you put too many images on a line, the browser will wrap the line and your images will appear on multiple lines. If you don't want images to appear on the same line, be sure to place a **
** or **<P>** between them.

Defining an Image's Border

Typically, an image is displayed with a border around it. This is the border that is set to the color blue when the image is part of an anchor. Using the **BORDER** modifier, you can specify a border width for any image you display. Here's an example that displays an image with a five pixel border:

```
<IMG SRC="logo.gif" BORDER=5>
```

ISMAP Parameter

The optional **ISMAP** parameter allows you to place hyperlinks to other documents "in" a bitmapped image. This technique is used to turn an image into a clickable map. (See the section *Using Many Anchors in an Image* for more detail.)

HORIZONTAL RULES

The **<HR>** tag draws a *horizontal rule*, or line, across the screen to separate parts of your text. It's fairly common to put a rule before and after a form, to help set off the user entry areas from the normal text.

Many people use small inline images for decoration and separation, instead of rules. While using images in this manner lets you customize how your pages look, it also makes them take longer to load—and it makes them look horrible with inline images turned off.

The original **<HR>** tag simply displayed an engraved rule across a Web page. A newer version of the tag has been extended to add additional features

Table A.3 Summary of <IMG> Parameters

Parameter	Required?	Settings
SRC	Yes	URL
ALT	No	A text string
ALIGN	No	top, middle, bottom, left, right, texttop, absmiddle, baseline, absbottom
HEIGHT	No	Pixel setting
WIDTH	No	Pixel setting
BORDER	No	Pixel setting
VSPACE	No	Pixel setting
HSPACE	No	Pixel setting
ISMAP	No	None

including sizing, alignment, and shading. The format for the extended version of **<HR>** is:

```
<HR SIZE=pixels
    WIDTH=pixels|percent
    ALIGN=left|right|center
    NOSHADE>
```

The **SIZE** modifier sets the width (thickness) of the line in pixel units. The **WIDTH** modifier specifies the length of the line in actual pixel units or a percentage of the width of the page. The **ALIGN** modifier specifies the alignment for the line (the default is center) and the **NOSHADE** modifier allows you to display a solid line.

As an example of how some of these new features are used, the following tag displays a solid line, five pixels thick. The line is left justified and spans 80 percent of the width of the page:

```
<HR SIZE=5 WIDTH=80% ALIGN="left" NOSHADE>
```

HYPERMEDIA LINKS

The ability to add links to other Web pages or to entirely different sorts of documents is what makes the Web a *hypermedia* system. The special sort of highlight that your reader clicks on to traverse a hypermedia link is called an *anchor*, and all links are created with the anchor tag, **<A>**. The basic format for this tag is:

```
<A HREF="URL"
   NAME="text"
   REL=next|previous|parent|made
   REV=next|previous|parent|made
   TITLE="text">

text</A>
```

Links to Other Documents

While you can define a link to another point within the current page, most links are to other documents. Links to points within a document are very similar to links to other documents, but they are slightly more complicated, so we will talk about them later. (See the section, *Links to Anchors*.)

Each link has two parts: The visible part, or *anchor*, which the user clicks on, and the invisible part, which tells the browser where to go. The anchor is the text between the **<A>** and **</A>** tags of the **<A>** tag pair, while the actual link data appears in the **<A>** tag.

Just as the **<IMG>** tag has a **SRC=** parameter that specifies an image file, so does the **<A>** tag have an **HREF=** parameter that specifies the **h**ypermedia **ref**erence. Thus, "**<A HREF=**SomeFile.Type>click here**</A>**" is a link to "someFile.Type" with the visible anchor "click here".

Browsers will generally use the linked document's file name extension to decide how to display the linked document. For example, HTML or HTM files will be interpreted and displayed as HTML, whether they come from an http server, an FTP server, or a gopher site. Conversely, a link can be to any sort of file—a large bitmap, sound file, or movie.

Images as Hotspots

Since inline images are in many ways just big characters, there's no problem with using an image in an anchor. The anchor can include text on either side of the image, or the image can be an anchor by itself. Most browsers show an image anchor by drawing a blue border around the image (or around the placeholder graphic). The image anchor can somehow be a picture of what is being linked to, or it can just point to another copy of itself: **<AHREF=**image. gif>**<IMG SRC=**image.gif>**</A>**.

Thumbnail Images

One sort of "picture of the link" is called a *thumbnail* image. This is a tiny image, perhaps 100 pixels, which is either a condensed version of a larger image or a section of the image. Thumbnail images can be transmitted quickly, even over slow lines, leaving it up to the reader to decide which larger images to request. A secondary issue is aesthetic: Large images take up a lot of screen space, smaller images don't.

Linking an Image to Itself

Many people turn off inline images to improve performance over a slow network link. If the inline image is an anchor for itself, these people can then click on the placeholder graphic to see what they missed.

Using Many Anchors in an Image

The **<IMG>** tag's optional **ISMAP** parameter allows you to turn rectangular regions of a bitmap image into clickable anchors. Clicking on these parts of the image will activate an appropriate URL. (A default URL is also usually provided for when the user clicks on an area outside of one of the predefined regions.) While forms let you do this a bit more flexibly, the **ISMAP** approach doesn't require any custom programming—just a simple text file that defines the rectangles and their URLs—and this technique may work with browsers that do not support forms. For more information about how to create and use image maps, go to:

```
http://sunsite.unc.edu/boutell/faq/imagemap.htm
```

Links to Anchors

When an **HREF** parameter specifies a file name, the link is to the whole document. If the document is an HTML file, it will replace the current document and the reader will be placed at the top of the new document. Often this is just what you want. But sometimes you'd rather have a link take the reader to a specific section of a document. Doing this requires two anchor tags: one that defines an *anchor name* for a location, and one that points to that name. These two tags can be in the same document or in different documents.

Defining an Anchor Name To define an anchor name, you need to use the **NAME** parameter: **<A NAME=**AnchorName**>**. You can attach this name to a phrase, not just a single point, by following the **<A>** tag with a **</A>** tag.

Linking to an Anchor in the Current Document To then use this name, you simply insert an **<A HREF=**...**>** tag as usual, except that instead of a file

Table A.4 Summary of the <A> Tag Syntax

To:	Use:
Link to another document	<A HREF="URL">highlighted anchor text</A>
Name an anchor	<A NAME="Anchor Name">normal text</A>
Link to a named anchor in this document	<A HREF="#Anchor Name">highlighted anchor text</A>
Link to a named anchor in another document	<A HREF="URL#Anchor Name">highlighted anchor text</A>

name, you use a **#** followed by an anchor name. For example, **<A HREF=#**AnchorName**>** refers to the example in the last paragraph.

Names do not have to be defined before they are used; it's actually fairly common for lengthy documents to have a table of contents with links to names defined later in the document. It's also worth noting that while tag and parameter names are not case sensitive, anchor names *are*; **<A HREF=#**anchorname**>** will not take you to the AnchorName example.

Linking to an Anchor in a Different Document You can also link to specific places in any other HTML document, anywhere in the world—provided, of course, that it contains named anchors. To do this, you simply add the **#** and the anchor name after the URL that tells where the document can be found. For example, to plant a link to the anchor named "Section 1" in a file named complex.html in the same directory as the current file, you could use **<A HREF=**"Complex.html**#**Section 1"**>**. Similarly, if the named anchor was in http://www.another.org/Complex.html, you'd use **<A HREF=**"http://www.another.org/Complex.html**#**Section 1"**>**.

USING URLS

Just as a complete DOS file name starts with a drive letter followed by a colon, so a full URL starts with a resource type—HTTP, FTP, GOPHER, and so on—followed by a colon. If the name doesn't have a colon in it, it's assumed to be a local *reference*, which is a file name on the same file system as the current document. Thus, **<A HREF=**Another.html**>** refers to the file "Another.html" in the same directory as the current file, while **<A HREF=**/html/File.html**>** refers to the file "File.html" in the top-level directory "html". One thing to note here is that a URL always uses "/", the Unix-style *forward* slash, as a directory separator even when the files are on a Windows machine, which normally uses "\", the DOS-style backslash.

Local URLs can be very convenient when you have several HTML files with links to each other, or when you have a large number of inline images. If you ever have to move them all to another directory, or to another machine, you don't have to change all the URLs.

<BASE> Tag

One drawback of local URLs is that if someone makes a copy of your document, the local URLs will no longer work. Adding the optional **<BASE>** tag to the **<HEAD>** section of your document will help eliminate this problem. While many browsers do not yet support it, the intent of the **<BASE>** tag is precisely to provide a context for local URLs.

The **<BASE>** tag is like the **<IMG>** tag in that it's a so-called empty tag. It requires an **HREF** parameter—for example, **<BASE HREF=**http://www.imaginary.org/index.html**>**—which should contain the URL of the document itself. When a browser that supports the **<BASE>** tag encounters a URL that doesn't contain a protocol and path, it will look for it relative to the base URL, instead of relative to the location from which it actually loaded the document. The format for the **<BASE>** tag is:

```
<BASE HREF="URL">
```

Reading and Constructing URLs

Where a local URL is just a file name, a global URL specifies an instance of one of several resource types, which may be located on any Internet machine in the world. The wide variety of resources is reflected in a complex URL syntax. For example, while most URLs consist of a resource type followed by a colon, *two* forward slashes, a machine name, another forward slash, and a resource name, others consist only of a resource type, a colon, and the resource name.

The resource-type://machine-name/resource-name URL form is used with centralized resources, where there's a single server that supplies the document to the rest of the net, using a particular protocol. Thus, "http://www.another.org/Complex.html" means 'use the Hypertext Transfer Protocol to get file Complex.html from the main www directory on the machine www.another.org', while "ftp://foo.bar.net/pub/www/editors/README" means

Table A.5 A Partial Table of URL Resource Types

Resource	Interpretation	Format
HTTP	Hypertext Transfer Protocol	http://machine-name/file-name
FTP	File Transfer Protocol	ftp://machine-name/file-name
GOPHER	Gopher	gopher://machine-name/file-name
NEWS	Internet News	news:group-name
TELNET	Log on to a remote system	telnet://machine-name
MAILTO	Normal Internet email	mailto:user-name@machine-name

'use the File Transfer Protocol to get the file /pub/www/editors/README from the machine foo.bar.net'.

Conversely, many resource types are distributed. We don't all get our news or mail from the same central server, but from the nearest one of many news and mail servers. URLs for distributed resources use the simpler form resource-type:resource-name. For example, "news:comp.infosystems.www.providers" refers to the Usenet newsgroup comp.infosystems.www.providers, which is a good place to look for further information about writing HTML.

Using www and Actual Machine Names

In the HTTP domain, you'll often see "machine names" like "www.coriolis.com". This usually does *not* mean there's a machine named www.coriolis.com that you can FTP or Telnet to; "www" is an alias that a Webmaster can set up when he or she registers the server. Using the www alias makes sense, because machines come and go, but sites (and, we hope, the Web) last for quite a while. If URLs refer to www at the site and not to a specific machine, the server and all the HTML files can be moved to a new machine simply by changing the www alias, without having to update all the URLs.

USING SPECIAL CHARACTERS

Since < and > have special meanings in HTML, there must be a way to represent characters like these as part of text. While the default character set for the Web is ISO Latin-1, which includes European language characters like é and ß in the range from 128 to 255, it's not uncommon to pass around snippets of HTML in 7-bit email, or to edit them on dumb terminals, so the escape mechanism also has to include a way to specify high-bit characters using only 7-bit characters.

Two Forms: Numeric and Symbolic

There are two ways to specify an arbitrary character: numeric and symbolic. To include the copyright symbol, ©, which is character number 169, you can use ©. That is, &#, then the number of the character you want to include, and a closing semicolon. The numeric method is very general, but not easy to read.

The symbolic form is much easier to read, but its use is restricted to the four low-bit characters with special meaning in HTML. To use the other symbols in the ISO Latin-1 character set, like ® and the various currency symbols, you have to use the numeric form. The symbolic escape is like the numeric escape, except there's no #. For example, to insert é, you would use é, or &, the character name, and a closing semicolon. You should be aware that symbol names are *case sensitive:* É is É, not é, while &EAcute; is no character at all, and will show up as &EAcute;!

PREFORMATTED AND OTHER SPECIAL PARAGRAPH TYPES

HTML supports three special "block" formats. Any normal text within a block format is supposed to appear in a distinctive font.

<BLOCKQUOTE> ... </BLOCKQUOTE> Tag

The block quote sets an extended quotation off from normal text. That is, a **<BLOCKQUOTE>** tag pair does *not* imply indented, single-spaced, and italicized; rather, it's just meant to change the default, plain text font. The format for this tag is:

```
<BLOCKQUOTE>text</BLOCKQUOTE>
```

<PRE> ... </PRE> Tag

Everything in a *preformatted* block will appear in a monospaced font. The **<PRE>** tag pair is also the only HTML element that pays any attention to the line breaks in the source file: Any line break in a preformatted block will be treated just as a **
** elsewhere. HTML tags can be used within a preformatted block, thus you can have anchors as well as bold or italic monospaced text. The format for this tag is:

```
<PRE WIDTH=value>text</PRE>
```

The initial **<PRE>** tag has an optional **WIDTH=** parameter. Browsers won't trim lines to this length; the intent is to allow the browser to select a monospaced font that will allow the maximum line length to fit in the browser window.

<ADDRESS> ... </ADDRESS> Tag

The third block format is the address format: **<ADDRESS>**. This is generally displayed in italics, and is intended for displaying information about a document, such as creation date, revision history, and how to contact the author. Official style guides say that every document should provide an address block. The format for this tag is:

```
<ADDRESS>text</ADDRESS>
```

Many people put a horizontal rule, **<HR>**, between the body of the document and the address block. If you include a link to your home page or to a page that lets the reader send mail to you, you don't have to include a lot of information on each individual page.

USING TABLES

Features like lists are great for organizing data; however, sometimes you need a more compact way of grouping related data. Fortunately, some of the newer browsers like Netscape have implemented the proposed HTML 3.0 specification for tables. Tables can contain a heading and row and column data. Each unit of a table is called a *cell* and cell data can be text and images.

<TABLE> ... </TABLE> Tag

This tag is used to define a new table. All of the table specific tags must be placed within the pair **<TABLE> ... </TABLE>**, otherwise they will be ignored. The format for the **<TABLE>** tag is:

```
<TABLE  BORDER= number in pixels
        WIDTH= percentage of page or number
        cellspacing= number in pixels
        cellpadding= number>
table text</TABLE>
```

The **BORDER** tag allows you to define the width of the table's border in pixels. If **BORDER** is not defined, the default setting is no border. **WIDTH** defines the width of the table within the page, as either a percentage of the page or a defined number. It's better to use a percentage, as different people have different sized browser windows, so a defined number may not look right on their screen.

Like it sounds, **CELLSPACING** is the amount of space inserted between individual cells in a table, defined in pixels. The default spacing is 2. **CELLPADDING** is the amount of space between the border of the table cell and the contents of that cell. Setting the **CELLPADDING** at zero is not a good idea, because text from on cell could run into text from the next.

Creating a Table Caption

Creating a title or caption for a table is easy using the **<CAPTION>** tag. This tag must be placed within the **<TABLE> ... </TABLE>** tags. Here is its general format:

```
<CAPTION ALIGN=top|bottom>caption text</CAPTION>
```

Notice that you can display the caption at the top or bottom of the table. By default, the caption will be displayed at the top of the table.

Defining Headings for Cells

In addition to displaying a table caption, you can include headings for a table's data cells. The tag for defining a heading looks very similar to the **<TD>** tag:

```
<TH ALIGN=left|center|right
    VALIGN=top|middle|bottom|baseline
    NOWRAP
    COLSPAN=number
    ROWSPAN=number>
text</TH>
```

Creating Table Rows

Every table you create will have one or more rows (otherwise it won't be much of a table!). The simple tag for creating a row is:

```
<TR ALIGN=left|center|right
    VALIGN=top|middle|bottom|baseline>
text</TR>
```

For each row that you want to add, you must place the **<TR>** tag inside the body of the table (between the **<TABLE> ... </TABLE>** tags).

Defining Table Data Cells

Within each **<TR> ... </TR>** tag pair come one or more **<TD>** tags to define the table cell data. You can think of the cell data as the column definitions for the table. Here is the format for a **<TD>** tag:

```
<TD ALIGN=left|center|right
```

```
    VALIGN=top|middle|bottom|baseline
    NOWRAP
    COLSPAN=number
    ROWSPAN=number>
text</TD>
```

The size for each cell is determined by the width or height of the data that is displayed. The **ALIGN** parameter can be used to center or left or right justify the data displayed in the cell. The **VALIGN** parameter, on the other hand, specifies how the data will align vertically. If you don't want the text to wrap within the cell, you can include the **NOWRAP** modifier.

When defining a cell, you can manually override the width and height of the cell by using the **COLSPAN** and **ROWSPAN** parameters. **COLSPAN** specifies the number of columns the table cell will span and **ROWSPAN** specifies the number of rows to span. The default setting for each of these parameters is 1.

USING FORMS

The HTML features presented so far correspond with traditional publishing practices: You create a hypermedia document, and others read it. With HTML forms, however, you can do much more. You can create a form that lets your readers search a database using any criteria *they* like. Or you can create a form that lets them critique your Web pages. Or—and this is what excites business people—you can use forms to *sell* things over the Internet.

Forms are easy to create. However, to *use* them you'll need a program that runs on your Web server to process the information that the user's client sends back to you. For simple things like a "comments page," you can probably use an existing program. For anything more complex, you'll probably need a custom program. While I will briefly describe the way form data looks to the receiving program, any discussion of forms programming is beyond this book's scope.

<FORM> ... </FORM> TAG

All input widgets—text boxes, check boxes, and radio buttons—must appear within a **<FORM>** tag pair. When a user clicks on a submit button or an image map, the contents of all the widgets in the form will be sent to the program that you specify in the **<FORM>** tag. HTML widgets include single and multiline text boxes, radio buttons, check boxes, pull down lists, image maps, a couple of standard buttons, and a *hidden* widget that might be used to identify the form to a program that can process several forms.

Within your form, you can use any other HTML elements, including headers, images, rules, and lists. This gives you a fair amount of control over your form's appearance, but you should always remember that the user's screen size and font choices will affect the actual appearance of your form.

While you can have more than one form on a page, you cannot nest one form within another.

The basic format for the **<FORM>** tag is as follows:

```
<FORM ACTION="URL"
      METHOD=get|post>
text</FORM>
```

Notice that text can be included as part of the form definition.

Form Action and Method Attributes

Nothing gets sent to your Web server until the user presses a Submit button or clicks on an image map. What happens then depends on the **ACTION**, **METHOD**, and **ENCTYPE** parameters of the **<FORM>** tag.

The **ACTION** parameter specifies which URL the form data should be sent to for further processing. This is most commonly in the cgi-bin directory of a Web server. If you do not specify an action parameter, the contents will be sent to the current document's URL.

The **METHOD** parameter tells how to send the form's contents. There are two possibilities here: Get and Post. If you do not specify a method, Get will be used. Get and Post both format the form's data identically; they differ only in how they pass the form's data to the program that uses that data.

Get and Post both send the form's contents as a single long text vector consisting of a list of WidgetName=WidgetValue pairs, each separated from its successor by an ampersand. For example:

```
"NAME=Jon Shemitz&Address=jon@armory.com"
```

(Any & or = sign in a widget name or value will be quoted using the standard ampersand escape; any bare "&" and any "=" sign can therefore be taken as a separator.) You will not necessarily get a name and value for every widget in the form; while empty text is explicitly sent as a WidgetName= with an empty value, unselected radio buttons and check boxes don't send even their name.

Where Get and Post differ is that the Get method creates a "query URL," which consists of the action URL, a question mark, and the formatted form data. The Post method, on the other hand, sends the formatted form data to the action URL in a special data block. The Web server parses the query URL that a Get method creates and passes the form data to the form processing program as a command line parameter. This creates a limitation on form data length that the Post method does not.

Currently, all form data is sent in plain text. This creates a security problem. The optional **ENCTYPE** parameter offers a possible solution: Although currently this only allows you to ratify the plain text default, in the future, values may be provided that call for an encrypted transmission.

Widgets

From a users' point of view, there are seven types of Web widgets; all of them are generated by one of three HTML tags. Except for the standard buttons, all widgets must be given a name.

<INPUT> Tag

The **<INPUT>** tag is the most versatile, and the most complex. It can create single-line text boxes, radio buttons, check boxes, image maps, the two standard buttons, and the hidden widget. It's somewhat like the **<IMG>** tag in that it appears by itself, not as part of a tag pair, and has some optional parameters. Of these, the **TYPE=** parameter determines both the widget type and the meaning of the other parameters. If no other parameters are provided, the **<INPUT>** tag generates a text box.

The format for the **<INPUT>** tag is:

```
<INPUT
TYPE="text"|"password"|"checkbox"|"radio"|"submit"|"reset"|"hidden"|"image"
        NAME="name"
        VALUE="value"
        SIZE="number"
        MAXLENGTH="number"
        CHECKED>
```

The **TYPE** parameter can be set to one of eight values. We'll look at each of these options shortly. Each input must contain a unique name defined with **NAME**. The **VALUE** parameter specifies the initial value of the input. This

Table A.6 Syntax of the Text and Password Input Types

Attribute	Required?	Format	Meaning
TYPE	No	TYPE="text" *or* TYPE="password"	Determines what type of widget this will be. Default is "text".
NAME	Yes	NAME="WidgetName"	Identifies the widget.
VALUE	No	VALUE="Default text"	You supply default value. Cannot contain HTML commands.
SIZE	No	SIZE=*Cols*	Width (in characters) of a single line text area. Default is 20.
SIZE	No	SIZE=*Cols,Rows*	Height and width (in characters) of a multi-line text area.
MAXLENGTH	No	MAXLENGTH=*Chars*	Longest value a single line text area can return. Default unlimited.

value is optional. The **SIZE** parameter defines the size of a text line and **MAXLENGTH** is the maximum size allowed for the returned text.

Text Boxes

If the **TYPE=** parameter is set to **text** (or no parameter is used), the input widget will be a text box. The **password** input type is just like the text type, except that the value shows only as a series of asterisks. All text areas must have a name. Text areas *always* report their value, even if it is empty.

Check Boxes and Radio Buttons

Check boxes and radio buttons are created by an **<INPUT>** tag with a **checkbox** or **radio** type. Both must have a name and a value parameter, and may be initially checked. The name parameter is the widget's *symbolic name*, used in returning a value to your Web server, not its onscreen tag. For that, you use normal HTML text next to the **<INPUT>** tag. Since the display tag is not part of the **<INPUT>** tag, Netscape check boxes and radio buttons operate differently from their dialog box kin; you cannot toggle a widget by clicking on its text; you have to click on the widget itself.

A group of radio buttons is associated by having identical names. Only one (or none) of the group can be checked at any one time; clicking a radio button will turn off whichever button in the name group was already on.

Check boxes and radio buttons return their value if and only if they are checked.

Table A.7 Syntax of the Check Box and Radio Types

Attribute	Required?	Format	Meaning
TYPE	Yes	TYPE=checkbox *or* TYPE=radio	Determines what type of widget this will be. Default is "text".
NAME	Yes	NAME="WidgetName"	A unique identifier for a checkbox; a group identifier for radio buttons.
VALUE	Yes	VALUE="WidgetValue"	The value is sent if the widget is checked.
CHECKED	No	CHECKED	If this attribute is present, the widget starts out checked.

Image Maps

Image maps are created with the **TYPE="image"** code. They return their name and a pair of numbers that represents the position that the user clicked on: The form handling program is responsible for interpreting this pair of numbers. Since this program can do anything you want with the click position, you are not restricted to rectangular anchors as with **<IMG ISMAP>**.

Clicking on an image map, like clicking on a Submit button, will send all form data to the Web server.

Submit/Reset Buttons

The **submit** and **reset** types let you create one of the two standard buttons. Clicking on a Submit button, like clicking on an image map, will send all form data to the Web server. Clicking on a Reset button resets all widgets in the form to their default values. These buttons are the only widgets that don't need to have names. By default, they will be labeled Submit and Reset; you can specify the button text by supplying a **VALUE** parameter.

Hidden Fields

A **hidden** type creates an invisible widget. This widget won't appear onscreen, but its name and value are included in the form's contents when the user

Table A.8 Syntax of the Image Type

Attribute	Required?	Format	Meaning
TYPE	Yes	TYPE=image	Determines what type of widget this will be. Default is "text".
NAME	Yes	NAME="WidgetName"	Identifies the widget.
SRC	Yes	SRC="URL"	The URL of a bitmapped image to display.

Table A.9 Syntax of the Submit and Reset Types

Attribute	Required?	Format	Meaning
TYPE	Yes	TYPE=submit *or* TYPE=reset	Determines what type of widget this will be. Default is "text".
NAME	No	NAME="WidgetName"	The buttons never return their values, so a name will never be used.
VALUE	No	VALUE="WidgetValue"	The button text. Default is Submit or Reset, respectively.

presses the Submit button or clicks on an image map. This feature might be used to identify the form to a program that processes several different forms.

<TEXTAREA> ... </TEXTAREA> Tag

The **<TEXTAREA>** tag pair is similar to a multi-line text input widget. The primary difference is that you always use a **<TEXTAREA>** tag pair and put any default text between the **<TEXTAREA>** and **</TEXTAREA>** tags. As with **<PRE>** blocks, any line breaks in the source file are honored, which lets you include line breaks in the default text. The ability to have a long, multi-line default text is the *only* functional difference between a **<TEXTAREA>** and a multi-line input widget.

Table A.10 Syntax of the Hidden Type

Attribute	Required?	Format	Meaning
TYPE	Yes	TYPE=hidden	Determines what type of widget this will be. Default is "text".
NAME	Yes	NAME="WidgetName"	Identifies the widget.
VALUE	Yes	VALUE="WidgetValue"	Whatever constant data you might want to include with the form.

Table A.11 Syntax of the <TEXTAREA> Tag

Attribute	Required?	Format	Meaning
NAME	Yes	NAME="WidgetName"	Identifies the widget.
ROWS	No	ROWS=*Rows*	TextArea height, in characters.
COLS	No	COLS=*Cols*	TextArea width, in characters. Default is 20.

The format for the **<TEXTAREA>** tag is:

```
<TEXTAREA NAME="name"
          ROWS="rows"
          COLS="cols"> </TEXTAREA>
```

<SELECT> ... </SELECT> Tag

The **<SELECT>** tag pair allows you to present your users with a set of choices. This is not unlike a set of check boxes, yet it takes less room on the screen.

Just as you can use check boxes for 0 to *N* selections, or radio buttons for 0 or 1 selection, you can specify the cardinality of selection behavior. Normally, select widgets act like a set of radio buttons: Your users can only select zero or one of the options. However, if you specify the **MULTIPLE** option, the select widget will act like a set of check boxes: Your users may select any or all of the options.

The format for the **<SELECT>** tag is:

```
<SELECT NAME="name"
        SIZE="rows"
        MULTIPLE>text/option list</SELECT>
```

Within the **<SELECT>** tag pair is a series of **<OPTION>** statements, followed by the option text. These are similar to **<LI>** list items, except that **<OPTION>** text *may not include any HTML markup*. The **<OPTION>** tag may include an optional selected attribute; more than one option may be selected if and only if the **<SELECT>** tag includes the **MULTIPLE** option.

For example:

```
Which Web browsers do you use?
<SELECT NAME="Web Browsers" MULTIPLE>
<OPTION>Netscape
<OPTION>Lynx
<OPTION>WinWeb
<OPTION>Cello
</SELECT>
```

FRAMES

One of the newest HTML features is the ability to have separate frames within a document. Each frame is separate from the others, and is controlled inde-

Table A.12 *Syntax of the <SELECT> Tag*

Attribute	Required?	Format	Meaning
NAME	Yes	NAME="WidgetName"	Identifies the widget.
SIZE	No	SIZE=*Rows*	This is the widget height, in character rows. If the size is 1, you get a pull-down list. If the size is greater than 1, you get a scrolling list. Default is 1.
MULTIPLE	No	MULTIPLE	Allows more than one option to be selected.

pendently. Frames are a way to completely change the look of your Web site, without having to learn another, more complicated language.

<FRAMESET> ... </FRAMESET>

When you define a set of frames, you enclose your frame code inside the **<FRAMESET>** tags. The **<FRAMESET>** tag replaces the normal **<BODY>** tag and helps to alert Netscape that the file is a frame file that will set up the overall layout of the screen. Within the **<FRAMESET>** tag you can have a number of tags, such as:

```
<FRAMESET ROWS="row info, row info, row info..."
          COLS="col info, col info, col info...">
```

The **ROWS** and **COLS** attributes use a comma-separated list of values, either specific pixel values, percentages of the screen (1 to 100), or a relative scaling value. The scaling value is used to divide a section of the screen into separate frames divided into rows or columns. If you leave out the **ROWS** attribute, Netscape assumes that you're dealing with a single row and it will automatically size the row to fit. The same applies to **COLS**.

Within the **<FRAMESET>** tags, you can have a number of **<FRAME>** attributes, which define each frame that is being created. The tag for creating a frame is:

```
<FRAME SRC="url"
       NAME="window_name"
       MARGINWIDTH=value
       MARGINHEIGHT=value
       SCROLLING="YES|NO|AUTO"
       NORESIZE>
```

First, the **<FRAME>** tag specifies a source URL (**SRC=**), which tells Netscape which HTML file or picture to load into the frame. **NAME** gives the frame an internal source, so you can refer to the frame later in your HTML code. **MARGINHEIGHT** and **MARGINWIDTH** define how much of a border you want between the displayed document and the actual borders of the frame. This value is specified in pixels and can range from 0 up to completely filling the frame. These settings are optional. If you don't use them, Netscape will set the appropriate margin width automatically.

When you define a frame you can choose to have it scroll or not scroll. The default setting is **AUTO**, which allows the browser to scroll if the document loaded to that frame is bigger than the frame size allows. If you set the scrolling attribute to **YES**, the scroll bar will always appear. If you assign it **NO**, it won't show up. And finally, adding **NORESIZE** to the **FRAME** tag denies the user the ability to resize the frame.

The TARGET Tag

The **TARGET** attribute is the main resource Netscape offers to direct exactly which frame is updated by a specific user action. **TARGET** uses the following basic syntax:

```
TARGET="window_name"
```

TARGET can be used in conjunction with several tags, including the **<A>**, **<BASE>**, and **<FORM>** tags. Adding the **TARGET** attribute to the **<A>** tag directs the hyperlink to load the document into a specific frame. Here's an example:

```
<A HREF="myhtml.html" TARGET="mywindow">update my window.</A>
```

You can use the **<BASE>** tag to establish your own default target that is only overridden by other specified targets. This is a good way to set up a list of pictures in one frame that is reserved just for that. Here's an example:

```
<BASE TARGET="pictureframe">
```

When you activate a form using the **<FORM ACTION>** tag, you can add **TARGET** to it to tell Netscape which frame gets the result from the submitted form, as shown below:

```
<FORM ACTION="/process.cgi" TARGET="verification_window">
```

All **TARGET** names need to begin with an alphanumeric character to be valid, except for four, _blank, _self, _parent, and _top, which Netscape calls "magic **TARGET** names."

THE CGI

The CGI, or *Common Gateway Interface,* defines how a form handling program on a Web server should act. This includes the name1=value1&name2=value2 format of the form data vector, as well as how these programs interact with remote Web clients. A CGI program can be any sort of executable code, but on Unix servers, the most common executable seems to be a *Perl* script.

SECURITY

You should be aware that it's always possible for people to intercept forms data bound for your Web server. This means that until forms with encrypted **ENCTYPES** are widely supported, forms data cannot be considered 100 percent reliable—or 100 percent confidential.

The problem is that anyone who loads your form can read the HTML source to see where the forms data goes. If that data includes any tempting information like a credit card number, a thief may be tempted to watch traffic to your server for credit card numbers to steal. Since it can be relatively easy to intercept TCP/IP packets, this is a problem that you shouldn't ignore!

Basically, if you want to do online sales, *don't* use a plain text form to ask for a credit card number unless you have secure sockets (SSL). This means that all transactions between the browser and the server are encrypted, so hackers should be unable to decipher them. If you don't have secure sockets, use a service that lets customers create accounts over the Web but will only accept credit card numbers and expiration dates via a voice phone call or through snail (physical letter) mail. When your customers want to place an order, they don't run the risk of having their credit card number stolen; they would only have to supply a name and address to let the order taking system look up their credit card number.

JAVA APPLETS

To allow Java applets to be played in Java-enabled browsers like Netscape, a new **<APPLET> ... </APPLET>** tag pair has been added. The format for this tag pair is:

```
<APPLET CODE = "appletclassfile"
                WIDTH = pixelwidth
                HEIGHT = pixelheight
                CODEBASE= "URL"
                ALT = "alternatetext"
                NAME = symbolicname
                ALIGN =
left|right|top|texttop|middle|absmiddle|baseline|bottom|absbottom
                VSPACE = vertspace
                HSPACE = hortspace
                <PARAM NAME = parametername VALUE = parametervalue> >
```

When this tag is encountered, the Java-enabled Web browser loads the applet having the name *appletclassfile*. This will usually be the applet name with the extension .class at the end. In Java, all applets are created using Java classes. The applet class file that is loaded must be a compiled Java file. To load an applet, you must also specify the width and height of the area you want to run the applet in. These values must be specified in units of pixels.

Table A.13 *Syntax of the <APPLET> Tag*

Attribute	Required?	Format	Meaning
CODE	Yes	NAME=*appletname*	Identifies the name of the Java applet to load.
WIDTH	Yes	WIDTH=*pixels*	Specifies the initial width of the applet in pixels.
HEIGHT	Yes	HEIGHT=*pixels*	Specifies the initial height of the applet in pixels.
CODEBASE	No	CODEBASE="URL"	Specifies the base Internet address (URL) of the applet.
ALT	No	ALT="Text"	Provides alternate text to be displayed by text-only browsers.
NAME	No	NAME=*symbolicname*	Specifies a symbolic name for the applet. This name can be used by other applets on the same page to reference the applet.
ALIGN	No	ALIGN=*alignment*	Specifies the alignment for the applet.
VSPACE	No	VSPACE=*pixels*	Specifies the vertical space around the applet.
HSPACE	No	HSPACE=*pixels*	Specifies the horizontal space around the applet.

Here's an example:

```
<APPLET CODE ="TickerTape.class"
                WIDTH = 300
                HEIGHT = 100
                ALIGN = left>
```

If you look closely at the **<APPLET>** tag you'll see that it includes a **<PARAM>** tag. This tag provides information about optional parameters that can be passed to an applet. For each parameter that is passed to an applet, a separate **<PARAM>** tag must be provided. The **NAME** attribute specifies the name of the parameter and the **VALUE** parameter specifies the value assigned to the parameter. Here's an example of an **<APPLET>** instruction that includes a couple **<PARAM>** tags:

```
<APPLET CODE="TickerTape.class" WIDTH=600 HEIGHT=50>
<PARAM NAME=TEXT VALUE="The Java TickerTape Applet...">
<PARAM NAME=SPEED VALUE="4">
</APPLET>
```

Appendix B

JavaScript Coding Essentials

One reason JavaScript is much easier to use than other programming languages, like C++ or Java, is because it's integrated into your HTML documents. You can easily write all of your JavaScript code, view it, and test it at the same time that you create, read, and test your HTML documents. This combination makes using JavaScript popular and intuitive, even for people who've never programmed before.

This reference guide is designed to give you an overview of the key features of JavaScript and how JavaScript code is added to your HTML documents. You can refer to it whenever you need to look up a built-in object, property, event, and so on. You'll also find reference material on the syntax of JavaScript and techniques for using the basic components like functions, variables, data types, control statements, and so on.

WRITING JAVASCRIPT CODE

You can embed JavaScript into your HTML using this simple HTML tag:

```
<SCRIPT>...</SCRIPT>
```

This tag tells a JavaScript-supported browser like the new Netscape that the text between **<SCRIPT>** and **</SCRIPT>** should be processed as script code. When the Web browser encounters this code it tries to run it line by line. An optional attribute can be included with this tag to specify the language that is used:

```
<SCRIPT LANGUAGE="JavaScript">...</SCRIPT>
```

This is perhaps the best way to open up a JavaScript section of any HTML document, because in the future there may be other new languages (for example, Microsoft's upcoming Visual Basic Script) that might require you to mix and match different scripting languages. Therefore, you should get into the habit of identifying the type of code you're using.

Hiding Your Code from Old Browsers

You can't expect everyone to be using the latest version of Netscape, or even Netscape for that matter. That's why it makes a lot of sense to hide your JavaScript code so that it doesn't display in incompatible browsers. JavaScript code placed inside comment fields doesn't display in old browsers, but is still executed by JavaScript-compatible browsers. Here's a quick example:

```
<HTML>
<HEAD>

<!-- Begin Javascript — Using <! tag to hide code

   <SCRIPT LANGUAGE="JavaScript">
      document.write("Testing Hidden Javascript Code.")
   </SCRIPT>

// End of Code. -->


</HEAD>
<BODY>
<P>
Did you see any code?
</BODY>
</HTML>
```

Notice that you must use the two slash symbols (//) at the beginning of the last comment line. This is one of the comment indicators for JavaScript. If these symbols are omitted, Netscape will treat the comment line as if it were a line of JavaScript code.

Dealing with Quotes in Code

Sometimes you may need to reference strings inside an element. This is to make sure Netscape doesn't abruptly close out an attribute. To do this, you need to use a single quote ('). Here's an example:

```
onClick="myfunc('<INPUT TYPE="button" VALUE="Press Me" astring')">
```

Be sure to alternate double quotes with single quotes. Since event handlers in HTML must be enclosed in quotes, you must use single quotes to delimit arguments. For example:

```
<FORM NAME="myform">
<INPUT TYPE="button" NAME="Button1" VALUE="Open Sesame!"
onClick="window.open('stmtsov.html', 'newWin', 'toolbar=no,directories=no')">
</FORM>
```

Alternatively, you can use escape quotes by preceding them by a backslash (\). You can insert quotes inside of strings by preceding them with a backslash. For example,

```
Myquote = "The other day I said \"Hello World!\""
document.write(Myquote)
```

When this code is executed, it would output the following:

```
The other day I said "Hello World!"
```

EXECUTING JAVASCRIPT CODE

When Netscape loads a page, it doesn't evaluate the code until after the page is loaded. However, a lot of JavaScript code is executed through functions that are executed when a certain "event" happens, such as a user clicking on a button or within a listbox. The following code shows an example of this.

```
<HEAD>
<SCRIPT LANGUAGE="JavaScript">
<!--  to hide script contents from old browsers

function square(i)
{
   document.write("The call passed ", i ," to the function.","<BR>")
   return i * i
}

document.write("The function returned ",square(5),".")

// end hiding contents from old browsers  -->
</SCRIPT>
</HEAD>
<BODY>
<BR>
All done.
</BODY>
```

This is how the above will appear on the screen.

```
The call passed 5 to the function.
```

```
The function returned 25.
All done.
```

Placement of JavaScript Code Is Important!

It's important where you place the JavaScript code in your document. Why? Well not everyone waits for a page to load completely before doing something with it. It's entirely possible that a user might click on a button that executes the code, but because the user hit ESC, the code hasn't loaded to tell Netscape what to do with it. Ouch!

This is easily overcome by placing your JavaScript code in the **<HEAD>**... **</HEAD>** tag section of your HTML code. This way, the JavaScript code is loaded before the user has a chance to do anything that might need a JavaScript response.

Updating Pages

You can't dynamically update pages very easily with JavaScript in Navigator. Once the page has been loaded and formatted, you can't change it without reloading the page. Currently, you cannot update a particular part of a page without updating the entire page. The way to work around this is to use frames and target updates directly into frames. You also can't currently print output created with JavaScript. For example, if you had the following in a page

```
<P>This is some text.
<SCRIPT>document.write("<P>And some generated text")</SCRIPT>
```

and you printed it, you would get only "This is some text," even though you would see both lines on your screen.

LANGUAGE ESSENTIALS

Some key component to any programming language are values, variables, data types, and expressions. In the remainder of this appendix we'll review these basic components to help you create useful JavaScript code.

Values (Data Types)

A programming language has to have the ability to set, store, and manipulate data via named variables. As you will learn, JavaScript has very few value or data types. This can be a curse or a blessing, depending on your previous programming experience. JavaScript works with several key types of values:

Numbers:	These are any type of number like 21 or 1.314.
Logical (Boolean):	These are True (-1) or False (0) values.
Strings:	Strings are any type of variable treated as text. "Hello." or "12/31/95" or "123456" would all be valid strings.
Null:	A null value is a special type of value which is used in certain situations.

Datatype Conversions

JavaScript is known as a loosely typed language. This means that you don't have to declare what type of value a variable is going to work with up front. This is both helpful and confusing. On the one hand this makes writing JavaScript programs easier. You can casually declare variables and stuff values in them as you code. On the other hand, you can easily get lost remembering which variables are which. This also means that at some point, say in the beginning of the script, variable R might be equal to the integer 12 and at the end it could be equal to "Eat at Joe's...."

My recommendation is that you watch your variables like a hawk and try to use some self control—JavaScript's flexibility could be a nightmare if you're not careful.

In expressions involving the combination of a string and a numeric value, the resulting value will always be a string. Here's an example.

```
Length=9
Width=9
Area=length*width
Answer="The Area is..."+Area
```

will result in the variable answer being a string equal to: "The Area is 81".

Naming Variables

JavaScript has the following rules when it comes to naming a variable:

1. A JavaScript identifier or name must start with either a letter or an underscore ("_"). After that the variable name can be constructed from both numbers (0-9) and letters like "A" or "a".
2. JavaScript is case sensitive! This means that the variable "TEST" is not the same as the variable "test" or "TeSt".

Integers

Integers can be expressed in decimal (base 10), hexadecimal (base 16), or octal (base 8) format. A decimal integer literal consists of a sequence of digits (optionally suffixed as described below) without a leading 0 (zero).

An integer can be expressed in octal or hexadecimal rather than decimal. A leading zero on an integer literal means it is in octal; a leading 0x (or 0X) means hexadecimal. Hexadecimal integers can include digits (0-9) and the letters a-f and A-F. Octal integers can include only the digits 0-7.

Floating Point Values

A floating point value is any decimal number or fraction. JavaScript works with floating points easily and uses scientific notation as shown in the following examples:

```
2.1564563
-2.5E10
.9e12
3E-16
```

Boolean Values

The boolean type has two literal values: true and false.

String Values

A string value is any set of characters enclosed in quotes, either double or single. Strings can be composed entirely of characters, such as "Hello World!", or even entirely of numbers, such as "124", or both, such as "Hello 124". Note, though, that if you have a string of just numbers, say "12", the string will not have the mathematical value of 12. Using the **eval()**, **parseInt()**, and **parseFloat()** functions you can turn a string of numbers into a numerical value for computational purposes.

Special Characters

You can use the following special characters in JavaScript string literals:

\b indicates a backspace

\f indicates a form feed

\n indicates a new line character

\r indicates a carriage return

\t indicates a tab character

Creating Arrays

An array is a series of values assigned to a single variable that all share the same characteristics. For example, assume you wanted to list all the names in a group of 20 people. Instead of creating a separate variable for each one, like **NameOne** and **NameTwo** and **NameThree**..., you could create an array called **Names** and assign the first name to **Names[1],** the second name to **Names[2]**, until you get to the final name on your list, which would be assigned to **Names[20]**.

UNDERSTANDING EXPRESSIONS

An expression is basically a formula of some sort. For example A=1, 1+1, Name="Urb" + "LeJeune", and 2>X are all types of expressions. The main types of expressions you can create with JavaScript include:

Arithmetic

These are basic numerical expressions, such as 2+2=4 or 81/9+23.

String

These expressions deal with text values, be they "Ben" or "3.14344"—anything that is being treated as text is a string (even if it's a number).

Logical

Logical expressions are formulas such as "does 2+3=5?". All logical expressions result in either a true or false answer.

Conditional

A conditional is somewhat like a logical expression. The difference is that in a logical expression the answer is either true or false, but with a conditional expression you provide the outcome choices, which can be different types of values.

Evaluating Expressions with JavaScript Operators

Tables B.1 and B.2 illustrate how different JavaScript expressions are constructed using the standard JavaScript operators, including assignment operators. For the purposes of Table B.1, assume that the variables A and B have been assigned these values: A=8 and B=2.

Table B.1 *Standard JavaScript Assignment Operators*

JavaScript Expression	Expression Represents	Resulting Value
A+=B	A=A+B	A=10
A-=B	A=A-B	A=6
A*=B	A=A*B	A=16
A/=B	A=A/B	A=4
A%=B	A=A%B	A=0
A=-B	A=-B	A=-2

Table B.2 *JavaScript Incrementing Operators*

JavaScript Expression	Expression Represents	Resulting Value
B=A++	B=A and A=A+1	B=3 and A=4
B=A--	B=A and A=A-1	B=3 and A=2
B=++A	B=A+1 and A=A+1	B=4 and A=4
B=--A	B=B-1 and A=A-1	B=2 and A=2

The **%** is a special operator called the modulus operator and it takes two values, in the above case A and B, and divides A by B and returns the value left over. In this example, 8/2 = 4, with no remainder. If the values were 41 and 10, or 41/10, the resulting value would be 1.

For the purposes of Table B.2, assume that the variables A and B have been assigned these values: B=0 and A=3

Comparing Expressions

You can create expressions in JavaScript for comparison purposes. For example, you might want to test if "A is greater than B" or if "B does not equal A". In each case you would set up a comparison expression using various comparison operators (==, >, >=, <, <=, !=) to tell JavaScript exactly what it is you want to know.

Many times these expressions are used in conjunction with an if-then statement. For example, the following simple code demonstrates the use of a few comparison expressions:

```
<HTML>
<HEAD>
<TITLE>Java Function Example</TITLE>
<SCRIPT LANGUAGE="JavaScript">
```

```
<!-- Beginning of JavaScript Applet ————————

A=5
B=6
C=5

document.write("<H3>Example JavaScript for Comparison Operators<HR><P></H3>")
document.write("A="+A+" B="+B+" C="+C+"<P><HR>")
if(A==B)
{
   document.write("A does equal B!<P>")
}

if(A!=B)
{
   document.write("A does not equal B!<P>")
}

if(A<B)
{
   document.write("A is less than B!<P>")
}

if(A>=C)
{
   document.write("A is greater than or equal to C!")
}

document.write("<HR><P><H3>You Can Also Set A Variable To Return The Result Of A
Comparison Expression!</H3><P>")

D=(A>C)

document.write("D equals:"+D+" when it is set to = the expression A>C")
document.write("<HR><P>")

D=(A==C)

document.write("D equals:"+D+" when it is set to = the expression A==C")

  // -- End of JavaScript code ———— -->

</SCRIPT>
</HEAD>

<BODY>
</BODY>

</HTML>
```

A comparison operator compares its operands and returns a logical value based on whether the comparison is true or not. While the previous demonstration works with numerical values, comparison expressions may also be used with strings. For example, you could check whether "Ben"="neB" to see if two strings matched each other. When used on string values, the comparisons are based on the standard lexicographical ordering.

Here's a quick review of the key comparison operators:

Equal (==): Returns true if the operands are equal.

Not equal (!=): Returns true if the operands are not equal.

Greater than (>): Returns true if the left operand is greater than the right operand.

Greater than or equal to (>=): Returns true if the left operand is greater than or equal to the right operand.

Less than (<): Returns true if the left operand is less than the right operand.

Less than or equal to (<=): Returns true if the left operand is less than or equal to the right operand.

String Operators

In addition to the comparison operators, which may be used on string values, you can also add strings together using a simple + operator. For example

```
"The" + "Coriolis" + "Group"
```

returns the string:

```
"The Coriolis Group"
```

You can add strings to existing strings by using the shorthand of +=. For example, if you had a string FIRSTPART which was equal to "This Book is", and then you added the following line of JavaScript code:

```
FIRSTPART+=" GREAT!"
```

If you printed out the string, you'd get:

```
"This Book is GREAT!"
```

JAVASCRIPT PROPERTIES

Table B.3 provides an alphabetical list of JavaScript's built-in properties and a brief explanation of each one.

Table B.3 *JavaScript's Built-in Properties*

Properties	Of	Explanation	Sample Code
action	form	You set the form.action property to a string that is the destination URL for data from that form when it is submitted.	myform.action="String"
alinkColor	document	You set the document.alinkcolor to a string that is a hexidecimal or color command that tells the browser what the color of an active link should look like in your document.	document.alinkcolor=""
appCodeName	navigator	By reading the navigator.appCodeName property you can see what the internal codename is for the current version of Navigator that the browser is using.	Codename= navigator.appcodename
appName	navigator	By reading the navigator.appName property you can see what the official name is for the current version of Navigator that the browser is using.	ApplicationName= navigator.appName
appVersion	navigator	By reading the navigator.appVersion property you get the exact version number of Navigator that the browser is using.	ApplicationVersion= navigator.appVersion
bgColor	document	You set the document.bgColor property to a string specifying the color of the document background.	document.bhColor=""
checked	checkbox, radio	Reading this property will return a Boolean value (true or false) that indicates the current state of a specific checkbox or radio button object.	checkvalue= checkbox.checked
cookie	document	Reading this property returns the string contents of the cookies.txt file.	cookietext= document.cookie
defaultChecked	checkbox, radio	Reading this property gives you a Boolean value which indicates the default selection state of a checkbox or radio button.	Currentvalue= checkbox. defaultChecked
defaultStatus	window	This property controls the default message displayed in the status bar at the bottom of a window in Navigator.	window.defaultStatus=" My Document!"
defaultValue	hidden, password, text, textarea	This property contols a string value which is equal to the default value of a password, text, or textarea object.	.text.defaultValue= "Coriolis"
E	Math	Reading this property returns Euler's constant, the base of natural logarithms, which approximately equals 2.718.	EulerConstant=math.E
encoding	form	This property refers to a string that indicates the type of MIME encoding used on a specific form.	TypeofEncoding= form.encoding
fgColor	document	This property controls the color of a document's text. It accepts a string value set to a hexidecimal indicator or a color command.	document.fgColor=""
hash	link, location	Reading this property of a link or a location returns a string which begins with a hash mark (#) that pulls out just the anchor name in the referred-to URL.	anchorname=link.hash
host	link, location	Reading this property of a link or a location returns a string that gives you the specific hostname:port part of the referred to URL.	nameofHost=link.host

Continued

Table B.3 JavaScript's Built-in Properties (continued)

Properties	Of	Explanation	Sample Code
hostname	link, location	Reading this property of a link or a location returns a string that gives you the specific host and domain name or IP address of the referred-to URL's network host.	Currenthostname= location.hostname
href	link, location	Reading this property returns a string equal to the entire referred-to URL.	hreference=link.href
length	frame, links, history, radio, select, string, window, objects, anchors, forms, frames, elements, arrays, options	This property returns an integer reading equal to the length of the object or array specified.	Lengthofstring= mystring.length
linkColor	document	This property accepts a string value of either a hexidecimal color indicator or specific color command to control the color of a document's hyperlinks.	document.linkColor=""
LN2	math	Reading this value returns the natural logarithm of two, equal to about 0.693.	LogofTwo=math.LN2
LN10	math	Reading this value returns the natural logarithm of ten, equal to about 2.302.	LogofTen=math.LN10
location	document	This property returns a string equal to the complete URL of the currently viewed document.	Currentlocation= document.location
LOG2E	math	Reading this property returns the base 2 logarithm of e equal to about 1.442.	LogofE=math.LOG2E
LOG10E	math	Reading this property returns the base 10 logarithm of e equal to about 0.434.	LogofTEN=math.LOG10E
method	form	Use this property to tell Navigator how to send field input from forms to the server.	form.method
name	button, frame, checkbox, hidden, radio, password, reset, select, submit, text, textarea, window, options array	Reading this property returns a string specifying the name of the referenced object.	Nameofbutton= button1.name
parent	frame, window	The parent property is a synonym for a window whose frameset contains the current frame.	Parentwindow= frame.parent
pathname	link, location	A string specifying the url-path portion of the URL. link.pathname.	pathofURL=
PI	math	The property of this math object returns a value equal to PI or about 3.14159...	Circumfrence= Diameter*math.PI
port	link, location	This string specifies the communications port the server to the referred-to link uses for communications	portoflink=link.port

Continued

Table B.3 JavaScript's Built-in Properties (continued)

Properties	Of	Explanation	Sample Code
protocol	link, location	This string specifies the protocol portion of a URL as specified by the referenced link or location. This is the part of a URL that takes place up to and including the first colon.	Protocoloflink= link.protocol
referrer	document	This property controls the URL of the calling document when a link is chosen by the user.	Callingdocument= document.referrer
search	link, location	This property returns a string that begins with a question mark. The string equals the query information in a specified URL.	searchofURL=link.search
selected	options array	This property controls a Boolean value (true or false) which specifies the current selection state of an option in a select object which is a select index as created by the **<SELECT>**...**</SELECT>** tags.	Currentlyselected= document.form. selectindex
SQRT1_2 property	math	This math object property returns the square root of one-half, roughly 0.707.	squarerootonehalf= math.SQRT1_2
sqrt2	math	This math object property returns the square root of two, which is equal to about 1.414.	squareroottwo= math.sqrt2
status	window	The status property of a window controls the message which is displayed on the status bar at the bottom of a window via a string.	window.status= "My Document!"
target	form, link, location	The target property works with forms, links, and locations. For a form it denotes the name of the window to send responses to when the form is submitted. For a link it tells Navigator which window to display the linked document in.	form.target= "TARGETFrame"
text	options array	This property controls via a string the text which follows an **<OPTION>** tag in a select object.	Selectedoption= document.myform. selectlist.options(X).text
title	document	This property controls the title of the document in the browser.	document.title= "Title is My Document!"
top	window	The top property is a synonym for the top-most Navigator window, which is a "document window"or "Web Browser window."	Topwindownow= window.top
userAgent	navigator	A string representing the value of the user-agent header sent in the HTTP protocol from client to server.	userAgentHeader= navigator.userAgent
value	button, radio, checkbox, hidden, password, reset, submit, text, textarea objects, options array	Reading this property returns a string equal to the value of the related object.	value=document. myform.text1.value
vlinkColor	document	This property controls the color of visited links. It accepts a hexidecimal string or color command string.	document.vlinkColor=""

JAVASCRIPT EVENTS

Table B.4 below offers a list of some of JavaScript's built-in events.

Table B.4 JavaScript's Built-in Events

Event Name	Event Happens When...	Event for...	Actual Syntax	Example Syntax
blur	User removes input focus from form element.	text fields, textareas, and selections	onBlur	<INPUT TYPE=INPUT NAME= "TEXT3" SIZE=20 onBlur= "blurry(object)">
click	User clicks on form element or link.	buttons, radio buttons, links, checkboxes, submit buttons, reset buttons	onClick	<INPUT TYPE="button" VALUE= "Test Click Here" onClick= "compute(object)">
change	User changes text or textarea, or selects element.	text fields, textareas, and selections	onChange	<INPUT TYPE=INPUT NAME= "TEXT2" SIZE=20 onChange="changed(object)">
focus	User gives form element input focus.	text fields, textareas, and selections	onFocus	<INPUT TYPE=INPUT NAME="TEXT3" SIZE=20 onFocus= "FocusOn(object)">
load	User loads an HTML document in Netscape.	Documents	onLoad	<BODY onLoad="JavaScript Code!">
mouseover	User moves mouse pointer over a link or anchor.	links	onMouseOver	<A HREF="http://home.netscape.com/" onMouseOver= "JavaScript Code!">
select	User selects form element's input field.	text fields, textareas	onSelect	<INPUT TYPE="text" VALUE= "" NAME=text1" onSelect= "JavaScript Code!">
submit	User submits a form.	Forms	onSubmit	form.onSubmit="JavaScript Code!"
unload	User exits the page.	Documents	onUnload	<BODY onUnload="JavaScript Code!”>

JAVASCRIPT OBJECTS

JavaScript contains a number of built-in objects for you to work with. Table B.5 lists most of the objects and their purposes.

Table B.5 *JavaScript Objects*

Object	Purpose	Associated Events
Anchors	Anchors are text which can be specifically linked to by a typical URL **<HREF>** statement.	None
Button	A Button object is created in the **<FORM>** ... **</FORM>** area of your document and displays a push-button on the form.	onClick
Check Box	A checkbox on an HTML form. A Checkbox is a toggle switch that lets the user set a value on or off.	onClick
Date	JavaScript's Date object is a non-visible object which gives you access to an array of methods and functions concerning time and dates.	None. Use the OnLoad and OnUnLoad events in the **<BODY>** tag of a document.
Document	The Document object is used to refer to the current document loaded into the current browser window. You can especially use the document object to output HTML via the document.write("string") method.	onClick
Form	A form is created in your document through the HTML command **<FORM NAME="formname">** ... **</FORM>** tag. This is an area in your document where you display other objects like buttons and text to facilitate input between the user and your site or server.	onSubmit
Frames	A frame created by the **<FRAME>** ... **</FRAME>** tag is a window that can display a document or contain other frames.	None. Use the OnLoad and OnUnLoad events in the **<FRAME>** tag of a document.
Hidden	A Hidden object is a special instance of a text object that isn't shown to the user, but might contain internal information created by JavaScript code. This code is then passed on when a form is submitted for processing.	None
History	This object contains information on which URLs the client has visited in the current window in action. The information is taken from the history list found by the menu and toolbar in the Navigator window.	None
Links	A link is a URL location in the current document as defined by the **<A HREF>** ...**<A>**HTML tag.	onClick onMouseOver
Location	This object refers to the current window's current URL location on the Web.	None
Math	A non-visible built-in Javascript object which is used to do an array of math functions.	None
Navigator	This object is used to refer to the actual Navigator program. Don't confuse this with a window. There is only one navigator object, while their can be multiple windows.	None
Password	This is a special object that creates a text field but displays any values with asterisks (*) to conceal the actual value from view.	None
Radio	A radio button is an object used to create a list of options, but allows the user to select only one of the given set at any time.	onClick
Reset	A reset button, which is placed in the **<FORM>** ... **</FORM>** area of a document is used to reset all form elements back to their original default values.	onClick

Continued

Table B.5 *JavaScript Objects (continued)*

Object	Purpose	Associated Events
Select	A select object is created via the HTML tag of **<SELECT>** ... **</SELECT>** and is placed in a forms area. The object creates a selection list (a scrolling list of items) for the user to choose from.	onBlur
String	Any variable containing a series of characters.	None
Submit	A submit button on a form is used to create a submission instance which sends form data to a program of some sort (perhaps a CGI script) which then processes the contained data.	OnClick
Text Box	A text input field is created via the HTML command **<INPUT TYPE= TEXT Name="TEXTNAME" SIZE=[number]>** tag. A text box can accept input or display text.	onBlur onChange
TextArea	The text area object is created in via the HTML syntax of **<TEXTAREA>** ... **</TEXTAREA>** tags and is a multiline input field which can accept input from the user or display output as well.	onBlur onChange
Window	A window is the specific instance of a browser window.	onLoad

Appendix C: A Survivor's Guide to Unix

The overwhelming majority of Internet accounts are set up on the Unix operating system, though Windows is becoming more and more popular. Unix is a system that is functionally similar to DOS, or System 7 on a Mac. But even if you are using a graphical interface like Netscape, there will be times when you'll need to confront Unix head on. For example, if you plan to write your own CGI scripts, you'll need to know how to at least fake your way around Unix.

Unix aficionados say Unix is more complex than DOS; however, it's less complex than operating systems found on IBM mainframes. Unix is also tough to learn and counter-intuitive. Therefore, I've put this appendix together to help you learn the basics. You can think of it as a crash course to get you through some of the more common commands once you come face-to-face with the dreaded Unix command line prompt.

Unix Commands

Unix will likely make you feel like you're traveling around in a foreign country because you're probably more familiar with a visual operating systems like Windows than a text-based command-line one. Basically, Unix is a system that requires you to enter commands manually. The difficult part, the part that tends to drive people crazy, is the exactness of the format of Unix commands. This means that if you make a mistake in typing in a command, you won't get any help from Unix. Fortunately, there are some general principles I can give you to help you get around in Unix.

Are Unix commands like DOS commands? You bet. In fact, both have highly structured component parts. You can think of a command as if it were a verb in English. Some examples include DOS's **copy**, **erase**, and **print** commands. The verb is the action part of the command—it tells the computer what to do.

The action verb *always* comes first. But many commands require additional information. For example, if you want to delete a file, you must provide the following:

- The name of the command to delete a file.
- The name of the file to delete.

Let's assume that we want to erase a DOS file named urb.txt. At the DOS prompt we enter:

```
C:> del urb.txt
```

This action or "verb" tells DOS what to do. In some cases the command all by itself is enough information. For example, the DOS **cls** (clear screen) tells DOS to clear everything currently on the screen. To delete a file, we need to provide an object for our verb—the name of the file to be deleted. In the world of commands, this object is called a *parameter.* If more than one parameter is required, the information following the verb is called a *parameter list.* One such operation requiring multiple parameters is that of copying a file. To do this, we need to tell the operating system the following three things: the fact that we want to copy (*action*), the name of the original file (*from-where*), and the name of the new file (*to-where*):

```
command from-where to-where
```

The Unix equivalent of the DOS **copy** command is **cp**. (Remember, you were forewarned—the designers of Unix did not go out of their way to make life easier for users.) If we want to copy a file named urb.txt to a new file having the name pat.txt, the command would be:

```
unix% cp urb.txt pat.txt
```

Here, the portion of the command that you enter is underlined. The prompt, precedes the part that you enter. (Your actual Unix prompt most likely will not be unix%.) The copy command (**cp**) used in this example requires three things:

- The name of the command to perform—**cp**.
- The name of the file to copy—urb.txt.
- The name of the new file—pat.txt.

One last and extremely important rule is that *each distinctive piece of information in a command must be separated by at least one space.* If a command contains a verb and one parameter, the parameter and the verb must be separated by one or more spaces. Likewise, if there are multiple parameters, each must be separated by at least one space. In the example copy command

```
unix% cp urb.txt  pat.txt
```

there must be at least one space between the **cp** and the filename urb.txt. Likewise, there must be at least one space between urb.txt and pat.txt. In computer jargon, *delimiter* is the technical term for these separators. Always remember, the computer is not nearly as smart as you are, so do all you can to help the poor thing do its task.

In summary, the key points for writing Unix commands include:

- The prompt, followed by a blinking cursor, is what greets you on the command line.
- A command instructs Unix to perform a specific action.
- The first component part of a command is always the action verb.
- The format of a command must be exact.
- Commands typically require additional information, which is specified using *parameters.*
- Each component of a command must be separated by at least one space.
- Unix commands are case sensitive.

CONVENTIONS YOU CANNOT IGNORE!

In this appendix, I'll use the following notation for our command-line prompt:

```
unix%
```

The prompt on your system will probably look different; it may be displayed with just the "%" character. Following the prompt is a command. Now the only catch is that *you must type a command exactly as you see it printed here.* One of the biggest problems new Unix users have is that they forget that Unix is case sensitive. **LS**, **ls**, and **Ls** are all different to Unix, and only **ls** represents a command. (I spent an agonizing five minutes trying to figure out why I was getting an "invalid command" message when trying to change directories by entering CD in caps.) Command parameters are shown enclosed between the "< >" or "[ ]" pairs. The parameter list enclosed between the "< >" pair must be supplied while the parameter list enclosed between the "[ ]" pair is optional.

The ellipsis (...) is used to indicate that the parameter may be repeated any number of times. The "!" character is used to indicate mutually exclusive parameters. To illustrate,

```
unix% cd  [directory-path]
```

indicates that the command **cd** may be entered all by itself (to return to your home directory from any working directory) or a directory path name may be entered. The parameter enclosed within the square brackets is optional. However, if optional parameters are used, they must be in exactly the form shown. Since *directory-path* is enclosed between the "[ ]" pair, you supply the desired path name. Multiple directory names may be entered at the same time such as:

```
unix% cd  /pub/ftp/Urb
```

Entering the **cd** command for each directory, although requiring fewer key strokes, is less error prone. The sequence

```
unix% cd  /pub
unix% cd  ftp
unix% cd  Urb
```

accomplishes the same function as the multiple directory names used in the previous example. This command

```
unix% rm  <file-name>  [...file-name]
```

illustrates that the **rm** (remove) command requires at least one filename, although any number may be entered, such as **rm temp.001 temp.002**. The command

```
unix% cd [  ..  !   <[directory-path]subdirectory-directory-name>]
```

indicates that the **cd** command doesn't require any parameters. **cd** entered without a parameter will change your current working directory from whatever it may be to your home directory. If a parameter is used, it must have one of two forms, either **cd ..** (cd and at least one space followed by two consecutive periods), or a subdirectory name optionally preceded by a directory path.

What's a File?

Unix stores information in terms of files. A file may be empty, or it may contain a collection of data. Text files primarily contain characters that may be entered from a keyboard. Binary files may contain characters that are not keyboard characters. Files are grouped together inside directories in much the same fashion as documents are grouped in a hanging folder. From a system standpoint, directories are also treated as files. (The same is true for DOS.) A directory may also contain one, or more, directories, which become subdirectories of the parent directory.

Files are stored within directories. The entire structure may be conceptualized as a file cabinet. The individual directories are drawers in the cabinet, with individual files like documents stored within the drawers. Executable programs and Unix scripts are also considered files. Unix considers nearly everything that stores or generates data a file.

DIRECTORIES

A directory structure is much like a family tree, with a specially designated directory, called the *root*, at the top of the structure. All references begin with the root directory. The root is designated as "/" (without the quotations). Directories subordinate to the root directory, also called child directories, may be added. The subdirectory may also have subdirectories. The entire structure is called a directory tree.

When you log on to your system, you are automatically placed into what Unix calls your *home directory*. Typically your home directory has the same name as your logon name. Although your directory is certainly not the root directory of the system, it is convenient to conceptualize it as your personal root directory. You will rarely need to access a directory that is closer to the system root directory than your personal directory.

Your Home Directory

Your *home directory* is where you are placed when you first log on to a Unix system. It may be referenced by the tilde character "~" or by the standard system variable $HOME. (Because not all Unix shells recognize $home, the uppercase version is safer.)

Your Working Directory

Your *working*, or *current, directory* is the one that is currently accessed. If you change directories (**cd**), your working directory changes. To find the complete directory path (from the root) of your working directory, you need only enter:

```
unix% pwd
```

The output will be in the form of:

```
/user/local/LeJeune
```

The leftmost "/" indicates the root directory. The directory user is a subdirectory of the root; the directory local is a subdirectory of user; and lastly, LeJeune is a subdirectory of local. Notice that the last subdirectory, LeJeune, has two capital letters. Entering the name without the capitals will produce the dreaded "/user/local/lejeune: No such file or directory" message. Keep an eye out for this—it's bound to happen to you now and then.

Moving around the Directory Structure

You may create a subdirectory using the **mkdir** (make directory) command. The syntax is:

```
unix% mkdir <[directory-path]new-directory-name>
```

If you omit the optional *directory-path* component, a subdirectory—using the name supplied as the new-directory-name parameter—is created immediately under the current working directory. If your working directory is /abc/def and you enter **mkdir** xxx, you will then have a path /abc/def/xxx. If you enter **mkdir** /abc/xxx, you will have path /abc/xxx.

The **rmdir** (remove directory) command is the complement of **mkdir**. The syntax is:

```
unix% rmdir <[directory-path]directory-name-to-delete>
```

Unix will not remove a directory unless it is empty, which means it doesn't contain any files or subdirectories.

The **cd** (change directory) comes in three flavors:

```
unix% cd [  ..   !   <[directory-path]subdirectory-directory-name>]
```

The syntax shown here indicates that the **cd** command may be entered without a parameter since everything else is optional. If a parameter is entered, the "!" indicates that it must take the form of either:

```
unix% cd ..
```

or

```
unix% cd   [directory-path]subdirectory-directory-name
```

If you enter **cd** with no parameters, you will be returned to your home directory. **cd ..** (cd followed by at least one space followed by two consecutive periods) will back up your working directory one level toward the root. If you don't use the **cd** option or the **cd ..** option, you must use the following option:

```
unix% cd  [directory-path]subdirectory-directory-name
```

Remember the syntax conventions, everything between the "[" and the "]" is optional. However, if a parameter is specified, it must take either of the two forms within the square brackets. The "!" indicates one or the other. **cd** (without a parameter), **cd $HOME**, and **cd ~** are all functionally the same thing.

FILE MANIPULATION COMMANDS

The terms *command* and *program* are used interchangeably in Unix parlance. Generally, issuing a command causes execution of the named program. The **ls** (list) command will provide a directory listing. The syntax is:

```
unix% ls  <[switches]  [directory-path]filename>
```

If *directory-path* is omitted, the working directory is assumed. The most common switch is in the form

```
unix% ls  -l
```

which provides a detailed listing. There must be at least one space between the command name and the start of any switches. Entering **ls** without any parameters produces a listing containing only filenames. The following is an example of an **ls** listing:

```
absent          mother-boards
acm.dat         musthave.txt
acy-bill        n
ad              ncsa
advertising     netinfo
amipro          nets
```

The use of the **-l** switch will produce a detailed listing similar to the following:

```
-rw-      1 lejeune users    33154   Jun23   12:16   1liners
-rw-      1 lejeune users    4559    Apr12   17:27   486
-rw-      1 lejeune users    29845   Jun20   19:24   Archie-Reference-Manual
```

```
-rw—      1 lejeune users   1387   Jun10   13:07   Internet-primer
drwx—     2 lejeune users   512    Mar28   17:46   Mail
drwx—     2 lejeune users   512    May12   11:17   News
-rw—      1 lejeune users   314    May12   14:01   blond
-rwx—     1 lejeune users   20     Jun22   07:15   borland
-rwx—     1 lejeune users   139    May13   13:57   garbo
drwx—     2 lejeune users   512    Jun23   14:55   gopher
```

The leftmost group of 10 columns deserves special attention. A "d" in the first position denotes a subdirectory. Mail, News, and gopher are directories in this listing. (Remember that case counts. If you want to change to directory Mail, you must enter **cd Mail**.) The remaining nine columns represent the Unix protection scheme. These nine columns are partitioned into logical sets of three each. The three sets, from left to right, are user (you), group, and others (the remainder of the world.) Unix is a multi-user network. Groups, which can be ignored for our purposes, represent work groups. Each set has the three components read, write, and execute. If you create a file, the protection scheme might initially be set to:

```
rw-                - - -    - - -
        User       Group    Others
```

The actual initial file creation protection scheme is determined by your system administrator. The groupings shown above would indicate that you have read and write privileges for this file but it cannot be executed. No one in your workgroup, or any others, has any access to the file. A dash in the listing simply means no privilege. If this file is to be an executable script, your executable privilege must be turned on. (More on this in a minute.) The listing would then be:

```
rwx             - - -           - - -
```

If you turn off the write protection for a specific file, you cannot accidentally delete that file. You may read a write-protected file but you will not be able to change or delete the file. If you give execution privilege to people in your group, and anyone else in the universe, your listing would be:

```
rwx             - - x           - - x
```

One caveat: A file must have read privilege as well as execute privilege before the system allows execution. A file listing with:

```
rwx             rwx             rwx
```

would give everyone everything.

You may ignore the next column. The next item is the owner of the file followed by the group. Next comes the file size, followed by the file's creation or modification date and time. The last entry is the file name.

CHANGING FILE AND DIRECTORY PROTECTION

The command used to change the protection for a file, or directory, is **chmod** (change mode.) The syntax is:

```
unix% chmod <[a][u][g][o]> <<-!+>[r][w][x]> file-name
```

u, g, and o indicate the three major categories of user, group, and other. The letter "a" indicates all three groups, which is also the default. The "+'" parameter enables and the "-" parameter disables. The r, w, and x parameters indicate read, write, and execute. Assume that you have recently created a file named garbo. Immediately after the creation of file garbo, it would probably have the following listing:

```
rw-  – –  [stuff removed]  garbo
```

The user has read and write privileges but no execute privilege. The group and the world have no privileges at all for file garbo. Let's assume first that the file garbo is to be an executable script; additionally, you want to get everyone (user, group, and others) to have the ability to execute the script. Execution requires both read and execute privileges. The command enabling file garbo to be executed by everyone would be:

```
unix% chmod ugo+rx garbo
```

or

```
unix% chmod a+rx garbo
```

Either of these commands would change the user, group, and others modes to executable and readable. The new listing would be:

```
rwx    r-x    r-x   [stuff  removed]    garbo
```

People in your workgroup, and anyone else in the universe, could execute this file, but only you could display, modify, or erase the file. The directory holding the file must also allow execution. The directory protection need only be changed once. Assuming that garbo is in your home directory, you could enter

```
unix% chmod a+rx  ~
```

or

```
unix% chmod a+rx  $HOME
```

That is, the enabled directory will now allow execution, for files that have been execute enabled, for all three groups.

Let's assume that file big-dummy has protection that gives everyone everything. The listing would be:

```
rwx  rwx  rwx  [stuff removed]  big-dummy
```

Also assume that you want to take away all privileges for the group "others." You would enter:

```
unix% chmod o-rwx dummy
```

The "-" parameter removes privileges. A listing for big-dummy would now be:

```
rwx  rwx  —  [stuff removed]  big-dummy
```

Copying and Moving Files

The Unix commands for copying and moving files are **cp** and **mv**. Here are the general formats for these commands:

```
unix% cp [source-path]source-filename  [destination-path]destination-filename
unix% mv [source-path]source-filename  [destination-path]destination-filename
```

The source and destination file names don't need to be the same. Actually, the move command (**mv**) is frequently used to rename a file. To move a file named Urb from your home directory to path /abc/def and change the name to Pat in the process, you'd enter:

```
unix% mv $HOME/Urb  /abc/def/Pat
```

Deleting Files

Unix files are removed using the **rm** command. Here's the syntax required:

```
unix% rm [-i] [path-name]file-name
```

The **-i** (interactive switch) tells the command to prompt the user to approve the operation before a file is deleted. I think it's a good idea to use this switch if you use wild cards as part of your file name. Unix wild cards tend to be more inclusive than DOS wild cards. The command

```
unix% rm  -i  temp*
```

deletes all file names beginning with the string "temp". However, the use of the **-i** switch causes the system to prompt for approval before deleting each file matching the mask. You are prompted with:

```
rm: remove 'temp001'?
```

Unless your reply is "y" or "yes" the system will not delete the file.

Unix Globs, aka Wild Cards

The "*" and "?" characters are called *glob constructs* in Unix. There once was a program named glob that functionally expanded names containing wild cards. However, no one seems to really know where the name originated. The asterisk "*" is a glob construct that expands to any string of zero or more characters. For example, the command

```
unix% ls g*
```

lists all files that begin with g. The file gaaa.xxx would be included in Unix but not in DOS, so be careful. Unix uses of globs tend to be more inclusive than their DOS counterparts. The "?" glob stands for any character in the same position. For example,

```
unix% ls ?abc
```

lists all files and directories that have any first letter and abc as the second, third, and fourth characters, respectively. Unix provides an additional glob that is lacking in DOS. The "[]" pair can match any one of the characters inside the brackets. As an example,

```
unix% ls [123]xyz
```

lists any file that has a 1, 2, or 3 in the first character position and xyz as the second through fourth characters. Thus, files with names like, 1xyz, 2xyz, and 3xyz would be listed. You may indicate a range of characters within the brackets by enclosing the first character and the last character between the character "-". The glob [a-z] would expand to any lowercase letter. Globs may be combined. For example, the command

```
unix% ls [a-z]*
```

lists all files in the current directory and all subdirectories having a lowercase first letter.

GET ME SOME 'MORE' 'CAT'

Two commands that may be used for viewing text files are **cat** (concatenate) and **more**. **cat** will display the entire contents of a file on your terminal without pausing. Unfortunately, the file will scroll merrily out of sight if it has more lines that you have lines on your terminal. On the other hand, when **more** is used, it will pause every time the screen is filled. Pressing Enter will advance one line while pressing the space bar will refill the screen. The syntax is:

```
unix% cat [path]file-name [...[path]file-name]
unix% more [path]file-name [...[path]file-name]
```

PIPING

Using the command **more** in conjunction with other commands will produce listings on the terminal that would otherwise scroll off the screen. Piping is the technical term for taking the output from one command and passing it to another command. The vertical bar (|) indicates piping. The command:

```
unix% ls -l  |  more
```

takes the output from the **ls** command and passes it to the command **more**.

MISDIRECTION AND REDIRECTION

The character < is used to redirect input to a command; the character > is employed to redirect output from a command. **echo** is a command that normally displays everything following the command on the terminal. Let's use the **echo** command, coupled with the > redirection symbol, to create a new command. In the following example

```
unix% echo "Now is the time" > text.tmp
```

the **echo** command's parameter "Now is the time" would normally be displayed on the screen. Adding the redirection symbol > will direct the parameter to the file text.tmp. The file is created if it does not exist; if the file already exists, it replaces and erases the old version. If you want the output appended to an existing file, use two consecutive >> symbols. The sequence

```
unix% echo  "Now is the time">text.tmp
unix% echo  "for everyone to party">> text.tmp
unix% more  text.tmp
unix% rm  text.tmp
```

would first create a file text.tmp with a line of text "Now is the time". Next, the line "for everyone to party" is appended to file text.tmp. File text.tmp will then be displayed as follows:

```
Now is the time
for everyone to party
```

and finally, the file text.tmp will be removed.

GETTING HELP

There are two Unix commands that will give you more help than you ever wanted. The **man** (manual) command will display documentation for a command. The form is:

```
unix% man <command>
```

The commands listed in this guide are short form. Use **man** to get all the options. The **man** command uses the **more** command without being told. Great people, these Unix programmers. Using redirection, you could get the online documentation for program mail and write it to a file, mail.doc. You could then transfer it to your home computer and subsequently print the file. Here's how to use the command **man** with redirection to file mail.doc:

```
unix% man mail > mail.doc
```

If you don't know the name of a command, but you have an idea of what it does, use the **apropos** command. (The use of the **apropos** command requires that the "whatis" database be installed on your system.) For example, if you don't know the specific command but you're sure that there must be a command that does what the DOS copy does, you would enter

```
unix% apropos copy
```

and you will be greeted with a flock of commands that have copy in their description. This list would include cp - copy files. You could then do a **man cp** to get the lowdown on the **cp** command.

ALIASES AND SCRIPTS

An *alias*, which is frequently called a macro, is typically a name substitution. One of the major uses of an alias allows substitution of familiar names for the frequently abstruse Unix command names. As an example, you could create an alias "dir" that would actually evoke the **ls** command.

Almost all operating systems contain the ability to create an executable file. A *script*, which is an executable file in Unix parlance, permits the entry and execution of a repetitive command series that might otherwise be entered, one at a time, at the command line prompt. The series of commands, contained within a script file, may then be executed by entering only a few keystrokes. Within DOS these executable files are called batch files and must have an extension of .BAT. Scripts are created using an editor and subsequently made executable script by using the **chmod** command. Scripts and DOS batch files are frequently used to reduce an extended command line sequence to a few keystrokes.

SUMMARY

So there you have it, DOS and Windows fans, not exactly everything that you wanted to know about Unix but were afraid to ask (sounds like a great name for a book), but a good start. If you are more comfortable with DOS than you are with Unix commands, you may want to create a series of aliases and scripts so you can use the names of the DOS commands you are familiar with. For example, you could create an alias "dir" that would actually evoke the **ls** command. Scripts, which are much like DOS batch files, are Unix executable files. A series of repetitive commands may be included in a script and executed by simply entering the name of the script. Many of the tips contained in this book are shortcut Unix scripts.

Appendix D: Web Publishing Resources

The collection of Web sites, HTML tools and utilities, and electronic and hardcopy books and magazines in this appendix gives you a varied and fairly extensive education with which to venture forth into the world of Web publishing.

When using the resources listed here, remember that Web sites can change location, or vanish altogether, literally overnight. Similarly, new ones are constantly being added. Don't be surprised, then, if you type the URL for one of these sites and get an error message or something totally different from what's described here.

If a really great HTML converter, Netscape helper, or other Web resource seems to be missing from those discussed here, it's probably because it's already included on the CD-ROM. To find out, review the highlights of the CD-ROM in Appendix F.

HOW THIS GUIDE IS ORGANIZED

Each item in this appendix was selected for its relevance to Web publishing and HTML. To specify which items you'll probably find most helpful, I've used a five-star rating system. Stars indicate *usefulness specifically for creating and managing Web pages*, not judgment of any other criteria.

General resources for creating Web pages are listed first, followed by Web-based HTML guides and documents, then sites for specific HTML tools and related utilities. Resources for specific issues related to Web publishing follow: CGI and VRML, sights and sounds, and legalities. Lastly, online and traditional magazines and books are reviewed. Note that resources are listed alphabetically within sections.

Sites for HTML Stuff

The sites listed in this section are those with extensive links to Web publishing and HTML resources throughout the Web. Several of these make excellent launching points for developing your own hotlist of Web pages.

☆☆☆☆ Best of the Web

`http://gnn.com/wic/botn/index.html`

Want to see how HTML should be done—or at least how GNN thinks it should be done? Surf on over here and save a few pages to disk. Pages are divided into amateur and professional. You'll be amazed at what's being done on the Web.

☆☆☆ Interesting Business Sites on the Web

`http://www.owi.com/netvalue`

You won't learn how to write HTML directly from this site, but you will learn what it can do for you and your business. The relatively small number of carefully selected links provide excellent examples of how organizations large and small are creating a presence on the Web. Save a few that you particularly like (or dislike) to disk and study their use of HTML.

☆☆☆☆ PC Week Navigator's World Wide Web Tools

`http://www.pcweek.ziff.com/~pcweek/WebTools.html`

A good site with links to all the essential HTML documents and products. Not as extensive as the Virtual Library site, but a good place for beginners looking to build a basic HTML library.

☆☆☆ Subjective Electronic Information Repository

`http://cbl.leeds.ac.uk/nikos/doc/repository.html`

Although you'd never be able to tell from the name, if it has to do with WWW or HTML, it's probably listed among the hundreds of links here. Finding a particular tool, site, or document could take some time and effort, however. This site can be slow, and there's little in the way of explanation, so you'll probably have to rely on trial and error. Also, some sections, particularly "Manuals and FAQs," are too Unix-oriented. If you decide to check this site out, be sure to peruse the links at "How to Do Fancy Stuff" and "About HTML."

☆☆☆ TECFA WWW and Internet Manuals, Demos, and Guides

http://tecfa.unige.ch/info-www.html

TECFA stands for "Technologies de Formation et Apprentissage," part of the University of Geneva, which explains why some of the links from this site are to French articles and software. Ignore the icons at the top of the page; it's hard to tell what they do, anyway. (For example, clicking on the icon of a bottle and trashcan takes you to the "ftp dump," an archive of mostly French files.) In fact, skip everything and go directly to "Help for WWW Information Providers." Here you'll find well-organized and helpfully annotated links, although the page could use some pruning to remove dead sites and revise changed ones. Links to icon archives, image-processing programs, and Netscape-specific sites are particularly helpful.

☆☆☆☆☆ The Web Developer's Virtual Library

http://www.stars.com/Vlib/

This extremely useful site contains hundreds of links to interesting resources for Web publishers, organized by topic. From *annotation* to *forms* to *VR*, if it has to do with Web development, you'll find it here. This is one for your hotlist.

☆☆☆☆ Web Communications Home Page

http://www.webcom.com

Unapologetically a marketing vehicle for Web Communications, a "WWW presence provider," it still provides lots of good information. Unlike many broader sites that devote only part of their space to Web publishing, this one is targeted strictly at those who want to set up a full-blown Web site. It's especially useful if you're interested in doing business on the Web, since it covers advanced Web topics like security, forms creation, and clickable image maps. You can also get a short manual from here, "Web Communication's Comprehensive Guide to Publishing on the Web." While I might not call this manual "comprehensive," it does have a few special sections that set it apart from similar guides, notably "How to Widely Publicize Your Site."

☆☆☆☆☆ The WebWeavers Page—Tools for Aspiring Web Authors

http://www.nas.nasa.gov/NAS/WebWeavers/

Starting with just this extremely helpful, well-organized site, you could get everything you'd need to learn HTML, and then design, publish, and manage your own Web pages. You'll find links to news, tools, tutorials, technical standards, documentation, and more. Fast and uncluttered, WebWeavers is a good example of efficient HTML design in its own right. Definitely one to add to your hotlist.

☆☆☆☆ The WWW and HTML Developers' Jumpstation

`http://oneworld.wa.com/htmldev/devpage/dev-page.html`

If you spend much time at all Web-surfing for HTML-related areas, you're sure to see lots of references to this one. Links to sites for art and graphics are particularly helpful. Note, though, that it deals more with the Mosaic Web browser than with Netscape.

Web and HTML FAQs and Docs

The following sites provide information about the history and use of HTML in varying degrees of detail and readability.

☆☆☆ Beginner's Guide to HTML

`http://www.ncsa.uiuc.edu/demoweb/html-primer.html`

This classic introductory guide from NCSA is quite well done, especially the section on troubleshooting. The site itself, however, can be very slow. Also, the material is geared toward NCSA's own Mosaic browser rather than Netscape, although this isn't too much of a problem in a basic text.

☆☆☆☆☆ Composing Good HTML

`http://www.cs.cmu.edu/~tilt/cgh`

This document should be required reading for would-be Web publishers. To make this as easy as possible, it's available online or can be downloaded as either a hypertext document or a standard text file. "Composing Good HTML" picks up where other style guides and primers leave off, with practical advice on good Web publishing practices, common errors, and things to avoid.

☆☆ How to Write HTML Files

`http://kcgl1.eng.ohio-state.edu/www/doc/htmldoc.html`

A little outdated, this document is still a good place to get started figuring out what HTML is and how to use it. The bulk of this site is divided into sections for beginning, intermediate, and advanced users, so you can dive in at the appropriate place. The writing is straightforward. Note that this can be a slow site.

☆☆☆ HTML Documentation Table of Contents

`http://www.utirc.utoronto.ca/HTMLdocs/NewHTML/htmlindex.html`

Just like it says, this is the home page for an introductory HTML guide by Ian Graham, a professor at the University of Toronto. A good, solid introduction.

☆ HyperText Mark Up Language

`http://www.w3.org/hypertext/WWW/MarkUp/MarkUp.html`

From CERN, the developers of the Web itself, this one is *the* technical paper describing the history and current status of existing and upcoming versions of HTML. If you're a Web historian or researcher, this is great; if you just want to put up a few Web pages as quickly and painlessly as possible, this is more than you need to know.

HTML Tools and Related Stuff

Here are the sites that are jam-packed with goodies to help you create HTML documents using a word processor such as Ami Pro or Word for Windows. Tools are also featured to help you write better HTML documents.

☆☆ Amiweb16.zip

`ftp://oak.oakland.edu/SimTel/win3/amipro/`

Are you an Ami Pro aficionado feeling left out by all the Word-to-HTML converters available for the downloading? Get this freeware Ami Pro add-on, amiweb16.zip, similar to the popular Word-based HTML Assistant, and join in the fun!

☆☆☆☆ HaL Software Systems

`http://www.webtechs.com/html-val-svc`

Once you've written a few HTML documents, go to this site by Mark Gaither to have them validated (checked to see whether they're in proper syntax). Just enter the URL of the page you want to check or type text in manually, select the level of standards that you want, and instantly see how well you've done.

☆☆ HTML Author

`http://www.salford.ac.uk/iti/gsc/htmlauth/summary.html`

HTML Author provides a Word for Windows 6.0 template and macros for writing HTML pages in Word. In addition to basic features, it supports simple tables, as well as non-English versions of Word. It also formats pages based on Netscape displays. That's the good news. The bad news: This site can be painfully slow.

☆☆☆ HTML Converters

`http://union.ncsa.uiuc.edu:80/HyperNews/get/www/html/converters.html`

You'll find links to dozens of sites for news, utilities, word processing macros, and conversion programs for HTML here. DOS/Windows, Mac, and Unix sites are included. Not very well organized, but lots of good links.

☆☆ Internet Assistant

`http://www.microsoft.com/msword/internet/ia`

This Word-to-HTML toolkit from Microsoft is available for English, French, and German versions of Word 6.0a and later. It automatically turns Word documents into simple Web pages, with *simple* being the operative word. If you want to do fancy stuff, you'll still have to write HTML code. It also allows Word to be used as a somewhat limited Web browser—but with Netscape around, why bother? Be warned: It can be a slow download.

☆☆☆☆☆ WWW Software for Windows PCs

`http://www.utirc.utoronto.ca/HTMLdocs/pc_tools.html`

Unlike other HTML-related sites, this one concentrates strictly on DOS and Windows. (Yes, there are a few DOS links, despite the name.) Frank explanations and reviews of its links are extremely helpful and can save a lot of online time. I have only one complaint: It's too short!

☆☆☆☆ Tools for World Wide Web Providers

`http://www.w3.org/hypertext/WWW/Tools/`

This popular, well-maintained Web space from CERN contains a large list of links to HTML filters, editors, validators, converters, and more.

CGI and VRML

You say you've completely mastered HTML and are looking for a new challenge? Check out the next generation of HTML, called *CGI* (the Common

Gateway Interface)—and the generation beyond that, called *VRML* (Virtual Reality Modeling Language)—at these sites.

☆☆☆☆ The Common Gateway Interface

`http://hoohoo.ncsa.uiuc.edu/cgi/overview.html`

If you're curious about CGI, which can serve as a way to allow greater interactivity between your Web site and its users, check out this page. With the help of the CGI programs and information archived here, visitors to your Web pages can fill out forms, take surveys, play games, and more. This NCSA site is not for beginners, but then, neither is CGI.

☆☆☆ WebSpace Home Page

`http://www.sgi.com`

Silicon Graphic's WebSpace is a 3-D browser for sites designed with VRML, possible heir to HTML. Presently, you'll only be able to use WebSpace if you're running Windows NT, but it's supposed to be available soon for the rest of the Windows family, as well as the Power Mac. Get the FAQs on VRML and WebSpace, download the software, and then sample some Doom-like VRML sites from here. Note, though, that the links at this site are definitely not for slow modems or computers, and are best explored during non-peak hours.

☆☆ *Wired*'s VRML Forum

`http://vrml.wired.com/`

An "open forum" from *Wired* magazine, this site contains a loose collection of VRML papers, proposals, and projects. If you're interested in the cutting edge of Web design and can follow the techno-jargon, this is the place to hang out with VRML researchers and programmers.

Adding Sights (and Sounds) to Your Site

To get in on the emerging multimedia Web publishing frontier, here are some useful tools, icons, art, and music.

☆☆☆☆ Graphics Viewers, Editors, Utilities, and Information

`http://www2.ncsu.edu:80/bae/people/faculty/walker/hotlist/graphics.html`

Yes, it's a long and clumsy URL to type in, but you'll probably only type it in once because you'll want to add it to your hotlist. You'll find over 100 links to great sources of help for working with graphics, video, and animation.

☆☆☆☆ Images, Icons, and Flags

http://www.nosc.mil/planet_earth/images.html

Most of the photographs and illustrations cataloged at this site have to do with nature and space, not surprisingly, since this page is part of the Planet Earth Web site. You can use a few GIFs directly from here, but you'll probably use it most for its comprehensive system of links to sources of art all over the Web. There's a lot to dig through here, but if you need images that can be processed into attractive icons and logos, it's worthwhile.

☆☆☆ Music Resources on the Net

http://www.music.indiana.edu/music_resources.html

Interested in adding some sounds to your sites? You'll find nearly 800 links to all kinds of music here, from accordions to ZZ Top. Many of the files here are in AU format, rather than the more commonly used WAV or MIDI formats, so you'll need to make your selections carefully. You'll also need to make sure you're not stepping on any musical toes: Much of the stuff here is copyrighted, so be sure to read those readme files thoroughly. (Also check out the resources listed in the "Legalities" section of this chapter.)

☆☆☆ The Transparent/Interlaced GIF Resource

http://dragon.jpl.nasa.gov/~adam/transparent.html

Download these tools and supporting documentation to create particularly cool-looking GIFs for any environment: DOS/Windows, Mac, or Unix.

☆ WWW Icon Collection

http://www.bsdi.com/icons/

This short page has only three links, but these links contain hundreds of icons, most in the public domain. However, almost all of them are in XPM or XBM format instead of GIF, making them of limited use for DOS/Windows.

☆☆☆☆ Yahoo's Music List

http://www.yahoo.com/Entertainment/Music

Links to thousands of sound and music resources, organized by type, are found here. If you can hear it and get it on the Net, you can get it from this site.

Free Art

If you're not an artist, you'll want to have a ready supply of free art that you can use. Here are some of the better stocked sites to help you spice up your Web pages.

☆☆☆☆ Clip Art Server

http://wwwin-vision.com/panda/c

This is the place to go if you are looking for great clip art. Here you'll find useful clip art collections from other archive sites on the Internet. The pictures were collected from a variety of sources, including various public-domain Amiga, Atari, PC, and Macintosh clip art collections. Many useful color clip art images are also available.

☆☆☆ Department of Computer Science Icon Browser

http://www.di.unipi.it/iconbrowser/icons.html

This site features a collection of useful icons that you can use to create your own Web pages. All of the icons are displayed in tables so that you can view all of them and find the one you want.

Legalities

Confused about who has the legal right to do what in cyberspace? You're not alone; law on the Net frontier is complicated and still being defined. If you're going to publish there or use what others have published, you'd better keep an eye on its evolving status, starting with these sites.

☆☆ Copyright Act of 1976, as Amended (1994)

http://www.law.cornell.edu:80/usc/17/overview.html

A hypertext version of the basic U.S. copyright law. It's surely not much fun, but you should browse through it anyway for a basic understanding of how to protect what you put on the Web, as well as legal use of what others have put there.

☆☆☆ Copyrights in Cyberspace

http://www.digital.com/gnn/bus/nolo/copy.html

This brief and readable article from Nolo Press's Web space explains how copyright law affects you as a user and publisher of online material. It also includes a link to an order form for the author's book, *The Copyright Handbook*.

Periodicals (Online and on Paper) Related to Web Publishing

You'll only find one magazine in this section that rated more than three stars (and that one is actually an online one, or *ezine*). It's not that there aren't good Net-related magazines—in fact, there's a glut of them, with a new one appearing almost every month. However, none is aimed directly and exclusively at Web publishers; most concentrate on articles that are variations of "Wow, check out this cool site I found" instead of "Wow, check out this cool site I made."

The magazines discussed in this section, therefore, vary from issue to issue in their attention to Web and HTML topics—great one month, negligible the next. Unless some enterprising publisher steps in to fill the gap, keep an eye on these at the newsstand (real or virtual), and buy or download them in the good months.

☆☆☆ *Boardwatch* (ISSN 1054-2760)

This magazine represents the opposite end of the design spectrum from other popular Net-related magazines, especially *Wired*, with their wild color and type combinations. In fact, it's downright plain, reminiscent of the *Commodore User* era of computer periodicals. But don't buy it for the pictures, buy it for the articles. *Boardwatch* is the only widely distributed magazine for the creators rather than the users of bulletin board systems and, by extension, Web sites. As such, you'll find it a good source for instruction, problem-solving ideas, and as a forum to share the experiences of running a site.

☆☆☆☆ *GNN NetNews*

`http://nearnet.gnn.com/gnn/index.html`

This weekly ezine is part of The Global Network Navigator, which won honorable mention for Most Important Service Concept from Best of the Web '94. *GNN NetNews* is small, but full of interesting and well-written articles.

☆☆ *Interactivity* (ISSN 1077-8047)

This new magazine is geared toward interactive publishing, including, but not limited to, the Web. You'll have to pick and choose among the articles in any given issue. In a recent issue, for example, instructions on CD-ROM mastering are of little use to the average Web publisher, while other articles like "Guide to File Formats" and "How to Put Together a Web Site" are great.

☆☆ *Internet World* (ISSN 1064-3923)

An interesting and fun magazine, *Internet World* covers all of the Net, with side-trips into commercial online services. General emphasis is on the Web most months, but topics that specifically affect Web publishers are discussed only occasionally. Most articles include source lists with Web sites to explore.

☆☆☆ *The Net* (ISSN 1080-2681)

This new monthly has just begun to define itself. At the moment, it's all over the place, in both style and content. It's less hyper-designed than *Wired*, but still desperately seeking hipness—the premiere June 1995 issue, for example, has the page numbers "scrawled" in someone's not-too-readable handwriting. Yes, it looks cool, but it takes a moment to figure out what page you're on. On the other hand, the articles themselves are (thankfully) readable, basic-black text on white paper. Much of the magazine is devoted to new and casual users, but the pull-no-punches evaluations of books, software, and Web sites make *The Net* worthwhile browsing for Web publishers. Also in its favor, HTML tools and Web utilities, including shareware and freeware that you can get online, are reviewed candidly and concisely.

☆☆☆ The *Netsurfer Digest* Home Page

`http://www.netsurf.com/nsd/index.html`

Here you can subscribe to free ezines, get back issues, and link to a few related sites. You'll want to browse through the weekly *Netsurfer Digest*, but the (more or less) monthly *Netsurfer Focus* is where the real value is for Web publishers.

☆☆☆ *PC Magazine* (ISSN 0888-8507)

Don't overlook this venerable font of computer knowledge and (especially) opinion. Make sure, however, to get the network edition for coverage of Web-related news and reviews beyond what's in the regular newsstand version, as well as special features on the state of the Net.

☆ *Publish* (ISSN 0897-6007)

A monthly that bills itself as "the magazine for electronic publishing professionals" should be just what the Web weaver ordered, right? Unfortunately not in this case, where "electronic publishing" means "high-end desktop publishing." There are a few Web-related reviews and news items, but even these don't include URLs. Save your money.

☆☆ *Wired* (ISSN 1059-1028)

You've probably seen this, um, attention-getting magazine if you've been following the evolution of the Net for any amount of time. Among the articles warning about government censorship, reviewing alternative music, and so on, you'll find reviews of Web-related products and the occasional helpful article for Web publishers. Unlike some other magazines about the Net, *Wired*'s articles include plenty of Web sites for more information. You can also check out the corresponding Web site, *HotWired*, at http://www.wired.com. It's free (right now, anyway), but you have to register.

Books

By the time you read this, there will probably be many more books on HTML and Web publishing than are currently available; publishers seem to be preparing an avalanche of them.

☆☆☆ *HTML Manual of Style*

by Larry Aronson (ZD Press, ISBN 1-56276-300-8)

Dry, text-heavy, and relatively short, this book is nevertheless a classic, and a good complement to *Teach Yourself Web Publishing*.

☆☆☆☆ *JavaScript & Netscape 2 Wizardry*

by Dan Shafer (Coriolis Group Books, ISBN 1-883577-86-1)

If you're interested in learning more about JavaScript and how to use it with Netscape, this new book is for you. It's filled with easy-to-understand tips on how to make your Web pages more dynamic by using JavaScript.

☆☆ *Managing Internet Information Services*

by Cricket Liu et al. (O'Reilly & Associates, ISBN 1-56592-062-7)

Geared too much toward Unix in its discussion of HTML tools and converters, this book nevertheless contains some helpful information on running a Net site, including a good (but too brief) discussion of legal issues and extensive sections on security.

☆☆☆☆ *Teach Yourself Web Publishing with HTML in a Week*
by Laura Lemay (Sams, ISBN 0-672-30667-0)

`http://slack.lne.com/lemay/theBook/index.html`

You *could* probably do all of this in a week, but it would be like cramming for college finals. If you take your time with this guide, you'll be richly rewarded by a thorough understanding of HTML. The extensive appendices are particularly good sources of reference material.

☆☆☆ *World Wide Web Bible*
by Bryan Pfaffenberger (MIS:Press, ISBN 1-55828-410-9)

A thorough general Web text, this book is generally well-written, with over 100 pages specifically on HTML. But hey, who drew the thumbs-down icon that shows up about every 10 pages? It's a good concept, but surely they could have found a better-looking piece of public-domain clip art on the Net!

Appendix E: Installing Netscape

The amount of work you'll have to do to get up on the Web depends heavily on what your provider offers you in addition to a dialup line. Many providers will give you an install diskette with a TCP/IP stack and a Web browser right on it, ready to install. That certainly makes your installation easier, but you can't always count on such technological generosity. In many cases, you'll just have to hunt down a browser on your own.

There's an additional wrinkle: The newer versions of Netscape may require prior installation of the latest version of Win32s. Netscape comes in 16- and 32-bit versions. If you're running Windows 95, don't worry--it already runs 32-bit applications. The 16-bit version, n16e201.exe, also doesn't require Win32s. Here's a word of caution concerning Netscape and Win32s. If you want to run the 16-bit version of Netscape without Win32s, and Win32s is already installed on your system, double check to insure no other applications are using Win32s before you attempt to delete it from your system.

To run one of the 32-bit versions of Netscape with 16-bit Windows 3.1, you must first install Microsoft's Win32s compatibility module. So before I explain how to install Netscape, I should explain more about Win32s, including where to find it and how to "mount" it.

Do You Need Win32s?

If you intend to run Netscape on a system that needs Win32s for other applications, you must install Win32s. There is no charge for the software if you are a licensed Windows or Windows for Workgroups user. If you are going to run Netscape on a system where other applications don't require Win32s, or if you are running Windows NT or Windows 95, you will not need to install Win32s.

Bear with me, at this point, because some of the details of Win32s tend to get confusing. For instance, there are several different versions of Win32s floating around. As an added complication, it's often difficult to distinguish among the different versions of Win32s just by looking at them on a name-by-name basis. On many FTP sites, the same name represents different versions of Win32s. You will need Win32s version 1.20 or later installed on your system.

First, check whether Win32s is already installed on your system. See if there is a win32s.ini file in your Windows system directory. (Try looking in c:\windows\system.) If Win32s is not installed, you will need to install it. If you find a win32s.ini file, check its contents. The first three lines should look something like this:

```
[Win32s]
Setup=1
Version=1.20.123.0
```

The third line specifies the version—in this case, 1.20. If you have version 1.20 or later installed, you're home free.

Installing Win32s

A later version of Win32s is provided on the companion CD-ROM so that you can install it on your computer. You can use the software provided on the CD-ROM or download a copy of Win32s from the Internet. Here is one reliable FTP site where you can get a copy of Win32s:

```
ftp.ncsa.uiuc.edu/Web/Mosaic/Windows/Win31x/Win32s
```

Once you have the Win32s software, follow these steps to install it:

1. Run the program setup.exe. (This program is stored on the companion CD-ROM in the directory \tools\win32s.)
2. The installation program then tries to determine the location of your Windows system files. Setup displays the c:\windows\system path, and informs you that it will create a subdirectory named WIN32S subordinate to the c:\windows\system path. If you click on Continue, a series of progress messages are displayed as the Setup program uncompresses the files and places these files in the appropriate places.

After the installation runs to its conclusion you'll receive a completion message. After those kind words, click on OK. The next dialog box asks if you want to install Freecell. Click on Continue to install this game. There are two reasons to install Freecell: It's a great game, and you can use it to verify the successful installation of Win32s.

After the installation of Win32s and Freecell are complete, Setup asks you to allow it to exit and restart Windows. After Windows restarts, take a few minutes to play Freecell. A brief aside: Freecell is a solitaire game that involves both luck and strategy. Strategy is more important than luck when playing Freecell, as opposed to regular Solitaire.

Before you install Netscape or any other WinSock-compliant Web browser, you need to ensure that both you and your system meet a few requirements:

- Microsoft Windows, version 3.1 or later, must be installed on your computer and properly configured.
- You need to know how to use FTP to transfer files from a remote location, unless you have a Web browsing client already installed on your PC.
- It would be nice if you know how to use an ASCII editor, such as DOS EDIT or Windows Notepad.
- A TCP/IP stack, such as the Internet Chameleon or Trumpet WinSock, needs to be installed on your PC and must be properly configured.
- You must have an Internet connection that supports transmissions to a TCP/IP stack.
- You may also need the prior installation of Win32s for some browsers.

INSTALLING NETSCAPE

Most Web browsers, including Netscape, are WinSock-compliant applications. This means that your computer must speak the language of networks—Transmission Control Protocol/Internet Protocol (TCP/IP). A TCP/IP stack is essentially a piece of "middleware" that allows your system to communicate with the Net. If you already have a TCP/IP stack, such as Trumpet or Chameleon installed, you're in good shape. Here's a good check to determine whether a TCP/IP stack is already installed on your system: Check your system for a file named WINSOCK.DLL. If you don't find this file, you're not yet ready to install a Web browser. If your TCP/IP stack is up and running, you're ready to forge ahead.

Before you begin the installation of any browser, you must have available your full email address, the domain name of your SMTP mail server, and the domain name of your NNTP news server. The domain names are available from your system administrator or Internet provider.

There are some common steps involved in obtaining and installing all Windows software from the Internet. To provide you with a conceptual model, I'll begin by using the procedures for locating and installing Netscape. In general, the installation process involves the following six steps:

1. Locate the Internet site that contains the desired program.
2. Download the file (FTP it) to a dedicated directory on your PC.
3. Uncompress the file, if necessary.
4. Add the program's parameters and icon to an existing Windows group.
5. Configure the program.
6. Test the program and, if necessary, debug the configuration.

Step 1 - Locate the Internet Site

To make this step as simple as possible, I'll provide you with the site where the desired browser package is stored. (I'll do this in Step 2.) This file is a standard HTML file and may be viewed by any Web browser. If you're relatively new at downloading files, you might want to review Chapter 9, *Finding and Retrieving Files*, before proceeding. Chapter 9 is a complete tutorial for developing the skills necessary to locate information and programs on the Internet.

Step 2 - Download the Desired File to Your PC

I've made this point elsewhere in this chapter and in other chapters, but it bears repeating before we continue: Since FTPed files are typically obtained from Unix-based computers, be precise in your use of uppercase and lowercase letters in specifying file and directory names.

In this demo example, version information is embedded in the file name, which helps in determining whether you're downloading the most current version of a file. The latest version of Netscape, as we go to press, is 2.01 Netscape also frequently has beta versions of the browser available. The naming convention previously used by Netscape is n16eVVbN.exe, where VV is the version number and N is the beta number. For example, n16e11b3 was the last beta before the alpha of version 1.1 was released. Should you use a beta or alpha version? This depends on if you like to live dangerously. I keep both versions on my system. Unfortunately, there is an abundance of obsolete software on the Internet. Try to download your browser of choice from the sites listed in this chapter because they are known for providing the most up-to-date versions.

The FTP domain name for downloading Netscape is ftp.netscape.com. The URL for downloading the file for the 16-bit Windows version is:

```
ftp://ftp.netscape.com/2.01/windows/n16e201.exe
```

The URL for the 32-bit version is:

```
ftp://ftp.netscape.com/2.01/windows/n32e201.exe
```

If you are downloading the Mac or Unix version of Netscape, back up one directory level by clicking on:

```
Up to higher level directory
```

The Unix and Mac files will then be listed.

I would suggest you enter the URL without the filename since it may have changed before you read this. Keep in mind that Netscape is a very busy site, especially after a new software release. It will often take a long time to get connected, so try to be patient.

Prior to downloading a new package, create a temporary directory to hold the compressed file. Let's assume we create a directory "temp" on our c: drive. If you are already cruising with Netscape or another Web browser and just want to get a different browser or an updated one, simply go to the Netscape home page and choose Download Software from the menu at the bottom of the page. At the next page click on Netscape Navigator. You'll then be presented with four pull-down menus asking you to specify what you want to download, what your operating system is, the desired language (English, French, etc.), and your location.

When you arrive at the directory listing, click on the latest version of Netscape. Since this file has an .EXE extension, Netscape realizes it cannot process the file and displays the Unknown File Type dialog box. Select the Save to Disk option. Next, you are prompted with a Save As dialog box. The file name defaults to the same name as the remote file, if it is in a legal DOS format. You select a target file name and directory path just as you would in any other Windows application. Click on OK and the transfer starts.

Step 3 - Uncompress the File

Almost without exception, large FTPable files are stored in compressed format to save disk space and transfer time. A compressed file is about 50 percent the size of its uncompressed version. In this case, the .EXE extension indicates that n16e201.exe is in self-extracting form. From the command line, enter

```
c:\TEMP>n16e201.exe
```

or click on the file in file manager, and the extraction process will begin. Most of the other programs mentioned in this chapter have a .ZIP extension. To uncompress these browsers, you will need a PKUNZIP, WinZip, or a PKZIP-compatible uncompression utility. If you don't have PKUNZIP, or if you're unsure of how to use it, read Chapter 9, *Finding and Retrieving Files.*

Step 4 - Add the Program's Icon to Windows

This step explains the Windows installation component. The details in this step generally apply to installing any Windows programs, not just Web browsers. There are two possible paths for this step:

1. The program may install into its own Windows group, which it creates during installation.
2. The program may allow itself to be copied into an existing Windows group.

Before proceeding with this step, play it safe and look for a file named readme.txt or install.txt. There could be some variation on these naming themes. Look for one of these instructional files in the directory where the uncompressed program components are stored. (The expansion of Mosaic produces a file named readme.wri. The .WRI extension tells us the file is in Windows Write format.) We will not always be lucky, though; many times there will be no readme.txt, install.txt, or any other installation or setup help file.

If the program creates its own Windows group, you almost always will find a file named setup.exe or install.exe in the directory listing. For our example, there is a setup.exe accompanying this collection of files. If you don't find either of these files, look for a file having an .EXE extension with the basic program name, such as netscape.exe. If there are multiple files with .EXE extensions, the main one should be fairly large.

Make a note of the major file's name and the current directory. Start Windows. If Windows is already running, it's usually a good idea to terminate all other programs before installing a new application.

Since we do have a setup.exe for our example, we will start by selecting the sequence File | Run. Enter the path and name of the program that will start the installation process and click on OK. Or you can simply go into File Manager and choose the setup.exe file from there.

Next, a notice appears stating the "Netscape Setup" has started, followed by an instruction to press Continue to install. The installation program will next ask for the path name to install Netscape. After some disk activity, the setup's next interaction is a request for a Program Group to hold the Netscape icon. I prefer to have all my Internet-related icons in the same program group.

Next, you're asked if you want to read the readme.txt file—a good idea if this is your first fling with Netscape. Finally, the ubiquitous license agreement and then your Netscape icon is displayed in the group you selected.

You can actually start to surf the Web at this point. Assuming that your TCP/IP stack is configured and tested, activate the stack. If you're using the Internet Chameleon or the Chameleon Sampler, activate Custom and click on Connect. After your SLIP/PPP connection has been established, click on Netscape and start surfing.

Step 5 - Configure the Program

Netscape is highly customizable. Read Chapter 4, *Setting Your Netscape Preferences*, to get the inside scoop on configuring Netscape. Most configuration options can wait until you get an idea of how you want the browser to look and act. However, it's a good idea to configure your mail and Usenet news server right away so you can send mail from within Netscape and access Usenet newsgroups. See Chapter 6 for more information about configuring mail, see Chapter 7 for Netscape News.

Step 6 - Test the Program and Configuration

Well, there you have it, Netscape is installed. The best way to test Netscape and its initial configuration is to go forth and surf.

III

Appendix F: Using the Web Surfing and Publishing CD-ROM

The companion CD-ROM contains over 130MB of the best programs and clips for getting the most out of the Web, especially if you're interested in HTML and Web publishing. A few of these shareware and freeware programs and resources are described here, but see the CD-ROM directory for the complete list.

You've probably heard of shareware described as "software on the honor system." Basically, if you try it and decide to keep it, you should register and pay for it. Basic registration instructions are given for each of the shareware programs discussed here, but more details can be found in the programs themselves, usually in the form of a readme file or screen.

Freeware is fully functional software that the author has generously made available to whomever wants it, no strings attached (although commercial versions, with more features, are sometimes available). Note, however, that the author almost always retains full rights to the program, and distribution policies vary, so read any copyright information carefully before you sell your favorite freeware program to a hundred of your closest friends.

The audio and visual clips and art, images, and icons on the CD-ROM are in the public domain, which means that no single person or organization claims copyright. That means you can do whatever you want with them and to them—except, of course, claim copyright.

Enjoy!

AUDIO, VIDEO, ANIMATION, AND CLIP ART

What: Hundreds of audio and visual clips to dress up your Web pages
Where on the CD-ROM: \clips
Where on the Net: Various sites

You'll find over 40MB worth of audio, video, animation, and image files on the CD. All the clips can be run directly from the CD as long as the appropriate player or viewer program is installed on your PC. They provide examples, inspirations, and the beginning of your own collection of multimedia goodies to add to your Web pages.

Audio

The audio files in WAV format provide sound effects for every conceivable situation, while the MIDI files provide pieces of music in styles ranging from classical to country. One especially nice thing about the MIDI files here is that they're not tiny pieces that seem to be over before they've begun—some play as long as 10 minutes! You can play the audio files with Windows' own Sound Recorder and Media Player accessories, or, for cooler-looking control panels and more playback options, use the Wham and Wplay programs in the \helper branch of the CD.

Images

If you've been looking longingly at all the nifty buttons, bullets, lines, and icons on other people's Web pages, check out the files in \clips\images and \clips\art. They're public domain and ready to use in GIF, BMP, and PCX formats. If one of these clips is almost, but not quite, right for your purpose, just install Paint Shop Pro from the CD and change it!

Video and Animation

The animation and video files in \clips\animatio and \clips\video will provide examples and inspiration when you're ready to add movement to your Web site. To run the FLC and FLI files, use the AAplayer program in \helpers\waaplay. You can play it right from the CD, or, if you prefer, copy it to the hard disk. In either case, run aawin.exe, choose File|Open Animation, select the one you want to watch, click the >> (play) button, and watch it go. You can even add WAV or MIDI sound effects if you like, using File|Get Sound. The Truespace animations can be run by the ViewSpace program, discussed later in this chapter.

Two types of video clips are included on the CD: AVI and MPEG. AVI videos can be run by Windows' Media Player accessory, but MPEG requires the MPEGplayer program discussed later in this chapter.

PROGRAMS INCLUDED ON THE CD-ROM

Please keep in mind that there are many more files on the CD-ROM than the few that are mentioned below. These files are meant to simply whet your appetite before you dig into the actual CD-ROM.

Clipart

What: collection of clip art
Where on the CD-ROM: \clips

This collection of clipart was gathered from many different places. You can find images here that can really spice up your Web pages. Check out the collections in \CLIPS\ART\COHEN and \CLIPS\ART\FUNET to see some really impressive line art pieces.

Some of the more useful images are in the \BARS, \DOTS, and \SYMBOLS directories. These simple images don't take up much space, but they can really liven up a Web page and give it that custom look. There are also many images that can be used as separator bars and custom list bullets. Why stick to what Netscape has to offer you? Use custom images to give your page a unique style. But, be careful. Too many images can really slow things down! In the \CLIPS\AUDIO directory, there are many sound effects and samples that you can use to give feedback to the people visiting your pages. Once again though, you need to be careful that you don't use too many. Sound and video are also not supported on everyone's systems, so you may want to consider the people who will visit your site before you load up your pages with multimedia files.

CuteFTP

What: FTP program
Where on the CD-ROM: \tools\ftp\cuteftp

CuteFTP is another stand-alone FTP program that expands on some of the features of WS_FTP. One of the best features of CuteFTP is its robust stop command, similar in nature to the stop button found on many web browsers. This command allows a user to stop any operation in progress while still maintaining the connection. Beyond the stop command, CuteFTP also integrates the file listing process with file descriptions obtained from the index files found at many anonymous FTP sites (extremely helpful for deciphering the cryptic file names found at many FTP sites). Caching of recently visited directories is another distinctive feature found in CuteFTP. In addition to fixing many bugs, the newer releases of CuteFTP have implemented WS-FTP's File Manageresque approach to listing both remote and local directories side-by-side, comprehensive login listings, selectable file viewers, and selectable colors, the ability to recursively download directory trees, and the ability to easily send multiple files at once.

HomePage Creator

What: Visual home page designer tool
Where on the CD-ROM: \tools\hpc

HomePage Creator is a brand new tool that is included with this book to help you automatically create your own page. It's not just another HTML editor. It allows you to insert a picture, text, and links to your favorite sites on the Web and then it does the dirty work of generating HTML tags for you. This program is covered in more detail in Chapter 9.

The installation procedure for HomePage Creator is easy: Just run the SETUP.EXE program in the directory \tools\hpc. You'll need to specify the directory where you want to install the HomePage Creator program. The developer of this program, Demetris Kafas, is currently developing a more feature-rich version of HomePage Creator that you'll be able to purchase in the future.

HotMetal

What: HTML editor
Where on the CD-ROM: \tools\hotmetal

HotMetal is a Windows-based, freeware HTML editor from SoftQuad. An HTML editor is a stand-alond program; it's used by itself to write Web pages, not added on to a word porcessor or other program.

HotMetal has several elements that make it a good choice for beginning HTML publishers. It sticks to the basic, standard features of HTML, so you won't be overwhelmed by dozens of different tags. In fact, selecting Hide Tags from the View menu lets you ignore the tags altogether, so you can read just the text on the page that, for example, you saved to disk from someone else's Web site. Also from the View menu, the Structure function creates an "outline" of your document, so you can keep track of its links without driving yourself crazy.

Best of all, HotMetal comes with 14 templates for typical documents like home pages, customer registration forms, and hotlists. Just choose File | Open Template, pick the appropriate one from the list, type your text in between the tags, save it as an HTM file, and voila!—instant HTML. Be sure to start with readme3.htm, a template that describes the other templates.

It is possible to run HotMetal straight from the CD, but installing it on your hard disk is more practical. It's not self-installing, so you'll have to copy the entire \hotmetal branch from the CD to the root directory of your hard drive, and then make an icon for it as follows:

1. In Program Manager, open the group in which you want HotMetal to belong.
2. Choose File | New. The Program Item option should be selected. Click OK, and the Program Item Properties dialog box should appear.
3. Type *Hot Metal* in the Description box.
4. Click Browse and navigate through your hard disk until you find sqhm.exe. Click on that file to select it, then click OK.
5. Click OK again, and the HotMetal icon should appear in your group.

HotMetal takes up only about 5MB of hard disk space, but is fairly greedy for memory, so unless you have plenty of RAM to spare, it's a good idea to shut down other programs when you run it.

HTML Assistant

What: HTML editor
Where on the CD-ROM: \tools\htmlasst

HTML Assistant is an extremely popular, freeware HTML editor for Windows. Like HotMetal, it's a stand-alone program for creating Web pages. The two differ, however, in their approach and specific set of features. HTML Assistant doesn't come with a wide variety of prewritten templates like HotMetal does, but makes up for it with an elegant interface and, especially, an easy-to-use Test function that lets you see how your page will actually look on the Web.

The installation procedure for HTML Assistant is basically the same as for Hot Metal: Copy the directory and create a program icon. The file that runs HTML

Assistant (step 4 in the installation instructions listed for HotMetal) is different from the one for HotMetal, of course; the one to browse for here is htmlasst.exe.

To create a page with HTML Assistant, start by choosing Command\Display Standard Document Template. This will bring up a skeleton Web page with basic codes. Add your text, and then add other elements by clicking on them from the toolbars or selecting them from the menus. When your page looks ready, choose Save and type in the filename, including the HTM extension. **Important:** You have to explicitly type *.htm*; it won't be added for you, and without it, your pages won't display properly.

The real fun starts after you've saved a document. Click the Test button. The first time you do this, you'll be asked for the test program name—the file name of the browser program you use. HTML Assistant will then run the browser, and your pages will appear just as they would on the Web! Note, however, that you have to end the browser yourself so HTML Assistant can restart it the next time you want to test a page. Once you've gotten the hang of basic HTML, dive into HTML Assistant's extensive support for URLs and start linking things up.

HTMLed

What: HTML editor
Where on the CD-ROM: \tools\htmled

HTMLed incorporates many advanced features into a program that is extremely easy to use. Intelligent tag insertion, tag removal, automatic saving with or without HTML tags, word wrap, and configurable floating toolbars are just a few of HTMLed's advanced features. In addition, the task of creating background images and identifying colors for your web pages is made easy with HTMLed. HTMLed also makes good use of right mouse button functionality.

MPEGplay version 1.65

What: Player for MPEG videos
Where on the CD-ROM: \helpers\mpegpla

MPEGplay is a very fast video player for Win32s and WinG. If you don't already have either of these Windows extensions, Win32s is available as freeware on the CD-ROM. Install it on your hard disk by running \win32s\disk1\setup.exe before installing MPEGplay.

MPEGplay's interface looks like a VCR, with the standard rewind, stop, and play buttons, plus an extra one that allows a video clip to be played frame-by-frame. To get the most out of any machine, MPEGplay gives the user control over the number of colors displayed in the clip and the size of the window. If you have a fast machine, you can set these options high for the best detail; if you have a slower machine, you can sacrifice a little detail for less jerky motion. You can even choose Movie | Time Play to find out how fast your PC is playing the video, in frames per second.

MPEGplay is shareware. The included register.txt file has more details.

Paint Shop Pro version 3.0

What: Image conversion and enhancement program
Where on the CD-ROM: \helpers\psp

Paint Shop Pro, from JASC Corporation, is a shareware program that gives you control of your graphics. You might use it, for example, to open a PCX file, copy a small part of it to a new window, resize and flip the new image, put a red border all around it, and save it as a GIF file. It would then be ready to use as an icon for your Web pages.

Paint Shop Pro has several features that have made it the standard shareware graphics-conversion program for several years:

- Screen capture
- Multiple document windows
- Filters for special effects
- Support for over file formats
- TWAIN scanner support
- Batch conversion, so you can, for example, turn ten WMF images into GIFs with a single click

Paint Shop Pro is self-installing; just run setup.exe from the CD.

ViewSpace

What: 3D animation program
Where on the CD-ROM: \helpers\viewspace\disk1

ViewSpace is a freeware 3D animation and rendering program from Caligari Corporation. You can use it with objects that have been created separately by a CAD program, or with Truespace animations. ViewSpace is relatively easy to use, but at first you'll probably want to make use of its online help. (You might need to resize the program window to see the Help menu. Unlike most Windows programs, ViewSpace's menu bar is at the bottom of the window.)

To run an animation, you simply choose File | Animation. To create an animation, you first position your wireframe objects in the 3D space by choosing File | Load Object. Then, using the tools at the bottom of the window, you can move, rotate, render (add surfaces and depth), and ultimately animate them.

ViewSpace is self-installing; just run vsetup.exe. Note, however, that ViewSpace is not for slower computers. To really use it, you'll need a fast 486 or a Pentium with plenty of RAM and a fast video card.

VocalTec Internet Phone

What: Internet phone
Where on the CD-ROM: \tools\phone

With Internet Phone, you can use the Internet to speak with any other user, from any point in the world! Real-time voice conversations over the Internet, at the price of a local phone call or even less! All you need is Internet Phone, a TCP\IP Internet connection, and a Windows-compatible audio device. Plug in a microphone and speaker, run Internet Phone, and, by clicking a button, get in touch with Internet users all over the world who are using the same software. A friendly graphic user interface and a Voice-Activation feature make conversation easy. VocalTec's sophisticated voice compression and voice transfer technology makes sure your voice gets across in a flash, using only a fraction of the available bandwidth. Internet Phone now also supports Full Duplex audio: it lets you speak and listen at the same time.

WebEdit

What: An HTML editor
Where on the CD-ROM: \tools\webedit1

WebEdit is a very intuitive and feature-packed HTML editor. Some of its features include: HTML 3.0 tags (math functions, icon entities, tables, and more), a Home Page Wizard, improved web browser support, and much more. WebEdit also saves every URL you enter, letting you choose from a list rather than having to retype the same URLs over and over. Also included are a tool for removing HTML tags from a document and one for quickly producing a template of tags commonly used in your HTML documents. WebEdit also features MDI—multiple-document interface—which allows you to work on up to ten different HTML documents simultaneously.

WebEdit does have some very interesting new features, like floating customizable toolbars, a Table Builder, and a multilingual spelling checker;

unfortunately, all of these features are crippled in the evaluation package, so you will have to register the product to get the full benefit of it's features. WebEdit also lets you call your favorite web browser to view the page you are currently working on so that you can see what it will look like. Additional features include word wrap, time/date stamping, search and replace, and almost every HTML command imaginable.

Web Spinner

What: HTML editor
Where on the CD-ROM: \tools\webspin

Web Spinner is the new kid on the block of HTML editors. It is a very powerful but easy-to-use editor for creating HTML documents. Web Spinner is a snap to install and get started with. You just need to make sure that you have Win32s installed on your computer if you are running Windows 3.1. If you are running Windows 95, you won't need Win32s to run Web Spinner. To learn more about how to use Web Spinner, see Chapter 10 where we use it to create a home page and a complete HTML style guide.

WinJammer

What: fully-featured MIDI sequencer
Where on the CD-ROM: \helpers\winjamr

WinJammer uses standard MIDI files, giving you access to a huge number of songs. WinJammer also contains a companion program called WinJammer Player, which is used to play MIDI song files in the background.

Major features of WinJammer include:

- imports Adlib ROL files
- up to 64 tracks
- runs in ALL Windows modes (including enhanced mode)
- very powerful editing commands
- uniquc piano roll style notation for editing
- full online help
- supports standard MIDI files
- supports MIDI system exclusive bulk dumps
- supports Windows Multimedia Extensions

Major features of WinJammer Player include:

- supports standard MIDI files
- up to 64 tracks
- runs in ALL Windows modes (including enhanced mode)
- in enhanced mode, will even play while in DOS
- full online help
- builds albums of songs to play (forever if desired)
- supports Windows Multimedia Extensions

WPlayAny

What: versatile sound file player
Where on the CD-ROM: \HELPERS\WPLANY

WPLANY is a compact utility that will detect and play almost any sound file you will run into on the Web. Use the Wham application to create and edit audio and use this one as a helper program for your Web browser. The proper drivers for your sound card (or PC speaker) must be loaded prior to using WPlayAny. This program does not have an interface, it simply plays files that it is sent by your browser.

Currently supported sound types:

- SoundBlaster .VOC
- Sun/NeXT/DEC .AU
- Windows .WAV
- Sounder/Soundtools .SND
- Amiga .8SVX .IFF

WS-FTP

What: program
Where on the CD-ROM:\tools\ftp\ws_ftp16 (16-bit)
\tools\ftp\ws_ftp32 (32-bit)

FTP remains one of the most widely used Internet applications, and WS-FTP makes this oft-used tool quick and painless. Configurability options include several alternative screen layouts, the ability to associate remote files with local programs, automatic logging, and quick screen sizing. WS-FTP also comes pre-configured with an extensive array of ftp sites to check out. Multiple copies of the program can be launched to download multiple files at the same time. WS-FTP comes in two varieties: a 16-bit app and a 32-bit app. The only features missing are drag 'n' drop capabilities between local and remote file listings. WS-FTP is another of the must-have Internet applications.

INDEX

I

N

O

P

Q

R

S

T

Y

Z

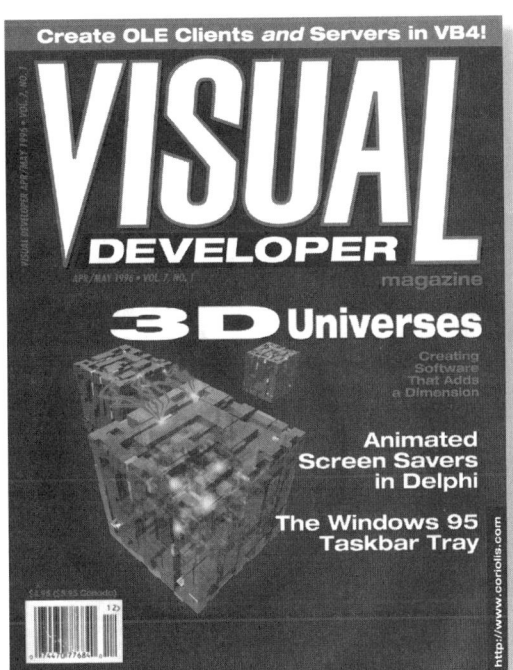

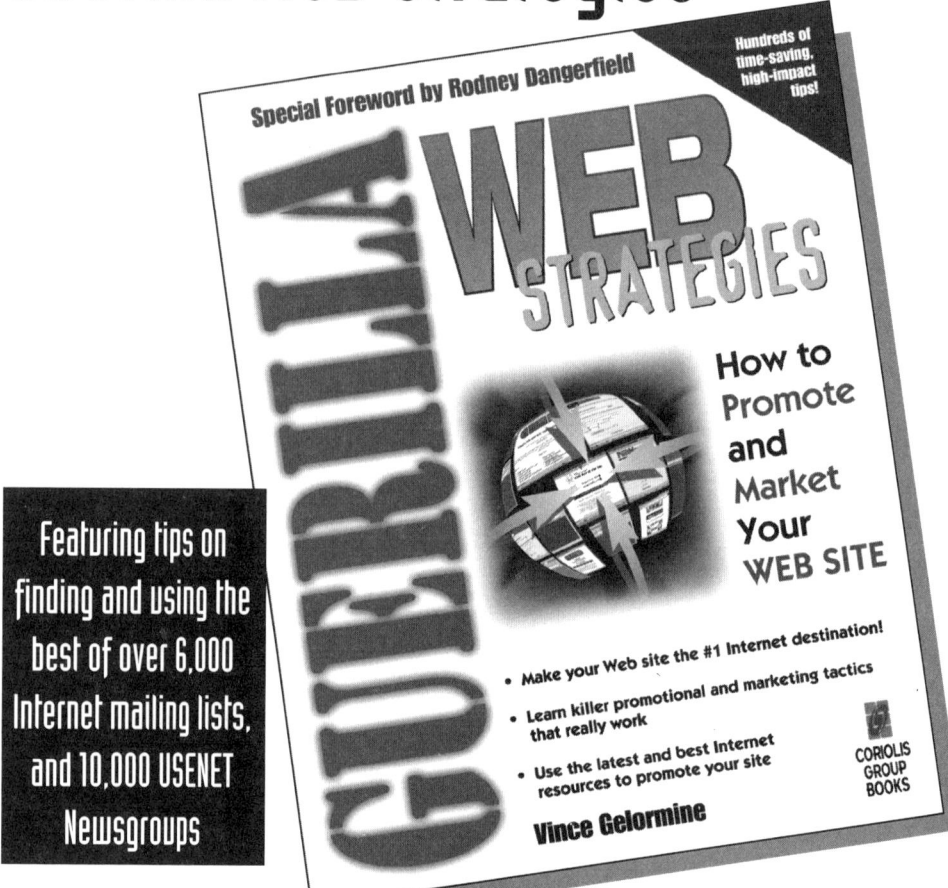

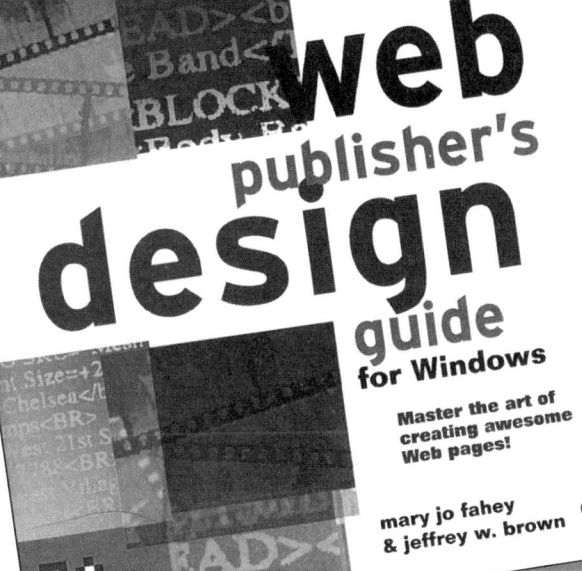

Coriolis Group World Wide Web Home page

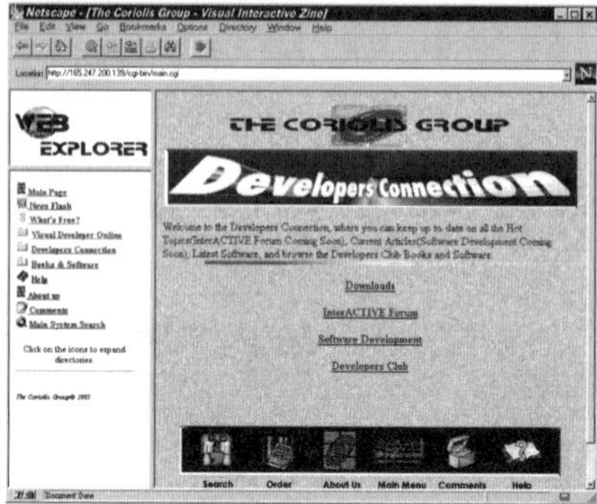

Delphi EXplorer—An incredible resource for Delphi programmers. Includes: commercial demos, dozens of shareware controls, sample code, articles, and two complete chapters from *Delphi Programming Explorer* by Jeff Duntemann, et al.

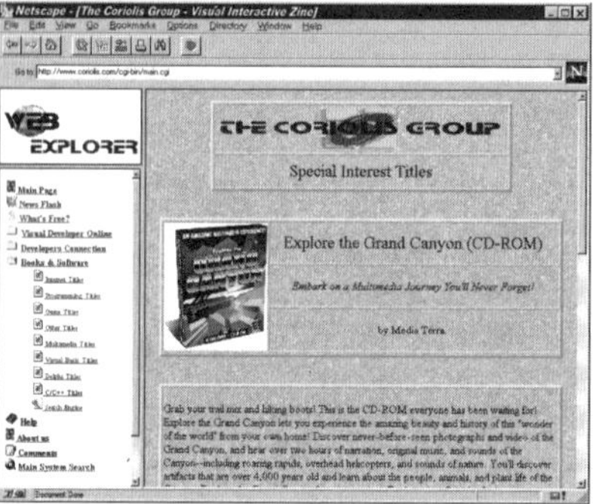

Explore the Grand Canyon—Take a Web wide view of this incredible new multimedia package produced by the Coriolis Group. Read the press releases, learn about amazing new NetSeeker technology, and view a few of the thousands of images from the software!

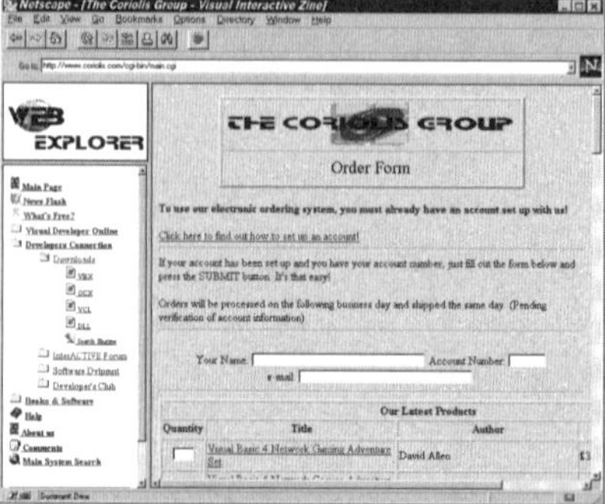

Online Ordering—Set up an account with the Coriolis Group and you can order all of your programming books over the Web. And not just Coriolis Group Books, you can order any of the books from our Developer's Club catalog!

Come visit us at:

http://www.coriolis.com